THE ART
OF QUESTIONING

THE ART OF QUESTIONING

Daniel E. Flage

Department of Philosophy and Religion

James Madison University

Harrisonburg, VA 22807

PEARSON

Prentice
Hall

Upper Saddle River, New Jersey 07458

Library of Congress Cataloging-in-Publication Data

Flage, Daniel E.
   The art of questioning : an introduction to critical thinking / Daniel
E. Flage.
      p.   cm.
Includes bibliographical references
   ISBN 0-13-093699-5
   1. Critical thinking   2. Questioning.   I. title.
   BF441.F55   2003
   160–dc21

                                                      2003008429

VP, Editorial Director: Charlyce Jones-Owen
Senior Acquisition Editor: Ross Miller
Assistant Editor: Wendy Yurash
Editorial Assistant: Carla Warner
Senior Managing Editor: Jan Stephan
Production Liaison: Fran Russello
Project Manager: Patty Donovan/Pine
   Tree Composition
Prepress and Manufacturing
   Buyer: Brian Mackey
Creative Design Director: Leslie Osher
Interior Design: Kathy Mystkowska

Director of Marketing: Beth Meija
Marketing Manager: Claire Bitting
Marketing Assistant: Kimberly Daum
Art Director: Jayne Conte
Cover designer: Bruce Kenselaar
Cover Art:
Director, Image Resource Center: Melinda Reo
Manager, Rights and Permissions: Zina Arabia
Interior Image Specialist: Beth Boyd-Brenzel
Cover Image Specialist: Karen Sanatar
Photo Researcher: Kathy Ringrose

This book was set in 10/12 Adobe Garamond Type face by Pine Tree Composition
and was printed and bound by Maple Vail. The cover was printed by Coral Graphics

 ©2004 by Pearson Education Inc.
Pearson Education Inc.
Upper Saddle River, New Jersey 07458

Printed in the United States of America
10 9 8 7 6 5 4 3 2 1

ISBN 0-13-093699-5

Pearson Education LTD., *London*
Pearson Education Australia PTY, Limited, *Sydney*
Pearson Education Singapore, Pte. Ltd
Pearson Education North Asia Ltd, *Hong Kong*
Pearson Education Canada, Ltd., *Toronto*
Pearson Educación de Mexico, S.A. de C.V.
Pearson Education – Japan, *Tokyo*
Pearson Education Malaysia, Pte. Ltd
Pearson Education, *Upper Saddle River, New Jersey*

TO TRISTAN AND ANGELA

There are two ways to slide easily through life: to believe everything and to doubt everything. Both ways save us from thinking.

—Alfred Korzybski

CONTENTS

PART VII   Informal Fallacies   319

PART VIII   Reading and Writing Essays   377

PREFACE

A Note to Instructors

This book provides a comprehensive and systematic approach to critical thinking. It begins with simple issues at the level of words and concludes with large-scale applications, applying all the skills discussed in this book to reading and writing essays. Throughout, there is a commitment to intellectual rigor and student-friendliness. Each topic begins with relatively simple and straightforward cases and moves systematically to the kinds of messy cases found in ordinary language. Each part is sufficiently self-contained that the instructor can choose to skip some of the later chapters in a part without posing difficulties for the student with respect to another part. For the same reason, the instructor can use the various parts in an alternative order without placing the student at a disadvantage.

Some critical-thinking books focus primarily on discussions in newspapers and magazines. Some critical-thinking books focus on political discussions. I have avoided doing both, even though there are some examples and exercises of both of those kinds. I believe critical thinking is a practical enterprise, so I have attempted to draw examples and exercises from a wide range of fields. If there is a tendency to choose exercises from a certain genre, they are drawn from classical and popular literature (novels). This means they are somewhat timeless. Nonetheless, some of the examples and exercises *are* current. For example, some concern the events of September 11, 2001, and the aftermath of those events.

The book contains over 1,200 exercises and discussion questions drawn from diverse sources and covering numerous distinct topics. Solutions to the odd-numbered exercises are included in the book, which will give your students immediate feedback on their work.

How to use this book. There are at least three ways in which this book can be used. (1) You might work through it from the beginning to the end. (2) You might want to use it as an anthology, choosing topics in some alternative order. (3) You might want to use this as a secondary text in a writing or writing-intensive course.

If your approach to critical thinking is like mine, you assume that there are two fundamental issues that must be addressed in a critical-thinking course. One has to do with statements: Are they true? The other has to do with arguments: Are their conclusions well-supported? To answer the first question, you need to look a bit at language. So, the book discusses uses of language before turning to its primary topic: argument. Some of the linguistic issues also are relevant to the evaluation of arguments. For example, arguments are sometimes persuasive, but weak or unacceptable, due to the emotional connotations of terms. So, the book begins with some basic considerations regarding language. It is arranged in such a way that the later chapters build on what was covered in the earlier chapters. For example, the discussions of informal fallacies include allusions back to earlier chapters. The chapters on evaluation of essays (Chapter 32) and writing argumentative essays (Chapter 33) pull together all the individual skills honed in the earlier chapters.

There is nothing sacred about the order of the chapters in the book. Some will want to skip various chapters. Some will want to cover informal fallacies early in the course. Informal fallacies are fun! Students enjoy them. If you cover informal fallacies early in your course, the allusions to earlier chapters will show your students how the informal fallacies are related to broader issues.

Some might want to use the book as a resource in a writing course. Chapters 32 and 33 focus on reading and writing essays.

On the contents. The first nine chapters are introductory. Chapters 1 through 4 concern issues regarding words and descriptions. Chapter 5 is an introduction to issues regarding explanations. While chapters 6 through 9 provide an introduction to arguments, they do *not* focus on evaluation. They are concerned with kinds of arguments, identification of arguments, and diagramming arguments.

Chapters 10 and 11 concern the evaluation of observational claims and testimony. Chapter 12 provides a brief introduction to arguments in ethics and aesthetics. The emphasis in these chapters is on inductive arguments.

The book examines categorical syllogisms (Chapters 13 through 19) both by means of a set of rules and by means of Venn diagrams. (A discussion of the Euler diagram approach to syllogisms is included in the Student Study Guide.) I have included both approaches because some students thrive on rules, while others are "visual learners" and find the Venn diagram approach more intuitive. The rules are based on a set proposed by Wesley Salmon.[1] They are *not* the six rules to which seven fallacies correspond that are found in some logic books.[2] I chose this set of rules because they're straightforward and easy to use when searching for missing premises.

Chapters 20 through 24 concern propositional logic. The approach is quasi-symbolic. When discussing simple and compound propositions in Chapter 20, the statement connectives are introduced in sidebars. Chapter 21, "Truth Tables," is purely symbolic. The remaining chapters return to the sidebar approach. This allows those students who find the symbols helpful to use them and those students who suffer from symbol-phobia to avoid them. Alternatively, it allows instructors to use or avoid symbols as they see fit.

Chapter 22 introduces a number of common argument forms and three common formal fallacies. Chapter 24 introduces five common logical equivalences. This is *not* a complete system of propositional logic, nor is it intended to be. The argument forms were chosen on the basis of what I believe students are most likely to find in ordinary life, as are the equivalences. So, when students confront enthymematic arguments, they are enthymematic relative to the list of argument forms given. A more robust system of logic would have a larger number of equivalences and perhaps fewer argument forms (rules). As *logic* students acknowledge, the dilemmas can be reduced to hypothetical syllogisms, and you can develop a complete system of logic

---

[1]Wesley C. Salmon, *Logic*, 2nd ed., Foundations of Philosophy Series (Englewood Cliffs, NJ: Prentice Hall, 1973), p. 53.

[2]See Daniel E. Flage, *Understanding Logic* (Upper Saddle River, NJ: Prentice Hall, 1995), pp. 165–168.

without arrows (material implication), but it gets tedious. Although critical thinking is closely related to logic, I assume its emphasis is on practical applications. Hence, there are no formal proofs in this book, although the "what follows?" problems in chapters 23 and 24 can be treated as simple proofs—you can simply provide the conclusion to be derived. The solutions for those problems include a step-by-step symbolic derivation of the conclusion.

Chapters 25, 26, and 27 focus on induction. Chapter 25 provides a systematic discussion of arguments by analogy. In Chapter 26 the focus is on generalizations and surveys. Chapter 27 concerns hypotheses and arguments to the best explanation. In addition to these chapters, the Student Study Guide includes discussions of the probability calculus and Mill's methods.

The discussion of informal fallacies is divided into four chapters: Chapter 28, "Fallacies of Ambiguity," Chapter 29, "Fallacies of Relevance," Chapter 30, "Fallacies of Presumption," and Chapter 31, "Fallacies of Weak Induction." Sometimes known as material fallacies, the problem posed by many arguments committing informal fallacies is that one of the premises is false. For example, fallacious slippery-slope arguments contain at least one false causal claim, but there are also nonfallacious slippery-slope arguments. There are both fallacious and nonfallacious cases of composition, division, and appeal to force, among others. So, the discussion stresses that care must be taken in examining the premises.

The discussion covers twenty-five fallacies, some of which are themselves subdivided into kinds. There is nothing magic about the number. Some would argue that there should be more. Others might contend that it's already a case of multiplying fallacy names beyond necessity. My hope is that the number is sufficient to sensitize students to the sorts of problems that arise when examining the content of arguments, while allowing them to recognize (and argue that) an argument is defective in some other way.

The book concludes with chapters on reading and writing essays. Chapter 32, "How to Read an Essay," gives guidelines for reading essays, analyses of a letter to an editor, of an editorial, and of a short essay, plus four additional essays for analysis. Chapter 33, "How to Write an Argumentative Essay," provides an approach to writing argumentative essays that stresses clarity. Both of these chapters draw on all the skills the students have honed while working through the book.

I hope this book will meet your needs.

A Note to Students

Critical thinking is a process that results in decisions regarding what to believe and what to do. Some of the material in this book you will have confronted before. Some will be new. Some will be familiar topics examined in new ways.

Each chapter begins with a paragraph called "The View." This is a preview of the topic discussed in the chapter. Key terms in the chapter are in **bold** type. These terms are also contained in the glossary at the end of the book, so if you find an unknown term, you might check the glossary. Solutions for all the odd-numbered problems are included at the end of the book.

In studying the topics in this book, start by reading "The View" in each chapter. Look for the topics mentioned in "The View" while reading through the chapter. Work through the odd-numbered exercises and check your answers. If you answer all the odd-numbered exercises correctly, there is good reason to believe you understand the material in the chapter. If your answer differs from that in the solutions section, ask yourself why.

I hope you will find this book useful and, occasionally, amusing.

Acknowledgments

Many people played a role in the writing this book. I wish to thank Dr. Linda Halpern and the other administrators of the James Madison University General Education Program for granting me the freedom to develop and use my own critical-thinking book. I wish to thank Dr. Don Fawkes, Dr. Tom Adajian, and my other colleagues for their many discussions of and suggestions regarding the topics covered in this book. I wish to thank various people who, with good humor, posed for icon pictures for "The View." I wish to thank my students, who not only tolerated the several versions of the manuscript used in class over the past several years, but offered suggestions for improvements. The book was significantly improved by comments from the following reviewers, to whom I give my thanks: Johann A. Klaassen, University of Central Arkansas; Heather Campbell, Arizona State University; Tim Schroeder, University of Manitoba; Michael Papazian, Berry College; Peter Dlugos, Bergen Community College; Christopher Trogan, John Jay College of Criminal Justice; Kenneth F. Rogerson, Florida International University; Bill Pamerleau, University of Pittsburgh at Greensburg; Keith Abney, California Polytechnic University, San Luis Obispo; Matt Schulte, Montgomery College; Stephen Turner, University of South Florida; David Kite, Champlain College; Paul Newberry, California State University, Bakersfield; John Nolu, University of Tennessee; and Pedro Blas Gonzalez, Barry University. I am deeply indebted to Dr. Ross Miller and Wendy Yurash, the philosophy and religion editors of Prentice Hall, for their suggestions, encouragement, and gentle prodding. Working with them was a joy! Finally, I wish to thank my family for their tolerance and love during the writing.

INTRODUCTION

If you want to be a critical thinker, you must learn to ask questions. You must learn to ask the right questions. You must be willing to search for the answers to those questions, and you must understand what counts as a reasonable answer to those questions. You must know where to search and how to search for answers. Sometimes you will need to "dig beneath the surface" to uncover information that is assumed but not stated. Sometimes you will need to look at a problem from many perspectives. And sometimes you will have to show that what initially *appears* to be a reasonable answer is not reasonable.

Critical thinking requires courage: Sometimes you will need to ask unpopular questions. Critical thinking requires persistence: Sometimes the search for answers will be long and hard. Critical thinking requires honesty: Sometimes—indeed, many times—you will need to admit that your proposed answers are wrong. But if you persist and fortune smiles upon you, you might ask a question that changes the way we look at the world.

This book is an introduction to critical thinking. So, the first question is, "What is critical thinking?"

Critical thinking is careful reasoning. It is a deliberate, efficient, and effective means for determining whether a **statement** or **claim** is, or probably is, true or false. If you cannot determine whether the claim is true or false, critical thinking helps you determine the degree of confidence you should place in the claim. Is it likely that the claim is true or likely that it is false? What reasons are given for you to accept the claim? Are they "good" reasons? What counts as a "good reason"? What reasons are there to question the truth of the claim? Should you suspend judgment regarding the truth of the claim? When and why should you suspend judgment?

Critical thinking is *not* fault-finding. A critical thinker provides reasons to believe claims are true or false. Film and book critics provide examples of this characteristic. A film critic might fault a film *because* (for the reason that) the plot is predictable, or the characters are not developed, or it is billed as a comedy but provides few laughs. A book critic might praise a novel *because* the plot contains unexpected twists and turns, or it gives you a sense of living in nineteenth-century London, or its characters are amusing.

> *It's just better to have action, isn't it, than to just sit on the fence? Not if you're not sure which way to go, it isn't.*
> —Richard P. Feynman, *The Meaning of It All* (Reading: Perseus Books, 1998), p. 100

A critical thinker is committed to **clarity, accuracy,** and **precision.** She will ask what words and sentences mean in an attempt to clearly understand them. She will arrange her writing so her reader will see the connections among its various elements. She craves accuracy, the avoidance of error. And she will be as precise as the situation requires. She will ask, for example, "Is 'In 1492' an adequate answer to the question, 'When did Columbus discover America?' or should I be more precise and say, 'On October 12, 1492'?" And she will recognize that some attempts at precision will fail in terms of accuracy. If she had answered, "Columbus discovered America at 10:33 a.m. eastern daylight time on October 12, 1492, according to the Julian calendar," she probably would be wrong.[1]

A critical thinker is **economical** in verbiage and evidence. He uses no more words than necessary to make a point, attempting to use precisely the right words. He recognizes that simpler explanations are more probably true.

A critical thinker is committed to **relevance** and **depth** in reasoning. In supporting her conclusions, she shows that all her evidence supports the conclusion. She seeks understanding of all aspects of an issue, a problem, or an argument.

A critical thinker craves **consistency**. Two propositions are consistent if it is possible for both to be true. He strives for consistency among his own beliefs and examines the works of others to see whether their positions are consistent.

A critical thinker is **open-minded**. She is willing to examine new ideas and reexamine her own claims if new facts come to light. This does *not* mean that she treats one idea as equal in value to another. A critical thinker considers new hypotheses and asks whether there are reasons to believe they are more probable than the old ones. She examines the evidence. She evaluates the arguments on each side of the issue.

A critical thinker is **willing to doubt**. He questions the evidence supporting claims, including claims he believes. He regularly asks, "Is there better evidence for this claim? Is there evidence for the denial of this claim? How strong is the evidence?" A critical thinker is one who inquires. He recognizes that the search for knowledge never is complete. The critical thinker recognizes that he often needs to act on the basis of probable truths, while seeking greater certainty. As a person willing to doubt, a critical thinker must be open-minded.

A critical thinker is **curious**. She has a desire to learn. She is a truth-seeker who recognizes that the certainty of obtaining that goal might be illusive. Curiosity and a willingness to doubt are companionable characteristics.

A critical thinker is **industrious**. He recognizes that the road to truth is often long and difficult. A critical thinker is willing to devote all his abilities to reach that goal. He is persistent. Industriousness is curiosity put into practice.

A critical thinker is **detached** from her subject of inquiry. She is willing to set aside her own interests and emotional attachments in seeking truth. Oedipus of *Oedipus Rex* displayed the characteristics of industriousness, detachment, and courage.

A critical thinker is **civil**. He treats the works of others with tolerance and respect even if he argues that their beliefs are misguided.

A critical thinker respects **humor**. She takes the search for truth more seriously than she takes herself. To a critical thinker, the search for truth is *not* a matter of ego-satisfaction.

This book is an introduction to critical thinking. Since most reasoning occurs in language, Part I concerns language. We consider issues concerning words, descrip-

---

[1] Since Spain did not adopt the Gregorian calendar until 1582, I *assume* the date is correct according to the *Julian* calendar. It probably wasn't at precisely 10:33. It *probably* took some time for the sailors to conclude that they'd actually sighted land.

tions, and explanations. In Part II we begin our discussion of arguments. We concern ourselves with characteristics of arguments and recognizing arguments. We also develop a simple way to diagram arguments. Part III concerns evaluating observation statements, testimony, and value claims. In each case we engage in arguments. Parts IV and V concern deductive arguments. We develop techniques for determining whether the conclusion *must* be true if the premises are. Part VI concerns inductive arguments. We examine criteria for evaluating analogies, generalizations, and hypotheses. Part VII concerns some common mistakes in reasoning called *informal fallacies*. We'll see how these mistakes in reasoning are related to the kinds of arguments we examined in the previous three parts. Part VIII shows how all the skills covered in the book are related to two everyday college tasks: reading essays and writing essays.

Critical thinking is a collection of skills you use every day. This book introduces some of those skills.[2] But critical thinking is like writing or playing a musical instrument. You won't be a Pulitzer Prize-winning writer after one writing or journalism course. You won't be a concert pianist after one semester of lessons. Similarly, the mastery of the skills in this book requires continual practice.

You'll find that critical-thinking skills are useful in all your other classes. They are essential for good citizenship. Their mastery is necessary for the full intellectual development of a person.

Daniel E. Fage
James Madison University

---

[2]For a more complete and regularly expanding list of critical-thinking skills, see Don Fawkes, "A Critical Thinking Inventory" at http://www.geocities.com/fawkesdx/ctINVENTORYhomeworld.htm.

PART

I

Some Uses of Language

We all speak and understand some language. Many of us understand several natural languages, such as English or Italian. We also might understand specialized "languages" such as the "language of mathematics" or the "language of philosophy." What do we do with language? How are thought and language related to one another?

Questions arise in language. Answers are given in language. Clarity of thought is often judged by clarity of linguistic expression. Many people believe that subtlety of thought is shown by subtlety of expression: the ability to find *exactly* the right word. So, while we may grant that infants and animals think, we will assume that most of our thinking occurs in language.

For critical thinkers, there are two questions that are of paramount importance. (1) Is a given statement true? (2) What reasons do you have to believe that a given statement is true? Does the **evidence** show that a statement is true or probably true? Before you can answer either question, you will sometimes need to ask, "What does this mean?" A primary concern in this part of the book is with meaning.

In Chapter 1 we examine statements. Statements are true or false. To determine what a statement claims, you often need to resolve ambiguities in the statement and reduce the amount of vagueness.

In Chapter 2 we examine commands. In addition to questions of ambiguity and vagueness, you must also ask whether the authority making the command had the right to do so. There also is a discussion of ways to convert statements to commands and commands to statements.

In Chapter 3 we examine the emotive connotations of terms. Since you might believe a statement is true because of the emotional impact of words, or you might do something because of the emotional impact of words, we look at alternative ways of making claims.

In Chapter 4 we begin our discussion of more complex functions of language. The most common use of language is descriptive. Descriptive passages answer the questions, Who? What? When? Where? and sometimes How? Descriptive passages are accurate and complete to a certain degree. We ask questions regarding the importance of accuracy and completeness. We also consider potential problems that arise when you make inferences on the basis of an inaccurate or incomplete description.

In Chapter 5 we examine explanations. Explanations answer the questions, Why or how did something happen? and How do you do something?

C H A P T E R 1

The Informative Function of Language

The View: When you use language to communicate, a fundamental question is whether statements are true. To answer that question, you might need to ask questions about what is said. Do you understand the meaning of each of the words in the statements? Are any of the words ambiguous? Are any of the words vague?

What do we do with language? What are some ways language can mislead us?

We use language to give each other information. We make **statements** or **claims**. A statement is a sentence that is **true** or **false**. It is true if it corresponds to the way the world is. It is false if it does not. Examples of statements include "Today is Tuesday," "It is raining," "The square of the length of the hypotenuse of any right triangle is equal to the sum of the squares of the lengths of the remaining two sides," "The expression 'critical thinking' has a clearly defined meaning." Some of those statements are true. The statement "Today is Tuesday" is true if today is Tuesday; otherwise it is false. How do you know whether it is true?

> **Saying the Same Thing**
>
> If today is Tuesday, each of the following statements is true: "Today is Tuesday," "Today is the day between Monday and Wednesday," "*Heute ist Dienstag.*" Some philosophers distinguish between statements and **propositions.** A statement is true, they say, in virtue of a true proposition it expresses. Each of the three statements quoted in the first sentence expresses the same proposition, just as any number of pictures might represent Mt. Everest. Whether propositions are distinct from statements is an interesting philosophical question. In *this* book, however, we shall use the words 'statement' and 'proposition' synonymously.

Check a calendar or ask a friend. To determine whether the statement "It is raining" is true, look outside. The geometrical statement can be proven true given the principles of geometry. To determine whether the statement "The expression 'critical thinking' has a clearly defined meaning" is true, you might look up 'critical thinking' in a recent unabridged dictionary or check to see whether all the people you know who use the expression define it in the same way. In each case, you appeal to a **criterion** or standard for judging whether the statement is true.

Criteria of truth differ for different kinds of statements. Sometimes you only have to "look and see." Sometimes you have to engage in careful reasoning. Sometimes you have to administer a test. Sometimes you have to construct a survey. Nonetheless, whenever you are dealing with a statement, several questions should be asked. Is the statement true? How do I find out whether it is true? Does it make a difference?

Let us start with the last question: Does it make a difference whether a statement is true or false? Sometimes it does. Sometimes it doesn't. Assume you are visiting Baltimore for the first time. You are looking for the National Aquarium. You know that the National Aquarium is at the harbor, but you are lost. You stop at a gas station to ask for directions. The attendant sells you a map and traces a path to the National Aquarium. Is the assumption that the attendant told you the truth important? It is if your objective is to reach the National Aquarium in a timely fashion. So, follow her directions. If you find your way to the Aquarium, she told you the truth.[1]

Now assume you are sitting in your dorm room and reading Sir Arthur Conan Doyle's *A Study in Scarlet*. In the second chapter you read that Sherlock Holmes and Dr. Watson rented a suite of rooms at 221B Baker Street. Is that claim true? Does it make a difference whether it is true? Neither question can be answered until it is clarified. If you are asking whether the statement "Holmes and Watson lived at 221B Baker Street" is true in the same sense that the statement "You are now reading a critical-thinking book" is true, then the statement is false. *A Study in Scarlet* is a piece of fiction. Neither Holmes nor Watson was a real person. There is not now, nor has there ever been, a 221B Baker Street in London. So, the statement "Holmes and Watson lived at 221B Baker Street" is properly false. But in the context of the book, the statement is true. A **context** is a set of assumptions made for the sake of a discussion. In the context of Doyle's stories, Holmes and Watson lived at 221B Baker Street. The "world" of Sherlock Holmes is exactly as Doyle describes it, and it does not need to correspond to anything outside of the stories. Is it important to distinguish between what is true in the "real world" and what is true in "the world of Sherlock Holmes"? This depends on the situation. If you are sitting in your room and reading *A Study in Scarlet* "just for fun," the truth of the claim makes little difference. If you are taking an English test and one of the questions reads, "True or false: Sherlock Holmes and Dr. Watson lived at 221B Baker Street," then you must recognize that the *implicit* context is Doyle's London. In *that* context, the statement is true, and the importance of the question will depend on the importance you attribute to your grade in English. If you are writing a term paper on the similarities and differences between Holmes's London and the actual city, then one issue is whether there actually was a residence at 221B Baker Street. Relative to that project, the issue is important.

Knowing the context is important. An amusing bit of fiction might be quite disturbing if taken as a claim of fact. On October 30, 1938, dance music on radio station WCBS was interrupted by a series of "news flashes" reporting the invasion of armed Martians. The result was widespread panic. Was the panic justified? No. Listeners were hearing the Mercury Theatre production of *The War of the Worlds*. The news flashes sounded like those that occasionally interrupt a radio broadcast. The panic

---

[1]If she didn't tell the truth, this does not necessarily imply that she lied. Perhaps she didn't know that one of the streets on which she directed you was closed. Were you to claim that she *lied*, you would need to show that she intentionally misled you.

resulted from incomplete information. Many listeners were not aware that they were listening to a radio drama and confused fiction with fact.

But even if you are reading a novel, sometimes claims can be taken as factual. In Gore Vidal's *Burr,* most of the situations described are rooted in historical fact. How do I know that? Vidal himself says so.[2] Reviewers remark on Vidal's commitment to historical accuracy, and each of the presumably factual claims I've checked against scholarly historical discussions has proven accurate. Similarly, if I read a description of a Los Angeles class nuclear submarine in a Tom Clancy novel, I can be fairly certain that the description is accurate. Why? Clancy has a reputation for technological accuracy. Indeed, he wrote a nonfiction book on submarines.[3] Does this mean that one should read novels to discover historical or technological facts? No. If you want to know facts, the best way is to read books and articles that claim to give accurate descriptions of history, or submarines, or whatever. But even there, you should look into the author's background to see whether she should be believed.[4]

What must you know to determine whether a statement is true? You need to know what is being said. This usually means you need to know the meanings of words in a sentence. So, if you do not know the meaning of a word, look it up in a dictionary. Does that solve the problem? Sometimes.

Ambiguity

Most words are **ambiguous**. A word is ambiguous if it has more than one **meaning**. Consider the sentence, "A cat walked across the street." The word 'cat' has many meanings. Taken in isolation, the sentence might mean any of the following. (1) A domesticated carnivore of the genus and species *Felis domestica* walked across the street. (2) A large carnivore of the family *Felidae* (such as a lion or tiger) walked across the street. (3) A jazz musician walked across the street.[5] Since the cat *walked* across the street, you probably are not concerned with a Caterpillar tractor, although if the cat had *crawled* across the street, that would have been another possibility. What does the author mean by the word 'cat'? That question usually can be answered by

> **Use and Mention**
>
> If I say, "A cat walked across the street," I'm *using* the word 'cat'. The statement probably makes a claim about a small furry animal. But sometimes I want to talk about the word 'cat'. When I talk about a word, I *mention* the word. There are several conventions used to show that I'm talking about the word 'cat'. In this book, the word is placed in single quotation marks ('cat'). Other people mention a word by placing it in double quotation marks ("cat") or in italics (*cat*). Which convention is used is seldom announced, so you need to infer the convention used from what you see.

---

[2] See Gore Vidal, *Burr: A Novel* (New York: Bantam Books, 1973), pp. 563–64.

[3] Tom Clancy, Jr., *Submarine: A Guided Tour Inside a Nuclear Warship* (New York: Berkley Books, 1993).

[4] We shall return to the ways to evaluate sources in Part III.

[5] These definitions are taken from *The Random House Dictionary of the English Language,* the unabridged edition, edited by Jess Stein and Lawrence Urdag (New York: Random House, 1966), p. 231.

Source: *Scott Adams,* Dilbert *reprinted by permission of United Feature Syndicate, Inc.*

considering the context in which the word is used. If the sentence is found in a story about a child's pet Tabby, 'cat' probably should be understood in the first sense. If it is in a story about a lion on the loose, 'cat' probably should be understood in the second sense. If it is in a story about a jazz musician, 'cat' is probably used in the last sense. Considering the context in which a word is used usually allows you to determine which meaning is assigned to the word.[6]

It is not only words that are ambiguous. Sometimes whole sentences are ambiguous. This is the result of loose sentence construction. In the movie *Animal Crackers,* Captain Spaulding (Groucho Marx) says, "One morning I shot an elephant in my pajamas. How he got in my pajamas I don't know."[7] (I bet you thought Groucho was in the pajamas!) Near an elevator I saw this sign:

In Case of Fire Elevators Are Out of Service

I thought they were being terribly cautious by having the elevators out of service *now* (note the present-tense verb) in case there would be a fire at some time. I watched people getting on and off the elevator. I concluded what they meant to say was, "If there is a fire, then (at that time) the elevator will be out of service." In 2001 I received the following message: "We are celebrating the 100th anniversary of the death of Giuseppe Verdi at JMU." I hadn't known that Verdi had ever been at James Madison University, let alone had died there. Then I realized that 1901 was seven years before the school had been founded. What they meant to say was, "We at JMU are celebrating the 100th anniversary of the death of Giuseppe

> **Was Alice Right?**
> ". . . you should say what you mean," the March Hare went on.
> "I do," Alice hastily replied; "at least—at least I mean what I say—that's the same thing, you know."
> — Lewis Carroll, *Alice in Wonderland,*
> Chapter 7.

---

[6]As we shall see in Parts V, VI, and VII, we must be aware of alternative meanings of a word, for there are errors in reasoning that are based on shifts in the meaning of a key word.

[7]*Animal Crackers,* Paramount Pictures, 1930; quoted in Joe Adamson, *Groucho, Harpo, Chico, and Sometimes Zeppo* (New York: Pocket Books, 1973), p. 105.

Verdi." By considering the context in which a sentence is made, we can usually figure out what the sentence means.[8]

Exercises

I. In each of the following sentences, is the <u>underscored</u> word is ambiguous. Give two meanings of the ambiguous word.

1. Chris is a <u>bookmaker</u>.
2. Lucinda found a ten-dollar bill on her <u>walk</u>.
3. Every time you write a check, you put your <u>name</u> on the line.
4. In school today, I learned how to string my <u>bow</u>.
5. Ms. Carpenter, whose profession corresponds with her name, removed a <u>horse</u> from her truck.
6. Golfers always like a good <u>lie</u>.
7. Our dog Fido is <u>mad</u>.
8. Stephan was <u>stoned</u>.
9. A <u>mouse</u> is on the table beside the computer.
10. John is a <u>rat</u>.

II. Explain why each of the following sentences is ambiguous.

1. Dr. Mata will give a lecture on the causes of cancer in the Biology Building.
2. People race horses at Churchill Downs.
3. Juan has been reading books on zebras in the wild.
4. Minister: Yesterday I had the honor to marry a couple people.
5. Angelica was interviewed for a job as a computer programmer in the personnel office.
6. Lost: American Tourister briefcase with eyeglasses.
7. Newspaper announcement: "The marriage of Henry Smith and Anita Hernandez, which we announced a couple weeks ago, was a mistake, and we wish to correct it."
8. Advertisement for a headache remedy: "Nothing is more effective for the relief of headache pain! Nothing!"
9. Don't let worry kill you—let the church help.
10. The eighth-graders will be presenting Shakespeare's *Hamlet* in the church basement on Friday at 7 p.m. The congregation is invited to attend this tragedy.

---

[8]In Chapter 28 we shall see that some defective arguments rest upon alternative meanings of sentences.

III. Headlines are sometimes ambiguous. Explain why each of the following headlines is ambiguous.[9]

1. Man Robs, Then Kills Himself

2. [President] Carter Plans Swell Deficit

3. Deer Kill 130,000

4. Bar Trying to Help Alcoholic Lawyers

5. Milk Drinkers Turn to Powder

6. Two Convicts Evade Noose; Jury Hung

7. Farmer Bill Dies in House

8. Town Okays Animal Rule

9. Lawmen from Mexico Barbeque Guests

10. Antique Stripper to Demonstrate Wares at Store

Vagueness

An additional problem with words is that some are **vague** or **obscure**. A word is vague when it has no precise meaning. Consider the word 'rich'. Members of the Democratic Party often claim that the Republican Party is the party of the rich. Who are "the rich"? How do you find out? Is a person deemed rich on the basis of his or her net worth, or on the basis of his or her income, or on some combination of both? Is a person with a net worth of $100,000 rich? Probably not. In many parts of the United States, a modest family home costs more than $100,000. What if she has a net worth of a quarter-million or a half-million dollars? Nor is it clear that we can determine who "the rich" are on the basis of annual income. You or I might believe that anyone making over $100,000 per year is at least well off. What if they squander it? What about people who live beyond their means? What about people with a modest income who manage to set aside a substantial nest egg? What about small business owners whose income is modest, but who have a great deal of money invested in their businesses? Are only those having an income or net worth above that of ninety percent of all Americans rich? If so, why ninety percent rather than eighty-nine percent or ninety-one percent? The expression "the rich" has no determinate

> **Family Values**
>
> Should anyone consider the discussion of "the rich" politically partisan, a similar account can be developed regarding one of the Republican Party's favorite expressions: 'family values'. What are they? Are they real values that are or were practiced by real people? Can they be applied in today's society? Is a single bread-winner compatible with a decent lifestyle? Is it right to suggest that only one parent should be a bread-winner, and the other should stay home with the family as a full-time parent? Is divorce always an evil?

---

[9]These are taken from The Bathroom Reader's Institute, *Uncle John's Biggest Ever Bathroom Reader* (Thunder Bay Press, 2002), p. 410.

meaning. It is vague. Any attempt to draw a hard line between "the rich" and those who are not rich is arbitrary. This is *not* to say that we cannot identify *some* rich people. By any standard, Bill Gates is rich and Sally Streetperson is not. But since 'the rich' is vague, a claim such as "The rich should be made to pay their fair share of taxes" has no determinate meaning.[10]

Politicians are not the only people who use vague terms. Nor is it only in our everyday language that we confront words with no determinate meaning. Sometimes common words are used **metaphorically**. A word is used metaphorically when its common meaning is extended in some way. If a sentence contains a vague word, you cannot determine whether the sentence is true or false until you clarify the meaning of the word in question. Sometimes you might need to propose various **conditional** or **hypothetical statements**, claiming that *if* a certain word has a certain meaning, *then* you could expect to find certain kinds of discussions later in the article. Then you look for the expected discussions. If you find them, your proposed meaning is probably correct. If you don't find them—if your proposed meaning does not help "make sense" of the passage—you probably should propose an alternative meaning of the term.

Vagueness is a serious problem. Unless you are able to make the meaning of vague words *fairly* precise, you cannot determine whether the statement containing the words is true or false. Of course, precision is a matter of degree. The man who said, "My son was born on June 29, 1983. My daughter was born on July 1, 1986. We wanted our kids three years apart, but we failed," assumes an unrealistically high degree of precision.

Exercises

IV. In each of the following, explain why the underscored word is vague.

1. <u>Many</u> people attended the concert Thursday night.

2. You should work on critical-thinking exercises for <u>some</u> time every day.

3. Everyone should do <u>well</u> in this course.

4. President Bush said that winning the war against terrorism could take a <u>long</u> time.

5. The exercises in this book are *not* <u>difficult</u>.

6. Jo was <u>sad</u>.

7. The author of this book is an <u>old</u> man.

8. Pike's Peak is a <u>tall</u> mountain.

---

[10]The statement, "The rich should be made to pay their fair share of taxes" is at least doubly vague. Not only is 'the rich' vague, so is 'their fair share', and the meaning of 'should' is at least ambiguous, if not vague. Of course, what is meant is fairly clear: Those in higher income brackets should pay proportionately more personal income tax than they are now paying.

9. Norman is <u>well educated</u>.

10. Maria is <u>erudite</u>.

V. Are the <u>underscored</u> words or phrases in the following sentences ambiguous, or vague, or both? How would you eliminate the ambiguity or vagueness?

1. Senator Short is a <u>liberal</u>.

2. It was <u>a hot day on Wall Street</u>.

3. Professor Smith is <u>bald</u>.

4. Mary Higgins Clark is a <u>prolific</u> author.

5. George sells <u>dogs</u> for $1.00 each at his stand.

6. Harrison Ford is a <u>great</u> actor.

7. Gene enjoys building <u>airplanes</u> from kits.

8. Richard Nixon was a <u>master politician</u>.

9. Watching television can be <u>harmful</u> to your <u>health</u>.

10. Children's <u>toys</u> are safer than adults' <u>toys</u>.

11. John is a <u>big man</u> on campus.

12. Professor S. hopes to nab at least one good <u>bass</u> today.

13. The face on the figure was <u>wooden</u>.

14. Samantha was constantly <u>pulling my leg</u> while we were on a walk.

15. It's a <u>long way</u> from Peoria to New York City.

Factual and Verbal Disputes ————

Ambiguity can play a role in disagreements. Sometimes people disagree about facts, about the way the world is. Sometimes apparent disagreements rest on ambiguous words. For example, assume you and I disagree about building materials for houses. You like brick. I like wood. You give your reasons why brick is the better material for building houses. I give my reasons why wood is the better material. Assume that we agree regarding our criteria for judging the quality of building materials and that we are concerned *solely* with the structural integrity of buildings. This implies that we are *not* concerned with several potentially important issues, such as differences in costs of building materials or the designs of buildings. Given this, there are various kinds of tests we can make, and given the results of those tests, we should agree regarding the preferable building material. Our disagreement is **factual**. We are concerned with the way the world is, and there is a specifiable way to resolve our dispute.

Now consider the exchange between Lynn and Chris:

Lynn: Fred is a real dolt.

Chris: I wouldn't say that. I just gave him an IQ test. He has an IQ of 101. That shows he's no genius, but he's certainly not a dolt.

Lynn: Oh, he's bright enough—I won't deny that. But he's one of the most foolish, senseless, and bizarre people I know, and that's enough to make him a dolt in my book!

Do Lynn and Chris disagree about the facts? No. They disagree about the meaning of the word 'dolt'. Chris appeals to the results of a standardized test to determine whether Fred is mentally challenged. Lynn is not concerned with Fred's mental abilities. She uses the word 'dolt' to refer to Fred's strange behavior. Lynn and Chris are involved in a **verbal dispute**. They disagree regarding alternative meanings of the word 'dolt'. Once the meanings of the term are clarified, the apparent disagreement disappears. The moral of this story is this: If you and someone else disagree, make sure you are assigning the same meanings to the key words you use. Make sure your dispute is factual and not merely verbal.

"It Is My Opinion That . . ."

Some people claim that opinions differ from beliefs. Beliefs might be true or false, but opinions—or *some* opinions—are neither true nor false. What does that mean? If I said, "I believe it's ninety-five degrees outside and snowing," you would say (correctly) that my belief is false. At ninety-five degrees Fahrenheit or Celsius it would be too warm to snow. At ninety-five degrees Kelvin it would be too cold to snow. Does this change if I say, "It is my opinion that it's ninety-five degrees outside and snowing"?

But some say that *some* opinions are neither true nor false. It might be your opinion that abortion is wrong. Posed as a *belief*, I could ask you for reasons to support your belief. How is it different if it is posed as an *opinion*? There are disagreements regarding the *criteria* for determining what makes an action wrong. But not *knowing* whether a belief is true does *not* entail that it is neither true nor false. Calling a belief an opinion changes nothing.

Exercises

VI. Which of the following disputes are verbal and which are factual? If the dispute is verbal, on which ambiguous word does the dispute rest? If the dispute is factual, describe a way in which the disagreement might be resolved.

1. **Merle:** It's a really hot day today. Why, it's better than ninety degrees in the shade.

   Maud: I'll grant that it's hot, but it's only forty degrees.

2. **Sam:** It's twenty miles to Winchester.

   Chris: No, that can't be right. I just saw a road sign that says it's only fifteen miles to Winchester.

3. **Jan:** There are 150 senators, since each state has three senators and there are fifty states.

   Jean: No, you've got that all wrong. Each state has only two senators, and since there are only forty-eight states, the total has to be ninety-six senators.

4. **Carter:** Franklin Roosevelt was the greatest president in American history, since no other president was elected to four consecutive terms.

Sydney: No, Lincoln was the greatest president in history, since he led the United States through the Civil War, the war in which there were the greatest number of American casualties.

5. **Jim:** Gas costs more today than it did in 1970. Why, back in seventy, you could buy a gallon of gas for only about thirty-five cents, and now it's over a dollar a gallon.

   Jen: No, gas is cheaper now than it was in 1970. While the price is higher now than it was then, a dollar today is worth less than thirty-five cents was worth in 1970.

6. **Jo:** Humphrey Bogart was one of the biggest actors in the history of the movies.

   Flo: You've got to be kidding! Both Stanley Greenstreet and William Conrad have him beat by at least 100 pounds.

7. **Juanita:** We should always come to the aid of people who are attacked by muggers. It's our moral duty to help those in need. By aiding them, we might even save a life.

   Jorge: If you *don't* help them, the life you save may be your own. There are cases in which those who tried to help a victim became victims themselves. What might have been a simple mugging became three or four funerals. We have a moral duty to avoid placing ourselves in danger. So the most we should do is call the police, and we should do that only from a safe distance.

8. **Fred:** We agree that in choosing the new computers for our business, if the computers are the same price, the most important points are the power of the processor, speed, storage capacity, and compatibility with our network software. Both the Wiz-Bang 3400FX and the Crackerjack F414QXZ are compatible with our network software. But the Wiz-Bang has the latest processor from Intel, so it's the computer we want to buy.

   Jed: No, I believe we should go with the Crackerjack. True, its processor is a generation out of date, but when networked, it's as fast as the Wiz-Bang, and we can buy twice as much storage capacity for the same money.

9. **Brodie:** Cookie stand's not part of the food court.

   T.S.: Sure it is.

   Brodie: The food court is downstairs, the cookie stand is upstairs. It's not like we're talking quantum physics here!

   T.S.: The cookie stand is an eatery; an eatery is part of the food court.

   Brodie: . . . Eateries that operate within the designated square downstairs qualify as food court, anything operating outside the said designated square is considered an autonomous unit for mid-mall snacking. (*Mallrats,* Universal Pictures, 1995.)

10. During the development of the Strategic Defense Initiative (Star Wars), then Secretary of Defense Caspar Weinberger asked Richard De Lauer, the Pentagon's

head of research and engineering, whether the x-ray lasers needed to destroy Soviet missiles would be generated by nuclear explosions.

"Is it a bomb?" Weinberger asked De Lauer. That was how you generated the laser beams, De Lauer explained, by detonating a nuclear device in space.

"But it's not a bomb, is it?" Weinberger asked, looking for semantic elbow room. De Lauer found a useful euphemism: "No, not a bomb, it would be a nuclear event." Thereafter, Weinberger in congressional testimony and elsewhere refused to admit that SDI required a nuclear blast. He would begin rolling two No. 2 yellow pencils between his fingers, a Captain Queeg talisman indicating that his mind had gone into combat mode. He preferred the word "generator" to "bomb."

Technically he was wrong. I feared that in his obstinacy he would look evasive. When the two of us were alone in his office, I tried to explain, "Mr. Secretary, a nuclear device does have to explode in space to generate the enormous energy required to make the system work. The power is not supplied by Con Edison."

"Generates energy, you say," he repeated with satisfaction. "Then you agree with me. It's not a bomb. It's a generator." (Colin Powell with Joseph E. Persico, *My American Journey* [New York: Random House, 1995], pp. 295–296.)

The Directive Function of Language

The View: A command tells you to do or believe something. A command, as such, is neither true nor false. Nonetheless, questions regarding ambiguity and vagueness arise regarding commands. Since commands are based on authority, we should consider what *justifies* the authority of the person making the command. While they are distinct linguistic forms, commands can be reformulated as statements, and statements can be reformulated as commands. Reformulating a command as a statement introduces an obligation-term.

What do we do with language other than state facts? How do these uses differ from the informative function? How are the different uses of language related to one another?

We do not talk only about facts. We also tell people to do things or how to do things. Call this the **directive** function of language. Examples include "Do not kill," "Do not walk on the grass," and "Place piece A in slot 1 of piece B and secure the two pieces to one another by means of one-inch by quarter-inch bolts inserted through holes a and b." Most questions also are directive.[1] In asking a question you are directing someone to give you information. Examples include "Is today Tuesday?" and "Is Professor Jones a good teacher?"

The directive function of language differs from the informative function of language in an important way. Sentences that direct are not statements. Sentences that direct are not true or false.[2] They tell you to do something or to refrain from doing something. They often take the form of **commands**: "Do this" or "Do not do that." "Believe this" or "Do not believe that." Commands are given by someone in a position of authority. While it is improper to ask whether a command is true or false, it is

---

[1]Rhetorical questions often are an exception to this. When the poet asks, "What is so rare as a day in June?" she is not directing you to reply; rather, she is asserting that June days are rare. The function is informative, although the function of the poem itself might be emotive (see Chapter 3).
[2]As we shall see, however, they can be restated in such a way that they may be taken as informative.

proper to ask *why* you should follow the command or instruction. In raising this question you are asking two questions: (1) On whose authority am I being told to do or refrain from doing something? (2) Why should I take that authority figure as a person whose command I should follow?

The directive function of language shares one aspect with the informative: You have to know what the words mean if you are going to follow the directions. And if you ask *why* you should follow a command, you must understand the words used in the answer you are given to that question. Let us consider the first of these issues.

Assume you are told "Do not kill." What does that mean? *What* are you told not to kill? How broadly or narrowly should you understand the command? And what counts as *killing*?

Generally, considerations of the context will answer these questions. At this point in history, "Do not kill" means "Do not intentionally kill human beings." Because this is the primary meaning of the command, some people argue for vegetarianism on the basis of similarities between humans and animals. While the command forbids running a knife through my heart while we are having a quiet dinner, other cases are less clear. If you kill me to protect yourself from attack, it is a case of self-defense. Here your *primary* intention was not to kill me. Most people believe acts of war are not covered by the command. Accidental deaths are not intentional, so they are not forbidden by the command. Nonetheless, if the accident could have been prevented, the person who caused the accident might be held *legally* responsible for a person's death. What about cases of euthanasia or "mercy killing"? That depends upon the authority making the command. The *legal* issue will depend upon the laws in your state. The *moral* issue will depend on many aspects of the situation.

Once you have clarified the command, the question remains whether it should be followed. Who made the command? Is that person—whether an individual or a corporate person, such as a government—an authority regarding the domain of the command? In short, why should you do what is commanded?

This question is sometimes easy to answer, although the answer might raise additional questions. Why should I follow the command "Do not kill"? Consider some answers to that question. It is morally right not to kill. This answer raises the question "What makes an action morally right or wrong?" Or is it a commandment made by God? This answer raises questions such as "Does God exist?" "If God exists, why should I follow God's commands?" Or is it a law established by the government of the state in which I reside? This answer might raise the question "Why should I follow the laws of the state?" Or "Why should I follow the laws of the state *in this particular case*?" If there are several answers to the question "Why should I obey this command?" it is possible that there are conflicts among those answers. During the Vietnam War, numerous men were told to report to their local draft boards for induction into the army. They were told to do so by the authority of the United States government. Some responded that there was another command, "Do not kill humans," given by a higher moral or religious authority, which forbade them from being inducted into the army. If there is a conflict of authorities, which should be followed? Often there is no clear answer, and you must provide an argument stating the reasons why one authority is superior to another.

Further, you should ask whether the authority figure in question has the right to direct you to act in the way you are instructed to act. Your drill sergeant in boot camp might have the authority to make you run drills, stand at attention in the rain, do endless numbers of pushups, and, in general, to make your life miserable, but there are limits to his or her authority. Your sergeant does *not* have the authority to command you to engage in sexual activities. Demanding sexual activities is outside the sergeant's domain of authority.

Not all alleged authorities tell you to act in certain ways. Some tell you to accept claims as true. You believe that the United States declared independence from England in 1776 because your history book says so. Your history book counts as an authority in this case. Why should you believe it? It was written by an expert in the field, and before it was published, the manuscript was examined and approved by other experts in the field. In short, experts in the field are in agreement that the United States declared independence from England in 1776. If these experts were pushed for more evidence, they would point to dated documents, such as the Declaration of Independence.[3] You might keep pushing the question "And why should I believe that?" further and further back. At some point you will conclude that given everything you know, it is likely that the claim is true. For example, human beings generally write the correct date on documents, particularly important documents. Further, when they err, it is usually unintentional. Thus, it is much more likely that the Declaration of Independence was written in 1776 than that, for example, the framers of the Declaration conspired to deceive future historians regarding the year in which the United States declared independence from England.

Exercises

I. Consider the following commands. Are any terms ambiguous or vague? On whose authority are the commands issued? Does he or she have the authority to make the command? Why?

1. "Drink at least three glasses of milk every day." The American Dairy Association.

2. "Write a three-page essay on what you did during summer vacation." Your English teacher.

3. "Drop and do twenty pushups!" Your drill sergeant.

4. "Get the pan from the stove." Your mother.

5. "Meet me at the theater at 9:00." Your friend Fred.

6. "Don't touch the cookies!" Your brother, who just baked three dozen cookies for his scout troop project.

7. "Practice vegetarianism!" Your ethics teacher.

---

[3]In Part III we examine criteria for judging the credentials of expert witnesses.

8. "Don't have sex with your interns!" Senate Ethics Committee.

9. "Love your neighbor as yourself." God (Leviticus 19:18).

10. "Don't pick the flowers!" University policies manual.

Statements and Commands

While statements and commands are distinct linguistic forms, every command can be reformulated as a statement, and every statement can be reformulated as a command. If your stock broker tells you, "This is going to be a good year on Wall Street," her statement is true or false. (You probably won't know which until the end of the year.) But she is also commanding or requesting belief: "Believe me: The statement 'This is going to be a good year on Wall Street' is true."

Similarly, commands can be reformulated as statements using obligation-words such as 'should', 'ought', 'are obliged to', 'are obligated to', or 'it is your duty to'. The command on the sign "Keep

> *Always do what's in your best interest. Why is the term 'best interest' ambiguous?*

off the grass!" is reflected in the statement, "You should keep off the grass." Obligation-words are ambiguous. There are many kinds of obligations. Should I keep off the grass because it's in my best interest to avoid the owner's ire? This is a prudential obligation. Should I keep off the grass to avoid being arrested for trespassing? This is a legal obligation, and it is usually prudent to fulfill your legal obligations. Should I keep off the grass because it would be morally wrong to walk on the grass? Or because it would be morally wrong to walk on the grass given the owner's request that I not do so? In addition to these, there are social obligations, civic duties (voting, serving on a jury), obligations that arise from being a member of an organization, and so forth. As in all cases of ambiguous words, you should determine the meaning or meanings of the obligation-word—often there are several meanings. And different kinds of obligations can conflict with one another. When they conflict, you should be able to give reasons why one kind of obligation takes precedence over another.

Exercises

II. Reformulate each of the following statements as a command.

1. You ought to drive on the right side of the road.

2. You should do some critical-thinking exercises every night.

3. You are obligated to respect your roommate's possessions.

4. You are obliged not to pick flowers from the university's flower beds.

5. All eligible voters are obligated to vote in the next election.

6. Noah, I want you to build an ark.

7. You should look after your own interests!

8. Smoking is forbidden in this building.

9. Writing should be done with great care.

10. You ought to cook your hamburgers until they are well-done.

III. Reformulate the following commands as statements. Remove the ambiguity in words such as 'ought' or 'should' by stating the *kind* of obligation (legal, moral, religious, prudential, etc.) to which you believe the command alludes.

1. "No Trespassing!" A sign on the gates of an army base.

2. "Thou shalt not steal." A sign seen in a courtroom.

3. "Don't take drugs!" A public service announcement in a health magazine.

4. "Do your homework!" A parent's remark to his child.

5. "Always read the fine print!" A lawyer's advice to her client.

6. "Write legibly!" A professor's remark before an essay exam.

7. "Take two tablets before bedtime." Instructions on a bottle of prescription medicine.

8. "Go to jail! Go directly to jail! Do not pass Go! Do not collect $200!" Instructions on a *Monopoly* card.

9. "Always keep two month's wages in a saving's account." Advice of a financial planner.

10. "Give ten percent of your income to the church." Remark of a minister.

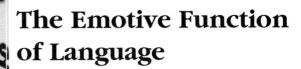

C H A P T E R 3

The Emotive Function of Language

The View: Many words have both cognitive meanings and emotional connotations. The emotional connotations can influence what we believe and do. By replacing emotionally charged words with emotionally neutral words, we can determine whether the emotional connotations are influencing our actions and beliefs.

Do our word choices make any difference? Does it make any difference whether I call a flower a rare bloom or a weed? If so, why does it make a difference?

Language is not always used to inform or direct. Sometimes it is used to express emotions. You do not do justice to an Emily Dickenson poem if you know what all the words mean and ignore their emotional impact. Nor is understanding the meaning of individual words always necessary for a poem to have an emotional impact. Lewis Carroll's "Jabberwocky" rouses feelings of excitement, even though it is liberally sprinkled with meaningless words. But it is not only in poetry that words have emotive meanings.

Discussions of the meanings of words are usually stated in terms of distinction between a word's **denotation** and its **connotation**. The denotation of a term consists of all those objects to which a term applies. For example, my cat Turbo and your cat Felix are included in the denotation of the term 'cat'. The connotation of a term consists of those properties an object has by virtue of which it is included in the denotation. If you look up 'cat' in a dictionary, you might find a list of properties, including its shape, its eating habits (it's a carnivore), its approximate size, and so forth. There might be more properties that all cats have in common. You or I might appeal to more or fewer properties in describing a cat. Let us call the connotation the **cognitive meaning** of a word.

Words also have **emotional connotations**. The emotional connotation of a word is the tendency of a word to cause a favorable or unfavorable emotional response. Consider the words 'democracy' and 'republic'. A democracy is a form of government in which the citizens rule, either directly or through representatives. A republic is a government controlled by representatives elected by the citizens. Both terms have favorable emotional connotations. The former communist East Germany—which was not a western-style democracy—was known as the German Democratic Republic.

Many words have emotive connotations. Assume John joined the army and was sent off to war. In the heat of a battle, he saved the lives of many members of his platoon by killing three enemy soldiers. Consider the following three descriptions of John, and notice the differences in the emotional connotations of the descriptive words. (1) John is a killer (negative). (2) John is a soldier (neutral). (3) John is a military hero (positive). Does it make a difference how we describe John? Military heroes are always soldiers. They are usually soldiers who have either given their lives for their fellow soldiers or have been exceptional on the field of battle; that is, they have successfully killed the enemy. So, in terms of its cognitive meaning, being a military hero usually implies being a soldier who has killed some enemy soldiers. But there is a significant difference regarding the emotional impact of the words 'killer', 'soldier', and 'military hero'. You might feel honored to have a hero accept an invitation to dinner. You probably would not invite a killer.

Or consider the following passage from the novel *Ishmael: An Adventure of the Mind and Spirit*. Ishmael and the narrator are discussing the words 'Takers' and 'Leavers':

"... if I call one group Takers and the other group Leavers, will that sound like I'm setting one to be good guys and the other to be bad guys?"

"No. They sound pretty neutral to me."

"Good. So henceforth I'm going to call the people of your culture Takers and the people of all other cultures Leavers."

I hmm'd a bit. "I have a problem with that."

"Speak."

"I don't see how you can lump everyone else in the world into one category like that."

"This is the way it's done in your culture, except that you use a pair of heavily loaded terms instead of these relatively neutral words. You call yourselves *civilized* and all the rest *primitive*."[1]

We all acknowledge that words have different emotional connotations. We don't like to talk about death, so we use euphemisms: "Joan passed away." "Hamlet shuffled off this mortal coil." Often, longer or less common words have a more favorable

In combing through the minutes of editorial meetings where editors and publishers gather to consider the week's offering of projects, one sees the same phrases repeated over and over. Encoded within them are what I call editorial rejection euphemisms: *not right for our list* (get it out of here), *pacing problems* (boring), *exhaustive* (academic/boring), *somewhat heavy-handed* (preachy), *not without charm* (too precious), *nicely written but ultimately unsatisfying* (plotless), *underdeveloped characters* (totally stock), *nice sense of place* (is this about anything?), *not enough tension* (mind-numbingly slow), *feels familiar* (yet another road-trip/coming-of-age/ugly-duckling/dysfunctional-family novel), *entertaining* (overwritten), *crowded marketplace* (not another!), and my personal favorite, *too special* (which of course means it won't sell).

—Betty Lerner, *The Forest for the Trees: An Editor's Advice to Writers* (New York: Riverhead Books, 2000), p. 174.

---

[1] Daniel Quinn, *Ishmael: An Adventure of the Mind and Spirit* (New York: Bantam/Turner Books, 1992), pp. 38–39. Notice that the author distinguishes mention from use by means of *italics*.

"To you they're networking. To me they're not working."

Source: Used with permission of Mike Shapiro.

emotional connotation. It is better to perspire than to sweat. It is better to be a glamour technician than a beautician, and it's better to be a beautician than a hair dresser. It is better to be a gourmand than a glutton. Some foreign words have more favorable connotations than their English counterparts. It is better for an object to have a certain *je ne sais quoi* than for it to have a certain indescribable something. But not all foreign words are more favorable than their ordinary English synonyms. For example, is it better if my computer is *kaput* than if it is broken?

We should pay attention to the emotional connotations of words, since the emotional connotations of words reflect a person's biases. As we shall see in Part III, it is important to determine what a person's biases are when evaluating observation statements and testimony. Assume a news broadcaster reports on "the President's new tax-cut scheme." The word 'scheme' has negative connotations. It suggests that the broadcaster either does not look favorably on the President's plan or the broadcaster has a negative bias regarding the President. A more neutral allusion would be to "the President's tax-cut proposal."

We also should pay attention to the emotional connotations of words when examining arguments. As we will see in Part II, arguments provide reasons for claiming that a statement is true. Only the cognitive meanings of words are relevant to truth. But emotional appeals can influence what you believe or do. Have you ever contributed to a charity based on an appeal to "poor starving children"? Have you ever contributed to a political candidate because she was going to "do the right thing" for the country? For any emotionally charged terms, there are other terms that are emotionally neutral or negative. Would the charity's appeal have the same impact if it had referred to "malnourished young people"? Would the candidate's appeal have the same impact if she replaced "do the right thing" with ten points from her political platform? When you find emotionally charged words in an argument, consider replacing them with neutral terms. This will help you determine whether you are influenced by the reasons given or the emotional connotations of the words used.[2]

> ### Ceremonial Language, Commissives, and Performatives
>
> There are other things we do with words. We use them in ceremonies. These range from greetings, such as "Hi! How are you?"—which is not a request for information—to wedding vows and oaths of office. In the latter two cases we commit ourselves to various actions. The words are used **commissively**. Sometimes words bring things into being. These are what J. L. Austin called **performative utterances**. We bring promises into existence by saying, "I promise that...." Marriages are brought into existence when the person presiding at a wedding says, "I now pronounce you husband and wife."

Exercises

I. Each of the following words has a favorable emotional connotation. Give another word which has approximately the same cognitive meaning but an emotively neutral or a negative connotation. For example, Given the word 'abortion', you might write, "killing unborn babies." (If you're puzzled, check a dictionary or a thesaurus.)

1. oeuvre
2. provoke
3. peruse
4. domestic engineer
5. encore performance (of a radio or television program)
6. sweltering
7. aficionado
8. embezzler
9. prevaricator
10. philanderer
11. pontificate
12. *Weltanschauung*
13. expectorate
14. choreography
15. calligraphy
16. cartography
17. narcissism

---

[2]In Chapter 29 we examine some roles of emotional appeals in arguments.

18. expletive

19. nom de plume

20. intellectual milieu

II. Each of the following words has a negative emotional connotation. Give another word which has approximately the same cognitive meaning but a more positive connotation. For example, given 'procrastinate', you might write, "to be time-management challenged." (If you're puzzled, check a dictionary or a thesaurus.)

1. jalopy

2. revenge

3. jungle

4. propaganda minister

5. retarded

6. drunk

7. fat

8. barf

9. monologue

10. road

11. oaf

12. lollygag

13. nag

14. tabloid

15. stubborn

16. preacher

17. a joker

18. a quack

19. lecture

20. a hobo

III. The emotive terms used often show the speaker's or writer's bias. For each of the following, read the passage to determine whether the writer is favorably or disfavorably disposed toward the person or topic discussed.

1. "It's true that we have problems with alcohol abuse, misuse and bingeing on campus, but perhaps our restrictive laws are partly to blame." (Elizabeth M. Whelan, "To Your Health, or . . . Maybe Not," *Wall Street Journal,* April 5, 2002, http://www.acsh.org/press/editorials/alcohol040502.html)

2. Speaking of a recent bill to limit automobile emissions in California: "This is an attempt to restrict Californians' freedom of choice," said Marlo Lewis, senior fellow at the Competitive Enterprise Institute. (http://www.cei.org/gencon/003,03008.cfm)

3. "... the Center for Food Safety opposes irradiation, which would kill dangerous bacteria and rot-encouraging organisms in your food." (Dennis Avery, "Anti-Biotech Group Scares *WSJ*," http://www.hudson.org/index.cfm?fuseaction=publication_details&id=1650)

4. Two big trends distinguished CEO pay in 2001: first, a dangerous and ongoing disconnect between performance and pay, and second, stark double standards on retirement security and job security for CEOs compared with workers. (http://www.aflcio.org/paywatch/index.htm)

5. "The federal government, I believe, has become too big, too complex, too bloated, too bureaucratic." (Elizabeth Dole, Speech to the American Farm Bureau Federation, quoted at http://www.fb.com/annual/amnews/nr/nr0201.html)

6. "Instead of relegating teachers to the role of production workers—with no say in organizing their schools for excellence—we need to enlist teachers as full partners, indeed, as co-managers of their schools." (Bob Chase, "The New Unionism—A Course for School Quality," http://www.nea.org/newunion/)

7. You have just taken one small step into trying to make sure that our planet does not go completely crazy with modern science and technology. (http://communities.msn.com/PeopleunitedagainstGeneticallyModifiedFoods)

8. Several of the Senate's most liberal members, including Hillary Clinton, Jim Jeffords, and Joe Lieberman are pushing for a bill that would allow federal bureaucrats to determine how land will be developed and used in local communities. This bold attack on our federalist society is titled the "Community Character Act" (S. 975). (American Policy Center, "S. 975: Eco-tyranny from Washington," http://www.americanpolicy.org/newswire/main.htm)

9. ... Global Climate Coalition is not advertising a product. Its propaganda budget serves solely to influence the news media and government policymakers on a single issue and comes on top of the marketing, lobbying, and campaign contributions that industry already spends in the regular course of doing business. (Sheldon Rampton and John Stauber, *Trust Us, We're Experts!: How Industry Manipulates Science and Gambles with Your Future* [New York: Jeremy P. Tarcher, 2001], p. 271)

10. The Valley may be a hunter's stew of companies—semiconductors, PCs, peripherals, software, and Internet commerce—but its one unifying ingredient is Microsoft, seven hundred miles due north. Microsoft is like oxygen. It's all around. If you're in business in the Valley, you can't inhale without getting a whiff. Many entrepreneurs hope that "innovative" Microsoft will knock on the door one day and buy them out for a fortune. That's what happened in 1997 to WebTV; its three cofounders walked away with tens of millions of dollars apiece. (David A. Kaplan, *The Silicon Boys and Their Valley of Dreams* [New York: William Morrow, 1999], p. 257)

CHAPTER 4

Descriptive Passages

The View: The descriptive function of language tells you who, what, when, where, or how something is or was. It is the most widely used function of language. Descriptive passages are usually deemed accurate or inaccurate to a certain degree. They are also complete or incomplete to a certain degree. The inferences we make based on a description are deemed reasonable or unreasonable depending upon the completeness of the information in conjunction with any background information you might have.

When we put sentences together, what are the characteristics of the resulting passages? What kinds of questions do they answer?

In the last three chapters we examined the fundamental elements of language: words and sentences. Words and sentences are like the cells and tissues of an organism. To understand the organism, you need to understand what happens at the level of cells and tissues. Problems sometimes arise at the level of cells and tissues. More interesting problems, however, often arise at the level of organs and organ systems. In this and the next several chapters, we examine some of these linguistic "organs": descriptions, explanations, and arguments. Understanding how these organs work together will allow us to examine the health of linguistic "organisms" such as essays and speeches.

The most common use of language is descriptive. The **descriptive function** of language is to tell you who, what, when, where, or how something is or was.[1] All statements are descriptive. All true statements describe the world. False statements claim to describe the world but fail to do so. Many sentences in fictitious works describe a world created in the author's imagination. For example, the following passage from *The Bridges of Madison County* describes one character and the thoughts of another:

> He was lithe; that was the word she had thought of while watching him. At fifty-two his body was all lean muscle, muscle that moved with the kind of inten-

---

[1] As we shall see below, the question "How?" is also used in explanations.

sity and power that comes only to men who work hard and take care of them-selves. He told her he had been a combat photographer in the Pacific, and Francesca could imagine him coming up smoke-drenched beaches with the marines, cameras banging against him, one to his eye, the shutter almost on fire with the speed of his picture taking.[2]

The passage tells you *what* the characteristics of the character are. He is limber (*what*). He is muscular (*what*). He is fifty-two years old (*what*). At some earlier time (*when*), he had been a photographer (*what*) in the Pacific (*where*). Francesca imag-ines *what* his characteristics and actions must have been like when he stormed the beaches.

Language is used descriptively in news reports, in the narrative portions of novels, stories, and poems, and in the purely informative portions of your textbooks. What you are now reading is descriptive. I am telling you *what* we mean by 'descrip-tive language'. I am telling you *how* to recognize descriptive uses of language. Ask yourself whether the passage you are examining answers the questions Who? What? When? Where? or sometimes How? If it does, language is being used descriptively.

Most textbook history consists of descriptive language. If you are studying American history, you might read the following account of the colonial reaction to the Stamp Act:

The stamps themselves were printed in England and shipped to stamp mas-ters (all Americans) in the colonies well in advance of November 1, 1765, the date the law was to go into effect. When the stamps reached New York harbor, all vessels in the port lowered their colors in protest. At Portsmouth, New Hamp-shire, "patriots" ceremoniously buried a copy of the law. Some of the stamps were quickly snatched up by mobs and put to the torch amid rejoicing. Others were locked up in secret by British officials or held on shipboard. For a time after November 1, no business requiring stamped paper was transacted; then, gradually, people began to defy the law by issuing and accepting unstamped doc-uments. Threatened by mob action should they resist, British officials stood by helplessly. The law was a dead letter.[3]

This tells you *where* the stamps were printed, *when* the stamps were shipped to the colonies, and *when* the Stamp Act went into effect. It tells you *how* some of the colonists reacted to the Stamp Act, that is, *what* their reactions were. It tells you *how* the British officials responded to the colonial resistance (*what* they did). It tells you *what* the effect of these reactions to the Stamp Act was: "The law was a dead letter."

---

[2]Robert James Waller, *The Bridges of Madison County* (New York: Warner Books, 1992), p. 26.
[3]John A. Garraty, *The American Nation: A History of the United States to 1877*, 2nd ed. (New York: Harper & Row, 1971), p. 117.

Exercises

I. In each of the following passages, indicate *who* or *what* is being discussed, *what* is said about the object of the discussion, *when* it happened, *where* it is set, and *how* things were. Sometimes you will not be able to note all of these characteristics.

1. The year is 1865. In one of the dismal taverns of a Far Rockies mining area known as Angel's Camp, a group of prospectors, miners, fortune hunters, and scalawags are gathered to while away a wintry afternoon. A man by the name of Ben Coon drawls his way through story after story—no one pays much attention—Ben is notorious for his inexhaustible stock of tales and his dreary, matter-of-fact way of telling them. He welcomes my ear, especially when there is the chance of a free drink, too. (Mark Twain, "The Celebrated Jumping Frog of Calaveras County")

2. And now it was that, being on some occasion made ashamed of my ignorance in figures, which I had twice failed in learning when at school, I took Cocker's book of *Arithmetick,* and went through the whole by myself with great ease. I also read Seller's and Shermy's books of *Navigation,* and became acquainted with the little geometry they contain; but never proceeded far in that science. And I read about this time Locke *On Human Understanding,* and *The Art of Thinking,* by Messrs. du Port Royal. (Benjamin Franklin, *The Autobiography of Benjamin Franklin*)

3. As Siddhartha left the grove in which the Buddha, the Perfect One, remained, in which Govinda remained, he felt that he had left his former life behind him in the grove. As he slowly went on his way, his head was full of this thought. He reflected deeply, until this feeling completely overwhelmed him and he reached a point where he recognized causes, for to recognize causes, it seemed to him, is to think, and through thought alone feelings become knowledge and are not lost, but become real and begin to mature. (Hermann Hesse, *Siddhartha,* translated by Hilda Rosner [New York: Bantam Books, 1951], p. 37)

4. Young Goodman Brown came forth at sunset into the street at Salem village; but put his head back, after crossing the threshold, to exchange a parting kiss with his young wife. And Faith, as the wife was aptly named, thrust her own pretty head into the street, letting the wind play with the pink ribbons of her cap while she called to Goodman Brown. (Nathanial Hawthorne, "Young Goodman Brown")

5. On the first Monday of the month of April, 1625, the town of Meung, in which the author of the *Romance of the Rose* was born, appeared to be in as perfect a state of revolution as if the Huguenots had just made a second Rochelle of it. Many citizens, seeing the women flying toward High Street, and hearing the children crying on the doorsteps, hastened to don their cuirasses, and supporting their somewhat uncertain courage with a musket or a partisan, directed their steps toward the hostelry of the Frank-Meunier, before which was gathered a

compact, vociferous, and curious group, increasing every minute. (Alexandre Dumas, *The Three Musketeers*, translated by W. Robson, Chapter 1)

6. The English poems [of John Milton], though they make no promise of *Paradise Lost,* have this evidence of genius, that they have a cast original and unborrowed. But their peculiarity is not excellence: if they differ from verses of others, they differ for the worse, for they are too often distinguished by repulsive harshness; the combinations of words are new, but they are not pleasing; the rhymes and epithets seem to be laboriously sought and violently applied. (Samuel Johnson, *Lives of the Poets*)

7. Lady Lynn was a large and stout personage of about forty; very erect, very haughty-looking, richly dressed in a satin robe of changeful sheen: her dark hair shown glossily under the shade of an azure plume, and within the circlet of a band of gems.

   Mrs. Colonel Dent was less showy; but, I thought, more lady-like. She had a slight figure, a pale, gentle face, and fair hair. Her black satin dress, her scarf of rich foreign lave, and her pearl ornaments, pleased me better than the rainbow radiance of the tilted dame. (Charlotte Brontë, *Jane Eyre*, Chapter 17)

8. When he was nearly thirteen, my brother Jem got his arm badly broken at the elbow. When it healed, and Jem's fears of never being able to play football were assuaged, he was seldom self-conscious of his injury. His left arm was somewhat shorter than his right; when he stood or walked, the back of his hand was at right angles to his body, his thumb parallel to his thigh. He couldn't have cared less, so long as he could pass and punt. (Harper Lee, *To Kill a Mockingbird* [New York: Popular Library, 1960], p. 7)

9. By eight o'clock the light was fading. The loud speakers in the tower of the Stoke Poges Club House began, in more than human tenor, to announce the closing of the [obstacle golf] courses. Lenina and Henry abandoned their game and walked back towards the Club. From the grounds of the Internal and External Secretion Trust came the lowing of those thousands of cattle which provided, with their hormones and their milk, the raw materials for the great factory at Farnham Royal. (Aldous Huxley, *Brave New World* [New York: Harper & Row, Perennial Classics, 1946], p. 48)

10. On an exceptionally hot evening early in July a young man came out of the garret in which he lodged and walked slowly, as though in hesitation, towards a bridge.

   He had successfully avoided meeting his landlady on the staircase. His garret was under the roof of a high, five-storied house and was more like a cupboard than a room. The landlady, who provided him with garret, dinners, and attendance, lived on the floor below, and every time he went out he was obliged to pass her kitchen, the door of which invariably stood open. And each time he passed, the young man had a sick, frightening feeling, which made him scowl and feel ashamed. He was hopelessly in debt to his landlady, and was afraid of meeting her. (Fydor Dostoevski, *Crime and Punishment*, translated by Constance Garett, Part I)

Accuracy

If you are looking at descriptions in works of fiction, questions of truth are secondary. If you are taking an English quiz on *1984,* you might need to know whether Orwell described Winston Smith as a thirty-nine-year-old,[4] but that description is true only within the context of *1984.* If you glance at Goethe's *Faust,* you might be surprised that Faust is old early in Part I, while he is young later in the same part. If you read the play, your puzzle will be resolved. But fictitious claims have little to do with the "real world."

If you are dealing with descriptions of the real world, you usually want the descriptions to be **accurate**. A description is accurate when it corresponds to the way the world is. Accuracy is to a descriptive passage what truth is to a statement with this difference: A statement is either true or false. A statement cannot be partially true.[5] Descriptions can vary in degrees of accuracy. You might have noticed that *one* thing your teachers take into account on an essay exam is the accuracy of your claims. While it is always a good idea to be as accurate as possible, there are times when accuracy is of little importance. Consider the following description of our family cat: "Our cat's name is Turbo. Turbo is a brown, short-haired tabby. She weighs about seven pounds. She's six years old and very bashful. She leaves our house only when she has to visit the vet."

If you walked into my house and saw Turbo, you'd recognize her. But the description is not completely accurate. Turbo is closer to *sixteen* than she is to six. Does that make any difference? Probably not. But there are cases in which an accurate description is important. In which of these would *you* suggest it is important? Why?

1. You heard that a prisoner escaped from the state penitentiary and should be considered armed and dangerous. The person was described as a Caucasian male, five feet, ten inches tall, about 165 pounds, with shoulder-length brown hair and an orange, lightning-shaped tattoo on his left cheek. Your doorbell rings. You look out the window, and the man at the door fits the description perfectly *except* he's only about five foot two. Should you answer the door?

2. You dined at Dave's last week. He prepared a sumptuous dish, a dish unlike any you had ever tasted. After your considerable begging, he wrote down the recipe for you—including his secret ingredients. Sadly, Dave was killed in an auto accident three days ago. As a way of dealing with your grief, you plan to prepare Dave's dish. Does the accuracy of the recipe make any difference? Are there circumstances in which the accuracy of the recipe would be more or less important?

3. Scientists at the Oak Ridge National Laboratories recently claimed to have produced a fusion reaction in a table-top device. There were some similarities to the "cold fusion" claims made by Stanley Pons and Martin Fleischmann in 1989.

---

[4]He did. See George Orwell, *1984* (New York: Signet Books, 1949), p. 5.
[5]We discuss this in Chapter 21.

The repeatable experiment is one of the pillars of modern science. Since Pons's and Fleischmann's results could not be duplicated by other scientists, their claims regarding "cold fusion" were rejected. If the scientists at Oak Ridge *have* produced a fusion reaction, how important is it that they provide an accurate description of their experimental procedures?

4. You have been feeling ill for the last few days, so you visit your local physician. Your physician asks you when you became ill and what your symptoms are. What you tell your physician will help her decide what medications to prescribe and whether various tests should be given. Is giving an accurate account of the history of your disease important?

5. You are out on a date for the first time. Neither of you knows the other very well, so you tell your date a bit about yourself. How important is it that your description of yourself be accurate? What circumstances, if any, would influence the importance you ascribe to the accuracy of the description you give of yourself?

6. You are in the Federal Witness Protection program. After testifying in a highly publicized trial in Boston, you have been resettled in Anchorage, Alaska. You have a new name. You have a new "history." You have dyed your hair and had plastic surgery. Your contact lenses have been replaced by glasses. You bear little resemblance to the person who helped send a major criminal "up the river." How important is it that any descriptions you provide of your past be accurate relative to your *new* history?

7. On September 11, 2001, airliners crashed into the Twin Towers of the World Trade Center in New York City and into the Pentagon. Another airliner crashed into a Pennsylvania field. Each had been hijacked by terrorists. Early in the day there were reports that the President had been assassinated, that there were bombs in the White House, and that car bombs were located outside the Department of the Treasury, reports that were later retracted. By evening, some commentators were suggesting that the number of dead would exceed the number killed in the Battle of Shiloh (over 20,000). The final death toll was under 5,000. Should greater care have been taken to assure accuracy of news reporting on September 11, 2001?

8. Recently a severe thunderstorm hit a town in the upper Midwest. Over two inches of rain fell in less than an hour. While the storm was severe, it was isolated. Afterwards, nearby towns reported little or no rain. As the storm approached, the local radio station reported that tornado clouds had been sighted. One tornado reportedly destroyed a barn several miles outside of town. The "victim" was later interviewed and said, "My barn's fine. We had clear skies all day." Should the radio station be faulted for its **inaccurate** report?

9. Sven applied for a job as a janitor with your firm. You requested a complete employment history. He's been employed as a janitor by several firms over the past twenty years. His employment record during that time is glowing, as the references from his previous two employers attest. There was a five-year period before that when he had been employed part-time as a janitor at the state prison. Would his application be inaccurate if he failed to mention that he had

been an inmate at the time? Would it make any difference? Would it make a difference if Sven had been chaplain at the prison—not an inmate—but he *said* he had been a janitor?

10. You've been dating the same person for some time now. Words such as 'marriage' have started slipping into your conversations. How important is it that you accurately describe your expectations regarding your career and family life before you marry?

Completeness

Sometimes descriptions are accurate, as far as they go, but they provide relatively little information, or are **incomplete**. If you want more information, you want the description to approach **completeness**.

Completeness, like accuracy, is a matter of degree. It seldom, if ever, happens that a description of an object is absolutely complete. A biologist might devote a lifetime to examining and describing the sex life of the bumble bee and die believing that there was much more to learn. Typically, what will count as sufficiently complete will depend upon your goals or purposes.

Assume you are trying to decide what classes to take next semester. You read the description of various courses in the college catalog. Course descriptions in the college catalog are "officially accurate," even though individual professors often depart from the descriptions. Are the descriptions in the catalog complete enough for you to decide which courses to take? Probably not. But they are probably complete enough to help you decide which courses *not* to take. If you have had no math since elementary algebra in high school, the description of MATH 435 Introduction to Topology might convince you to look for a different course. (It is generally wise not to take a course whose catalog description you can't understand.) Once you have limited the field, you might need more information before you decide which courses to take. You might want to examine syllabi. You might want to know something about various professors' teaching styles. At some point you will have gathered enough information—the description you have developed of the actual course taught by a particular professor will be sufficiently complete and (you hope) fairly accurate—for you to choose a class. Of course, additional information could cause you not to act on your decision. Aren't "course closed" signs at registration frustrating?

Concerns with completeness also come up regarding information you read or hear. Assume Peter Jennings reports on the *ABC Evening News*, "There was rioting in Jerusalem today." Assume he shows you film clips of the rioting. You have no reason to doubt his claim. Nonetheless, it might prove misleading. You might take his report to mean that there were riots throughout Jerusalem, while the riots were confined to a very small part of the city. You might take the news story to mean that the riots continued throughout the day, even if they were short-lived. All the claims made in the news story are true. The news story was accurate but not complete. If you **inferred** that the rioting was general and continued throughout the day, while it was very localized and short-lived, you are "reading more" into the news story than was presented. An **inference** is a psychological state in which you draw a conclusion on the basis of a certain body of information. If you read more into the situation than had been presented in the news story, would your inference be **reasonable**? Perhaps. Perhaps not. The conclusion that rioting was widespread is **consistent** with the information presented; that is, it is possible that both the information given and your conclusion are true. But the information is also consistent with the possibility that the riots were localized

> We often make erroneous inferences on the basis of the information presented. On October 19, 1998, the lead story on *Good Morning America* concerned flooding in Texas. Pictures were shown of a flood-plagued San Antonio. Lisa McCree interviewed the mayor of San Antonio. Part of the exchange was along the following lines:
>
> **McCree:** "It looks like most of the city is under water."
>
> **Mayor:** "No. Flooding is confined to only a very small part of the city."

and short-lived. Whether the conclusion is reasonable or **unreasonable** depends in part on other available information. For example, if you have reason to believe that the news media tend to sensationalize events, then it would *not* be reasonable for you to conclude that there was widespread rioting in Jerusalem all day.

One more point needs to be mentioned. All the descriptions we have considered to this point might be called *direct*. They are based on characteristics that a thing or action has. There are also indirect descriptions. These are based on **analogies**. Analogies are based on similarities between the thing or event described and something else. If you read in a story that the desert sizzled like bacon in a pan, you have a nice **simile**. It presents an understandable picture, although you

> Why is it unreasonable to claim that *all* teaching is based on analogies?

might need to ask questions about precisely, *how*, the desert and the bacon are similar. Nor are analogies used only for literary effect. The science teacher who suggests that an atom is like a tiny solar system provides an initial understanding of the structure of the atom. Further, understanding of the structure of the atom comes, in part, by exploring the limits of the analogy, that is, the ways in which it is like and is not like a tiny solar system. Much teaching is done by showing similarities between something well-known and some new object or concept. Advancing beyond that point, you explore the limits of the analogy, the differences between the two things.

Exercises

II. Questions of accuracy or completeness arise regarding each of the following. Where might you question the accuracy of the claims? Given the information available, when might you claim it is sufficiently complete for your purposes? When might you request additional information?

1. The French and Indian War involved the French and Native Americans.

2. Van Gogh painted pictures of sunflowers.

3. Abe Lincoln was so honest that when he gave a customer the wrong amount of change, he walked ten miles through the snow to return the additional three cents to the customer.

4. The White House is at 1600 Pennsylvania Avenue in Washington, D.C. It's called "the White House" because it was designed by and originally owned by George Henry White.

5. On November 22, 1963, John F. Kennedy, the youngest person ever elected President of the United States, died in Dallas, Texas.

6. You're thinking of buying a computer. You talk to your friend Raul, who says, with a twinkle in his eye, "You should buy a Cray. It is extremely fast and reliable. You would have no trouble with the size of its memory or its storage capacity." Should you ask anything else?

7. You received an offer in the mail from a credit card company. It says, "You have been preapproved for our credit card. There is no yearly fee for the first year, and you may transfer your outstanding accounts from other cards for a rate as low as 4.8% for the first six months." Is that a good deal or what?

8. The Exacto Telephone Company has contacted you, suggesting that you switch your long-distance service to them. "There is no monthly service charge. We charge nothing for switching you to our service, and our rates are less than half those of AT&T." Should you switch?

9. You are thinking about buying a used car. Looking through the newspaper, you find the following ad:

   For sale: 1987 Volvo 240DL—4 door, 4 cyl., auto., 30 mpg., new brakes all around.

   Where might you raise questions of accuracy? For what is the information sufficiently complete? Give at least one additional fact you might need before deciding to buy the car.

10. Several years ago, the news media claimed that there was a race riot at a small midwestern college. Several African-American students at the predominantly white school had asked the faculty senate to permit them to forgo final exams. The school responded by canceling final exams for everyone. That was the extent of the "riot." Was the news report either inaccurate or incomplete?

Explanations

The View: Explanations answer the questions Why? and How? You know that an event or a phenomenon has occurred, and you seek information to tell you why it occurred. You may also explain *how to* do something or *how something happened*. Explanations can be based on facts about nature or facts about people who act.

Why do events happen? How do things work? What do we explain, and how do we explain it?

The six journalistic questions are Who? What? When? Where? Why? and How? The first four questions concern descriptions. The questions Why? and sometimes How? concern the explanations. Some explanations tell you why something is as it is. Other explanations tell you how to do something or how something happened. Explanations do *not* tell you how something is: That is another way to ask *what* it is.

Explanations come in many forms. You can explain why an event occurs on the basis of natural laws. Why is the water on the stove boiling? The water is boiling because all water heated to 212°F boils (law), and the water on the stove is water heated to 212°F. Or you can explain it by appealing to the objectives (purposes) that people have in doing something. "I'm planning to make spaghetti for supper. I set a pan of water on the stove to boil so I could cook the spaghetti." Either of these would be good explanations. The statement, "All pure water at a pressure of 29.92 inches of mercury when heated to 212°F boils" correctly describes the world. People commonly boil water to cook spaghetti, so you would find my purposive explanation plausible.

Not all explanations are plausible. Assume I explained why the water is boiling as follows. "Invisible gremlins are bathing in the water. Whenever invisible gremlins bathe, the water in which they bathe boils." What's wrong with the explanation? We have no reason to believe that there are gremlins. When we explain, we do so on the basis of what we reasonably believe. If there are no gremlins, we cannot appeal to them in an explanation.

When we ask for an explanation, we are often asking for the **cause** of something we already know exists. I was the cause that started a process that led to the water

33

boiling on the stove. The cause of my action might have been a desire to eat spaghetti for supper together with the recognition that we must boil water to cook spaghetti. Or the cause of the water's boiling depends on various properties of water, heat transfer, and so on. In explaining why something is as it is, you might appeal to any number of different causes or possible causes.

> What counts as a reasonable explanation at one time might not count as a reasonable explanation at another. Four hundred years ago, witchcraft was a commonly accepted explanation of hysteria. A hundred years ago, Freud explained hysteria in terms of a conflict between the id, the ego, and the superego in conjunction with repressed memories. Today, most psychologists explain hysteria in terms of electrochemical imbalances in the brain.

Nonetheless, some explanations are better than others. We discuss some issues relevant to the evaluation of an explanation in Chapter 27.

Sometimes we explain something unfamiliar by comparing it with something familiar. When we do this, we construct an analogy. For example, Anne Frank explains in her diary why one of the cats was named Bosche:

> A bottle of preserved sole has gone bad; gala dinner for Mouschi and Boche [the cats]. You haven't met Boche yet, although she was here before we went into hiding. She is the warehouse cat and the office cat and keeps down the rats in the storerooms. Her odd political name requires an explanation. For some time the firm had two cats; one for the warehouse and one for the attic. Now it occasionally happened that the two cats met; and the result was always a terrible fight. The aggressor was always the warehouse cat; yet it was always the attic cat who managed to win—just like among nations. So the storehouse cat was named the German or "Bosche" and the attic cat the English or "Tommy." Tommy was got rid of later; we are all entertained by Bosche when we go downstairs.[1]

Everything before and including "Her odd political name requires an explanation," as well as the last sentence, are descriptive. The explanation of why the cats were named Bosche and Tommy rests on their similarities to the behavior of Germany and England.

Regardless how you explain an event, you start at the same point. You know that something has happened or is happening. A statement describes that event. What you're seeking is an answer to the question "Why did that event occur?" or "How did it occur?" You answer that question in terms of general properties of the world or characteristics of the person or thing that acts. Taken individually, each element of an explanation is descriptive.

> There are technical terms for the parts of an explanation. The event or **phenomenon** to be explained is called the **explanandum**. That which does the explaining—that which answers the question "Why?" the phenomenon is as it is—is called the **explanans**. So, in the explanation, "Stacy went across the street [Why?] so he could buy groceries," "Stacy went across the street" is the explanandum, and "so he could buy groceries" is the explanans.

---

[1] *Anne Frank: The Diary of a Young Girl,* translated by B. M. Mooyaart-Doubleday (New York: Pocket Books, 1952), p. 62.

Source: Seth Casana, Academia Nuts. *Used with permission of the author.*

As a statement, it is either true or false. It is only when a set of such sentences is taken together that you have an explanation. The event or phenomenon to be explained is known or believed or assumed at the outset of your inquiry. What you seek is the answer to the question why or how the phenomenon occurred. As we shall see, the place you begin—what you take as initially known—is one of the elements used in distinguishing an explanation from an argument. But before we turn to arguments, it might be useful to examine a few more examples of explanations.

Explanations can be quite brief or extremely detailed. Sometimes there are perfectly adequate explanations, but not the kind of explanation that is wanted. When a Sunday School teacher asked her class, "Why was Jesus born in Bethlehem?" one of her students answered, "That's where his mother was." This is an adequate explanation. Jesus *could not* have been born in Bethlehem had his mother been anywhere else at the time! Of course, the teacher probably had an entirely different kind of explanation in mind, presumably a religious explanation. The student provided a naturalistic explanation.

Exercises

I. In each of the following, ⟨circle⟩ the description of the event or phenomenon that is explained (the explanandum). **Underline** the sentences that do the explaining (the explanans).

1. My car wouldn't start this morning. The battery was dead.

2. Jessica received an "A" in critical thinking because she worked on the material every day and slowly mastered it.

3. Why don't your juries hang murderers? Because they're afraid the man's friends will shoot them in the back, in the dark—and it's just what they would do. (Mark Twain, *The Adventures of Huckleberry Finn*, Chapter 22)

4. Everyone working in radio believed it would be too tough to do a regular show on television. On TV, we heard, actors had to work without scripts. That meant, as the great comedy writer John P. Medbury pointed out, "You certainly couldn't do a show every week. There just isn't enough time to write, rehearse, memorize, and broadcast." (George Burns, *Gracie: A Love Story* [New York: G. P. Putnam's Sons, 1988], p. 240)

5. "How did you manage to get hold of all these things?"

"It's all Inner Party stuff. There's nothing those swine don't have, nothing. But of course waiters and servants and people pinch things, and—look, I've got a little packet of tea as well." (George Orwell, *1984* [New York: Signet Classics, 1949], p. 117)

6. If you want to put the bicycle together, all you will need is an adjustable wrench and a screwdriver. Put the front wheel into the proper place and tighten the bolts on either side. Put the back wheel in its place, place the chain on the sprocket, and tighten the bolts on the wheel. Place the handle bar onto its place, and tighten it with your wrench. Bolt the kick stand to the frame. Finally, attach the shifting levers and the brake handles to the handle bar and tighten them with a screwdriver. Now all you need to do is ride off into the sunset.

7. "Why do you constantly accuse me of being the warden's friend?" Highbourne said, petulant.

"Why? Because your cheeks are shaven. You coat's brushed, your linen's clean. Someone's feeding you well. Who would do all those favors when you claim you're too poor to offer bribes? Everyone knows you're in the warden's quarters nearly every day. Does that answer you, Mason? If so, please take yourself out of my sight." (John Jakes, *On Secret Service* [New York: Dutton, 2000], p. 172)

8. Thus much for my general intention in favour of matrimony; it remains to be told why my views were directed to Longbourn instead of my own neighbourhood, where I assure you there are many amiable young women. But the fact is, that being, as I am, to inherit this estate after the death of your honoured father (who, however, may live many years longer), I could not satisfy myself without resolving to chuse a wife from among his daughters, that the loss to them might be as little as possible, when the melancholy event takes place—which, however, as I have already said, may not be for several years. This has been my motive, my fair cousin, and I flatter myself it will not sink me in your esteem. (Jane Austen, *Pride and Prejudice*)

9. The release of Volkswagen's New Beetle has unquestionably ushered in a new wave of Beetlemania. The look is unmistakeable in its nostalgic appeal. Yet, well beyond its retro inspiration, this car's styling is an innovative mix of past, present, and future, melding its classic shape with a unique new-millennium influence, along with the current realities of 5-mph bumpers and side airbags. Yet, most significant of all, the New Beetle is much more than just a clever design. This VW delivers throughout. It's genuinely fun to drive. It has segment-leading safety features, as well as a surprisingly roomy interior for its class size. Plus, with a base price of under $16,000 that includes a long list of standards more typical of higher-cost models, it's an outstanding value. For all these reasons and more,

we're proud to name the Volkswagen New Beetle as *Motor Trend*'s '99 Import Car of the Year. (Editors of *Motor Trend*, "*Motor Trend* '99 Import Car of the Year Volkswagen New Beetle," *Motor Trend* [February 1999], p. 57)

10. "I was just wondering," said the Savage, ". . . Why don't you make everybody an Alpha Double Plus while you're at it?"

Mustapha Mond laughed. "Because we have no wish to have our throats cut," he answered. "We believe in happiness and stability. A society of Alphas couldn't fail to be unstable and miserable. Imagine a factory staffed by Alphas—that is to say by separate and unrelated individuals of good heredity and conditioned so as to be capable (within limits) of free choice and assuming responsibilities. Imagine it!" he repeated. (Aldous Huxley, *Brave New World* [New York: Perennial Classic, Harper & Row, 1946], p. 151)

An Extended Example

Often, explanations are quite involved, and one explanation builds on earlier explanations. In his *Chemical History of a Candle,* the nineteenth-century chemist Michael Faraday provides an extended explanation of why candles burn as they do. Let us look at a paragraph from that work and sort out the explanatory and other elements in that paragraph.[2]

Faraday's *Chemical History of a Candle* is a set of lectures he delivered to a group of children during the 1860–1861 Christmas holidays. He talked about how candles are made. He discussed the differences between candles and lamps. He talked about the usefulness of placing a chimney around a candle to prevent air currents from affecting the flame. Then he lighted a candle and observed it.

> You see then, in the first instance, that a beautiful cup is formed. As the air comes to the candle, it moves upward by the force of the current which the heat of the candle produces, and it also cools all the sides of the wax, tallow, or fuel as to keep the edge much cooler than the part within; the part within melts by the flame that runs down the wick as far as it can before it is extinguished, but the part on the outside does not melt. If I made a current in one direction, my cup would be lop-sided, and the fluid would consequently run over; for the same force of gravity which holds worlds together holds this fluid in a horizontal position, and if the cup is not horizontal, the fluid will run away in guttering. You see, therefore, that the cup is formed by this beautifully regular ascending current of the air playing upon all sides, which keeps the exterior of the candle cool.

Faraday focuses on the "beautiful cup" that is formed at the top of a burning candle. His concern is with *why* the cup is formed. The flame burns down the wick until

---

[2]The paragraph we shall examine is from Michael Faraday, *The Chemical History of a Candle*, introduction by L. Pearce Williams (New York: Collier Books, 1962), Lecture I, pp. 24–25.

it is extinguished, that is, until it reaches the solid candle. The cup is formed because the flame causes air currents to rise along the sides of the candle. These currents cool the sides of the candle. This keeps the sides of the candle below the melting point. Faraday goes further and says that if the room were breezy, the flame would unevenly melt the top of the candle. The edge of the cup would melt and the wax would run down the side of the candle. (It would be like the motions of the flames of the candles on a lighted birthday cake being carried into a room.) It is the absence of horizontal air currents, the cooling of the sides of the candle and the gravitational attraction on the melted wax (which explains why the wax remains horizontal in the cup) that explain why the "beautiful cup" of melted wax is formed at the top of the candle.

Faraday continues by noting that the nature of the fuel and the shape of the candle both play a role in the formation of the cup. He also tells us what he means by such emotionally charged terms as 'beautiful' and 'good' or 'bad'. He continues:

> No fuel would serve for a candle which has not the property of giving this cup, except such fuel as the Irish bog-wood, where the material itself is like a sponge and holds its own fuel. You see now why you would have had such a bad result if you were to burn these beautiful candles that I have shown you, which are irregular, intermittent in their shape, and cannot therefore, have that nicely-formed edge to the cup which is the great beauty in a candle. I hope you will now see that the perfection of a process—that is, its utility—is the better point of beauty about it. It is not the best looking thing, but the best acting thing, which is the most advantageous to us. This good-looking candle is a bad-burning one. There will be a guttering round about it because of the irregularity of the stream of air and the badness of the cup which is formed thereby.

For the cup to form, the material must be of the correct kind. The wax or tallow from which candles are made have the property of cooling sufficiently from the air currents that go up their sides for the cup to form. The shape of the candle is relevant. The uniformity of air-flow along the sides of a tapered candle is more conducive to the formation of a uniform cup at the top of the candle than other, sometimes very attractive, shapes. Then Faraday tells us what he means by 'beautiful' or 'good'. He understands beauty and goodness in terms of the utility or usefulness for a certain purpose. If your objective is to receive light from a candle, the candle that most efficiently produces the light is the best candle. Notice that the remarks on beauty, goodness, and utility are strictly *descriptive*. In the last sentence, however, he explains why the good-looking candle is the bad-burning one: The airstream around it is irregular and the cup is "bad." These factors explain the guttering, the tendency of the cup to be irregular and wax to melt down the side of the candle.

Faraday concludes his paragraph by pointing to what can be learned from "bad" candles. He says:

> You may see some pretty examples (and I trust you will notice these instances) of the action of the ascending current when you have a little gutter run down the side of a candle, making it thicker there than it is elsewhere. As the candle

goes on burning, that keeps its place and forms a little pillar sticking up by the side, because, as it rises higher above the rest of the wax or fuel, the air gets better round it, and it is more cooled and better able to resist the action of the heat at a little distance. Now the greatest mistakes and faults with regard to candles, as in many other things, often bring with them instruction which we should not receive if they had not occurred. We come here to be philosophers, and I hope you will always remember that whenever a result happens, especially if it be new, you should say, "What is the cause? Why does it occur?" and you will, in the course of time, find out the reason.

Much of this is purely descriptive. Faraday describes what you see when a "bad" candle burns. He *explains*, on the basis of cooling air currents, why the wax that had melted down the side of the candle forms a pillar. And he describes what you can learn and how you should go about learning from mistakes or faults in candles and other things. You learn by looking for the cause of the phenomenon; that is, you learn by looking for an explanation.

Exercises

II. Find five examples of explanations. At least one of these should be drawn from the natural sciences (biology, chemistry, physics, geology, etc.). At least one should be drawn from the social sciences (sociology, psychology, history, etc.). At least one should be drawn from ordinary life.

III. Each of the following is either a description or an explanation. Indicate whether it is a description or an explanation. If it is a description, indicate how it answers the questions "Who?" "What?" "When?" "Where?" or "How?" If it is an explanation, circle the description of the phenomenon that is explained (the explanandum). **Underline** the sentences that do the explaining (the explanans).

1. I think Watanye liked me a good deal, because he often used to take me out alone to fish or hunt, and he was always teaching me things. Also, he liked to tell me stories, mostly funny ones, when he did not have sore lips. (*Black Elk Speaks*, as told through John G. Niehardt [New York: Pocket Books, 1972], p. 55)

2. The bad news is that none of the bikes [six-foot, seven-inch Brian Hahl tried] felt like a perfect fit. This could be for two reasons: They didn't fit, or Brian's never ridden a bike that fit perfectly, so he didn't realize it. ("Size Matters . . . Bikes for the Massive (and the Tiny)," *Mountain Bike* 13 [April 1997], pp. 111–112)

3. Despite her achievements, neither [Mary Antoinette] Perry's acting nor her directing skills explain the high esteem in which she was held by the theater community. Rather, it was her efforts as an activist, organizer, and promoter of causes that benefitted and uplifted her Broadway "family." As [Brock] Pemberton put it, "Probably about a third of her life was given to our work, the other two-thirds to helping people individually or through the organizations she headed." (Joseph Gustaitis, "The Woman Behind the 'Tony'," *American History*, [March/April 1997], p. 19)

4. Christina [of Sweden] first expressed her desire to abdicate the throne in August 1651. However, there was so much opposition to the move that she was persuaded to wait for almost three years before carrying out her plan. On June 6, 1654, the twenty-seven-year-old queen abdicated the throne and set out for Rome. Only a few days after her departure she had her hair cut short, put on the coat and trousers of a man, and continued on horseback, calling herself Count Dohna. (Ruth K. Westheimer with Steven Kaplan, *Power: The Ultimate Aphrodisiac* [Lanham: Madison Books, 2001], p. 145)

5. I'm closer to my notebook computer than to some of my friends. That may sound sick, but think about it: No matter where I am, my portable PC is there to help keep track of my thoughts, to tell me jokes, to educate and entertain me. It keeps me on schedule and within my budget. And it knows when to stay out of the way too. When my buddies come over for Monday-night football, I simply slip my computer out of sight in a desk drawer. (Don Trivette, "How to Buy Notebooks," *Computer Life,* [February 1997], p. 91)

6. When Gregor Samsa woke up one morning from unsettling dreams, he found himself changed in his bed into a monstrous vermin. He was lying on his back as hard as armor plate, and when he lifted his head a little, he saw his vaulted brown belly, sectioned by arch-shaped ribs, to whose dome the cover, about to slide off completely, could barely cling. His many legs, pitifully thin things compared with the size of the rest of him, were waving helplessly before his eyes. (Franz Kafka, *The Metamorphosis*, translated and edited by Stanley Corngold [New York: Bantam Books, 1972], p. 3)

7. All forms of orgiastic union have three characteristics: they are intense, even violent; they occur in the total personality, mind *and* body; they are transitory and periodical. Exactly the opposite holds true for the form of union which is by far the most frequent solution chosen by man in the past and in the present: the union based on *conformity* with the group, its customs, practices and beliefs. (Erich Fromm, *The Art of Loving* [New York: Perennial Library, 1956], p. 10)

8. I have always believed in the death penalty for murderers, and I still do. We show our respect for the dead and proclaim the value of human life human life by taking the trouble to execute murderers. The families of the murdered dead are chained down with grief forever. If an execution relieves them even in the slightest, and I think it does, then we ought to do it—and if you want to call that vengeance, fine. I call it plain decency. Another word for it is justice. (David Gelernter, "Surviving the Unibomber," *Reader's Digest* [December 1997], p. 32)

9. The band almost didn't survive long enough to enjoy this moment [the release of *Nine Lives*]. There were tumultuous times last year when Aerosmith seemed to have used up all nine lives and a few bonus rounds to boot. Between a publicly traumatic group/manager split, the exit of one member in the throes of depression, squabbling over musical direction, a producer change, an entire scrapped album, and—most damningly and doggedly—rumors about renewed drug use, 1996 was the Year of Recording Dangerously. (Chris Willman, "Sweet Commotion," *Entertainment Week* #371 [March 21, 1997], p. 24)

10. It was the beginning of November. I had become used to taking short meditative walks during all kinds of weather, walks on which I often enjoyed a kind of rapture tinged with melancholy, scorn of the world and self-hatred. Thus I roamed in the foggy dusk on evening through the town. The broad avenue of a public park stood deserted beckoning me to enter; the path lay thickly carpeted with fallen leaves which I stirred angrily with my feet. There was a damp, bitter smell, and distant trees, shadowy as ghosts, loomed huge out of the mist. (Hermann Hesse, *Demian*, translated by Michael Roloff and Michael Lebeck [New York: Bantam Books, 1965], p. 58)

PART II

Arguments

An **argument** is a complex discourse in which one or more statements, the **premises**, are taken as providing evidence for (reasons for accepting) the truth of another statement, the **conclusion**. Arguments are used to persuade. Arguments are used to instruct. Arguments are used to clarify. Arguments are used to investigate. Arguments are the life-blood of the examined life.

Arguments always are found in language. Every argument is either a valid deductive argument or an inductive argument. A valid deductive argument with true premises provides conclusive evidence for the truth of its conclusion. An inductive argument with true premises provides *some,* but not conclusive, evidence for the truth of its conclusion.

In Part II we begin by discussing deductive arguments (Chapter 6). In a valid deductive argument, the conclusion is "contained in" the premises. If the premises are consistent, the conclusion provides no new information that is not found in the premises.

In Chapter 7 we turn to inductive arguments. The conclusion of an inductive argument goes beyond the information given in the premises. So, while it is impossible for a valid deductive argument to have all true premises and a false conclusion, it *is* possible for all the premises of an inductive argument to be true and the conclusion false.

In Chapter 8 we examine techniques for finding arguments and their elements, premises and conclusions. In Chapter 9, we develop a technique for diagramming arguments.

Deduction

The View: A valid deductive argument with true premises provides conclusive evidence for the truth of its conclusion. Validity is a formal characteristic of an argument. It is concerned with the form or structure of an argument. Valid arguments can have false premises. A sound argument is a valid deductive argument in which all the premises are true.

What kinds of arguments provide the strongest evidence for the truth of their conclusions? Why do they do so?

An argument is a **valid deductive argument** if and only if it is logically impossible for all the premises to be true and the conclusion false. **Validity** is a **formal** characteristic of an argument. The **form** of an argument is the structure or pattern found in an argument. More than one argument can have the same form, in much the same way that more than one house can have the same design. The following two arguments have the same form:

All dogs are carnivores.
All collies are dogs.
So, all collies are carnivores.

All cats are mousers.
All Persians are cats.
So, all Persians are mousers.

Notice that the words 'dogs' and 'cats' have the same positions in the two arguments, as do the words 'collies' and 'Persians', and 'carnivores' and 'mousers'. We can represent the common form of the two arguments by replacing the terms in the argument—'dogs', 'carnivores', 'collies', 'cats', 'mousers', and 'Persians'—with variables:

All Ms are Ps.
All Ss are Ms.
So, all Ss are Ps.

This argument form is valid. Regardless what you plug in for the variables *S*, *P*, and *M*, the resulting argument will be valid. Whether or not the premises are true, you are guaranteed that *if* the premises are true, then the conclusion is true as well, but you might need to do some research to determine whether the premises are true. Notice, however, that validity does not guarantee that the premises are true. The following argument is valid, but all the premises are false:

> All mice are carnivores.
> All dogs are mice.
> So, all dogs are carnivores.

Argument Forms and Form 1040

An argument form is a pattern or design that is common to many arguments. We might understand this better by comparing it with two other kinds of forms.

When you do your taxes, you use Form 1040. When you start, the form is blank. You fill in the relevant information. The information *you* write onto Form 1040 is different from that *I* write on it, but the *organization* of the information is the same. The *organization* is dictated by Form 1040.

The argument form affirming the antecedent looks like this:

> If *p*, then *q*.
> *p*. Therefore, *q*.

p and *q* are variables. They are like the blanks on Form 1040. By replacing the variables with statements, you obtain an *argument* of the form affirming the antecedent. *p* is replaced by one statement throughout. *q* is replaced by some other statement throughout. *What* statements replace *p* and *q* is irrelevant to the argument form, just as what information is inserted into the blanks on Form 1040 is irrelevant to the form. (The IRS never complains about the form, only about the information you fill in.)

Consider a different kind of form. When you pour cement, you start by building a form of boards or metal. The form determines the shape the cement will assume. Similarly, argument forms determine what results. If you "pour" statements of the forms "If *p*, then *q*" and "*p*," the result will be a statement of the form "*q*."

This argument is valid but **unsound**. An argument is **sound** if, and only if, it is valid *and* all its premises are true. In the above case, the premises are false, but the argument is valid. There are also unsound arguments in which premises are true, but the form is invalid. Let us look at some invalid argument forms.

An argument form is **invalid** if, and only if, it is possible for all the premises to be true and the conclusion false. The following two arguments are of the same form. In one case the premises and the conclusion are true. In the other case the premises are true but the conclusion is false.

All dogs are carnivores.	All collies are carnivores.
All collies are carnivores.	All dogs are carnivores.
So, all collies are dogs.	All dogs are collies.

The two arguments share the same form:

> All *P*s are *M*s.
> All *S*s are *M*s.
> So, all *S*s are *P*s.

The second argument shows that the form of the argument does *not* guarantee that if the premises are true, the conclusion also will be true. The argument is invalid. The second argument *demonstrates* that the argument is invalid, for it shows that it is possible to have an argument of that form with all true premises and a false conclusion. The second argument is a **deductive counterexample** to the first. You construct a deductive counterexample to an argument of a given form by constructing another argument of the same form in which all the premises are true and the conclusion is false. A deductive counterexample shows that *any* argument of that form is invalid.

Constructing a deductive counterexample has a great deal of rhetorical force, but there are two reasons why it is not an efficient way to test the validity of an argument form. First, it can only demonstrate invalidity. It cannot demonstrate validity. Second, there is a certain amount of luck in finding a good deductive counterexample. In Parts IV and V we examine some ways conclusively to determine whether an argument form is valid.

The type of deductive argument at which we have looked so far is a **categorical syllogism**. A categorical syllogism is a deductive argument composed of two premises and a conclusion, each of which is a **categorical proposition** (a proposition expressing a relation among sets or classes of things) and has exactly three distinct terms. In each of the examples, we were concerned with relationships among three classes of objects represented by terms such as 'collies', 'dogs', and 'carnivores'. In some deductive arguments, the concern is with relationships among statements. For example, consider the following argument:

> If this course is easy, then I'll receive an A.
> This course is easy.
> So, I'll receive an A.

This argument contains two simple statements: "This course is easy" and "I'll receive an A," and a compound statement (a statement that has a simple statement as a proper part), "If this course is easy, then I'll receive an A." Where *p* and *q* are variables that can be replaced by simple statements, the form of the argument is

> If *p*, then *q*.
> *p*.
> So, *q*.

That argument form is valid. It is known as affirming the antecedent.

Just as in the case of categorical syllogisms, there are many invalid argument forms in which statements are the fundamental components. Consider the following form:

$$\text{If } p, \text{ then } q.$$
$$\underline{q.\hspace{3cm}}$$
$$\text{So, } p.$$

Let us assume your critical-thinking class meets on Monday, Wednesday, and Friday. Now consider an instance of an argument of that form:

If today is Monday, then we have critical thinking today.
We have critical thinking today.
So, today is Monday.

Do the premises guarantee the truth of the conclusion? No. Assuming your critical-thinking class meets on Monday, Wednesday, and Friday, all the premises are true so long as it is a Monday, a Wednesday, or a Friday. But the conclusion is true only if it is a Monday. Let us assume today is Wednesday. Then you have an argument with two true premises and a false conclusion, which is sufficient to show that the argument is invalid. And this argument form is *always* invalid (even on Monday!). It does not guarantee that if all the premises are true, the conclusion will be true as well.

Exercises

I. Each of the following is a valid deductive argument. State another argument of the same form. The conclusion is <u>underlined</u>.

1. No dogs are cats. Some cats are tabbies. So, <u>some tabbies are not dogs</u>.

2. No sharks are mammals. All elephants are mammals. So, <u>no elephants are sharks</u>.

3. All scorpions are arachnids. Some scorpions are creepy things. So, <u>some creepy things are arachnids</u>.

4. If Jan went to the movie, then Luis went to the game. If Luis went to the game, then Chris went dancing. Therefore, <u>if Jan went to the movie, then Chris went dancing</u>.

5. Either Chris went to the game or Lucinda went to the concert. Chris did not go to the game. Thus, <u>Lucinda went to the concert</u>.

6. Anna went to the dance. So, <u>either Anna went to the dance or Jorge went to the game</u>.

7. Angelica went to the dance. Jean spent the evening in the library. Hence, <u>Angelica went to the dance and Jean spent the evening studying in the library</u>.

8. If Umberto attends Harvard, then Sophia attends Yale. Hence, <u>if Umberto attends Harvard, then both Umberto attends Harvard and Sophia attends Yale.</u>

9. If pretentious problems are perfectly perplexing, then tumultuous times are readily realized; and if murder mysteries are mostly mundane, then riveting reading is seldom silly. Either pretentious problems are perfectly perplexing or murder mysteries are mostly mundane. So, <u>either tumultuous times are readily realized or riveting reading is seldom silly.</u>

10. If silly sisters are seldom serious, then boorish brothers are really revolting; and if elderly educators are easily in error, then serious students are seldom satisfied. Either boorish brothers are not really revolting, or it is not the case that serious students are seldom satisfied. Therefore, <u>either it is not the case that silly sisters are seldom serious, or elderly educators are not easily in error.</u>

II. The forms of the following arguments are invalid. For each argument, construct a deductive counterexample to show that the argument form is invalid; that is, construct another argument of the same form in which all the premises are true and the conclusion is false. The conclusion of each argument is <u>underlined</u>.

1. Since all professors are scholars, and no aardvarks are professors, it follows that <u>no aardvarks are scholars.</u>

2. Either Samantha had soup with dinner or she had salad. She had soup. So, <u>she didn't have salad.</u>

3. If Chris took a trip to Germany, then he took an excursion on the Rhine. Chris did not take a trip to Germany. So, <u>he did not take an excursion on the Rhine.</u>

4. <u>Some cats are not dogs,</u> for no dogs are tabbies and some cats are not tabbies.

5. Since all cats are mammals and all tabbies are cats, it follows that <u>some tabbies are mammals.</u> (Hint: The word 'some' means there is at least one, so a conclusion alluding to a mythical animal would be false.)

6. If John went to the movies, then either Samantha or Ingrid went to the movie. So, <u>if John went to the movie, Samantha went to the movie.</u>

7. Not both Gottfried and Lars went to Norway. So, <u>Lars did not go to Norway.</u>

8. Neither Gottfried nor Lars went to Iceland. Gottfried did not go. So, <u>Lars did go.</u>

9. No cats are dogs. No cats are aardvarks. So, <u>no aardvarks are dogs.</u>

10. Some popular songs are love songs. Some popular songs are ballads. So, <u>some ballads are love songs.</u>

11. Some Cadillacs are not Chevrolets. Some Fords are not Cadillacs. So, <u>some Fords are not Chevrolets.</u>

12. All cats are vertebrates. All cats are mammals. So, <u>all mammals are vertebrates.</u>

13. All cats are mammals. All tabbies are mammals. So, <u>all tabbies are cats.</u>

14. No dogs are cats. Some cats are not tabbies. So, <u>some tabbies are not dogs.</u>

15. "I opened the glove compartment and took out the dark glasses. If there had been a gun there I *certainly* would have seen it, and if I'd seen it, I naturally would have demanded what Edward was doing with a gun."

"And you're sure there was no gun in there?"

"Absolutely certain." [So, <u>I didn't see a gun</u>.]

(Erle Stanley Gardner, *The Case of the Dubious Bridegroom* [New York: Ballantine Books, 1949], p. 119)

Induction

The View: The conclusion of an inductive argument contains information that is not found in the premises. Inductive arguments include inductive generalizations, arguments by analogy, and arguments to the best explanation.

Do some invalid arguments provide evidence for the truth of their conclusions? If so, how strong is that evidence? What are some common kinds of those arguments?

All the information in the conclusion of a valid deductive argument is contained in the premises. A valid argument form, in effect, sieves out some of the information in the premises in such a way that it guarantees that *if* the premises are true, the conclusion also is true.

As we will see in later chapters, relatively few argument forms are valid. Nonetheless, some invalid arguments provide evidence for the truth of their conclusions. In an **inductive argument**, the conclusion provides information that is *not* contained in the premises. So, it is always possible for the premises of an inductive argument to be true and the conclusion to be false. Inductive arguments range from strong to weak, depending upon the quality of the evidence they provide in support of their conclusions.[1]

Most of the arguments you find every day are inductive arguments. You have probably heard an ad for some organization that goes something like this:

> We do good deeds.
>
> <u>We cannot survive without contributions from people like you</u>.
>
> Send your donations to . . .

There might be very good reasons *not* to send your donations. Lack of cash might be one.[2] Advertisers usually give you *some* reason to buy their products, but it is sel-

---

[1]All invalid deductive arguments are inductive arguments. Nonetheless, most invalid arguments are so weak that they can be ignored. In Part III we examine some common inductive arguments. In Part VI we examine criteria for judging the strength of inductive arguments.

[2]We examine other reasons in Chapter 29.

dom a conclusive reason. Their arguments are inductive. In this chapter we look at three common kinds of inductive arguments: (1) inductive generalizations, (2) arguments by analogy, and (3) arguments to the best explanation. Let's consider some examples of each.

Warning: Not Everyone Uses 'Deduction' and 'Induction' in the Same Way!

The words 'deductive' and 'deduction' are used in several ways. When Sherlock Holmes and many other heroes of the mystery novel claim something "follows by deduction" they often allude to a strong inductive argument. More commonly, people distinguish between an inductive and a deductive argument on the basis of the claim, "In an inductive argument, you go from particular premises to a general conclusion, and in a deductive argument, you go from general premises to a particular conclusion." This description cannot be right.

Everyone will grant that the following is a valid deductive argument:

All mortals are things that die.

All humans are mortals.

All humans are things that die.

Notice that here you go from general premises to a general conclusion. Everyone will grant that the following is a valid deductive argument:

If Sydney sleeps in class, then she will fail the test.

Sydney sleeps in class.

Sydney will fail the test.

Here *no* statement is general—each is concerned only with Sydney. And, as we shall see below, analogies are inductive arguments in which one often goes from premises concerning a very limited number of things to a conclusion concerning exactly one thing. So, one of the standard ways of distinguishing between inductive and deductive arguments is inadequate given what anyone proposing the distinction will grant.

(Notice: The author has provided an *argument* that the proposed account is inadequate. Notice also that the author has provided two inductive counterexamples to the proposed account of the distinction between induction and deduction.)

A common use of *inductive reasoning* is to reach a general conclusion. If I spend several years observing ravens, I might notice that each raven I observe is black. This might provide the basis for a conclusion that all ravens are black or that most ravens are black. I have observed only several hundred or several thousand ravens. If I conclude that all (or most) ravens are black, I am going beyond my experience, for I am making a claim about all presently existing ravens, all past ravens, and all future ravens. My conclusion goes far beyond the experience I have had or could have. If I claim that *all* ravens are black, one raven that is not black would be sufficient to show that conclusion is false. One raven that is not black would constitute an **inductive counterexample** to my conclusion. An inductive counterexample is a true statement that is sufficient to show that the conclusion of an inductive argument is false. The truth of the statement "One raven is not black" is sufficient to show that my conclusion, "All ravens are black" is false. If I concluded that most ravens are black, I am more probably correct. The conclusion is weaker, since it would be shown false only if more than half of the ravens that have existed, now exist, or will exist are not black. Of course, even that could happen. Imagine that two hundred years from now there is a cosmic accident that changes the genetic makeup of ravens. All ravens after that point in time are green. And imagine that these green ravens are fruitful and multiply and continue to exist as a species for twice as long as ravens have existed up to that point. Were this to happen, my present inference that most ravens are black probably would be false. Nonetheless, given the evidence on which I have based my conclusion, namely, a vast number of observations of ravens, it is reasonable to claim that at least most ravens are black: All the ravens I observed were black, and what *might* happen in the future is no evidence at all.

A special case of an inference to a general conclusion is found in the scientific method. The scientist proposes a **hypothesis**. The hypothesis takes the form of a conditional statement: "If x occurs, then y occurs." The hypothesis is a prediction, and the scientist attempts to construct an experiment in which all conditions are controlled, so that when condition x is introduced and x is followed by y, she is reasonably certain that the occurrence of x is a sufficient condition for the occurrence of y. The experiment must be repeatable, and if the results are consistent, each repetition tends to provide more evidence for the truth of the conditional statement, "If x occurs, then y occurs." Nonetheless, it is impossible to control *all* the conditions under which an experiment is undertaken. It is *possible* that some factor z was overlooked and that it is only when both x and z are present that y occurs. It is also *possible* that x is a complex phenomenon, and it is only some aspect of x that is responsible for the occurrence of y. Repetitions of the experiment—repetitions that eliminate factor z or include only some aspect of factor x—will allow you to determine whether the original hypothesis was correct. Consider an example.

When the Panama Canal was being constructed in the early 1900s, many of the workers suffered from yellow fever. Dr. Walter Reed constructed a series of experiments to determine how the disease was spread. One hypothesis was that the disease was spread by means of the bedding used by people who had suffered from the disease. Reed placed a number of people who had not been exposed to yellow fever in a closed house with bedding used by yellow fever patients. None came down with the disease. Another hypothesis was that the disease was spread by mosquitoes. Reed placed a number of people who had not been exposed to yellow fever in a closed house containing mosquitoes that had bitten yellow fever patients. Most of those people came down with yellow fever. Several of them died. This tended to confirm his hypothesis that yellow fever is spread by mosquitoes.

Arguments by analogy are comparisons of particular cases in which the fact that the objects compared are similar in a significant number of ways provides reason to believe that they are similar in yet another. The general form of an argument by analogy is as follows: Both X and Y share certain properties—for example, *a, b, c,* and *d*. *X* also has some additional property *e*, so it is likely that *Y* also has property *e*. Consider some examples.

You are wondering whether you would enjoy the latest Tom Clancy novel. This novel is similar to *The Hunt for Red October, Patriot Games, Clear and Present Danger, The Cardinal of the Kremlin, The Sum of All Fears,* and *Debt of Honor* insofar as (1) it is written by Clancy, (2) it describes actions undertaken by submarines,

(3) it contains many of the same characters found in the earlier novels, and (4) it describes various covert operations undertaken by the CIA. You enjoyed all the other novels, so you have reason to believe you will enjoy this one too.

You are planning to tell your friend Jena to expect that her car will develop a certain kind of mechanical difficulty. You reason as follows. You and Jena have the same make and model car. Your driving habits are similar, and you both have your cars serviced with approximately the same regularity. Your car has developed a certain kind of problem. So, you have some reason to suggest that Jena's car will develop the same kind of problem. But you might have even better grounds for your conclusion if it also happened that your friends Fritz, Hilda, Chris, Ostafar, Jean, Jan, and Josephine also have the same make and model car, and each of them experienced the same mechanical problem you are going to mention to Jena.

Notice what you are doing here. You are comparing individual objects and arguing that since two or more objects are similar in a number of ways, it is likely that they will be similar in yet another. The more objects you compare and the more ways in which they are similar, the more likely it is that they will be similar in yet another way. Notice also what you are *not* doing. You do *not* generalize and then reach an additional conclusion on the basis of that generalization. For example, you are *not* arguing from the fact that all the people you have met who owned a Chevrolet Vega experienced problems with the car's engine to the conclusion that most or all Vegas develop engine problems, and then applying that conclusion to Jena's Vega. In an argument from analogy, you are making specific comparisons regarding specific objects. There is no generalization.

An *explanation* often is given in terms of a conditional statement plus a statement of initial conditions. For example,

> If the air pressure is dropping, we will have precipitation.
> The air pressure is dropping.
> We will have precipitation.

If we know we are going to have precipitation, the conditional (If . . ., then . . .) statement together with the statement of conditions explains why we will have precipitation. This explanation is deductive. When we are *looking for* an explanation, we do not know what conditional statement will explain the phenomenon in question. We propose a hypothesis stating that *if* certain conditions occur, then the phenomenon in question occurs. The argument we give might be something like this:

> If the air pressure is dropping, we will have precipitation.
> We will have precipitation.
> So, the air pressure is dropping.

This is an *invalid* deductive argument known as affirming the consequent (the "then" phrase of the conditional.) Since it is an invalid deductive argument, it can provide nothing more than limited evidence for the truth of the conclusion.

To make matters worse, there are an indefinitely large number of explanations for any given phenomenon. Consider the following hypotheses:

1. If the gods are bowling in heaven, then we will have precipitation.

2. If my father is doing his rain dance, then we will have precipitation.

3. If the Boy Scouts are going camping (or we're going on a picnic, or I've just washed and waxed my car, or the weather forecaster has predicted sunshine, or . . .), then we will have precipitation.

4. If silver nitrate has been seeded in the clouds, then we will have precipitation.

5. If the air pressure is dropping and there is an adequate source of moisture, then we will have precipitation.

In asking the question "Why is it raining?" certain kinds of explanations will be acceptable. Others will not be acceptable. What will count as an acceptable explanation depends upon the **conceptual framework** that is assumed. A conceptual framework is a set of assumptions operative in presenting an argument or explanation. In this case you *probably* will be seeking a naturalistic explanation. A **naturalistic explanation** is an explanation based upon facts about nature. It assumes that *if* certain natural phenomena occur, then they will be followed by other natural events or that other natural events occur at the same time. Scientists assume a naturalistic framework. They assume that all natural phenomena can be explained on the basis of other natural phenomena, including natural laws. Given such a framework, hypothesis 1, "If the gods are bowling in heaven, then we will have precipitation," is unacceptable. The gods—if there are gods—are supernatural beings. An explanation based on appeals to actions of the gods is outside the naturalistic framework. So, if you are assuming a naturalistic framework, the explanation is unacceptable.

Hypothesis 2, "If my father is doing his rain dance, then we will have precipitation," is unacceptable for a different reason. While my father's dance might be a natural phenomenon, there is no reason to believe that there is any *causal* relationship between his gyrations and the occurrence of rain. You might even find cases in which Dad dances and there is no rain, and you will certainly find cases in which it rained and Dad did not dance. The same can be said regarding hypothesis 3, "If the Boy Scouts are going camping (or we're going on a picnic, or I've just washed and waxed my car, or the weather forecaster has predicted sunshine, or . . .), then we will have precipitation." While we have all claimed that the only sure guarantee that it is going to rain is making plans to engage in an enjoyable outdoor activity, there is no causal relation between our plans and the occurrence of precipitation. If you have any question regarding that claim, all you need do is recognize that *sometimes* you make outdoor plans and it does not rain, and sometimes it rains even though you have no plans for outdoor activities. Hypothesis 4, "If silver nitrate has been seeded in the clouds, then we will have precipitation," is more interesting. Here we have a naturalistic explanation. Let us assume—contrary to fact—that it *always* happens that when silver nitrate is seeded into clouds, precipitation follows. This would show that cloud seeding is a sufficient condition for precipitation. This would not show that it is a necessary condition; that is, it would not show that every time there is precipitation there

Source: Cassett and Brookins, Shoe. *Used with permission of Tribune Media Services.*

has been cloud seeding. So, if you are looking for a very general explanation of why it rained, the explanation will not do. If you are looking for a very general explanation, you are looking for both necessary and sufficient conditions—that is, the (assumed) law would be "Silver nitrate has been seeded in the clouds if, and only if, we will have precipitation."[3] Nonetheless, it might be the basis for an adequate explanation of why it rained on a particular day. Imagine the following situation. It is the middle of July, and there has been no measurable precipitation since late April. You and some friends know that, if silver nitrate is seeded in clouds, it usually rains. So, you hire a pilot to seed the clouds around your ranch. It rains. To explain why it rained *at that time,* the following explanation would be adequate.

> If silver nitrate is seeded in the clouds, then it (usually) rains.
> <u>Silver nitrate was seeded in the clouds today.</u>
> It rained today.

Since cloud seeding usually, but not always, results in rain, you have a highly probable explanation of why it rained today.

Hypothesis 5, "If the air pressure is dropping and there is an adequate source of moisture, then we will have precipitation," is also interesting. Recall that in our original explanation we appealed to the hypothesis "If the air pressure is dropping, we will have precipitation." Hypothesis 5 is more complex. It specifies an additional condition that must be realized if we are going to explain why we will have precipitation. As anyone who has lived in an arid region will attest, low atmospheric pressure alone does not assure rain. So, explaining why we will have precipitation on the basis of hypothesis 5 and the antecedent conditions that the atmospheric pressure is dropping *and* adequate moisture is present will be a *better* explanation than that based only on dropping air pressure. It specifies more conditions that must be realized if the phenomenon in question is to occur.

---

[3] If you prefer, "If silver nitrate has been seeded in the clouds, then we will have precipitation, and if we will have precipitation, then silver nitrate was seeded in the clouds." For a more complete discussion of necessary and sufficient conditions, see Chapter 22.

In the sciences, choices are often made among theoretical explanations based on which of the two explanations is "better." This can mean any of a number of things. The better of two explanations will explain phenomena that cannot be explained by the alternative explanation. The case we have just considered—explaining why we will have precipitation on the basis of both dropping atmospheric pressure and the presence of moisture—is an example of this sense of 'better'. Similarly, Einstein's theory provides a better explanation of the physical world than does Newton's theory, since it explains everything Newton's theory explains and makes successful predictions in cases where Newton's theory does not. The Copernican hypothesis provides a better explanation of the movement of the planets than does its earth-centered predecessor, the Ptolemaic theory, since it is simpler. It does not require the introduction of epicycles to account for the observed movements of the planets.[4]

What About Jokes?

Does the division of complex language uses into description, argument, and explanation cover the entire spectrum of language uses? No. Poetry, particularly lyric poetry—poetry that expresses feelings—falls under none of these classes. The criteria for evaluating descriptions, explanations, and arguments do not apply to the aesthetic elements of literature. Thus, even retelling a narrative (descriptive) poem—such as "The Raven"—in prose will "leave something out."

But the threefold distinction applies to most other forms of discourse. Many jokes and riddles have a descriptive or explanatory element, but there is some unexpected twist. The old (I didn't say funny) joke, "Why did the chicken cross the road? To get to the other side," is explanatory in form. Often there is a double meaning, as in the riddle, "When is a door not a door? When it's ajar." There is always an assumed context—even something so simple as knowing the difference between 'a jar' and 'ajar'—and without knowing the context you will not "get the joke." Thus, a would-be wit's description of the breakdown in salary negotiations at a school, "Never in the field of academic affairs was so little owed by so few to so many," will not draw a (sickly) smile unless you recognize that it is a parody of Winston Churchill's tribute to the Royal Air Force, "Never in the field of human conflict was so much owed by so many to so few."

Exercises

I. Are the following examples of inductive generalizations, arguments by analogy, or arguments to the best explanation? The conclusion is <u>underlined</u>.

1. Chris, a member of ΘΔΓ, went to the dance. Jan, a member of ΘΔΓ, went to the dance. Ashley, a member of ΘΔΓ, went to the dance. So, <u>all members of ΘΔΓ went to the dance</u>.

2. Your computer and my computer are similar. Your computer and mine are both Micron GoBooks. We've both owned our computers for three years. We both take our computers wherever we go. We both use our computers for at least eight hours every day. My hard disk crashed. So, <u>it's likely that your hard disk will crash too</u>.

---

[4]Peter Lipton presents a thorough discussion of argument to the best explanation in his *Inference to the Best Explanation* (London: Routledge, 1991). See also Chapter 27.

3. I made an appointment to see Dr. Dan today, but he didn't show up. He might have been ill, but then the secretary should have known, and she didn't. It might be that he overslept, but the appointment was for noon, and he's usually on campus by 8:00 a.m. It might be that he forgot to write down the appointment. He seldom misses an appointment when he writes it down, but the only memory he has is a "paper memory." Of course, he could have been detained by a student after class, but I waited a full half hour. Or he could have been run down by a truck or hit by lightning, but neither is likely. So, <u>he must have forgotten to write down my appointment</u>.

4. Old watches are like old-fashioned clocks insofar as they both have mechanical movements. Old watches needed to be wound regularly. So, <u>old clocks needed to be wound regularly</u>.

5. Paper books and e-books are similar in various ways. They are both divided into pages. If a paper book has an illustration, the same illustration is found in the e-book version. If I'm writing a paper for class and want to quote a passage from a paper book, I have to type it. So, <u>if I'm writing a paper for class and want to quote a passage from an e-book, I'll have to type it</u>.

6. I've taken two classes from Professor Hernandez and enjoyed both. Both classes focused on European history, but I took a European history class from Professor Holder and it was not enjoyable. Professor Hernandez required us to write papers, but so did Professor Koenig, and Koenig's class was *anything* but fun. It can't be that Hernandez insists on teaching at 8:00 a.m., for I regularly slept through Professor Latham's eight o'clock class. <u>It must be Professor Hernandez herself that makes her classes enjoyable</u>.

7. I enjoyed Introduction to Philosophy. I enjoyed the history of ancient and history of modern philosophy courses. I enjoyed the metaphysics class, the ethics class, and the epistemology class. I even enjoyed logic. All I can conclude is <u>I like virtually all philosophy classes</u>.

8. A recent poll of 1,000 Americans indicated that 69 percent of those polled approved of the President's domestic policy. So, <u>69 percent of Americans approved of the President's domestic policy</u>.

9. My car won't start. It could be that I'm out of gas. It could be that the starter has played out. It could be that the battery is dead. <u>I'm inclined to go with the battery hypothesis</u>, since that would also explain why the lights and the radio won't work.

10. When my desk lamp wouldn't work, the problem was with the light bulb. When the kitchen light wouldn't work, the problem was with the light bulb. When the light in the bedroom wouldn't work, the problem was with the light bulb. My reading lamp doesn't work. Since it is like my desk lamp, the light in the kitchen, and the light in the bedroom in terms of all its working components, I conclude that <u>the light bulb is most probably the reason my reading lamp won't work</u>.

Recognizing Arguments

The View: Premise indicators and conclusion indicators provide *some* reason to believe that you are in the presence of an argument. You must also ask whether any premises are left unstated. You might need to examine the context to determine whether you are confronting an argument or an explanation.

How can you distinguish arguments from explanations and descriptions? Are there ways to distinguish premises from conclusions? Are there any guidelines for distinguishing inductive from deductive arguments?

Distinctions between arguments, explanations, and descriptions are important. We need a practical way to recognize them when we find them. If we have ways of finding arguments and explanations, we may assume that all other passages are descriptive. Further, we need a practical way to distinguish between inductive and deductive arguments.

Looking for arguments is like looking for anything else. It is a lot easier to find them in some places than in others. Arguments are commonly found in essays, editorials, letters to editors, persuasive speeches, and advertisements. But even if you know the general places to look, that alone does not guarantee that you will find them. Fortunately, there are some words that *tend* to show that you are in the presence of an argument. These are known as **premise indicators** and **conclusion indicators**.

The following is a partial list of premise indicators—that is, words indicating that the statement *following* them is a premise of an argument:

> A distinction should be drawn between an argument and an *intended argument*. Some people "accidentally" construct arguments. You yourself probably have given reasons why someone should accept a conclusion without consciously realizing that you were doing so. Generally, when people set forth arguments, they intend to show that a certain conclusion is supported by a certain set of evidence, or they attempt to convince you that you should hold a belief or act in a certain way. Regardless of the quality of the argument, the premise and conclusion indicators tend to show what the *intended* argument is.

since	because	*may be deduced from
for	as	*is shown by
given (that)	assuming (that)	*is entailed by
inasmuch as	insofar as	*may be derived from
due to	whereas (in formal motions)	

Sometimes premises are numbered, and the numbers can be taken as indicators. What *precedes* the indicators marked with an asterisk (*) is always a conclusion.

The following is a partial list of conclusion indicators—that is, words indicating that the statement *following* them is the conclusion of an argument:

thus	we may conclude that	it follows that
therefore	it follows that	*is a reason to believe that
hence	it is entailed that	*is a reason to hold that
so	we may infer that	*is evidence that
consequently	accordingly	*implies that
wherefore	whence	*means [that]
ergo	be it therefore resolved (in formal motions)	
be it resolved that (in formal motions)		

What *precedes* the indicators marked with an asterisk (*) is always a premise.

Further, conditional statements are often found in arguments. A conditional statement is a statement of the form "If . . ., then . . . ." A conditional statement might be either a premise or a conclusion. *A conditional statement by itself is not an argument*, and conditional statements are often used in explanations as well as arguments.

Exercises

I. In each of the following, circle the premise indicators and put a box around the conclusion indicators.

1. Since Heinrich Böll won the Nobel Prize for Literature in 1972, we may conclude that his books and short stories are significant pieces of literature.

2. Insofar as the last day of classes is June 7, and given that my last final is over at 3:30, it follows that vacation begins at 3:30 on June 7.

3. The fact that today is Friday implies that I'll have two relatively uninterrupted days to study for the test on Monday.

4. We may infer that the last chapter we'll cover this semester is Chapter 29, because (1) we just started on Chapter 29, (2) it's already the last week of classes, (3) we never cover more than two chapters in a week, (4) we meet only three days each week, and (5) the last day of classes will be a big exam.

5. Assuming that the clock runs properly, it follows that the current time is 10:50, for the clock was set to the correct time yesterday.

6. Inasmuch as all dogs have fleas, and as Fido is a dog, it is entailed that Fido has fleas.

7. The fact that Tom Clancy has published a new novel means that Jack Ryan is still "alive and well," since Jack Ryan is a major character in the novel.

8. That Silent Bob is still keeping his peace is shown by the fact that he's a major character is Kevin Smith's new movie.

9. Because the old educational wing of the church was torn down, and since a basement was dug, and insofar far as cement, bricks, and other building materials were delivered to the site, we may conclude that the church is building a new educational wing.

10. Jorge was at the football game this afternoon. Therefore, Jorge did not spend the afternoon studying in the library, due to the fact that it is impossible for Jorge to be at the football game and in the library at the same time.

Indicator Words Are Not Enough

While it is useful to have a list of premise and conclusion indicators, they alone will not allow you to say, "Ah! Here are the premises and conclusions of an argument." There are two reasons for this. First, all the single-word premise and conclusion indicators have uses other than marking the premise or conclusion of an argument. Second, not all premises and conclusions are marked by indicator words.

'Since' can be used to mark a point in time: "Since the demise of the Soviet Union, people have come to believe that the threat of a nuclear war is greatly decreased." 'For' has several uses. 'For' can mark a goal or purpose: "She ran for fun." "George W. Bush ran for President." 'For' can express the object of a desire: "After three days lost in the desert, she longed for a bowl of Ben and Jerry's Ice Cream." 'For' can mark a rate of exchange: "She bought three birthday cards for $5." 'For' can be used in a dedication: "For Elise" (*Für Elise*) is a Beethoven piano composition." 'Given' can allude to a gift: "John was given a bicycle for his birthday." 'Because' can allude to a cause: "Chris drove off the road because she fell asleep." 'As' can be used to make comparisons: "Joan is now as tall as her father." 'Assuming' can mean to play a role: "The criminal managed to avoid capture by assuming the role of a poor peasant." When used as premise indicators, these words are taken as shorthand for more complex claims: "since it is true that ...," "because it is true that ...," "for the following reason ...," "as it is true that ...," "given that it is true that ...," "assuming it is true that ...," "inasmuch as it is true that ...," "insofar as it is true that ...," "whereas it is true that ...."

Similarly, the single-word conclusion indicators 'thus,' 'therefore,' 'hence,' 'so,' and 'consequently' can mark the phenomenon to be explained in an explanation. In explaining why a cup is formed at the top of the candle, Faraday concluded his explanation with the words, "You see, therefore, that the cup is formed by this beautifully regular ascending current of the air playing upon all sides, which keeps the exterior of the candle cool."[1] Here the word 'therefore' marks only a summary of the explanation. Similarly, the word 'thus' can mean "in this manner," as it does in the following passage from the Koran:

> If a childless man have two sisters, they shall inherit two-thirds of his estate; but if he have both brothers and sisters, the share of each male shall be that of two females.
>
> Thus [in this way] God makes plain to you His precepts so that you may not err. God has knowledge of all things.[2]

Further, many premises and conclusions are not marked by indicator words. Generally, you are fortunate if one premise and the conclusion have indicators. Nonetheless, if you can find the conclusion, you should be able to find the premises by asking the question, *What reasons are given for me to accept this statement as true?*

It is always important to find the conclusion and ask, What reasons are given for me to accept this statement as true? since it makes no difference whether the premises of an argument are given first, or the conclusion is given first, or the conclusion is nestled somewhere among the premises. The same argument is given in each of the following passages.

Since all cats are carnivores, and Tabby is a cat, it follows that Tabby is a carnivore.

Tabby is a carnivore, since Tabby is a cat and all cats are carnivores.

Tabby is a cat, so Tabby is a carnivore, for all cats are carnivores.

Sometimes not all the premises of an argument are given. The author of an argument might consider it an obvious truth that "All cats are carnivores," and simply state the following:

> Tabby is a cat. So, Tabby is a carnivore.[3]

Sometimes the conclusion is left unstated:

> Tabby is a cat, and all cats are carnivores.

And sometimes the premises of an argument are scattered throughout a very long discourse. An argumentative essay is an extended argument that a certain thesis is true. When reading an essay, you need to keep track of the statements used to support the thesis.[4]

---

[1] Faraday, *The Chemical History of a Candle*, introduction by L. Pearce Williams (New York: Collier Books, 1962), Lecture I, p. 24.
[2] Koran 4:174, translated with notes by N. J. Dawood (New York: Penguin Books 1997), p. 78.
[3] In Chapters 18 and 23 we look at ways of "finding" missing or unstated premises.
[4] We examine the art of reading an essay in Chapter 32.

So, in looking for an argument, the first step is to look for premise and conclusion indicators. They *suggest* that an argument is being presented. But there is nothing "automatic" about this. You will need to ask yourself *whether* the words are being used as premise and conclusion indicators. You will have to ask whether the discourse is an argument or an explanation.

As we noticed above, when you are providing an explanation for a phenomenon (stated as the explanandum), what you know at the outset is that the phenomenon has occurred or is occurring. What you are looking for is the explanans, that which explains the phenomenon. The explanandum corresponds to the conclusion of an argument. The explanans correspond to the premises of an argument. But in an *argument* the premises are known or accepted as true at the outset. In an *explanation* the explanandum is known or accepted as true at the outset. Taken simply as a piece of discourse, they are not distinguishable. So, let us consider the following and tell two stories: In one it will be an explanation, and in the other it will be an argument.

> All water heated to 212° F boils.
> The water on the stove is heated to 212°F.
> The water on the stove is boiling.

Story 1. You walk into my house and notice that there is a pan of boiling water on the stove. You know that the water is boiling. You ask why the water is boiling. You are looking for an explanation. The discourse above *explains why* the water is boiling, although it might not be the kind of explanation you were after, especially if you had thoughts of inviting yourself to supper.

Story 2. I am sitting in the living room watching the news. I have a pot of water on the stove. In the water is a thermometer that broadcasts the temperature of the water to my television. I am planning to cook spaghetti for supper, so I want to know whether the water is boiling. I push a button, and for a moment the following message is displayed on my TV screen:

212°F/100°C

Since I know that all water heated to 212°F boils, and the water in the pan is heated to 212°F, I *conclude* that the water is boiling.

The point of these stories is that you need to know something about the context if you are to determine whether the discourse is an argument or an explanation. If you *know* that the water is boiling and you ask why it is doing so, the discourse above is an explanation. It tells you *why* the water is boiling. If you want to know *whether* the water is boiling and you *know* that water heated to 212°F boils and the temperature of the water on the stove is 212°F, the claim that the water is boiling is the conclusion of an argument.

If you find a discourse in ordinary life, and you are asked to determine whether it is an argument or an explanation, you might need to do a bit of research to determine what is taken as known. Without doing so, you cannot determine whether the discourse is an argument or an explanation. Nonetheless, there are certain locutions that virtually guarantee that a discourse is an explanation. If Fran says, "I took critical thinking because I wanted to fulfill one of my general education requirements," you have an explanation. Fran *knows* that she is taking critical thinking, and she is telling you why. In virtually any case in which a person says, "I *did* such-and-such because . . ." you have an explanation. *But* if someone tells you why she *holds a belief,* it might be an explanation of how she came to hold the belief, or the *explanation* itself might be an argument she accepts in supporting the belief. If Fran says, "I believe in the existence of God because I was regularly taken to religious services as a child," this is an explanation of how the belief was developed. But when John Nash was asked why he held beliefs regarding extraterrestrial beings, he indicated that he was convinced by an argument by analogy.

> "How could you," began Mackey, "how could you, a mathematician, a man devoted to reason and logical proof . . . how could you believe that extraterrestrials are sending you messages? How could you believe that you are being recruited by aliens from outer space to save the world? How could you . . .?"
>
> Nash looked up at last and fixed Mackey with an unblinking stare as cool and dispassionate as that of any bird or snake. "Because," Nash said slowly in his soft, reasonable southern drawl, as if talking to himself, "the ideas I had about supernatural beings came to me the same way that my mathematical ideas did. So I took them seriously."[5]

The *source* of the ideas about extraterrestrials was the same as the *source* of his mathematical ideas. The mathematical ideas were important and provable. But the source itself does not guarantee that all ideas from that source are equally reliable.[6] And there are cases in which *I* might explain why I hold a belief, and *you* would take my explanation as an argument. If I told you I believe Paul Cézanne's *The Card Players* is an excellent work of art, you might ask why. I might reply in terms of the vibrant colors, the bold lines, and other qualities of the work. You might take my *explanation* as an *argument* that *The Card Players* is an excellent work or art.

Finally, we need a practical way to determine whether an argument is inductive or deductive. Generally, if adding a premise or increasing the strength of a premise (short of universality) can either strengthen or weaken the argument, the argument is inductive. Consider some examples.

The following argument concludes that Shannon will enjoy this course.

> John, Jane, Chris, Liz, and Waldo are all math majors, and they all enjoyed this course. Shannon is a math major. So, it is likely that Shannon also will enjoy this course.

This is an inductive argument—an analogy. If you stated the argument very formally, it might be stated as follows:

> John is a math major and enjoyed this course.
>
> Jane is a math major and enjoyed this course.
>
> Chris is a math major and enjoyed this course.
>
> Liz is a math major and enjoyed this course.

---

[5]Sylvia Nasar, *A Beautiful Mind: The Life of Mathematical Genius and Nobel Prize Laureate John Nash* (New York: Simon & Schuster, A Touchstone Book, 1998), p. 11.

[6]Historically, there have been odd sources of some very fruitful ideas. But the source of the idea (hypothesis) and its verification are distinct issues. See Chapter 27.

> Waldo is a math major and enjoyed this course.
>
> Shannon is a math major. _____
>
> Shannon will enjoy this course.

You will notice that the conclusion that Shannon will enjoy the course is strengthened if she is compared with an additional person:

> John, Jane, Chris, Liz, Waldo, and Sam are all math majors, and they all enjoyed this course. Shannon is a math major. So, it is likely that Shannon also will enjoy this course.

The argument also will be strengthened if Shannon shares an additional characteristic with John, Jane, Chris, Liz, and Waldo:

> John, Jane, Chris, Liz, and Waldo are all math majors, they all enjoy brain-teasers, and they all enjoyed this course. Shannon is a math major who enjoys brainteasers. So, it is likely that Shannon also will enjoy this course.

Notice that the argument by analogy is strengthened either by comparing Shannon with an additional math major or by noting that Shannon is similar to other enjoyers of this class in another way.

The same holds for other types of inductive arguments. If I conclude that all (or most) ravens are black because I have seen a thousand ravens and each one was black, I have better evidence for my conclusion if I have seen two thousand ravens, all of which were black. On the other hand, if I observed one raven that was white, I would have *conclusive* evidence that not all ravens are black, and it would slightly weaken my conclusion that *most* ravens are black.

If you have arguments with statistical premises, increasing the probability stated in a premise is another way to increase the probability of the conclusion.

> Fifty-one percent of all business majors at State U. are members of βββ fraternity.
>
> Lucinda is a business major at State U. _____
>
> So, Lucinda is a member of βββ fraternity.

Do you know that Lucinda is a member of βββ? No, but the chances are *slightly* better that she is a member than that she is not. If the probability stated in the first premise were higher—"Sixty percent of all business majors at State U. are members of βββ fraternity," or "Eighty percent of all business majors at State U. are members of βββ fraternity"—you have a stronger argument for the conclusion that Lucinda is a member of βββ. There is a limit, however. When you reach 100 percent—when you claim that *all* business majors at State U. are members of βββ fraternity—the argument becomes a *valid deductive* argument.

If you have a sound deductive argument (a valid deductive argument with all true premises), you have conclusive evidence for the truth of its conclusion. The truth of the conclusion is *entailed* by the premises. The truth of the conclusion follows *with necessity* from the truth of the premises. Adding additional premises *cannot* strengthen or weaken the evidence for the conclusion.

But what do you do when there are missing premises? As we have noticed, sometimes it is easy to supply a missing premise. Other times it is not. Consider the following argument:

> Imhotep's pyramid was not much good, really, for the steps, or terraces, were not filled in, and it was less than 200 feet high.[7]

The conclusion is that Imhotep's pyramid was not much good, and the reasons given to support this claim are that its terraces were not filled in and it was less than 200 feet high. You might be able to give additional reasons why Imhotep's pyramid "was not much good," which suggests that the argument is inductive. For example, assume that it was made of sandstone rather than of granite. Assume that its foundation was on sand rather than on rock. Assume that its burial chamber was six inches too short to hold the mummified King Zoser.[8] Any of those considerations might provide more reasons why it was not a great pyramid. But at a certain point you might find yourself asking the question, "What makes for a really good pyramid, anyway?" When you ask *that* question, you might come to believe that it is a valid deductive argument with a missing premise:

> No pyramid that is less than 200 feet tall and does not have filled steps is a good pyramid.
>
> Imhotep's pyramid is a pyramid that is less than 200 feet tall and does not have filled steps.
> _____
>
> Imhotep's pyramid is not a good pyramid.

The argument is valid. *If* the first premise accurately states the criteria for deeming a pyramid not much good, then you have conclusive evidence that Imhotep's pyramid was not a good pyramid. Of course, it is not clear that the first premise is true. Nor is it clear how you would find out whether it is true, or at least widely accepted. You might pose the question to a number of Egyptologists. Obviously, asking your mummy won't do.

It is often possible to state an argument in more than one way. Since a sound deductive argument is stronger than an inductive argument, you will want to ask yourself whether a premise is assumed that will yield a valid deductive argument with true premises. You should *always* state the strongest argument you can. This might be called the **principle of charity**. The reason you want to treat another's argument with intellectual respect is that you would hope that others would treat your argu-

---

[7]Will Cuppy, *The Decline and Fall of Practically Everybody* (New York: Dell, 1950), p. 14.
[8]I wish to thank Lisa Storer for informing me that Imhotep was the architect, not the king.

ments in the same way.[9] Notice that 'charity' does *not* mean anything goes. In your "charitable" moment you will point out the ambiguities and *give reasons why* (argue that) *your* account of the missing premise yields the strongest argument. In being charitable, you're implicitly criticizing the way the argument was stated. The principle of charity commits you to "tough love."

Exercises

II. For each of the following, determine whether the passage is a description, an explanation, or an argument. If it is an argument, circle the premise indicators and put a box around the conclusion indicators. If it is an argument, is it inductive or deductive? If the passage presents an explanation, double underline the explanandum. Give reasons to support your analysis.

1. These men are not drunk, as you imagine; for it is only nine in the morning. (Acts 2:15 [New English Bible])

2. Consider, for example, the character named Carin (Monica Potter), who is one of Patch's fellow students. She appears too late in the movie to be a major love interest. Yet Patch does love her. Therefore, she's obviously in the movie for one purpose: to die. (Roger Ebert, "Patch Adams," in his *I Hated, Hated, Hated That Movie* [Kansas City: Andrews McMeel, 2000], p. 272)

3. I believe in a journeyman period in any profession. It was so in the Army. It was so in farm life. You apprenticed with your elders, your parents, and learned how to do the work. It should be so in the theatre. (James Earl Jones and Penelope Niven, *James Earl Jones: Voices and Silences* [New York: Charles Scribner's Sons, 1993], p. 91)

4. Sea ice is not the same as fresh-water ice. The salt-water ice is stronger, more elastic, isn't as slippery. Also the sea ice moves all the time, even when it is thick. (Gary Paulsen, *Dogsong* [New York: Bradbury Press, 1985], p. 51)

5. "Don't ever fool yourself that facts don't fit if you get the right explanation. They're just like jigsaw puzzles—when you get them right, they're all going to fit together." (Erle Stanley Gardner, *The Case of the Howling Dog* [Philadelphia: The Blakiston Company, 1934], p. 150)

6. Since about three-fourths of the earth's surface is water and about one-fourth land, it stands to reason that the good Lord intended for man to spend three times

---

[9]If you do not like to be charitable, there is another reason. Making someone else's argument as strong as you can avoids the charge that you have committed the straw person fallacy. The straw person fallacy consists of either assuming that the conclusion is stronger than it is and attacking the stronger conclusion, or assuming that the arguer has assumed a clearly false premise and attacking the premise (see Chapter 29). If you are charged with a straw person fallacy, you will lose credibility. So, out of self-interest, you should be charitable in interpreting the arguments of others.

as much time fishing as he does plowing. (Cal and Rose Samra, *More Holy Humor: Inspirational Wit and Cartoons* [Carmel, NY: Guideposts, 1997], p. 116)

7. One day I met him [Kierkegaard] as he was walking with a hymnal in his hand. I don't know how it came to me, but I asked him which of the city's pastors he preferred to hear. He answered instantly: "Visby, and I will tell you why. When one of the other pastors has written his sermon counting on sunshine, he will talk about sunshine, even if it pours rain, but when Visby preaches, and a ray of sunshine comes into the church, he grasps that ray and speaks about it at such length, and so beautifully and edifyingly, that you leave with a ray of sunshine in your heart. He is the only improviser of them all. (Letter from H. P. Holst to H. P. Barfod, September 14, 1869, in *Encounters with Kierkegaard: A Life as Seen by His Contemporaries*, edited by Bruce H. Kirmmse, translated by Bruce H. Kirmmse and Virginia R. Laursen [Princeton: Princeton University Press, 1996], p. 13.)

8. When I found myself on my feet, I looked about me, and must confess I never beheld a more entertaining prospect. The country round appeared like a continued garden, and the inclosed fields, which were generally forty feet square, resembled so many beds of flowers. These fields were intermingled with woods of half a stang, and the tallest trees, as I could judge, appeared to be seven foot high. I viewed the town on my left hand, which looked like the painted scene of a city in a theater. (Jonathan Swift, *Gulliver's Travels*, Chapter 2)

9. Therefore all should work. First because it is impossible that you have *no* creative gift. Second: the only way to make it live and increase is to use it. Third: you cannot be sure that it is not a *great* gift. (Brenda Ueland, *If You Want to Write: A Book about Art, Independence and Spirit* [Saint Paul: Graywolf Press, 1987], p. 158)

10. Racist acts are as apparent today as a century ago, evidenced by the recent burnings of Southern black churches and the discovery that top Texaco employees frequently referred to fellow employees using racially derogatory words. ("Discrimination Still a Threat," *The Breeze,* James Madison University, Harrisonburg, VA [January 20, 1997], p. 12)

11. For a long time I was reporter to a journal, of no very wide circulation, whose editor has never yet seen fit to print the bulk of my contributions, and, as is too common with writers, I got only my labor for my pains. (Henry David Thoreau, *Walden*)

12. Christ our Lord invites to his table all who love him,

    who earnestly repent of their sin

    and seek to live in peace with one another.

    Therefore, let us confess our sin before God and one another. (*The United Methodist Hymnal* [Nashville, TN: United Methodist Publishing House, 1989], p. 12)

13. I have always believed in the death penalty for murderers, and I still do. We show our respect for the dead and proclaim the value of human life human life by tak-

ing the trouble to execute murderers. The families of the murdered dead are chained down with grief forever. If an execution relieves them even in the slightest, and I think it does, then we ought to do it—and if you want to call that vengeance, fine. I call it plain decency. Another word for it is justice. (David Gelernter, "Surviving the Unibomber," *Reader's Digest* [December 1997], p. 32)

14. **Example I** Suppose that a certain school of economists modeled the Gross National Product of the United States at time t (measured in years from January 1, 1990) by the formula

$$f(t) = 3.4 + .04 - .13e^{-t},$$

where the Gross National Product is measured in trillions of dollars. What was the predicted percentage rate of growth (or decline) of the economy at $t = 0$ and $t = 1$?

Solution   Since

$$f'(t) = .04 - .13e^{-t},$$

we see that

$$\frac{f'(0)}{f(0)} = \frac{.04 - .13}{3.4 + .13} = \frac{.09}{3.53} \approx -2.6\%$$

$$\frac{f'(1)}{f(1)} = \frac{.04 - .13e^{-1}}{3.4 + .04 + .13e^{-1}} = \frac{-.00782}{3.4878} \approx -.2\%$$

So on January 1, 1990, the economy is predicted to contract at a relative rate of 2.6% per year; on January 1, 1991, the economy is predicted to be still contracting but only at a relative rate of .2% per year. (Larry J. Goldstein, David C. Lay, and David I. Schneider, *Calculus and its Applications*, 7th ed. [Upper Saddle River, NJ: Prentice Hall, 1996], p. 348)

15. "There's two reasons a car won't start. Either you're not getting fuel or you're not getting fire. You've got fire." (Benny Pearl in *Benny and Joon*, Metro Goldwyn Mayer, 1993)

16. The ability to change hand positions and speed—and the confidence to do it in the appropriate situations—is the most productive asset in bowling. Norm Duke and Bryan Goebel are two prime examples of players who were transformed from mediocrity to superstar status by virtue of their ability to master hand positions and speed. Mike Aulby, Dave Husted, Amelio Monacelli, David Ozio, Brian Voss, Mark Williams, Danny Wiseman, and Walter Ray Williams Jr. all have escalated their stature due to their artistic touch in this phase of the game. (John Jowdy, "The Coach's Corner: Your Best Equipment Is in Your Head," *Bowling Digest* [June 1996], p. 39)

17. I have read everywhere that Africa means sexual license. Perhaps it does. Most folk who talk sex frantically have all too seldom revealed their source material. I was in West Africa only two months, but with both eyes wide. I saw children

quite naked and women usually naked to the waist—with bare bosom and limbs. And in those sixty days I saw less of sex dalliance and appeal than I see daily on Fifth Avenue. This does not mean much, but it is an interesting fact. (W. E. B. Du Bois, *Dusk of Dawn: An Essay toward an Autobiography of a Race Concept* [New York: Schocken Books, 1968], pp. 127–128)

18. "Silencing Floors From Below"

1. Enlist a helper to walk on the finished floor above while you look for move-ment of the floor joists and of the subfloor from below. When you locate the problem area, first check to make sure that diagonal bridging between your floor joists (if any is nearby) is firm. Snuggling it up may solve the problem.

   If the noise comes from between the joists, drive a tight-fitting piece of solid bridging up between the joists until it makes contact with the subfloor, and then end-nail it in place.

2. To silence a subfloor that has worked away from the joists, drive glue-coated shims into the gaps between subfloor and the joists. (*Better Homes and Gardens*® *Step-By-Step Household Repairs* [New York: Bantam Books, 1983], p. 26)

19. "And unless we do get into that house we shall never get him off your track. I beg you to make no mistake over that. I have more knowledge on this particular psy-chology than, if I may say so, you are likely to have. At the proper range, with his perfect shot, he is as determined to get you, as a golfer who won't go on to the third green until he has holed out on the second. You are No. 2 on his score." (H. F. Heard, *A Taste of Honey* [1941, 1969], in *The Amazing Mycroft Mysteries* [New York: The Vanguard Press, 1980], p. 123)

20. Chief Engineer Montgomery Scott celebrated the birth of his niece by passing out cigars to the crew of the Starship *Enterprise*. Mr. Spock examined the cigar:

He raised it, sniffed it, drew it quickly from his nose. "This is tobacco, Mr. Scott. It contains noxious chemicals."

"Aye, 'tis true," Scott admitted. "But 'tis the *tradition*, d'ye see?"

Spock regarded the cigar a moment longer. "I believe I understand," he said. "During a time of critical overpopulation, the birth of a child would have required an adult to die. The adults resorted to this sort of lottery to decide who must make way. Your customs . . . fascinating. Not efficient, but fascinating."

"It wasna quite like that, Mr. Spock—"

Spock handed him the cigar. "I am sure you meant it to compliment me, but I should prefer not to participate in your lottery." (Vonda N. McIntyre, *Star Trek: Enterprise, The First Adventure* [New York: Pocket Books, 1986], pp. 25–26)

Tree Diagrams for Arguments

The View: This chapter develops a system of line diagrams for representing arguments. Premises and conclusions are represented by numbers. Lines are drawn to show how premises individually or jointly support a conclusion.

Is there a convenient way to represent the relations between the premises and conclusion of an argument? Is there a way to represent the relations among several arguments in a single passage?

It is useful to have a means to represent the relations between the premises and conclusion of an argument. Many passages contain several arguments. Often, the conclusion of one argument is a premise of another. It is useful to develop a "map" to see how the arguments are related to one another.

In this chapter we develop a method for diagramming arguments. We represent each statement by means of a number in parentheses and show the relationships between the various premises and conclusions by means of lines. Sometimes premises individually support a conclusion. Sometimes two or more premises support a conclusion only when they are taken together. The argument trees we develop reflect these differences.

How to Build an Argument Tree —————

When constructing a tree diagram for an argument, begin by finding the premise(s) and conclusion of the argument. Sometimes the argument is clearly stated. Sometimes it is not. If the argument is not clearly stated, restate the premises and conclusion in as clear a way as possible. Number the premises and conclusion. For purposes of uniformity, number the statements in the order in which they are presented in the passage you examine. In some passages there will be descriptive or explanatory claims that are *not* parts of an argument, so there will be times when your restatement of the argument will *not* contain all statements in the passage. If there is an assumed premise or conclusion, place it in square brackets ([]) and number it with the rest of the premises or conclusions. Place the number of the conclusion at bottom of the diagram, and place the numbers of the premises above the conclusion, showing how the premises support the conclusion. If two or more premises support a conclusion only when taken together, connect the two premises by a line. Use a diagram that looks like a football goal post: ⌐⊤⌐. Numbers representing the premises go at the top of the uprights. The number representing the conclusion goes at the bottom. Sometimes three or more premises jointly support a conclusion, so your "goal post" might look like this ⌐⊥⌐, or this ⌐⌐⊤⌐⌐, or this ⌐⌐⊥⌐⌐. If premises support a conclusion individually, not jointly, draw a line from the numbers representing the premises directly to the number representing the conclusion. If there is only one premise supporting a conclusion, there will be a straight line from the premise number (at the top) to the conclusion number. If two premises each support a conclusion, the diagram will look like this: V. A premise number will be at the top of each line, and the conclusion will be at the bottom. The number of lines will be determined by the number of premises. We can see how this works by considering some examples.

In discussing the interviewing process, Ronald B. Adler and George Rodman propose the following argument:

> Physical attractiveness is a major influence on how applicants are rated, so it makes sense to do everything possible to look your best.[1]

There is one premise and a conclusion. So, you might begin by numbering the statements in the passage:

> (1) Physical attractiveness is a major influence on how applicants are rated, so (2) it makes sense to do everything possible to look your best.

The argument may be set forth as follows:

> (1) Physical attractiveness is a major influence on how applicants are rated [in an interview].
>
> (2) [You should] do everything possible to look your best.[2]

The words in square brackets are added to show the context in (1) and to yield a grammatical sentence in (2). The conclusion is (2). The argument is diagramed as follows:

(1)

|

(2)

[1]Ronald B. Adler and George Rodman, *Understanding Human Communication*, 6th ed. (Fort Worth: Harcourt Brace, 1997), p. 269.
[2]You might suggest that in this case the premise and conclusion are so obvious that it makes little sense to rewrite the argument. If you believe it is unnecessary to rewrite the argument, you may skip this step and simply number the premise and conclusion in the sentence that presents the argument.

This is an inductive argument. If there were another premise, there might be better support for the conclusion. If there were another premise, for example, "(3) Interviewers give $50 bills to well-dressed interviewees," both premises would support the conclusion individually. The diagram would look like this:

There are some deductive arguments in which the conclusion follows from a single premise. For example, consider this argument. (1) All sumo wrestlers are heavyweights. So, (2) if Tomoji is a sumo wrestler, then Tomoji is a heavyweight. The diagram will look just like the first argument above:

Typically, in a deductive argument, two or more premises taken together support the truth of the conclusion. Consider the following:

Students going to college have to start budgeting their money, so everyone in this critical-thinking class needs to budget his or her money, for everyone in this critical-thinking class is a college student.

Number the statements in the passage:

(1) Students going to college have to start budgeting their money, so (2) everyone in this critical-thinking class needs to budget his or her money, for (3) everyone in this critical-thinking class is a college student.

The conclusion is (2). The argument may be set forth as follows:

(1) [All] college students are people who have to start budgeting their money.

(3) <u>All people in this critical-thinking class are college students.</u>

Therefore, (2) all people in this critical-thinking class are people who have to start budgeting their money.

We have restated the argument in such a way that we take into account what *seems* to be the argument. Premise (1) does not indicate whether we are concerned with all or most or only many students. Statements (2) and (3) are general (universal) statements. So, it seems reasonable to believe that (1) also should be understood as a universal statement. We have **reconstructed** the argument. We have restated it in what we take to be the correct argument form. If we are correct, the argument is deductive. We would diagram it as follows:

But this cannot be right! Look again at premise (1). Understood as a universal state-ment, (1) is false. Surely you know someone—call him J. P. Moneybags—who is so wealthy that he has no need to budget his money. So, a better reconstruction of the argument might be:

(1) Most [many? the overwhelming majority of?] college students are people who have to start budgeting their money.

(3) <u>All people in this critical-thinking class are college students.</u>

Therefore, (2) all people in this critical-thinking class are people who have to start budgeting their money.

Now the premises are probably all true. But this is *not* a deductive argument. The premises might all be true and the conclusion false—it would be false if J. P. were in this class. The argument is inductive. The truth of the premises provides *some* evi-dence for the truth of the conclusion, and the evidence for the truth of the conclu-sion will be stronger depending upon whether we are concerned in (1) with "many" (but perhaps not even the majority) or "most" (at least half) or "the overwhelming majority of" college students. Nonetheless, there is no evidence for (2) unless you are given both (1) and (3), so the diagram for the argument is identical with that for the deductive argument:

There are other cases in which premises individually support a conclusion. Consider the following:

"I can't marry you," he continued slowly, "not now, because we've no money, and they depend on me at home."[3]

Notice that there are three statements:

"(1) I can't marry you," he continued slowly, "not now, because (2) we've no money, and (3) they depend on me at home."

[3]D. H. Lawrence, *Sons and Lovers* (New York: Viking Press, 1958), p. 281. Anyone who would sug-gest that this is more probably an explanation than an argument is invited to examine the con-text in which the passage is given and provide an *argument* that the speaker is providing an explanation.

The argument can be restated as follows:

(2) We have no money.

(3) <u>My family depends on me.</u>

Therefore, (1) I cannot marry you now.

Do the premises support the conclusion individually or only when taken together? The fact that "We have no money" is *a* reason that "I cannot marry you now." The fact that "My family depends on me" is *another* reason "I cannot marry you now." They are independent reasons. Each provides some evidence that they cannot marry now, and together they strengthen the evidence for the conclusion. The diagram looks like this:

The argument is inductive. Clearly you could propose other premises that would strengthen the conclusion: (4) "I'm going to spend the next twenty years in prison," (5) "I'm currently married to someone else," and so forth.

Exercises

I. For each of the following, restate the argument clearly. Number the premises and conclusion. Construct an argument tree to show the relations between the premises and the conclusion.

1. Either I'll figure out argument trees without much trouble, or I'll become perplexed. I won't become perplexed. So, I'll figure out argument trees without much trouble.

2. If I figure out argument trees before supper, I can go to a movie tonight. I'll figure out argument trees before supper. Therefore, I can go to a movie tonight.

3. Everyone who studied for an hour mastered argument trees. Angel studied for an hour and mastered argument trees. Leticia studied for an hour and mastered argument trees. Dimitri studied for an hour and mastered argument trees. Solvig studied for an hour and mastered argument trees.

4. If Erica mastered argument trees, Baruch mastered argument trees. Hence, if Alejandro mastered argument trees, then Baruch mastered argument trees. Since if Alejandro mastered argument trees, then Erica mastered argument trees.

5. We should go to the movie, since it's based on a Robert Ludlum book, it stars Demi Moore, and Woody Allen has a cameo appearance. Further, *I'll* buy the popcorn.

6. If I complete my homework, then we can go to the movie; but if I cook my own supper, I'll have to visit the hospital. So, either we can go to the movie or I'll have to visit the hospital, since either I'll complete my homework or I'll cook my own supper.

7. Everyone who goes to the movie will receive a free mask. No one who receives a free mask will be able to eat popcorn. Therefore, no one who goes to the movie will be able to eat popcorn.

8. Rolf is like Daphne insofar as they are both students in this class. Daphne likes movies. So, Rolf likes movies too.

9. Giralda likes sports cars. Giralda is like Ackley insofar as they are both students at the same school. Giralda is like Ackley insofar as they both play in the orchestra. Giralda is like Ackley insofar as they both water ski. Gidalda is like Ackley insofar as they both like to vacation on the French Riviera. We may conclude, therefore, that Ackley likes sports cars.

10. Geraldo cannot afford to skip class. Geraldo plays trumpet. Geraldo plays piano. Geraldo is active in the theatre. Geraldo is active in student government. Geraldo is running for city council. No one who plays trumpet, plays piano, is active in the theatre, is active in student government, and is running for city council is a person who can afford to skip class.

Longer Passages

So far we have looked at passages in which there was only one argument. In many passages there are several arguments that are related in such a way that the conclusion of one argument is the premise of another. In other passages there is considerable information that might not be relevant to the argument. Consider the following:

> The handsome volume you are now holding in your (recently washed, I trust) hands—*Leslie Nielsen's Bad Golf My Way*—is the book you have been waiting for, and thanks to modern publishing technology, it has been produced so speedily that you may not even have had time to realize that you were waiting for it before it appeared on the shelves of your local bookstore!
> And if I may say so, it was worth the wait, even if you were not actually waiting for it, because *Leslie Nielsen's Bad Golf My Way* is the first golf text to describe fully the ins and outs of the game that the vast majority of golfers really play and the only one they have any hope of mastering—bad golf.[4]

First, you have to find the argument or arguments. The first paragraph is amusing, but there is no argument. There is a short argument in the second paragraph. It may be represented as follows:

---

[4]Leslie Nielsen and Henry Beard, *Bad Golf My Way* (York: Doubleday, 1996), p. xi.

1. The book was worth waiting for.

2. *Leslie Nielsen's Bad Golf My Way* is the first golf text to describe fully the ins and outs of the game that the vast majority of golfers really play and the only one they have any hope of mastering—bad golf.

The conclusion is (1). The premise is (2). The tree looks like this:

(2)

|

(1)

   In the following passage there are several arguments in which the conclusion of one argument is a premise of another.

   (1) Chris, a member of ΘΔΓ, went to the dance. (2) Jan, a member of ΘΔΓ, went to the dance. (3) Ashley, a member of ΘΔΓ, went to the dance. So, (4) all members of ΘΔΓ went to the dance. (5) If all members of ΘΔΓ went to the dance, then all members of KΞN went to the dance. So, (6) all members of KΞN went to the dance. (7) Kit is a member of KΞN. So, (8) Kit went to the dance.

We have three arguments, conveniently marked by three conclusion indicators. The first argument is:

1. Chris, a member of ΘΔΓ, went to the dance.

2. Jan, a member of ΘΔΓ, went to the dance.

3. Ashley, a member of ΘΔΓ, went to the dance.

4. All members of ΘΔΓ went to the dance.

This is an inductive generalization. (If you have any question about that, ask whether the evidence for the conclusion would be strengthened if Lynn was a member of ΘΔΓ and went to the dance.) Each of the first three premises individually provides *some* evidence for the truth of (4). The diagram for the first argument looks like this:

(1) (2) (3)

(4)

But (4) is not merely the conclusion of the first argument. It's also a premise for another argument. Statements (4) and (5) jointly support (6).

(4) All members of ΘΔΓ went to the dance.

(5) If all members of ΘΔΓ went to the dance, then all members of KΞN went to the dance.

(6) All members of KΞN went to the dance.

So, that can be added to the diagram.

Nor are we finished now. Statements (6) and (7) jointly support (8).

> (6) All members of KΞN went to the dance.
>
> (7) <u>Kit is a member of KΞN.</u>
>
> (8) Kit went to the dance.

So, this also is added to the diagram.

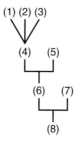

This is the diagram of the complex argument in the passage.

The previous case was fairly straightforward. The premises and conclusions were in a nice, neat order. Everything in the paragraph connected to the final conclusion, (8). This is not always so. Sometimes there is extra information, so you have to figure out what's relevant. Sometimes the premises and conclusions are scattered throughout a passage. You always have to find the individual arguments and figure out how they fit together. And sometimes premises or conclusions are unstated. This said, consider the following:

> (1) Logicians like to play with symbols. So, (2) this course is easy. (3) Critical-thinking problems are like logic problems insofar as they both focus on the evaluation of arguments. (4) Mathematicians see the world as composed of numbers. (5) Fran herds cats all night long. (6) Logic problems are easy. (7) If critical-thinking problems are easy, then this course is easy. (8) If math problems are like critical-thinking problems insofar as both are easy, then mathematicians see the world as composed of numbers. So, (9) critical-thinking problems are easy.

A good way to begin is by looking for premise and conclusion indicators, but that *does not guarantee* that you have found all the arguments. There are two conclusion indicators, so you can be pretty sure that (2) and (9) are conclusions of arguments. If you read the passage through, you probably were puzzled by (5). Statement (5) is unrelated to anything else in the paragraph, so it can be ignored. So, you probably want to concentrate on (2) and (9) and see how they are related to other statements in the paragraph.

If you start with (2), you will notice that (2) is contained in (7). Statement (2) is the consequent (*then* clause) of (7), and (9) is the antecedent (*if* clause) of (7). So, *part* of the argument in the passage has to go like this:

> (7) If critical-thinking problems are easy, then this course is easy.
>
> (9) <u>Critical-thinking problems are easy.</u>
>
> (2) This course is easy.

Statements (7) and (9) jointly support (2), so you will draw the following diagram:

We have already noted that (9) is graced with a conclusion indicator, so it is probably the conclusion of another argument. Is there a premise to which (9) is related? Yes. Statement (3) talks about the similarities between critical-thinking problems and logic problems. Statement (6) tells you that logic problems are easy. If critical-thinking problems are like logic problems in some way (they deal with argumentation), and logic problems are easy, then you have reason to believe that critical-thinking problems are easy. It is an argument by analogy. It may be represented as follows:

(3) Critical-thinking problems are like logic problems insofar as they both focus on the evaluation of arguments.

(6) <u>Logic problems are easy.</u>

(9) Critical-thinking problems are easy.

The tree for this argument looks like this:

Since (9) is a premise of the first argument for which we drew a tree, we may put them together as follows:

Are these arguments related to anything else in the paragraph? Is there, perhaps, another, independent argument in the paragraph? Let's look and see.

Statement (1), "Logicians like to play with symbols," is like (5). It is unconnected to anything else in the paragraph. Unlike (5), (1) at least talks about some of the same things the other statements talk about. Nonetheless, (1) stands in no argumentative relation to the other statements in the paragraph. What about (4) and (8)? Statement (4) is the consequent (*then* clause) of (8). Does it mean it follows from (8)? No. If (4) could be derived from (8), you would need the additional premise [10] Math problems are like critical-thinking problems insofar as both are easy.

Statements (8) and [10] jointly entail (4). But the truth of [10] is questionable, since some of us find most math problems anything but easy. Assumed premises should be pieces of *common knowledge.* Common knowledge consists of statements that virtually everyone assumes are true. So, there is little reason to believe that [10] is assumed. So, there is good reason to believe that there is *no* additional argument.[5]

Let's look at a passage from John Grisham's *The Runaway Jury*:

> **Common Knowledge**
>
> There are statements that virtually everyone takes to be true. At this point in history, "The earth is round" might be one. Simple arithmetic truths are others. And there is common knowledge that applies to certain areas. For example, if you're called to serve on a jury, and if serving would cause personal hardship, the judge might accept that as a reason to excuse you.
>
> There is a problem with common knowledge. Sometimes what virtually everyone assumes to be true is actually false. In 1400, it was common knowledge that the earth is flat, for example. So, while appeals to common knowledge provide some guidance regarding what can *reasonably* be accepted as an assumed premise, it does not guarantee that the assumed premise is true.

The second attempt [to be excused from the jury] was by a middle-aged woman who operated an unlicensed day care center in her home. "I keep kids, Your Honor," she whispered, fighting back tears. "It's all I can do. I collect two hundred dollars a week, and I barely get by. If I have to serve on this jury, then I'll have to hire a stranger to keep the kids. Their parents won't like this, plus I can't afford to hire anyone. I'll go busted."[6]

We may begin by numbering the various statements in the passage and noting that the conclusion, namely, "I should be excused from jury duty," is unstated:

(1) The second attempt [to be excused from the jury] was by a middle-aged woman who operated an unlicensed day care center in her home. "(2) I keep

---

[5]If you wished to be extremely cautious, you might introduce [10], draw the tree including (8), [10], and (4), and then state your misgivings regarding the truth, and therefore the assumption, of [10].

[6]John Grisham, *The Runaway Jury* (New York: Doubleday, 1996), p. 45.

kids, Your Honor," she whispered, fighting back tears. "(3) It's all I can do. (4) I collect two hundred dollars a week, and (5) I barely get by. (6) If I have to serve on this jury, then I'll have to hire a stranger to keep the kids. (7) Their parents won't like this, plus (8) I can't afford to hire anyone. (9) I'll go busted."

Statement (1) is not part of the argument. But without (1) there would be no way to recognize the implicit conclusion, [(10) I should be excused from jury duty]. Statements (2), (3), and (4) set the stage for the argument. Statements (5) and (8) say virtually the same thing. It is a general principle that hardship is a reason for being excluded from serving on jury. What constitutes hardship is left to the judge's discretion. So, the potential juror presents an argument to show that she should be excused. We may reconstruct the argument as follows:

(6) If I have to serve on this jury, then I'll have to hire a stranger to keep the kids.

[(11) If I have to hire a stranger to keep the kids, then I have to be able to afford to hire a stranger to keep the kids.]

Therefore, [(12) if I have to serve on this jury, then I have to be able to afford to hire a stranger to keep the kids].

(8) I cannot afford to hire a stranger to keep the kids.

Therefore, [(10) I do not have to serve on this jury].

Notice that we have taken considerable liberty in reconstructing the argument. Statement [11] may be called the hardship premise. It reflects the principle that causing hardship is a reason to be excused from jury duty. So, given this reconstruction, the diagram would be as follows:

But if we can take this much liberty in reconstructing the argument, why not cut it down to an even simpler form, a form that explicitly recognizes the principle that if serving on a jury causes hardship, then one should be excused? Why not state it as follows?

If serving on this jury will cause extreme hardship then I should be excused.

Serving on this jury will cause extreme hardship.

Therefore, I should be excused.

Certainly, this is the gist of the argument. Why not leave it at that?

A principle that should be employed in reconstructing an argument is that *you should preserve as much of the original language as is possible*. Insofar as you preserve the original language—you *must* at least preserve the original meaning when restating a statement in your own words—the reconstruction retains the "richness" of the original argument. Nonetheless, this is a fairly loose principle. As you learn more about arguments, you will learn that there are several valid deductive argument forms. A valid deductive argument form with all true premises provides conclusive evidence for the truth of

---

In My Own Words

Wouldn't it be better to restate the argument in my own words? Wouldn't I understand the argument better if I stated it in my own words?

If you state the argument in your own words, you show *your* understanding of the argument. *That's important!* But you are also trying to reconstruct *someone else's* argument. Words are important. So, by retaining the verbiage, you are giving a good reconstruction.

In *practice,* you might start with a very simple reconstruction and ask several times, "What more is said in the argument?" Ultimately, such a practice might yield the *best* reconstruction. It would be accompanied by additional arguments that the way *you* restate the premises is reasonable.

---

its conclusion. So, if you can reconstruct an argument as a valid deductive argument with true premises, do so. If this involves introducing a *true premise to yield the valid form,* introduce it. But be sure you have introduced a *true* premise, or one you have good reason to believe is true. *Never* introduce an obviously false premise. As we saw above, this means that sometimes you will need to replace a statement such as "All crows are black" with a statement such as "Most crows are black," thereby changing an argument from an unsound deductive argument (in this case, a valid argument with a false premise) to a strong inductive argument. By providing as strong a reconstruction of any argument as you can, and by retaining as much of the original verbiage as you can, you demonstrate your respect to both the person presenting the argument and the argumentative enterprise.[7]

Exercises

II. Construct an argument tree for each of the following.

1. (1) If this problem is hard, I'll get a headache. (2) If I get a headache, I'll have to take aspirin. (3) But I won't have to take aspirin. (4) So, I won't get a headache. (5) So, this problem it not hard. (6) If this problem is not hard, then I'll be able to celebrate tonight. (7) So, I'll be able to celebrate tonight. (8) If my professor has an evil grin, then I will not be able to celebrate tonight. (9) So, my professor does not have an evil grin.

2. (1) Old watches are like old-fashioned clocks insofar as they both have mechanical movements. (2) Old watches needed to be wound regularly. (3) So, old clocks needed to be wound regularly. (4) Nothing that needed to be wound regularly

---

[7]The author is not wholly satisfied with his reconstruction of the last argumentative passage. Can you do better?

contains computer chips. (5) So, old watches do not contain computer chips. (6) Model-T Fords are old and do not contain computer chips. (7) My stalk of celery is old and does not contain computer chips. (8) So, no old things contain computer chips.

3. (1) Fran went to the party and became ill. (2) Joe went to the party and became ill. (3) Chris went to the party and became ill. (4) If Jan became ill, Jan visited the doctor. (5) Jan did not visit the doctor. (6) So, everyone who went to the party became ill. (7) So, if Jan went to the party, Jan became ill. (8) So, if Jan went to the party, Jan visited the doctor. (9) So Jan did not go to the party.

4. (1) If John went to the game, then either Frieda went to the library or Johanna wrote problems for this test. (2) Johanna did not write problems for this test. (3) If Frieda went to the library, then Chris was behind the reference desk. (4) If Chris was behind the reference desk, then if Theophilus received a letter from Luke, then Josephus wrote jazz quartets. (5) John went to the game. (6) So, if Theophilus received a letter from Luke, then Josephus wrote jazz quartets. (7) So, Frieda went to the library. (9) So, Chris was behind the reference desk. (9) So, either Frieda went to the library or Johanna wrote problems for this test.

5. (1) So, the coach will probably be in trouble. (2) The Mighty Mice lost this week. (3) We may conclude that the Mighty Mice have learned how to lose (with style). (4) If the Mighty Mice have learned to lose (with style), then they won't be in the playoffs. (5) The Mighty Mice lost the week before last. (6) If the Mighty Mice won't be in the playoffs, the coach will probably be in trouble. (7) The Mighty Mice lost last week. (8) The Mighty Mice won't be in the playoffs.

6. (1) The lamp doesn't work. (2) The electricity is on. (3) So, either the electricity is off, or a fuse is blown, or the bulb has burned out. (4) If the lamp doesn't work, then either the electricity is off, or a fuse is blown, or the bulb has burned out. (5) No fuse has blown. (6) So, we'll be sitting in the dark. (7) So, the bulb has burned out. (8) So, the bulb has burned out and we don't have another bulb. (9) If the bulb has burned out and we don't have another bulb, then we'll be sitting in the dark. (10) We don't have another bulb.

7. (1) If today is Saturday, then I'll attend the big game; and if today is Sunday, I'll spend the morning at St. Mattress. (2) Either today is Saturday or today is Sunday. (3) So, either I'll attend the big game or I'll spend the morning at St. Mattress. (4) If I have to study for a big test, then I won't attend the big game; and if my parents are coming to visit, then I won't spend the morning at St. Mattress. (5) So, either I don't have to study for a big test, or my parents are not coming to visit. (6) My parents are coming to visit. (7) So, I don't have to study for a big test. (8) If I don't have to study for a big test, I'll have lunch at Red Lobster. (9) So, I'll have lunch at Red Lobster.

8. (1) If Fran went to the party, she became ill. (2) If Joe went to the party, he became ill. (3) If Chris went to the party, she became ill. (4) If Jan went to the party, Jan became ill. (5) If Jan became ill, Jan visited the doctor. (6) So, if Jan went to the party, then Jan visited the doctor. (7) So, Jan did not go to the party. (8) Everyone who went to the party became ill. (9) Jan did not visit the doctor.

9. (1) Aristotle's scientific theories have been proven wrong. (2) Virtually all the scientific theories of the twelfth century have been proven wrong. (3) Descartes's scientific theories have been proven wrong. (4) If Einstein's theory is correct, then Newton's theory has been proven wrong. (5) Einstein's theory is correct. (6) So, Newton's theory has been proven wrong. (7) Therefore, many scientific theories have been proven wrong. (8) If many scientific theories have been proven wrong, then it is likely that some of the scientific theories that are current today will be proven wrong. (9) Therefore, it is likely that some of the scientific theories that are current today will be proven wrong.

10. (1) If today is Saturday, then there will be a big game. (2) If there is a big game, then fans will be out in large numbers. (3) If the fans are out in large numbers, then the library will be deserted. (4) If the library is deserted, then it will be a good place to study. (5) But if the library is deserted, then keeping it open would not be cost effective. (6) If keeping the library open would not be cost effective, then the bookkeepers will insist that it be closed. (7) If the bookkeepers insist that the library be closed, then the library will be closed. (8) So, if today is Saturday, then the fans will be out in large numbers. (9) So, if today is Saturday, then the library will be deserted. (10) So, the library would be a good place to study. (11) Today is Saturday. (12) So, the library will be deserted. (13) So, keeping the library open will not be cost effective. (14) So, the bookkeepers will insist the library be closed. (15) So, the library will be closed. (16) So, the library would be a good place to study, and the library will be closed.

One More *Real* Argument

Consider the following:

> (1) Fiber is important in the diet because (2) it binds water, causing a softer and bulkier stool that increases peristalsis (involuntary muscle contractions of intestinal walls that force the stool forward) and (3) allows food residues to pass through the intestinal tract more quickly. (4) Many researchers believe that speeding up passage of food residues through the intestines lowers the risk for colon cancer, mainly because (5) cancer-causing agents are not in contact as long with the intestinal wall. (6) Fiber also is thought to bind the carcinogens (cancer-producing substances), and (7) more water in the stool may dilute the cancer-causing agents, lessening their potency.[8]

There is a lot going on here. There is *at least one* explanation: (5) explains why many researchers believe (4) is true. Is the entire paragraph merely an explanation? Taken in isolation, there is no way to tell. If (1) were taken as a known truth, (2), (3), (6), and (7) would explain why fiber is important. But the passage is taken from a textbook on health. You might reasonably expect that one of the authors' goals is to convince

---

[8]Werner W. K. Hoeger and Sharon A. Hoeger, *Lifetime Physical Fitness and Wellness: A Personalized Program,* 5th ed. (Englewood: Morton Publishing, 1998), p. 163.

you that consuming a fair amount of fiber is important to your health. So understood, we can reconstruct an argument as follows:

(2) Fiber binds water, causing a softer and bulkier stool that increases peristalsis (involuntary muscle contractions of intestinal walls that force the stool forward).

(3) Fiber allows food residues to pass through the intestinal tract more quickly.

(6) Fiber binds the carcinogens (cancer-producing substances).

(7) More water in the stool may dilute the cancer-causing agents, lessening their potency.
_____

Therefore, [(8) fiber helps prevent cancer.]

[(9) Anything in the diet that helps prevent cancer is an important element in the diet.]
_____

Therefore, (1) fiber is an important element in the diet.

Notice that there are two arguments. The first is inductive: (2), (3), (6), and (7) each provide some evidence that (8), consuming fiber, helps prevent cancer. The diagram would look like this:

The second argument is strictly deductive:

So, the reconstruction of the argument in the passage would look like this:

Is our reconstruction correct? Maybe. Some might suggest that there is something missing in the first argument, since there is nothing that "connects" the premises with conclusion. No explicit reason is given that ties the various effects of fiber consumption with the prevention of cancer. So, you might suggest that there is another implicit premise [(10) If (2), (4), (6), and (7), then (8).] This would convert the first argument into a deductive argument, and the diagram for the arguments in the entire passage would look like this:

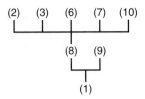

Is this reconstruction better? Maybe. One problem is that some might question the truth of [(10)]. Others might suggest that there are two separate arguments, that premises (2) and (3) are not explicitly linked to the prevention of cancer. These might suggest that (2) and (3) each provide some evidence for (1) and that (6) and (7) each assume a premise that ties fiber consumption to the prevention of cancer:

[(10*) If (6) then (8).]

[(10**) If (7) then (9).]

These might suggest that the argumentative structure of the paragraph looks like this:

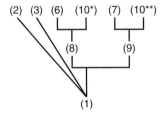

Others might suggest that if (2) and (3) are related to the prevention of cancer, they are linked by way of (4). Statement (4) might be restated as (4*): Anything that speeds the passage of food residues through the intestines helps prevent cancer. Such a person might also suggest that (2) *explains why* (3) is the case, so (2) is not part of the argument as such. Hence, the argumentative structure of the paragraph is as follows:

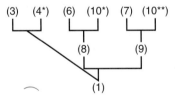

But, which of these reconstructions RIGHT? you ask. One problem with real-life uses of English is that speakers and writers do not always say precisely what they mean. Arguments often are presented in a rather loose way, as they are in the paragraph under consideration. It is clear that (1) is the conclusion. It *seems* clear that the primary reason one should accept (1) is that fiber helps prevent cancer of the intestines. Anyone who has followed the medical discussions of the virtues of fiber over the past several decades would be quick to acknowledge that health professionals have consistently pointed to the virtues of fiber as a means of preventing cancer.[9] Since the passage was taken from a health textbook, it is reasonable to assume that the authors are concerned with fiber as a cancer preventative. So, I am inclined to believe that our last reconstruction of the argument is superior to the others.

Notice what was done in the last paragraph. An argument has been presented that the last reconstruction of the argument is probably superior to the earlier formulations. *That* argument can itself be reconstructed as follows:

(1) Most health professionals promote the virtues of fiber as a means of preventing cancer.

(2) The argument was presented by a health professional.

(3) The last reconstruction of the argument most clearly shows the relationship between eating fiber and preventing cancer.

Therefore, (4) the last reconstruction of the argument probably represents the authors' intended argument more accurately than the earlier ones.

The argument is inductive, and it may be represented as follows:

The point of all this is that arguments can be reconstructed in various ways. Some reconstructions seem to be superior to others. Which reconstruction is the best can be a matter of dispute. So, you might need to give—you always should be prepared to give—an argument defending your reconstruction of a given argumentative passage.

Exercises

III. Advertisements can be understood as arguments to the conclusion "Buy our stuff." This "stuff" might be a product, a service, or a system of beliefs. Sometimes the conclusion is stated. Often it is not. For each of the following advertisements, state the argument, numbering the premises and conclusions, and construct a diagram to show how the premises are related to the conclusion or conclusions.

---

[9]Until recently, the assumption that a high-fiber diet prevents cancer of the colon was virtually taken as a truism. This recently was challenged. See Charles S. Fuchs, Edward L. Giovannucci, Graham A. Colditz, David J. Hunter, Meir J. Stampfer, Bernard Rosner, Frank E. Speizer, Walter C. Willett, "Dietary Fiber and the Risk of Colorectal Cancer and Adenoma in Women." *The New England Journal of Medicine*, 340 (January 21, 1999): 169–76; Jeff Don, "Disease Diet Doubts: Study: Anti-Cancer Benefits of High-Fiber Diet Questionable," Associated Press, April 20, 2000.

1.

Source: Used with permission of Environmental Defense.

2.

Source: Used with permission of Environmental Defense.

3.

Source: Reprinted with permission from the Natural Resources Defense Council.

4.

Source: Used by permission of the National Action Council for Minorities in Engineering, (NACME) Inc.

5.

With Army ROTC, you'll get to fuel your desire to be the best. In the process, you'll learn how to think on your feet, stay cool under pressure, really take charge. *Register for an Army ROTC course today.* It's time to stoke that fire.

ARMY ROTC
Unlike any other college course you can take.

Source: Used with permission of U. S. Army Cadet Command.

6.

Jesus Christ was a liar.

Either that or a complete raving lunatic. Oh yeah, there's one other option (and only one): He was and is God, just like he claimed.

Many people prefer to think he was a good moral teacher, but if you think through it, that's not logically possible. Jesus, in the midst of a fiercely monotheistic culture, through his actions and overt statements claimed to be God in the flesh.

If the claim was false, then either Jesus knew that, or he didn't. If it was false and he knew it, then by his intentional deception he has scammed the world with the greatest hoax ever conceived. Liars don't tend to make particularly good moral teachers.

If, on the other hand, he honestly was convinced in his own mind that he was God (and wasn't) then it's pretty clear that he was a lunatic. If your roommate really thought she was God, what would you think of her?

The only remaining possibility, as implausible as it sounds, is that the claim was true: Jesus really is God. He really does love you. And He really can forgive your sins.

Liar, Lunatic, or Lord. There is no other option.

What do you believe?

wcucrusade.org • Campus Crusade for Christ • Thursdays at 8 • Schmucker 100

Source: Used with permission of Tim Henderson of Campus Crusade for Christ.

7.

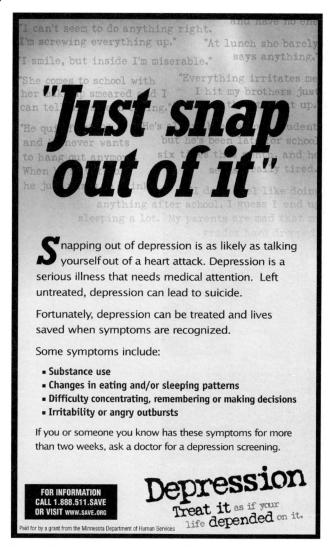

Source: Used with permission of SA\VE: Suicide Awareness Voices of Education.

8.

Source: Used with permission of Alleycat Tattoo and Body Piercing.

IV. Examine each of the following passages. Number the statements in the passage, and state the arguments as clearly as you can, adding assumed premises and unstated conclusions as necessary. Then construct a tree diagram to show the argumentative structure of the passage.

1. "Hirsch and Lancaster are the same people. Hirsch and Easter are the same people. Therefore, Lancaster and Easter must be the same." (John Grisham, *The Runaway Jury* [New York: Doubleday, 1996], p. 321).

2. There are only three things in this world with that kind of unconditional acceptance: dogs, donuts, and money. Only money is better [than dogs or donuts]. You

know why? Because it don't make you fat, and it don't poop all over the living room floor. (Lawrence Garfield, in *Other People's Money*, Warner Bros. 1992)

3. It is pretty clear that screenwriter Mitch Glazer and director Alfonso Cuaron never quite discovered what Dickens' novel [*Great Expectations*] is about, for they've created a movie so lost in its own ambiguity and obsessed with its own beauty that the emptiness at its center is crystal-clear. (Brent Bowles, "Nothing great about new 'Expectations'," *The Breeze*, James Madison University, February 6, 1998, p. 17)

4. After mentioning that the victim, Gilbert Adrian, kept a large sum of money in his safe, a safe that was emptied on the night of Adrian's murder, Megan Calder continues: "There was no mention in the news about any money disappearing, so I don't think anyone knew about it. Am I right?" (Thomas Chastain, *Perry Mason in The Case of Too Many Murders* [New York: William Morrow and Company, 1989], p. 99)

5. Heather Lodovico, who graduated in December, joined the group surrounding Mark and said, "He's speaking the truth. If we're not with God, we're in hell. That's what [Mark] is preaching. A lot of people don't want to hear that." (Kristen Heiss, "Man on commons tells students to seek Christ," *The Breeze,* James Madison University, [February 12, 1998], p. 3)

6. As the volume of the food is increased, the time required to cook or heat the item increases proportionately. If twice the amount of food is placed in the range, it will take almost twice as long to cook. For example, if one strip of bacon requires 1 minute, two strips of the same size will require 1 minute, 45 seconds. (*The Amana Radarange Microwave Oven Cook Book,* [Amana, Iowa: Amana Refrigeration, Inc., 1975], p. 3)

7. As for tasting other people's cones, never do it. The reason here is that if it tastes good, you'll wish you had it; if it tastes bad, you'll have had a taste of something that tastes bad; if it doesn't taste either good or bad, you won't have missed anything. Of course no person in his right mind ever *would* want to taste anyone else's cone, but it's useful to have good, logical reasons for hating the thought of it. (L. Rust Hills, "How to Eat an Ice Cream Cone," in *Russell Baker's Book of American Humor,* edited by Russell Baker [New York: W. W. Norton & Company, 1993], p. 291)

8. It's a universal law—*when we do more than we are paid to do, eventually we will be paid more for what we do.* When we accept additional responsibilities, we become in essence like sailing vessels. On a sailing vessel, the more sail that is hoisted, the faster and farther it will go. In life, if we want to go faster and farther, we must hoist more sail or put more of ourselves into a project. (Zig Ziglar, *Raising Positive Kids in a Negative World* [New York: Ballantine Books, 1989], p. 69)

9. Swine are, among other things, miraculously efficient converters of grain to meat. Hence too, they help farmers hold grain off the market, "add to its value" by eating it, until the price improves. Then, as the saying goes, "the corn walks itself to market." Since grains seldom fetch their cost of production, that fatal walk helps

keep food affordable and agriculture solvent. (Richard Horwitz, "Hogs and the Meaning of Life in Iowa," *The University of Iowa Spectator* 31, #1 [Fall 1997], p. 10. Used with permission of the author.)

10. "Why did you say 'careless'?" I asked, conciliatingly.

"Well," he replied, not looking up from the final task of taking the last stones off the dead man's feet, "it is careless not to bury more carefully when you have murdered."

"You're sure?" I asked.

"Look at the skin. It's perfectly unbroken anywhere else. But there is a tear in the chest and I think that darker color on the piece of shirt is pretty certainly blood." (H. F. Heard, *Reply Paid* [1942, 1970], in *The Amazing Mycroft Mysteries* [New York: The Vanguard Press, 1980], p. 297)

11. The excellent performance of the equity and bond markets in 1995 through the third quarter of 1997 was followed by a correction in equity markets. Once again, the driving force for the correction came from an unanticipated source—the currency and credit crises in Southeast Asia.

Equity markets should benefit from steady or declining rates, and earnings will drive divergence in the market. As currency devaluations make American goods more expensive, large multinational companies will likely find reduced demand for their products in Asia. Subsequently, less expensive imports from Asia will put pressure on American companies to lower prices on goods such as automobiles. In this scenario, small and medium-sized companies would benefit because lower prices for imported goods increase real disposable income. (AGSPC President's Letter, *American General Series Portfolio Company Semi-Annual Report* [November 30, 1997] p. 1)

12. There is virtually no evidence to support [the view that immigrants take jobs from U.S. citizens], probably the most widespread misunderstanding about immigrants. . . . The jobs immigrants take are of course easier to see, but immigrants are often highly productive, [they] run their own businesses, and [they] employ both immigrants and citizens. One study found that Mexican immigration to Los Angeles County between 1970 and 1980 was responsible for 78,000 new jobs. Governor Mario Cuomo reports that immigrants own more than 40,000 companies in New York, which provide thousands of jobs and $3.5 billion to the state's economy every year. (David Cole, "Five Myths about Immigration," in *Current Issues and Enduring Questions*, edited by Sylvan Barnet and Hugo Bedeu, 4th ed. [Boston: Bedford Books, 1996], p. 99)

13. **Sampson.** I strike quickly, being moved.

Gregory. But thou art not quickly moved to strike.

Sam. A dog of the house of Montague shall move me to stand.

Gre. To move is to stir; and to be valiant is to stand: therefore, if thou art moved, thou runn'st away.

Sam. A dog of that house shall move me to stand: I will take the wall of any man or maid of Montague's.

Gre. That shows thee a weak slave; for the weakest goes to the wall.

Sam. True; and therefore women, being the weaker vessels, are ever thrust to the wall: therefore I push Montague's men from the wall and thrust his maids to the wall. (William Shakespeare, *Romeo and Juliet*, Act 1, Scene 1)

14. Infant's flesh will be in season throughout the year, but [it will be] more plentiful in March and a little before and after: for we are told by a grave author, an eminent French physician, that fish being a prolific diet, there are more children born in Roman Catholic countries about nine months after Lent than at any other season; therefore, reckoning a year after Lent, the markets will be more glutted than usual, because the number of popish infants is at least three to one in this kingdom. . . . [March and a little before and after is a year after Lent.] (Jonathan Swift, "A Modest Proposal")

15. Judging by the time she and her grooms and her maid had passed by in the forest, Cadfael reckoned, Adelais must have arrived here that same day, two days previously. They would have no need to halt for a night between Chenet and Elford, for on horseback the distance was easy. Therefore she must already have seen and talked with her son. What she had to communicate to him now, as soon as he returned from riding, might well have to do with whatever was new this day at the manor of Elford. And what was new but the arrival of the two monks from Shrewsbury, and their reason for being here, a reason she would interpret with discretion for his ears. For he had been here at Elford when his sister died at Hales, for the world's ears—and her brother also?—of a fever. That must be all he had ever known of it, a simple, sad death, such as may happen in any household, even to one in the bloom of youth. No, that strong and resolute woman would never have let her son into the secret. An old, trusted, confidential maidservant, maybe. She must have needed such a one, now perhaps dead. But her son, no, never. (Ellis Peters, *The Confession of Brother Haluin* [New York: The Mysterious Press, 1988], p. 62)

16. Perry Mason and Lt. Tragg are discussing the California marriage laws pertaining to Mason's current case:

"Notice that language again," Mason said. "I'll read it to you once more. He held up the paper and read, "*All* marriages contracted without this state, which would be valid by the laws of the country in which the same were contracted, are valid in this state."

. . .

"There you are," Mason said. "The marriage is legal in Mexico. Therefore, it's legal in every other country, particularly in the state of California, because the California law specifically so provides."

"But look here," Tragg said. "It'll be possible to prove that these two people left California in order to perpetrate a fraud on the marriage laws of California and. . . ."

Mason smiled and shook his head. "Read the case of McDonald versus McDonald, 6 California (Second) 457. It's also reported and discussed in 106 A. L. R. 1290 and is reported in the Pacific Reporter in 58 Pacific (Second) page 163. That case holds squarely and fairly that where people leave California for the sole purpose of contracting a marriage, in defiance of the laws of California, and go to another state, and, as part of that general scheme, a marriage is contracted in that state, that marriage is valid. It is a legal and binding ceremony regardless of the fact that such marriage is not only contrary to the *laws* of California but contrary to the underlying policy of the laws of California."

"Well, . . . ," Tragg said, "the divorce in Mexico is no good in California, you have to admit that."

"I don't have to admit it, but I'm willing to concede it for the purpose of the argument."

"Then the marriage has to be bigamous."

"The marriage is as good as gold," Mason said.

"You mean that this man has two wives and . . ."

"He doesn't now," Mason said, "but until an early hour this morning [when his first wife was killed] he did have. He's in the rather unique position of having committed bigamy and having had two perfectly legal wives." (Erle Stanley Gardner, *The Case of the Dubious Bridegroom* [New York: Ballantine Books, 1949], pp. 116-17)

17. "Of course there have always been apostles of peace and men who have risked a bold and quotable word against war. Permit me to remind the High Womenal [Women's Tribunal] of the poet Opitz, who during the Thirty Years' War—how vainly, we know—attempted to foment peace. Or Old Man Bebel's antiwar speech. It was in the spring of 1913, and the Socialist International cheered him. We know that in religious songs and philosophical treatises peace has been sung, longed for, spun into allegory, and meditated upon *ad nauseam*. But since no one ever tried seriously to resolve the conflicts of human society while forswearing the categories of masculine thinking, nothing was ever accomplished beyond protestation of peaceful intent and sophistical distinctions between just and unjust wars. Crusaders have always managed to massacre people in the name of brotherly love. Wars of liberation are still very much in vogue, and the principle of the free market has meant undernourishment for millions of people: hunger, too, is war." (Günter Grass, *The Flounder*, translated by Ralph Manheim [New York: Harcourt Brace Jovanovich, 1978], pp. 520-521)

18. Christian theology speaks of 'revelation', when on the ground of the Easter appearances of the risen Lord it perceives and proclaims the identity of the risen one with the crucified one. Jesus is recognized in the Easter appearances as what he really *was*. That is the ground of faith's 'historical' remembrance of the life and work, claims and sufferings of Jesus of Nazareth. But the messianic titles, in which this identity of Jesus in cross and resurrection is claimed and described, all anticipate at the same time the not yet apparent future of the risen Lord. This means that the Easter appearances and revelations of the risen Lord are manifestly understood as foretaste and promise of his still future glory and lordship. Jesus is recognized in the Easter appearances as what he really *will be*. This 'vital point' for a Christian view of revelation accordingly lies neither in 'that which came to expression in the man Jesus' (Ebeling) nor in the 'destiny of Jesus' (Pannenberg) but—combining both of these—in the fact that in all the qualitative difference of

cross and resurrection Jesus is the same. This identity in infinite contraction is theologically understood as an event of identification, and act of the faithfulness of God. It is this that forms the ground of the promise of the still outstanding future of Jesus Christ. It is this that is the ground of the hope which carries faith through the trials of the god-forsaken world and of death. (Jürgen Moltmann, *Theology of Hope: On the Ground and Implications of Christian Eschatology*, translated by James W. Leitch [New York: Harper & Row, 1967], pp. 84–85)

19. Cool Mesh comes with hemmed or banded sleeves pocket or plain . . .

First, let's narrow the field. There are a lot of mesh knit shirts out there, all the way from discount warehouses to specialty shops and department stores. Most of them fall short of our standards for quality, fabric, and construction. Sad but true.

The fact is, we've been making mesh shirts for about 15 years now. That's long enough to perfect everything—from buttons to bottom vents and all seams in between.

A few worthy competitors.

What about our worthy competitors, those who make "pretty good" polos? Most of them use single-piqué mesh rather than our airier, more luxurious double-piqué. Some use fabric softeners, and get stiff and "boardy" after a wash or two. Some fade easily.

Differences in the details.

All but one have chosen a less expensive, less stylish placket than we have. None have our same clean-finished "treetop" side vents. Ours has our elegant single-needle topstitching. Despite these differences, some ask you to pay more than twice our price.

When the smoke clears . . .

All things considered, we're confident we offer you the best mesh at any price. (*Lands' End Direct Merchants,* June 1998, pp. 4–5)

20. "Anyway, the book has vanished. . . ."

"This is the most unlikely thing," William said, as we arrived at the chapter house. "If it was there, as Severinus told us it was, either it's been taken away or it's there still."

"And since it isn't there, someone has taken it away," I concluded.

"It is also possible that the argument should proceed from another minor premise. Since everything confirms the fact that nobody can have taken it away . . ."

"Then it should be there still. But it is not there."

"Just a moment. We say it isn't there because we didn't find it. But perhaps we didn't find it because we haven't seen where it was."

"But we looked everywhere!"

"We looked, but did not see. Or else saw, but did not recognize. . . . Adso, how did Severinus describe that book to us? What words did he use?"

"He said he had found a book that was not one of his, in Greek. . . ."

"No! Now I remember. He said a *strange* book. Severinus was a man of learning, and for a man of learning a book in Greek is not strange; even if that scholar doesn't know Greek, he would at least recognize the alphabet. And a scholar wouldn't' call a book in Arabic strange, either, even if he doesn't know Arabic. . . ." He broke off. "And what was an Arabic book doing in Severinus's laboratory?"

"But why should he have called an Arabic book strange?"

"This is the problem. If he called it strange it was because it had an unusual appearance, unusual at least for him, who was an herbalist and not a librarian. . . . And in libraries it can happen that several ancient manuscripts are bound together, collecting in one volume various and curious texts, one in Greek, or in Aramaic. . . ."

". . . and one in Arabic!" I cried, dazzled by this illumination. (Umberto Eco, *The Name of the Rose*, translated by William Weaver [New York: Warner Books, 1980], pp. 440–41)

PART III

Checking the Evidence

Whom should you trust and why? Are your beliefs true? How do you go about determining whether your beliefs are true? Can you ever *know* that your beliefs are true?

In Part III we examine the sources of some of our common beliefs and the criteria for judging whether those beliefs are true. Many of our beliefs rest on observation. If you saw Chris in class, you are likely to claim that the statement, "Chris was in class" is true. Could you be wrong?

Many of our beliefs are based on the testimony of others. If a noted historian tells you that the intervention of the French navy was responsible for the victory at Yorktown during the American Revolution, you probably would believe her. But you might not believe this if your neighbor or your younger brother made the same claim. Why should you believe one person but not the other? Should you believe either of them? And what role should what you already know play in other claims you accept as true?

Some actions are said to be good or bad, right or wrong. What justifies such a claim? Are there moral rules? If so, why should one follow them? If not, is there any basis for making decisions regarding what you should do in a given set of circumstances? And what about aesthetic values? Are there criteria for evaluating works of art?

In Chapter 10 we examine the criteria for evaluating observation statements. In Chapter 11 we examine the criteria for evaluating testimony. In Chapter 12 we examine arguments supporting moral and aesthetic claims.

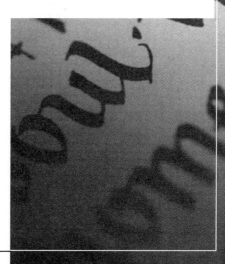

When Should Seeing Be Believing?

The View: The chapter examines the criteria for evaluating the probable truth of observation statements. The criteria provide inductive evidence that the claim is true or false.

When should we believe what we see? What criteria guide our judgments regarding the probable truth of observation claims?

Sense experience is a primary source of knowledge. You might look out the window and see that it is raining. You might look out the window and see a robbery in progress. Or you might see Frank steal Audrey's purse. You might look through a microscope, see an amoeba, and conclude that the water you drink is polluted. Are the activities the same in each case?

In each of these cases, we take what we see as evidence that a statement is true: "It is raining." "There was a robbery on such-and-such a date at such-and-such a location." "Frank stole Audrey's purse." "The water I drink is polluted." Your observations provide **evidence** (reasons for you to believe) that the statement is true. How do we weigh this evidence?

There are five questions you should ask in judging whether an observation statement—whether your own or another's[1]—is probably true.

O1. Was the observer in a position to make the observation?

O2. Were the observation conditions adequate for making an accurate observation?

O3. Did the observer have the appropriate technology to make the observation? If so, did the observer know how to use that technology?

O4. Does the observer have the background knowledge needed to interpret what was observed? Does the observer's claim make sense? That is, is it consistent with or supported by what you know from other sources?

---

[1] If it is the observation claim of another, there are additional questions to ask. We look at those questions in Chapter 11.

O5. Is the observer free from bias that might influence what he or she believes was observed?

Answers to these questions provide *inductive evidence* that an observation statement is true or false. *Whether* a statement is true or false depends upon the facts. For example, the statement "A rabbit lives under my shed" might be true even if no one has ever seen the rabbit in its domicile. A concern with evidence indicates that you are drawing a *conclusion* on the basis of observations. This is not how we ordinarily speak. If Officer Carter visits a crime scene, we usually say she *sees* the body on the floor, while she *concludes* that a crime has been committed. Ordinarily, we would say she *concluded* that there was a *body* on the floor only if there had been some reason for doubt. (Assume the police recently had found several life-like mannequins covered with animal blood.) Generally, where you draw the distinction between observing something and concluding that someone has observed something is relatively unimportant. You are clearly drawing a conclusion when you go beyond the observational evidence, as when Officer Carter concludes that a crime had been committed.

The five questions are interrelated. An answer given to any one of them might need to be revised on the basis of the answers to others. Nonetheless, if the answer to **O1** is negative, the conditions probably are sufficient to show that an observation claim is false. If Smith says he saw Frank steal Audrey's purse at 12:30 on the corner of First Street and Maple, but at the time Smith was halfway across town, he was not in a position to make the observation. So, his observation statement should be judged false, right? Probably. At the very least there is a shift in the **burden of proof**. Smith must explain how it was possible for him to make the observation given his location at the time. Perhaps he saw the crime on a surveillance tape sometime after the crime occurred. Not all observations are direct and unaided. For example, most of us have *seen* an airplane hit one of the World Trade Center towers on September 11, 2001, because we saw it on television.

On the other hand, if you were present when and where the event occurred, this does not guarantee that you saw it. You can probably remember an occasion when you were watching a movie or a sporting event while talking with a friend, and you missed seeing a significant event in the movie or the "big play" in the game. So, while being physically present or present by way of some technological device might be a necessary condition for deeming the claim "I saw . . ." true, it is not a sufficient condition.

O2 is a judgment call. If you claim to see something that was adequately illuminated on a sunny day, the observation conditions generally are more favorable than if you claimed to see something in a dark corner at night. Rain can reduce visibility. The size and color of the object in certain conditions can affect the visibility. And the conditions of the observer might be relevant. An intoxicated observer or a person just waking from a sound sleep might not be trusted to the degree of a sober or wide awake person. So here your judgment might be one of degree: definitely adequate, somewhat adequate, probably inadequate, or definitely inadequate.

O3 will vary with the situation. Different objects can be seen in different ways. Different people must use different technologies to support their claims. If you are nearsighted, you may need to wear glasses to observe objects at a distance. If you wear bifocals, you may need to "learn how to see through them" before you can trust your observation claims. If you are looking at very small things, you may need to learn how to use a magnifying glass or a microscope before your observations can be trusted. A person looking through a microscope will not see an amoeba unless she knows what patterns of light are evidence for seeing an amoeba. A person looking through a telescope at one of the moons of Jupiter will not recognize it as a moon unless he knows what counts as "seeing a moon of Jupiter." As in the case of **O2**, answering **O3** might require a judgment of degree.

We already have considered some of the issues concerning background knowledge that is necessary to interpret what you observe. But **O4** is broader and applies even when little or no technology is involved. At bottom, it is the ability to recognize things and to draw careful conclusions about what you see. Is what you *believe* you see **consistent** with what you know from other sources? Two statements are consistent if it is possible for both to be true at the same time. If you're driving down a road on a hot summer day and you seem to see water on the road ahead, experience suggests that it is probably a reflection of light off the pavement. Of course, if the area has recently been subject to flooding, it might be consistent to suggest that the apparent puddle is actually water. More complicated cases include seeing wormlike creatures in a calm body of water. If you have some background in biology, you might judge that the "worms" are mosquito larva. (Keeping a sample of the water in a closed jar for a few days might confirm this.) You often need some understanding of how things work, and you might need to make observations over a number of days to reach a conclusion. Galileo observed and plotted the movements of the moons of Jupiter for some time before concluding that they were moons. Before you claim to have seen a "flying saucer" (not to be confused with a Frisbee™), you might ask whether you can come up with an alternative explanation of what you have seen. Generally, the more background knowledge you have, the more likely it is that you will be able to correctly interpret what you observe.

But there is another side to this. Sometimes we "see" what we expect to see. Sometimes—perhaps more often than we realize—we draw conclusions without being certain that all aspects of the observational situation have been taken into account. At one time, the university where I worked set up a new heating plant. The heating plant was about five hundred yards from my office. A prevalent feature of the new plant was a tall smokestack. The top of the smokestack was painted white, and there was an object on a scaffold near the top of the smokestack. I observed this phenomenon in the ordinary way: I saw it with the aid of my glasses. Seeing this for the first time, I said to myself, "Ah, there is a person on the scaffold painting the chimney." That evening I went to my office and was surprised to notice that the "person" on the scaffold was flashing off and on in bright red. At that point I realized that I had drawn a conclusion on the basis of my observation. Given my distance from the smokestack and the fact that I had not used any optical instruments (such as binoculars) to improve my normal vision, observational conditions were far from optimal (**O2**). I had seen *something* on a scaffold. The chimney that had been brick-colored a few days before was now white. Given my past experience with scaffolding, I *inferred* that the thing on the scaffold must be a person—what else would be on a scaffold? Given that the chimney that had been brick-colored was now (turning?) white, the assumption that the person was painting the chimney *explained* why the chimney was changing colors (**O4**). My *conclusion* made

This is only a picture of a wizard, right?

a coherent story. And I learned something the evening I visited my office: Airplane beacons, as well as painters, stand on scaffolds.

Bias (**O5**) is an interesting issue. Typically, bias is viewed an observational defect. Assume Grandma Jones regularly refers to her neighbor Fred as a "young hoodlum." Grandma Jones sees someone steal Audrey's purse. If the robber bears some resemblance to Fred, she might jump to the conclusion that she saw *Fred* rob Audrey. Here Grandma Jones's bias might have led to a misidentification. Or assume that Yves is a big fan of flying saucer stories. If one night he sees a "mysterious light" in the sky, he might conclude that he saw a flying saucer, even though it was an elaborate hoax you concocted to fool him. In these cases, Grandma's and Yves's beliefs affected what they believed they saw.

But there also are positive biases. A scientist who is testing a hypothesis is *not* a disinterested (unbiased) observer. Scientific observations are "guided by" hypotheses. Hypotheses tell you where to look and for what to look. Given such guidance, the scientist might see things that others do not see. Is this bad? No. Were it not for such "biased observations," many discoveries would not have been made. But the scientist is in a situation somewhat like that in which Grandma Jones identifies Fred as the robber. If the scientist's conclusion that her experiment confirms a certain hypothesis is acceptable, other scientists must be able to repeat the experiment and make similar observations. Similarly, if the police are to accept Grandma Jones's conclusion that Fred robbed Audrey, that claim must be consistent with the rest of the evidence they gather (**O4**).

Examples

Situation 1. Assume that Sam sees Jan walking down the street. It is a bright sunny day, and Sam has known Jan for years. Further, assume that Sam makes her observations from about twenty feet away, and she is able to see Jan's face as he walks by. Sam has 20-20 vision. Is Sam's claim that she saw Jan justified? Sam is in the right place (**O1**). The observational conditions are good (**O2**). She uses the technology appropriate for the situation—which is none (**O3**). She has the background knowledge necessary to identify Jan when she sees him (**O4**). Jan told Sam yesterday that he would be visiting his friend Chong that afternoon, and Chong lives three blocks down the street, so seeing Jan walking down the street coheres with other information Sam has (**O4**). And while she and Jan are friends, Sam has no tendencies to "see Jan" wherever she happens to look (**O5**). It is reasonable to accept her claim that she saw Jan walking down the street.

Of course the situation can be changed a bit, and Sam would have less reason to "believe her eyes" when she seems to see Jan walking down the street. Assume that

Source: Seth Casana, Academia Nuts. *Used with permission of the author.*

Jan had told Sam last month that he was going to spend the next several months in France. Consistent with this, Sam recently had received a letter from Jan with a French stamp and a Paris postmark. The letter said that Jan planned to extend his stay in France for at least another two months. The day after receiving the letter, Sam sees someone walking down the street who looks just like Jan. "That can't be Jan," Sam reasons, "since Jan is in Paris." What she seems to see is *inconsistent* with what she believes on other grounds (**O4**). At least, Sam could be expected to do a double-take. She might be so surprised at what she seems to see that she looks more carefully to see if the person she sees has all Jan's characteristics. If Sam concludes that the person looks just like Jan, she might attempt to talk with him. She might find (1) that it is indeed Jan. He explains that he had to cut his trip short due to a family emergency, thereby resolving the inconsistency. Or she might find (2) that he is Jan's younger brother Jon, who is in town for the weekend and is staying with Chong. If it is the latter, Sam might notice various ways in which Jon differs from Jan as the two converse.

Situation 2.   Pat has just returned from a trip to Chicago. She visited the Field Museum and saw a picture in a brochure that looks like her friend Chris. She shows the picture to Chris, saying, "Your picture is in a Field Museum brochure, see?!" Chris looks at the picture and, sure enough, the person has the same color hair and wears his hair in the same style as Chris. The pictured person even is wearing a shirt that looks exactly like one Chris often wears. So, it is not unreasonable to identify the person in the picture with Chris. It is consistent with information Pat had (**O4**). But Pat's information is limited. Chris responds, "I see the similarities, but it is not I. I've never been in Chicago."

This situation illustrates several things. First, Pat's observation was "biased" in a way in which most people's observations are biased (**O5**). We generally tend to "see" things in terms of things with which we are familiar. Just as Grandma Jones "saw" Fred rob Audrey, Pat "saw" Chris in the picture. In each case, there was a degree of similarity between the person seen and the person identified. In each case, the person seen was acting in a way that the observer considered consistent with the character of the person identified (**O4**): Grandma Jones considered Fred a "young hoodlum." Pat knew Chris well enough to *assume* that if he visited Chicago he would surely visit the Field Museum. Second, there is a general problem with pictures. Pictures are often small and the details are unclear. This alone makes observation conditions short of ideal (**O2**). Had Pat had a life-size picture of the person in the Field Museum, she might have noticed significant differences between the person in the picture and Chris.

> WHEN YOU CAREFULLY READ THE
> THE WORDS IN A PARAGRAPH LIKE
> LIKE THIS ONE IT IS EASY TO
> TO MAKE A MISTAKE. IN
> IN FACT YOU MIGHT BE
> BE MAKING ONE RIGHT NOW
> NOW UNLESS YOU ARE
> ARE READING VERY, VERY SLOWLY.

Situation 3.   Assume Moe asks Jo out for dinner. Jo likes Moe, but she really needs to study for her critical-thinking test. So, she asks her identical twin sister Flo, of whom Moe does not know, to take her place for the evening. Jo does not bother to tell Moe that he will be going out with Flo. So, when Moe arrives, he sees Flo, but he believes he is seeing Jo. Everything goes well for a time, until Moe asks Flo about something that happened in the critical-thinking class he attends with Jo. Since Flo is not Jo, she does not know what to say. This sort of thing happens several times until Moe is quite confused. Although the visual evidence suggests that Moe sees Jo, "Jo" does not know what she should know if she really is Jo. The visual evidence does not **cohere** with other things Moe knows about Jo; that is, it doesn't make sense that "Jo" doesn't know what she should know if she's really Jo. So, Moe asks Flo whether she really is Jo. She replies no and explains the switch. Flo thinks it was a good joke. Moe feels like a *shmo* and eventually marries Gertrude O. They have thirty-seven kids. Moral: Never ask anyone out to dinner on the night before a critical-thinking test—study instead!

Again coherence (**O4**) plays a major role in the evaluation of the observation claim, "I (Moe) am seeing Jo." A person who looks like Jo is at the place where Moe and Jo had agreed to meet. There are no problems with **O1, O2,** or **O3**. Moe is where he should be to see Jo (but he's being deceived). We may assume that the observational conditions were adequate. There is no reason to use any extraordinary technology. (Afterwards, however, Moe might have wished he had brought along his fingerprinting kit.) It was only that Flo didn't know what Jo should know that caused Moe to question his belief that he was out with Jo.

This story illustrates that even if the visual cues tend to support a conclusion—in this case that Moe saw Jo—there are times when you will need to revise your conclusions. And this is so even if your judgment should be good on the basis of all the other criteria for judging the reliability of an observation claim.

Situation 4.   Officer Max of the Police Department investigated the scene of a murder. This is the same Officer Max who, a year earlier, had been instrumental in solving a triple homicide in the city. She wrote in her notebook that the victim had been shot three times in the chest. Using her magnifying glass, she noted that there were traces of white powder on and around the victim's body. A small taste of the powder assured her that it was a controlled substance. All this was recorded in her notebook and included in her report. At the trial, she said, "I went to the scene of the crime and saw that it was a drug deal that had gone bad."

Officer Max was at the crime scene (**O1**). We may safely assume that the observation conditions were favorable (**O2**). She used the appropriate technology (**O3**), and she has sufficient background information (a) to know a controlled substance when she observes one (**O4**) and (b) to accurately use a magnifying glass (**O3**). We might even stipulate that Officer Max is free from observational bias (**O5**). Can we accept her claim that it was a drug deal that had gone bad? No. This is something she certainly *did not* observe. It is a conclusion based on what she saw. Had she been present when the victim was killed, she might have seen that the victim and another were involved in a drug deal, and she would at least have been justified in claiming that the murder occurred in the course of a drug deal. As things stand, she was *not* in the appropriate place at the appropriate time to make *that* observation (**O1**). It is consistent with the evidence she observed to suggest that the killer made it look as if it was a drug deal that had gone bad—the killer might have spread drugs around the room so it would look as if that happened. So, Officer Max's remark "it was a drug deal that had gone bad" goes beyond what she observed. Insofar as she was asked what she observed, the defendant's lawyer would object. Nonetheless, what she claimed might be true. Given other information available to the jury, the suggestion that the murder had occurred in the course of a drug deal might provide the best (most reasonable) explanation of what happened. But Officer Max did not *observe* that the crime occurred under such conditions.

Exercises

I. Evaluate the observation statements made in each of the following cases on the basis of the five questions above. Explain why you believe the observational conditions support or fail to support the proposed observation statement.

1. Solvig is mountain climbing with her friend Bruno. It is a lovely spring day. The flowers are in bloom, and goats are frolicking in the meadows. As they climb further up the mountain, however, visibility is impaired by thick fog. As they approach the summit, Solvig sees what appears to be a large humanoid creature deftly climbing down the mountain about fifty feet to her right. Should she conclude that she has had a fleeting glance at Bigfoot? Should she conclude that she has seen a person?

2. Captain Ahab had finally caught up with his nemesis Moby Dick, the great whale that in an earlier encounter had removed something more than a foot from his stature. The Captain himself leads the attack on the whale. Ahab becomes tangled in the various ropes connected to the harpoons before the whale dives. Several minutes later the whale surfaces and Ahab's arm moves up and down as if he is beckoning the harpoonists to resume the attack. Should the harpoonists conclude that Ahab is, in fact, beckoning them to attack?

3. I'm very nearsighted, but I never wear my glasses before breakfast, and I never eat breakfast before 6:45 a.m. I got out of bed at 5:30 this morning and looked out the window. I saw what appeared to be a large white ox in my garden. Since the city in which I live has ordinances against keeping livestock within the city limits, I'm a bit surprised. But surely, seeing is believing! Should I conclude there is an ox in my garden?

4. The prosecutor was given the following information: On the morning of November 3, Granny Smith was roused from a deep sleep by a loud noise. She jumped from bed and ran to the window of her apartment. In the dawn's early light, she saw what appeared to be a white male running away from her apartment building. Granny is 83. She has lived in the neighborhood all of her life and knows virtually everyone in the neighborhood. Upon listening to the news later in the day, she heard that her neighbor had been killed and that the police were holding a white male, Fred Fritz, for questioning. It is known that Granny frequently called Fred a "young hooligan." She phoned the police station and said that she'd seen him running away from the building. Why might the prosecutor question her credibility as a witness?

5. Natalie reports that she saw Horace at the political convention in Houston. Natalie was not in Houston during the convention—indeed, she never left her house in Dallas during the entire time the convention was in session. Give a scenario under which her claim might be plausible. Can you create alternative scenarios under which the plausibility of her claim would increase?

6. In his story "The Catbird Seat" James Thurber introduces two characters, Mr. Martin and Mrs. Ulgine Barrows. Mr. Martin is a very quiet, respectful person. He neither smokes nor drinks. He also despises Mrs. Barrows. Mr. Martin was a twenty-two-year employee of F&S, and his quiet habits are very well-known to all the employees. One morning Mrs. Barrows arrives at work, claiming that Mr. Martin had visited her the previous evening. She said he smoked, he drank a highball, claimed he took heroin, and described his plans to blow up "that old windbag" Mr. Fitweiler, their boss. Mr. Fitweiler did not believe Mrs. Barrows's observation report. If you were Mr. Fitweiler, would you have believed her?

7. Bob is going deer hunting one night. Bob is a great hunter, as is evidenced by the numerous deer heads in his den. Since it is a moonless night, he dons his night-vision goggles, goggles he has used on many previous occasions. Would you be willing to go hunting with Bob under such conditions?

8. Sharon Science is in her lab one evening testing her hypothesis that a certain bacterium causes a certain disease. She's been actively engaged in medical research for over ten years, and her objective this evening is to examine several dozen tissue samples from people having the disease to determine whether the bacterium is present. She's particularly excited about her evening's work, since it will be the first time she will use a new high-powered optical microscope. After her work, she reports that each of the samples contained the bacterium in question. Should she be believed?

9. Look again at number 8, but this time assume that Sharon is one of your classmates in Biology 101. Again she claims to find the bacterium in each sample she examines. Should she be believed?

10. Your friend Sam claims that she looked out her window one evening and saw an altercation between two people under a street lamp half a block away. She says that, given the distance and the fact that it was at night, she took out her night-vision binoculars and was able to identify the two people as Moe and Jo, two peo-

ple who were in her critical-thinking class last semester. Should you believe her report?

11. It was sunny day. Jan was walking down the street, talking with his friend Joan, when he noticed out of the corner of his eye that someone had grabbed the brief-case of an executive-type in front of him. The briefcase snatcher ran into Jan and knocked him down. Jan reported to the police that the perpetrator of the crime was a Caucasian male, about sixteen or eighteen years old, five feet nine inches tall, with short red hair. Should the police believe his report?

12. It was a cold and snowy day. Felicia looked out her window and saw something red moving down the street. As she stared at the object, she concluded that it was her neighbor Fred, since the size of the red object from her vantage point corre-sponded to the size of a stocking cap, and her neighbor Fred owned such a cap. Should she be believed?

13. It was a cold and snowy day. There was little traffic on the street outside Felicia's window, but she saw a large red object that seemed to be stuck in the snow. The size was right for a car, and her neighbor Fred had a red car of the appropriate size. Felicia later claimed that she saw Fred's car stuck in the snow at the same time that other witnesses claimed that his car was involved in a robbery on the other side of town. Should Felicia be believed?

14. It was a dark and stormy night. Shawn was driving home from a party and saw what appeared to be a streaker running along the road. Shawn tells you this. Should he be believed? Does it make any difference what kind of party Shawn attended?

15. Carter tells you that she saw Sydney at the Beethoven concert last night. Carter was sitting in the third row of the balcony. She says she saw Sydney sitting in the front row on the main floor at just the point that the lights were dimmed. You've known Sydney for many years, and you know that she's not a big fan of Beethoven's music. Should you believe Carter? Would it make a difference if you knew that Sydney was dating Jorge, that Jorge was a big Beethovan fan, and that Carter also claimed to see Jorge just before the lights dimmed? Would it make any difference if you also knew that Carter has 20-20 vision?

CHAPTER 11

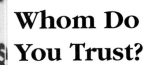

Whom Do You Trust?

The View: This chapter examines five criteria for evaluating testimony. It includes a discussion of evaluating library sources and Internet sources.

Should you believe everything you hear or read? If not, how can you decide what to believe?

Much of what we know, or believe we know, is based upon the testimony of others. You are currently paying an institution of higher education a significant amount of money to have people tell you things. Do your professors always tell you the truth? Probably not.[1] Are you justified in accepting the claims your professors make regarding their disciplines? Almost certainly. Are there guidelines that help us decide whom we should trust?

There are several questions you need to ask when evaluating the testimony a person has given.

T1 Is the person offering the testimony generally reliable?

T2 Is the person offering the testimony trained in or does he or she have experience regarding the subject about which he or she is offering testimony?

T3 Does the person stand to gain financially or in terms of status, prestige, or reputation by being believed? Does the person stand to lose financially or in terms of status, prestige, or reputation if he or she is wrong?

---

[1] This is not to say that your professors intentionally attempt to deceive you (lie). No one is perfect. Even the very best professor occasionally slips. And there are cases in which a professor might reasonably judge that you are not intellectually prepared to understand all the details of a certain situation, so she gives you a "simplified" version of the situation. Physics teachers still teach Newton's laws of gravity and motion as if they are true. At best, Newton's laws hold only with respect to "medium-sized objects," objects larger than a subatomic particle and smaller than objects in interstellar space.

T4 Is the testimony consistent with what you know from other equally reliable sources? For example, is it consistent with the testimony of equally qualified experts?

T5 Is the person offering the testimony biased?

As in the case of the questions asked regarding observational evidence, these questions do *not* show that a proposition is true or false. They provide inductive evidence that the person offering the testimony is reliable and limited evidence that the claim made is true. As in any case of inductive reasoning, the testimony under consideration can be evaluated positively according to each of these criteria and still turn out to be false. Assume the year is 1300 and you're a student at the University of Paris. One of your professors—a professor who has an outstanding reputation for the quality of his scholarship and honesty—tells you that the earth is flat. At that time, such a claim would be consistent with what virtually all learned persons claimed. And, of course, the claim was as false then as it is now. Let us look at these questions.

> ### Hearsay Evidence
>
> Did you ever play "telephone"? The first person in a line whispers something to the second. The second whispers it to the third, and so on down the line. Often, what the last person reports differs significantly from what the first whispered. Hearsay evidence is testimony that is passed from one person to the next. One *hears* it and *says* it to the next. Hearsay evidence is unreliable. As in the game of telephone, in passing a message from one person to another, the message often becomes distorted. So, if Jan said that Sam said that Chris said that . . ., you are being given hearsay evidence, and it should be considered untrustworthy (**T1**). If someone begins, "They say that . . ." or "Rumor has it that . . .," the message should be deemed unreliable for the same reason.
>
> Forwarded email, as such, is not hearsay evidence, since there is little chance of change in the message by forwarding it. You must, of course, ask whether the original sender or the persons who forwarded it are reliable.

T1 is a difficult question. Often it cannot be answered. Assume you met a person a few days ago, and she introduced herself, "I'm Sabrina O'Tool. I'm from Hoboken, New Jersey." You have never met her before. You know nothing about her reputation for honesty or reliability. Should you believe her? Probably. Most people tell the truth—or what they believe is the truth—most of the time. Her name and address are the sorts of information you would expect her to know. All things being equal, there is no reason she should deceive you. Of course, she might not want you to know anything about her. If she is in the federal witness protection program, "Sabrina O'Tool" might not give you accurate information. If she never wanted to hear from you, "her phone number" might connect you with Dial-A-Prayer. On the other hand, there are many times when you might know a person quite well, and the first question discredits that person's testimony. Assume you have known Vaudra for many years and she has a reputation for misrepresenting the facts. If Vaudra tells you that she won $10 million in the Publishers' Clearing House Sweepstakes, you might want to check some other source before believing her.

Ordinarily, you wouldn't visit a carpenter to receive advice on your health. Ordinarily, you wouldn't visit your philosophy professor for advice on fixing your car. The second question, **T2**, concerns the academic or vocational credentials of the person giving the testimony. You usually should believe your history professor when she is talking about history. She probably has a doctorate in history. Her research has focused on that history. She is someone who would probably know the territory if anyone does. So, if she tells you that the French Navy was responsible for the American victory at Yorktown, you probably should believe her. If you question her claim, she probably will be able to give you evidence that supports it. A person making claims about his or her area of expertise is usually reliable. Furthermore, a person speaking regarding his or her specialty either is attempting to build a reputation in an area or has a reputation to maintain it, so according to **T3**, this person also has more credibility than someone outside the area.

Nonetheless, you must be careful regarding question **T2**. You might reasonably believe that a sports figure advertising beer or breakfast cereal probably doesn't have strong credentials in the area. If Tiger Woods is on the Wheaties box, this does not imply that he is an expert on nutrition. But before you discount his endorsement as nothing more than an advertising gimmick, fairness requires that you look into his academic background. Imagine Lucent Technologies created a commercial in which the late Hedy Lamarr talked about the virtues of Lucent's cellular phones. Hedy Lamarr was an actress in the 1930s, 1940s, and 1950s. Assume the commercial manifested the wonders of film editing, so the Miss Lamarr you saw was the young, attractive actress of *Ecstasy* (1933). You wouldn't—*and shouldn't*—believe her claims regarding cellular phones, right? While it is always prudent to be skeptical regarding claims made in a commercial, Hedy Lamarr's credentials regarding cellular phones are quite good. She invented the technology that led to the cellular phone.

Consider another case. In the late 1970s Linus Pauling proposed that taking massive doses of vitamin C would prevent the common cold. Linus Pauling was a chemist. He won the Nobel Prize for chemistry in 1954, as well as the Nobel Peace Prize in 1962. So, he obviously has the proper credentials for making claims regarding the medicinal virtues of vitamin C, right? Wrong! Research in medicine is very specialized. Being an outstanding chemist does not make you an authority in medicine. As research has shown, Pauling's vitamin C hypothesis was wrong.

Returning to your history professor, there are credentials—and there are credentials. If your professor's research and publications have focused on colonial American history, she has *excellent* credentials in that area. On the other hand, if her primary background is in ancient Greek intellectual history, but this semester she was assigned an American history course, she is a less credible authority than someone whose research focused on early American history. Nonetheless, she probably has far better credentials in colonial American history than either your philosophy professor or your physics professor.

Question **T2** requires that you look into the background of the person making a claim. Famous actors and sports personalities often appear in commercials or support certain social causes. Do they have credentials that make them authoritative in those areas? Generally not. If you believe that you should shop at Ace Hardware simply because John Madden—former professional football player—says so, or that you or your aged relatives should buy Colonial Penn Life Insurance simply because Ed McMahon—former announcer on the *Tonight Show*—says so, you have fallen victim to the informal fallacy known as *appeal to authority*.[2] You either commit or fall victim to this fallacy when you assume that just because a person is an authority (has good credentials) in one field, he or she is also an authority in another field. Madden might be an authority on professional football, but that doesn't make him an authority on hardware. McMahon might be a good source for finding out some of the inside information on how the *Tonight Show* was produced during the Johnny Carson years, but there is little reason to believe he's an authority on life insurance. So look into the background of those who make authoritative claims.

One more point should be made. There are areas in which *no one* is an authority, even though many people—the "critics"—might have sterling credentials. Before Gene Siskel's untimely death, if you were thinking about going to a movie, you might have sat down and watched *Siskel and Ebert at the Movies* to see movie clips and hear their reviews. Gene Siskel and Roger Ebert reviewed movies for decades. They saw more movies in a week than some of us see in a year. Doesn't this mean that when they gave a movie their sign of mutual approval, "two big thumbs up," it had to have been a good movie? No, but this is for reasons other than those we have considered up to this point. What makes a movie a good movie? There is no simple answer. If *Titanic* and *George of the Jungle* are both good movies—Siskel and Ebert gave each a thumbs up—they're not good for all (if any) of the same reasons. *Titanic* is historical drama/romance. *George of the Jungle* is a cartoon reconstructed with people. How do you compare movies that are so different? Presumably, there are different criteria for judging the quality of different kinds of movies. If you want to know what these criteria are, you'll have to ask Ebert, and Gene Shalit *(Today),* and Joel Siegel *(Good Morning America),* and Jeffrey Lyons *(Sneak Previews),* and the film critics of the *New York Times, Washington Post, San Francisco Chronicle, Time,* and *Newsweek.* In each category, I suspect there will be a great deal of agreement, but you'll find some disagreement as well. If you ask what the relative weight of each of the criteria in a category is, you can expect more disagreement. Or they may say that the criteria for judging the quality of a movie of a certain genre are like the criteria for judging the probable truth of an observation statement (**O1–O5**): The weight assigned to one depends, in part, on the judgments made regarding the others. So, what can you tell about a movie if Siskel and Ebert each gave it thumbs up? They both liked it. And if you were a devoted watcher of their program—or a devoted follower of any other film critic or group of film (or book, theater, art, food, and so on) critics—you could come up with a reasonable judgment regarding whether you'll like it. I tended to like the movies Ebert liked but Siskel didn't. But that was not a perfect guide. *Both* Siskel and Ebert liked that cinematic masterpiece *George of the Jungle.*

Two people are advising you to use Pennzoil in your car. One is Arnold Palmer, seated on his old tractor in a Pennzoil commercial. The other person is your neighbor, who happens to be a philosophy professor. Whom should you believe? On the face of it, neither Palmer nor your neighbor has obvious credentials regarding automotive products. Palmer is known for his golfing prowess. Your neighbor is known for talking about philosophical problems. So, in terms of **T2**, the two seem to be

---

[2]We shall discuss this at greater length in Chapter 31.

equal: They're both duds. But **T3** gives the edge to your neighbor. Arnold Palmer—and virtually anyone else who makes a sales pitch in a commercial—is giving a *paid* endorsement. If someone is being paid to say something, there is a potential **conflict of interest**. You cannot be sure that the person is making the endorsement because he or she believes it or simply because he or she is being paid to say it. Your neighbor, on the other hand, probably stands to gain nothing from your choice of motor oil, but if she gives you bad advice, her reputation in the neighborhood might be sullied. So, you probably should take your neighbor's advice—although your best bet might be to check a reliable source on motor oils or perhaps an issue of *Consumer Reports*.

T3 generally should be considered in conjunction with **T2**. If a person is an expert in a certain area, he stands to lose in reputation if he gives you incorrect information. So, if your sociology professor is talking about an issue in sociology, she should be believed because she has credentials in the area (**T2**) and her reputation as an expert in the field is at stake (**T3**). On the other hand, if your friend Max tells you he saw a flying saucer, you probably shouldn't believe him. In that case, there is probably an alternative explanation of what Max saw that does not assume extraterrestrial creatures (**T4**). Further, Max stands to gain in reputation by being believed (**T3**).

Conflict of interest is interesting, since there are cases in which a person *appears* to have a conflict of interest in telling you something, and that is a reason why you should believe her. The automotive authorities contend that one of the most important things you can do to keep your car working well for many years is to change the oil regularly. So, at one point in my life I followed or exceeded the manufacturer's recommendations and changed the oil in my car every three months or two thousand miles. One day the owner of the shop where I had my car serviced asked, "Why do you change your oil so often? Every three thousand miles is often enough, and oil doesn't break down just because it gets older. It's your money, so you can do as you wish, but changing the oil every three thousand miles is generally enough." I assumed this was good advice. The owner of the shop had good credentials in automotive maintenance and repair: The appropriate "master mechanic" designations were posted on the walls (**T2**). He stood to *lose* financially by providing the information (**T3**), since I would spend less on oil changes. Nonetheless, he might have gained in reputation (**T3**), since I tended to trust that his judgment was not based solely on *immediate* financial gain. If a conflict of interest is based in part on self-

> **Does the fact that the following was unsolicited speak to its credibility?**
>
> I'm also interested in the area of critical thinking. From your description, I imagine the practice of law (parts of it, in any event) would constitute a practical application of critical thinking. Building and making arguments and finding weakness in those made by opponents is a daily function for us. I'm convinced that my background in philosophy helps me analyze arguments in ways that others don't. When I hear or read an argument that is somehow flawed (whether I'm making it or someone else is), there is always a bell that goes off in the back of my head that tells me something just isn't right. Knowing where the holes are helps me hide my weaknesses and jump all over someone else's (which I likely do with a little too much glee).
>
> *Used with permission of Duffy Doyle Keever, Attorney at Law*

Source: Bill Watterson, Calvin and Hobbes. *Used with permission of Universal Press Syndicate.*

interest, cases in which someone is willing to sacrifice short-term self-interest in favor of long-term self-interest—which might not be realized—are cases in which credibility increases.

You should notice that there are cases in which **T2** and **T3** seem to give mixed messages. For example, assume your stock broker tells you that XYZ Corporation would be a good investment. Assume that your stock broker is well-trained in finance and investment, so you give her a positive rating regarding **T2**. But *if* you invest in XYZ Corporation, your stock broker will benefit financially. She receives a commission on all the stock she sells. So, it seems, she receives a negative rating on **T3**. But since she is an expert, her reputation as a financial consultant is at stake. If she gives you bad advice, she probably will receive more business from neither you nor those friends you tell. So, she receives a positive rating on **T3.** Let us also assume that your stock broker is fresh out of school, so she has no track record. Her previous reliability plays no role in your judgment (**T1** is neither positive nor negative). Should you take her advice?

Probably. In the case of professionals, the fact that they are paid for their services usually should not be seen as a negative point. You don't begrudge your physician and your dentist their fees for an evaluation of your health, do you? What you are buying is their knowledge. The mere fact that someone is paid to do something does not itself constitute a conflict of interest. But if your doctor tells you that you're seriously ill—if you are advised to undergo major surgery, for example—you are well-advised to seek a second opinion. This is the issue brought up by **T4.** If you seek advice from an expert in a field, that person has background in the field, and he or she has a reputation to maintain, but even experts make mistakes. So, you are well-advised to determine whether an expert's claims are consistent with the claims of others who are equally qualified. To determine *who* is equally qualified, you might need to do some research. If you are seeking a second medical opinion, you should seek a specialist with a good reputation. If you are wondering whether a certain book is a reliable source for your psychology paper, you might want to read some reviews of the book.[3] If you are wondering whether you should believe your stock broker, you might

---

[3]We examine criteria for evaluating academic books and articles near the end of this chapter.

want to do some background reading on the company in an attempt to determine whether your broker's advice seems reasonable and examine the reputation (track record) of the brokerage firm of which she is a part.

But being a professional and having some credentials in a field are not sufficient to discount possible conflicts of interest. Some experts are better than others. Expert witnesses at a civil trial and expert witnesses for the defense at a criminal trial are carefully chosen and often paid for their testimony. And those who hire expert witnesses know what their expert witnesses are going to say. Jurors are not in a position to examine the credentials of such an expert. They are not in a position to determine whether their research is respected in their fields. Here is a case in which any juror who knows how the system works must *assume* that there is a potential conflict of interest.

> The following is a passage from Robert Traver's *Anatomy of a Murder* (New York: St. Martin's Press, 1958, p. 62), which comes close to describing how expert witnesses are chosen. "Well, you can't prove insanity without a medical expert, you tell me. Yet you and I have already decided I was insane, we know that we're going to plead insanity—you tell me it's the only legal defense I've got. And even I can see that now. In other words, you a mere lawyer and I a dumb soldier have between us decided that I was medically and legally insane. Having decided that, we must now go out and shop around for a medical expert to confirm *our* settled conclusion. Yet you tell me an ordinary medical doctor won't do," The Lieutenant shook his head. "It all sounds . . . unscientific to me."

Similarly, when virtually anyone tries to sell you something, he or she has a conflict of interest, and a typical salesperson probably also will have a bias in favor of his or her product (**T5**). For example, your neighborhood New York Life Insurance agent has some knowledge of the insurance industry. In most states he or she must be licensed to sell insurance, and this alone guarantees that he or she has some understanding of the industry, the terms used in the industry, and his or her legal obligations with respect to potential clients. She might have extensive background knowledge. A life insurance agent who places the letters CLU behind his or her name is a certified life underwriter, which means he or she has completed a course of study and passed a series of tests to obtain the designation.[4] Still, Ms. Life, CLU, is attempting to sell you life insurance. She will show you the products available from the company she represents. It is unlikely that she will tell you that you can purchase a comparable product from a different company for less money.[5] And if *you* were to point out that you could purchase a comparable policy for less elsewhere, she probably would speak about the strengths of the company she represents, the services she could provide as your "personal agent," and so on. No sales person is unbiased. Most successful salespersons believe—with or without justification—that the product they sell is the best product on the market. If you are a careful consumer, you must recognize that the salesperson has a conflict of interest (**T3**) and that some of the

---

[4]This is a designation comparable to C.P.A. in the accounting industry.

[5]There is a book available in many libraries called *Best's Flitcraft Compend* that provides a cost/benefits index which allows you to compare life insurance policies across company lines as well as different policies issued by any given company. This index is based upon cost per $1,000 of coverage and might not reflect all the objectives one has in the choice of a policy.

information you receive from the salesperson is biased (**T5**). To protect your interests, you must check the claims made by the salesperson against other sources (**T4**), and those sources also must be evaluated in terms of the five questions.

While used car dealers and insurance agents might be among those of whom you should be wary, they are not the only persons who might attempt to "sell you a bill of goods." If you are taking a course on the history of the religious reformation of the sixteenth century, virtually any secondary source you read will have a certain bias.[6] A Protestant historian might be inclined to write more favorably about Martin Luther and John Calvin than might a Roman Catholic historian. Is this inherently bad? No, but it is one of the things you should recognize in reading the literature. A bias can blind a writer to historical facts that others would recognize. So, if you want to know "what really happened," you should be aware of a writer's bias. Pay attention to the emotional connotations of the descriptive words used. Ask whether the picture changes if you replace emotionally charged terms with emotionally neutral words. Find out as much as you can about the period in which the work was written. How Stalin is portrayed in Russian histories of the Soviet Union depends, in part, on whether the history was written during a period of "deStalinization." Or follow *Time* magazine's descriptions of Stalin before World War II, during World War II (when we were allies), and after World War II. Examining little more than their cover art reflects shifts in the magazine's editorial attitude toward Stalin during the period. By detecting a writer's bias, you should find yourself asking questions about whether certain facts are ignored and others receive excessive emphasis.

> **The News Is Objective, Right?**
> There are numerous types of bias that can affect news coverage. One is simply the choice of stories to be covered. This often reflects nothing more than the presumed interests of the audience. On any day, if you compare what is on American news broadcasts with stories on the BBC or some other non-American news service, this becomes obvious. In addition, there is the question of *how* the stories are presented. What are the emotional connotations of the words used to describe events? Who is portrayed in a favorable light?
>
> For many years conservative politicians have suggested that the news media have a liberal bias. Do you believe that is true? Why or why not?

Evaluating Research Sources

Assume you are doing research for a paper. There are numerous sources you could consult. Will the guidelines on testimony help you decide what to examine carefully and what to ignore? Are some guidelines more important than others?

---

[6]Filipe Fernández-Armesto and Derek Wilson, *Reformations: A Radical Interpretation of Christianity and the World, 1500–2000* (New York: Scribner, 1996) might appear to be an exception. One of the authors is a Protestant and the other is a Roman Catholic historian. Their objective is to show that the Reformation of the sixteenth century was neither as radical nor as unique as many historians have suggested. Their scholarship is impressive. Yet, before accepting their conclusions, you should ask whether their hypothesis (thesis) has blinded them to significant changes that resulted directly from the Reformation. To answer *that* question might require twenty or thirty years of careful scholarship.

First, be certain your sources are relevant and suitable. If you're writing a paper on the impact of a recent recession on the export of agricultural products, there are three issues: (1) Make sure the statistics you use are timely, that is, that they apply to the relevant period. Statistics regarding the recessions of the 1970s are not relevant to the recession of 2000–2002. (2) Economic theories are more timeless, but you probably want to work with fairly recent approaches. Your textbook and your professors are good sources of advice. (3) Use sources you can understand. A brilliant mathematical analysis of economic data is useless if you cannot understand the mathematics.

Second, you have to evaluate the sources themselves. Several questions should be asked regarding the author: (1) What is the reputation of the author? Here your professor might be able to help you. (2) What is the author's background? You might be able to find information on the author's educational background and recent work in biographical works such as *Who's Who in America*. (3) Is the work respected by experts in the field? If you're using a book, you might check some reviews in scholarly journals to see how the book was received by other scholars. (4) To what school of thought does the author belong? Every discipline has several approaches. If an author assumes Keynesian theories of economics, this will tell you something about the author's biases.

Several questions also should be asked about the publisher: (1) What is the reputation of the publisher? Some book publishers have superb reputations. In any given field, certain journals are reputed as outstanding. Here your professor or a reference librarian should be able to help. (2) Does the publisher "referee" manuscripts? That is, does the publisher send the manuscript to authorities in the field for evaluation before publishing? (3) Does the publisher reflect a certain school of thought? Some academic journals are quite specialized. If you go outside the academy and read such things as corporate annual reports or publications of professional organizations, the narrative might be biased. Beware!

Finally, the document itself might provide clues to its credibility. *Generally*, books and articles that are well documented are more trustworthy than those that are not. Footnotes (or endnotes) or a bibliography suggest that the author is well informed and careful.

Consistent with all of this, you might find an unknown scholar who publishes an excellent article in a minor journal, or an important article might have virtually no documentation. If you paged through *Annalen der Physik* 17 (1905) and used the "Is there extensive documentation?" approach, you would ignore a little article called *"Zur Elekrodynamik bewegter Körper"* ("On the Electrodynamics of Moving Bodies") by a Swiss patent clerk named A. Einstein. (It is the original statement of the Special Theory of Relativity.) Similarly, a well-known person occasionally publishes a poor book with a well-respected press. The guidelines for evaluating sources are like the general guidelines for evaluating testimony. They provide considerations that more often than not correspond to reliability.

"But," I hear some of you saying, "Your remarks suggest we go to the library. This is the age of the Internet! We can get everything we need from the Internet, can't we?"

No. First, most books, and many good journals, are not available in electronic form. Second, *anyone*—even your twelve-year-old brother—can publish on the

Internet. All you need is a Web page. While there are some refereed Internet journals, most of what you'll find is just thrown up on a Web page. For Web pages, there is no "court" of experts that have passed judgment on the piece. So, if it is always wise to examine the credentials of the authors you read, it is *imperative* to do so when taking information from the Internet. If, as your professors will

> On the Web page for my modern philosophy class there are a number of files that appear to be chapters from a book called *A Look at the Moderns* by H. Hans von Denkmüller of *Neuealtzeiter Universität*. What can you find out about Hermann Hans Heinrich Friedrich Franz Josef Ludwig Johann von Denkmüller? You might want to start by checking into the academic credentials of *Neuealtzeiter Universität*. (If you find *anything*, please let me know, because you *shouldn't* find anything.)

probably tell you, *much* of what is published in good refereed journals is not all that good, the situation is *much worse* on the Internet. So, if you are looking for articles and discussions, it is wise to follow the guidelines above religiously.

This is not to say that you should trust nothing on the Internet. If you are looking for census data, you should be able to trust the Bureau of the Census. If you are looking for economic data, reliable data should be available from various government agencies. Numerous historical documents are available on the Internet. In general, however, if it is information on a personal Web page or the Web page of an organization with some political agenda, you should be very careful. Your professors are probably your best source for guidance regarding reliable Web pages.

Exercises

I. Use the criteria for evaluating testimony to answer the following questions.

1. You are going to write a paper for your German literature class on Goethe's *Faust*. You come upon a book called *Faust: A Marxist Interpretation* by G. I. M. Smart. Using the criteria for evaluating testimony, how would you determine whether the book is probably a reliable source?

2. Professor Smith recently published a book entitled *Quantum Mechanics and the Physics of Grocery Shopping* with Oxford University Press. Professor Smith holds an endowed chair in physics at Princeton University, and she has published numerous articles in well-respected physics journals. Oxford University Press is considered one of the world's premier publishers of academic books. Given this information, do you have grounds for believing that Professor Smith's book is probably a reliable source on applications of physics to everyday life? Explain.

3. Duracell commercials claim that Duracells last longer than Energizers, and, of course, they'd have no reason to lie, would they? And Energizer commercials claim that Energizers last longer than Duracells, and, of course, they'd have no reason to lie, would they? So, Duracells must last longer than Energizers, and Energizers must last longer than Duracells. Why should you doubt the truth of the conclusion?

4. John claims he saw an alien spacecraft land in his back yard. Indeed, he has what he claims are pictures of the craft. If he is believed, he can sell the pictures to the *National Enquirer* for a significant sum. John has been interested in extraterrestrial life for many years and is quite excited by his observations. Should you believe his report?

5. Several years ago, NBA basketball player Michael Jordan advertised Nike athletic shoes. (a) Give one reason why one should be inclined to deem Jordan a credible witness. (b) Give one reason why one should be inclined to doubt Jordan's credibility.

6. Professor Jones is a physicist at Princeton. She has published numerous articles in very well-respected scientific journals. For the past two years she has been taking massive doses of vitamin C and has suffered from far fewer head colds than during any comparable period in the past twenty years. Is she justified in concluding that massive doses of vitamin C prevents head colds? Why or why not?

7. Dr. K. has been practicing medicine in a small town for over twenty-five years. Dr. K. is well respected in his community and in the larger medical community. One of his young patients is terribly ill. The child had measles and is now running a fever in excess of 107 degrees. Although he has never treated a case of encephalitis, Dr. K. knows that encephalitis can be a complication of measles, and the child's symptoms are consistent with those of encephalitis. He concludes that the child has encephalitis and has the child transported to a major medical center for treatment. Are there good reasons for the medical center personnel to accept Dr. K.'s diagnosis? What are those reasons?

8. Looking again at the case in question 7, if the personnel at the medical center concur with Dr. K's diagnosis, why do you have even more reason to believe that the child has encephalitis?

9. John told you that Amy said she had seen Joan with Fred last night at a table for two in the Red Nose, a fashionable nightclub downtown. The club is so popular that one must make table reservations at least a week in advance. You happen to know that Joan is engaged to Andy: Joan told you of her engagement three weeks ago, and you received an invitation to her wedding in today's mail. Should you believe that Joan is seeing Fred? Why or why not?

10. Assume that Pat Smith, a noted agricultural economist, has just given testimony before Congress that without a continued farm subsidy, American agriculture will be unable to compete in international markets. In support of her claim, she cited (a) practices in France and Holland that keep prices for domestically produced farm goods artificially low, (b) attempts by Japan to retain a closed market, and (c) the escalating cost of production of agricultural goods in the United States. Senator Short replied to her argument by saying, "I happen to know that Pat Smith is not merely an agricultural economist, she runs one of the largest agricultural enterprises in her state. Obviously, she has a conflict of interest. Her 'reasons' are merely rationalizations!" Should you accept Senator Short's argument? Why or why not?

11. Dr. Jones is a noted heart specialist at State University Hospital. He was the director of research for a new heart drug tentatively called Nozak, which, if approved by the FDA, will be marketed by the McDeven-Graegor Pharmaceutical Company, a company on whose board of directors Dr. Jones sits. If approved, Nozak promises to be a major source of income for McDeven-Graegor. In his testimony before the FDA, Dr. Jones claimed that the new drug has no adverse side effects. Do you have any tentative misgivings regarding his testimony?

12. Jonas Salk developed the first effective polio vaccine, a vaccine for which he became famous, even though he himself gained little financially from its development. At an AIDS conference in the early 1990s, Dr. Salk discussed his research on a vaccine for AIDS, indicating that he was guardedly optimistic that an effective AIDS vaccine will be available within the next decade. Should you believe him?

13. Mark Twain once said that drinking two hot Scotches every night before bed prevents toothache, remarking, "I only drink them as a preventative of toothache, and I've never had the toothache." Since Scotch is readily available and Twain was not heavily invested in Scottish distilleries, we may conclude that he had no vested interest in the effectiveness of Scotch as a health aide. So, should we accept Twain's word regarding the medicinal virtues of Scotch?

14. Your friend Fred says he saw Abigail flirting with John. Fred claims to have made the observation on a sunny day from about 500 feet through a pair of high-powered binoculars. Fred and Abigail have been informally dating for several months. Fred tends to be a very jealous person. Should you accept his conclusion?

15. Dr. F. recently finished a book on Descartes, a book that will be published by Routledge, a well-respected British publisher. The manuscript was examined and approved by a number of specialists in the area. Dr. F's area of specialization is history of modern philosophy, and Descartes is known as the father of modern philosophy. Most of Dr. F's earlier research focused on eighteenth-century British empirical philosophers: Locke, Berkeley, and Hume. Descartes is a seventeenth-century French rationalist. Among the theses Dr. F. defends in his book is the claim that Descartes *did not* hold that all innate ideas are true, a claim that puts Dr. F. at odds with virtually all Descartes scholars. By publishing a book, Dr. F. is virtually assured of a raise, and he might even receive a promotion in rank. Given this information, do you have reason to believe that Dr. F's book probably will be a reliable source on Descartes?

16. Professor Smith is a philosopher who, after a careful examination of all the available evidence, concluded that there is no reason to believe that intelligent extraterrestrial beings visit our planet. She neither smokes, nor drinks, nor takes drugs. Her character is impeccable. She has excellent vision. She says that while driving home one clear evening, she saw strange lights in the sky which appeared to land, and then she saw beings resembling some of those in *Men in Black*. The next day, she checked with the weather service and other agencies to see if she could provide an explanation of what she saw. If she concludes that she saw extraterrestrials, should you believe her?

17. Joan said that John said that Fred said that Sam said she'd heard a rumor that the instructor is ill and the critical-thinking test is going to be postponed from tomorrow until some time next week. So, you don't have to study for the exam tonight, right?

18. Rosetta Stone is president of the American Association for Colon Health. On a recent radio show, she stressed that periodic purgings of the digestive tract are essential for colon health. She also mentioned that her company carries an excellent purgative. Given her outstanding credentials, I'm sure you'll agree that purging your digestive track is something you should look into at your earliest convenience, right? (I already have it on *my* calendar for August 4, 2294.)

19. Several weeks ago, I received an email from a student in my critical-thinking class warning me of a virus on my computer called bogus.exe. She had sent this message to all people with whom she had communicated by email. The message had been forwarded to her from another of her correspondents. The message assured me that it was not a hoax and said that bogus.exe had been forwarded with some email messages. It could not be detected by any of the standard antivirus programs, such as the Norton AntiVirus, but it would sit innocently in my computer for a time and then suddenly destroy all the programs on my hard disk. The only way to rid the computer of the virus was to find it, send it to the recycle bin, and then empty the bin. That sounded serious! So, I immediately did a search for the program, deleted it, and emptied my recycle bin. That was reasonable, wasn't it? Since then, I've had no problems except that my computer won't boot.

20. Last week I received an official-looking email from the Office of the Vice President of the University. It contained a message forwarded from the University's Office of Computer Affairs. The message said that there was a hoax going around campus, an email warning that bogus.exe is an undetectable virus that should be deleted. "*Ignore any such email!*" the message said emphatically. "Bogus.exe is an essential part of your operating system, and if it is deleted, your computer will fail to function." I deleted the message, since there was little reason to believe what it claimed. After all, doesn't forwarded email provide only hearsay evidence?

II. Use the criteria for evaluating observations, the criteria for evaluating testimony, or both to answer the following questions.

1. John told you he saw a large pink elephant wearing a black tophat outside a supper club in Marquette, Iowa. He said he'd been driving north on Iowa Highway 13 on a clear, sunny day intending to visit Effigy Mounds National Monument, and when he entered Marquette he saw this . . . this . . . pink elephant. John said, "I've read enough philosophy to know that pink elephants and pink rats are philosophers' favorite examples of nonexistent objects, so I had to stop. I rubbed my eyes. I'd been driving a while, but I was still alert. When this strange apparition remained after I rubbed my eyes, I went up and touched it. I tapped it, and it sounded hollow. I concluded that, sure enough, there is at least one real pink elephant, even though it's a statue." You've known John for a good number of years, and while he's honest as the day is long, he occasionally tells a real whopper. On those occasions, he appears dead earnest until you say, "Wow!" then he laughs at you for being gullible. This time he held his ground after you said "Wow!," even promising to show you pictures. Should you believe him?

2. While walking through the park yesterday at dusk, Kate says she saw two people engaged in amorous acts. "I peeked around a tree," she said in a trembling voice, "and there was Uri making out with some tart." Kate and Uri had been going together for several years, but they broke up last week. Kate did not take the breakup very well and has been hitting the sauce rather hard since then. (As she's talking with you, in fact, you think she really should put up signs prohibiting open flames in her presence.) You've known Kate for years. She has 20-20 vision, and you've never known her to tell a lie. But you bumped into Uri shortly after supper last night, and he said he was heading to the library to study for a big exam. So, it's reasonable for you to disregard Kate's claim, right?

3. It was a perfect day for a football game. John and Joe were sitting in the fifty-eighth row of the stadium. Each brought his copy of Berkeley's *Principles* (*PHK*), but neither brought binoculars. Having briefly discussed issues facing the Society of Midgets—in which both are active members—they were deep in a discussion of *PHK* §7 when, late in the game, the entire crowd came to its feet. It was the game-winning play. You were in the library studying for a test. Assuming that John and Joe both have perfect eye sight and that both are honest as the day is long, you should be able to rely on them to give you a complete account of the big play, right?

4. You're driving along the Blue Ridge Parkway just north of Roanoke, Virginia. Much to your surprise—and delight!—while scanning the radio dial, you managed to pick up WLS Radio from Chicago, and you've been tuned to it for well over an hour now. The day is clear. The breeze is balmy. It's a typical trip down the shaded lanes of the Parkway, zipping along at 40 miles per hour. Suddenly, you believe you smell smoke, and there seems to be an orange glow up ahead. The weather seems to have grown measurably warmer. But, you say to yourself, if there any problems on the Parkway, they *surely* would have said something on the radio. You've heard nothing, so you proceed blithely on your way. This is reasonable, right?

5. Elwood is telling Dr. Sanderson how he met Harvey, the six foot, three-and-a-half-inch-tall white rabbit. Elwood is well liked and has a reputation for honesty. What would you question in his account and why?

Elwood: One night several years go, I was walking early in the evening along Fairfax Street—between 18th and 19th. . . . I had just helped Ed Hickey into a taxi. Ed had been mixing his rye with his gin, and I felt he needed conveying. I started to walk down the street when I heard a voice saying: "Good evening, Mr. Dowd." I turned and there was this great white rabbit leaning against a lamp-post. Well, I thought nothing of that, because when you have lived in a town as long as I have lived in this one, you get used to the fact that everybody knows your name. Naturally, I went over to chat with him. He said to me: "Ed Hickey is a little spiffed this evening, or could I be mistaken?" Well, of course he was not mistaken. I think the world and all of Ed but he was spiffed. Well, anyway, we stood there and talked, and finally I said—"You have the advantage of me. You know my name and I don't know yours." Right back at me he said: "What name do you like?" Well, I didn't even have to think a minute: Harvey has always been my favorite name. So I said, "Harvey," and this is the interesting part of the whole thing. He said—"What a coincidence! My name happens to be Harvey." (Mary Chase, *Harvey: Comedy in Three Acts*, Act II, Scene 2 [New York: Dramatists Play Service, 1944], p. 55)

Discussion Questions

Use the criteria for evaluating testimony as the basis for discussing the following.

1. Do the criteria for evaluating testimony provide grounds for questioning the claims made on television commercials? If so, what kinds of claims should be questioned? Explain.

2. Given that the Nielsen Ratings apply as much to network television news programs as to entertainment programs, do you have grounds for questioning what you hear on the news? If so, what kinds of issues do the criteria for evaluating testimony raise? Explain.

3. A person is said to have a **vested interest** in something if he or she is closely involved with it and that thing promotes some kind of personal advantage. The president of a company has a vested interest in the success of the company. You have a vested interest in your success as a student. Does having a vested interest constitute a conflict of interest? Why or why not?

4. A person is open-minded when he or she is willing to consider new ideas. We're told it's good to be open-minded, since open-minded people are free of prejudice. Does this mean all ideas should be treated as equal?

5. Why is it reasonable to suggest that the best way to become a person who can evaluate sources on a given topic is to become an authority on that topic? Is it reasonable to suggest that authorities on a topic are probably biased?

Values and Obligations

The View: This chapter examines claims of moral value and obligation, and claims of aesthetic value. It concerns issues regarding the basis for value claims and their objectivity.

Are moral claims true or false? Is Thomas Gainsborough's *The Blue Boy* a better painting than Grant Wood's *American Gothic*? If someone says that Shakespeare's *Hamlet* is a better piece of literature than Frederick Forsyth's *The Fourth Protocol*,[1] is he or she merely making a claim about his or her personal tastes? If there are disagreements regarding questions of value or obligation, is there a way our critical-thinking skills can help resolve it?

We describe things in many ways. (1) The cabinet is square. (2) The book is green. (3) The story is interesting. (4) The painting is exquisite. (5) In refraining from murder and theft, you do as you morally ought. Not all of these are descriptions of the same kind. The last three are **evaluative** descriptions. The fourth concerns aesthetic value. The fifth concerns moral obligation. Are we doing the same sorts of things when describe in each of these ways?

The quick answer is no. Anyone whose senses are operating properly and knows how to recognize things to which the words 'square' and 'green' apply should agree that the table is square and that the book is green.[2] If there is disagreement, differences in appearance can be explained, and arguments can be bolstered to resolve the dispute. "The cabinet against the wall might look square, but it is actually rectangular. A careful measurement of its dimensions shows that it is two inches higher than it is wide." "The book *looks* green, but it is actually blue. You are looking at the book under a strong yellow light. If you take it out into the sunlight or place it under a pure white light, it will appear to be blue. The 'color of an object' is the color it appears (to nor-

---

[1] Frederick Forsyth, *The Fourth Protocol* (New York: Viking Penguin, 1984).

[2] Of course, it can be argued that we do not *know* that what has been green in the past will be green in the future. See Nelson Goodman, "The New Problem of Induction," in his *Fact, Fiction, & Forecast* (Cambridge: Harvard University Press, 1955), pp. 63–86.

mally sighted people) under white light." There are recognized criteria for determining the shape or color of an object. If we disagree, we appeal to the criteria and resolve the dispute. In the case of moral and aesthetic judgments, there is less agreement regarding the criteria. Does this mean that there are no truths regarding value and obligation? No.

In this chapter we examine questions concerning value and obligation. Since there are things we all call "good" in neither a moral nor an aesthetic sense—for example, good apples and good cars—we will explore whether they provide any clues to understanding moral or aesthetic goodness and moral obligation. Before turning to these issues, however, we look briefly at moral and aesthetic arguments.

Moral and Aesthetic Arguments

We develop arguments about what is right or wrong. Some argue that abortion is always wrong. Others argue that, at least in some situations, abortion is morally permissible. We might argue (give reasons to believe) that Paul Cézanne's paintings are better than Jackson Pollack's. So, are moral and aesthetic arguments possible? Sure, but this doesn't mean we'll

> **Matters of Multiple Judgment**
> Some of the details of the scientific account of matter are matters of multiple judgment. These are cases in which there are several *defendable* answers to a question, but there is no one answer that is clearly correct. These are not uncommon. Should you invest in the stock market? Should you put Granny in a nursing home? There are several defendable answers to these questions.

reach an agreement regarding the permissibility of abortion or the relative merits of paintings. Does this mean that moral and aesthetic arguments are fundamentally different from arguments in other fields? No. Scientists have been examining the structure of matter for thousands of years. They support their conclusions with arguments. We probably know more about the structure of matter now than we knew three hundred or even a hundred years ago. Does that mean that scientific arguments have conclusively established what the nature of matter is? No.

In many ways, moral and aesthetic arguments are like any others. Assume you're given the following argument.

> John lied about his relationship with Veronica. So, John's action (lying) was wrong.

Does the conclusion follow? No.

In a famous discussion, the eighteenth-century philosopher David Hume argued that claims of moral obligation (rightness and wrongness, ought-claims) do not follow from claims of fact (is-claims).[3] Hume's contention is *at least* that if you are going to

---

[3]See David Hume, *A Treatise of Human Nature*, edited by L. A. Selby-Bigge, 2nd ed., revised by P. H. Nidditch (Oxford: Clarendon Press,1978), pp. 469-70. See also Daniel E. Flage, "Hume's Deontology," *International Studies in Philosophy* 26 (1994): 29-46, and Daniel E. Flage and Ronald J. Glass, "Hume's Problem and the Possibility of Normative Ethics," *Journal of Value Inquiry* 29 (1995): 231-239.

reach a conclusion about the moral quality of John's action, you need another premise. The statement "John lied about his relationship with Veronica" tells us nothing about the rightness or wrongness of the action. If you add the premise, "All cases of lying are wrong actions" or "If John lied, then John's action was wrong," you have a deductive argument.

> All cases of lying are wrong actions.
>
> John's action was a case of lying.
> _____
>
> John's action was wrong.
>
> If John lied, then John's action was wrong.
>
> John lied.
> _____
>
> John's action was wrong.

If there are cases in which lying is morally permissible or right, then the missing premise is "Most cases of lying are wrong actions," and you have an inductive argument.

> Most cases of lying are wrong actions.
>
> John's action was a case of lying.
> _____
>
> John's action was wrong.

As we will see in chapters 17 and 23, there are easy ways to find missing premises.

But what about the missing premise? Can we know or have reason to believe that the premise is true? To answer that question we ask whether moral attributes are fundamentally different from other attributes. Are the ways you know moral goodness fundamentally different from the ways you know nonmoral goodness?

On Morals —————————————————————

You are in the supermarket. You are looking for apples. You want to bring home "good" apples. Which apples are those? You have eaten enough apples to know that there are rituals you perform at the fruit counter to determine whether the apples are (probably) good. You sniff the apple to see if it has the appropriate scent. You look at its color to see if it is shiny red if it is a Delicious, or shiny green if a Granny Smith, or the appropriate color if some other variety. You check to see if the skin of the apple is smooth. You feel the surface of the apple to be sure it is firm without being hard. If it passes all these tests, it is probably a good apple. What does that mean? Is the goodness of the apple identical with all the characteristics you observed?

No. All the characteristics you observed are **signs** that the apple is good. A good apple is one that has a certain flavor or one that is nutritious. You do not see or feel or smell the flavor. Unless you are a chemist and do the appropriate tests, you have no grounds for claiming that the apple contains various nutrients beyond knowing that apples possessing a certain color, aroma, texture, and flavor have been nutritious in the past. (And your evidence that apples have been nutritious in the past is probably based on the testimony of a health book.) Does the fact that moral goodness cannot be observed by the senses mean that it is fundamentally different from the goodness of apples?

I tell you that I have a good computer. You ask, "What do you mean by a 'good' computer?" I reply, "It does all the things I need a computer to do—word processing, email, spreadsheets—and it's reliable: It seldom crashes more than three times per day." The computer is good insofar as it fulfills some of my needs. These needs are not observable. If some morally good actions also fulfill certain needs, does that mean they are fundamentally different from the goodness of my computer?

Notice that in talking about apples as nutritious and the goodness of my computer, you are not saying that something is good as such. You are saying it is "good for" something else. It is a **means** (a way to reach) to an **end** (purpose or goal), which itself is considered good. Nutrition is a necessary condition for health. Is health good *as such*, or is it merely a necessary condition for doing other things? Isn't health the sort of thing you appreciate only when it's absent? If you come down with a disease, you are unable to do the things you normally do and there is often some kind of pain or discomfort. Physical pain might be a **natural evil**. Pain might be something you would like to avoid as such.[4] But if health is good only as a necessary condition for doing other things, it is not good as such. Health is not an ultimate end. Is there some other ultimate end? Individual pleasure? Group cohesion? Are there any ultimate ends?

Over the years, various people have claimed that while we might be able to discover criteria for determining that, for example, an apple is good, the same does not hold for moral claims. Some have claimed that we cannot discover criteria for claiming actions are morally good or obligatory because there are no such criteria. In what follows I argue that neither claim is reasonable. I shall *not* defend a particular moral theory (see sidebar), although I shall conclude by showing how my account is related to various moral theories. Let's start by talking about food.

If you have taken a health class, you have probably been told that you should eat lots of fruits and vegetables. Why should you do that? Because it is good for your health. Some people—health teachers come to mind—seem to believe that health or life is an ultimate end, something that is good as such. Those who question the ultimacy of the end would still grant that life and health are at least a necessary means to other ends. Is it true that eating fruits and vegetables is a good means to living a healthy life? Sure. Is it the only reason you eat fruits and vegetables? No. I trust all of you believe that *some* fruits and *some* vegetables are tasty some of the time. Some of us grew up in households where eating one's vegetables also was a means to avoiding various unpleasantries. Similarly, you might refrain from theft because you "wouldn't

---

[4]If you think about it for a time, however, you'll discover that physical pain is not something that is evil as such. If you suffered no pain, you would not know that there is a problem in your body and the consequences could be dire. Victims of leprosy (Hansen's disease) are unable to sense pain in various parts of their bodies. They can be attacked by various kinds of vermin without knowing they've been attacked.

Moral Theories

There is a moral theory that is *not* a theory of obligation. This is **virtue ethics**. The moral quality of the action depends upon the moral quality of the character or motive from which it arises. Virtue theorists construct moral rules which, if followed, *tend* to yield a virtuous character. They are rules known by induction. They are *not* rules the following of which make an action right or wrong. They only tell you what, more often than not, will result in a virtuous character. Aristotle was a virtue theorist.

Philosophers distinguish among several theories of moral obligation. The **divine command theory** holds that moral obligations are based on commands of God.

Ethical egoism assumes the principle that you ought to do that which is in your best interest. If this is plausible, the egoist must be concerned with long-term self-interest. Long-term self-interest must take the interests of other people into account. **Utilitarianism** assumes the principle that one ought act in a way that yields the greatest good (or pleasure or happiness) to the greatest number of people. The egoistic principle or the utilitarian principle can be applied to actions directly or can be used to decide what rules are moral rules (rules that tend to maximize the principle). Both egoism and utilitarianism are **consequentialist (teleological)** theories. It is the consequences of the actions (the goods produced) that determine whether an action is right or wrong.

Nonconsequentialist (deontological) theories maintain that the rightness or wrongness of an action is independent of its consequences. Most of these are theories based on moral rules (they are rule-deontological theories). Rule-deontologists maintain that doing what is morally right consists of nothing but following a moral rule. Immanuel Kant's categorial imperative, "Act only on that maxim whereby thou canst at the same time will that it should become a universal law," is a rule for rationally choosing moral rules. Rules said to follow from this include, "Keep your promises," "Do not steal," and "Do not commit murder." These rules are taken to determine actual obligations that hold at all times. So, if you can prevent a murder by breaking a promise, you must decide which duty not to fulfill. Some moralists consider such a strict notion implausible. W. D. Ross suggests that there are only *prima facie* rules of moral obligation. When rules conflict, you must determine (by reason) which of the conflicting rules actually applies in the situation. Act-deontologists, on the other hand, maintain that there is a method whereby one can determine the moral value or obligation of a specific action without appealing to rules. The consequences of an action can play *some* role, but not the only role, in determining the moral property of an action or state. (For an example of such a method, see the sidebar called "On Resolving Disputes.") Act-deontologists maintain that the moral rules we might be taught as children are merely summary rules. They are inductive generalizations from particular cases.

feel right" if you stole or to avoid possibly unpleasant consequences. The term 'should' in "You should eat your vegetables" is an evaluative term. It specifies an obligation, though not a moral obligation. It is a "for-your-health" obligation.[5] I have also suggested that the statement "You should (in the for-your-health sense) eat your vegetables" is true. How do we know that?

The human body is interesting and complex. People have been studying it for centuries. Knowledge of how the body works, what it needs, and what can be done to keep it working well is, like virtually any other kind of knowledge, something that has been slowly developed over the centuries. We all know that we should eat fruits,

---

[5]It might be deemed a *prudential* obligation. It is something that is wise or prudent to do. It is in your long-term best interest.

in part to obtain our daily requirement of vitamin C. We also know that if we go without vitamin C for a significant period of time, we will develop scurvy. Scurvy has been around for a long time. It was described during the medieval Crusades. Scurvy became a cause of serious illness and death among sailors beginning in the late fifteenth century. It was only in 1753 that James Lind showed that eating citrus fruits could prevent scurvy. Does this imply that before 1753 the statement, "You should (for-your-health) eat citrus fruit every day" was false, or neither true nor false? No. It simply wasn't known to be true. Just as, "You should ingest a significant amount of vitamin C every day" was not known until the early 1930s, since vitamin C wasn't isolated until 1928 and its connection with scurvy was not established until 1932.

"But what does this have to do with ethics?" you ask. To answer that question, consider an analogy between a human body and a society. The human body is a complex machine. It is composed of cells, tissues, organs, and systems of organs. What happens at the cellular level can eventually have an impact on the whole. Somewhere in your body there is almost certainly a cancerous or precancerous cell. Coursing through your bloodstream are globs of cholesterol. If the cancerous cells multiply unchecked, you will die. If the cholesterol blocks the major arteries in your heart, you will die. The various dietary rules pushed by your health teacher and your physician reflect what the current evidence suggests will reduce the chances that you'll die sooner rather than later. So, eat your fruits and vegetables. They prevent diseases caused by vitamin deficiencies, and current research suggests that the antioxidants in fruits and vegetables help prevent some forms of cancer. Don't eat lots of sugars and saturated fats. The body converts sugars and saturated fats into cholesterol. Don't smoke. Tobacco contains or produces chemicals known to cause cancer. Exercise. Sleep for six or seven hours per night. And be sure to look both ways before you cross the street—even if you follow the rules of diet and exercise, you could still be killed by a fast-moving truck.

Human beings are social animals. No one can live all her life without other people—infants abandoned in the snow don't survive. Most of us, most of the time, could not survive long without others. We need the goods and services provided by others. We need emotional support from one another. And we need some assurance that our lives, our persons, and our property are safe. A society is like a body. There are individuals (cells) and groups of varying degrees of complexity (comparable to tissues, organs, and organ systems). Just as centuries of experience have taught us that eating various foods, exercising, and refraining from various activities

> H. L. A. Hart explains why there must be certain kinds of moral rules and, in a political society, positive (enacted) laws on the basis of five facts about human beings. (1) Humans are vulnerable; that is, every human is potentially subject to harm at the hands of others. (2) Humans are approximately equal in strength and intellectual ability. Even those who are superior in either way are vulnerable—and therefore made equal—during periods of sleep. (3) Humans possess only limited altruism. They're neither entirely self-interested nor solely interested in the welfare of others. (4) Resources are limited. Resources to meet our needs and wants are not available in abundance. (5) We have limited understandings and limited strength of will. We often do not recognize what is in our long-term interests, and we sometimes have problems restraining our desires to available resources.
>
> See H. L. A. Hart, *The Concept of Law* (Oxford: Clarendon Press, 1961), pp. 189–195.

tends to increase the probability that one's body will continue functioning fairly well for a relatively long period of time, so we have learned that certain kinds of social relationships are good for the health and longevity of the society on which most of us depend. So, in virtually any society, there are moral rules concerning murder, theft, and promises (which are needed for many exchanges and agreements). One may understand a **moral rule** (a rule stating a moral obligation) as a prescription to act or refrain from acting in a certain way to further societal "health".[6]

On Resolving Disputes

You'll often find yourself in disputes with friends. Appeals to general principles will point in different directions. How do you resolve the disputes? The following method should help clarify the issues and allow you and your friends to come to at least a *conditional agreement*. A conditional agreement is an agreement that *if* certain facts hold, then a moral or aesthetic or some other property applies in the case.

1. Avoid verbal disputes. Make sure that all parties to the dispute are using key words in the same ways. This may need to be checked at several times during your discussions.
2. Try to determine all the facts that are relevant to the case. These should be *both* facts that you know apply and facts that *would* be relevant *if* they did apply.
3. Construct and discuss conditional statements of the forms "If x is F_1, then x is P" and "If x is F_2, then x is not P," where x is an action, F is a factual predicate, and P is a moral, aesthetic, or some other predicate (such as "is morally permissible" or "is aesthetically good" or "is guilty").
4. Continue constructing conditional statements of those forms until all parties to the dispute agree that "If x is F_1 and F_2 and F_3 ... F_m, then x is P, and if x is F_i and F_{ii} and F_{iii} ... F_n, then x is not P."
5. Be willing to revise your conditionals if additional factual considerations come to light.

This will resolve the dispute regarding P insofar as you come to *agreement* regarding the application of P or not P to the action. It resolves disputes regarding the criterion. It will *not* guarantee that the disputants will agree regarding what facts actually apply. It will *not* guarantee that you have reached a *correct* conclusion. Sometimes this is the best we can do. For example, in a jury trial, members of the jury are given guidelines for determining whether the defendant should be found guilty or innocent. They must reach additional agreement on what facts would count as indicating that the defendant committed the crime *and* agreement that those facts hold. If there is agreement on what would count but no agreement on what facts hold, the jury is "hung." If there is agreement on both, it still sometimes happens that they reach a wrong verdict.

You need not study much history or anthropology to discover that, as a matter of fact, different societies accept different collections of moral rules. This fact is called the **cultural relativity of morals**. Doesn't the fact of cultural relativity imply that what is morally right for us today is not the same as what was morally right for the ancient Roman aristocracy and probably is not the same as what will be right for Europeans or certain groups of Europeans two hundred years hence? That is, doesn't cultural relativity imply **moral relativity**, the thesis that there are no moral rules *as such,* that what actions are moral varies from culture to culture? Indeed, doesn't this

---

[6]This is a teleological account of moral law. We consider other accounts below.

imply that I could declare myself a culture of one and it would be literally the case that what is true for me is not true for you? No. To see why not, let us return to our analogy to the human body.

Three hundred years ago, we did not know that we should eat citrus fruit to prevent scurvy. The fact that James Lind did not discover the connection between eating citrus fruit and preventing scurvy until 1753 does *not* constitute a change in the natural world. It constitutes a change in what we know. A society is a very complex body. Discovering the rules that yield societal health is no small task. The moral rules in a given culture reflect the current understanding of what yields societal health. Murder, theft, and lying (at least in some circumstances) are like a cancer which, if allowed to grow (increase in significant numbers), could destroy the proper working of the societal body. Just as not all organs of a body need be cancerous in order for a person to die, an entire society need be morally corrupt to destroy the society. (When you replied to a moralist's question, "What if everyone did that?" by saying, "But everyone won't," your remark was insightful but irrelevant.) Not all diseases are fatal. Some diseases are merely uncomfortable. We have all suffered from a cold. To avoid colds, you should wash your hands regularly. Similarly, while some moral rules are essential for the health of society, others help avoid various societal discomforts.

But, you might say, there are some societies in which activities are condoned that we would never condone. A common example used in this case concerns Eskimos. Eskimos once considered it morally permissible to set aged parents out on ice floes.[7] *We* would never do something like that, much to the relief of our aged relatives. Doesn't this show that there are fundamental differences in moral principles? No. It was only in times of extreme shortage that aged relatives were placed on ice floes. It was recognized by all that the measure was extreme but necessary for the survival of the society (village).

Just as we come to know—or, as various disputes in the medical community suggest, come to believe—that certain kinds of activities are harmful to the health of the body, the same can be said regarding the development of moral knowledge. Four hundred years ago there were no recognized moral obligations with respect to nonhuman animals. Analogies between human suffering and suffering in the higher animals were responsible for the recognition that cruelty to animals is wrong.

Moral principles sometimes conflict. It is a moral principle that you ought not kill. It is also a moral principle that you should do what you can to reduce suffering. If there is a patient suffering severely from a disease that almost certainly will be fatal, is it morally permissible for a medical professional to end the patient's suffering with an overdose of morphine? If it is your relative, is it morally permissible for you to relieve the suffering with a blast from a

> Heart patients are told to reduce their intake of salt (sodium) and fat. They are advised to look for the "reduced fat" or "no fat" varieties of food at the supermarket. The sodium levels in most reduced fat foods are higher than the sodium levels in the common varieties. What should heart patients do?

---

[7]Whether the Eskimos themselves would have answered this question in terms of obligations is a factual question more properly answered by an anthropologist than an ethicist. So, I leave that question open.

shotgun? Do the patient's wishes make a difference? If the patient's wishes make a difference, at what point can you be certain that the patient consents? If she wrote a "living will" two years ago while in good health, should you assume that this gives consent in the current situation? If there is sound medical evidence that she will slip into a coma within the next few days, does that make a difference?[8] If funds for paying the hospital have been exhausted, does that make a difference? What do you do?

You argue. You do your best to determine which principles take precedence over the others on the basis of strong inductive arguments. How do various facts tend to support your claim that principle A takes precedence over principle B? Construct analogies to clear cases. For example, normally if Jan indicates that he wants something done to him, then that is sufficient to indicate that it is morally permissible to do that to him. How is the present similar and different from the typical case? Discuss your arguments with other people who are affected by Jan's condition, including, if possible, Jan. If you come to an agreement, you have some reason to believe that the conclusion is correct.

You will notice that, except for a sidebar a few pages back, there have been no allusions to theories of moral obligation, so I conclude this discussion with a few words on moral theories.

Proponents of the **divine command theory** maintain that moral rules are right because God says so. Religious skeptics discount this theory on the ground that there is insufficient evidence to establish the existence of God, so there are no grounds for accepting the commands. Let's set aside that consideration for the moment. The divine command theory is based on an analogy to an absolute ruler who sets down laws. We can either assume that this ruler is purely arbitrary or that the ruler is wise and benevolent. (Of course, the ruler could be somewhere between these extremes.) Those who take the divine command theory seriously generally contend that God is wise, benevolent, and looking out for the welfare of his or her "children." If this is the case, then it is entirely reasonable that God would give commands that would be to the overall benefit of society. So, it is not unreasonable to suggest that the same general principles could be discovered over an extended period of time by empirical means.

Ethical egoism maintains that you should do that which is in your best interest. If this has any plausibility, you have to be concerned with long-term self-interest, and long-term self interest has to take the interests and desires of other people into account. In effect, it reduces to utilitarianism. **Utilitarianism** maintains that one should act in such a way that yields the greatest good (or pleasure

> Those familiar with the Judeo-Christian tradition know that, in addition to moral rules, tradition has it that God instituted a number of dietary rules. Eating pork was prohibited, for example. In an age when food-borne parasites were common, these dietary laws were reasonable on medical grounds. (And, as some of my friends discovered a few years ago, it is still reasonable to cook pork to an internal temperature of 160°F to avoid trichinosis.)

---

[8]As a person who was once comatose, my experience suggests that once a person slips into a coma, there is no pain.

or happiness) to the greatest number of people. The problem with utilitarianism is that, properly speaking, you cannot quantify goodness (or pleasure or happiness), so you cannot properly do the calculations. Nonetheless, you will notice that the account I have proposed has similarities to utilitarianism.

I have little to say regarding the **nonconsequentialist** rule theories—I'll leave their defense to your ethics teacher. Suffice it to say that occidental rule-deontologists propose moral rules very much like those of the divine command theory and those proposed by most rule-utilitarians. At least one act-deontologist suggests that resolving moral disputes in a manner like that in the "On Resolving Disputes" sidebar (while making no appeals to moral rules) is sufficient for obtaining moral knowledge. While I question whether consensus alone is a sufficient condition for moral truth, I believe it is a reasonable method to use to resolve moral disputes.

Discussion Questions

1. You are marooned on a desert island. Does that fact affect the moral rules you would assume? Would it make any difference whether you were assured that you would be alone on the island for the rest of your natural life or you had a reasonable hope of being rescued?

2. You are marooned on a desert island with the person with whom you would most like to be marooned on a desert island. Would the moral rules you would assume be the same as those you assumed when you were marooned alone?

3. You are marooned on a desert island with an android made to look and act like the person with whom you would most like to be marooned on a desert island. Would you assume the same moral rules as you would assume if you were marooned with a real person?

4. If you knew that you had only six months to live, would you assume the same moral principles you had previously assumed? Why or why not?

5. Does a person's motive or purpose in doing something play any role in the moral evaluation of the resulting action? If so, does it always play a role? Does what a person knows (or what he or she should know) play any role in evaluating the moral worth of a motive?

6. Consider the following two moral principles: (1) You should not kill human beings. (2) Individuals have a right to control what happens to their bodies. Explain how these two principles might seem to conflict with respect to abortion issues. Are there grounds for resolving the apparent conflict with respect to abortion in general, or do you need to look at things on a case-by-case basis? If you need to look at things on a case-by-case basis, what considerations tend to show that abortion is permissible? What considerations tend to show that abortion is impermissible?

7. Moral rules are arguably ranked in terms of importance. Moral rules prohibiting murder, assault, and theft are rules for which there seem to be few exceptions.

Certain "white lies," such as complimenting the host of a (dull) party, might be morally permissible insofar as they are required by the rules of etiquette. Where do moral rules regarding drugs or sexual behavior rank in this hierarchy? Does the fact that one can transmit AIDS by needles or sexual intercourse imply that there might be a shift in the ranking of these moral rules relative to their position prior to AIDS? Why or why not?

8. Zelda is 92. She has recently been in an automobile accident. In the hospital, she is unconscious. She is being kept alive by various medical devices. Furthermore, she was recently diagnosed as suffering from inoperable cancer. Before the accident, her doctor had given her no more than six months to live. Is it morally permissible to turn off the machines that are keeping her alive? If Zelda were 29, would that make a difference?

9. Dale, a child of seven, has been admitted to the hospital with a severe case of viral encephalitis. He is comatose. He has been running a fever in excess of 107°F for several days. His doctor remarked, "He'll probably die. If he lives, he'll suffer severe mental or physical challenges for life, probably both." Should efforts be taken to keep him alive?

10. Let us grant that murder is generally wrong. Nonetheless, virtually everyone will grant that if the various plots to assassinate Adolph Hitler had succeeded, the perpetrators would have been (or were in spite of their failure) moral heroes. (If you don't like considering Adolph Hitler, choose your favorite villain.) How can this be? If there are exceptions to moral rules, why is that?

Aesthetics

Our evaluations are not limited to the morality of actions. We evaluate works of art. Indeed, in claiming that something is a work of art, we are making an evaluative claim. We claim that Shakespeare's *Hamlet* is a great play. We claim that Beethovan's Ninth Symphony is a superb piece of music. We claim that Seurat's *An Afternoon at La Grande Jatte* is an excellent painting. What do these claims mean?

Many philosophers claim that there are close ties between our emotions and our *moral* judgments. Some claim moral goodness consists of nothing but a certain kind of emotional approval. Others claim that all human beings are "hardwired" in the same way, and our emotional responses to actions and pieces of art are signs of moral or aesthetic properties in the action or object. If the latter are correct, then moral or aesthetic goodness is like blueness. When we see an object as blue, the surface of the object reflects light of a certain wavelength, and the mind "sees" the object as blue. The blueness in the object is what causes the light to be reflected. It is not what we "see." The blueness that we see is a sign of the structure in the object. Does the same hold regarding moral and aesthetic properties?

Regardless how you understand aesthetic goodness, an emotional response almost certainly plays some role in deeming an object aesthetically good. If no one responded to a work by saying, "I like it!" no one would claim the work is aesthetically good. Of course, the fact that you don't "appreciate" Bach's Organ Concerto no. 4 in C Major

(BWV 595) and that I don't "appreciate" Jackson Pollock's *Male and Female* doesn't mean neither is aesthetically valuable. How do you assess aesthetic value?

In many ways assessing aesthetic value is like assessing moral value. Centuries of experience tell us that (generally) murder is not good. Centuries of experience tell us that *Oedipus Rex* is an excellent play. But there also seem to be differences. If I transported myself back to Sophocles' Athens and surveyed the citizens on the question, "Is murder wrong?" I suspect they would agree that murder is wrong. If there were disagreements, I suspect they would have to do with whether the potential victim was a Greek or a barbarian (a non-Greek). On the other hand, if Sophocles had been born in 1970 (rather than 496 BCE) and submitted *Oedipus Rex* to a Broadway producer, I doubt that it would be produced. At best, the producer might say, "The story has possibilities, but either we gotta get rid of the chorus or give them something to *do*." Or if I went to a Kabuki play, I might leave saying, "It was fascinating" but have no views on whether the play itself or the performance of it was good. Why is that?

There seem to be several reasons. What counts as a "classic" work depends, in part, upon what has been accepted as an important or artistically significant work in the past. And it is not majority opinion that determines that something is a work of art. Norman Rockwell was one of the most popular American painters of the twentieth century. Few would claim that Rockwell's paintings have artistic merit comparable to paintings by Jackson Pollack, even though most Americans would find Pollack's paintings a bit strange. Many people would prefer reading Robert Ludlum's *The Bourne Identity*[9] to Geoffrey Chaucer's *The Canterbury Tales,* even though Chaucer's work will remain forever a "classic," while Ludlum's book will probably be forgotten within a century. As your literature teachers probably tell you, classical literature teaches you something about the human condition.[10] Of course, while lost in *Paradise Lost* or agonizing over the *Odyssey,* you might have thought Mark Twain had it right: ". . . a classic—something that everybody wants to have read and nobody wants to read." *Art*—as opposed to drawings and songs—and *literature*—as opposed to stories—are what are deemed "good" by the "cultured" members of a society. Neither you nor I might ever be quite clear what that certain *je ne sais quoi* is that makes one cultured, but there are certain elements that we can discuss. Understanding these elements will allow us to appreciate works of art.

> Is "folk art" an oxymoron?

Elements of Art

A work of art is something made by a human. Most human artifacts and all works of art are intentionally produced. The creator wants to fulfill certain objectives. This applies to mundane things as well as to works of art. I might decide to build a porch

---

[9]Robert Ludlum, *The Bourne Identity* (New York: R. Marek Publishers, 1980).

[10]I've always found the expression "the human condition" vague. *Which* human condition? Isn't there more than one? I assume it has something to do with "timeless" attributes ascribed to humanity. Are these *moral* attributes? Are these *behavioral* attributes? Surely, they cannot be *physical* attributes. What kinds of attributes are these, and why are those attributes important?

swing. I draw a sketch. I buy lumber. I go into my woodshop and cut, sand, glue, and nail. If, when I'm done, I can hang it on my porch and people can sit in it and swing, it is "good" in one sense of that term. The object does what it is supposed to do. It fulfills the modest purpose for which it was built. If it had collapsed when my wife sat in it, it would not have been a good swing. If I had been unable to hang it on the porch, it would not have been a good swing. It might be "good" in another sense as well. It resembles what most people would call a porch swing. But there are also senses in which it is not good. Good porch swings are symmetrical. Mine isn't, but it's close enough to hang well. Good porch swings look cheery and inviting. Battleship gray might not be the best color to fulfill that objective. Good porch swings allow you to sit comfortably for hours at a time.

Element 1: What are the artist's objectives? Artists have objectives. Common objectives and common means to reach those objectives define a "style." A typical objective of portrait painters is to recognizably represent the subject while occasionally flattering the subject. Cubist painters, such as Picasso, have other objectives. To understand and appreciate Picasso—or any other artist—you need some understanding of his objectives and how he went about fulfilling them. One element in judging aesthetic worth is judging the artist's success in fulfilling her objectives. So, it is not merely a matter of what you or I might like. It is consistent to say, "I really don't like Cézanne, but his landscapes are excellent examples of French impressionism." That is, Cézanne's paintings fulfill the common objectives of the French impressionists. Of course, some people must "like" Cézanne's paintings—they must speak to someone's aesthetic sentiments—or no one would ascribe them aesthetic worth.

So, **Element 2: Does *someone* ascribe aesthetic worth to the object?** Typically they are ascribed aesthetic value by the "cultured" members of society, and it often takes some time for a new art form to be accepted. Similarly, ordinary objects can be converted into objects of art as people begin to appreciate their aesthetic value. There is a growing recognition of the aesthetic value of quilts, for example, as is shown by the growing number of quilt museums and quilt exhibits.

Element 3: How well does the artist fulfill his or her objectives? One element of aesthetic worth is that an artist fulfills his or her objectives. When these objectives and the methods by which those objectives are reached become common to a number of artists, you have a style or school of art. Once you have a style or school of art, it is easy to compare pieces of art in terms of fulfillment of common objectives. Is Paul Cézanne's landscape *Paysage a Auvers* (1873; http://www.artchive .com/artchive/C/cezanne/auvers.jpg.html) a better example of French Impressionism than Claude Monet's *Le bateau-atelier* (1876; http://www.artchive.com/artchive/M/monet/monet.jpg.html)? You will argue for your answer on the basis of common objectives of the impressionists and the skills with which the artists exemplify those objectives in their paintings. Of course, it is possible that an artist has individual objectives that differ from those of the school to which she belongs. So, it is possible that an artist is an imperfect representative of a school and that the work does an excellent job of fulfilling the artist's individual objectives. Which takes precedence?

Literature provides us with insights into the human condition. It has a point (it fulfills the author's objectives). It is not just a matter of telling a story well, although that is also required. (The words should paint memorable images.) One task for the reader of literature is determining what the writer's objective is. What does the author want you to learn about yourself or the world? As in the case of a graphic artist, some evidence may be drawn from the work itself. Evidence also might be drawn from facts about the writer's life as well as about the historical period in which it was written. If *Gulliver's Travels* is a satire, what does this tell us about Swift's views of his times? Are the presumed satirical elements consistent with what you might discover about Swift in a good biography or in his letters? If you can find evidence in, for example, Swift's letters that he intended the work to be a satire, how successful was he? Does the quality of his work depend upon his success as a satirical writer? Does his work illustrate truths that are as important for understanding people in the twenty-first century as they were for understanding people in the eighteenth century? Present arguments to support your claims.

Element 4: In performance art, is an individual performance aesthetically valuable? What should be taken into account in reaching a judgment? Pieces of performance art, such as plays and musical compositions, are judged in two ways. The aesthetic worth of the piece itself is judged, as is the aesthetic worth of the performance. Shakespeare's *Hamlet* is an excellent play on all those grounds by which one judges excellence in literature. Is Cedric Messina's 1980 production for the BBC as good as Sir Laurence Olivier's 1948 cinematic production? Is either as good as an actual stage production? Could anything compare with a production by the eighth graders at a neighborhood church? (Might the last be "charming" but "tragic" in more than one sense?) How do you judge the quality of a performance?

Consider two performances of Haydn's Concerto for Trumpet in B-flat. In 1964, Al Hirt, noted for renditions of popular music on his trumpet ("Java" was his signature piece at the time), recorded the Haydn Concerto with the Boston Pops.[11] In 1983, Wynton Marsalis recorded the Concerto with the National Philharmonic.[12] Which is the better performance (assuming you can compare analog and digital recordings)? How do you decide?

In comparing two pieces of music, one issue is technical precision. Which of the two performers gets more of the notes right, follows the marked dynamics more closely, and so on? (As some of you know, judges at music contests follow the score to check these things.) Both were good, but Marsalis was a bit better. In wind instruments, the clarity of the tone is important. Here the kudos go to Marsalis. The high E-flat at three measures before Ⓑ⑨ was exactly on target.[13] In general, Marsalis's tone was purer, that is, there was less (virtually no) "wavering" of pitch. Finally, the Haydn Concerto contains a cadenza. A cadenza is an unaccompanied, improvised solo passage. Marsalis's cadenza is musically more interesting, and it more fully highlighted his

---

[11]Al Hirt, soloist, Arthur Fiedler, conductor, *"Pops" Goes the Trumpet*, Boston Pops, (Radio Corporation of America, 1964).

[12]Wynton Marsalis, soloist, Raymond Leppard, conductor, *Trumpet Concertos*, National Philharmonic Orchestra, (CBS, Inc., 1983).

[13]Joseph Haydn, *Concerto, Transcribed for Cornet (Trumpet) in B-flat*, with piano accompaniment and variations and cadenzas by A. Goeyens (New York: Carl Fisher, W1834).

talents. So, if you're going to buy only one of these recordings of the Haydn Concerto for Trumpet, I'd recommend Marsalis's.

So, is judging the quality of a musical performance largely a matter of getting the notes right? No, although that is an element to be taken into consideration. Technical precision does not always make a great performance.

In 1951, Albert Schweitzer recorded a number of J. S. Bach's organ pieces. At the time, Schweitzer was best known for his work as a medical missionary in Africa, although he was also a noted theologian, had written a highly acclaimed biography of Bach (published in 1905), and was an accomplished organist. In 1951, Albert Schweitzer was 76 years old. At 76, one's coordination is not what it is at 26. Schweitzer's recordings are *not* the most technically precise recordings of Bach's organ works. The organ he played was *not* the most technologically advanced organ in Europe. But *oh, the music!* Schweitzer knew Bach. He instilled emotion into the works that goes beyond the demands of technical precision. They're superb (and historically important) recordings. Are they better than recordings by E. Power Biggs, who was noted for his musical precision? Is either a Schweitzer or Biggs performance better than a performance by Virgil Fox, who was noted for taking liberties with the score but always provided an exciting performance? Was Schweitzer's interpretation of Bach excellent given the musical and scholarly standards *of the time,* but *now* they have been superseded? I'll let you develop arguments on these issues.

So, we can reason about issues in ethics and aesthetics, since we do argue about such things. In each case, there are some guidelines that are established by "historical wisdom." Murder is generally wrong, but there are cases in which we can provide strong inductive evidence that the intentional taking of a human life is justified. Technical precision in painting or music is an element to take into account in considering the value of the work, but it is not the only element to take into consideration. Sometimes it is not the most important element to take into account. As in all inductive arguments, the conclusions you reach will be open to further investigation. Arguments may need to be developed that the criteria you apply are reasonable. Perfect agreement might never be reached. These facts, however, do not make ethical and aesthetic issues fundamentally different from most issues in ordinary life.

Discussion Questions

1. *West Side Story* is a contemporary musical setting of *Romeo and Juliet.* Does it do justice to Shakespeare's play? What considerations do you believe should be taken into account when Shakespeare is placed in a contemporary setting? Why?

2. Arnold Schönberg was noted for his atonal music (music in which a key signature is of little importance). He was one of the pioneers of the 12-tone musical scale. If you attend a concert featuring a Schönberg piece, you probably won't leave "whistling the tune." Are Schönberg's atonal works of aesthetic worth? Why or why not?

3. You are at an auction one day and buy a trunk and all its contents. Inside the trunk you find a folder containing a number of finger paintings done by a child

of four or five. After some investigation you are able to establish that the finger paintings were not done by just any four- or five-year-old. They were finger paintings by Jackson Pollack, who was one of the great American painters of the twentieth century. If you sell the finger paintings, you probably could pay for at least a year of college. Does this imply they have aesthetic worth? How would you judge the aesthetic worth of the finger paintings?

4. Listen to two orchestras led by different conductors play the opening movement of Beethoven's Fifth Symphony. Which provides the better interpretation of the work? Why?

5. Andy Warhol was famous for painting pictures of soup cans. Examine an Andy Warhol painting (http://imv.aau.dk/~jfogde/gallery/art/13.html). Is it aesthetically valuable? If you can find information on his artistic intentions, do they change your judgment regarding the aesthetic value of the Warhol painting?

6. We often claim that natural objects are beautiful. There are beautiful flowers (as opposed to beautiful arrangements). There are beautiful horses. Is this aesthetic beauty?

7. Can one reasonably compare art of radically different styles? For example, can you make comparative judgments regarding the works of Peter Paul Rubens (1577–1640) and Edvard Munch (1863–1944)? What arguments could be developed to support the claim that Rubens's *The Lamentation* (1609–1611) is a better painting than Munch's *The Scream* (1893)? What arguments could be developed to support the claim that Munch's *Madonna* (1894–95) is a better painting then Rubens's *Virgin and Child Enthroned with Saints* (1627–28)? Or is it only reasonable to make comparative evaluations of art within a single style? (Images may be found at http://artchive.com/ftp_site.htm)

8. Is it possible to compare artistic works across media? For example, could you develop arguments that Molière's play *The Imaginary Invalid* (*Le Malade Imaginaire*) is a better piece of comedy than a musical composition by P. D. Q. Bach (Peter Schickele)? Would the evaluations be different if you compared performances of each?

9. Several years ago the National Endowment for the Arts was embroiled in controversy for supporting artists whose work was deemed "pornographic." Is pornography an aesthetic concept or a moral concept? If it is a moral concept, can moral notions be relevant to evaluations of aesthetic value?

10. Can whimsical or comedic works constitute serious art? Would *A Midsummer Night's Dream* be a great work even if Shakespeare had written neither *Romeo and Juliet* nor *Hamlet*? Is Mozart's *Magic Flute* a great opera? If it is, would it be considered great even if Mozart had written no "serious" operas? Why?

PART IV

Categorical Syllogisms

In Part IV we begin our examination of deductive arguments. As we noticed in Chapter 6, a valid deductive argument with true premises provides conclusive evidence for the truth of its conclusion. The **form** of an argument is its structure. The form of an argument is like the design of a house. Just as many houses can have the same design, many arguments have the same form. If you want a solid house, you need a good design. If the design of your house is defective—even if it is made of the finest materials—eventually there will be problems. Similarly, if the form of an argument is defective—if it is invalid—there is no guarantee that *if* the premises are true, the conclusion will be as well. Although we shall be primarily concerned with the form of the argument, in ordinary life we cannot ignore the content. A **sound** argument is a valid argument with true premises, so the truth of the conclusion is guaranteed. So, at various points we shall need to ask whether the premises are true. Just as a house with a fine design but constructed of poor materials is defective, similarly, a valid argument with one or more false premises does not guarantee that the conclusion is true.

Categorical syllogisms are deductive arguments concerning relations among classes of things. The study of categorical syllogisms dates back to Aristotle (384-322 BCE), and for centuries the study of argument was identified with the study of categorical syllogisms. In this part we examine two ways to evaluate the validity of categorical syllogisms. In Chapter 13, we examine the characteristics of categorical propositions. In Chapter 14, we examine some of the characteristics of categorical syllogisms. In Chapter 15, we evaluate categorical syllogisms on the basis of a system of rules. In Chapter 16, we evaluate categorical syllogisms on the basis of Venn diagrams. In Chapter 17, we develop techniques for finding missing premises on the basis of rules and on the basis of Venn diagrams. In Chapter 18, we examine equivalent forms of categorical statements and immediate inferences (squares of opposition). Finally, in Chapter 19, we turn to ways of dealing with arguments in ordinary language.

Categorical Propositions

The View: Sometimes we discuss the relationships between classes of objects. These are called categorical propositions. We say that all members of one class are members of another, or that none are, or that some are, or that some are not. The various properties and elements of categorical propositions are discussed in this chapter.

What are the relationships between classes (sets) of objects? How are they expressed?

Sometimes we are concerned with relationships between classes of things. These relationships are expressed by **categorical propositions**. Assume there are two classes: Call them *S* (for 'subject') and *P* (for 'predicate'). There are four possible relationships between these classes. (1) All members of *S* are members of *P*; for example, "All collies are dogs." (2) No members of *S* are members of *P*; for example, "No dogs are cats." (3) Some members of *S* are members of *P*; for example, "Some dogs are collies." (4) Some members of *S* are *not* members of *P*; for example, "Some cats are not Siamese."

> The statement "Some dogs are not cats" is true because there is at least one dog that is not a cat. *Do not be tempted to claim that* "Some dogs are not cats" is false because the statement "No dogs are cats" is true! "No unicorns are one-horned horses" is *true* because there are no unicorns. "Some unicorns are one-horned horses" is *false* because there are no unicorns."

Categorical propositions have two characteristics: **quantity** and **quality**. The quantity of a categorical proposition refers to the number of objects about which we are concerned. Categorical propositions are either **universal** or **particular**. A universal proposition refers to all the members of a class. A particular proposition refers only to some members of a class. What does 'some' mean? In ordinary English, 'some' usually means "a few." (Here we are replacing one vague term with another.) Following a long tradition, we stipulate that 'some' means "at least one." So, for our purposes, the statement "Some critical-thinking teachers are people who enjoy woodworking" is true even if I am the *only* critical-thinking teacher who ever has or ever

142

will enjoy woodworking. In addition to universal and particular propositions, there are **singular propositions**. A singular proposition refers to an individual. "Lassie is a dog" or "Flage is a woodworker" are examples of singular propositions. Given our meaning of 'some', if the statement "Lassie is a collie" is true, and the statement "Lassie is a dog" is true, it follows that "Some (at least one—for example, Lassie) collies are dogs" is true.

The quality of a categorical proposition is either **affirmative** or **negative**. An affirmative proposition makes a positive claim. "All collies are dogs" and "Some dogs are collies" are affirmative propositions. A negative proposition includes a denial: It asserts that all or some members of one class are *not* members of another class. "No cats are dogs" and "Some cats are not Siamese" are negative propositions.

So, we can name the types of propositions in terms of quantity and quality. (1) A proposition asserting that all members of one class are

> The letter-names of categorical propositions are derived from the Latin words 'AffIrmo', meaning "I affirm," and 'nEgO', meaning "I deny."

members of another, for example, "All Siamese are cats," is a **universal affirmative** proposition. This is sometimes known as an **A** proposition. (2) A proposition denying that two classes have any members in common, for example, "No elephants are aardvarks," is a **universal negative** proposition. This is sometimes known as an **E** proposition. (3) A proposition asserting that two classes have some members in common, for example, "Some dogs are great Danes," is a **particular affirmative** proposition. This is sometimes known as an **I** proposition. (4) A proposition asserting that there is at least one member of the first class that is *not* a member of the second class, for example, "Some aardvarks are not weasels," is a **particular negative** proposition. This is sometimes known as an **O** proposition.

There are many ways we can assert a universal affirmative proposition. The statements, "All collies are dogs," "Every collie is a dog," "Any collie is a dog," and "Collies are dogs" say the same thing. To simplify matters— at least for the time being—we introduce the notion of a **standard form categorical proposition**. A standard form categorical proposition has four distinct parts.

> **Ways to Say All, No, and Some**
> While 'all', 'no', and 'some' are the only quantifiers used in *standard form* categorical propositions, other words are commonly used to represent universal or particular propositions. These are among the most common.
>
> For all: every, any, each.
> For no: not any, none.
> For some: at least one, there is a, there are, there exists a.
> For some . . . are not . . .: not every, not all.
>
> In Chapter 19 we examine other words that mean all, no, and some.

1. It has a **quantifier**, which is either 'all', 'no', or 'some'.

2. It has a **subject term**. A **term** is a word or phrase that can function as the subject of a sentence (a noun or noun phrase). The subject term is immediately to the right of the quantifier.

3. It has a form of the verb 'to be,' which is immediately to the right of the subject term.

4. It has a **predicate term**, which is immediately to the right of the verb.

So, where *S* stands for the subject term and *P* stands for the predicate term, our four standard form categorical propositions are as follows:

Universal affirmative (**A**): All *S* is *P*.

Universal negative (**E**): No *S* is *P*.

Particular affirmative (**I**): Some *S* is *P*.

Particular negative (**O**): Some *S* is not *P*.

The subject and predicate terms can be either a single word, such as 'cats', or a complex phrase, such as 'cats who play post office on rainy days in June'.

Exercises

I. In each of the following, circle the subject term and **underline** the predicate term. Indicate whether the proposition is a universal affirmative (**A**), a universal negative (**E**), a particular affirmative (**I**), or a particular negative (**O**). If the statement is *not* a standard form categorical proposition, rewrite it so that it is a standard form categorical proposition. This might mean that you will need to replace the given quantifier with 'all', 'no', or 'some'. In some cases you might need to introduce a form of the verb 'to be'. For example, if given "No professor oversleeps," you would write, "No professor is a person who oversleeps." Indicate whether the statements are true or false.

1. All cats are pets.

2. No dogs are cats.

3. Some horses are palominos.

4. Some horses are not thoroughbreds.

5. No mutts are purebred Afghan hounds.

6. Some members of Parliament are not Democrats.

7. All teachers at this school are people born before 2000.

8. Some people who lived during the twentieth century are people who are still alive.

9. No aardvarks that occasionally enjoy a tasty ant are kangaroos.

10. Some books written by people who are now dead are not books written by witty women.

11. All products that are featured in infomercials are products that are useful around the house.

12. Some books that are deemed classics are not books you'll probably read.

13. At least one insomniac is a person who would like to have a full night's sleep.

14. None of the exercises in the book are exercises about aardvarks.

15. Not every play by William Shakespeare is a tragedy.

16. Every person who reads this book is a redhead.

17. There is a light bulb that has lasted more than three years.

18. Not any person will fly faster than the speed of light.

19. Each person who has robbed a bank has been caught.

20. There exists a dog that does not live outdoors.

21. Anyone who writes in the margins of library books can expect a cross word from the librarian if he or she is caught.

22. No one who skips all the tests in this class can expect an A.

23. There is a person who is not President of the United States who sells books in London.

24. Not every witty woman fricassees fowl to form fabulous fare.

25. Everyone who understands everything that is in this chapter is prepared for the next chapter.

Categorical Syllogisms

The View: Categorical syllogisms are deductive arguments that demonstrate the relationships among classes of things. A categorical syllogism has two premises, a conclusion, and exactly three terms.

How do we reason about classes of objects? What are the general characteristics of such arguments?

Categorical syllogisms are deductive arguments concerning relations among classes of things. They consist of two premises and a conclusion, each of which is a categorical proposition. Categorical syllogisms have *exactly* three terms. The **major term** is the predicate term of the conclusion. In a standard form categorical proposition, the predicate term of the conclusion is to the right of 'is' or 'are'. The **minor term** is the subject term of the conclusion. In a standard form categorical proposition, the subject term of the conclusion is to the right of the quantifier and to the left of 'is' or 'are'. The **middle term** is the term that is found in the premises but not in the conclusion. The **major premise** is the premise containing the major term. The **minor premise** is the premise containing the minor term.

So, if you're going to find the three distinct terms of a syllogism, you must start by finding the conclusion. Notice which terms are major, minor, and middle in the following syllogisms.

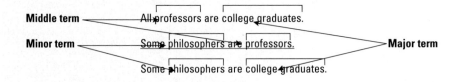

'Professors' is the middle term. 'Philosophers' is the minor term. 'College graduates' is the major term.

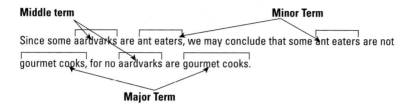

'Aardvarks' is the middle term. 'Ant eaters' is the minor term. 'Gourmet cooks' is the major term.

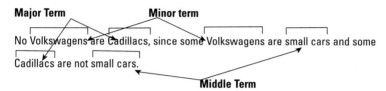

'Cadillacs' is the major term. 'Volkswagens' is the minor term. 'Small cars' is the middle term.

Ordinarily, you might suggest that there are various procedures that can help you find the conclusion. For example, if you find the conclusion, you can ask, What reasons are given for me to accept this statement as true? In the case of categorical syllogisms, it is both easier and harder than this. It is easier, since a categorical syllogism must have exactly three terms. If you find the conclusion, each of the premises must have exactly one of the terms in the conclusion. It is harder, since the forms the overwhelming majority of categorical syllogisms are invalid. The premise and conclusion indicators may be your only clues to what the author of the argument *intended* to be the conclusion. For example, assume you are given the following three categorical propositions: "Some collies are dogs," "Some dogs are gentle beasts," and "Some collies are gentle beasts." Regardless which statement you choose as the conclusion, the other two statements will *not* successfully show that the proposed conclusion is true. However you understand the argument, the argument form will be invalid. So, it becomes important to pay close attention to the indicators if you are to correctly determine the *intended* conclusion.

Exercises

I. For each of the following, draw a (circle) around the major term, draw a box around the minor term, and **underline** the middle term.

> Is it important to know the meanings of all the words in these exercises? For the purposes of *these* exercises, would it make any difference if the major, minor, and middle terms of the syllogisms were in German, Spanish, Russian, or Swahili?

1. All collies are dogs, so no collies are cats, since no cats are dogs.

2. Since some spiders are not poisonous animals, and no spiders are animals featured characters in yogurt commercials, we may conclude that some poisonous animals are not animals featured characters in yogurt commercials.

3. No pampered pets are portly pooches, since some portly pooches are massive mastiffs, and all massive mastiffs are pampered pets.

4. All felonious felines are curious cats, since some felonious felines are not malicious mutts, and no malicious mutts are curious cats.

5. Some wise wombats are wretched rascals, so no wise wombats are portly pooches, since no portly pooches are wretched rascals.

6. Some ridiculous rodents are not ludicrous louts, for some squirrelly squirrels are ludicrous louts, and some ridiculous rodents are squirrelly squirrels.

7. Some fastidious felines are ambitious Angoras, and some ambitious Angoras are cantankerous kitties, so some fastidious felines are cantankerous kitties.

8. Some cautious canines are not rambunctious rabbits, so no finicky felines are cautious canines, since some rambunctious rabbits are not finicky felines.

9. All ferocious fruit flies are preposterously persistent pests. Therefore, no dastardly dangerous dogs are preposterously persistent pests, because some ferocious fruit flies are not dastardly dangerous dogs.

10. Since some perpetually pernicious pythons are not mightily malicious mastodons, and all mightily malicious mastodons are eminently extinct entities, it follows that no eminently extinct entities are perpetually pernicious pythons.

Standard Form Categorical Syllogisms

Just as there is a standard form for categorical propositions, there is a standard form for categorical syllogisms. In a **standard form categorical syllogism**, each statement is a standard form categorical proposition, the major premise is given first, the minor premise is given second, and the conclusion is given last. The pattern looks like this:

Major premise

<u>Minor premise</u>

Conclusion

As they are found in ordinary English, the premises and conclusions can be in any order. You must use premise indicators and conclusion indicators to help sort out which statements are premises and which is the conclusion. So, if you are given the following argument,

All elephants are heavy animals, so some dormice are not elephants, since some dormice are not heavy animals.

you would state it in standard form as follows:

All elephants are heavy animals.

Some dormice are not heavy animals.

Some dormice are not elephants.

If a premise or conclusion is not given in standard form, you restate it as a standard form categorial proposition and then put the syllogism in standard form. So, if you were given

There is an arachnid that is not poisonous, since every spider is an arachnid, and not every spider is a poisonous animal.

you would rewrite it as follows:

Some spiders are not poisonous animals.

All spiders are arachnids.

Some arachnids are not poisonous animals.

Categorical syllogisms are deductive arguments. In deductive arguments, our primary concern is with the **validity** of the argument's form. Recall that the **form** of an argument is the argument pattern, regardless of its content. The following two syllogisms have the same form:

All dogs are mammals.	All horses are fish.
All collies are dogs.	All aardvarks are horses.
All collies arc mammals.	All aardvarks are fish.

Where P represents the major term, S represents the minor term, and M represents the middle term, both arguments are of the form:

All M are P.

All S are M

All S are P.

The argument *form* is valid. If the premises are true, the conclusion is guaranteed to be true (it is logically impossible for all the premises to be true and the conclusion false). But while the premises and the conclusion of the dogs-mammals-collies argument are true, the premises and the conclusion of the horses-fish-aardvarks argument are false. *Validity is one thing; truth is something else.* So, in terms of validity, the first two arguments are equally acceptable. Both arguments are valid. In terms of **soundness**—an argument is sound if, and only if, it is valid and all of its premise are true—the second argument is defective. The second argument is unsound, since at least one of its premises is false.

There are 256 syllogistic forms, of which fifteen are valid. In the next two chapters, we explore ways to determine whether a syllogism is valid.

Can you show that there are exactly 256 syllogistic forms? Start with a syllogism in which all the premises and the conclusion are universal affirmatives. Notice that there are four positions in which you can place the middle term: (1) subject term of the major premise and predicate term of the minor premise; (2) predicate term of both premises; (3) subject term of both premises; and (4) predicate term of the major premise and subject term of the minor premise. Now systematically replace the universal affirmative propositions with the other kinds of categorical propositions. Where A, E, I, and O are the names of the categorical propositions, and where we represent syllogisms in standard form (major premise, minor premise, conclusion), you will have four versions of each of the following: AAA, AAE, AAO, AAO, AEA, AEE, AEI, AEO, AIA, AIE, AIO, AIA, AIE, AII, AIO, AOA, AOE, AOI, AOO, EAA, EEA, EIA, EOA, EAE, EEE, EIE, EOE, and so on.

Exercises

II. Restate each of the following syllogisms in standard form (major premise, minor premise, conclusion). If one of more of the propositions given is *not* a standard form categorical proposition, restate it as a standard form categorical proposition.

1. Some cows are pets, so all Herefords are cows, since some Herefords are pets.

2. No dogs are cats, no cats are spaniels, so some dogs are spaniels.

3. Some aardvarks are not eight-legged animals, since no aardvarks are spiders, and all spiders are eight-legged animals.

4. Some ludicrous landlubbers are not silly shipmates, so all silly shipmates are devotees of dubious dogmas, since some ludicrous landlubbers are devotees of dubious dogmas.

5. Since some studious stenographers are not practitioners of pecuniary peccadilloes, and since all serious scribes are studious stenographers, we must conclude that some serious scribes are practitioners of pecuniary peccadilloes.

6. All acrimonious acrobats are folks fated for a fatal fall, for all acrimonious acrobats are temperamental tumblers, and all folks fated for a fatal fall are temperamental tumblers.

7. All attenuated attendants are folks who have wasted away. So, some hefty humans are folks who have wasted away, since no hefty humans are attenuated attendants.

8. Since some glamorous gorillas are petite primates, and some petite primates are not slithery snakes, we may conclude that no slithery snakes are glamorous gorillas.

9. No gregarious goats are solitary sheep, for some restive rodents are not gregarious goats, and some restive rodents are not solitary sheep.

10. Some sumptuous snacks are not pepperoni pizzas, so some luscious libations are not pepperoni pizzas, for some luscious libations are not sumptuous snacks.

11. There is a lecherous leopard who talks turkey with turtles. So, not every elegant elephant is a lecherous leopard, for some animals that talk turkey with turtles are not elegant elephants.

12. Not any pious pachyderm is a lugubrious lion, for at least one happy hyena is not a lugubrious lion, and there is not a single happy hyena that is a pious pachyderm.

13. Every tumultuous tiger is a cool cat. But not any perplexed primate is a cool cat. So, at least one perplexed primate is not a tumultuous tiger.

14. Not every reticent ruminant is a benevolent bovine, since every joyous Jersey is a benevolent bovine, and any joyous Jersey is a reticent ruminant.

15. There is a boisterous buffalo that elicits emotions from elegant elk. But since no cantankerous carnivore is a boisterous buffalo, we may conclude that every cantankerous carnivore elicits emotions from elegant elk.

16. At least one enormous eucalyptus is a truncated tree, for not every puny pine is an enormous eucalyptus, and there is a puny pine that is a truncated tree.

17. Some burnished brass is not tarnished titanium, and not any amalgamated aluminum is tarnished titanium, so some amalgamated aluminum is not burnished brass.

18. Not every wicked wizard writes tantalizing tales on tree trunks, for some malicious magicians do not write tantalizing tales on tree trunks, and at least one wicked wizard is a malicious magician.

19. There is an awful author who writes exasperating exercises to torment tenacious tutees, since no malicious madmen are awful authors, and at least one malicious madman writes exasperating exercises to torment tenacious tutees.

20. None of the gilded gargoyles on the conquered castle are worthy of trite tributes by traveling troubadours. So, not any gargoyles worthy of trite tributes by traveling troubadours are pretentious pieces of pottery, since every pretentious piece of pottery is a gilded gargoyle on the conquered castle.

CHAPTER 15

Rules for Judging Validity

The View: This chapter introduces six rules for judging the validity of categorical syllogisms according to the Boolean interpretation of categorical logic. Violating any rule is a sufficient condition for deeming the syllogistic form invalid.

How can you judge the validity of a categorical syllogism? What are the sufficient conditions for deeming a syllogistic form invalid?

The traditional way to determine whether an argument is valid is by a set of rules. To understand how the rules work, we need to introduce the notion of **distribution**. A term in a categorical syllogism is distributed if it refers to *all* members of a class. If you think about, you'll conclude that the subject term of a universal affirmative proposition refers to all the members of the subject class, that both terms of a universal negative proposition refer to all the members of both classes, and that the predicate term of a particular negative proposition refers to all the members of a class. Where S and P represent to the subject term and the predicate term in any categorical syllogism, D means distributed, and U means undistributed, we may summarize the distribution of terms in a categorical syllogism as follows:

$$\text{All } S^{D} \text{ are } P^{U}.$$

$$\text{No } S^{D} \text{ are } P^{D}.$$

$$\text{Some } S^{U} \text{ are } P^{U}.$$

$$\text{Some } S^{U} \text{ are not } P^{D}.$$

Now for the rules.

1. All valid standard-form categorical syllogisms have *exactly* three terms that are used with the same meaning throughout the syllogism.

2. The middle term of a valid standard-form categorical syllogism must be distributed *exactly once*.

3. The major term of a valid standard-form categorical syllogism is either distributed twice (in both the premise and the conclusion) or not at all.

4. The minor term of a valid standard-form categorical syllogism is either distributed twice (in both the premise and the conclusion) or not at all.

5. There must be as many negative premises as negative conclusions.

6. There must be as many particular premises as particular conclusions.

The rules need a few comments.

The first rule is unique. It says, "Make sure you have a categorical syllogism!" If you don't have exactly three terms, you don't have a categorical syllogism and none of the other rules applies. For example, in the following argument, two meanings are ascribed to the expression "people to my right":

> As we shall see in Chapter 19, there are cases in which a valid categorical syllogism has more than three terms, but it is possible to "reduce" the number of terms to three.

All people to my right are arch-conservatives.

All the students on the northern half of this room are people to my right.

All the students on the northern half of this room are arch-conservatives.

In the major premise, the term 'people to my right' concerns political views. In the minor premise, the term 'people to my right' concerns spatial relations. Except when said from the appropriate point in the House of Commons, there is no reason to correlate political ideology with spatial relations. So, the term 'people to my right' is assigned two meanings. The argument involves an **equivocation** on the term 'people to my right', so we don't have a categorical syllogism.

If an argument contains exactly three terms, all you need do is go through the list and see if any other rules are violated. If *any* rule is violated, the argument is invalid. And it is possible for a syllogism to violate more than one of the last five rules. For example, the following syllogism violates each of rules 2 through 6:

But When Is It an Equivocation?

Consider the argument

All conductors are ticket-takers.

No pieces of wood are conductors.

No pieces of wood are ticket-takers.

Does the argument assign two meanings to 'conductor,' one having to do with railroad workers and the other conductors of electricity? It might seem so, *but* both premises are true if we understand 'conductor' to mean railroad worker. Accepting the conclusion does *not* require a shift in meaning. Breaking rule 1 is very serious, arguably more serious than breaking any of the others. So, *unless* accepting the conclusion *requires* that you assign two meanings to one of the terms, you should *not* conclude a proposed syllogism violates rule 1.

No students in this class are college graduates.

No students in this class are railroad engineers.

Some railroad engineers are college graduates.

Notice that the middle term, 'students in this class,' is distributed twice (rule 2). The major term, 'college graduates,' is distributed in the premise but not in the conclusion (rule 3). The minor term, 'railroad engineers,' is distributed in the premise but not in the conclusion (rule 4). There are two negative premises but no negative conclusion (rule 5), and there are no particular premises, but there is a particular conclusion (rule 6). Although this argument breaks five of the six rules, it is neither more nor less invalid than the "people to my right" argument. Validity is like a light switch. Just as the switch is either on (it completes the circuit) or off (it doesn't complete the circuit), a deductive argument is either valid or invalid. Breaking one rule is a sufficient condition for deeming an argument invalid.

Examples

Since initially we are concerned only with the forms of arguments, we will abbreviate the terms as follows: **P** is the major term (the predicate term of the conclusion), **S** is the minor term (the subject term of the conclusion), and **M** is the middle term (the term that is in both premises but not in the conclusion). **P, S**, and **M** are **variables**. You obtain an actual syllogism by replacing the variables with terms. When we are working with variables, it is impossible to violate rule 1.

Consider the following argument form:

All *M* are P.

All *S* are *M*.

All *S* are *P*.

Go down the list of rules and see if any are broken. Since we are dealing with variables, it is impossible to violate rule 1. The middle term (**M**) is distributed in the major premise, but not in the minor premise, so the form follows rule 2. The major term (**P**) is distributed in neither the major premise nor in the conclusion, so the form follows rule 3. The minor term (**S**) is distributed in both the minor premise and the conclusion, so the form follows rule 4. There are no negative premises and no negative conclusions, so the form follows rule 5. There are no particular premises and no particular conclusions, so the form follows rule 6. No rules are broken, so the argument form is valid.

Consider the following argument form:

Some *M* are *P*.

All *M* are *S*.

Some *S* are *P*.

Since we are dealing with variables, it is impossible to violate rule 1. The middle term (**M**) is distributed in the minor premise, but not in the major premise, so the form follows rule 2. The major term (**P**) is distributed in neither the major premise nor the conclusion, so the form follows rule 3. The minor term (**S**) is distributed in neither the minor premise nor the conclusion, so the form follows rule 4. There are no negative premises and no negative conclusions, so the form follows rule 5. There is one particular premise and one particular conclusion, so the form follows rule 6. No rules are broken, so the argument is valid.

Consider the following argument form:

> Some *P* are not *M*.
>
> All *M* are S.
> _____
>
> Some *S* are not *P*.

This argument is invalid. While rule 1 is not violated, the middle term is distributed in both premises, so the form violates rule 2. Further, the major term is distributed in the conclusion, but it is not distributed in the major premise, so rule 3 is violated. The minor term is undistributed in both premises, so rule 4 is *not* violated. The number of negative premises and conclusions is the same (none), so the form follows rule 5. The number of particular premises and conclusions is the same (one), so rule 6 is not violated. But since at least one rule (in this case, rules 2 and 3) is violated, the argument form is invalid.

Consider the following argument:

> All *M* are *P*.
>
> Some *M* are not *S*.
> _____
>
> Some *S* are *P*.

This argument is invalid. Since we are dealing with variables, rule 1 is not violated. The middle term is distributed exactly once, so rule 2 is unviolated. The major term is undistributed in both the premise and the conclusion, so rule 3 is unviolated. The minor term is distributed in the minor premise but not in the conclusion, so the form violates rule 4. There is a negative premise but no negative conclusion, so rule 5 is violated. The number of particular premises and conclusions is the same, so the form does not violate rule 6. Nonetheless, since at least one rule is broken (rules 4 and 5), the argument form is invalid.

Exercises

I. Are the following argument forms valid? Remember, since you are given only the *form* of the argument, you cannot violate rule 1. If the argument form is invalid, name all the rules that are violated.

1. All *M* are *P*.
All M are S.
_____
All *S* are *P*.

2. Some *M* are *P*.
Some S are not M.
_____
Some *S* are not *P*.

3. No *P* are *M*.
Some S are M.
_____
Some *S* are not *P*.

4. Some *P* are not *M*.
All S are M.
_____
Some *S* are not *P*.

5. Some *M* are not *P*.
All S are M.
_____
Some *S* are not *P*.

6. Some *M* are not *P*.
All M are S.
_____
Some *S* are not *P*.

7. Some *M* are *P*.

No S are M.

Some *S* are not *P*.

8. All *M* are *P*.

No M are S.

No *S* are *P*.

9. All *P* are *M*.

No S are M.

No *S* are *P*.

10. Some *M* are not *P*.

No S are M.

Some *S* are not *P*.

11. Some *P* are not *M*.

Some S are M.

Some *S* are not *P*.

12. All *P* are *M*.

No M are S.

No *S* are *P*.

13. All *M* are *P*.

No S are M.

Some *S* are not *P*.

14. No *M* are *P*.

Some M are not S.

All *S* are *P*.

15. No *P* are *M*.

Some M are S.

Some *S* are *P*.

16. Some *P* are *M*.

All M are S.

Some *S* are *P*.

17. Some *M* are *P*.

All S are M.

Some *S* are *P*.

18. All *M* are *P*.

Some M are not S.

Some *S* are not *P*.

19. All *P* are *M*.

Some M are not S.

Some *S* are not *P*.

20. All *P* are *M*.

Some S are not M.

Some *S* are not *P*.

21. All *M* are *P*.

Some S are M.

Some *S* are not *P*.

22. All *M* are *P*.

Some M are S.

Some *S* are not *P*.

23. No *M* are *P*.

No M are S.

No *S* are *P*.

24. No *M* are *P*.

No M are S.

Some *S* are not *P*.

25. No *M* are *P*.

Some M are S.

Some *S* are not *P*.

26. All *M* are *P*.

All S are M.

Some *S* are *P*.

27. All *M* are *P*.

All S are M.

Some *S* are not *P*.

28. All *P* are *M*.

No M are S.

Some *S* are not *P*.

29. All *M* are *P*.

Some M are S.

No *S* are *P*.

30. No *M* are *P*.

All S are M.

Some *S* are *P*.

II. Evaluate each of the following syllogisms on the basis of the rules. If the argument is invalid, name all the rules that are violated. *Remember,* however, if the syllogism violates rule 1, it can violate no others. If the syllogism violates rule 1, explain the equivocation.

1. All felines who spend the winter outside are real cool cats.

All jazz musicians are real cool cats.

All jazz musicians are felines who spend the winter outside.

2. All collies are dogs.

No schnauzers are collies.

No schnauzers are dogs.

3. All dogs are collies.
    Some friendly beasts are collies.

    Some friendly beasts are not dogs.

4. No cats are dogs.
    Some dogs are friendly beasts.

    Some friendly beasts are not cats.

5. Some aardvarks are anteaters.
    Some anteaters are gourmets.

    Some gourmets are aardvarks.

6. All novas are astronomical phenomena.
    Some Chevrolets are Novas.

    Some Chevrolets are astronomical phenomena.

7. Some dogs are not schnauzers.
    Some dogs are collies.

    Some collies are not schnauzers.

8. No aardvarks are collies.
    No collies are schnauzers.

    No schnauzers are aardvarks.

9. Some dogs are collies.
    No dogs are turtles.

    Some turtles are not collies.

10. Some dogs are not collies.
    No collies are aardvarks.

    Some aardvarks are not dogs.

III. The following arguments are not in standard form. *Pay attention to premise and conclusion indicators.* Restate each argument in standard form (major premise, minor premise, conclusion). Evaluate each argument according to the rules. If the argument violates rule 1, explain the equivocation.

1. Since no collies are felines, we may conclude that some longhairs are not collies, since all longhairs are felines.

2. All collies are vicious beasts, since some dogs are collies, and no dogs are vicious beasts.

3. Since no dogs are cats and no cats are aardvarks, we may conclude that all aardvarks are dogs.

4. Since no aardvarks are cats, it follows that all longhairs are cats, since no longhairs are aardvarks.

5. All cats are mammals, so no mammals are reptiles, since all cats are reptiles.

6. Since all collies are dogs, and all sheep-herding animals are dogs, it follows that all collies are sheep-herding animals.

7. All participants at the conference are members of the Society, and all members of the Society are scholars of the first rank. Therefore, some scholars of the first rank are participants at the conference.

8. No breeders of aardvarks are members of the Society. Thus, no breeders of aardvarks are professional polo players, since no professional polo players are members of the Society.

9. Since no professional polo players are members of the Society, and since no breeders of aardvarks are members of the Society, we may conclude that some breeders of aardvarks are professional polo players.

10. Some people who do these problems are not master magicians, because some aardvark fans are not people who do these problems, and no master magicians are aardvark fans.

11. No aardvark fans are master magicians, so some people who do these problems are not aardvark fans, for some people who do these problems are not master magicians.

12. Some aardvark fans are not accomplished linguists, for some aardvark fans are people who are obsessed with double vowels, and no people who are obsessed with double vowels are accomplished linguists.

13. All editors and publishers are bookmakers, and all people who are in the business of taking bets are bookmakers. Hence, some people who are in the business of taking bets are editors and publishers.

14. Since all editors are people of integrity, it follows that some liars are not people of integrity, since no editors are liars.

15. Some editors are gamblers, since some people who take chances are editors and all people who take chances are gamblers.

16. Some authors are editors, since no editors are lunatics and some authors are not lunatics.

17. Some people who act strangely on bright moonlit nights are not lunatics. So some authors are lunatics, since all authors are people who act strangely on bright moonlit nights.

18. Some people who spend warm sunny days in cold dark rooms are not authors. Some people who spend warm sunny days in cold dark rooms are not people of at least average intelligence. Therefore, some authors are not people of at least average intelligence.

19. Some gardeners are not authors. Therefore, no authors are pianists, given that some pianists are gardeners.

20. All conductors are ticket-takers on trains. Some pieces of copper wire are conductors. So, some pieces of copper wire are ticket-takers on trains.

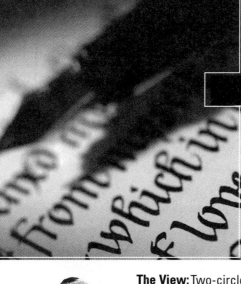

Venn
Diagrams

The View: Two-circle Venn diagrams represent categorical propositions. Three-circle Venn diagrams represent categorical syllogisms.
When constructing a Venn diagram for a universal proposition, you
shade the areas that are empty. When constructing a Venn diagram
for a particular proposition, you place an *X* in the area where the
proposition indicates that something is found. When constructing a
Venn diagram for a categorical syllogism containing a particular proposition, you should (a)
always diagram any universal proposition first, and (b) place the *X* for the particular proposition on the line representing the term not mentioned in the premise *unless* an area on
either side of that line is shaded. If an area on either side of the line of the circle representing the term not mentioned in the premise is shaded, place the *X* in the area that is *not*
shaded.

Is there a way to evaluate syllogisms that does not require rules?

About a century ago, the British logician and mathematician John Venn developed a method for evaluating the validity of categorical syllogisms based on spatial
relations among circles. He was not the first to develop a system of diagrams for evaluating syllogisms, but his has become virtually the standard method. In this chapter
we examine Venn diagrams and show how they can be used to demonstrate the validity or invalidity of any standard form categorical syllogism.

Venn diagrams represent sets by circles. In the case of a universal proposition,
you shade the portion of the diagram that represents an empty set. A proposition of
the form "All *S* are *P*" indicates that all the members of the class of things that are *S*
are contained in the class of things that are *P*. If you prefer, it shows that the class of
things that are *S* but not *P* is empty.[1] Similarly, in the case of a universal negative you
shade the area in which *S* and *P* overlap. A universal negative asserts that the class of
things that are both *S* and *P* is empty. The diagrams look like this:

---

[1] As we see in Chapter 18, "All *S* are *P*" is logically equivalent to the statement "No *S* is *non-P*,"
where the set of things that are *non-P* contains *everything* that is not *P*.

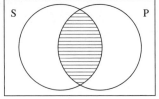

All *S* are *P*.

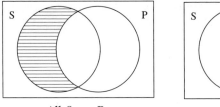

No *S* are *P*.

The diagrams for "All *P* is *S*" and "No *P* is *S*" are as follows:

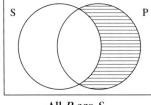

All *P* are *S*.

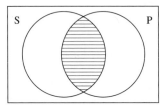

No *P* are *S*.

In the case of particular propositions, you claim either that there is at least one thing *S* that is *P* ("Some *S* is *P*") or there is at least one thing *S* that is not *P* ("Some *S* is not *P*"). Look at a Venn diagram as a treasure map. In all good pirate stories, an *X* marks the spot in which the treasure is buried. So let an *X* mark the spot in which the "something" is "buried" on a Venn diagram. The diagrams look like this:

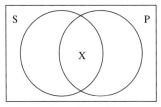

Some *S* are *P*.

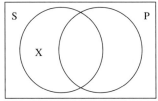

Some *S* are not *P*.

The diagrams for "Some *P* is *S*" and "Some *P* is not *S*" look like this:

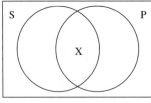

Some *P* are *S*.

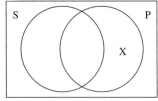

Some *P* are not *S*.

When diagramming a syllogism, you diagram the premises to see if, in so doing, you have also diagrammed the conclusion. If you have diagrammed the conclusion in the course of diagramming the premises, the argument is valid. If you do not diagram the conclusion, the argument is invalid. This requires three interlocking circles.

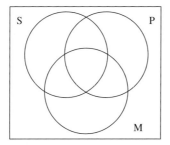

Two Interpretations of Categorical Syllogisms

Venn diagrams assume what is known as the Boolean interpretation of categorical logic. The **Boolean interpretation** assumes that *neither* a universal affirmative *nor* a universal negative entails the truth of a corresponding particular proposition. Thus, on the Boolean interpretation, both the statements "All unicorns are one-horned horses" and "No unicorns are one-horned horses" are true; since there are no unicorns, the corresponding particulars are both false. There is an older interpretation, the traditional or **Aristotelian interpretation**, according to which the truth of a universal proposition *does* entail the truth of its corresponding particular. According to the Aristotelian interpretation, the truth of the statement "All collies are dogs" entails the truth of the statement "Some collies are dogs." Those who favor the Aristotelian interpretation tend to prefer Euler diagrams, the traditional versions of which assume that interpretation of categorical logic. Traditional Euler diagrams are complicated, which is a reason many favor Venn diagrams.

But surely, you are thinking, one of these two interpretations must be correct, and we should follow whichever interpretation is correct. Hence, if we are going to do diagrams, we should do either Venns or traditional Eulers, depending on which interpretation is correct. But it is not that easy. You cannot appeal to ordinary English usage, since ordinary English points in both directions. Assume the statement "All musicians are real cool cats" is true. Doesn't that show that the statement "Some musicians are real cool cats" is also true? Certainly the particular statement is true, and as we *sometimes* talk, we would be perfectly willing to allow that its truth follows from the truth of the universal. This points in favor of the Aristotelian interpretation. But we also grant that Newton's first law is true: "All objects in uniform rectilinear motion or at rest will remain in uniform rectilinear motion or at rest unless they are acted upon by an outside force," which may be restated, "For all objects *o*, if *o* is not acted upon by an outside force, then *o* will remain in uniform rectilinear motion if it is in motion or at rest if it is at rest." The problem is that *there is no object that is* not *acted upon by some outside force*. So, if we accept Newton's first law of motion, this tends to indicate that the Boolean interpretation is assumed. But if ordinary English usage cannot be our guide, what can be?

There is a *pragmatic* consideration that points toward the Boolean interpretation. The Boolean interpretation allows us to handle everything we need to handle, and the Venn diagram technique provides us with a very straightforward means of evaluating arguments on this interpretation. (The rules that were introduced earlier also *assume* the Boolean interpretation.) In those cases when we know, based on some source distinct from the premises of the argument, that the subject-class introduced by a universal proposition has members, we can treat the universal statement as *both* a universal and a particular and construct diagrams for both readings of the premise. The argument containing such a universal will be deemed valid if the conclusion follows from *either* the universal premise *or* the corresponding particular. Generally, the difference between the two interpretations makes no difference. We return to this issue when we look at ways of dealing with syllogisms in ordinary English.

The three circles within the universe defined by the square divides itself into eight regions. A bar over a letter $(\bar{S}, \bar{P}, \bar{M})$ represents not-S, not-P, or not-M. The Venn diagram is divided into eight distinct regions:

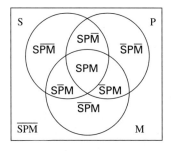

To see how these interlocking circles allow us to examine the validity of a syllogism, let us consider some examples.

Consider the argument

All mammals are vertebrates.	All M are P
All cats are mammals.	All S are M.
All cats are vertebrates.	All S are P.

We diagram the major premise first:

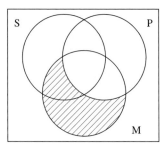

Now we diagram the minor premise:

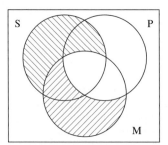

Notice that the only area of the class representing *cats* (*S*) that can have members is contained in the area of the circle representing *vertebrates* (*P*). This is what is claimed by the statement "All cats are vertebrates"—compare what is diagrammed in the top two circles with the diagram for "All *S* is *P*." The argument is valid.

Consider the argument

No dogs are aardvarks.	No *M* are *P*.
All collies are dogs.	All *S* are *M*.
No collies are aardvarks.	No *S* are *P*.

Diagram the major premise:

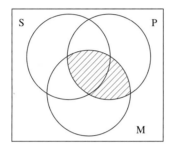

Now diagram of the minor premise:

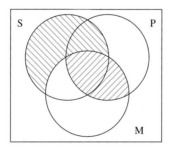

Compare the top two circles in the resulting diagram to that for "No *S* is *P*." The argument is valid.

Now consider the argument

No cows are aardvarks.	No *M* are *P*
No ravens are cows.	No *S* are *M*.
No ravens are aardvarks.	No *S* are *P*.

Here we diagram both premises and discover that the conclusion is *not* diagrammed

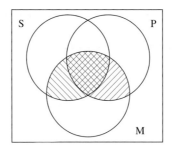

The argument is invalid.

The same procedure is followed when diagramming arguments with particular premises. However, if there is both a universal premise and a particular premise, you should diagram the universal premise first.[2] Consider the syllogism

All cats are mammals.	All *M* are *P*.
Some cats are Siamese.	Some *M* are *S*.
Some Siamese are mammals.	Some *S* are *P*.

Diagram the universal premise first:

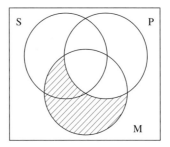

Now determine where the *X* should go in diagramming the minor premise. It has to be in the part of the diagram where *S* and *M* overlap.[3] So, the diagram looks like this:

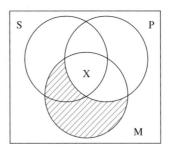

---

[2]As we see below, many times in diagramming a particular premise you will place an *X* "on the line." By diagramming the universal first, you sometimes avoid the need to move an *X* from a line in diagramming a syllogism.

[3]In classes in formal logic, the statement "Some *S* are *M*" is represented by the following set of symbols: $(\exists x)(Sx \ \& \ Mx)$, which is sometimes read, "There is an *x* such that *x* is *S* and *x* is *P*."

Look at the two-circle diagram for "Some *S* is *P*." We have diagrammed the conclusion. The argument is valid.

It does not always (it does not usually) work so neatly. Consider this syllogism:

All mammals are vertebrates.   All *P* are *M*.
<u>Some animals are vertebrates.</u>   <u>Some *S* are *M*.</u>
Some animals are mammals.   Some *S* are *P*.

Diagram the universal premise:

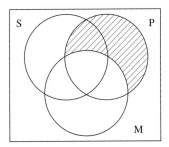

Now diagram the particular. Where does the *X* go? It has to go where *S* and *M* overlap, but there are two such areas. One area is in *P*. The other area is not. So you put the *X* on the *P* circle in the area where *S* and *M* overlap.

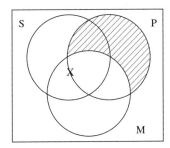

Whenever you place an *X* on the line of a circle, the syllogism is invalid.

Consider one more. As we noticed when looking at the rules, whenever there are two particular premises, the syllogism is invalid (rule 6). You will reach the same conclusion with Venn diagrams. If there are two particular premises, the *X* for each premise will be "on the line." Consider the following:

While you might consider that a very stilted reading of "Some *S* is *M*," we might reformulate it in such a way that it tells us where to put the *x* in the diagram: "There is an *x* such that *x* is <u>in</u> *S* and *x* is <u>in</u> *M*." Similarly, we might read "Some *S* is not *M*" as "There is an *x* such that *x* is <u>in</u> *S* and *x* is not <u>in</u> *M*." And, of course, you could come up with similar readings in terms of *S* and *P*, and *P* and *M*.

Some cows are Jerseys.	Some M are P.
Some cows are Holsteins.	Some *M* are *S*.
Some Holsteins are Jerseys.	Some S are M.

The Venn diagram looks like this:

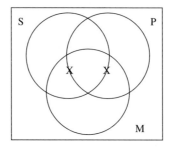

The argument is invalid.

Some students are perplexed when called to place an *X* on a line. "Which line?" they ask. *It is always placed on the line of the circle* not *mentioned in the premise.* So, if you are given a premise of the form, "Some *S* are *M*," you diagram it for only those two terms. On a three-circle diagram, the circle for *P* divides the area where the *S* circle and the *M* circle overlap into two parts. In the area where *S* and *M* overlap, if neither the area inside *P* nor the area outside *P* is shaded, you place the *X* on the *P* circle.

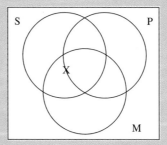

Similarly, if the premise is "Some M is not *P*," the *X* goes in *M* outside of *P*. In the area where *M* is outside of *P*, if neither the area inside *S* nor the area outside *S* is shaded, you place the *X* on the *S* circle.

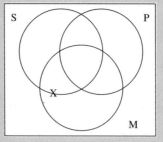

Exercises

I. For each of the following, draw a three-circle Venn diagram (for *S*, *P*, and *M*), and diagram the premise given.

1. All *S* are *M*.
2. All *P* are *M*.
3. All *M* are *S*.
4. All *M* are *P*.
5. No *S* are *M*.
6. No *P* are *M*.
7. No *M* are *S*.
8. No *M* are *P*.
9. Some *S* are *M*.
10. Some *P* are *M*.
11. Some *M* are *S*.
12. Some *M* are *P*.
13. Some *S* are not M.
14. Some *P* are not *S*.
15. Some *M* are not *S*.
16. Some *M* are not *P*.

II. Construct a Venn diagram for each of the exercises in Chapter 15, Exercise set I.
III. Construct a Venn diagram for each of the exercises in Chapter 15, Exercise set II. In some cases there are more than three terms. If there are more than three terms, *it is impossible to construct a Venn diagram,* so explain the alternative meanings of one of the terms.
IV. Construct a Venn diagram for each of the exercises in Chapter 15, Exercise set III. Restate each syllogism in standard form. In some cases there are more than three terms. If there are more than three terms, *it is impossible to construct a Venn diagram,* so explain the alternative meanings of one of the terms.

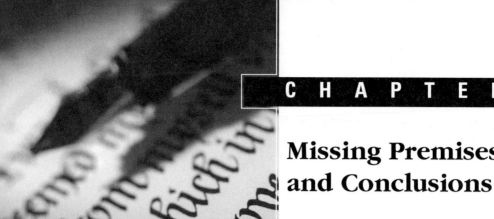

CHAPTER 17

Missing Premises and Conclusions

The View: People often leave a premise or the conclusion of a syllogism unstated. If the conclusion is unstated, simply use the rules or construct a Venn diagram to determine the conclusion. If a premise is missing, you can use the rules or Venn diagrams to determine what premise, if any, will yield a valid syllogism. If there is a premise that will yield a valid syllogism, you must ask whether the premise is true.

What do you do if part of a syllogism is missing?

So far, the syllogisms we have examined have been quite pure. We have been concerned with *standard-form* categorical propositions and *standard-form* categorical syllogisms. There is nothing wrong with these. Indeed, if you construct standard-form categorical syllogisms in the papers you write, your reader will be able to understand precisely what your intended argument is. But the glory and the misery of English is that there are many ways to say the same thing. Further, there are many times when either a premise or the conclusion of a syllogism is unstated. This is known as an **enthymeme** or an **enthymematic argument**. There are various reasons why people leave parts of syllogisms unstated. Sometimes, if the conclusion is unstated, the argument has more *rhetorical* force. Sometimes, if a premise is unstated, the person reading or hearing the argument will not notice that either the premise is false or the argument form is invalid.

In this and the following two chapters we look at various ways of surviving in ordinary English. In this chapter we examine two ways to find a missing premise or a missing conclusion. One of these is based on the rules. The other is based on Venn diagrams. Regarding missing premises, we ask two distinct questions. (1) What premise, if any, will yield a valid syllogism? (2) If there is a premise that yields a valid syllogism, is that premise true?

168

Rules

If you are given the premises but not the conclusion of a syllogism, the rules allow you to read off the conclusion. Assume you are given these premises:

> All dogs are mammals.
>
> <u>All schnauzers are dogs.</u>
>
> So, _____.

Look at the rules. Rule 2 says that the middle term must be distributed exactly once, which it is. So, there is some reason to believe that a conclusion follows from the premises. Rule 6 says that there must be the same number of particular premises as conclusions. Both premises are universal, so the conclusion has to be universal as well. The quantifier must be either "All" or "No." Rule 5 says that there must be the same number of negative premises as conclusions. Both premises are affirmative, so the conclusion has to be affirmative as well. Given rules 5 and 6, the missing premises must be either "All mammals are schnauzers" or "All schnauzers are mammals." Which is it? To answer that question, look at rules 3 and 4. The major term, 'mammals', is undistributed in the premise, so it must be undistributed in the conclusion. So, the conclusion *should* be "All schnauzers are mammals." Checking rule 4 confirms that the conclusion is "All schnauzers are mammals," since 'schnauzers' is then distributed in the minor premise and the conclusion. So, given the premises and the conclusion "All schnauzers are mammals," the argument is valid. Validity is good, but soundness is better. Is the conclusion true? Sure. Whenever you determine that a conclusion follows from a pair of premises—or a certain premise, if assumed, will yield a valid syllogism—you always should ask whether each statement in the argument is true. Validity and truth are separate issues and should be treated as such.

Now consider this argument:

> No cats are dogs.
>
> <u>Some rats are not cats.</u>
>
> So, _____.

Nothing follows: The argument violates rule 5. If a pair of premises violates a rule, it indicates that the argument is invalid and *nothing* follows from the premises.

The procedure is the same if you are looking for a missing premise given the other premise and conclusion. Consider the following:

> All longhairs are cats.
>
> So, some dogs are not longhairs.

When looking at a premise and a conclusion, begin by making sure no rules are violated. Are the terms given the same meaning throughout the argument? If not, the syllogism violates rule 1 and is invalid.[1] If you have a universal conclusion and a particular premise, rule 6 is violated. If you have an affirmative conclusion and a negative premise, rule 5 is violated. Make sure that the major or minor term in the premise has the same distribution as the term has in the conclusion. *If there are any of these problems, indicate that no premise will yield a valid argument and cite the rule.* If there are none of these problems—there are none of these in the case we are considering—then it is possible to find a premise that will yield a valid argument. Start with rule 6. The conclusion is particular. The given premise is universal, so the missing premise must be particular. Then go to rule 5. The conclusion is negative. The given premise is affirmative, so the missing premise must be negative. Now you have to worry about the distribution rules. We are concerned with the terms 'dogs' and 'cats'. The missing premise is either "Some cats are not dogs" or "Some dogs are not cats." Looking at rule 4 and noticing that 'dogs' is not distributed in the conclusion, you will see that the missing premise must be "Some dogs are not cats." Looking at rule 2, we notice that the conclusion must be "Some dogs are not cats," for that yields a middle term that is distributed exactly once. So, the conclusion must be "Some dogs are not cats." Is that statement true? *Of course!* Remember, all the statement claims is that there is at least one dog that is not a cat—which is true.

Now consider this premise and conclusion:

> All cows are bovines.
>
> So, some bovines are Jerseys.

We are using the terms consistently throughout the syllogism (rule 1). We do not have a universal conclusion from a particular premise (rule 6). We do not have an affirmative conclusion from a negative premise (rule 5). And the minor term, 'bovines', is undistributed in both the premise and the conclusion (rule 4). So, it is possible to find a statement that will yield a valid syllogism. The conclusion is particular. The premise is universal, so the missing premise must be particular (rule 6). The conclusion is affirmative, so the missing premise must be affirmative (rule 5). So the missing premise must be either "Some Jerseys are cows" or "Some cows are Jerseys." In either case, the distribution of the major term, 'Jerseys', will be the same: undistributed (rule 3). In either case, the middle term, 'cows', will be distributed exactly once, since it is distributed in the given premise (rule 2). So, the major premise is either—take your pick—"Some Jerseys are cows" or "Some cows are Jerseys." Is the premise true? Sure.

Now consider this premise and conclusion:

> All cats are vertebrates.
>
> So, all cats are mammals.

The terms are used consistently throughout (rule 1). Both the conclusion and the given premise are universal (rule 6), and neither is negative (rule 5). So, the premise will need

---

[1]Whether or not terms are given the same meaning is not always obvious when first considering an enthymematic argument. In many cases you must double-check when you are done.

to be a universal affirmative: either "All mammals are vertebrates" or "All vertebrates are mammals." The major term, 'mammals', must be undistributed in the premise, since it is undistributed in the conclusion (rule 3). The middle term must be distributed in the missing premise, since it is undistributed in the given premise (rule 2). So, the missing premise must be "All vertebrates are mammals." Is the premise true? No. Vertebrates are animals with backbones. Mammals are vertebrates that have additional characteristics, such as that they are warm blooded. So, while we can find a statement that yields a valid argument, the premise is false. If it were replaced with the true premise, "All mammals are vertebrates," the premise would be true, but the syllogism would then violate rules 2 and 3. In either case, the argument is unsound.

Now try this one:

> All cats are domestic animals.
>
> So, some lions are domestic animals.

Do we violate rule 1? Yes, but to see that, you will need to work out the missing premise. There are no initial problems with rules 3, 5, or 6. Since the conclusion is particular and affirmative, the missing premise must be either "Some lions are cats" or "Some cats are lions." Since the middle term, 'cats', is distributed in the given premise but in neither of the proposed premises, either premise will work equally well. But there is a problem: The argument is unsound. While either of the proposed premises is true, so long as 'cat' is used to represent a broad category that includes cats of all sizes and types, the given premise cannot be true if the term 'cat' is so understood. So, there is reason to believe that the word 'cat' is assigned two distinct meanings, and the argument violates rule 1. The alternative is to suggest that the given premise is false, since lions, tigers, and cougars are not domestic animals. In either case the argument is unsound: It cannot be valid and have all true premises.

Let us try one more. You are given

> All collies are dogs.
>
> So, no cats are dogs.

Source: Seth Casana, Academia Nuts. *Used with permission of the author.*

It is impossible to find a premise that will yield a valid syllogism. Notice that rule 3 is already broken. The major term, 'dogs', is undistributed in the premise, but it is distributed in the conclusion, so the syllogism is invalid. All you need do is point out that the argument is invalid due to the violation of rule 3: You *should not* introduce a missing premise.

Venn Diagrams

You also can look for missing premises or conclusions by means of Venn diagrams. If you are given both premises, simply construct a Venn diagram and read off the conclusion. For example, assume you are given the argument

> Some students who are visually oriented are good critical thinkers.
>
> All students who are visually oriented are fans of Venn diagrams.
>
> So, _____.

Just construct the Venn diagram and see what the conclusion is:

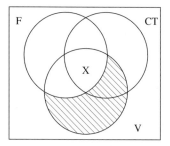

The X is in the section where the circles representing students who are visually oriented, good critical thinkers, and fans of Venn diagrams overlap. So, the conclusion is either—take your pick—"Some fans of Venn diagrams are good critical thinkers" or "Some good critical thinkers are fans of Venn diagrams."

To find a missing premise, we introduce some procedural rules and some rules of interpretation.

Procedural Rules

1. Diagram the premise and the conclusion.

2. If either the premise or the conclusion is a particular proposition, place an X in *every* (unshaded) portion of the diagram warranted by the statement: *Never place an X on the line.*

3. Interpret the diagram.

4. If you were able to interpret the diagram in such a way that the syllogism appears to be valid, check your interpretation by constructing a Venn diagram for the given premise and the proposed premise.

Rules of Interpretation

1. If you have a universal premise and a universal conclusion, then if you have shaded one area of the diagram twice, determine which premise containing the middle and the major or minor term, as is relevant, has been partially diagrammed.[2]

2. If both the premise and the conclusion are particulars, appeal to the diagrams for universal propositions involving the terms in the missing premise to see which of them, if diagrammed, would reduce the number of sections in which *X*s are found to *two*.

3. If the conclusion is a particular and the premise is a universal, consult the diagrams for the particular propositions involving the terms in the missing premise to see which of them, if diagrammed, would introduce *one* of the two *X*s diagrammed in diagramming the conclusion.

4. *No* premise will yield a valid conclusion if (1) the conclusion is a universal statement and you shade either more or fewer than three interior regions of the diagram, or (2) the conclusion is a particular proposition, and you either place an *X* in only one region of the diagram or you place *X*s in four regions of the diagram.

To see how this works, let's consider some examples.

You are given the following premise and conclusion:

> All mammals are vertebrates.
>
> So, all cats are vertebrates.

Diagram the premise and the conclusion:

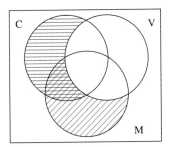

Notice that in diagramming the premise and the conclusion, you have shaded the area representing things that are cats and mammals, but not vertebrates, twice. The missing premise contains the terms cats and mammals. *Any area that has been shaded twice* in the course of shading the premise and conclusion will *not* be

---

[2]If you're a "very visual person," you might want to consult the three-circle diagrams for universal and particular propositions that you constructed in Chapter 16, Exercise I.

shaded when introducing the relevant premise. Notice that the area representing things that are cats but are neither vertebrates nor mammals has been shaded. This is *part* of what you should shade if the missing premise were "All cats are mammals," so "All cats are mammals" must be the missing premise. The premise is true, and by diagramming the premises you would find that you have diagrammed the conclusion.

Consider the following argument:

> No cats are rats.
>
> So, no dogs are cats.

Diagram the premise and the conclusion:

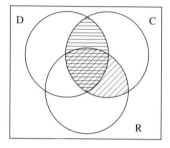

The portion of the diagram representing things that are dogs, cats, and rats has been shaded twice, so it *cannot* be shaded by the missing premise. The area representing dogs and cats, but not rats, has been shaded. That is part of the diagram for the statement, "All dogs are rats," and if you construct a Venn diagram for the propositions "No cats are rats" and "All dogs are rats," you will have diagrammed the conclusion. The statement "All dogs are rats," however, is false, so the syllogism is valid but unsound.

Consider the following argument:

> All longhairs are cats.
>
> So, some dogs are not longhairs.

Again, diagram the premise and the conclusion:

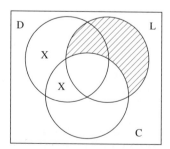

Notice that you have introduced two *X*s into the diagram. *One* of those *X*s would be introduced by the missing premise. The missing premise must contain the terms 'dogs' and 'cats'. The premise is either "Some dogs are cats" or "Some dogs are not cats." It cannot be "Some dogs are cats," since that would introduce an additional *X*—or an *X* on the line. So, it must be "Some dogs are not cats," which will account for the *X* in the area that represents dogs that are neither cats nor longhairs. Construct a Venn diagram for the premises, and you will see that the conclusion is diagrammed—the "extra" *X* that was involved in diagramming the premise and the conclusion disappears. The premise "Some (at least one) dogs are not cats" is true. The argument is sound.

Now consider this premise and conclusion:

> All cows are bovines.
>
> So, some bovines are Jerseys.

Again, diagram the premise and the conclusion:

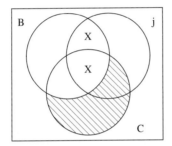

We are concerned with Jerseys and cows. The missing premise must be particular to account for one of the *X*s. It cannot introduce an additional *X*. It has to be "Some Jerseys are cows" or "Some cows are Jerseys"—take your pick. Again, diagramming the premises yields the conclusion: The extra *X* disappears. The syllogism is valid. The statement is true. The argument is sound.

Now consider this syllogism:

> Some flowers are petunias.
>
> So, some flowers are plants.

Construct the diagram for the premise and the conclusion:

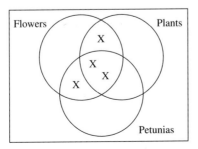

Notice that you have introduced *two* Xs in the middle region. It is that region that will contain an *X* when you diagram the premises. You need to introduce a universal premise that will reduce the number of Xs to two, either of which could represent the conclusion. Clearly, the extra *X* is in the region representing things that are flowers and petunias, but not plants. The premise must concern petunias and plants. So the missing premise must be "All petunias are plants": Only that universal premise will show that the area representing flowers and petunias, but not plants, is empty. Diagramming the premises yields the conclusion. The missing premise is true. The argument is sound.

If the syllogism is valid and you have a particular premise and a particular conclusion, you will always introduce a second *X* into one area when diagramming the conclusion. The other *X* you introduce when diagramming the conclusion will disappear if you diagram the premises to be sure the conclusion follows. You might find it helpful to circle the *X* that disappears so that you know which *X* must be eliminated by the missing premise. For the petunias syllogism, the diagram would look like this:

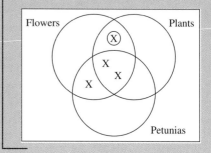

Of course, there are times when it is impossible to find a premise that yields a valid syllogism. Consider the following:

All flowers are plants.

So, some flowers are petunias.

Construct the diagram for the premise and the conclusion:

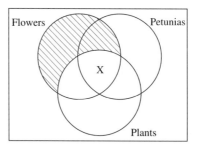

Notice that you have introduced only one *X*. By the last rule of interpretation, this argument is invalid.

Consider this premise and conclusion:

All mice are rodents.

So, all rodents are animals.

Construct the diagram for the premise and the conclusion:

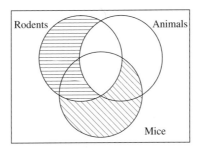

You have shaded four areas of the diagram. By the last rule of interpretation, the argument is invalid.

Consider the following:

> Some mice are not cats.
>
> So, some Siamese are cats.

Construct the diagram for the premise and the conclusion:

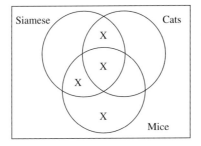

Here you have introduced four Xs in four distinct regions. By the last rule of interpretation, the argument is invalid.

There is one hazard, however, that you cannot cover by simply appealing to Venn diagrams. That is the possibility that a term has more than one meaning in the syllogism. Consider the following:

> All cats are domestic animals.
>
> So, some lions are domestic animals.

Construct the diagram for the premise and the conclusion:

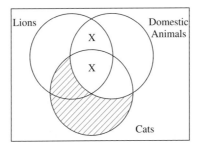

The missing premise has to be "Some lions are cats" or "Some cats are lions"—take your pick. Both are true. But if the missing premise is true, then either the given premise is false, since lions, tigers, and cougars are not domestic animals, or the word 'cat' has been assigned two different meanings. So, either the argument is invalid due to a shift in the meaning of one of the terms ('cats'), or the argument is valid but unsound due to a false premise. You always must pay some attention to the meaning of the words in the syllogism.

Exercises

Use the rules or Venn diagrams to determine what premise, if any, would yield a valid syllogism or what conclusion, if any, follows from the premises. If no premise will yield a valid syllogism or no conclusion is entailed by the given premises, explain why: Cite the rule or explain your diagram. If you can find the missing premise or conclusion, is that statement true?

1. Since some millionaires are stingy, and no millionaires are poor, the conclusion is obvious.

2. Since all professors are intelligent, and some intelligent persons are rich, I'll let you draw your own conclusions.

3. Some creepy things are arachnids, since some creepy things are spiders.

4. All people who read *A Christmas Carol* in the middle of July are Dickens buffs, so all members of the Charles Dickens Memorial Committee are Dickens buffs.

5. Some Presbyterians are not Lutherans, so some Presbyterians are not Methodists.

6. All people who master the art of the syllogism are people who enjoy playing logical games, so some who enjoy playing logical games are mathematicians.

7. Some people who play syllogistic games are not people who find them enjoyable, for no one who finds syllogisms utterly perplexing is a person who enjoys syllogistic games.

8. No Protestants are Catholics, since no Baptists are Catholics.

9. Since no Protestants are Catholics, it follows that no Presbyterians are Catholics.

10. Since some people who do these problems are not people who are mathematically disposed, we may conclude that some who enjoy these problems are not people who are mathematically disposed.

11. Since no aardvarks are cats, and no cats are dogs, the conclusion should be obvious.

12. Given that some philosophers are not men, we may conclude that some women are not philosophers.

13. Insofar as some aardvarks are anteaters, we may conclude that some mammals are anteaters.

14. Some aardvarks are not cows, for some aardvarks are not birds.

15. No dogs are cows, since no cows are schnauzers.

16. Some people who do these exercises are confused people, since some people who do these exercises are students.

17. Some people who do these exercises are not confused people, since some students are people who do these exercises.

18. Some people who do these exercises are not confused people, because some students are confused people.

19. No confused people are people who do these exercises, since no people who do these exercises are aardvarks.

20. Since all people who do these exercises are people who enjoy these exercises, and no people who enjoy these exercises are aardvarks, the conclusion is obvious.

21. Some authors are interesting people, inasmuch as some interesting people are people who do not work fewer than fifteen hours per day.

22. All aardvarks are interesting animals, so all interesting animals are anteaters.

23. Inasmuch as all aardvarks are interesting animals, and no aardvarks are animals that eat tree bark, the conclusion should be obvious.

24. Assuming that some aardvarks are not cows, we may conclude that some cows are not horses.

25. Given that no cows are carnivores, we may conclude that some cows are not aardvarks.

26. Some people who talk on the telephone for hours are adolescents, so some people who talk on the telephone for hours are not cell-phone owners.

27. Some people who talk on the telephone for hours are adolescents, and some adolescents are people who drive sports cars, so the conclusion is obvious.

28. Some young adults are people who like jazz, for some people who like jazz are musicians.

29. No jazz lovers are trumpet afficionados. So, some classical music buffs are not trumpet afficionados.

30. Some Backstreet Boys fans are old people, so some old people are people of good taste.

31. Some aardvarks are gentle animals, so all aardvarks are cows.

32. Some aardvarks are vicious animals, since some aardvarks are not gentle animals.

33. No trombone players are chemists, for no musicians are chemists.

34. No musicians are chemists, for all trombone players are chemists.

35. All singers are musicians, thus some musicians are not trumpeters.

36. Some operatic sopranos are cellists, so some steelworkers are not operatic sopranos.

37. All cellists are musicians, since all musicians are fans of the fine arts.

38. No chemists are alchemists, so no chemists are people who change lead into gold.

39. No alchemists are people who turn lead into gold, but some physicists are people who turn lead into gold, so . . .

40. Some people who have completed these problems are exhausted people, since some people who have completed these problems are diligent students.

Conversion, Obversion, and Squares of Opposition

The View: There are logically equivalent forms of categorical propositions. In this chapter we examine conversion, obversion, and to a lesser extent contraposition. We also discuss some of the immediate inferences that can be drawn from categorical propositions on both the Boolean and Aristotelian interpretations of categorical syllogisms.

What are the relationships among the four standard-form categorical propositions? Can an affirmative proposition be restated as a negative, or vice versa? If you know the truth or falsehood of one categorical proposition, can you deduce the truth value of any other categorical proposition with the same content?

Before turning to the remaining hazards found in ordinary language, we must introduce some **logically equivalent forms** of standard-form categorical propositions. Two statement forms are logically equivalent if and only if they are true or false under exactly the same circumstances. The first of these is **conversion**. To **convert** a categorical proposition, switch the places of the subject and predicate terms. For example, the **converse** of "All collies are dogs" is "All dogs are collies." Here, clearly, the converse is *not* logically equivalent to the original proposition, since the first proposition is true and the second is false. Similarly, the converse of "Some dogs are not collies," namely, "Some collies are not dogs," is *not* logically equivalent to the original proposition. But in the cases of universal negative propositions and particular affirmative propositions the original proposition is logically equivalent to its converse. You are saying the same thing, whether you say "No cats are aardvarks" or "No aardvarks are cats." You are saying that the two classes have no members in common. You are saying the same thing whether you say "Some dogs are mammals" or "Some mammals are dogs." You are claiming that the two classes have at least one member in common. So, conversion may be summarized in the following table:

Conversion

Given Propositional Form	Converse
All *S* is *P*.	not logically equivalent
No *S* is *P*.	No *P* is *S*.
Some *S* is *P*.	Some *P* is *S*.
Some *S* is not *P*.	not logically equivalent

If you are a fan of Venn diagrams, you will notice that the Venn diagram for a universal negative and its converse are identical, as they are for a particular affirmative and its converse.

To understand the notion of **obversion**, we must first understand the notion of a complementary class. One class is the **complement** of another if it contains all and only those things that are *not* contained in the original class. For example, the complement of the class of professors contains everything that is not a professor: students, tables, chairs, dust bunnies, and so on. Two terms are **complementary terms** if the class of objects picked out by one term is the complement of the class of objects picked out by the other term. Let us represent the complement of the term *T* as *non-T*. So the complement of the term 'red things' is 'nonred things'.[1]

You form the **obverse** of a given categorical proposition by changing the quality of the proposition from affirmative to negative (or negative to affirmative) and replacing the predicate term with its complement. For example, the obverse of the proposition "Some professors are humane persons" is "Some professors are not nonhumane (inhumane) persons."[2] Every standard-form categorical proposition is logically equivalent to its obverse. Obversion is summarized in the following table:

Obversion

Given Categorical Proposition	Obverse
All *S* is *P*.	No *S* is non-*P*.
No *S* is *P*.	All *S* is non-*P*.
Some *S* is *P*.	Some *S* is not non-*P*.
Some *S* is not *P*.	Some *S* is non-*P*.

Conversion and obversion can be used in succession to generate four logically equivalent forms for each of the categorical propositions:

---

[1]There are numerous prefixes that usually mark the complement of a certain class: 'un-', 'in-', and so on. For example, the complement of the term 'educated people' is 'uneducated people', although it might be difficult to determine precisely where to draw the line between those two classes of people (the terms 'educated' and 'uneducated' are vague). But, except in the case of the prefix 'non-', you can't simply look at the prefix and immediately assume that you have the complement of the given term. For example, the terms 'flammable' and 'inflammable' are synonymous.
[2]We are here concerned with the denotative meanings of words. There is a difference in the emotional connotation depending whether you say, "Professor Charlot is a humane teacher" or "Professor Charlot is not an inhumane teacher." The former is a better compliment.

All *S* is *P* obverts to

> No *S* is non-*P*, which converts to
>
> No non-*P* is *S*, which obverts to
>
> All non-*P* is non-*S*.

No *S* is *P* converts to

> No *P* is *S*, which obverts to
>
> All *P* is non-*S*.
>
> No *S* is *P* obverts to All *S* is non-*P*

Some *S* is *P* converts to

> Some *P* is *S*, which obverts to
>
> Some *P* is not non-*S*.
>
> Some *S* is *P* obverts to Some *S* is not non-*P*.

Some *S* is not *P* obverts to

> Some *S* is non-*P*, which converts to
>
> Some non-*P* is *S*, which obverts to
>
> Some non-*P* is not non-*S*.

Contraposition

There is a third equivalent form known as contraposition. To form the contrapositive of a given proposition, replace the subject and predicate terms with their complements and convert the resulting proposition. The contrapositive of universal affirmative and a particular negative are logically equivalent to the original proposition. The resulting contrapositives of a universal affirmative and a particular negative are the fourth propositions in the chart to the left. The contrapositive of a universal negative and a particular affirmative are not logically equivalent to the original propositions. Can you give an example of each to show that?

Why are we doing this? I hear you ask. Is it just another one of those weird things critical-thinking teachers do to torment their students? No. As we shall see in the next chapter, one of the joys of ordinary English is that sometimes we need to reduce the number of terms in a syllogism to three by dealing with a term and its antonym. Obversion and conversion are sometimes needed to reduce the number of terms in a syllogism to three.

Squares of Opposition: The Boolean Square

Given the truth or falsehood of a categorical proposition, it is possible to immediately (without appealing to another proposition) infer the truth value of at least one other categorical proposition with the same content. Whether it is *only* one proposition depends upon the interpretation of categorical propositions that is assumed.

In Chapter 16, we noticed the distinction between the Boolean and the Aristotelian interpretations of categorical syllogisms. The Boolean interpretation, which is assumed by both our set of rules and Venn diagrams, does *not* assign **existential import** to universal propositions. A statement has existential import if and only if its truth assumes that there is at least one object of which the proposition is true. On the Boolean interpretation, particular propositions have existential import, but universal propositions do not. So, on the Boolean interpretation, the statement, "All unicorns are one-horned horses" is true. The statements, "Some unicorns are one-horned horses" and "Some unicorns are not one-horned horses" are false because there are no unicorns. On the Boolean interpretation, universal affirmatives are the contradictories of particular negatives, and universal negatives are the contradictories of particular affirmatives. Two statements are **contradictories** if and only if it is logically impossible for both to be true under the same conditions *and* it is logically impossible for both to be false under the same conditions. So, if you know that one statement is true, you can infer that its contradictory is false, and vice versa. This is summarized in a diagram known as the **Boolean square of opposition**.

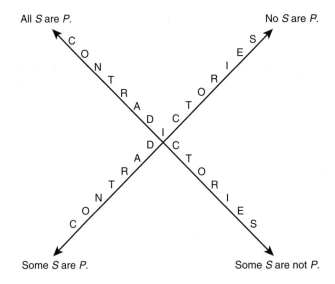

So, given that the statement "Some collies are dogs" is true, it follows that the statement "No collies are dogs" is false. You cannot *infer* anything regarding the truth value of "All collies are dogs" or "Some collies are not dogs," although you might know their truth values on some other basis. Given that the statement "Some rodents are not rats" is true, you can infer that the statement "All rodents are rats" is false. You cannot *infer* anything regarding the truth value of "No rodents are rats" or "Some rodents are not rats," although you might know their truth values on some other basis.

You can combine considerations of the Boolean square of opposition with the equivalent forms of each of the four logically equivalent forms of the categorical propositions to answer questions regarding entailment. Assume that the statement

"No Jerseys are noncattle" is true, and you are asked what, if anything, follows regarding the truth value of "Some Jerseys are not cattle." "No Jerseys are noncattle" is equivalent to (the obverse of) "All Jerseys are cattle." So, since "All Jerseys are cattle" is true, it follows that "Some Jerseys are not cattle" is false, since the two statements are contradictories. Assume that "Some mice are not noncats" is false, and you are asked what, if anything, follows regarding the truth value of "No cats are mice." "Some mice are not noncats" is equivalent to (is the obverse of) "Some mice are cats," which converts to "Some cats are mice." So, since "Some cats are mice" is the contradictory of "No cats are mice," and "Some cats are mice" is false, it follows that "No cats are mice" is true. Assume that "All aardvarks are anteaters" is true, and you are asked what, if anything, follows regarding the truth value of "All aardvarks are non-anteaters." "All aardvarks are non-anteaters" is the obverse of "No aardvarks are anteaters." On the Boolean interpretation, the *only* inference you can draw from the truth of "All aardvarks are anteaters" is that "Some aardvarks are not anteaters" (in all of its logically equivalent forms) is false. You can draw *no* inferences regarding the truth or falsehood of "No aardvarks are anteaters." You would indicate that the truth value of "No aardvarks are anteaters" and its equivalent "All aardvarks are non-anteaters" *cannot be determined*.

Exercises

I. Assuming the Boolean square of opposition, and assuming that the first statement (a) is *true*, what can you infer regarding the truth value of the second statement (b)?

1. (a) All tabbies are cats. (b) Some tabbies are not cats.
2. (a) Some dogs are collies. (b) All collies are dogs.
3. (a) No Scottish terriers are Irish setters. (b) Some Scottish terriers are Irish setters.
4. (a) Some spiders are not electric eels. (b) All spiders are electric eels.
5. (a) Some cats are not pests. (b) No cats are nonpests.
6. (a) No unicorns are nonmythical beasts. (b) Some unicorns are mythical beasts.
7. (a) No aardvarks are tree frogs. (b) All aardvarks are tree frogs.
8. (a) All electric eels are shocking fish. (b) Some electric eels are nonshocking fish.
9. (a) Some spiders are not nonarachnids. (b) Some spiders are arachnids.
10. (a) All nonhumans are nonprimates. (b) Some primates are nonhumans.
11. (a) No unicorns are hippogriffs. (b) Some nonunicorn is a hippogriff.
12. (a) No nondogs are collies. (b) Some collies are dogs.
13. (a) All nondogs are noncollies. (b) Some collies are not nondogs.

14. (a) Some nondogs are not cats. (b) Some cats are dogs.

15. (a) Some nonaardvarks are anteaters. (b) Some non-anteaters are not nonaardvarks.

II. Assuming the Boolean square of opposition, and assuming that the first statement (a) is *false*, what can you infer regarding the truth value of the second statement (b)?

1. (a) Some unicorns are hippogriffs. (b) All unicorns are hippogriffs.

2. (a) All terriers are cats. (b) Some terriers are not cats.

3. (a) No tabbies are cats. (b) Some tabbies are not cats.

4. (a) Some tabbies are not cats. (b) Some tabbies are cats.

5. (a) All collies are nondogs. (b) Some nondogs are not noncollies.

6. (a) Some plants are not nondogs. (b) All dogs are nonplants.

7. (a) Some dogs are not nonplants. (b) Some dogs are not plants.

8. (a) No nonplants are aardvarks. (b) Some aardvarks are nonplants.

9. (a) Some antelope are deer. (b) Some nondeer are not nonantelope.

10. (a) Some hippogriffs are not noncentaurs. (b) All centaurs are nonhippogriffs.

11. (a) All centaurs are nonmythical beasts. (b) Some nonmythical beasts are not noncentaurs.

12. (a) Some flytraps are animals. (b) All animals are nonflytraps.

13. (a) Some flytraps are animals. (b) Some nonflytraps are not nonanimals.

14. (a) Some nonanimals are not nonflytraps. (b) All nonflytraps are nonanimals.

15. (a) No dogs are cats. (b) No noncats are dogs.

Squares of Opposition: The Aristotelian Square

On the Boolean interpretation, the only inference that can be drawn from the truth or falsehood of any categorical proposition is that its contradictory has the opposite truth value. So, if "All aardvarks are anteaters" is true, the *only* immediate inference that can be drawn is that the statement "Some aardvarks are not anteaters" is false. On the Boolean interpretation, you can infer *neither* that the statement "No aardvarks are anteaters" is false *nor* that the statement "Some aardvarks are anteaters" is true. This is because the Boolean interpretation does *not* attribute existential import to universal propositions. On the Boolean interpretation, "All aardvarks are anteaters" is understood as saying, "If anything is an aardvark, then it is an anteater." As we'll see in Chapter 20, conditional statements are true except when the antecedent (*if* clause) is true and the consequent (*then* clause) is false. So, on the

Boolean interpretation, a universal affirmative proposition is trivially true if it refers to an empty set.

There is an alternative interpretation of categorical logic. The Aristotelian interpretation ascribes existential import to universal propositions. In effect, the Aristotelian interpretation treats a universal affirmative proposition as asserting *both* "All *S* are *P*" *and* "Some *S* are *P*." It treats a universal negative proposition as asserting *both* "No *S* are *P*" *and* "Some *S* are not *P*." This interpretation increases the number of immediate inferences that can be drawn. It also corresponds to *some* ordinary assumptions. Many universal propositions represent nonempty sets. The statement "All collies are dogs" is true, and we know that there are collies. So, when we know that a universal is true and that the classes to which the terms refer have members, we reasonably can draw inferences according to the Aristotelian interpretation. The odd element of the Aristotelian interpretation is that it requires that a statement such as "All unicorns are horned horses" is false—since there are no unicorns—even though the word 'unicorn' is defined as a horned horse.

The Aristotelian square of opposition looks like this:

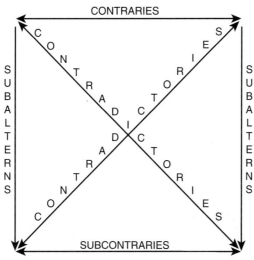

All *S* are *P* and Some *S* are *P*.   No *S* are *P* and Some *S* are not *P*.

Some *S* are *P*.   Some *S* are not *P*.

Two statements are **contraries** if it is possible for both to be false, but it is not possible for both to be true. If one of two contraries is true, the other must be false. If one of two contraries is false, you can draw no inferences regarding the truth or falsehood of the other. Two statements are **contradictories** if they both cannot be true *and* they both cannot be false in the same circumstances. If a statement is true, its contradictory is false. If a statement is false, its contradictory is true. **Subalternation** is a relation between a universal and its corresponding particular such that if the universal is true, the corresponding particular is also true. The relation goes *only* from the universal to the particular. If you know that a particular proposition is true, you cannot infer anything regarding the corresponding universal. Two statements are **subcontraries** if it is possible for both to be true, but it is not possible for both to be false. So, if you know that one particular affirmative proposition is *false,* the corresponding particular negative must be true. If you know that a particular negative is *false,* the corresponding particular affirmative must be true. The Aristotelian square of opposition summarizes these relations.

If a universal affirmative proposition is true, the Aristotelian interpretation allows you to infer the truth values of all the other propositions on the square. If a universal affirmative is true, then the corresponding universal negative (its contrary) must be false, the corresponding particular negative (its contradictory) must be false, and the corresponding particular affirmative (its subaltern) must be true. You can read this off of the square as follows:

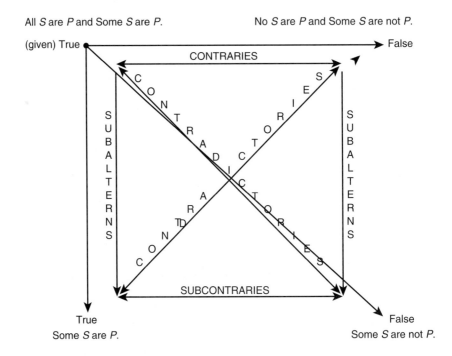

The same relations would be found if a given universal negative is true, although it would be the universal affirmative that is false, the particular affirmative that is false, and the particular negative that is true.

If a particular proposition is *false,* you can similarly infer the truth values of all the corresponding propositions on the square. For example, if a particular negative is false, then the corresponding particular affirmative (its subcontrary) is true, the corresponding universal affirmative (its contradictory) is true, and the corresponding universal negative must be false (it is the contradictory of the particular affirmative). You can read this off the square as follows:

All *S* are *P* and Some *S* are *P.*   No *S* are *P* and Some *S* are not *P.*

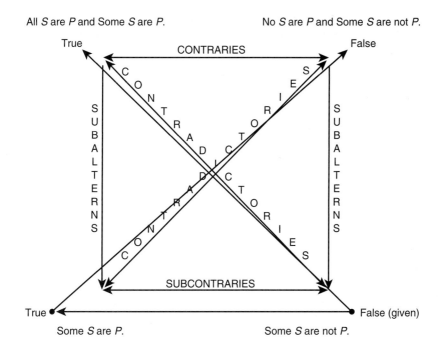

If a universal proposition is *false,* the *only* inference the square allows is that its contradictory is true. If a particular proposition is *true,* the only inference the square allows is that its contradictory is false. And, of course, if the given is a logically equivalent form of one of the standard-form categorical propositions, your first task is to restate it in standard form. So, if you are given, "All nonunicorns are nonhippogriffs," you replace it with its contrapositive, "All hippogriffs are unicorns."

Exercises

III. Do exercise set I above assuming the Aristotelian square of opposition. Assuming that the first statement (a) is *true,* what can you infer regarding the truth value of the second statement (b)?

IV. Do exercise set II above assuming the Aristotelian square of opposition. Assuming that the first statement (a) is *false,* what can you infer regarding the truth value of the second statement (b)?

Living
in the Real World

The View Confronting syllogisms in ordinary English provides numerous challenges. Quantifiers are not standard. Premises often are missing. There *appear* to be four distinct terms or more, although some of the terms are synonyms or antonyms. This chapter presents guidelines for restating ordinary-English syllogisms in—"reducing" them to—standard form.

Of what must one be aware when dealing with syllogisms found in ordinary life? Are there additional quantifiers? If syllogisms are not always presented with exactly three terms, what do we do?

Categorical syllogisms are wonderful things. If everyone presenting categorical syllogisms stated them with the quantifiers 'All', 'No', 'Some', and 'Some . . . not', if they stated their syllogisms with exactly three terms used in the same sense throughout, and if all syllogisms were presented completely (no missing premises, no missing conclusions), there should be little question regarding what arguments are presented.[1] Part of the joy of language is that we can say the same thing in many different ways. The only disadvantage is that we have to figure out what is being said. In this chapter we examine issues that arise when examining syllogisms ordinary English.

Nonstandard Quantifiers

In ordinary English, we don't always use the quantifiers 'All', 'No', and 'Some'. We noticed some of these in Chapter 13. Here is a more complete list.

Ways to say All: every, whatever, any (except in an expression such as "If any . . . ," when it means 'some'), the only, the as in "The cat is a mammal," sometimes a or an as in "A cat is a mammal."

---

[1] Such writing is clear. We discuss the virtues of stylistic clarity in Chapter 33.

Ways to say No: not any, none, not even one, and so on.

Ways to say Some ... are ...: at least one, a few, more than none, there is a, there exists a, many, several, diverse, numerous, various, a or an (usually) and sometimes the.[2]

Ways to say Some ... are not ...: not all, not every.

Only and None but are All with a twist: If you say "None but the brave deserve the fair," it means "All deservers of the fair are brave people." *Notice that the position of subject and predicate terms is reversed.* 'Only' is like 'none but'. If you say "Only those who study hard pass," you mean "All those who pass are those who study hard." But 'only' can mean more than that. Sometimes a statement such as "Only those who study hard pass," *also* means "All those who study hard are those who pass." You have to ask two questions. (1) Which statement is true? (2) Which statement will yield a valid syllogism? If one statement is true but the other yields a valid syllogism, you point this out.

Sometimes you might have to think about what is being said. "Racehorses are all thoroughbreds" means "All racehorses are thoroughbreds," *not* "All thoroughbreds are racehorses," since *some* thoroughbreds are injured or too young or too old or too slow to race.

Unless: "No person takes this course unless he or she is a student" means "All people who take this course are students." 'Unless' introduces the negation of the predicate, so "No person takes this course unless he or she is a student" is equivalent to "No person who takes this course is a non-student," which obverts to the universal affirmative, "All people who take this course are students."[3]

Complex quantifiers: "All but (or all except) employees may enter the contest" means *both* "All nonemployees may enter the contest" *and* "No employees may enter the contest." 'Almost all', 'not quite all', and 'only some' mean *both* some are *and* some are not. If you have a premise with a complex quantifier, use whichever of the two meanings will give you a valid argument. If a complex quantifier is the conclusion

---

Can an argument with 'only some' in the conclusion be valid?

Assume you are given the argument

Only some M are P.
All M are S.
Only some S are P.

If you interpret the argument *charitably*, you will interpret it as *two* distinct arguments:

Some M are P.	Some M are not P.
All M are S	All M are S.
Some S are P.	Some S are not P.

Each of these argument forms is valid.

---

[2] We can treat statements with quantifiers such as 'many' or 'most' as categorical statements by replacing those terms with 'some'. This is not the most natural treatment of those terms. It is more natural to take them as expressing stronger than "at least one," and to treat the arguments as inductive. See Part VI.

[3] In Chapter 20, we will see that there is an alterative understanding of 'unless' when dealing with propositional arguments.

of an argument, you can show that the argument is invalid by showing that *one* form of the conclusion does *not* follow from the premises.

No quantifier: If no quantifier is given, you should ask yourself what statement is true. "Cats are mammals" probably means "All cats are mammals." "The cat is on the mat" probably means "Some cat is on the mat."

Exercises

I. Restate each of the following syllogisms in standard form and use rules or Venn diagrams to determine whether they are valid.

1. Every aardvark is an interesting animal. So, there is not an aardvark that is a warthog, since not any warthog is an interesting animal.

2. The shark has pretty teeth. Anything with pretty teeth is loved by dentists. So, everything loved by dentists is a shark.

3. There is a scorpion that does not chase cats. Not every thing that chases cats is a dog. So, not all dogs are scorpions.

4. Only some electric eels are light bulbs, since every bright thing at night is a light bulb, and several electric eels are bright things at night.

5. No one will figure out this problem unless he or she thinks, so various primates will not figure out this problem, since not every primate thinks.

6. None but anteaters are aardvarks. Not quite all aardvarks are pets suitable for children under six. So, various pets suitable for children under six are anteaters.

7. Not every viper is a snake. There is a Viper that is made by Dodge. So, nothing made by Dodge is a snake.

8. There is not a tree toad that is an elephant. So, not any elephant is an amphibian, since only amphibians are tree toads.

9. Almost all mammals are land animals. Therefore, at least one mammal lives in a tree, since many land animals are animals that live in a tree.

10. Only those who understand what we have been doing are prepared to look at a few new wrinkles. No one who has ignored these problems is a person who understands what we have been doing. Therefore, not anyone who has ignored these problems is a person prepared for a few new wrinkles.

Reducing the Number of Terms

As we have noticed regarding quantifiers, one of the hazards of ordinary language is that we can say the same thing with many different words. The same holds regarding the terms in a syllogism. Look at the following argument:

Since a few victors are not cheaters, we may conclude that none but the strong will win the race, for not any charlatans are powerful.

If you count the number of terms—(1) victors, (2) cheaters, (3) strong things, (4) winners of the race, (5) charlatans, (6) powerful things—you might say, "Ah! More than three terms. It's invalid: Rule 1." But here we have a number of synonyms: 'victors' and 'winners', 'cheaters' and 'charlatans', and 'strong things' and 'powerful things' are synonymous terms. So, replace one term with its synonym, replace the nonstandard quantifiers with standard quantifiers, and restate the argument in standard form:

> No cheaters are strong things.
>
> <u>Some winners are not cheaters.</u>
>
> All winners are strong things.

The argument is invalid, but the invalidity has nothing to do with rule 1. The argument violates rules 2, 3, 4, 5, and 6!

Similarly you must look for antonyms. Consider the following argument:

No valid argument is an argument with true premises and a false conclusion.

<u>All invalid arguments are unsound arguments.</u>

No sound argument is an argument with true premises and a false conclusion.

Here you need to use obversion and conversion to reduce the number of terms to three. Obvert the second premise to "No invalid arguments are sound arguments." Convert that statement to "No sound arguments are invalid arguments," which you obvert to "All sound arguments are valid arguments." (To put it differently, contrapose the second premise.) Plug that into the argument in place of the second premise, and you get this:

No valid argument is an argument with true premises and a false conclusion.

<u>All sound arguments are valid arguments.</u>

No sound argument is an argument with true premises and a false conclusion.

The argument is valid.

Sometimes you have to deal with complementary terms marked by prefixes such as in- or un-. This is not something that can be done automatically, since a negative prefix does not always mark the complement. For example, which is more dangerous: flammable materials or inflammable materials?[4] Sometimes you must recognize the context in which an argument is presented. The proper complement of the 'senator' is 'nonsenator'—which includes all of us, as well as tables and trees. But if you're talking about members of Congress—if members of Congress is the **context** assumed by the argument—then the complement of 'senator' is 'representative'. Hence,

---

[4]If you're uncertain, consult your dictionary.

> All representatives have two-year terms.
>
> <u>No members of the tax committee are senators.</u>
>
> So, all members of the tax committee have two-year terms.

is understood as

> All representatives have two-year terms.
>
> <u>No members of the tax committee are nonrepresentatives.</u>
>
> So, all members of the tax committee have two-year terms.

which, by obverting the major premise, becomes

> All representatives have two-year terms.
>
> <u>All members of the tax committee are representatives.</u>
>
> So, all members of the tax committee have two-year terms.

The argument is valid.

Singular Propositions

A singular proposition talks about one person or thing. Treat it as either a universal proposition or a particular proposition, whichever makes the argument valid. So "Jones is a senator" would be treated as either "Some things identical with Jones are senators" or "All things identical with Jones are senators." You must be consistent. If you treat a singular premise as a universal proposition, you must treat the corresponding singular conclusion as a universal. If you treat a singular premise as a particular proposition, you must treat the corresponding singular conclusion as a particular. So,

> **Name-Like Expressions**
> There are various complex linguistic expressions that, like names, pick out one thing. 'The' in the phrase "The cat on the mat" picks out one thing, perhaps, Fluffy. 'This' in "This problem is easy" refers to exactly one problem.

> All students in this class are enthusiastic persons.
>
> <u>Jessica is a student in this class.</u>
>
> So, Jessica is an enthusiastic person.

Can be treated as either

> All students in this class are enthusiastic persons.
>
> <u>All things identical with Jessica are students in this class.</u>
>
> So, all things identical with Jessica are enthusiastic persons.

or:

> All students in this class are enthusiastic persons.
>
> Some things identical with Jessica are students in this class.
>
> So, some things identical with Jessica are enthusiastic persons.

> **Important**
>
> If you *treat* "Jessica is a member of this class" as a universal, it *does not become* a universal. "(All) Jessica is a member of this class" does *not* claim that all Jessicas are members of this class. "(All) This problem is easy" does *not* claim that all problems are easy.

While you might *treat* the singular proposition in either of these two ways, it is unnecessary to use the elaborate locution "All things identical with Jessica" or "Some things identical with Jessica." Just put 'All' or 'Some' in parentheses before the word 'Jessica': "(All) Jessica. . . . "

There is one exception to this general rule. Consider the following argument:

> Fran is a member of Phi Beta Kappa.
>
> Fran is a member of Phi Alpha Theta.
>
> So, some members of Phi Alpha Theta are members of Phi Beta Kappa.

Given the premises, the conclusion is undoubtedly true. There is at least one person, namely Fran, who is a member of both Phi Alpha Theta and Phi Beta Kappa. So, to reach the conclusion, treat one premise mentioning Fran as a universal and the other as a particular.

> All people identical with Fran are members of Phi Beta Kappa.
>
> Some people identical with Fran are members of Phi Alpha Theta.
>
> So, some members of Phi Alpha Theta are members of Phi Beta Kappa.

Exercises

II. Show that each of the following is a valid categorical syllogism.

1. Dogs that do tricks are not kangaroos, so some zoo animals are not dogs that do tricks, for some kangaroos live in zoos.

2. Since some coins desired by coin collectors are circulating, and no coin coveted by a numismatist is common, we may conclude that a few rare coins are in circulation.

3. Since no scholars are cowards and John isn't brave, it follows that John does not devote his life to intellectual pursuits.

4. Some people who ride cows lose the race, for none but the swift win and a few cow-riders are not swift.

5. Since racehorses are all thoroughbreds and many racehorses do not win at Belmont, it follows that some thoroughbreds don't win at Belmont.

6. Since the cat is a carnivore, it follows that Frisky is not a feline, since Frisky doesn't eat meat.

7. Only those who hoard money are misers. So, some counting-house executives hoard money for its own sake, since some counting-house executives are real scrooges.

8. Since only inorganic compounds contain no carbon, it follows that not every stable substance is a compound that contains no carbon, for at least some organic compounds are not unstable.

9. Every mean person is inhumane. Therefore, nurses are nice, since only humane folks are trained to care for the sick.

10. Any all-terrain vehicle is designed for travel off the road. Limousines are intended solely for travel on streets and highways. So, limos aren't small, three- or four-wheeled vehicles with one seat and big tires.

11. Not every prison inmate cows before authority, for many jailbirds are tough, and whoever is intimidated is weak of will.

12. Only strangely enlightened students do these problems. So, Jeanne isn't doing these exercises, since she has no special insight, strange or otherwise.

13. Most people who do these problems are not working under constraint. No one who freely and willingly undertakes doing these problems is ignorant of logic. Hence, some of those laboring on these exercises are logicians.

14. Anyone who puts on the dog is likely to be ostracized from his or her peer group. Some of those who put on the ritz are absolute boors. Therefore, at least one person who is excluded from groups of his or her equals is a dolt.

15. "Tell me, what have they done with Mrs. Hardisty?" Harley Raymond asked.

    "I've got a writ of *habeas corpus* for her. They're going to have to bring her out in the open now. They've had her buried in some outlying town . . . . Were you people looking for something?" (Erle Stanley Gardner, The Case of the Buried Clock [New York: Ballantine Books, 1943], p. 70)

III. Check the validity of the following by means of the rules or a Venn diagram, if it is possible to do so. If you cannot construct a Venn diagram for the argument, explain why not.

1. This cat isn't a tabby, so this tabby isn't a mammal, for cats are mammals.

2. A few cats smile when they disappear, so some hedgehogs are not cats, for not everything that smiles when it disappears is a hedgehog.

3. Everyone who believes that the best government is one elected by a majority is a democrat, so no Republicans believe in majority rule, since no Republicans are Democrats.

4. A few coins of the realm are not valuable to coin collectors, since every coin in circulation is a coin of the realm and only some coins in circulation are of numismatic value.

5. Dogs are not cats, for a few rats are not cats, and not any dog is a rat.

6. Not every scoundrel is a coward, but since at least one traitor is a scoundrel, it follows that some traitors are not cowards.

7. Not a single Lincoln is a compact, so some presidents were not small, for one Lincoln was a president.

8. At least one cat is Siamese, so only some dogs are Siamese, for not any canines are felines.

9. None but stone bridges are standing bridges constructed by the Romans, so a bridge in Koblenz was built by the Romans, for a bridge in Koblenz is made of stone.

10. Not every dog is a hound, and not any hound is a schnauzer, so every schnauzer is a dog.

11. No one watches the news who is uninterested in current affairs, so every presidential candidate watches the news, given that anyone who runs for president is interested in current events.

12. No reader of Shakespeare reads mysteries, for not everyone who likes to solve problems reads Shakespeare, and no one reads mysteries unless he or she likes to solve puzzles.

13. "Lying is fiction," this crusty old reptile had proclaimed with a dry and cynical grin, "fiction is art, and therefore all art is a lie." (Stephen King, *Desperation* [New York: Penguin Books, 1996], p. 623)

14. In 1938, surrealist art was very controversial. Nobody really understood what surrealism was, and since no one understood what Gracie's paintings were either, they had to be surrealist. (George Burns, *Gracie: A Love Story* [New York: G. P. Putnam's Sons, 1988], p. 180)

15. "Soldiers don't murder people. Criminals do that, and a soldier isn't a criminal." (Tom Clancy, *Rainbow Six* [New York: G. P. Putnam's Sons, 1998], p. 531)

IV. A sorites is a chain of enthymematic categorical syllogisms. The conclusion of one syllogism is taken as a premise for the next. In the following you are given a series of premises and a conclusion. Use two premises to draw a conclusion. Use that conclusion with an additional premise to draw another conclusion. Follow that pattern until you reach the conclusion of the sorites. Each of the following sorites is valid.[5]

Example: You are given

(1) Babies are illogical.

(2) Nobody is despised who can manage a crocodile.

(3) Illogical persons are despised.

Therefore, no crocodile managers are babies.

---

[5]All the exercises are from Lewis Carroll, *Symbolic Logic and the Game of Logic* (New York: Dover Publications, 1958), pp. 112, 113, 117, 118, 119, 121, 123.

And you rewrite it as follows, reducing the number of terms to three in each of two arguments:

(3) All illogical persons are despised persons.

<u>(1) All babies are illogical persons.</u>

All babies are despised persons.

<u>(2) No despised persons are crocodile managers.</u>

No crocodile managers are babies.

Here both arguments are valid, but at least some of the premises are false. Now you try your hand at these.

1. (1) My saucepans are the only things I have that are made of tin.

   (2) I find *your* presents very useful.

   (3) None of my saucepans are of the slightest use.

   Therefore, *your* presents to me are not made of tin.

2. (1) No ducks waltz.

   (2) No officers ever decline to waltz.

   (3) All my poultry are ducks.

   Therefore, my poultry are not officers.

3. (1) All puddings are nice.

   (2) This dish is a pudding.

   (3) No nice things are wholesome.

   Therefore, this dish is unwholesome.

4. (1) Things sold in the street are of no great value.

   (2) Nothing but rubbish can be had for a song.

   (3) Eggs of the Great Auk are very valuable.

   (4) It is only what is sold in the street that is really *rubbish*.

   Therefore, an egg of the Great Auk is not to be had for a song.

5. (1) No birds, except ostriches, are nine feet high.

   (2) There are no birds in this aviary that belong to any one but *me*.

   (3) No ostrich lives on mince pies.

   (4) I have no birds less than nine feet high.

   Therefore, no bird in this aviary lives on mince pies.

6. (1) A plum pudding that is not really solid is mere porridge.

   (2) Every plum pudding served at my table has been boiled in a cloth.

(3) A plum pudding that is mere porridge is indistinguishable from soup.

(4) No plum puddings are really solid, except what is served at *my* table.

Therefore, no plum pudding that has not been boiled in a cloth can be distinguished from soup.

7. (1) No interesting poems are unpopular among people of real taste.

   (2) No modern poetry is free from affectation.

   (3) All your poems are on the subject of soap bubbles.

   (4) No affected poetry is popular among people of real taste.

   (5) No ancient poem is on the subject of soap bubbles.

   Therefore, all *your* poems are uninteresting.

8. (1) Promise-beakers are untrustworthy.

   (2) Wine drinkers are very communicative.

   (3) A person who keeps his or her promise is honest.

   (4) No teetotalers are pawnbrokers.

   (5) One can always trust a very communicative person.

   Therefore, no pawnbroker is dishonest.

9. (1) Animals that do not kick are always unexcitable.

   (2) Donkeys have no horns.

   (3) A buffalo can always toss one over a gate.

   (4) No animals that kick are easy to swallow.

   (5) No hornless animal can toss one over a gate.

   (6) All animals are excitable except buffaloes.

   Therefore, donkeys are not easy to swallow.

10. (1) I trust every animal that belongs to me.

    (2) Dogs gnaw bones.

    (3) I admit no animals to my study, unless they will beg when told to do so.

    (4) All the animals in the yard are mine.

    (5) I admit every animal that I trust into my study.

    (6) The only animals that are really willing to beg when told to do so are dogs.

    Therefore, all the animals in the yard gnaw bones.

Part V

Propositional Arguments

Not all deductive arguments are categorical syllogisms. Indeed, many of the most common deductive arguments take propositions or statements as their fundamental elements. For example, the following is an example of affirming the antecedent, an argument form you will find almost every day:

> If Ashley went to the mall, then Carol spent the afternoon at the movies.
>
> Ashley went to the mall.
> _____
>
> So, Carol spent the afternoon at the movies.

In this part we examine some of the most common valid argument forms as well as a number of common fallacies. We examine the ways in which some of these forms fit together to form more complex arguments. And we examine some logically equivalent statement forms, which will allow us to examine even more complex arguments.

In Chapter 20 we look at **truth-functionally compound statements**. We examine how simple statements can be combined together in such a way that the truth value of the compound statement depends upon the truth values of its parts. In Chapter 21 we examine the truth table method for determining the validity of propositional argument forms. In Chapter 22 we examine eight common valid argument forms and three common formal fallacies. In Chapter 23 we examine ways of finding missing premises or a missing conclusion. We also see how arguments of these forms can fit together—the conclusion of one being a premise for another—to form more complex argument chains. In Chapter 24 we discuss five common logically equivalent statement forms, that is, alternative ways of representing statements with the same truth value. These allow us to examine more complex arguments.

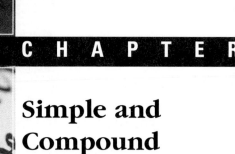

CHAPTER 20

Simple and Compound Statements

The View: Some of the most common deductive arguments are based on the relationships among propositions. In this chapter we set the stage for examining such arguments by examining a number of truth-functionally compound statements, that is, compound statements whose truth or falsehood depends upon the truth or falsehood of the statements of which it is composed.

How can statements be put together to form more complex statements? Can you know the truth values of some compound statements based on the truth values of their components?

A **compound statement** is a statement having another statement as a component. Compound statements are of two sorts. They are either **truth-functionally compound statements** or **nontruth-functionally compound statements**. The **truth value** (truth or falsity) of a truth-functionally compound statement depends upon the truth values of its component statements. The truth value of a nontruth-functionally compound statement does *not* depend on the truth values of its component statements. "John assumes that the critical thinking test will be easy" is a nontruth-functionally compound statement. It is compound because it contains the statement "The critical thinking test will be easy" as a component part. The compound proposition is nontruth-functional because the truth of the compound statement does *not* depend on the truth value of the component statement. The statement tells you something about John. It tells you nothing about the difficulty of the test. Our concern in this chapter is with five kinds of truth-functionally compound statements.

> In the twentieth century, a method of notion for representing propositional arguments was developed. This is to logic what algebraic notion is to mathematics. This gives very precise definitions to various symbols as well as approximate translations of English words into symbolese. The accounts of compound statements given in this chapter follow the definitions of the symbols. The symbols will be introduced in sidebars together with the **truth tables** defining the symbols.

A **negative statement** or **denial** is formed by denying the truth of a statement. If you are given the statement "Today is Tuesday," its denial is "Today is not Tuesday." If the statement "Today is Tuesday" is true, its denial is false; if the statement "Today is Tuesday" is false, its denial is true. Words that mark a denial include 'not', 'it is not the case that', 'no', and so forth.

Negation. The tilde (~), which represents negation, is defined as follows:

p	$\sim p$
T	F
F	T

A **conjunction** is formed by joining two or more statements with words such as 'and', 'but', 'yet', 'although', 'however', 'nevertheless', 'even though', and so forth.[1] A conjunction is true if and only if each of its component statements (**conjuncts**) is true. If the statements "Today is Tuesday" and "Today it is sunny" are both true, the statement "Today is Tuesday, and today it is sunny" is true; if either conjunct is false, the conjunction is false.

Conjunction. The ampersand (&), which represents conjunction, is defined as follows:

p	q	p & q
T	T	T
T	F	F
F	T	F
F	F	F

A **disjunction** is formed by joining two or more statements with words such as 'or' or 'unless'. A disjunction is true if and only if at least one of its component statements (**disjuncts**) is true. So, if it is true that today is Tuesday, or it is true that today is sunny, or it is both Tuesday and sunny, then the statement "Either today is Tuesday or today it is sunny" is true. Disjunction reflects what is commonly called an *inclusive* sense of the word 'or'. This is not the only meaning of the word 'or'. There is also what is called the *exclusive* sense of 'or'. If a restaurant menu says, "Soup or salad is included in the price of lunch," it does not mean that the price of both soup and salad is included in the lunch price. It means that the price includes one or the other but not both ($[p \lor q]$ & $\sim[p$ & $q]$). If you bump into other situations where the meaning of 'or' is clearly "one or the other but not both," restate it that way. In all other situations you can assume that the disjunction is true so long as at least one of its disjuncts is true. But this does not mean that every time you find the word 'or' you have found a disjunction.

Disjunction. The wedge ($\lor$), which represents disjunction, is defined as follows:

p	q	$p \lor q$
T	T	T
T	F	T
F	T	T
F	F	F

---

[1]As used in ordinary English, there are subtle differences in the connotations of these words. Generally, if you say that "Joan was an honors student, and she belonged to a sorority," you might mean something a bit different from "Joan was an honors student even though she belonged to a sorority." Nonetheless, the two statements are true under the same conditions, and this is the only relevant consideration when dealing with propositional arguments.

The world would be a nicer place if expressions such as 'either . . . or . . .' always had the same meaning. But there are *at least some* occasions on which 'either' means both. Consider the following passage from Sir Arthur Conan Doyle's *The Lost World*:

> The woods on either side were primeval, which are more easily penetrated than woods of the second growth, and we had no great difficulty in carrying our canoes through them.

"The woods on either side were primeval" means "The woods on *both* sides were primeval." Such uses of 'either' might be rare, but they occur, so you must ask yourself what the author means rather than automatically assuming that if you find the word 'either', you have a disjunction.

A **conditional** statement is of the form 'If . . ., then . . .'. The if clause is known as the **antecedent**. The then clause is known as the **consequent**. A conditional statement is true *except* when the antecedent is true and the consequent is false. So, the conditional statement "If today is Sunday, then we have a critical-thinking class" is probably false on any Sunday,[2] but it is true

Conditionals. The arrow (→), which represents material conditionality, is defined as follows:

p	q	$p \to q$
T	T	T
T	F	F
F	T	T
F	F	T

every other day of the week. There are many words that mean 'if'. Were I to say, "Today is Tuesday only if we have critical thinking," that means the same as "If today is Tuesday, then we have critical thinking." On the other hand, were I to say, "Today is Tuesday if we have critical thinking," that means the same as "If we have critical thinking, then today is Tuesday." The statement "If Chris goes to the movie, then Sam goes to the movie" can also be stated in each of the following ways:

> Chris goes to the movie only if Sam goes to the movie.
>
> Only if Sam goes to the movie, Chris goes to the movie.
>
> Sam goes to the movie if Chris goes to the movie.
>
> Provided that Chris goes to the movie, Sam goes to the movie.
>
> Sam goes to the movie provided that Chris goes to the movie.
>
> Sam goes to the movie on the condition that Chris goes to the movie.
>
> When Chris goes to the movie, Sam goes to the movie.[3]
>
> In case Chris goes to the movie, Sam goes to the movie.

---

[2]This assumes that your school is like any school I've ever attended insofar as there are seldom classes on Saturday, and there are never classes on Sunday.

[3]This also may be stated as "All times that are times when Chris goes to the movie are times when Sam goes to the movie." There is a close conceptual relationship between conditional statements and universal affirmative propositions.

Sam goes to the movie in case Chris goes to the movie.

Chris goes to the movie, in which case Sam goes to the movie.

Chris goes to the movie, in which event Sam goes to the movie.

Had Chris gone to the movie, Sam also would have gone.

The fact that Sam goes to the movie is a necessary condition for Chris to go to the movie.

The fact that Chris goes to the movie is a sufficient condition for Sam to go to the movie.[4]

You should notice that the *consequent* is whatever statement immediately follows 'only if'. You also should notice that the *antecedent* is whatever statement immediately follows the 'if' (so long as the 'if' is *not* preceded by 'only') or synonymous term such as 'provided that' or 'on the condition that'.

A **biconditional** statement is of the form '. . . if and only if . . .'. If I say, "Today is sunny if and only if there is a high pressure system dominating the area," this means "If today is sunny, then there is a high pressure system dominating the area; and if there is a high pressure area dominating the area, then it is sunny." The statement is true if "Today is sunny" and "There is a high pressure system dominating the area" have the same truth value, that is, if they are either both true or both false. Other ways to say '. . . if and only if . . .' are '. . . just in case . . .' and '. . . is a necessary and sufficient condition for . . .'.

Compound statements often are components of more complex statements. We already have noticed that the exclusive sense of 'or' is compound. If you are using the exclusive sense of 'or' and say, "Either Carol went to the movie or Carol went to the play," this can be restated using the inclusive sense of 'or' as follows: "Either Carol went to the movie or Carol went to the play, and it is not the case that both Carol went to the movie and Carol went to the play" ([M ∨ P] & ~[M & P]). Here are a few

---

Biconditionals. The double-arrow (↔), which represents material equivalence, is defined as follows:

p	q	$p \leftrightarrow q$
T	T	T
T	F	F
F	T	F
F	F	T

English to Symbols

Simple sentences should be abbreviated as capital letters. So, "Lucas drives a Ford" might be abbreviated 'L'.

Statements containing two-place connectives (&, ∨, →, ↔) must be grouped two statements at a time. You do this with a combination of parentheses, square brackets ([]), and braces ({}). These **grouping indicators** are to propositional logic what punctuation marks are to English. So, the statement "Either Jan went to the show or Carmen went to the play, only if Umberto wrote lyric poetry" would be represented as: (J ∨ C) → U. Additional examples of translations are given in parentheses in the main text.

---

[4]We discuss the terms 'necessary condition' and 'sufficient condition' in Chapter 22.

other examples in which a compound statement is a component of a more complex statement. "If both Jorge and Eric went to the game, then Dominique studied in the library" ([J & E] → D). "Lucinda went to the movie, and either Umberto did not go to the game or Beatrix rebuilt the engine of her car" (L & [~U ∨ B]). "Although Flo played tennis if and only if Bertie repainted her car, Julio knitted an afghan unless Gus wrote poetry" ([F ↔ B] & [J ∨ G]). "Juanita wrote a novel just in case either Hector wrote sonnets or César studies philosophy only if Alicia studies nuclear physics" (J ↔ {H ∨ [C → A]}). "Juanita wrote a novel just in case Hector wrote sonnets, unless César studies philosophy only if Alicia studies nuclear physics" ([J ↔ H] ∨ [C → A]). "It it not the case that if both Raul and Dimitri wrote music, then Colette rides horses unless Lucinda does not rebuild cars" (~ {[R & D] → [C ∨ ~L]}).

The compound statements with which we are concerned in this chapter are truth-functionally compound. The truth of the whole statement depends upon the truth values of its components. So, to determine the truth value of the compound statement, determine the truth values of the component statements, then use those to determine the truth value of the compound statement. If the statement is composed of one or more compound statements, you must start with the component statements. Let's consider some examples.

"Either South Dakota is north of North Dakota or New York City is a larger town than Peoria, Illinois" (S ∨ N). The statement, "South Dakota is north of North Dakota" is false. The statement, "New York City is a larger town than Peoria, Illinois" is true. A disjunction is true if either disjunct is true. So, the statement is true.

"If Bill Clinton was elected President in 1923, then George W. Bush was born in 1804" (B → G). The statement, "Bill Clinton was elected president in 1923" is false. Whenever the antecedent of a conditional statement is false, the statement is true. So, the statement is true.

"If the Second World War ended during the 1940s, then either London is the capital or France or Paris is the capital of Norway" (S → [L ∨ P]). The antecedent is true, so you have to look at the consequent. The statement "London is the capital of France" is false. The statement "Paris is the capital of Norway" is false. So, the disjunction is false, and the consequent is false. Whenever the antecedent of a conditional is true and the conclusion is false, the conditional is false. So, the statement is false.

"Either snakes are reptiles or trout are fish if and only if both flies are insects and dogs are cats" ([S ∨ T] ↔ [F & D]). Since a biconditional is true if and only if both component statements are true or both component

As statements become more complex, it might be useful to replace the component statements with T and F to represent the truth values of the component statements. So, if you're given, "It is not the case that if either George W. Bush was President in 2002 or Paris is the capital of Rhodesia, then coffee is a meat product if and only if books are made of soap bubbles" (~ [G ∨ P] → (C ↔ B]). So, you replace the statements with their truth values and determine the truth values of the component statements and the truth value of the entire statement. You might chart it as follows:

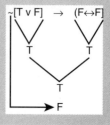

statements are false, you have to check the truth values of both statements. The statement "Snakes are reptiles" is true. A disjunction is true if either of its disjuncts is true. So, the statement "Either snakes are reptiles or trout are fish" is true. The statement "Flies are insects" is true. The statement "Dogs are cats" is false. A conjunction is true if and only if both of its conjuncts are true. Since one of the conjuncts is false, the conjunction is false. So, since the disjunction is true and the conjunction is false, the biconditional is false.

Exercises

Determine the truth value of each of the following statements. If your teacher is treating compound statements symbolically, begin by translating each using the suggested abbreviations.

1. Either <u>D</u> es Moines is the capital of Sweden or <u>C</u> alvin Coolidge was elected President in 2000. (D, C)

2. Both <u>C</u> openhagen is in Sweden and <u>P</u> aris is in France. (C, P)

3. If <u>D</u> allas is a city in Texas, then <u>I</u> celand is a tropical paradise. (D, I)

4. <u>R</u> obert E. Lee was a Confederate general if and only if <u>U</u> .S. Grant was a German general. (R, U)

5. It is not the case that if <u>H</u> awaii is north of Alaska then <u>C</u> Ds are popular among college students. (H, C)

6. If <u>H</u> awaii is not north of Alaska, then <u>C</u> Ds are popular among college students. (H, C)

7. <u>M</u> arie Antoinette was Queen of France only if <u>G</u> eorge Washington was President of Rhodesia. (M, G)

8. <u>M</u> arie Antoinette was Queen of France provided that <u>G</u> eorge Washington was President of Rhodesia. (M, G)

9. If <u>H</u> ollywood is in California, then <u>P</u> eoria is in Sweden only if <u>C</u> hicago is in Illinois. (H, P, C)

10. If <u>H</u> ollywood is in California, then <u>P</u> eoria is in Sweden if <u>C</u> hicago is in Illinois.

11. If <u>D</u> enver is in Colorado if and only if <u>N</u> orway is in Asia, then <u>b</u> eer is popular in Munich. (D, N, B)

12. <u>S</u> an Francisco is in California unless <u>Ne</u> w York City is in Brazil, just in case <u>M</u> oscow is the capital of Virginia. (S, N, M)

13. <u>S</u> an Francisco is in California, unless <u>N</u> ew York City is in Brazil just in case <u>M</u> oscow is the capital of Virginia. (S, N, M)

14. It is not the case the <u>S</u> an Francisco is in California unless <u>Ne</u> w York City is in Brazil, just in case <u>M</u> oscow is the capital of Virginia. (S, N, M)

15. If <u>P</u> atton was a general and <u>N</u> imitz was an admiral, then <u>C</u> uster won the Battle of Little Big Horn, unless <u>A</u> ustin is the capital of Texas. (P, N, C, A)

16. If neither Paris is in France nor Stockholm is in Sweden, then Tuscaloosa is in Iowa; or there are no Democrats in Washington, D.C. (P, S, T, D)

17. If the fact that neither Paris is in France nor Stockholm is in Sweden implies that Tuscaloosa is in Iowa, then there are no Democrats in Washington, D.C. (P, S, T, D)

18. London is in England just in case Moscow is in Russia; but it is not the case that if Johannesburg is in South Africa then Brussels is in New Jersey. (L, M, J, B)

19. Moscow is in Russia provided that London is in England, unless Johannesburg is in South Africa only if it is not the case that Brussels is in New Jersey. (L, M, J, B)

20. Being under two feet tall is a sufficient condition for an adult human being to be short; even though giraffes have long necks if and only if either zebras in the wild wear pajamas or Indian elephants vote a straight Republican ticket. (U, A, G, Z, E)

C H A P T E R   2 1

Truth Tables

The View: The truth table method provides a simple method for determining the validity of any propositional argument form. This chapter introduces the truth table technique.

Is there a systematic way to determine whether arguments based on propositions are valid?

There is a process by which you can determine whether any propositional argument form is valid. This is called the **truth table** method. A truth table shows all possible combinations of truth values for the statements in an argument. We used truth tables in the last chapter to define the connectives ($\sim, \&, \vee, \rightarrow,$ and $\leftrightarrow$). Since the truth table method shows all possible combinations of truth values in an argument, it shows us whether it is possible for all the premises to be true and the conclusion false. Since an argument form is valid unless it is possible for all the premises to be true and the conclusion false, it provides a systematic way to determine the validity of an argument form.

You represent the form of an argument by replacing the statements with variables. So, if you're given the argument

If Lucinda pays volleyball, then either Julio plays squash or Raul plays football.

Lucinda pays volleyball, but Raul does not play football. Therefore, Julio plays squash.

you can represent the argument by replacing the statements with statement abbreviations (capital letters) and introducing symbols to represent 'if . . . , then . . . ' and 'but'. Where the symbol '/∴' replaces the conclusion indicator, the symbolic representation of the argument looks like this:

$$L \rightarrow (J \vee R)$$
$$L \ \& \ \sim R \ / \therefore \ J$$

You can represent the form of the argument by replacing each simple statement with a variable. Where lowercase letters are used as variables, the form of the argument can be represented as follows:

$$p \rightarrow (q \vee r)$$
$$p \mathbin{\&} {\sim}r \mathbin{/} \therefore q$$

As we will see below, this argument form is valid.

A truth table consists of two parts: (1) **guide columns**, which show all possible combinations of the truth values of the simple statements in the argument, and (2) columns for the premises, any component statements of the premises, and the conclusion. If we set up the guide columns correctly and fill in the truth values for the premises and conclusion of an argument, we can determine whether it is possible that (whether there is any row in which) all the premises are true and the conclusion is false.

How many combinations of truth values are there? A statement is either true or false, so if there is one simple statement in an argument, there are two rows. In one row the statement is true. In the other row the statement is false. If there are two simple statements (p and q), there are four rows. In one row both p and q are true. In one row p is true and q is false. In one row p is false and q is true. In one row both p and q are false. If there are three simple statements, there are eight rows. If there are four simple statements, there are sixteen rows. In general, where n is the number of simple statements in an argument, there are 2^n rows in the truth table.

You can *guarantee* that you will include all possible combinations of truth values if you set up your truth table in a systematic way. Introduce columns for each simple variable: p, q, r, s, and so on. Determine the number of rows that will be in the truth table. However many rows are in the truth table, start with the left-hand column and put a T in successive rows until *half* the number of rows in the column are marked with a T, and put an F in the remaining rows. Move to the right, and double the frequency with which you vary Ts and Fs with each column. The rightmost guide column will vary Ts and Fs every other row. So, if you have two simple statements, p and q, the column for p will have Ts in two rows followed by Fs in two rows. The column for q will have T in the first row, F in the second row, T in the third row, and F in the last row. The same pattern is followed as the number of simple statements (and therefore rows) increases. So, the guide columns for arguments with two, three, and four simple statements will *always* look like this:

Where p and q are statements of any degree of complexity,

p	$\sim p$	p	q	$p \mathbin{\&} q$	$p \vee q$	$p \rightarrow q$	$p \leftrightarrow q$
T	F	T	T	T	T	T	T
F	T	T	F	F	T	F	F
		F	T	F	T	T	F
		F	F	F	F	T	T

p	q
T	T
T	F
F	T
F	F

p	q	r
T	T	T
T	T	F
T	F	T
T	F	F
F	T	T
F	T	F
F	F	T
F	F	F

p	q	r	s
T	T	T	T
T	T	T	F
T	T	F	T
T	T	F	F
T	F	T	T
T	F	T	F
T	F	F	T
T	F	F	F
F	T	T	T
F	T	T	F
F	T	F	T
F	T	F	F
F	F	T	T
F	F	T	F
F	F	F	T
F	F	F	F

Once you've filled in the guide columns, you appeal to the definitions of the connectives to determine the truth values for the premises and conclusion *given* the truth values for the simple statements in a given row. To see how this works, consider an argument form named affirming the antecedent. The form of the argument is

$$p \rightarrow q$$
$$p \, / \therefore q$$

You construct a truth table with guide columns for p and q and a column for each premise and the conclusion:

p	q	$p \rightarrow q$	p	q
T	T	T	T	T
T	F	F	T	F
F	T	T	F	T
F	F	T	F	F

You then check to see whether there are any rows in which all the premises are true and the conclusion is false. I find it convenient to go down the column for the conclusion and place a check mark beside any row in which the conclusion is false.

p	q	$p \rightarrow q$	p	q
T	T	T	T	T
T	F	F	T	F ✓
F	T	T	F	T
F	F	T	F	F ✓

Since the argument form is valid *unless* there is a row in which all the premises are true and the conclusion is false, the checked rows are the only ones that *could* show that the argument form is invalid. If you look at those rows, you will notice that in row two, the first premise is false. In row four, the second premise is false. There is no row in which all the premises are true and the conclusion is false. So, the argument form is valid.

Now consider an argument form called affirming the consequent:

$$p \rightarrow q$$
$$q / \therefore p$$

Construct the truth table:

p	q	$p \rightarrow q$	q	p
T	T	T	T	T
T	F	F	F	T
F	T	T	T	F ✓
F	F	T	F	F ✓

In the last two rows the conclusion is false. In the third row both premises are true. The argument form is invalid. By a longstanding tradition, if a truth table shows that an argument or argument form is invalid, you circle the row or rows in which all the premises are true and the conclusion is false.

p	q	$p \rightarrow q$	q	p
T	T	T	T	T
T	F	F	F	T
F	T	T	T	F ✓
F	F	T	F	F ✓

As the number of simple statements increases, there are more rows in the truth table, but the procedure is the same. Consider the argument form called hypothetical syllogism:

$$p \rightarrow q$$
$$q \rightarrow r / \therefore p \rightarrow r$$

We have three simple statements, so the truth table will have eight rows. In the column for each of the premises and the conclusion, you fill in truth values according to the guide columns.

p	q	r	$p \rightarrow q$	$q \rightarrow r$	$p \rightarrow r$
T	T	T	T	T	T
T	T	F	T	F	F ✓
T	F	T	F	T	T
T	F	F	F	T	F ✓
F	T	T	T	T	T
F	T	F	T	F	T
F	F	T	T	T	T
F	F	F	T	T	T

Notice that in the second and fourth rows the conclusion is false. In row two the second premise is false. In row four the first premise is false. There are no cases in which all the premises are true and the conclusion is false. The argument form is valid.

Now consider the argument form at which we looked early in the chapter:

$$p \rightarrow (q \vee r)$$

$$p \ \& \sim r \ / \therefore \ q$$

Notice how this differs from those we have examined so far. The consequent of the first premise and the second conjunct of the second premise are themselves compound statements. In order to determine the truth values of the premises, you must first determine the truth values of the compound component parts. So, you introduce a column for each of the compound statements. The truth table will look like this:[1]

p	q	r	$q \vee r$	$p \rightarrow (q \vee r)$	$\sim r$	$p \ \& \sim r$	q
T	T	T	T	T	F	F	T
T	T	F	T	T	T	T	T
T	F	T	T	T	F	F	F ✓
T	F	F	F	F	T	T	F ✓
F	T	T	T	T	F	F	T
F	T	F	T	T	T	F	T
F	F	T	T	T	F	F	F ✓
F	F	F	F	T	T	F	F ✓

Notice that in determining the truth values for the first premise (second column beyond the guide columns), you use the column for p and the column for $q \vee r$. In determining the truth value for the second premise, you use the column for p and the column for $\sim r$. You are now finished with the column for $q \vee r$ and the column for $\sim r$. *Only* the columns for the premises and conclusion are relevant for validity, so to keep yourself from looking at irrelevant columns, draw a line through the columns for $q \vee r$ and $\sim r$.

p	q	r	$q \vee r$	$p \rightarrow (q \vee r)$	$\sim r$	$p \ \& \sim r$	q
T	T	T	T	T	F	F	T
T	T	F	T	T	T	T	T
T	F	T	T	T	F	F	F ✓
T	F	F	F	F	T	T	F ✓
F	T	T	T	T	F	F	T
F	T	F	T	T	T	F	T
F	F	T	T	T	F	F	F ✓
F	F	F	F	T	T	F	F ✓

Now look at the rows in which the conclusion is false. In row three the second premise is false. In row four the first premise is false. In rows seven and eight the second premise is false. There is no row in which all the premises are true and the conclusion is false. Therefore, the argument form is valid.

---

[1]We will look at a different arrangement below. The difference is merely cosmetic.

There is a slight variation on this which might be called the columns-under-the-connectives approach. In this approach you write the premises and conclusion at the top of the truth table, and when there's a compound component of a premise, you construct a column for that component directly under the component. Do the column for the component *before* you do the column for the entire statement, then do a column for the entire statement and draw a line through the column for the component. To see how this works, consider the following argument form:

$$p \rightarrow q$$
$$(p \ \& \ q) \rightarrow r \ / \therefore \ {\sim}r \rightarrow p$$

Set up the truth table and construct a column for the first premise.

p	q	r	$p \rightarrow q$	$(p \ \& \ q) \rightarrow r$	$\sim r \rightarrow p$
T	T	T	T		
T	T	F	T		
T	F	T	F		
T	F	F	F		
F	T	T	T		
F	T	F	T		
F	F	T	T		
F	F	F	T		

Now construct a column for $p \ \& \ q$ under the ampersand.

p	q	r	$p \rightarrow q$	$(p \ \& \ q) \rightarrow r$	$\sim r \rightarrow p$
T	T	T	T	T	
T	T	F	T	T	
T	F	T	F	F	
T	F	F	F	F	
F	T	T	T	F	
F	T	F	T	F	
F	F	T	T	F	
F	F	F	T	F	

Now use that column to determine the truth value of $(p \ \& \ q) \rightarrow r$ and draw a line through the column for $p \ \& \ q$ when you have finished with the column for the premise.

p	q	r	$p \rightarrow q$	$(p \ \& \ q) \rightarrow r$	$\sim r \rightarrow p$
T	T	T	T	T	T
T	T	F	T	T	F
T	F	T	F	F	T
T	F	F	F	F	T
F	T	T	T	F	T
F	T	F	T	F	T
F	F	T	T	F	T
F	F	F	T	F	T

Proceed the same way with the conclusion and judge the validity of the argument.

p	q	r	$p \rightarrow q$	$(p \& q) \rightarrow r$	$\sim r \rightarrow p$
T	T	T	T	T	T T
T	T	F	T	F	T T
T	F	T	F	T	T T
T	F	F	F	T	T T
F	T	T	T	T	T T
F	T	F	T	T	T F ✓
F	F	T	T	T	T T
F	F	F	T	T	T F ✓

In both rows six and eight the premises are true and the conclusion is false. The argument form is invalid.

Exercises

I. Construct a truth table to determine whether each of the following argument forms is valid. If it is invalid, circle the line or lines showing that the argument form is invalid. Indicate whether it is valid or invalid. (Some of these forms have names. Names are given in parentheses.)

1. $p \& q /\therefore p$ (simplification)

2. $p \& q /\therefore q$ (simplification)

3. $p \rightarrow q$ (denying the consequent)
$\sim q /\therefore \sim p$

4. $p \rightarrow q$ (affirming the consequent)
$q /\therefore p$

5. $p \vee q$ (improper exclusive disjunctive syllogism)
$p /\therefore \sim q$

6. $p \vee q$ (disjunctive syllogism)
$\sim p /\therefore q$

7. $p \vee q$ (disjunctive syllogism)
$\sim q /\therefore p$

8. p (conjunction)
$q /\therefore p \& q$

9. $p \rightarrow (p \& q)$
$q \rightarrow r /\therefore \sim r \rightarrow \sim p$

10. $(p \& q) \rightarrow r$
$\sim r \rightarrow q /\therefore p \vee r$

11. $(\sim p \vee q) \& (q \rightarrow r) /\therefore p \rightarrow r$

12. $(p \vee q) \& \sim (p \& q)$
$p /\therefore q \rightarrow r$

13. $(p \rightarrow q) \,\&\, (r \rightarrow s)$
$p \vee q \,/\therefore\, r \vee s$

14. $(p \rightarrow q) \,\&\, (r \rightarrow s)$ (constructive dilemma)
$p \vee r \,/\therefore\, q \vee s$

15. $(p \rightarrow q) \,\&\, (r \rightarrow s)$ (destructive dilemma)
$\sim q \vee \sim s \,/\therefore\, \sim p \vee \sim r$

II. Translate and construct a truth table for each of the following problems using the statement abbreviations suggested. Note that the solutions in the back of the book are given for the *argument,* not for the argument form. If your instructor asks you to do them for the *form,* substitute *p, q, r,* and *s* (as required) for the statement variables in the order given at the end of each exercise.

1. If Angie went to the dance, then Cleo stayed home. If Cleo stayed home, then Luis went to the library. Either Angie went to the dance or Luis went to the library. So, Cleo stayed home. (A, C, L)

2. If both Angie did not go to the dance and Cleo did not go to the dance, then Luis went to the dance. If Luis went to the dance, then Cleo went to the dance. So, Angie went to the dance. (A, C, L)

3. If Angie went to the dance, then Cleo went to the dance; and if Cleo went to the dance, then Luis went to the dance. Luis did not go to the dance. So, Angie didn't go to the dance. (A, C, L)

4. Luis went to the dance if and only if either Angie or Cleo went to the dance. Angie did not go to the dance. So, if Cleo went to the dance, then Luis went to the dance. (L, A, C)

5. Angie went to the dance and Cleo did not go to the dance if and only if Luis went to the dance. So, if Angie went to the dance, Luis went to the dance; and if Luis did not go to the dance, then Cleo went to the dance. (A, C, L)

6. Angie went to the dance or Cleo did not go to the dance if and only if Luis went to the dance. So, if Angie went to the dance, Luis went to the dance; and if Luis did not go to the dance, then Cleo went to the dance. (A, C, L)

7. If Horatio went to the party, then if Angie went to the dance, then both Cleo and Luis went to the football game. Horatio went to the party, but Angie did not go to the dance. So, Cleo did not go to the football game. (H, A, C, L)

8. Either Juanita sings arias or Ashley dances the polka. If Ashley dances the polka, then Hortense rebuilds cars; and if Drusilla does not write novels, then Hortense does not rebuild cars. Therefore, if Juanita does not sing arias, then Drusilla writes novels. (J, A, H, D)

9. If Sally sells seashells by the seashore, then either Anna or Jose writes editorials for the *Times.* Although Anna does not write editorials for the *Times,* Pierre passes his time playing polo. So, if Sally sells seashells by the seashore, then Jose writes editorials for the *Times* and Pierre passes his time playing polo. (S, A, J, P)

10. Svetlana sings silly syncopated songs just in case Drusilla drugs druids on dry days. Svetlana sings silly syncopated songs unless either Rosetta rides roughshod

over ruinous roads or Carla catches cats with canine cunningness. Rosetta does not ride roughshod over ruinous roads. Thus, Drusilla does not drug druids on dry days. (S, D, R, C)

Tautologies, Contradictions, and Contingent Statements

Statements are of three types. The truth value of a **contingent statement** depends upon the facts. Some days it rains. Some days it does not rain. The truth value of the statement "It is raining" depends upon the weather conditions. Almost all the statements you find in everyday life are contingent statements. The guide columns for any simple statements in a truth table represent contingent statements.

Tautologies are statements that are true in virtue of their forms. Tautologies are always compound statements. The statement "Either it is raining or it is not raining" is a tautology. While the statement is true, it tells you nothing about current weather conditions. Nor does the content make any difference. That it is true in virtue of its form can be shown by a truth table. The column indicating the truth of a tautologous statement will have Ts all the way down. The form of the statement "Either it is raining or it is not raining" is $p \lor \sim p$. The truth table for that statement form looks like this:

p	$p \lor \sim p$
T	T F
F	T T

Regardless what is substituted for p, a statement of the form $p \lor \sim p$ will be true.

Contradictions are statements that are false in virtue of their form. Contradictions are always compound statements. The statement "It is raining, and it is not raining" is a contradiction. What is expressed by a contradiction is logically impossible. That a contradiction is false in virtue of its form can be shown by a truth table. The column indicating the truth of a contradictory statement will have Fs all the way down. The form of the statement "It is raining, and it is not raining," is $p \ \& \sim p$. Its truth table looks like this:

p	$p \ \& \sim p$
T	F F
F	F T

Truth tables can be used to determine whether any statement is a tautology, a contradiction, or a contingent statement. If the column for the statement contains only Ts, the statement is a tautology. If the column for the statement contains only Fs, it is a contradiction. If the column for the statement contains both Ts and Fs, it is a contingent statement.

Exercises

III. Construct a truth table to determine whether each of the following statement forms is tautologous, contradictory, or contingent. Indicate whether it is a tautology, a contradiction, or a contingent statement.

1. $p \rightarrow p$
2. $p \rightarrow \sim p$
3. $p \rightarrow (p \,\&\, q)$
4. $p \rightarrow (p \vee q)$
5. $(p \rightarrow q) \,\&\, (q \rightarrow p)$
6. $(p \leftrightarrow q) \rightarrow (\sim p \leftrightarrow \sim q)$
7. $[(p \vee q) \,\&\, (\sim p \vee q)] \,\&\, [(p \vee \sim q) \,\&\, (\sim p \vee \sim q)]$
8. $[(p \rightarrow q) \,\&\, (\sim q \vee r)] \,\&\, (p \,\&\, \sim r)$
9. $\sim \{(\sim p \,\&\, r) \,\&\, [(p \vee q) \,\&\, (q \rightarrow r)]\}$
10. $\sim \{\sim(\sim p \vee r) \,\&\, [(p \rightarrow q) \,\&\, (\sim q \vee r)]\}$

Logical Equivalence

Two statements are **logically equivalent** if they are true under the same circumstances. This is a matter of the logical form of the two statements. One of your English teachers probably told you that two negatives make a positive. We can show this by means of a truth table. Remember that a biconditional (a statement of material equivalence) is true when the statements on either side of the double-arrow have the same truth value. You can show that two statements are logically equivalent if joining them by a double-arrow is a tautology. So, if your English teacher was right, any statement p should be logically equivalent to not-not-p. Any statement of the form $p \leftrightarrow \sim(\sim p)$ should be a tautology. Let's do the truth table:

p	$p \leftrightarrow \sim (\sim p)$
T	T T F
F	T F T

The biconditional is a tautology. Your English teacher was right, of course.

"Why are we concerned with logical equivalences? Is this just one of those weird things critical-thinking teachers introduce to make our lives more difficult?" I hear you asking yourself. No. Just as we needed to look at equivalent forms of categorical propositions to deal with arguments in ordinary English, we'll see in Chapter 24 that knowing a number of logical equivalences is necessary to sort through propositional arguments. By recognizing that claims of logical equivalence can be tested by truth tables, you will not have to take the claims of logical equivalence in Chapter 24 on faith. Further, should you confront an argument that assumes a claim of logical equivalence that is not included in Chapter 24, you'll have a means to determine whether the statements that the arguer *assumes* are equivalent actually are.

Exercises

IV. Construct a truth table for each of the following to determine whether the biconditional is a tautology (whether the statements flanking the double-arrow are logically equivalent). Indicate whether they are logically equivalent. (The names of some equivalences are given in parentheses.)

1. $\sim(p \vee q) \leftrightarrow (\sim p \mathbin{\&} \sim q)$ (DeMorgan's theorem)

2. $\sim(p \mathbin{\&} q) \leftrightarrow (\sim p \vee \sim q)$ (DeMorgan's theorem)

3. $\sim(p \vee q) \leftrightarrow (\sim p \vee \sim q)$

4. $\sim(p \mathbin{\&} q) \leftrightarrow (\sim p \mathbin{\&} \sim q)$

5. $(p \rightarrow q) \leftrightarrow (\sim p \vee q)$ (material implication)

6. $(p \leftrightarrow q) \leftrightarrow [(p \rightarrow q) \mathbin{\&} (q \rightarrow p)]$ (material equivalence)

7. $(p \leftrightarrow q) \leftrightarrow [(p \mathbin{\&} q) \vee (\sim p \mathbin{\&} \sim q)]$ (material equivalence)

8. $(p \rightarrow q) \leftrightarrow (\sim q \rightarrow \sim p)$ (contraposition, transposition)

9. $[p \rightarrow (q \rightarrow r)] \leftrightarrow [(p \mathbin{\&} q) \rightarrow r]$ (exportation)

10. $[p \rightarrow (q \rightarrow r)] \leftrightarrow [(p \rightarrow q) \rightarrow r]$

CHAPTER 22

Common Propositional Argument Forms

The View: This chapter examines eight of the most common valid propositional argument forms: simplification, conjunction, affirming the antecedent, denying the consequent, hypothetical syllogism, disjunctive syllogism, constructive dilemma, and destructive dilemma. In addition, we examine three common invalid argument forms (fallacies): denying the antecedent, affirming the consequent, and improper exclusive disjunctive syllogism.

Do we always have to construct truth tables to evaluate arguments? Since validity is a formal property, can we use what we learn from truth tables to evaluate arguments in everyday life?

Just as there are valid argument forms (patterns) for categorical arguments, there are a number of common valid propositional argument forms.[1] Let us introduce some variables: *p, q, r,* and *s*. These variables can be replaced by *any* statement. In one instance of an argument form *p* might be replaced by "Today is Tuesday," while in another instance of an argument of the same form *p* might be replaced by "Today is Tuesday, and we will have a test today if and only if our critical-thinking teacher is not ill." In yet another case *p* might be replaced by a negative statement, such as "Today is not Tuesday" or "It is not the case that if today is Tuesday and the sum of the interior angles of a triangle is not equal to 260 degrees, then XYZ Corporation will declare a significant dividend if and only if there is not a bear market on Wall Street and AT&T declares a three-for-two split." What counts as *p* or *q* or *r* or *s* is relative to a given argument. *All* you do is look for a pattern. This will become clear with some examples.

---

[1]We will not look at *all* the valid forms, since there are an infinite number of such forms. It is possible, however, to show that any valid propositional argument form is valid on the basis of a limited number of argument forms plus some cases of logical equivalence. If you are interested in such a set of argument forms, see Daniel E. Flage, *Understanding Logic* (Engelwood Cliffs, NJ: Prentice-Hall, 1995).

Simplification

A conjunction is true if and only if both conjuncts—statements from which it is composed—are true. If you are given the truth of a conjunction of the form p and q, it follows that p is true, and it follows that q is true. So, if you are given the statement "Gene is in class, and Joan is in class if and only if Jan is in class,"

> **Simplification (Simp.)**
> $p \& q /\therefore p$
> $p \& q /\therefore q$

you can conclude "Gene is in class" and you can conclude "Joan is in class if and only if Jan is in class." The forms may be stated as follows:

> p and (yet, but, even though, although, . . .) q.
>
> Therefore, p.
>
> p and (yet, but, even though, although, . . .) q.
>
> Therefore, q.

Conjunction

Conjunction is the flip side of simplification. Its form is

> p
>
> q Therefore, p. and q.

> **Conjunction (Conj.)**
> p
> $q /\therefore p \& q$

If you are given that p is true and you are given that q is true, you can conclude that the statement "Both p and q" is true. So, if you are given "Carter is going to the movies" and you are given "Jayne is going to the movies," you can conclude "Carter is going to the movies, and Jayne is going to the movies," or if you prefer, "Both Carter and Jayne are going to the movies" or "Carter and Jayne are (both) going to the movies."

Affirming the Antecedent

Affirming the antecedent (***modus ponens***) is one of the most common argument forms found in everyday English. Where p and q are any statements, its form is

> If p then q.
>
> p. Therefore, q.

> **Affirming the Antecedent (AA)**
> $p \rightarrow q$
> $p /\therefore q$

An example is

> If Chris went to the movie, then Lynn went to the movie.
>
> Chris went to the movie.
>
> Therefore, Lynn went to the movie.

Another example is

> If both Andre and Heidi are in class, then the instructor will have to keep on her toes.
>
> <u>Both Andre and Heidi are in class.</u>
>
> Therefore, the instructor will have to keep on her toes.

Of course, you might be given the two statements "Andre is in class" and "Heidi is in class" and conjoin them to form the second premise. And, just as in the case of categorical syllogisms, sometimes one of the premises is not stated. If you are given the argument

> <u>If this class is easy, I'll ace it.</u>
>
> Therefore, I'll ace the class.

the premise, "This class is easy," is unstated, but given the conclusion, it has to have been assumed. Knowing what the form of the argument is will guide you to the missing premise. Once you have found the missing premise, then you should ask whether it is true.

Denying the Consequent

Denying the consequent (***modus tollens***) is the flip side of affirming the antecedent. Where p and q are any statements, its form is

If p, then q.

Not q. Therefore, not p.

> **Denying the Consequent (DC)**
> $p \rightarrow q$
> $\sim q / \therefore \sim p$

An example is

> If Sam is in class, then Rosie is in class.
>
> <u>Rosie is not in class.</u>
>
> Therefore, Sam is not in class.

Another example is

> If Sam is in class only if Rosie is in class, then both Lorna and Delores have overslept.
>
> <u>It is not the case that both Lorna and Delores have overslept.</u>
>
> Therefore, it is not the case that Sam is in class only if Rosie is in class.

As in the case of affirming the antecedent, you will find cases in which a premise is unstated:

> <u>If this class is easy, then I'll ace it.</u>
>
> So, this class is not easy.

The missing premise is "I won't ace this class." And sometimes, both a premise and the conclusion are left unstated, but then you will need to show that assuming a premise and a conclusion are warranted by the context in which the conditional statement is given. By itself, a conditional statement is *never* an argument. In the following passage there are a number of conditional statements, but there is no argument:

> Always be careful before you retrieve a file, erase a worksheet, or end a 1-2-3 session that you save the current worksheet if you want to use it again. If you do not save it, you will lose it.
>
> If you want to leave 1-2-3 at this time, issue the following command:
>
> **/Quit Yes**
>
> If you are using a two-disk system, you may see the message "Insert disk with COMMAND.COM in drive A and strike any key when ready." To exit properly and return to the DOS prompt, follow these instructions. (*Note:* COMMAND.COM is on your DOS disk.)[2]

But consider the following:

> A woman called her daughter at college. Her daughter was not home, so the woman left a message on an answering machine. Part of the woman's message was: "If you were in the bathroom, you would have answered by now, so I suppose you're...."

Is there an argument? Sure. It goes like this:

> If you were in the bathroom, you would have answered by now.
>
> You have not answered by now.
> ———————————————————————
> So, you were not in the bathroom.

The context makes clear that no one had answered the phone, and given the conditional statement and the assumed premise, the conclusion follows.

Hypothetical Syllogism ————————————————

Where p, q, and r are statements, the form of a hypothetical syllogism is

> **Hypothetical Syllogism (HS)**
> $p \to q$
> $q \to r \,/\therefore p \to r$

———————————————

[2]Timothy J. O'Leary and Linda I. O'Leary, *The Student Edition of Lotus 1-2-3 Release 2.2: User's Manual* (Reading, MA: Addison-Wesley Publishing Company, 1990), p. 101.

If p, then q.

If q, then r.

Therefore, if p, then r.

An example is

If Fred went to the movie, then Jan went bowling.

If Jan went bowling, then Chris went to the dance.

So, if Fred went to the movie, then Chris went to the dance.

Often there is a long chain of conditional statements. Sometimes there will be an additional premise that either affirms the antecedent of the first conditional or denies the consequent of the last. So, you use that premise in conjunction with affirming the antecedent or denying the consequent to reach the consequent of the final conditional or the denial of the antecedent of the first conditional as a conclusion. For example, if you are given

(1) If today is Friday, then we have a test.

(2) If we have a test, then we party tonight.

(3) Today is Friday.

So, (4) we party tonight.

From (1) and (2) we may conclude that (5), "If today is Friday, then we party tonight," by hypothetical syllogism. Given (5) and (3), we may conclude that (4), "We party tonight," by affirming the antecedent.

Necessary and Sufficient Conditions

If you read scholarly literature for a time, you are almost certain to bump into the terms 'necessary condition' and 'sufficient condition'. Given our understanding of conditional statements and the valid argument forms we have examined, it is easy to draw the distinction.

A **necessary condition** corresponds to the *consequent* of a conditional. It is a condition in the absence of which something will not occur. In a science class you might read that the combustible materials, heat, and the presence of oxygen are all necessary conditions for fire. If you take any one of them away, you will not have a fire. Notice that this reflects the argument form *denying the consequent*.

A **sufficient condition** corresponds to the *antecedent* of a conditional. It is a condition which, if met, guarantees that some other condition holds. Using Lewis M. Terman's scale, having an IQ in excess of 150 is a sufficient condition for being a potential genius; that is, if you have an IQ in excess of 150, then you are a potential genius. (Having an IQ of at least 140 is a necessary condition, according to the Terman scale.) Notice that this reflects the argument form *affirming the antecedent*.

If you are told that p is both a **necessary and a sufficient condition** for q, it is claimed that if p happens, then q happens, and if q happens, then p happens. This corresponds to a *biconditional*.

Disjunctive Syllogism

Where *p* and *q* are statements, the form of a disjunctive syllogism is

Either *p* or *q*.

Not *p*. Therefore, q.

> **Disjunctive Syllogism (DS)**
> $p \vee q$ $p \vee q$
> $\sim p / \therefore q$ $\sim q / \therefore p$

or

Either *p* or *q*.

Not *q*. Therefore, *p*.

An example is

Either Fred or Hilda went to the hockey game.

Fred didn't go to the hockey game.

So, Hilda went to the hockey game.

And sometimes there are more than three disjuncts:

Professor Smith determined that either hypothesis A, hypothesis B, or hypothesis C is true. But she determined that hypothesis A is false, and she determined that hypothesis C is false. So, she concluded that hypothesis B is true.

A significant problem that you will have with disjunctive syllogism is showing that the disjunctive premise is true. It has to cover *all* the relevant possibilities. If it does not, you commit the informal fallacy of false dichotomy.[3] Consider this example. You do not know much about Dana's political views, but you present the following argument:

Either Dana is a Republican or she is a Communist.

She is not a Republican.

So she is a Communist.

Assume the second premise is true. Is the conclusion true? Probably not. The disjunctive premise is probably false. It does not cover all the possibilities. Dana could be a Democrat, a Socialist, a member of the Green Peace Party or of any other party, or she might have no political affiliations. The argument is a valid deductive argument, but since there is no reason to believe that the disjunctive premise is true, there is no reason to believe the conclusion. The argument commits the informal fallacy of false dichotomy. The argument is deductively valid, but assuming the disjunctive premise is false, it is unsound.

---

[3]We discuss this at greater length in Chapter 30.

Constructive Dilemma ————————————————

Where p, q, r, and s are statements, the form of a constructive dilemma is

If p, then q, and if r, then s.

p or r.

So, q or s.

> **Constructive Dilemma (CD)** ————
> $(p \rightarrow q)$ & $(r \rightarrow s)$
> $p \lor r / \therefore q \lor s$

An example is

If today is Wednesday, then we have critical thinking, and if today is Saturday, then we can sleep late.

Either today is Wednesday or today is Saturday.

So, either we have critical thinking or we can sleep late.

Often the consequent of both conditionals is the same, so the argument will have the form

If p, then q, and if r, then q.

Either p or r.

Therefore, q.

Consider the following:

The comedian Mark Lowry once wrote about attempting to skip church as a kid.

"When the church doors were open," I continued, "the Lowry family was all right there. But don't think I didn't try to get out of going, like any normal kid. Many times I'd say, 'Daddy, I'm too sick to go to church.'

"He'd say, 'Throw up and prove it.' If I couldn't throw up, I went to church. And if I *did* throw up, he'd say, 'Now don't you feel better? Let's go to church.' "[4]

Lowry's situation can be restated in the form of a dilemma:

If I throw up, I shall go to church, and if I do not throw up, I shall go to church.

Either I shall throw up or I won't.

So, I shall go to church.

That gives it a bit of a punch.

———————

[4]Mark Lowry, "Gifts in Disguise," *Guideposts*, September 1997, p. 5.

Destructive Dilemma

Where *p, q, r,* and *s* are statements, the form of a destructive dilemma is

If *p,* then *q,* and if *r,* then *s.*

Either not *q* or not *s.*

So, either not *p* or not *r.*

> **Destructive Dilemma (DD)**
> $(p \rightarrow q) \mathbin{\&} (r \rightarrow s)$
> $\sim q \vee \sim s\ /\therefore\ \sim p \vee \sim r$

An example is

If today is Wednesday, then we have critical thinking, and if today is Saturday, then we can sleep late.

Either we do not have critical thinking or we cannot sleep late.

So, either today is not Wednesday or today is not Saturday.

There are a couple things to notice about the dilemmas. First, a constructive dilemma is like a complex affirming the antecedent, and a destructive dilemma is like a complex denying the consequent. Second, since both forms of the dilemma are valid, an attack on the dilemma must take the form of an attack on the premises. This can take any of three forms. (1) If you attack the disjunctive premise (the "or" premise), you are attempting to "go between the horns": You are attacking the assumption that the disjunction covers all possibilities. This was the problem with the example of Dana's political affiliation. (2) If you "grasp the dilemma by the horns," you attempt to show that the conjunctive premise (the "and" premise) is false by showing that one of its components is false. (3) You might construct a counterdilemma. Consider the following. An Athenian mother was attempting to convince her son not to enter politics:

If you say what is just, men will hate you; and if you say what is unjust, the gods will hate you. But you must either say what is just or what is unjust. So, you will be hated.

The son replied:

If I say what is just, the gods will love me; and if I say what is unjust, men will love me. I must say what is just or what is unjust. So, I will be loved.

The problem here is that the conclusion of both the original dilemma and the counterdilemma are compatible: Both could be true at the same time. This is often a problem with attempted refutations by counterdilemmas.

Common Invalid Argument Forms

An invalid deductive argument form is known as a **formal fallacy**. There are two common invalid argument forms that are similar to affirming the antecedent and denying the consequent. These are the formal fallacies of **denying the antecedent** and **affirming the consequent**. Where p and q are statements, the form of denying the antecedent is

If p, then q.

Not p.

Therefore, not q.

> **Fallacy: Denying the Antecedent**
> $$p \rightarrow q$$
> $$\sim p \: / \therefore \: \sim q$$

An example is

If I had all the money made by the movie *Titanic,* then I would be rich.

I do not have all the money made by the movie *Titanic.*

So, I am not rich.

The premises and the conclusion are true. We can show that the argument is invalid by means of a **deductive counterexample**. To construct a deductive counterexample, construct an argument of the same form in which the premises are true and the conclusion is false. The following will do:

If Bill Gates had all the money made by the movie *Titanic,* he would be rich.

Bill Gates does not have all the money made by the movie *Titanic.*

Therefore, Bill Gates is not rich.

The premises are true. As of the writing of this book, Bill Gates, chairman of Microsoft, was one of the wealthiest people in the world, so the conclusion is false. This shows that the form of denying the antecedent is invalid.

Where p and q are statements, the form of **affirming the consequent** is

If p, then q.

q.

Therefore, p.

> **Fallacy: Affirming the Consequent**
> $$p \rightarrow q$$
> $$q \: / \therefore \: p$$

I leave it as an exercise for you to provide a counterexample showing that this form is invalid.

There is also a variant on disjunctive syllogism that some students find tempting. This may be called **improper exclusive disjunctive syllogism**. As we note in Chapter 20, there are cases in which the sense of 'or' is exclusive. In such cases you might argue,

I am having either soup or salad with lunch (but not both).

I am having soup.

So, I am not having salad.

This form is valid. The form of the argument is

Either p or q, and not both p and q.

p.

Not q.

> $$(p \vee q) \: \& \: \sim(p \: \& \: q)$$
> $$p \: / \therefore \: \sim q$$

If you question whether this form is valid, construct a truth table.

We usually do not use the exclusive sense of 'or'. If you argue in the same way using the *inclusive* sense of 'or', you commit the fallacy of **improper exclusive disjunctive syllogism**. The form of that fallacious argument is as follows:

<table>
<tr><td>

p or *q*.

p.____

So, not *q*.

</td><td>

Fallacy: Improper Exclusive Disjunctive Syllogism _____

$p \vee q$ $p \vee q$

$p / \therefore \sim q$ $q / \sim p$

</td></tr>
</table>

But it is easy to show that *this* form is invalid. Consider the following:

> Either the author of this book is over forty or he has a large bald spot.
>
> The author of this book is over forty._____
>
> So, the author of this book does not have a large bald spot.

The premises are true. The conclusion, alas, is false. The argument form is invalid.

As in the case of disjunctive syllogism, there is a second version of improper exclusive disjunctive syllogism:

> *p* or *q*.
>
> *q*._____
>
> Therefore, not *p*.

If you have any doubt that this form is also invalid, redo the previous deductive counterexample beginning with the premise, "Either the author of this book has a large bald spot or he is over forty."

Exercises

Identify the argument forms by letter according to the following scheme: (A) affirming the antecedent, (B) denying the consequent, (C) hypothetical syllogism, (D) disjunctive syllogism, (E) simplification, (F) conjunction, (G) constructive dilemma, (H) destructive dilemma, (I) the fallacy of denying the antecedent, (J) the fallacy of affirming the consequent, or (K) the fallacy of improper exclusive disjunctive syllogism.

1. John went to the dance, and Joan went to the dance. So, John went to the dance.

2. If Sam went to the dance, then Chris went to the dance. Chris did not go to the dance. So, Sam did not go to the dance.

3. Either Carter aced the test or Sydney slept through class. Sydney did not sleep through class. So, Carter aced the test.

4. Either Carter is a student at this school or she is enrolled in this critical-thinking class. Carter is enrolled in this class. Therefore, Carter is not a student at this school.

5. If Sydney is a sophomore, then she has at least thirty hours of academic credit, and if Sydney is a freshman, then she has fewer than thirty hours of academic credit. Either Sydney is a sophomore or Sydney is a freshman. So, either Sydney has more than thirty hours of academic credit or she has fewer than thirty hours of academic credit.

6. If Jan is registered in this course, then Jean is registered in this course. Jan is not registered in this course. So, Jean is not registered in this course.

7. If Dan writes a paper, then Jan writes a paper; and if Jan writes a paper, then Sam is confused. So, if Dan writes a paper, Sam is confused.

8. Jan writes a paper only if Sam is confused. Jan writes a paper. Thus, Sam is confused.

9. If Lynn writes songs, then Theodora is a famous singer; and if Wilfred writes plays, then Theodora is a famous actress. Either Theodora is not a famous singer or she is not a famous actress. So, either Lynn does not write songs or Wilfred does not write plays.

10. Either some people from the planet Vulcan were presenters at the Academy Awards presentation (which might explain the green tinge and pointed ears of some presenters) or some people need new makeup artists. No people from the planet Vulcan were presenters at the Academy Awards. Hence, some people need new makeup artists.

11. If Clare is a math major, then I can trust her to do the calculations for my income tax. But Clare is not a math major. Ergo, I cannot trust Clare to do the calculations for my income tax.

12. Merle is a woman. Merle is a teacher. So, we may conclude that Merle is a woman and a teacher.

13. If Clare is a math major, then I can trust her to do the calculations for my income tax. I can trust Clare to do the calculations for my income tax. So, Clare is a math major.

14. If Jerry is a tax accountant, then I can trust her to complete my income tax forms. I cannot trust Jerry to complete my income tax forms. Therefore, Jerry is not a tax accountant.

15. If Herb is not a philosopher, then I cannot assume that Herb has an adequate understanding of Descartes's ontological argument for the existence of God. Herb is not a philosopher. Hence, I cannot assume Herb has an adequate understanding of Descartes's ontological argument for the existence of God.

16. Chris is not a *Star Trek* fan unless she has pointed ears. Chris is not a *Star Trek* fan, from whence it follows that Chris does not have pointed ears.

17. Provided that Zola plays the tuba, Zola plays in the band; and Ola attends the university on a tuba scholarship provided that she plays the tuba. Either Zola or Ola plays the tuba. So, either Zola plays in the band or Ola attends the university on a tuba scholarship.

18. Fred goes to the movies provided that Chris goes to the movies. Fred goes to the movies only if Jan goes to the movies. Hence, Jan goes to the movies on the condition that Chris goes to the movies.

19. Ima is the governor's daughter even though she is a graduate of the university. So, Ima is a graduate of the university.

20. Ima is the governor's daughter unless she is a graduate of Smith. Ima is not a graduate of Smith. Therefore, Ima is the governor's daughter.

21. In the event that Chris writes books in her spare time, John is Chris's literary agent; and Cassandra is Lulu's editor if Lulu writes books. But John is not Chris's literary agent unless Cassandra is not Lulu's editor. So, either Chris does not write books in her spare time or Lulu does not write books.

22. If either Jan or Jean is enrolled in this class, then Fran has a study partner. But it is not the case that either Jan or Jean is enrolled in this class. Hence, Fran does not have a study partner.

23. The fact that Merle does not smoke cheap cigars is a necessary condition for Merle's healthy life style. Merle has a healthy life style. Thus, Merle does not smoke cheap cigars.

24. The fact that Merle smokes cheap cigars is a sufficient condition for her to be avoided by her friends. Merle is avoided by her friends. So, Merle smokes cheap cigars.

25. If Lynn does not do well in this class, then she is seeking a tutor; and Sam is making ten dollars an hour provided that she is freelancing as a computer programmer. But Lynn is not seeking a tutor unless Sam is not making ten dollars an hour. So, either it is not the case that Lynn does not do well in this class or Sam is not freelancing as a computer programmer.

26. Since Carter studies computer science provided that Sydney studies religion, and since Jean studies nuclear physics if Carter studies computer science, we may conclude that if Sydney studies religion, then Jean studies nuclear physics.

27. Sam is not a physics major, for Lynn is a psychology major only if Sam is a physics major, and Lynn is not a psychology major.

28. Sam is not a physics major, for Lynn is a psychology major on the condition that Sam is a physics major, and Lynn is not a psychology major.

29. Unless Sam is a physics major, Lynn is a psychology major. Sam is not a physics major. So, Lynn is a psychology major.

30. Jen finds this exercise confusing on the condition that George is her study partner, and Kat considers these exercises fun only if Jill is confused. But either Jen does not find this exercise confusing or Jill is not confused. So, either George is not Jen's study partner or Kat does not consider these exercises fun.

31. The British Ambassador in Berlin handed the German government a final note stating that unless we heard from them, . . . they were prepared at once to withdraw their troops from Poland, and a state of war would exist between us. No

such undertaking has been received. Consequently, as of today, September the 3, 1939, this country is at war with Germany.   (*The X-Files: Triangle*, originally broadcast on the Fox Broadcasting Company, November 22, 1998)

32. "No blood on the walls. It was a single slash, very strong, cutting jugular and carotid. There wouldn't have been a gusher, so to speak, but some significant blood would have hit the walls if he'd been facing in or out." She pointed in, "And it wasn't back there either."

"Rain," the chief reminded her. "And it was at least an hour before he was found."

She nodded, "But the trail, even after that time, seemed pretty clear, at least from the pictures." She looked up, squinting, using her chin to show the chief the opposing roof's slight overhang, bulging with sagging copper gutters; it may have been raining, but only a downpour would have made the alley as soaked as the street. "He was facing the wall." (Charles Grant, *The X-Files: Goblins* [New York: HarperPrism, 1994], pp. 97–98)

33. "You can *see* that the area is thoroughly stable—if seismic tremors occurred frequently, these ruins would have been leveled centuries ago. The mere fact that Xitaclan remains standing provides incontrovertible evidence that this land is phenomenally stable."   (Kevin J. Anderson, *The X-Files: Ruins* [New York: HarperPrism, 1996], p. 115)

34. "We lost bouyancy," Suzanne reported.

"We suddenly got heavier or the water got lighter," Donald said as he scanned the instrumentation.

"What does that mean?" Perry demanded.

"Since we obviously didn't get heavier, the water indeed got lighter." (Robin Cook, *Abduction* [New York: Berkley Books, 2000], p. 51)

35. "If you don't serve your clients well, you can't serve your shareholders well; if you don't serve your people well, you can't serve your clients well. To serve your people well means being effective in the community that they work in and that they live in, and it's just reductive and tunnel vision to think otherwise. You have to think of the linkages to long-term shareholder value across all your stakeholder commmmunities." (Dennis Weatherstone, quoted in Charles J. Fombrun, *Reputation: Realizing Value from the Corporate Image* [Boston: Harvard Business School Press, 1996], p. 128)

Enthymemes, Argument Chains, and Other Hazards

The View: Sometimes arguments are not fully stated. If you know the forms that were introduced in the last chapter, you will be able to fill in an unstated premise or the conclusion if given the premises. Just as simple statements can be put together to form compound statements, arguments can be put together to form more complex arguments. The conclusion of one argument will be a premise for the next. Arguments can form chains.

Are there the same pitfalls for propositional arguments that we noticed when examining syllogisms? Are arguments always fully stated? What do we do if they are not? Can the argument forms we have examined be parts of more complex arguments?

As we noted when discussing categorical syllogisms, there are occasions when a given argument leaves a premise or its conclusion unstated. This also holds regarding propositional arguments. You must ask yourself the same kinds of questions as you did when dealing with categorical syllogisms: What premise would yield a valid argument? What conclusion, if any, follows with necessity from the premises? Is the missing premise or conclusion true?

If a premise is missing, the procedure is straightforward. Compare what you have with the argument forms to determine what the missing premise *must* be if the form is valid or if it commits one of the formal fallacies. Consider the following:

> Either Jean went to the movie (*M*) or he went to the dance (*D*). So, he went to the dance.

What you have is

> Either *M* or *D*.
>
> So, *D*.

The first premise is a disjunction. The only argument forms involving disjunctions are disjunctive syllogism, the dilemmas, and the fallacy of improper exclusive disjunctive syllogism. The conclusion is not a disjunction, so it cannot be one of the dilemmas. So, you are confronting either a disjunctive syllogism or an improper exclusive disjunctive syllogism. The conclusion is the affirmation of the second disjunct in the premise rather than its denial, so it cannot be an improper exclusive disjunctive syllogism. Hence, it must be a disjunctive syllogism. So, the missing premise must be not-M: "Jean did not go to the movie."[1]

Now consider this one:

> If Sydney (S) went to the movie, then Chris (C) went to the dance.
>
> So, Chris went to the dance.

You have this:

$$\text{If } S, \text{ then } C.$$
$$\text{So, } C.$$

The only forms that include a conditional statement as a premise and either the antecedent or the consequent of that conditional as the conclusion are affirming the antecedent, denying the consequent, and the fallacies denying the antecedent and affirming the consequent. The consequent of the given conditional is the conclusion. The only one of those forms in which the consequent is the conclusion is affirming the antecedent, so that has to be the form of the argument assumed. So, the assumed premise must be S: "Sydney went to the movie."

Now consider this one:

> If Sydney (S) went to the movie, then Chris (C) went to the dance.
>
> So, Sydney went to the movie.

You have this:

$$\text{If } S, \text{ then } C.$$
$$\text{So, } S.$$

The possibilities are the same as in the previous case, but here your conclusion is the antecedent of the conditional. The only form in which the conclusion is the antecedent of the conditional is the fallacy of affirming the consequent. Affirming the consequent is a *fallacy*. So, indicate that the argument commits the fallacy of affirming the consequent and explain why it is reasonable to hold that the argument does so.

And, of course, English is as rich a language when you are dealing with propositional arguments as it is when you are dealing with syllogisms. You must be aware of

---

[1]Notice also that this *solution* was reached by successive applications of disjunctive syllogism.

synonyms, antonyms, complementary terms, contexts, and so forth. The following argument is an example of denying the antecedent:

> "I understand you," Scrooge returned, "and I would do it, if I could. But I have not the power, Spirit. I have not the power."[2]

Notice that "I have not the power" is a fancy way to say, "I can't."

There are times when an argument is presented, but it is not presented in a standard way. **Rhetorical questions**, that is, questions that presuppose an answer, can be an effective way to make a point. So, if you confront a rhetorical question, treat it as a statement. At other times, you will have questions that presuppose an answer even if they are not typical rhetorical questions. Consider the following argument:

> My response to those who say racism is a thing of the past is to say that if we have eliminated racism, why doesn't the American workplace look like the face of America?
>
> If racism does not exist, why, in 1992, did 46.1 percent of black children under age 18 live in poverty, compared to 16.9 percent of European American children?
>
> If racism does not exist, why are black babies in America twice as likely to die within the first year of life as European American babies?
>
> If racism does not exist, why, in November 1994, were 31.7 percent of black teenagers in the labor force out of work, while only 12.9 percent of European American youths faced with the same plight?
>
> These statistics, compiled by the U.S. government, make a lie out of claims that reverse discrimination has made blacks a privileged class in America.[3]

We have a series of conditional *questions,* but the author's point is clearly that these questions are to be understood as conditional *statements* together with the denial of the consequent. So, for example, the question, "If racism does not exist, why, in November 1994, were 31.7 percent of black teenagers in the labor force out of work, while only 12.9 percent of European American youths faced with the same plight?" is to be understood as the following argument:

If racism does not exist, then it is not the case that 31.7 percent of black teenagers in the labor force are out of work, while only 12.9 percent of European American youths face the same plight.

But it is the case that 31.7 percent of black teenagers in the labor force are out of work, while only 12.9 percent of European American youths face the same plight.

Therefore, racism does exist.

---

[2]Charles Dickens, *A Christmas Carol.*
[3]Terry Jones, "The Quest for Convenient Scapegoats and Other Foolish Errands," *Academe: Bulletin of the American Association of University Professors* 81 (November–December 1994): p. 15.

> **Racism still exists and that is why we still need affirmative action.**

Were there any question that this is the author's intended conclusion, any doubt is set aside by the presence of a text box on the same page as the series of questions:

Dilemmas are often enthymematic. Often the disjunctive premise is missing. Further, sometimes the context shows that one—or in the case of a more complex dilemma, several—of the disjuncts in the conclusion are to be rejected. So, in the following exchange you must conclude that the only viable option is that spelled out by Eragian:

> "Allow me to explain," said Picard. "As the Federation sees it, your empire is in a no-win situation. If you keep the prisoners, they become symbols of oppression to all those who already sympathize with their movement. If you kill them, they become martyrs, and the pot of discontent gets stirred even more quickly. But if you turn them over to us . . ."
>
> "I see your point now," Eragian replied—though of course he must have seen it from the beginning. "If I release the prisoners, they will be seen as exiles. Examples of Federation weakness, who couldn't make it in the Empire."[4]

The disjunctive premise is "Either you keep the prisoners, or you kill them, or you release them." From this you conclude, "Either the prisoners become symbols of oppression to all those who already sympathize with their movement, or they become martyrs, and the pot of discontent gets stirred even more quickly, or they will be seen as exiles." Neither of the first two options in the conclusion could be acceptable to the Empire. So, Eragian should accept the last disjunct in the conclusion.

Finally, there are cases in which the argument form is present, but the argument is stated in such a way that the premises are not clear. In other cases you are given information that is not directly relevant to the argument. Consider the following argument from Frederick Copleston's *A History of Philosophy*:

> It may be objected that in this case St. Bonaventure is simply a theologian and not a philosopher at all; but one can give a similar answer in the case of Bonaventure as in that of Augustine. If one were to define a philosopher as one who pursues the study of being or ultimate causes, or whatever other object one is pleased to assign the philosopher, without reference to revelation and prescinding *completely* from dogmatic philosophy, the Christian dispensation and supernatural order, then of course neither Augustine nor Bonaventure could be termed a philosopher; but **if one is willing to admit into the ranks of philosophers all those who pursue what are generally recognized as philosophical themes, then both men must be recognized as philosophers.** Bonaventure may sometimes treat, for instance, the stages of the soul's assent from knowledge of God through creatures to immediate and interior experience of God and he may speak of the stages without demarcation of what is

---

[4]Michael Jan Friedman, *Star Trek: The Next Generation: Crossover* (New York: Pocket Books, 1995), p. 111.

proper to theology and what is proper to philosophy; but that does not alter the fact that in treating of knowledge of God through creatures, he develops proofs of God's existence and that these proofs are reasoned arguments and so can be termed philosophical arguments. Again, Bonaventure's interest in the material world may be principally an interest in that world as the manifestation of God and he may delight to see therein *vestigia* of the Triune God, but that does not alter the fact that he holds certain opinions about the nature of the world and its constitution which are cosmological, philosophical, in character. It is true that to isolate Bonaventure's doctrines is in a sense to impair the integrity of his system; but there are philosophical doctrines in his system and this fact entitles him to a place in the history of philosophy.[5]

I have boldfaced the conditional statement with which we initially shall be concerned. Can you take the statement at face value? Perhaps not. What the *passage* makes clear is that Copleston is arguing that Bonaventure should be considered a philosopher. If you include the phrase "one is willing to admit into the ranks of philosophers" as a proper part of the antecedent, Copleston does *not* show that Bonaventure is a philosopher: Who can determine what "one is willing to admit"? But the *sense* of the conditional can be stated this way: "If anyone who pursues generally recognized philosophical themes is a philosopher, then Bonaventure was a philosopher," or as an instance thereof, "If Bonaventure pursued recognized philosophical themes, then Bonaventure was a philosopher." But Copleston does not *say* that Bonaventure is a person who pursued generally recognized philosophical themes. Rather, he gives examples of generally recognized philosophical themes Bonaventure pursued, namely, arguments for the existence of God and cosmological arguments. So *implicit* in the passage is the premise, "Bonaventure pursued recognized philosophical themes." Taking this into account, we can restate Copleston's argument as follows:

If Bonaventure pursued generally recognized philosophical themes, then Bonaventure was a philosopher.

Bonaventure pursued recognized philosophical themes.

So, Bonaventure was a philosopher.

This is a nice case of affirming the antecedent. As in the case of categorical syllogisms in ordinary English, you have to pay attention not only to the words that are actually used, but to what appears to be the author's intent. Copleston's *intent* was almost certainly to convince the reader that Bonaventure was a philosopher. (Some reason to believe this may be drawn from the title of his book: *A History of Philosophy*.) Recognizing this, and recognizing that Copleston gives examples of philosophical themes Bonaventure pursued, one can *reconstruct* his implicit argument as a case of affirming the antecedent. One's *reconstruction* shows what Copleston *meant* in offering the argument.

---

[5]Frederick Copleston, *A History of Philosophy*, vol. 2, *Medieval Philosophy*, part 1 (Garden City, NY: Doubleday Image Books, 1962), p. 273, emphasis added.

Is the affirming the antecedent the only argument in the paragraph? No, but again, some rewording is necessary. Copleston sets forth his argument in terms of a comparison to Augustine. Indeed, in the conditional statements in sentence two, Augustine and Bonaventure would seem to stand or fall together as philosophers. Since virtually everyone would consider Augustine a philosopher, one might claim that there is an implicit argument by analogy, an inductive argument.[6] The argument might be put as follows:

Augustine was a philosopher.

Bonaventure is like Augustine in terms of the topics and issues he pursued (they were alike in all the relevant ways).

So Bonaventure is a philosopher.[7]

Nor is it clear that this is the only additional argument in the passage. Notice that the sentence from which the conditional statement that provided the basis for our previous affirming the antecedent contained another conditional statement: "If one were to define a philosopher as one who pursues the study of being or ultimate causes, or whatever other object one is pleased to assign the philosopher, without reference to revelation and prescinding *completely* from dogmatic philosophy, the Christian dispensation and supernatural order, then of course neither Augustine nor Bonaventure could be termed a philosopher." Recognizing the conclusion that Bonaventure is a philosopher, and reformulating this second conditional to apply only to Bonaventure, one might suggest that Copleston is drawing an implicit conclusion on the basis of denying the consequent:

If a philosopher is one who pursues the study of being or ultimate causes, or whatever other object one is pleased to assign the philosopher, without reference to revelation and prescinding *completely* from dogmatic philosophy, the Christian dispensation, and supernatural order, then Bonaventure was not a philosopher.

Bonaventure was a philosopher (it is not the case that Bonaventure was not a philosopher).

So, it is not the case that a philosopher is one who pursues the study of being or ultimate causes, or whatever other object one is pleased to assign the philosopher, without reference to revelation and prescinding *completely* from dogmatic philosophy, the Christian dispensation, and supernatural order.[8]

When you find a complex passage, you should look for *all* the arguments in the passage. Since you will sometimes need to reformulate the arguments so that they are

---

[6]We examine criteria for evaluating arguments by analogy in Chapter 25.

[7]You might even suggest that there is an additional case of affirming the antecedent. If Augustine was a philosopher, then Bonaventure was a philosopher. Augustine was a philosopher. So, Bonaventure was a philosopher. When *reconstructing* arguments, there often are several possible ways to proceed.

[8]I wish to thank Kimberly Criner for bringing this implicit argument to my attention.

clearly of a particular form, the arguments you present will not always correspond directly to the wording in the passage. In this way, propositional arguments are like categorical syllogisms in ordinary English. Further, sometimes when you draw one conclusion, it becomes clear that other elements of the passage provide the basis for an additional conclusion. Passages often contain *chains* of arguments. The conclusion of one argument is a premise for another argument.

As our previous example illustrates, sometimes you will have a set of premises and you will draw a conclusion from them using several argument forms in succession. Here is an example:

Either today is <u>S</u>aturday or this <u>e</u>xercise is easy. If today is <u>F</u>riday, then it is not <u>S</u>aturday. Today is <u>F</u>riday. So, ...

1.	S ∨ E	
2.	F → ~ S	
3.	F	
4.	~ S	2, 3 AA
5.	E	1, 4 DS

Given the second and third premise, we can conclude that "Today is not Saturday" by affirming the antecedent. Given the first premise and the statement "Today is not Saturday," we can conclude that "The exercise is easy" by disjunctive syllogism.

Exercises

I. Identify the argument forms by letter according to the following scheme: (A) affirming the antecedent, (B) denying the consequent, (C) hypothetical syllogism, (D) disjunctive syllogism, (E) simplification, (F) conjunction, (G) constructive dilemma, (H) destructive dilemma, (I) the fallacy of denying the antecedent, (J) the fallacy of affirming the consequent, or (K) the fallacy of improper exclusive disjunctive syllogism. In some cases, a premise or conclusion is missing. If a premise or conclusion is missing, state it.

1. If the test is easy, then I'll do well. If I do well, I'll make the dean's list. So, if the test is easy, I'll make the dean's list.

2. Joan is both bright and popular. So, Joan is bright.

3. The test is short, if I complete it in the assigned time. But the test is not short. So, I won't complete it in the assigned time.

4. Either the test is short or I'll have trouble finishing it before the end of the hour. But I won't have trouble completing it before the end of the hour. So, the test is short.

5. If the instructor is kind, then he has written an easy test. But he has not written an easy test. So, you know what follows!

6. If the test is easy, I'll do well. So, I'll do well.

7. Either this test is easy or the instructor is a mean old man. So, this test is easy.

8. If Chris is a philosophy major, then Chris has read Plato; and if Chris is an English major, then Chris has read Milton. So, either Chris has read Plato or Chris has read Milton.

9. The Scottish philosopher David Hume defined the word *miracle* as "a violation of a law of nature." His definition implies that miracles do not occur, for either there are laws of nature or there are not. If there are laws of nature, then miracles are impossible, since it makes no sense to violate a law of nature (such as the law of universal gravitation). But if there are no laws of nature, then there can be no miracles, since there is nothing to violate. So, there are no miracles.

10. "So I told Della Street that if I wasn't back in five minutes to call the police. I didn't get back in five minutes, and she called the police." (Erle Stanley Gardner, *The Case of the Grinning Gorilla* [New York: Pocket Books, 1952], p. 97)

11. Alas! Why does man boast of sensibilities superior to those apparent in the brute; it only renders them more necessary beings. If our impulses were confined to hunger, thirst, and desire, we might be nearly free; but now we are moved by every wind that blows, and a chance word or scene that that word may convey to us. (Mary W. Shelley, *Frankenstein*)

12. Reiteration is essential in persuading the reader to practice; to try and try again. If water wears away a stone, so does emphasis, even at the danger of repetition, wear away our apathy toward self-betterment. (Norman Vincent Peale, *A Guide to Confident Living* [New York: Prentice-Hall, 1948], p. viii)

13. "From the time I first began to check through the Helen Cadmus diaries I have been impressed by two things. One of them is that no member of the crew specifically mentioned seeing Helen Cadmus aboard the yacht after they got down to the outer harbor. The other one is that you can't explain what became of the papers she had been typing. Either she took them to Benjamin Addicks, in which event Benjamin Addicks' story to the police was false; or else they were left in the stateroom, in which event someone else surreptitiously removed them. (Erle Stanley Gardner, *The Case of the Grinning Gorilla* [New York: Pocket Books, 1952], p. 158)

14. If he had been anxious for secrecy, he would not have left the paper while I was by; but he rather pushed it towards me than towards you. (Jane Austen, *Emma*)

15. "Had the volume been an unusual one, he would have sent it to me. Instead of that, he had intended, before his plans were nipped, to send me the clue in this envelope. He says so in his note. This would seem to indicate that the book is one which he thought I would have no difficulty in finding for myself. He had it—and he imagined that I would have it, too. In short, Watson, it is a very common book." (Sir Arthur Conan Doyle, *Valley of Fear*)

16. Ceremony, and even, silence, from whatever motive they may arise, have a hurtful tendency, when they give the least degree of countenance to base and wicked performances; wherefore, if this maxim be admitted, it naturally follows, that the King's Speech, as being a piece of finished villainy, deserved, and still deserves, a general execration both by the Congress and the people. (Thomas Paine, *Common Sense*)

17. "Don't you be afraid of that," returned the woman. "I ain't so fond of his company that I'd loiter about him for such things, if he did. Ah. You may look through that

shirt till your eyes ache; but you won't find a hole in it, nor a threadbare place. It's the best he had, and a fine one too. They'd have wasted it, if it hadn't been for me."

"What do you call wasting of it?" asked old Joe.

"Putting it on him to be buried in, to be sure," replied the woman with a laugh. "Somebody was fool enough to do it, but I took it off again. If calico ain't good enough for such a purpose, it isn't good enough for anything. It's quite as becoming to the body. He can't look uglier than he did in that one." (Charles Dickens, *A Christmas Carol*)

18. "Now, of course he may have reasoned the way Paul did, that the gun would be somewhere in my desk. But the way the thing was planned this man had to *know* where the gun was."

"I don't follow you on that," Della Street said.

"If he had anticipated a long search," Mason explained, "he'd have told the cleaning woman he had some work to do and didn't want to be disturbed.

"He didn't do that. He told her he was catching a plane and had stopped in to get some papers. That meant he had committed himself to quick action, a hurried in-and-out affair." (Erle Stanley Gardner, *The Case of the Daring Divorcee* [New York: Pocket Books, 1964], p. 93)

19. It may be that when we reach Para we shall stop to refit. If we do, this letter will be a mail ahead. If not, it will reach London on the very day that I do. In either case, my dear Mr. McArdle, I hope very soon to shake you by the hand. (Sir Arthur Conan Doyle, *The Lost World*)

20. "You mean that someone waded across the moat?"

"Exactly!"

"Then if you were in the room within half a minute of the crime [as you were], he must have been in the water at that very moment."

"I have not a doubt of it. I wish to heaven that I had rushed to the window! But the curtain screened it, as you can see, and so it never occurred to me. Then I heard the step of Mrs. Douglas, and I could not let her enter the room. It would have been too horrible." (Sir Arthur Conan Doyle, *Valley of Fear*)

21. "Sir, if I tell you the true tale you will kill me, though there are many other witnesses and you cannot hope to find them all. But if I tell you a lie, you will find some of the witnesses and discover that I lied, and you will kill me. So my only choice is which tale will give me the quicker death. Perhaps I should hold my tongue altogether." (Vonda N. McIntyre, *Star Trek: Enterprise: The First Adventure* [New York: Pocket Books, 1986], p. 185)

22. If we were clever enough to anticipate nature's twists and turns, we might be able to store all the genes we need. But we have overestimated our own omniscience and underestimated the complexity and subtlety of the natural system with which we are interfering. (Al Gore, *Earth in the Balance* [Boston: Houghton Mifflin, 1992], p. 130)

23. "This is an alliance which, whoever—whatever your friends may be, must be agreeable to them, provided at least they have common sense; and we are not to

be addressing our conduct to fools. If they are anxious to see you happily married, here is a man whose amiable character gives every assurance of it;—if they wish to have you settled in the same country and circle which they have chosen to place you in, here it will be accomplished; and if their only object is that you should, in the common phrase, be well married, here is the comfortable fortune, the respectable establishment, the rise in the world which must satisfy them." (Jane Austen, *Emma*)

24. All she needed was someone to challenge Spock when the time came: and Stonn, who had desired her then, had been willing.

    If you lost, then Stonn would be mine. If you won, then you would release me because I had challenged, and still there would be Stonn. And if your captain won, then he would release me because he did not want me, and Stonn would still be there.... (Diane Duane, *Star Trek: Spock's World* [New York: Pocket Books, 1988], p. 282)

25. The gods either have power or they have not. If they have not, why pray to them? If they have, then instead of praying to be granted to be spared such-and-such a thing, why not rather pray to be delivered from dreading it, or lusting for it, or grieving over it? Clearly, if they can help a man at all, they can help him in this way. (Marcus Aurelius, *Meditations*, trans. by Maxwell Staniforth [Baltimore: Penguin Books, 1964], Book 9, §40, p. 147)

26. After dinner on Sundays, my Grandpa Bemis would take a nap, with the *Times,* or something, thrown over his face to keep out the glare. If he was in a good humor when he awoke, he would take us youngsters up to Dick Canfield's to play games, but as he was never in a good humor when he awoke, we never went to Dick Canfield's to play games. (Frank Sullivan, "The Night the Old Nostalgia Burned Down," in *Russell Baker's Book of American Humor*, Ed. Russell Baker [New York: W. W. Norton, 1993], p. 526)

27. **Bernardo:** You look so much like your mother.

    Elena: How would you know that?

    Bernardo: Well ... I don't see much of Don Rafael [her father] in you. (*The Mask of Zorro* [Culver City, CA: Columbia-Tri Star Home Video, 1998])

28. **Spock:** According to our data banks, this ship fired those torpedoes. If we did, the killers are here. If we did not, whoever altered the data banks is here. In either case, what we are looking for is here. (*Star Trek VI: The Undiscovered Country*, Paramount Pictures, 1991)

29. The second major myth about laughter is that we laugh because we are happy, when the reality is we're happy because we laugh. I ask my groups how many feel better after they have laughed, and there is always a unanimous show of hands....

    I think that laughter has been assigned the job of indicating happiness because we have been so desperate for some outward sign of this vague, undefined, but treasured state. Actually, most people (I am certainly one of them) don't know what happiness is. We know the Declaration of Independence directs us to pursue it, but judging by our national behavior, we are somewhat confused about where happiness lies. If we feel better after we laugh, then laughter must come from a source other than happiness. (Annette Goodheart, *Laughter Therapy: How to Laugh About Everything in Your Life That Isn't Really Funny* [Santa Barbara: Less Stress Press, 1994], pp. 31-32)

30. "If you're under interrogation by an advanced race, I have one piece of advice for you: talk. Tell them anything and everything they want to know."

... "But sir," a cadet had asked, "what if that costs lives?"

The instructor had answered without thinking. "There is nothing you can do about that. If you're captured by someone like the Klingons, you no longer have any control over the situation. No matter how tough you are—or *think* you are—you will eventually tell them what they want to know.

"If you do it without subjecting yourself to debilitating or even lethal torture," the man had said, "then you will be preserving a valuable Starfleet asset: yourself. If you remain alive, then there is the possibility of escape or a negotiated release. But if you allow yourself to be killed protecting secrets you are going to give up anyway, you will not have done Starfleet, or yourself, any favors." (Michael Jan Friedman, *Star Trek: The Next Generation: Crossover* [New York: Pocket Books, 1995], pp. 124-125)

II. What is the *final* conclusion of each of the following sets of premises? Treat a conclusion as the *final conclusion* if it is derived by using *all* the premises. Typically, the final conclusion will either be one of the simple statements in the premises or the denial of such a premise or the denial of a compound component that cannot be broken down further. If there is a fallacy, name it and explain how the fallacy is committed. **Before declaring that there is a fallacy, always consider alternative arrangements to determine whether there is one that yields a valid argument.** Intermediate conclusions are *not* given. If you are treating these arguments symbolically, please use the suggested abbreviations.

1. If today is Friday, then we have a test. If we have a test, the instructor will spend the weekend grading. So, ... (F, T, I)

2. If today is Saturday, then I can sleep late. Today's not Saturday. So, ... (S, I)

3. If today is Friday, then we have a test; and if today is Saturday, then we can sleep late. Either today is Friday, or today is Saturday. So, ... (F, T, S, W)

4. Your instructor will be charged with grade inflation if the test is easy. Your instructor will be charged with grade inflation. So, ... (I, E)

5. If the instructor is sane and there are no trick questions, then the test will be easy. If the test is easy, the instructor will be charged with grade inflation. The instructor will not be charged with grade inflation. So, ... (S, T, E, G)

6. If there is a test tomorrow, I'll study all night. If I study all night, I'll sleep through my first-period class. If I sleep through my first period class, I'll miss the test. But I won't miss the test. So, ... (T, N, S, M)

7. Either I'll go to the movie or I'll go to the dance. If I go to the movie, I'll pay seven bucks to sleep for two hours, and if I go to the dance, I'll be hard of

hearing before morning. I won't be <u>h</u>ard of hearing by morning. So,. . . . (M, D, P, H)

8. If I <u>p</u>ass this test, I'll spend the night <u>c</u>elebrating. If I spend the night <u>c</u>elebrating, I'll have a <u>h</u>eadache in the morning. If I have a <u>h</u>eadache in the morning, I'll either take <u>a</u>spirin or I'll <u>s</u>tay in bed until noon. So,. . . . (P, C, H, A, S)

9. Queen <u>E</u>lizabeth will *not* have the "Festive Overture" played at her birthday party. Either <u>H</u>oltz or <u>S</u>hostakovich wrote the "Festive Overture." If <u>S</u>hostakovich wrote the Festive Overture, then the "Festive Overture" is a <u>c</u>lassic of contemporary Russian music. If <u>H</u>oltz wrote the "Festive Overture," then Queen <u>E</u>lizabeth will have it played at her birthday party. So,. . . . (E, H, S, C)

10. If <u>S</u>am is a math major, then <u>J</u>o majors in chemistry. Either <u>S</u>am is not a math major, or <u>H</u>einrich is studying for the bar exam. If <u>H</u>einrich is studying for the bar exam, then <u>D</u>rusilla drugs druids on dry days or <u>G</u>ertrude teaches nuclear physics. <u>G</u>ertrude teaches nuclear physics. <u>J</u>o majors in chemistry. So,. . . . (S, J, H, D, G)

11. If <u>G</u>rainger wrote "Lincolnshire Posy," then "<u>L</u>incolnshire Posy" features a number of British folk songs. Either <u>G</u>rainger wrote "Lincolnshire Posy" or <u>S</u>travinsky wrote "La Fiesta Mexicana." If "<u>L</u>incolnshire Posy" features a number of British folk songs, then "Lincolnshire Posy" has a light and breezy <u>a</u>ir about it. <u>S</u>travinsky did *not* write "La Fiesta Mexicana." So,. . . . (G, L, S, A)

12. If <u>A</u>manda went to the movies, then <u>S</u>amantha went to the movies; and if <u>G</u>eorge went to the theater, then <u>H</u>enry went to the theater. It is not the case that <u>A</u>manda did not go to the movies. Either Samantha did not go to the movies or Henry did not go to the theater. So,. . . . (A, S, G, H)

13. If <u>A</u>na plays poker, then <u>B</u>oris sings tenor; and if <u>C</u>ecelia likes opera, then <u>D</u>ominic drives a truck. If <u>E</u>ve works in a cattle drive, then <u>F</u>ran favors fabulous foods. Either <u>B</u>oris does not sing tenor or <u>F</u>ran does not favor fabulous foods. So,. . . . (A, B, C, D, E, F)

14. If <u>L</u>orinda plays drums, then <u>A</u>ngela plays marimba; and if <u>A</u>ngela plays marimba, then <u>D</u>anielle plays saxophone. If <u>D</u>anielle plays saxophone, then <u>T</u>ristan plays baritone. <u>T</u>ristan does not play baritone. So,. . . . (L, A, D, T)

15. If <u>A</u>mos ambles amiably through artful arboretums, then <u>B</u>rutus bags billions of bright bugs; and if <u>A</u>mos does not amble amiably through artful arboretums, then <u>C</u>assandra catches calico cats in cavernous caves. If <u>D</u>rew drags delightful dogs from dirty ditches, then <u>E</u>lmira eats elegant eel hors d'oeuvres; and if <u>D</u>rew does not drag delightful dogs from dirty ditches, then <u>F</u>rançois fences furiously for fifty francs. Either <u>B</u>rutus does not bag billions of bright bugs or <u>E</u>lmira does not eat elegant eel hors d'oeuvres. So,. . . . (A, B, C, D, E)

Some Logical Equivalences

The View: Statements are logically equivalent if they are true under exactly the same circumstances. By examining a number of logically equivalent statements, we shall be able to work our way through arguments of greater complexity.

Do we need to supplement the argument forms to deal with arguments in ordinary English? Do we need to concern ourselves with logically equivalent forms of statements, as we did when examining categorical syllogisms?

Two statements are logically equivalent if they are true or false under exactly the same circumstances. As we saw in Chapter 21, if two statements are logically equivalent, the statement that they are materially equivalent is a tautology. Using logically equivalent statements in conjunction with valid argument forms allows us to draw further conclusions from a set of premises. We shall consider five common logical equivalences:

1. "Not both p and q" is logically equivalent to "Either not p or not q."

2. "Not either p or q" is logically equivalent to "Not p and not q." (This is sometimes said as "neither p nor q.")

3. "Not not p" is logically equivalent to "p."

4. "p if and only if q" is logically equivalent to "If p, then q, and if q, then p."

5. "If p, then q" is logically equivalent to "If not q, then not p." This is called **contraposition** (or **transposition**).

> Where p and q are variables representing statements of any degree of complexity,
>
> **De Morgan's Theorems (DeM)**
>
> $\sim(p \ \& \ q) \leftrightarrow (\sim p \lor \sim q)$
>
> $\sim(p \lor q) \leftrightarrow (\sim p \ \& \ \sim q)$
>
> **Double Negation (DN)**
>
> $p \leftrightarrow \sim\sim p$
>
> **Material Equivalence (Equiv.)**
>
> $(p \leftrightarrow q) \leftrightarrow [(p \to q) \ \& \ (q \to p)]$
>
> **Transposition (Trans.)**
>
> $(p \to q) \leftrightarrow (\sim q \to \sim p)$

245

Now we can consider how these allow us to deal with more complex arguments. Consider the following argument:

> If both Fred and Joanne go to the movie, then Tristan will have a lonely evening. But Tristan will not have a lonely evening, and Joanne will go to the movie. What can we conclude?

The second premise, "Tristan will not have a lonely evening, and Joanne will go the movie," is a conjunction. We can simplify and conclude that two statements are true: "Tristan will not have a lonely evening" and "Joanne will go to the movie." Given the conclusion that "Tristan will not have a lonely evening" and the conditional premise,

1.	(F & J) → T	
2.	~T & J	
3.	~T	2 Simp.
4.	J	2 Simp.
5.	~(F & J)	1,3 DC
6.	~F ∨ ~J	5 DeM
7.	~~J	4 DN
8.	~F	7,6 DS

we can conclude by denying the consequent that the statement "It is not the case that both Fred and Joanne will go to the movie" is true. That statement is logically equivalent to "Either Fred will not go to the movie or Joanne will not go to the movie." But the statement "Joanne will go to the movie" is true, which is equivalent to "It is not the case that Joanne will not go to the movie." Given that "Either Fred will not go to the movie or Joanne will not go to the movie" and that "It is not the case that Joanne will not go to the movie," it follows that "Fred will not go to the movie" is true by disjunctive syllogism.

Now consider this argument:

> Either Jan will spend the night in the library or Dana will go dancing, if and only if Aggie does not bowl a perfect game. Aggie bowls a perfect game. Will Dana go dancing?

Whenever you have a biconditional, you must recognize its equivalent form to allow you to draw conclusions on the basis of the other argument forms. Notice that "Either Jan will spend the night in the library or Dana will go dancing, if and only if Aggie does not bowl a perfect game" is equivalent to "If either Jan will spend

1.	(J ∨ D) ↔ ~A	
2.	A	
3.	[(J ∨ D) → ~A] & (~A → (J ∨ D)	1 Equiv.
4.	(J ∨ D) → ~A	3 Simp.
5.	~~A	2 DN
6.	~(J ∨ D)	4,5 DC
7.	~J & ~D	6 DeM
8.	~D	7 Simp.

the night in the library or Dana will go dancing, Aggie does not bowl a perfect game; and if Aggie does not bowl a perfect game, then either Jan will spend the night in the library or Dana will go dancing." We are concerned with Dana's activities. If we simplify the previous sentence, we may conclude that "If either Jan will spend the night in the library or Dana will go dancing, Aggie does not bowl a perfect game." The statement "Aggie bowls a perfect game" is equivalent to "It is not the case that Aggie does not bowl a perfect game." That statement, together with the previous conditional, allows us to conclude that "It is not the case that either Jan will spend the night in the library or Dana will go dancing." The statement "It is not the case that either Jan will spend the night in the library or Dana will go dancing" is equivalent to "Jan will not spend the night in the library and Dana will not go dancing." That statement simplifies to "Dana will not go dancing." So, the answer to the question at the end of the problem is no.

Exercises

I. Identify the argument forms by letter according to the following scheme: (A) affirming the antecedent, (B) denying the consequent, (C) hypothetical syllogism, (D) disjunctive syllogism, (E) simplification, (F) conjunction, (G) constructive dilemma, (H) destructive dilemma, (I) the fallacy of denying the antecedent, (J) the fallacy of affirming the consequent, or (K) the fallacy of improper exclusive disjunctive syllogism. In many cases, the identification of the form will require restating one or more of the premises in terms of logically equivalent forms. In some cases more than one of these argument forms might be used in conjunction with logically equivalent statement forms.

1. If Robin went to the dance, then Luis went to the dance. If Chris did not go to the dance, then Luis did not go to the dance. So, if Robin went to the dance, Chris went to the dance.

2. It is not the case that both Sam enjoys this problem and Jan enjoys this problem. Sam enjoys this problem. So, Jan does not enjoy this problem.

3. Sam enjoys these problems if and only if Jan enjoys these problems. So, if Jan enjoys these problems, then Sam enjoys these problems.

4. Neither Sam nor Chris expects to ace this course. So, Sam does not expect to ace this course.

5. Not both Sam and Chris expect to ace this course. If Sam does not expect to ace this course, then she plans an exciting career flipping burgers at McDonald's; and if Chris does not expect to ace this course, then he expects to be all that he can be in the Army. So, either Sam plans an exciting career flipping burgers at McDonald's or Chris expects to be all that he can be in the Army.

6. If Sam is planning a vacation in the Swiss Alps, then she expects to ace this course; and if Chris is planning a wild end-of-the-semester party at the Golden Horseshoe, then he expects to ace this course. Not both Sam and Chris expect to ace this course. So, either Sam is not planning a vacation in the Swiss Alps or Chris is not planning a wild end-of-the-semester party at the Golden Horseshoe.

7. If this problem is easy, then Sam is not perplexed and Lynn is not perplexed. But either Sam is perplexed or Lynn is perplexed. So, this problem is not easy.

8. It is not the case that either Jerry is perplexed or Sherry is confused. If Sherry is confused, then Harry is puzzled. So, Harry is not puzzled.

9. John enjoys these exercises if and only if Jen enjoys these problems. But John does not enjoy these problems. So, Jen does not enjoy these problems.

10. Ramon enjoys these exercises if and only if Jen does not enjoy these problems. If Ramon does not enjoy these exercises, then Sam is puzzled. So, if Sam is not puzzled, then Jen does not enjoy these problems.

II. What is the final conclusion that follows from each set of premises? Typically, the final conclusion will either be one of the simple statements in the premises or the denial of such a premise. It *could* be the denial of a compound statement found in the premises. If nothing follows, name the fallacy committed.

1. If Carlos goes to the movie, then either Joan or Fred will stay home alone. But Fred will not stay home alone, even though Carlos goes to the movie. So,.... (C, J, F)

2. Neither Carlos nor Jean goes to the movie. If Carlos does not go to the movie, then Fred will go. So,.... (C, J, F)

3. Jean went to the movies if and only if Alicia did. But Alicia went to the movies. So,.... (J, A)

4. Angel went to the movies if and only if Jan did. But Jan did not go to the movies. So,.... (A, J)

5. If Matio went to the dance, then Belinda went to the dance if and only if Chris went to the dance. Matio went to the dance, but Chris did not go to the dance. So,....

6. If Fred passed the course, then Amy passed the course. If Fred did not pass the course, then Jan did not pass the course. So,.... (F, A, J)

7. If Franz passed the course if and only if Amy passed the course, then Juan passed the course. Franz passed the course if Amy did; and if Franz passed the course, then so did Amy. So,.... (F, A, J)

8. If both Carmenza and Dottie have a new car, then Jean will eat his hat. But Jean will not eat his hat, even though Dottie has a new car. So,.... (C, D, J)

9. Either John is a student in this class or John is a history major, but he is not both a student in this class and a history major. John is a history major. So,.... (S, H)

10. If Jess wrote an essay on the complexity of critical-thinking courses, then Rene wrote an essay on the simplicity of critical-thinking courses. If Rene wrote an essay on the simplicity of critical-thinking courses, then Sam will believe she need not study in the course. Jess wrote an essay on the complexity of critical-thinking courses. So,.... (J, R, S)

11. Jess believes she need not study for the exam provided that Lucinda believes she need not study for the exam. George will receive an A in the course only if he studies for the exam. Jess believes she needs to study the exam unless George does not study for the exam. So,....

12. Jane is a music major provided that she studies piano. Jane does not study piano only if she is a chemistry major. Jane is a music major. So,.... (M, P, C)

13. If Sam had lunch at D-Hall, then Jan went out for hot dogs; and if Chris had lunch downtown, then Len is on a hunger strike. Jan did not go out for hot dogs. So,.... (S, J, C, L)

14. It is not the case that neither *die Walküre* went for a wild ride on the Rhine nor Siegfried bathed in dragon's blood. If *die Walküre* went for a wild ride on the Rhine, then R. W. is certain to have a perpetual hit, and if Siegfried bathed in dragon's blood, then he shouldn't have bathed under a tree. So, ... (W, S, R, B)

15. It is not the case that either *die Walküre* went for a wild ride on the Rhine or Siegfried bathed in dragon's blood. *Die Walküre* went for a wild ride on the Rhine, provided that R. W. is certain to have a perpetual hit; and Siegfried bathed in dragon's blood on the condition that he shouldn't have bathed under a tree. So, ... (W, S, R, B)

16. The orchestra will play music from *Gotterdämmerung* only if there is a divine banquet in Valhalla. If there is divine banquet in Valhalla, then the opera must be by Wagner. John attends the opera provided that Toscanini is conducting the orchestra. But it is not the case that both John attends the opera and the opera must be by Wagner. So, ... (O, B, W, J, T)

17. If Ura will attend the concert and Ima will be surprised, then Toscanini will direct the orchestra. The fact that Toscanini is dead is a sufficient condition for Ima to be surprised, and Toscanini is dead. The concert will be a sellout provided that Toscanini will direct the orchestra. Ura will attend the concert. So, ...

18. Either Carter enjoys this class or she doesn't. If Carter enjoys this class, then she will sign up for symbolic logic in the fall; and if Carter does not enjoy this class, she will complain about her grade. If either Carter takes symbolic logic in the fall or she complains about her grade, the instructor will eat his hat. So, ... (E, S, C, I)

19. If today is Monday, then we have an exam, and if today is Wednesday, the instructor will put me to sleep. It is either not the case that we have an exam or it is not the case that the instructor will put me to sleep. If it is not Monday, then I have time to study for my test; and if it is not Wednesday, then I can party tonight. I cannot party tonight. So, ... (W, E, W, I T, P)

20. If the *Walküre* are a bunch of serious sopranos, then the opera is by Wagner. The *Walküre* are a bunch of serious sopranos, even though Professor Hernandez purchased a set of ear plugs. Excedrin headache number 435 can be expected provided that Professor Hernandez has purchased a set of ear plugs. If the opera is by Wagner and Excedrin headache number 435 can be expected, then the listener is not a serious fan of opera. Either the listener is a serious fan of opera or *you* just want these problems to end. So, ... (W, O, H, E, F, P)

PART V

Inductive Arguments

Arguments are of two kinds: They are valid deductive arguments or they are inductive arguments. All *invalid* deductive arguments are inductive arguments. The conclusion of an inductive argument is a claim that goes beyond the information in the premises. An inductive argument with true premises provides *some*, but not conclusive, evidence for the truth of its conclusion. Inductive arguments range from weak to strong. Some are much stronger than others.

We all *reason* inductively all the time. Most of what we learn from experience is based on inductive reasoning. Even when presenting a valid deductive argument, the evidence for the truth of the premises often is based on induction.

Some of the syllogisms we examined in Chapter 19—those involving quantifiers such as 'most' or 'many'—also can be treated as inductive arguments. The natural reading of 'most' is more than half. So, if you have the argument

> Most fraternity members drink beer.
>
> <u>Fred is a fraternity member.</u>
>
> So, Fred drinks beer.

you have pretty good reason to believe that Fred drinks beer, but there is no guarantee. Taking 'most' to mean more than half, rather than some (at least one), you no longer have a categorical syllogism. You have a **loose derivation**. We use loose derivations all the time. When was the last time you attributed a characteristic to a person because she had some other characteristic, and *most* people with the second characteristic have the first?

In this part we examine three types of inductive arguments. In Chapter 25, we examine analogies, which are based on a direct comparison between two or more things. In Chapter 26, we examine generalizations and surveys. We also devote some space to statistical arguments. In Chapter 27, we examine hypotheses and arguments to the best explanation.

Analogies

The View: An analogy is a claim of similarity between two or more objects. In an argument by analogy you compare two or more things on the basis of the respects in which they are similar, arguing that since two things are similar with respect to properties *a, b,* and *c,* it is also likely that they are similar with respect to some additional property *d.* The chapter focuses on criteria for evaluating arguments by analogy.

Why do we make comparisons? What can we learn from comparisons? Are there times when all we know about something is derived from comparisons?

An **analogy** is a comparison between two or more objects. Analogies can be used to describe, to explain, and to argue.

In literature, analogies often are used to describe. As you learned in English, these analogies take the form of similes and metaphors. A **simile** makes an explicit comparison by using the words 'like' or 'as'. The following passage from Gore Vidal's *Burr* provides a simile between skirts and flags:

> I like the Battery best in high summer: trees too green, roses overblown, sailboats tacking on the gray river while pale muslin dresses of promenading girls furl and unfurl like flags in the flower and sea-scented wind.[1]

Descriptive **metaphors** are like similes except there is no explicit use of a comparative word such as 'like.' An author might metaphorically describe an angry character by saying, "He was a raging bull." The author might have made the same point by saying, "He behaved like a raging bull." The use of descriptive similes or metaphors often yields vivid literary images:" ... the rosy-fingered dawn appeared...."[2] "He shivered inwardly like a small animal, like a bird or a hare, when he realized how alone he was."[3] "K.... kissed her first on the lips, than all over the face, like some thirsty ani-

---

[1]Gore Vidal, *Burr: A Novel* (New York: Bantam Books, 1973), p. 30. You should notice that the *passage* is the character's explanation of why he likes summer best, although the analogy is descriptive.

[2]Homer, *The Odyssey,* translated by George H. Palmer.

[3]Hermann Hesse, *Siddhartha,* translated by Hilda Rosner (New York: Bantam Books, 1951), p. 41.

Metaphor

While discussion of metaphor goes back at least to Aristotle, it has become a topic of significant philosophical discussion within the last century. Aristotle's insight provided the basis for the discussion. In a metaphor, an object of one sort is described as an object of some other sort. The metaphorical claim, if taken literally, is false. To be understood, a metaphorical claim must be understood as an implicit analogy. Your English teachers might have said that a metaphor is a condensed simile, that is, a simile without an explicit claim of likeness. A metaphor must be "unpacked," that is, the assumed similarity should be made explicit. At one time, some assumed that it was possible to substitute a literal term for the metaphorical term. There are several problems with this approach. (1) The distinction between literal and metaphorical terms is imprecise and changes over time. There are river currents, and there are electrical currents. Both uses of 'current' we *now* understand as literal, but the application of 'current' to electricity was originally a metaphorical extension of the term. (2) In a literary work, you can gain *some* insight into a metaphor if you find evidence of the author's intended used of the metaphorical term. The author might have intended more than one analogy, or she might maintain that her use of the term it is not merely metaphorical. (3) There often are good reasons to argue that whatever the author intended does not exhaust the metaphor. Many metaphors are "rich." When Ludwig Wittgenstein said that language is a picture of the world, insight into the nature of language was gained by looking for ways in which the language is like, and *unlike*, a picture. We come to understand the metaphor by interacting with it, by looking for similarities and dissimilarities. And like any case of induction, we can never be certain that we have "mined" all the insightful similarities from the metaphor.

mal lapping greedily at a spring of long-sought fresh water."[4] Or when the comparison is unexpected, an analogy can have comic effect: "Love is a lot like a backache, it doesn't show up on X-rays, but you know when it's there."[5] And it is not only in literature that analogies are used to describe. When the concept of an atom was originally introduced to you in a science class, your teacher probably said it was like a miniature solar system or used models of atoms that looked like miniature solar systems. As you studied further, you discovered the limits of the analogy.

In some cases, virtually everything we know about an object is based on analogies. At least since the Middle Ages, philosophers and theologians have argued that any understanding of the Judeo-Christian God rests on analogies. God is described as a king, a parent, and as wise and loving. Most of us have some understanding of what a king is, and we all know what parents are. We have some understanding of what it is to be wise and loving. Insofar as we understand these words, they apply to human beings. God is not a human being. So, our understanding of God is analogical (metaphorical).[6]

Analogies are also used to explain. If you are working on a math problem and become stumped, a friend might explain how to do the problem by comparing the

---

[4]Franz Kafka, *The Trial,* translated by Willa and Edwin Muir, revised by E. M. Butler (New York: Vantage Books, 1964), p. 38.

[5]George Burns, *Gracie: A Love Story* (New York: G. P. Putnum's Sons, 1988), pp. 58–59.

[6]In movies angels or benevolent extraterrestrials often say, "I have assumed this form, since it is a form you can understand." This reflects a metaphorical understanding of things whose nature is fundamentally different from their appearances.

puzzling problem with one you know how to solve. If you are learning a new computer program, someone might teach you how to use it by way of comparisons to other programs you already know. If you know how to use *Lotus 1-2-3* but your new job requires that you learn *Microsoft Excel,* your teacher might look for analogies between the two programs.[7]

The previous examples used analogies to explain *how* to do something. Analogies can also explain *why* two things are as they are. In the following passage Stephen Bloom explains why long-time residents of a small Midwestern town were mesmerized by the yarmulkes worn by members of the Jewish community that had recently immigrated to the town.

> Sex acts are mystics' clichés for conveying the sublime nature of a spiritual climax. When St. John of the Cross escaped from prison, his first thought was to read his *Dark Night of the Soul* to the nuns among whom he took refuge. The pious virgins and their superiors apparently had no difficulty in understanding or at least excusing the incandescently erotic language. Spiritual fulfillment is not, presumably, much like sexual satisfaction; but writers who try to express its mystical form have been driven to the farthest margins of metaphor in the effort to evoke the experience for those who have never had it. "One makes these comparisons," St. Teresa said, "because there are no other suitable ones."
>
> Filipe Fernández-Armesto and Derek Wilson, *Reformations: A Radical Interpretation of Christianity and the World, 1500–2000* (New York: Scribner, 1996), pp. 50–51.

Then it struck me why Dawn, Stanley, and all the locals seemed so mesmerized by the Jews' yarmulkes. Both farmer and Jew would never go anywhere without their heads covered. The skullcaps were something like what the farmers wore on their heads. Yarmulkes were symbolic badges of honor, a constant reminder that the wearer pays homage to the Lord's continual presence. The farmers' caps shielded them from the scorching sun and from the rain when the heavens opened up and let loose a downpour. In a sense, the caps, too, were homages to the power of nature, the power of the Lord. No one needed any protection against the sun, heat, or rain in the middle of Ginger's this morning. These men wore hats because they were supposed to wear hats. As with the Jews, hats were an essential part of their uniform: both groups felt naked without them. Neither would ever think of going anywhere without them. Neither would ever think of going anywhere without wearing a head covering, whether it was a handstitched yarmulke or a cap with John Deere green colors.[8]

Analogies are used to inquire. You may propose a hypothesis that something is very like something else. Consider the metaphor "Language is a picture of the world." There is an implicit claim that language is like a picture. How are they alike? How are they different? You may need to **unpack** the metaphor; that is, you might need to enumerate the various similarities between language and a picture if you are going to

---

[7]Of course, you might teach yourself new programs by *arguing* that since the programs are similar in various ways, they must be similar in others as well.

[8]Stephen G. Bloom, *Postville: A Clash of Cultures in Heartland America* (New York: Harcourt, 2000), p. 93.

understand the point being made. Such unpacking—you often must construct arguments to show that the proposed similarities and differences are there—often yields significant insights into the subject investigated.

And analogies are used to argue. The general structure of an argument by analogy is

> Consider objects *A* and *B*. *A* and *B* share characteristics *a, b, c,* and *d*. *A* also has characteristic *e*. So, it is likely that *B* also has characteristic *e*.

For example, assume Sydney and Carter are both members of this class. Assume that they are similar in the following ways: Both are 18. Both are freshmen at the university. Both are from moderately affluent families. Both are products of the public school system in this state. Both took the college-bound curriculum in high school. Both are presently chemistry majors at the university. Assume Sydney finds the study of argument fascinating. Since Sydney and Carter are alike in many ways, you might conclude *by analogy* that Carter also finds the study of argument fascinating. Is the conclusion true? The only way you might know for sure is to ask Carter. The analogy provides only *some* reason to believe the conclusion. And the analogy could be strengthened if you found other *relevant* ways in which Sydney and Carter are similar. The argument might be *strengthened* if both were also majoring in philosophy, since argument is at the heart of philosophical discourse. The analogy would *not* be strengthened, however, if they were similar in the following ways, since none of the following is likely to influence their interest in argument: They are both redheads. They are both five feet, six inches tall. They are both females. They both drive 1995 Chevrolets. The analogy could be *weakened* if there were relevant differences. Assume Sydney attended a very large high school, which offered a wide variety of college-bound courses, and she was active on the debate team. Carter is from a very small high school, which offered only the most basic college-bound courses, and she had no interest in debate. Assume further that while Sydney's second major is in philosophy, Carter's second major is in drama. Under such conditions, it seems that there is less reason to believe that Carter is fascinated with argument, since there are the kinds of differences in their backgrounds that would seem to be relevant regarding an interest in argumentation.

Consider another case. I have a car; you have a car. My car and your car are similar in certain ways—as is reflected by the fact that they are both called cars. But there are cars and there are cars. If you drive a new BMW and I drive an old Chevy (where "old" means several years older than however old you happen to be), there are probably as many differences as there are similarities. So, if I told you some of the economic horrors you may expect with respect to your car by comparing it to mine, you could properly reply, "Bah! I deem your 'vehicle' a car only as a linguistic courtesy!" On the other hand, if we had the same make and model car, we took similar care of our vehicles, and our driving habits were similar, my litany of automotive lamentations might give you pause. And should it be that we had numerous friends who also owned cars of the same make and model, and we all complained about similar shortcomings in our vehicles, you would have much better reason to look out for similar problems with your car.

Exercises

I. Are the analogies in each of the following passages used to describe, to explain, to inquire, or to argue? If there is an *argument* by analogy, evaluate the strength of the analogy.

1. Cold, frosty daylight was a gray mantle on the lake. (Erle Stanley Gardner, *The Case of the Angry Mourner* [New York: Pocket Books, 1951], p. 16)

2. "When I was a kid, on the Fourth of July, the kids in the neighborhood would toss little cherry bombs to explode on the sidewalk around the feet of the other little kids, which made them jump." He grinned. "That's what I've been doing [in my cross-examinations] so far today. The cherry bombs didn't exactly do any real damage but they sure kept you hopping and off-balance." (Thomas Chastain, *Perry Mason in The Case of Too Many Murders* [New York: William Morrow and Company, 1989], p. 127)

3. "What . . . is a good terrorist?"
    "He's a businessman whose business is killing people to make a political point . . . almost like advertising. They serve a larger purpose, at least in their own minds. They believe in something, not like kids in a catechism class, more like reasoned adults in a Bible study. Crummy simile, I suppose, but it's the best I have at the moment. Long day, Mr. Chavez," Dr. Bellow concluded, while the stew topped off his glass. (Tom Clancy, *Rainbow Six* [New York: G. P. Putnam's Sons, 1998], p. 72)

4. Time is a river, the restless flow of all created things. One thing no sooner comes in sight than it is hurried past and another is borne along, only to be swept away in its turn. (Marcus Aurelius, *Meditations,* trans. by Maxwell Staniforth [Baltimore: Penguin Books, 1964], Book 4, §43, p. 73)

5. A bad joke is like a bad egg—all the worse for having been cracked. Since you don't want to crack bad eggs, you don't want to crack bad jokes.

6. But why should children be thankful—unless we train them to be? Ingratitude is natural—like weeds. Gratitude is like a rose. It has to be fed and watered and cultivated and loved and protected. (Dale Carnegie, *How to Stop Worrying and Start Living,* rev. ed. [New York: Pocket Books, 1984], p. 142)

7. As I remained in the Savior's glow, in his absolute love, I realized that when I had feared him as a child I had actually moved myself further from him. When I thought he didn't love me, I was moving my love from him. He never moved. I saw now that he was like a sun in my galaxy. I moved around him, sometimes nearer and sometimes farther away, but his love never failed. (Betty J. Eadie, *Embraced by the Light* [New York: Bantam Books, 1992], p. 60)

8. Tax loopholes are like parking spaces—they all seem to disappear by the time you get there. But if one is diligent and takes one's time, one can usually find a parking space. So, if one is diligent and takes one's time, one should be able to find a tax loophole.

9. Nature's way is like the bending of a bow:

    The top which is high is lowered while the bottom which is low is raised, And the width which is narrow is widened while the length which is long is shortened. Nature's way is to take away from those that have too much and give to those that have too little.   (Lao Tzu, *Tao Teh King,* Interpreted as Nature and Intelligence by Archie J. Bahm, 2nd ed. [Albuquerque: World Books, 1986], §LXXVII, p. 66)

10. When the . . . Chinese wanted to torture their prisoners, they would tie their prisoners hand and foot and put them under a bag of water that constantly dripped . . . dripped . . . dripped . . . day and night. These drops of water constantly falling on the head became like hammer blows—and drove men insane. This same method of torture was used during the Spanish Inquisition and in German concentration camps under Hitler.

    Worry is like the constant drip, drip, drip of water; and the constant drip, drip, drip of worry often drives men to insanity and suicide.   (Dale Carnegie, *How to Stop Worrying and Start Living,* rev. ed. [New York: Pocket Books, 1984], p. 33)

11. "Think of our tunnel under the slates at home. It isn't a room in any of the houses. In a way, it isn't really part of any of the houses. But once you're in the tunnel, you can go along it and come out into any of the houses in the row. Mightn't this wood be the same?—a place that isn't in any of the worlds, but once you've found that place you can get into them all."

    "Well, even if you can—" began Polly, but Digory went on as if he hadn't heard her.

    "And of course that explains everything," he said. "That's why it is so quiet and sleepy here. Nothing ever happens here. Like at home. It's in the houses that people talk, do things, and have meals. Nothing goes on in the in-between places, behind the walls and above the ceilings and under the floor, or in our own tunnel. When you come out of the tunnel you may find yourself in *any* house. I think we can get out of this place into jolly well Anywhere! We don't need to jump back into the same pool we came up by. Or not just yet."   (C. S. Lewis, *The Magician's Nephew* [New York, Macmillan, 1955], pp. 30-31)

12. " . . . I'll prepare no document designed for approval by a group!" Benjamin Franklin declared three evenings later, over coffee and tea cups at The Sovereign near the State House. "I can foresee the surgery that'll be done upon it."

    "Ben, don't be so confounded stubborn!" John Adams said.

    "On this, I will be stubborn. Let me tell you a story—"

    "I hope it's pertinent," Adams snapped.

    "Extremely. I once knew a fellow here in Philadelphia who desired to open a hatter's shop. He put hours of energy and effort into designing and finishing the most important feature of such a shop—the signboard for attracting customers. He meticulously painted a hat on it, and the inscription, 'John Thompson, hatter, makes and sells hats for ready money.' Then the poor fool consulted his friends. One said that because of the drawing, the word 'hatter' was superfluous. Out it went with a stroke of the brush! Someone else said that 'makes' should be deleted, since people who purchase hats didn't give a damn who made 'em. 'Ready money' was wasteful wordage—everyone knew Thompson never extended credit. Thus, his precious board was reduced to 'John Thompson sells hats.' Ah, said another helpful soul, but who will be dunce enough to believe you'd give 'em away? So all the hours of work and thought produced nothing more than a worthless piece of wood with all of its legend brushed over, save for 'John Thompson' and the hat drawing, which was poorly done in the first place. Spare me from editorial congresses of any sort!" Franklin completed cheerily. "I'll yield the labor—and the later discomfort produced by disemboweling of every other phrase—to our more eloquent and hardy gentlemen of Virginia." (John Jakes, *The Rebels,* The Kent Chronicles, vol. 2 [Garden City, NY: Nelson Doubleday, 1975], pp. 123–124)

13. We drove back onto the main road in silence. I was glad of the spot of quiet because I took it that a little constructive thinking was overdue. I am not one of these intellectual sleuths, I'm afraid. My mind does not work like an adding machine, taking the facts in nearly one by one and doing the work as it goes. I am more like the bloke with the sack and spiked stick. I collect all the odds and ends I can see and turn out the bag at the lunch hour. (Margery Allingham, "The Case of the Late Pig," from *Mr. Campion: Criminologist* [Doubleday, 1937])

14. Planning the expository paragraph is similar to constructing a shack. First, you must know why you want to build the shack: you cannot pour the foundation until you know what purpose the shack is to serve. Second, you must draw careful plans to assure that the shack will serve the intended purpose. It would be rather foolhardy to discover during construction that you did not leave enough room for a door. Then, once you have carefully reviewed the plans and made certain that they meet your purpose, you are finally ready to pour the foundation, which is the support for your shack. Now build on that foundation while carefully following your plans. Should you decide to make any modifications, you must first modify your plans to see if the changes conform to the purpose and overall plan. Organizing the paragraph is done is the same manner as constructing a shack. It would be just as foolhardy to begin with a topic sentence without first having a purpose—a thesis. Once you have a clear thesis statement, you are ready to outline, making certain that every sentence is well thought out and relevant to the thesis. Now you are ready to write the paragraph, carefully choosing the method best suited for developing your idea. Much as the builder puts on the finishing touches, so must you write an effective concluding sentence. (John McCall, *How to Write Themes and Essays,* 2nd ed. revised by Harry Teiteltbaum [New York: Macmillan, 1989], p. 16)

15. "Shucks, it ain't calling you anything. It's only saying do you know how to talk French."

　　"Well, den, why couldn't he say it?"

　　"Why, he is a-saying it. That's a Frenchman's way of saying it."

　　"Well, it's a blame' ridicklous way, en I doan' want to hear no mo' 'bout it. Dey ain' no sense in it."

　　"Looky here, Jim; does a cat talk like we do?"

"No, a cat don't."

"Well, does a cow?"

"No, a cow don't, nuther."

"Does a cat talk like a cow, or a cow talk like a cat?"

"No, dey don't."

"It's natural and right for 'em to talk different from each other, ain't it?"

"Course."

"And ain't it natural and right for a cat and a cow to talk different from *us*?"

"Why, mos' sholy it is."

"Well, then, why ain't it natural and right for a *Frenchman* to talk different from us? You answer me that."

"Is a cat a man, Huck?"

"No."

"Well, den, dey ain't no sense in a cat talkin' like a man. Is a cow a man?—er is a cow a cat?"

"No, she ain't either of them."

"Well, den, she ain' got no business to talk like either one or the yuther of 'em. Is a Frenchman a man?"

"Yes."

"*Well*, den! Dad blame it, why doan' he *talk* like a man? You answer me *dat!*" (Mark Twain, *The Adventures of Huckleberry Finn*, Chapter 14)

Evaluating Arguments by Analogy————

In an argument by analogy, you compare two or more things on the basis of the respects in which they are similar, arguing that since those things are similar with respect to a certain number of properties, it is also likely that they are similar with respect to some additional property. The objects compared are divided into kinds. Let us call the **ground for the analogy** those objects having *all* the properties under consideration. So, if you have three objects, A, B, and C, both A and B have properties a, b, c, and d, and the question is whether C also has property d, A and B are the ground for the analogy. Let us call the **objective extension of the analogy** the object compared to the ground of the analogy and which is known to have a number of properties in common with the objects in the ground. In the case above C would be the objective extension. The **basis of an analogy** consists of those properties known to be common to the ground and the objective extension of the analogy. In the case above a, b, and c are the basis of the analogy. The **problematic extension of an analogy** is that property common to objects in the ground but not known to be a property of the objective extension. In the case above the problematic extension is d. When evaluating an argument by analogy, some of the issues pertain to the ground for the analogy and the basis of it.

The basis of an analogy consists of all properties known to be common to the ground and the objective extension. Are all those properties relevant? Assume you are thinking about buying a car, and you are comparing my car with a car you are thinking about buying. If your concern is with having a dependable form of transportation

Source: *Charles M. Schulz*, PEANUTS. *Peanuts reprinted by permission of United Feature Syndicate, Inc.*

for a number of years, it will make little difference if you and I both drive red cars. If the issue is probable dependability, mechanical similarities are relevant, maintenance issues are relevant, some driving habits probably are relevant, and perhaps where we drive and how much we drive are relevant. Stop-and-go driving is said to be hard on cars. So, if I generally drive my car for fewer than four miles in town on a trip, and your average trip is at least ten miles at highway speeds, there is a relevant difference. My automotive woes might not be the same kinds of woes you could expect, even if our cars were similar in many other respects. If you drive in Virginia and I drive in northern Minnesota, the body of your car can be expected to last longer than the body of mine. The State of Minnesota spreads salt on its highways during the winter. The Commonwealth of Virginia does not. Since salt tends to "eat" metal away, the body of a car in Virginia has a longer life expectancy than one is Minnesota.

In general there are six things to take into account in judging the strength of an analogy. Some of these apply to other types of inductive arguments as well.

1. **The more respects in which things being compared are similar (the larger the basis is), the stronger the argument is.** Your new Lexus and my 1972 Chevy probably aren't much alike. Your 1952 Chevy and my 1952 Chevy are probably more alike than your 1992 Chevy Caprice Classic and my 1992 Chevy Cavalier even if your 1952 Chevy has an automatic transmission and a V-8 engine, and my 1952 Chevy has a standard transmission and a six-cylinder engine. Cars of the same make were not that different from one another in 1952.

2. **The respects in which things are compared (the properties included in the basis) must be relevant to the conclusion.** The color of a car generally is not relevant to its life-expectancy—although if it is a comparison of cars to be driven *exclusively* during snowstorms, color could play a role.

3. **The analogy is stronger if more things are compared (if the ground of the analogy is larger).** If you and thirty-two of your closest friends all own the same make and model car I own, and all of you had transmission problems at about 45,000 miles, I have much better grounds for believing I also will have such problems at about that time than I would have if I were comparing my car only to yours. In general, as the ground of the analogy increases in size, the probability decreases that the ground consists of typical cases.

4. **Relevant differences between things compared (the ground and the objective extension) tend to weaken the analogy.** Sure, we have the same make and model of car, but you religiously have your car serviced according to the manu-

facturer's prescribed schedule, while I think that a visit to the shop for a "check-up" is needed only once every 100,000 miles (no oil change, etc.). This makes a difference in the life expectancy of the car. Given this difference, if I tell you I had various troubles at 50,000 miles, you might have little reason to believe that you would have the same problems.

5. **When a significant number of things are similar in a significant number of respects (when the ground and the basis are strong), differences among objects in the ground can *strengthen* the evidence for the conclusion of the analogy.** You and thirty-two of your friends have the same make and model car I am thinking about buying. Your friends treat their cars in any number of ways, yet each of you has found the car to be very reliable for its first 75,000 miles. These differences might be relevant, but they tend to show that the car is reliable in spite of the various differences in care. Hence, the differences strengthen the conclusion of the argument. This is relevant to criterion number three, since if there are a significant number of things compared, it is increasingly likely that there will be a significant number of differences in spite of the similarities. In such cases, the differences will tend to strengthen the analogy.

6. **The stronger the conclusion is relative to the premises, the weaker the argument is.** If I had engine problems at 40,000 miles and claimed you would have engine problems at 40,000 miles, I would probably be wrong. It is more likely I would be right if I said, "You'll have trouble before you hit 60,000 miles." It might be more likely still that you will have problems before you hit 100,000 miles.

All these considerations show you some of the significant differences between inductive and valid deductive arguments. In a valid deductive argument the conclusion follows, period. In an inductive argument, you often can strengthen or weaken the argument by introducing more evidence. Inductive arguments are strong or weak, and additional premises can make them stronger or weaker. The six criteria help you judge the degree of strength or weakness, but they *do not* allow you to say "Ah! This is strong!" or "Ah! This is weak!" Two people looking at the same evidence can reach significantly different conclusions regarding the strength of the evidence. Should you and I disagree regarding the general evaluation of an analogy, we should discuss our differences. You might need to provide an argument (give reasons) why one or another of the criteria should weigh more heavily than another. Or, one of us might have unconsciously introduced an additional comparison which, when made explicit, will shift the other's analysis of the argument.

Two more points should be mentioned. Arguments from analogy are not only used to show that insofar as

---

Analogy and Deduction

To convert an argument by analogy to a valid deductive argument, add a premise of the form, "If *A* and *B* (or however many objects you are comparing) are similar in some number *n* ways, and *A* (or however many objects *other than B*) also has another characteristic, then it is likely (certain, probable, possible) that *B* has that characteristic as well." The issue, then, is whether the conditional premise is true. You check the truth (or probable truth) of the premise on the basis of the criteria for evaluating an argument by analogy. If characteristics in which things are similar are irrelevant, scratch them off your list. If the consequent is too strong, weaken it and compare the resulting conclusion with the original conclusion.

two or more things are similar in a number of respects, they are also similar in another. Sometimes two things are taken to be similar—the structure of the atom was at one time taken to be similar to a solar system—but you might question the analogy on the basis of criterion four. Important discoveries are sometimes made by showing that things believed to be similar are dissimilar in important ways. Or, in teaching a particular subject, your instructor might *begin* by claiming a certain set of similarities between something you know and something you do not know. As your understanding increases, she might introduce a number of respects in which the similar things differ. By approaching a subject by way of various approximations, you might slowly develop a deep understanding of a very complex subject.

Finally, while analogies are always based on comparisons, the respects in which two or more things are similar are not always spelled out in detail. Often you must think carefully about the things being compared and explore the basis for the analogy. You must look for the unstated respects in which two things are (or are not) similar before you can adequately assess the strength of an argument by analogy.

Let's look at a few examples.

> "And how do you know that you're mad?"
>
> "To begin with," said the [Cheshire] Cat, "a dog's not mad. You grant that?"
>
> "I suppose so," said Alice.
>
> "Well, then," the Cat went on, "you see a dog growls when it's angry, and wags its tail when it's pleased. Now *I* growl when I'm pleased, and wag my tail when I'm angry. Therefore I'm mad."
>
> "*I* call it purring, not growling," said Alice.[9]

The Cheshire Cat is comparing himself to dogs. There are many dogs, so the ground of the analogy is very large (criterion 3). Since canine and feline anatomies are very similar, the basis of the analogy is also very large (criterion 1). But, the only *relevant* similarities between the ground and the objective extension are *behavioral* characteristics (criterion 2). So, when you reduce the properties in the basis to only the relevant properties, the basis becomes very small (criterion 1). Finally, as Alice suggests, the properties in the basis that are said to support the problematic extension are relevant *differences* (criterion 4). So, the analogy is very weak. (You might also suggest that the word 'mad' is at least ambiguous. You might argue that there is an equivocation on 'mad' between angry and insane.)

> Showing our writing to hostile or undiscerning readers is like lending money to people with terrible fiscal pasts. We will not be repaid as we wish. Our work will not be valued. They will respond in dangerous extremes, "brilliant" or "awful." (Long experience teaches that extremes of any kind, high or low, are dangerous to the writing process because they create self-consciousness.) Even if our readers are enthusiastic, they may do so generically, and that, too, is dangerous.[10]

---

[9]Lewis Carroll, *Alice's Adventures in Wonderland*, Chapter 6.
[10]Julia Cameron, *The Right to Write* (New York: Jeremy P. Tarcher/Putnum, 1998), pp. 177–178.

The ground is the class of people with bad financial pasts to whom you could loan money, which is a large class (criterion 3). The objective extension is people whom you might let read your writing. The basis is unstated. It presumably is that those in the ground and the objective extension are unreliable people. If this is correct, then there are numerous similarities insofar as you are concerned with people (criterion 1), but unreliability is the only relevant one (criterion 2). Are there relevant differences (criterion 4)? That is hard to determine, since it is not clear what would be relevant or irrelevant. The conclusion is, in effect, "Never loan your writing to hostile or undiscerning readers," which is quite strong. So, the evidence the analogy provides for its conclusion seems to be weak.

This requires an additional remark, however. Anyone who has done any writing will grant that *sometimes* the conclusion gives very good advice, and it might always be good advice regarding *undiscerning* readers. If you are writing fiction, for example, the hostile critic will be discouraging and provide you with few insights. If you are writing an argumentative essay, a hostile reader—a reader supporting the denial of your thesis—might do a very good job of pointing out the weaknesses in your arguments. But in either case the reader must be *discerning*. She must be a careful, well-informed critic. She must be willing to give arguments supporting her criticisms. So, there might be good grounds for claiming that you should never show your writings to undiscerning readers, and regarding *some* kinds of writing, you should not show your writing to hostile readers. But since the basis for the analogy above is weak or unclear and the conclusion is strong, the analogical argument is weak.

Now consider this one.

> "I'm glad we've begun asking riddles—I believe I can guess that," she added aloud.
>
> "Do you mean that you think you can find out the answer to it?" said the March Hare.
>
> "Exactly so," said Alice.
>
> "Then you should say what you mean," the March Hare went on.
>
> "I do," Alice hastily replied; "at least—at least I mean what I say—that's the same thing, you know."
>
> "Not the same thing a bit!" said the Hatter. "Why, you might just as well say that 'I see what I eat' is the same as 'I eat what I see'!"
>
> "You might just as well say," added the March Hare, "that 'I like what I get' is the same thing as 'I get what I like'!"
>
> "You might just as well say," added the Dormouse, which seemed to be talking in its sleep, "that 'I breathe when I sleep' is the same thing as 'I sleep when I breathe'!"
>
> "It *is* the same thing with you," said the Hatter, . . .[11]

Here there are three objects in the ground. There is one characteristic in the basis. All the pairs of propositions in the basis are similar to the pair of propositions in the objective extension insofar as the second proposition is the converse of the first.

---

[11]Lewis Carroll, *Alice's Adventures in Wonderland*, Chapter 7.

(They are of the form, "I *x* when I *y*" and "I *y* when I *x*" or, if you prefer, "All times when I *y* are times when I *x*" and "All times when I *x* are times when I *y*.") The problematic extension is since the pairs of propositions in the ground do not have the same meanings, "I say what I mean" and "I mean what I say" do not have the same meanings. It is a good analogy. You are concerned with only one property (criterion 1), but it is the only property that is relevant to the analogy (criteria 2 and 4). There are only three instances in the ground (criterion 3), but it could easily be extended indefinitely. (As we noted in Chapter 18, a universal affirmative is *not* logically equivalent to its converse.) So, even though the conclusion is fairly strong (criterion 6), it is well-supported by the analogy.

Here is one more:

> Not everyone with a desire to write, after all, becomes a writer, and that is not necessarily because of a lack of inherent talent or an inability to communicate with words. Many avid readers harbor a secret desire to be a writer because they believe the pleasure to be gained from writing is identical with that gained from reading. But to be a writer, a person must first actually write, and write a great deal.
>
> If this definition sounds simpleminded, consider. A long-distance runner is someone who runs. Runs long distances, in fact. A long-distance runner is not a person who *desires* to run. A long-distance runner actually runs, and usually runs every day. If I announce to my friends that I want to run the Boston marathon, they might reasonably ask, "What steps are you taking to achieve this goal?" I might answer, "Well, I'm training ten miles every other day this year. I want to run a few fourteen-kilometer races first to see how I do under pressure. Next year I'll increase my training to fifteen miles. If I can maintain that distance in a good time for another year, maybe then I'll be ready."
>
> But suppose I answered instead, "I'm not running at all right now. I just thought I'd like to try it." Pressed further, I admit, "I thought I'd start with the Boston marathon to see if I like running or not." My friends might justifiably consider me not merely mad but a likely candidate for shin splints or a heart attack. Just think, then, how benevolently we let slide in casual conversation that famous wish-announcement: "I've got a novel in me. Someday I'm going to write it." [12]

While there are many words, the analogy is straightforward. Writing a novel is like running in a marathon. If you are going to run in a marathon, then you should train over a period of time, starting with short sprints and working up to long-distance running. So, if you are going to write a novel, you should train over a period of time, starting with short works and working up to a novel. The ground consists of training for marathon running. The objective extension consists of "training" to write a novel. There are numerous cases in the ground (criterion 3). The basis, however, is hard to state. Is the respect in which running marathons and writing novels are similar only

---

[12]Victoria Nelson, *On Writer's Block: A New Approach to Creativity* (Boston: Houghton Mifflin, 1993), pp. 11–12.

that they are "major projects"? If that is the only similarity, is that enough (criterion 1)? There are clearly differences—if your first venture into writing is a novel, you will suffer neither shin splints nor a heart attack, but you probably will not finish and publish it—but do the differences make a difference (criteria 2 and 4)? And the conclusion is rather strong (criterion 6).

While a simple consideration of the analogy suggests that it is rather weak, I am inclined to believe it is compelling. Those who *do not* run recognize that runners have to train incrementally if they are going to run a marathon. The ground could be expanded. If you are going to play Beethoven sonatas on the piano, you work up to them by starting with far simpler works. If you are going to do calculus problems, you work up to them from simple arithmetic problems. If you are going to build an elaborate china cabinet, you hone your woodworking skills on simpler projects (probably made with less expensive wood). Writing a novel is a large and intricate project. In this way it is similar to running a marathon, playing Beethoven sonatas, doing calculus problems, and building elaborate furniture. All the cases in the ground are cases up to which you need to work by engaging in similar but less intricate and demanding activities. So, it is reasonable to believe that you need to engage in less elaborate writing projects while "training" to write a novel.

Exercises

II. Follow the instructions for each of the following.

1. You are invited to Lynn's house for dinner. You have attended dinner at Lynn's twice before. Once Lynn prepared a traditional turkey dinner with all the trimmings. The other time Lynn prepared a German dinner: *sauerbraten*, Bavarian cabbage, and various other delicacies including Black Forest cherry cake. Both dinners were exquisite, and your mouth waters as you read the invitation. State two additional considerations which, if true, should *strengthen* your belief that the evening will be a culinary delight.

2. Consider the situation in number 1 again and state two additional considerations which, if true, should *weaken* your belief that the evening will be a dining delight.

3. Situation: You are planning to buy a computer. I have owned a number of computers of various makes and models. I have been most happy with my new Micron *GoBook²* with a Pentium II processor. Therefore, you conclude that if you buy a new Micron *GoBook²* with a Pentium II processor, you will be pleased with your purchase. Give two additional considerations that would tend to strengthen your conclusion.

4. Looking again at the situation in number 3, give two additional considerations that would tend to weaken your conclusion.

5. A recipe for fudge was published in the *Des Moines Register*. The *Register* claimed that fudge made from that recipe had won first place at the Iowa State Fair. The recipe was reprinted by the *Washington Post* in its holiday foods sec-

tion. Do you have good reasons to believe that if your culinary skills are equal to the task and if you make fudge from that recipe, the fudge probably will be liked by your holiday guests? Spell out the similarities and differences you consider implicit in the analogy.

6. Until relatively recently, classifications of plants and animals were based on analogies.[13] Assume you and a friend were arguing about whether dolphins should be classified as mammals or fish. Construct two analogies, one posing similarities between dolphins and fish, the other posing similarities between dolphins and mammals. Which is the stronger? Why?

7. My coffee pot died, and I went hunting for a new one. Since I drink several pots of coffee each day, it was imperative that I find a new and reliable coffee maker. My old coffee machine, a Mr. Coffee, had lasted for only twenty years. As I was examining the various brands of coffee makers, I noticed that there was one made by Black and Decker. I have owned a Black and Decker drill for nearly twenty years. I use it several times every year, and it has never given me any trouble. Within the past five years, I have purchased a Black and Decker circular saw, and it has served me well in each of the several dozen times I used it. And certainly my new Black and Decker Workmate is a veritable godsend. So, I bought a Black and Decker coffee maker. Given all the analogies, wouldn't you have done the same? Explain why or why not.

8. My daughter, who is both a cat lover and a *Star Trek* fan, concluded that cats are alien beings. "Siamese cats are Romulans, since they have pointed ears and are rather temperamental. Tabbies are Klingons, since they have those jagged Klingon-markings on their foreheads. Rag dolls are Vulcans, since they are very calm and never show any emotion." State at least two *disanalogies* that tend to show that cats are not aliens.

9. In the case of the *National Labor Relations Board* v. *Yeshiva University,* the Supreme Court ruled that the faculty at private universities cannot engage in collective bargaining, since university faculty have the status of managers, and according to the provisions of the Taft-Hartley Act, no managers can unionize. Part of the Court's reasoning was as follows:

> The controlling consideration in this case is that the faculty of Yeshiva University exercise authority which in any other context unquestionably would be managerial. Their authority in academic matters is absolute. They decide what courses will be taught. They debate and determine teaching methods, grading policies, and matriculation standards. They effectively decide which students will be admitted, retained, and graduated. On occasion their views have determined the size of the student body, the tuition charged, and the location of the school.

---

[13]While debates continue regarding the proper basis for biological taxonomy, there has been a move away from classifications based on analogies among plants and animals toward what is called cladistic classification. Cladistic classification is based, in part, upon theories of evolutionary descent. See Willi Hennig, *Phylogentic Systematics,* translated by D. Dwight Davis and Rainer Zangerl (Urbana: University of Illinois Press, 1966).

When one considers the function of a university, it is difficult to imagine decisions more managerial than these. To the extent the industrial analogy applies, the faculty determines within each school the product to be produced, the terms upon which it will be offered, and the customers who will be served. [Therefore, according to the terms of the Taft-Hartley Act, professors are managers and cannot legally unionize.]

State two respects in which one might argue that there are significant *differences* between professors and industrial managers.

10. Is the following argument by analogy strong or weak? Explain.

> Not every priest can do without a woman, not only on account of weakness of the flesh, but much more because of the necessities of the household. If he, then, may have a woman, and the pope grants him that, and yet may not have her in marriage—what is that but leaving a man and a woman alone and forbidding them to fall? It is as though one were to put fire and straw together and command that it shall neither burn nor smoke. (Martin Luther, *An Open Letter to the Christian Nobility of the German Nation,* trans. C. M. Jacobs, in Martin Luther, Three Treatises [Philadelphia: Muhlenberg Press, 1943], p. 68)

III. Reconstruct the arguments by analogy in each of the following passages. Make explicit the points of similarity and difference. Is the argument strong or a weak? Why?

1. Marshall was happy to note, "A president was not entirely like a king...."

"I mention two essential differences," said Marshall, most mildly, but speaking more loudly than usual. "The king can do no wrong, that no blame can be imputed to him, that he cannot be named in a debate. Since a president can do wrong and since he can be named in a debate, he is not an anointed king and so like any man is answerable to the law." (Gore Vidal, *Burr: A Novel* [New York: Bantam Books, 1973], p. 476)

2. Although [Boston District Attorney] Flanagan and other critics are correct when they say that the aim of a newspaper or television station is to make money, he and the other critics are dead wrong when they say that the issue is uppermost in the minds of those who make the everyday news decisions....

Many critics seems to think that the need to make a profit is the engine that drives a news operation. In reality, it is the opposite: it is the integrity of the news-gathering force that drives the economics. A wise (and financially successful) publisher or owner is a salesman for the product delivered by his news crew rather than the other way around. A rough analogy, in Flanagan's context, would be to accuse the district attorney's office of drumming up crimes so the staff could perpetuate their jobs. (Ken Englade, *Murder in Boston* [New York: St. Martin's Paperbacks, 1990], p. 221)

3. There's a funny moment in Fredric Dannen's book *Hit Men* when the legendary Clive Davis returns to CBS Records' New York headquarters from the Monterey Pop Festival with the hot news that a rock "revolution" is in the offing. This is, mind you, 1967, 11 years after Elvis burst on the scene and three after the Beatles held all five top spots on the singles charts. Three decades later, in a year in which hip-hop—or hip-hop-flavored R&B—week after week took as many as eight of the top ten spots on the *Billboard 200* album charts, a year in which the Beastie Boys sold 680,000 records their first week out, in which Lauryn Hill *wowed* everyone, it seems obvious that we see hip-hop the same way our elders saw rock 30 years ago: the mix tape to our lives, the loud, undifferentiated noise adults just don't understand.   (Craig Seymour, "Lauryn Hill," *Spin Magazine,* January 1999, p. 64)

4. "Life *is* a game, boy. Life *is* a game that one plays according to the rules."

    "Yes, sir. I know it is. I know it."

    . . . Some game. If you get on the side where all the hot-shots are, then it's a game, all right—I admit that. But if you're on the *other* side, where there aren't any hot-shots, what's the game about? Nothing. No game.   (J. D. Salinger, *The Catcher in the Rye* [Boston: Little, Brown, 1951], p. 8)

5. The human mind can be compared to the guidance system of a missile on automatic pilot. Once the target is set, the self-adjusting feedback system constantly monitors the course of its own navigation, making whatever corrections necessary to stay on target. But if it is not specifically set or is too far out of range, the missile will wander erratically until its propulsion system fails or it self-destructs.

    The human mind behaves in a similar manner. Once a goal is set, the mind constantly monitors self-talk and environmental feedback, both positive and negative, making adjustments along the way in order to score its target. But when the mind is programmed with vague expectations, or the goal is too far out of sight, the individual will wander aimlessly until he gives up in fatigue and frustration or he self-destructs with liquor, drugs, and other sources of immediate sensual gratification.   (Denis Waitley and Reni L. Witt, *The Joy of Working: The 30-Day System to Success, Wealth, and Happiness on the Job* [New York: Ballantine, 1985], p. 42)

6. . . . when Kate [Mulgrew] paused to take notice of an absolutely adorable little baby in the front row, even the infant provided material.

    Kate: *Look at that extraordinary baby—that beautiful baby has not stirred.* . . .

    Bill: It looks like a little alien. . . .

    Kate: *Bill!! That's terrible!*

    Bill: What? It looks like a *cute* alien? Y'know? Kinda like the ones in Roswell.

    Kate: *BILL!*

    Bill: What? Babies have big heads, and big eyes, and tiny little bodies with tiny little arms and legs. So did the aliens at Roswell! I rest my case.   (William Shatner, *Get a Life!* [New York: Pocket Books, 1999], pp. 180–181)

7. "All right then," Picard told him, ignoring the comparison [to Kirk]. "Forget how long I've been doing this. Think of the officers you're sending out in that shuttle. Think of the lives you're playing fast and loose with."

McCoy's nostrils flared. "I *am* thinking of lives," he replied, his anger boiling over. "I'm a doctor, dammit. I've never thought of anything *else*."

"Then act like it," the captain told him. "Give up this . . . this plan of yours."

"Not a chance," the admiral insisted. "To save a patient, you've got to act quickly sometimes. You've got to make choices. And you've got to live with the choices you make." He stuck his thumb in his chest. "This is a choice I can live with." (Michael Jan Friedman, *Star Trek: The Next Generation: Crossover* [New York: Pocket Books, 1995], p. 148)

8. If life is, in fact, a river, then you have very few options. You're in a canoe. You can try to paddle upstream and live in the past, looking backward. Then you're going to hit something, and you'll keep wondering why life keeps hitting you in the back. Or you can fight the current but face forward, and not get anywhere. Or you can casually go with the flow and think about pulling over to the side now and then to explore the land. Smell the roses. And some people want to go as fast as they possibly can, straight to hell.

I think I was backpaddling and the canoe tipped over. I had no idea about looking forward and setting a goal. Then I met a guy in prison, at one of those groups, who summoned up the best. The greatest missile in the world is useless, he said, unless it's targeted. A torpedo is adrift unless it has someplace to go. An arrow is pointless unless it hits something.

So it's important for kids—for everyone, even if we fail at first—to target something and head in that direction.

With all your might. (Tim Allen, *Don't Stand Too Close to a Naked Man* [New York: Hyperion, 1994], pp. 95–96)

9. Despite some ingenious suggestions by orthodox Darwinians . . . , there is no convincing Darwinian history for the emergence of sexual reproduction. However, evolutionary theorists believe the problem will be solved without abandoning the main Darwinian insights just as nineteenth-century astronomers believed that the problem of the motion of Uranus could be overcome without major modifications of Newton's celestial mechanics.

The comparison is apt. Like Newton's physics in 1800, evolutionary theory today rests on a huge record of successes. In both cases, we find a unified theory whose problem-solving strategies are applied to illuminate a host of diverse phenomena. Both theories offer problem solutions that can be subjected to rigorous independent checks. Both open new lines of inquiry and have a history of surmounting apparent obstacles. The virtues of successful science are clearly displayed in both. (Philip Kitcher, *Abusing Science: The Case Against Creationism* [Cambridge: MIT Press, 1982], p. 54)

10. On *Good Morning America* one day in June 1999, Diane Sawyer presented a pair of analogies she had received from her friend Leslie Stahl (at CBS):

Women perceive their computers to be a male because they are supposed to have all of the data but are generally clueless. They are supposed to help you with your problems but half of the time, they *are* the problem. And whenever you finally commit to one, you realize that if you had waited a little longer, you could have gotten a better model.

Men, it was concluded, felt their computer was female because only their "creator" could possibly understand their internal logic. Whenever you commit to one, you have to buy it a lot of accessories and even your smallest mistakes get stored in its long-term memory.[14]

11. Setting: King David had an affair with Bathsheba, Uriah's only wife. David had a harem. David arranged to have Uriah killed in battle, after which David married Bathsheba. One day Nathan the prophet visits David and tells him a story.

"There were two men in a certain city, the one rich and the other poor. The rich man had very many flocks and herds; but the poor man had nothing but one little ewe lamb, which he had bought. And he brought it up, and it grew up with him and with his children; it used to eat of his morsel, and drink from his cup, and lie in his bosom, and it was like a daughter to him. Now there came a traveler to the rich man, and he was unwilling to take one of his own flock or herd to prepare for the wayfarer who had come to him, but he took the poor man's lamb, and prepared it for the man who had come to him." David's anger was greatly kindled against the man; and he said to Nathan, "As the Lord lives, the man who has done this deserves to die; and he shall restore the lamb fourfold, because he did this thing, and because he had no pity."

Nathan said to David, "You are the man." (2 Samuel 12:1–7 [Revised Standard Version])

12. One of the main reasons gift receivers typically think of themselves as being financially well-off is because they receive parental subsidies. And people who think they are financially well-off tend to spend. In fact, statistically they are just as likely to view themselves as being affluent as are truly affluent non-gift receivers. This is the case in spite of earning 91 percent of the income and having 81 percent of the wealth of nonreceivers.

Look at the situation from a gift receiver's side of the equation. During each year of his adult life, William receives an annual tax-free gift of $10,000 from his parents. William is forty-eight years of age. Ten thousand dollars of tax-free income could be viewed as the product of what amount of capital? Assume an 8 percent return. This would equate to $125,000 in capital. Add this amount to his actual net worth. What is the result? William perceives himself as having $125,000 more in capital than he does.

Consider this analogy. Have you ever been confronted by an eight-year-old youngster standing in the front yard of their parents' home? If you, a stranger, attempt to walk on the property, Billy or Janie will likely say, "You can't come into *my yard*. This is *my property*." Billy and Janie think that it is their property. At the age of eight they may be correct. After all, they are children living at home. At this age kids feel that the yard, the home, the car are family property. But as the majority of Billys and Janies mature, they become properly socialized by their parents. They grow into independent adults, adults who can easily distinguish between

---

[14]I wish to thank Audience Information, ABC Inc., for providing me with a transcript of what Ms. Sawyer read.

what is theirs and what is not. Their parents teach them independence. (Thomas J. Stanley and William D. Danko, *The Millionaire Next Door: The Surprising Secrets of America's Wealth* [Atlanta: Longstreet Press, 1996], p. 155)

13. I was a good Christian; born and bred in the bosom of the infallible Presbyterian Church. How then could I unite with this wild idolater in worshiping his piece of wood? But what is worship? thought I. Do you suppose now, Ishmael, that the magnanimous God of heaven and earth—pagans and all included—can possibly be jealous of an insignificant bit of black wood? Impossible! But what is worship?—to do the will of God—that is worship. And what is the will of God?—to do to my fellow man what I would have my fellow man to do to me—that is the will of God. Now, Queequeg is my fellow man. And what do I wish that this Queequeg would do to me? Why, unite with me in my particular Presbyterian form of worship. Consequently, I must then unite with him in his; ergo, I must turn idolater. (Herman Melville, *Moby Dick*)

14. Cigarette ads are no different from others. Their purpose is to reinforce a person's desire to buy and use the product. Good ads stimulate the natural response to rush out and purchase what's being advertised. Ineffective ads do not, and normally are quickly pulled. She used the example of McDonald's, a company she had studied, and she just happened to have a report handy in the event the jury wanted to peruse it. By the time a child is three, the child can hum, whistle, or sing whatever the current McDonald's jingle happens to be. The child's first trip to McDonald's is a momentous occasion. This is no accident. The corporation spends billions to hook children before its competitors do. American children consume more fat and cholesterol than the last generation. They eat more cheeseburgers, fries, and pizza, and drink more sodas and sugared fruit drinks. Do we charge McDonald's and Pizza Hut with devious advertising practices for targeting the young? Do we sue them because our kids are fatter?

No. We as consumers make informed choices about the foods we feed our children. No one can argue that we make the best choices.

And we as consumers make informed choices about smoking. (John Grisham, *The Runaway Jury* [New York: Doubleday, 1996], p. 471)

15. If I were to sell the reader a barrel of molasses, and he, instead of sweetening his substantial dinner with the same at judicious intervals, should eat the entire barrel at one sitting, and then abuse me for making him sick, I would say that he deserved to be made sick for not knowing any better how to utilize the blessings this world affords. And if I sell to the reader this volume of nonsense, and he, instead of seasoning his graver reading with a chapter of it now and then, when his mind demands such relaxation, unwisely overdoses himself with several chapters of it at a single sitting, he will deserve to be nauseated, and he will have nobody to blame but himself if he is. There is no more sin in publishing an entire volume of nonsense than there is in keeping a candy-store with no hardware in it. It lies wholly with the customer whether he will injure himself by means of either, or will derive from them the benefits which they will afford him if he uses their possibilities judiciously.   (Mark Twain, Preface to *Mark Twain's Speeches* [New York: Harper and Brothers, 1910])

16. Imagine that you are a lover of the theater in London in the early 17th century, and you have just learned that Will Shakespeare has hung up his quill. You know instantly what this means. . . . Going to the Globe will never be quite as exciting or quite as interesting again. If this seems an excruciatingly hyperbolic analogy to Michael Jordan's retirement on January 13, well, this is the time for excruciatingly hyperbolic analogies. Shakespeare's nonpareil brilliance and versatility have resonated for more than 400 years—you can even see a young, love-struck Will being portrayed at your local multiplex right now!—and it's easy to imagine Jordan's legacy enduring for generations as well.   (Jack McCallum, "Indelible Impression," *Sports Illustrated* 90 [January 25, 1999], p. 84)

17. If you take a magnet and hold it over a paper clip, the paper clip will jump up to meet the magnet. Now hold that paper clip close to another paper clip. What happens? The second paper clip attaches itself to the first paper clip. But if you hold the first paper clip over a rubber band, the rubber band won't be attracted to the paper clip no matter how close the two get. *Any object that is attracted to a magnet becomes a magnet itself as long as it remains in contact with the real magnet.*

Look for friendships with those who are involved in life! Listen for "I can!" "Let me do it!" "Let's try it this way." Surround yourself with these people and you will be more likely to maintain a positive attitude.

Positive attitude and negative attitude are both magnets. They attract the same thing.   (Judy Zerafa, *Go for It!* [New York: Workman Publishing, 1982], p. 28)

18. Yet Earnshaw Rusk, like many thinking men and women across the state, knew that the twentieth century could not possibly begin until 31 December 1900; logic, history and mathematics all proved they were correct, but these zealots had a difficult task persuading their fellow citizens to delay celebrating until the proper date. . . . 'Any idiot knows the new century begins like we say [at the beginning of 1900], and I'm gonna be ringin' that church bell come New Year's Eve and Jim Bob Lomis is gonna be lightin' the fire.'

Rusk found such plans an insult to intelligence. 'Tell me,' he asked Jim Bob, 'now I want you to just tell me, how many years in a century?'. . . .

'A hunnert,' Jim Bob said.

'At the time of Christ, when this all began, was there ever a year zero?'

'Not that I heerd of.'

'So the first century must have begun with the year 1.'

'I think it did.'

'So when we reached the year 99, how may years had the first century had?'

'Sounds like ninety-nine.'

'It was ninety-nine, so the year 100 had nothing special about it. The second century couldn't have begun until the beginning of 101.'   (James A. Michener, *Texas: A Novel* [New York: Random House, 1985], pp. 825–826)

19. "In conclusion, I'd like to return for a moment to the example of the genie. Would I like it put back in the lamp, the lamp itself sealed away from the eyes, the very *awareness*, of man? My life's work is evidence to the contrary. As I interpret the story, it wasn't the genie's power to work wonders that heaped so much pain and trouble upon poor Aladdin. The cause, I think, was Aladdin's lack of judgment about how to use his gift, a failure to understand the exceeding degree of caution and restraint with which it needed to be managed. Power itself is never to be feared. Its uses are determined by the hands into which it falls. With passion and intelligence anything is truly possible.

"But as evolving technologies create new possibilities for us, as in a sense we use science to work magic, our eternal responsibility is to choose those uses which will build rather than destroy, liberate rather than imprison, bring gain rather than loss on us as a species. It's a responsibility that hasn't changed in essence since the discovery of fire or the wheel, although as the tools become more complex, so do our choices. Mistakes are inevitable, but I hope and believe we will learn from them, and be wise enough to correct those we can. If so, then you can take my word for it . . . the genie belongs among us. And he's in the very best of hands." (Tom Clancy and Martin Greenburg, *Tom Clancy's Power Plays: ruthless.com* [New York: Berkley Books, 1998], pp. 280-281)

20. The surface of the earth is, in a sense, its skin—a thin but crucial layer protecting the rest of the planet contained within it. Far more than a simple boundary, it interacts in complex ways with the volatile atmosphere above and the raw earth below. It may seem hard to imagine it as a crucial component of the ecological balance, but in fact, the health of the earth's surface is vital to the health of the global environment as a whole.

To use our own skin as an analogy, we may be surprised when anatomists describe it as the largest organ of our bodies; our skin seems to be first of all merely the boundary of our physical being and far too thin and attenuated to qualify as anything quite so complex as an organ. Yet it constantly renews itself and plays a complex role in shielding us from the harm we would otherwise suffer from the world around us; without it, even the air would corrode our raw innards.

Similarly, the surface of the earth—though it seems to be an insignificant layer of soil and rock, forest and desert, snow and ice, water and living things—serves as a vital protective skin. Just below the surface, the roots draw their nutrients from the soil and, in the process, hold it firmly in place, allowing it to absorb moisture and preventing the wind and rain from carrying it toward the sea. Aboveground, the characteristics of the surface determine how much light is absorbed or reflected and thus help to define the planet's relationship to the sun.
(Al Gore, *Earth in the Balance* [Boston: Houghton Mifflin, 1992], p. 115)

IV. For each of the following analogical arguments, use the six criteria to determine whether the additional considerations strengthen or weaken the argument. In each case, indicate which criteria support your judgment.

1. Hormella Kies is deciding which courses to take next semester. She is considering History 492: The History of England from Earliest Times to A.D. 1000. She has liked all the history courses she has taken in the past, and as she adds this to her tentative course schedule, she fully expects to enjoy it.

a) What if Hormella has taken only History 101 and 102 in the past, and History 492 is a senior seminar?

b) What if Hormella has taken courses in world history, oriental history, U.S. history, South American history, and European history and has enjoyed all those courses?

c) What if all the history courses she has previously taken required only a reading knowledge of modern English, but this course requires a reading knowledge of Anglo-Saxon and Old English?

d) What if Hormella has taken all the courses on English history except this one and found each at least as interesting as the one before?

e) What if Hormella was very interested in the history of the Vikings, and a good portion of the course was going to focus on the influence of Viking invasions of England in the ninth century?

f) What if Hormella thinks this is going to be the most interesting history course she has ever taken?

g) What if the courses Hormella has taken before were all courses in intellectual history, and this was a course in social and political history?

h) What if Professor Bjornsen was teaching this course, and she has enjoyed other courses she has taken with Professor Bjornsen?

i) What if this course was being offered at 8:00 a.m. and Hormella has never before taken a class in the morning?

j) What if Hormella's roommate was also going to take the course, Hormella has never been in a class with her roommate, and her roommate has no aptitude in history?

2. Ostafar Neumathesque is planning a trip on Trans-Transylvanian Airlines to Northern Slovobia. He has flown Trans-Transylvanian once every year for the past six years to visit his aged mother. In each case, he found that the cabin attendants provided exceptional service, the plane arrived at its destination within an hour of the scheduled arrival time, and the pilot added to the excitement of the trip by occasionally "buzzing" flocks of sheep. Ostafar was particularly taken by the airline's policy of "serving a hogshead of wine on every flight," always consuming at least his fair share of the wine. As he packs his bags, Ostafar looks forward to an enjoyable and moderately exciting flight.

a) What if Trans-Transylvanian Airlines has recently lost a court fight with the Northern Slovobian Sheep Farmer's Association and agreed to quit "buzzing" flocks of sheep?

b) What if Ostafar booked his previous flights with Count Dracula's Travel Service, but this time he booked his flight through Frank N. Stein Travel, Inc.?

c) What if there had been a different flight crew on each of his previous trips?

d) What if Ostafar recently joined Alcoholics Anonymous and takes his membership seriously?

e) What if the Amisglof-435 robotic flight attendant had been on all the previous flights and will be on this flight as well?

f) What if Ostafar has flown Trans-Transylvanian Airlines three times a year for the last ten years?

g) What if Ostafar's mother has eloped with the butcher and moved to Southern Slovobia?

h) What if Ostafar is a glutton and on previous flights the meals had consisted of sandwiches whereas on this flight the menu consists of a seven-course dinner?

i) What if all Trans-Transylvanian's cabin attendants are out on strike?

j) What if Ostafar expects this to be the most enjoyable flight he has ever taken?

3. Siegfried Hubbelschnitz is visiting the library, planning to check out a book for some light reading. Siegfried is a nuclear physicist and an avid reader of science fiction. He discovers that his favorite science-fiction author, Ostafar Neumathesque, has published a new book. Siegfried checks it out, fully expecting a moderately enjoyable evening of reading.

a) What if Siegfried has read all of Ostafar's previous books and has found each new book more enjoyable than those written earlier?

b) What if all of Ostafar's previous books were works of science fiction, but this one is an autobiography?

c) What if Siegfried finds his work extremely enjoyable and the main character in the book he checked out is a nuclear physicist?

d) What if Siegfried has read all of Ostafar's previous books, has found each new book more enjoyable than those written earlier, and therefore expects this to be the most enjoyable book Ostafar has written?

e) What if Siegfried has read hundreds of science-fiction books, he has never read a work in science fiction he didn't like, and the book he checked out is science fiction?

f) What if Siegfried has recently met Ostafar Neumathesque while on a trip to Northern Slovobia?

g) What if Siegfried has recently been married?

h) What if the books Siegfried has previously read by Ostafar Neumethesque included several works of science fiction, several biographies of famous physicists, and a history of Trans-Transylvanian Airlines?

i) What if all the books by Ostafar that Siegfried has previously read were written in Rumanian, and this one is also written in Rumanian?

j) What if Siegfried has always read in the privacy of his own home, but on his way home from the library he is kidnapped by South Slovobian terrorists?

4. Ingrid is planning her winter vacation. Since she has enjoyed skiing in the Blue Ridge Mountains, the Rockies, and the Swiss Alps, she decides to go on a skiing vacation. Since she likes to travel and there are some similarities between the mountains in Norway and those she has previously skied, she decides to go to Norway. She expects to enjoy her trip.

a) What if Ingrid speaks fluent English, German, French, and Italian, and therefore had no trouble communicating on her previous trips, but she doesn't speak a word of Norwegian?

b) What if the best skiing is in northern Norway, where it is almost perpetually dark in winter?

    c) What if Ingrid formerly went skiing with some of her closest friends, but they will not be coming along on this trip?

    d) What if on other trips Ingrid has gone to a ski resort and this time she is staying in a private family home?

    e) What if she expects it will be less enjoyable than her trip to Switzerland, which was her favorite trip?

    f) What if she has been accompanied on previous skiing trips by a group of her closest friends, and she will be accompanied by the same group this time?

    g) What if Ingrid recently broke her leg and she has never before gone skiing with a broken leg?

    h) What if the fjords in Norway will be frozen when she is there?

    i) What if Ingrid's best friend prefers ice skating to skiing?

    j) What if the Norwegian ski patrol replaces the brandy in its St. Bernards' barrels with diet cola?

5. Agatha is wondering how the university football team will do this year. Last year they had a record of eight wins and three losses. Half of their starting players are returning this year. The coaching staff is the same. So, she expects that they should have a winning season again this year.

    a) What if one of the returning players is their All-American quarterback Hank Hands?

    b) What if one of their new recruits was the top high-school fullback in the state last year?

    c) What if the grass in the stadium has been replaced with astroturf?

    d) What if all the roughest games on the schedule are home games?

    e) What if Agatha expects their record to be at least ten wins and one loss this year?

    f) What if their star receiver broke his leg in practice and will be out for the season?

    g) What if all the returning starters are in the offensive line, none in the defensive line?

    h) What if an Associated Press preseason poll has rated the team fourth in the country?

    i) What if the coach plans to change the offense from a ground game to a passing game?

    j) What if the NCAA placed the team on probation for recruiting violations?

6. On the last trading day of the year for each of the past ten years, Milan has invested in 100 shares of the XYZ Telephone Company stock. Over that time, she has observed that the stock provides dividends of approximately 6 percent on her investment and has appreciated in value at an average rate of 8 percent per year. As the last trading day of the year approaches, she plans to invest again, expecting comparable returns.

    a) What if she expects her stock to appreciate in value at the rate of 15 percent per year?

    b) What if in years past the price of the stock dropped before the last trading day of the year, and it dropped again this year?

c) What if the phone company is planning a three-for-one split?

d) What if the phone company is being investigated by the Federal Communications Commission for violations of several federal laws?

e) What if the phone company has recently sold its long-distance services to another company?

f) What if the economy has fallen into a severe recession in the last year?

g) What if she expected only a 3 percent dividend on her investment?

h) What if the company has a new chairman of the board?

i) What if the value of oil company stocks are appreciating at a greater rate than phone company stocks?

j) What if Milan decided to invest in 1,000 shares of stock rather than 100?

7. Josiah is working on his tenth book. His previous books have sold fairly well, and each has provided him with a reasonably good livelihood for about two years. As he finishes the final chapter, he expects this book will allow him to retain his current standard of living for another year or two.

a) What if Josiah had written his previous books in Indiana, and he is writing this book in Hawaii?

b) What if his previous books were murder mysteries, and this one is also a murder mystery?

c) What if his previous books were novels, and this book is an autobiography?

d) What if the same publisher that published his previous books is going to publish this book?

e) What if each of his previous books was published by a different publisher, but this book will be published by the same company that published his last book?

f) What if each of his previous books was published under a pseudonym but this book will be published under his own name?

g) What if Josiah recently has been divorced?

h) What if Josiah's book features the same hero as that in his previous nine books?

i) What if each of Josiah's previous books was more successful than its predecessor?

j) What if each of Josiah's previous books was more successful than its predecessor and Josiah expects this to be at least as successful as his second book?

8. Lucinda and Hector are planning to go dancing. They have gone dancing three times, and Lucinda enjoyed both Hector's quick wit and his "grace" on the dance floor. (At least his dance steps had done her no *permanent* damage.) As Lucinda puts on her new, steel-toed dance slippers, she looks forward to an enjoyable evening.

a) What if Hector has taken dance lessons since the last time he and Lucinda went dancing?

b) What if the last time they went dancing, they danced the fandango, the tango, the polka, and the schottische, and they will be dancing the same types of dance this time?

c) What if Hector has laryngitis?

d) Does the fact that Lucinda will be wearing *steel-toed* dance slippers tonight, unlike the previous times she went dancing with Hector, make any difference?

e) What if Hector picks up Lucinda in his "new" 1969 Chevy pickup? (On previous occasions he drove his parents' 2000 Lexus.)

f) What if the same band will be playing tonight that played the last three times they went dancing?

g) What if Lucinda's Aunt Alicia has finally given Hector her blessing, so Aunt Alicia will *not* be chaperoning tonight?

h) What if Lucinda and Hector had been dancing ten times before?

i) What if Lucinda picks up Hector in her new Porsche?

j) What if the other times the dances had been in the school gym, but this time the dance will be in the ballroom at the Hilton?

9. You are going to buy a house. You have been looking at a four-bedroom, two-and-a-half bath split-foyer home built by Sanchez Family Builders. You have compared it with ten other homes built by Sanchez, homes of various designs, and you have discovered that the home you are considering is similar to each of the ten insofar as they have six-inch walls that are thoroughly insulated, they are tastefully decorated, they have vinyl siding, they have heat pumps, and they have a Jacuzzi. You have talked with the owners of the ten homes in the ground, and they said their homes were comfortable, low-maintenance homes. So, as you submit your bid on the four-bedroom, two-and-a-half bath split-foyer, you assume it will be a comfortable, low-maintenance home.

a) What if the house on which you submit your bid were a five-bedroom Cape Cod home built by Sanchez?

b) What if you were comparing your prospective home to twenty other houses built by Sanchez?

c) What if all the houses in the ground were about twenty years old, and the house you are considering is also about twenty years old?

d) What if all the houses in the ground were four-bedroom, two-and-a-half bath split-foyer homes?

e) What if all the houses in the ground had vinyl siding, but the one you are looking at has a brick façade?

f) What if all the houses in the ground have blue vinyl siding, and the house you are considering also has blue vinyl siding?

g) What if the houses in the ground differed from one another insofar as some are brick, some are wood framed with vinyl siding, and some are underground houses?

h) What if the ownership of Sanchez Family Builders has changed and the houses in the ground were built by the original Sanchez Builders, but the house you are looking at was built by Sanchez Family Builders, a subsidiary of Build 'Em Cheap, Inc.?

i) What if all the houses in the ground were owned by their occupants, while the house you are considering has been a rental property for the past ten years?

j) What if each house in the ground has an attached two-car garage, and the house you are considering also has an attached two-car garage?

10. You are asking yourself whether you should attend the latest Denzel Washington movie. You have seen six of his movies, and have liked every one. So, you expect to enjoy the next Denzel Washington movie as well.

a) What if you expect it to be the best Denzel Washington movie ever?

b) What if in every movie in which you have seen him he played a serious dramatic role, and he will be playing a serious dramatic role in the next movie as well?

c) What if in every movie in which you have seen him he played a serious dramatic role, but in his new movie he has the lead in a comedy?

d) What if you had seen twelve of his movies and had enjoyed every one?

e) What if some of the movies you saw were serious dramas, some were action-adventure movies, and one was a comedy?

f) What if Washington won an Academy Award for one of the movies you saw?

g) What if the same director directed the new movie who directed your favorite three of the earlier movies?

h) What if the new movie differs from earlier movies insofar as it is a movie based on a video game?

i) What if the new movie is a sequel to *Crimson Tide,* and you enjoyed *Crimson Tide?*

j) What if the movie also stars Harrison Ford, and you are *not* a big Harrison Ford fan?

Discussion Questions

Explain how arguments by analogy play a role in each of the following.

1. You are choosing a roommate for next year. What kinds of similarities and differences between past roommates, friends, and family members would be relevant in choosing a roommate? Why and how are they relevant?

2. If you choose a major or a career, you always go beyond the kinds of experiences you have had. How can analogical arguments help clarify what the major or career would be like and whether it is likely you would enjoy it?

3. How can analogical arguments play a role in choosing among political candidates?

4. You are learning a new computer program. You have already mastered a word-processing program, a spreadsheet program, and a graphics program. How can analogical considerations probably help you figure out the various aspects of the new program? How will considerations of similarities and difference between operating systems (for example, DOS, Windows, and Linux) affect the analogies?

5. In his *Life of Reason,* the American philosopher George Santayana wrote, "Those who cannot remember the past are condemned to repeat it." How can reasoning by analogy help keep us from being "condemned to repeat" the past?

Generalizations and Surveys

The View: In some cases we argue from what is true of a certain number of things to what is true of a class of things. We generalize. In this chapter we examine the criteria used to evaluate generalizations.

How do you evaluate arguments to generalizations? How are surveys similar to and different from arguments to a universal generalization? Are there ways in which surveys can mislead?

In an argument by analogy you go directly from a comparison of two or more things to a conclusion about properties of one of those things. In reaching an inductive generalization, you go from claims that are true of a certain number of particular objects to a claim that is said to be true of a certain class of objects. Your conclusion might concern all objects of a kind, or most objects, or many objects, or a certain percentage of all objects of a kind.

The criteria for evaluating a generalization are similar to those used in evaluating an argument by analogy.

1. As the number of objects taken into account increases, the generalization is strengthened.

2. Care must be taken to show that the cases upon which you make your generalization are typical.

3. The more diverse the sample is, the better the basis for the generalization is.

4. The stronger the conclusion is, the weaker the argument is.

The first three criteria are related to one another. The first criterion concerns the size of the **sample**, the group of objects that provides the basis for the generalization. If you are going to talk about a class of objects, the larger the proportion of the class you examine, the more probable your conclusion is. So, all things being equal, the larger the number of objects you examine, the better the evidence is for the conclusion. If you have owned two IBM computers and had trouble with each, the sample is far too small to make any general claims regarding the quality of IBM computers.

As the number of objects in the sample increases, the probability that the objects sampled are typical increases. Assume you have a box of 100 balls. You are wondering what color or colors the balls in the box are. You reach in the box and pull out a red ball. Is it a typical ball? Are all the balls or most of the balls red? There is no way to tell. So, you set the ball aside, shake the box (to mix up the balls), draw out another ball, set it aside, and repeat the procedure until you have drawn out twenty balls. Each ball you drew out was red. At that point you have reason to believe that the first ball you drew out was typical. You probably would conclude that all or most of the balls in the box are red.

The size of the sample, however, will *not* assure the cases are typical unless questions of diversity are also taken into account. Assume you are studying the characteristics of rabbits. You have examined 200 rabbits found in a fifty-square-mile area. What can you conclude? If you are going to draw conclusions regarding *all* the different kinds of rabbits found in the area—jackrabbits, cottontails, marsh rabbits, swamp rabbits, and so on—care must be taken to make sure that the various kinds of rabbits found in the habitat are included in the sample. But you cannot say much about rabbits living outside that fifty-square-mile area. If you want to make a general claim about rabbits in the United States, you will need to sample rabbits of the relevant kinds from numerous places in the United States. The genetic pool for each species of rabbit in northern Minnesota might differ from those in Texas, California, Oregon, and Florida. The various habitats might select in favor of certain genetic characteristics or influence the size and development of rabbits in other ways. So, as the sample becomes more diverse, the generalization reached becomes more probable.

The fourth criterion differs from the other three. A conclusion is strong relative to the evidence needed to show that it is false. If I drew twenty red balls from a box of 100 and concluded that *all* the balls in the box are red, the conclusion is very strong. The conclusion would be false if there were only one ball in the box that was *not* red. The conclusion would be much weaker if I claimed that most (at least fifty-one) of the balls in the box are red. For that conclusion to be false, at least fifty of the 100 would have to be some color other than red. And the conclusion would be weaker still if I claimed that at least twenty-one balls are red.

> You are visiting your physician. To test the iron level in your blood, she pricks your finger and squeezes out a few cubic millimeters of blood. The sample is small. The blood is drawn from one place. Why is the sample typical? The bloodstream is a closed system. The rate of blood cell production is fairly uniform. If there are differences in the amount of iron in the blood cells produced from day to day, the cells are uniformly distributed throughout the system. So, a small amount of blood is a uniform sample.

Given these considerations, let's look at some examples.

Dan owned two IBM computers. He bought his first IBM computer in 1990, and within six months he had to replace a disk drive. He bought his second IBM computer in 1994. The hard disk crashed within the first three months. The main board cracked within the first six months. Can you draw any general conclusions? No. IBM has made millions of computers, and the sample is much too small to make any generalization (criterion 1). Further, the computer Dan bought in 1990 was not typical (criterion 2). It was a seven-year-old portable computer, and, consistent with the experience of vast numbers of people, old things (including computers) occasionally break down. The second computer, a laptop, was purchased new. While you might be surprised that it had two major problems within the first six months, it is consistent with the experience of many people that new things occasionally break down. Further, the sample is limited to two variations on portable computers. IBM makes desktop computers as well as mainframes. The sample lacks diversity (criterion 3). So, beyond the claims "Dan had some problems with his IBM computers" and "Some people have had some problems with their IBM computers"—which are *deductively entailed* by the evidence—Dan's experience provides no basis for a general evaluation of IBM computers. This also illustrates the fourth criterion. The statement "Some people have had some problems with their IBM computers" is extremely weak. Its truth requires only that at least one person had at least one problem with at least one IBM computer that he or she owned.[1]

There are many times when you will want to make a general statement. As we see in the next chapter, one of those is when looking for the cause of an event or phenomenon. Another might be when you are looking for a general premise to use in a syllogism. A third is when politicians or advertisers want to know how popular they or their products are. We begin with considerations of very broad generalizations. Then we turn to considerations of surveys.

Are all crows black birds? How do you find out? You look. You identify crows on the basis of their shape, size, behavior, and sounds, *not* in terms of their color. You look at birds near your home, at school, on trips to other cities, on trips to other countries. You even make a special trip to Australia, since Australia has a reputation for having animals that are a bit different from animals anywhere else. This helps assure diversity. Let's assume you have observed 1,000 crows, and each crow was black. What can you conclude? You can conclude that every crow you have seen is black,[2] that some crows are black, and, if you have observed no individual crow twice, that at least 1,000 crows are black. None of these conclusions take you beyond the data. Each follows with deductive certainty. But the question posed takes you beyond the data. You must reach a conclusion by induction.

You might conclude that *many* crows that existed during your period of observations are black. The word 'many' is vague. How many crows do you need to observe

---

[1] If you make a fairly strong generalization—one claiming that all or most things of one sort are things of another—from a small number of cases, especially from atypical cases, you commit the informal fallacy of hasty generalization. This is discussed in Chapter 31. There are exceptions to this general claim. If you are dealing with an object that is already well known, you might be able legitimately to generalize from a single case. If you already have grounds for determining that something is a piece of gold and you discover that that one piece of gold is tasteless, you have good grounds for claiming that any other piece of gold would be tasteless as well.

[2] Every proposition entails itself. So, if you begin with the premise "Every crow I have seen is black," you can conclude—with deductive certainty—that "Every crow I have seen is black." Of course, the conclusion provides you with neither new information nor insight into what is entailed by the premises. It is a useless argument. It is an example of the informal fallacy **begging the question**. More will be said about begging the question in Chapter 30.

before you claim that many crows are black? There are lots of crows. So, in proportion to the number of crows that existed during your period of observation, it would be reasonable to suggest that 1,000 crows do not count as "many." Your conclusion goes beyond the evidence. It is a strong inductive inference, since the conclusion is fairly weak. If you say *most* crows that existed during your period of observation were black, it is a weaker inference. If you say that *all* crows that existed during your period of observation were black, it would be weaker still. It would take only one nonblack crow to show that your inference is false, since the statements "All crows are black" and "Some crows are not black" are **contradictory propositions**. Two propositions are contradictory propositions if the truth of one validly implies the falsehood of the other. One of two contradictory propositions is true, although you might not know which one is true. But your question was broader still. In asking whether all crows are black, you are concerned with all crows that existed in the past, all presently existing crows, and all crows that will exist in the future. Again, it would take only one nonblack crow to establish that the conclusion is false. The conclusion is very strong. Therefore, the inference is very weak. The inference would be stronger if the conclusion were weaker, that is, if you concluded either that many or most past, present, and future crows are black, but the conclusion still might be false.

Assume that the vast majority of crows that have existed prior to 2041 were black, but in 2041 there is a disaster that results in a mutation of the crow's color gene. Assume that crows hatched after 2041 are green and that green crows are extremely prolific. Assume further that in the entire history of the crow, the period dominated by green crows is fifty times longer than the period dominated by black crows. Under such circumstances, the evidence you gather on the basis of 1,000 crows would not show that *most* crows are black, and relative to the population of crows throughout the history of the bird, it might not even show that *many* crows are black.

The example shows us several things. First, all generalizations are made relative to some class of objects—a sample—and the strength of the generalization varies relative to the sample. Given 1,000 or 10,000 instances of black crows observed in diverse places, you have fairly strong evidence that most currently existing crows are black. You have weaker evidence that most of the crows that have existed and will exist are black. If you had observed all 1,000 crows from your kitchen window, you would have less evidence that most currently existing crows are black, but you might have fairly good evidence that most (or all) of the crows in your neighborhood are black.

Second, the example illustrates an assumption made that, *at some level,* the future will resemble the past. This is sometimes called the **principle of the uniformity of nature**. The principle of the uniformity of nature is assumed regarding natural laws. For example, it is assumed that the principles of thermodynamics have always applied and will always apply to the material world. Our hypothetical case that after 2041 the overwhelming majority of crows are green still assumes that the principles of genetics and natural selection hold—these principles explain why the overwhelming majority of crows would be green. But in drawing an inductive inference—such as that all crows are black—we often assume uniformity at a less general level. For example, in the early days of rock 'n' roll, the swing-band leader

Benny Goodman predicted that rock 'n' roll would not become the dominant form of popular music. His implicit argument seems to have gone like this: Swing music has been the most popular form of music for the past twenty years. The future will resemble the past. So, swing will continue to be the most popular form of music. Goodman was wrong—at least, swing did *not* retain its place at the top of the pop charts—but this does not speak against the principle of the uniformity of nature. A more sophisticated argument might have predicted the downfall of swing. Swing music has been popular for about twenty years. Assume history shows that tastes in popular music change every twenty years. So, the popularity of swing music will decline in favor of some other musical form (for example, rock).[3]

Exercises

1. I have observed exactly 500 ravens and they were all black. Which of the following conclusions are justified on the basis of this evidence (choose all the correct answers by letter): (A) All ravens are black. (B) All the ravens I observed are black. (C) There are at least 500 black ravens. (D) Some ravens are black. (E) The majority of ravens are black. Why are your choices justified?

2. Walter Cronkite, the veteran CBS news broadcaster, was a college dropout. Michael Dell, founder and president of Dell Computers, was a college dropout. Harrison Ford, the actor, never completed college. Neither Danny Thomas, the actor who founded St. Jude's Children's Hospital, nor the veteran actors George Burns and Danny Kay completed high school. So, getting a good education will not help you become a success in your chosen field.

3. My doctor was wondering whether I was suffering from anemia, so she drew a sample of blood from my left arm and sent me on my way. Wouldn't the test be more accurate if she drew blood from several places in my body?

4. In 1981 I bought a Dodge Omni. In the fourteen years I owned it, I replaced virtually every moving part except the transmission and its Volkswagen engine. I vowed I would never again buy a Chrysler product, since they are not reliable. Why is my vow unreasonable?

5. I called Dial-a-Psychic, and they predicted that my car would break down last year. It did. I called Dial-a-Psychic during my senior year in college, and they predicted I would graduate. I did. I called Dial-a-Psychic, and they predicted I would meet a mysterious person. I did. So, I can always trust Dial-a-Psychic to tell me what to expect!

---

[3]There are problems with the principle of the uniformity of nature. There seems to be no means by which it can be proven true. See David Hume, *An Enquiry concerning Human Understanding*, in David Hume, *Enquiries concerning the Human Understanding and concerning the Principles of Morals*, ed. L. A. Selby-Bigge, 3rd ed. revised by P. H. Nidditch (Oxford: Clarendon Press, 1975), pp. 32–9. Nonetheless, the principle is assumed by us, all the time, in making inductive inferences.

Sampling and Surveys

We are often interested in generalizations that are less than universal. Sometimes we want a "snapshot" of how things appear at the present time. Politicians want to know how many people are likely to support them in an election. Advertisers want to know who buys a product and what the best places to advertise a product are. Political scientists might want to know what correlations are between religious beliefs and voting patterns so they can develop a theoretical explanation of that correlation. To answer these kinds of questions, we construct a survey.

You have probably participated in a survey. You are eating supper. The phone rings. You are asked, "Are you planning to vote in the next election? Are you planning to vote for Candidate A or Candidate B?" The next morning you read in the newspaper, "Forty-eight percent of voters surveyed who plan to vote in the next election favor Candidate A. Forty-seven percent favor Candidate B. Five percent are undecided. The survey had a margin of error of ± 4 percent." What does that mean? Should you believe it? To answer these questions, we need to draw some distinctions and ask some additional questions.

Surveys are of two types. There are **purposive sampling models** and **probability (random) sampling models**. A sample is **random** if every member of a population has an equal chance of being chosen to be included in the sample. If you are told the number of people who favor Candidates A or B, or if you are told the President's current approval rating, you *assume* the sample was random. As we shall see below, randomness is often an unrealizable ideal. Before turning to randomness, we shall look briefly at purposive sampling models.

Any sample that is *not* random is **biased**. In this sense, all purposive samples are biased. Nonetheless, there are times that it is either impossible or impractical to obtain a random sample. Assume that you are trying to determine the average life expectancy of people in the nineteenth century American West. You could do so by checking birth and death records in courthouses, or by checking baptismal and funeral records at churches, or by examining tombstones. The first two kinds of records are incomplete. Tombstones are more promising, since they often contain both birth and death dates. But many settlers in the American West were buried with

Source: Seth Casana, Academia Nuts. *Used with permission of the author.*

no marker or with a wooden marker, which has fallen victim to rot and decay. Tombstones made from soft stones have been eroded by wind and weather and are often illegible. So, your survey is limited to tombstones that are made of hard materials, such as marble and granite. The survey is **haphazard**. It is limited to the objects that present themselves for the study. Since there is probably a correlation between costly memorials and wealth, it is unlikely that the survey will tell you the life expectancy of a typical person in the nineteenth century American West.

Not only surveys of historical artifacts are haphazard. When I was in college, participants for a psychological study were recruited with signs saying, "Participate in this study and receive $5 for less than an hour of your time." When I was in college, $5 was equal to more than three hours of work-study, so I participated. The study was haphazard. It might still be a valuable study if there were other grounds for claiming that we money-poor students did not differ in relevant respects from our wealthier friends.

Homogeneous samples are drawn from a narrow range of a theoretical variable. Either extreme cases or rare cases are overrepresented. Extreme case samples are often used to determine the boundaries of human action or institutions. If you are interested in the relationship between stress and excitement, your subjects might be limited to members of sky diving clubs. You might do additional surveys focusing on other groups—people in other cultures or in other economic groups—to see whether the first study holds more generally. Rare case studies might focus on an issue such as the impact of parents on antidepressants on family life. To sample parents generally to find those who are on antidepressants would be costly and time consuming. So, you might turn to a medical database. But given confidentiality considerations, it is likely that only a small portion of the population could be identified as the basis for the sample. This raises questions of typicality and therefore whether the sample is random.

Quota sampling divides a population into relevant groups and samples the population in proportion to its prevalence in a population. So, if you are interested in questions regarding, for example, voting preferences with respect to gender and incomes above and below $50,000 per year, you would divide the population into males making more than $50,000 per year, females making more than $50,000 per year, males making less than $50,000 per year, and females making less than $50,000 per year. One problem with this is that the numbers in one or more of the groups might be so small that it could not be random.[4]

Structural samples are made regarding relationships in a structure. For example, if you are concerned with the tendencies of people in an organization to form small groups, you might focus on persons in a college community. What holds for a college community might not hold for a corporate community or a legislative community. To reach a general conclusion, you would need to do structural surveys regarding different kinds of communities to see whether the tendencies are similar across kinds of communities.

---

[4]As we shall see, there are similarities between this and a stratified random sample, and there are ways to overcome these problems.

Sometimes a survey group is hard to identify, and you increase the sample by requesting references from those in the original sample. This is called **snowball sampling**. If you are concerned with a characteristic regarding bridge players, you might identify an initial group, construct an interview, and ask for the names of other bridge players. Bridge players are likely to know other bridge players. So, with each interview, your sample is likely to increase.

Expert choice sampling assumes that experts in a certain area have some special understanding of what is typical. If a person were doing a comparative study of Shakespearian plays and plays by Thornton Wilder, she might choose one play by each—perhaps, *King Lear* and *Our Town*—as typical works of each playwright and base her comparison on those two plays alone. Why only two plays? The analysis would become exceptionally complex if the comparison covered all of Shakespeare's and Wilder's plays. There is only so much a person can do in one lifetime!

In each case of purposive sampling, there was some choice made regarding the sample. Since in a random sample every member of a population has an equal chance of being surveyed, purposive samples are not random. Does this mean they should be ignored? No, but you need to be aware of the limitations. A primary concern with surveys, as with all arguments to a generalization, is that the sample be typical. If the bridge-players sample with which you begin is drawn from the membership of the Millionaires' Bridge Club, chances are good that the snowball sample that develops will be composed of well-to-do bridge players. If the initial sample is from the College Faculty Bridge Club, chances are good that most of the people in the snowball sample will be well educated. So, to have a basis on which to judge the conclusions of the survey, you need to know something about the sample. A snowball sample that began with members of the Millionaires' Bridge Club would not be a good basis for concluding that 53 percent of *all* bridge players have at least a six-figure annual income.

> In 1936 *Literary Digest* constructed a poll to determine whether Alf Landon or Franklin Roosevelt was the favorite candidate for President. Landon "won" the poll. Roosevelt won the election. The survey was biased. It was a telephone poll constructed at a time when only wealthier Americans owned telephones.

When you hear that a recent poll shows that the 72 percent of Americans approve of the President's performance, you *assume* that the survey was random. If the survey was random, then *every* American had an equal chance of being contained in the sample. But that can't be right. Young children are never included in the sample. So, is it 72 percent of adult Americans? No. Most of the surveys reported in the news are telephone polls. While the overwhelming majority of adult Americans have telephones, street people usually do not. Some people have unlisted numbers. So, some adult Americans are systematically excluded. So, is it 72 percent of adult Americans who have listed telephones? No, not quite. Pollsters tell us that about 1 to 2 percent of people contacted refuse to participate in polls. So, is it 72 percent of adult Americans with telephones who agree to participate in polls? Well, the entire statement is 72 percent, ±5 percent with a 95 percent level of confidence. That means that there is a 95 percent chance that somewhere between 67 percent and 77 percent of all Americans who have telephones and agree to participate in polls approve of the President's performance. What's going on?

A simple random survey is one in which everything in the population surveyed has an equal chance of being chosen. Anything short of that is biased to some degree. Randomness is an *ideal* that is seldom realized or realizable. If a purely random survey is possible, the pollster must have a complete list of objects in the population. No such list is available for the population of the United States. So, any list will be biased. If you are surveying a national organization, you might have a membership list, but even if it is up-to-the-minute, it probably will contain names of persons who have died. So, for most surveys, at least some bias is built in. The goal in a random survey is to minimize the bias.

There must be a means by which one can assure that the choice of things in the sample is random. Common ways to do so include drawing names from a hat, randomly choosing where to begin on a list (perhaps by a throw of dice) and contacting every so-manyeth name on the list or object in a line, by draws of a card from well-shuffled deck, by use of a lotto machine, and so forth. Statisticians suggest that there are empirical grounds for claiming that each of the previous methods is not purely random. They suggest that the best method is by means of a computer-generated table of random numbers such as the following:[5]

Table of Random Numbers

	A	B	C	D	E	F	G	H	I	J
1	30646	54517	37759	33695	73405	4567	60481	53950	4850	54402
2	90636	5210	3583	43711	82662	29087	24153	87293	40023	37473
3	81154	9577	17675	64219	79355	42150	71858	52423	10175	58903
4	85514	52028	37698	5103	22379	46411	47208	98475	84022	1646
5	4621	33956	26190	22208	35109	40201	43572	25234	64790	34685
6	70096	23943	71663	65981	17386	43661	64042	72003	70283	98875
7	98379	39892	7343	59198	20175	99175	62883	99780	48883	14075
8	51257	64212	63735	95565	13530	70460	1095	84266	82167	59084
9	54703	33595	23339	41768	56463	50294	81756	53911	14218	13196
10	37989	50129	3109	35534	7720	32908	81235	5851	45248	82754

Assume you have a population of 100 objects. You have them numbered from 1 to 100. You want a sample of twenty objects. Choose a row—any row—and using the last two digits in the number, pick the object or person corresponding to each number and include it in your sample. If the final two digits are 00, it is number 100. If you prefer columns to rows, choose a column—any column—work down it, and then work down the one to its right.

You should notice something about this procedure. The final two digits of both cell 6J and 7J are 75. So, if you had chosen to use rows six and seven, item number 75 would be surveyed twice. This reflects what is called a **simple random sample with replacement**. In a simple random sample with replacement, any individual that

---

[5]Published tables of random numbers are typically larger than this, often having a hundred or more rows. This is strictly for purposes of illustration.

is drawn from the population is sampled (interviewed, examined) and then returned to the population from which the sample is drawn. In a simple random sample with replacement, an individual can be sampled multiple times. This is commonly used for an indefinitely large population. In a **simple random sample without replacement**, any individual that is drawn from the population is sampled (interviewed, examined) and *not* returned to the population from which the sample is drawn. In a simple random sample without replacement, no individual can be sampled multiple times. This is commonly used for a finitely large population. If you were using a table of random numbers with simple random sampling without replacement, when a given number came up twice, you would ignore the second instance and continue on to the next row or column.

> ## Generating Tables of Random Numbers
>
> If you have a spreadsheet program, it probably will include a function that allows you to generate a table of random numbers. In *Microsoft Excel*, for example, you type =rand()˙100000 in the first cell of the spreadsheet and copy it to as many additional cells as are needed to generate numbers up to five digits. Since the numbers generated are random, if you are doing simple sampling with replacement and want a sample of twenty objects, you need only twenty cells. If you are doing simple sampling without replacement, you might want thirty or forty cells. If you want a sample of 1,000 objects, you might want to generate larger numbers (=rand()˙1000000 would generate six-digit numbers) and construct a table of 1,000 to 1,500 cells.

But what does this tell you? As such, it tells you very little. You need to know how the survey was taken so there is reason to believe that no group has been systematically excluded. (It will not do to say, "Street people and people under 18 have no political opinions." It *might* be more reasonable to say, "Political opinions of people under 18 don't count, since they can't vote," but history shows that *some* people too young to vote have influenced political decisions.) You also need to know how many people are in the sample. The larger the sample, the more probable it is that the sample represents the population. Further, the more accurate (confident) you want to be, the larger the sample needs to be. If you have a population of 200 people and you want to be 99 percent sure that your conclusion is correct, you need to sample 171 people (85.5 percent of the population). If you settled for 98 percent confidence, it would take only 105 (52.5 percent of the population). If the population were

> The next kind of technique is statistical sampling. I referred to that idea when I said they tried to arrange things so that they had one in twenty odds.... The general idea is kind of obvious. If you want to know how many people are taller than six feet tall, then you just pick people out at random, and you see that maybe forty of them are more than six feet so you guess that maybe everybody is. Sounds stupid. Well, it is and it isn't. If you pick the hundred out by seeing which ones come through a low door, you get it wrong. If pick them out by looking at your friends you'll get it wrong because they're all in one place in the country. But if you pick out a way that as far as anybody can figure out has no connection with their height at all, then if you find forty out of a hundred, then, in a hundred million there will be more or less forty million. How much more or how much less can be worked out quite accurately. In fact, it turns out that to be more or less correct to 1 percent, you have to have 10,000 samples. People don't realize how difficult it is to get the accuracy high. For only 1 or 2 percent you need 10,000 tries.
>
> —Richard P. Feynman, *The Meaning of It All* (Reading: Perseus Books, 1998), p. 84.

100,000 people and you wanted to be 99 percent confident of your results, it would take 1,173 people (1.2 percent). For a confidence level of 98 percent, it would take only 217 people (0.2 percent of the population).[6] The **confidence level** is the degree of accuracy which experience indicates can be assumed on the basis of a sample of a certain size for a population of a certain size. Most surveys assume a confidence level of 95 percent. Most surveys also state a **margin of error** in terms of percentage points. The margin of error is the percentage by

The following chart shows the Gallup Organization's experience regarding margins of error calculations for U.S. adult survey samples.

Number of Interviews	Margin of Error (in percentage points)
4,000	±2
1,500	±3
1,000	±4
750	±4
600	±5
400	±6
200	±8
100	±11

which past experience suggests actual behavior might deviate from the results of a survey within a certain confidence level. So, if 72 percent ±5 percent approve of the President's performance, according to a survey with a confidence level of 95 percent, then it is 95 percent probable that between 67 percent and 77 percent of the population approves of the President's performance.

Most reports of surveys you hear on the news are (or approach) simple random surveys. Regarding such surveys, it is always appropriate to ask how the sample was constructed, how large the population is, how large the sample is, and, if you are not told, what the margin of error and the confidence level are.

Not all random surveys are simple random surveys. If you know something about divisions in the population—by gender, race, age, education level, and so on—you might construct a **stratified random survey**. In a stratified random survey, the population is divided into categories (strata), and each stratum is surveyed randomly. Social scientists often are interested in the correlations between age or gender or race and such things as economic status. There is an office at your college or university that thrives on such statistical correlations. This type of survey is also undertaken by many companies that sell durable goods. Remember the last time you sent in a warranty card? You were probably asked to fill in information regarding age, income, at what kind of store the product was purchased, how you came to know of the product, and so forth. Such information is used in marketing decisions. If most of those who purchase light-weight tennis rackets with enlarged heads are persons over fifty with an annual income in excess of $60,000, the advertising for the product will be more prevalent in magazines read by that group, and the advertisements will feature middle-aged people rather than teenagers.

There are a couple things we should note about stratified random sampling. If you are comparing the views of Christians, Jews, Buddhists, and atheists on how to

---

[6] See Morris James Slonim, *Sampling in a Nutshell* (New York: Simon & Schuster, 1960), pp. 74–75.

respond to terrorism, it is important that the samples in each stratum be of the same size. This helps assure randomness within the stratum. If you are doing marketing research on the basis of information on warranty cards, the sample is haphazard. You can deal only with those cards that are returned, and those cards will be completed to varying degrees. We all know people who say, "It's no one's business how much money I make," for example. So, in the case of the warranty cards, the sample is *not* random, although it might be as close to random as you could reasonably expect.

Systematic sampling consists of choosing every so-manyeth object after a random choice of the first object. The Census Bureau uses this approach, in part, since every so-manyeth form sent out is the long form, which requests more information than the short form. This is common in quality-control studies. Here care must be taken to assure that there are no hidden biases. For example, if you are the quality-control officer at a factory and you decide to check every twentieth widget on the conveyor belt, you want to be sure that the various machines that deposit widgets on the belt are equally represented. If there are five machines and they deposit widgets on the conveyor belt at the same rate, you would *not* want to choose a so-manyeth that is divisible by five.

So, what should you do when you hear the results of a survey? You should ask questions. What population was surveyed? Is it the same population to which the results are presumably applied? If a survey is undertaken by a certain small college and the subjects of the survey are students at that college, it probably will tell you little about student views nationwide. How was the sample chosen? Is it random? All things being equal, random surveys provide more accurate information than nonrandom (purposive) surveys. If it is not random, are there reasons why it could not be? How large was the sample? What is the confidence level? What is the margin of error? If you can ask the questions of those who constructed the survey, do so. The answers will sometimes surprise you.

And be wary if the person or company presenting the data stands to gain by being believed. A number of years ago, Camel Cigarettes ran a television ad indicating that based on a nationwide survey, more doctors smoke Camels than any other cigarette. Do you believe it was a random survey? We might have heard on a commercial that more hospitals use Tylenol than any other pain reliever. Many companies make acetaminophen, the stuff of which Tylenol is made. There often are good reasons to use acetaminophen rather than aspirin; for example, it does not reduce blood clotting. Does this mean that more hospitals use the Johnson & Johnson-produced acetaminophen (Tylenol) than acetaminophen produced by all other companies?

Ask yourself exactly what is being said. If you are being asked to believe something based on a survey, be willing to ask questions about the survey.

Exercises

1. Assume that ABC News reports that based response to a poll taken on its Web page, 68 percent of respondents believe that the economy is improving, 20 percent believe it is getting worse, and 12 percent are undecided. Is this a random survey? Why or why not?

2. State U. conducted a survey on the Honor System. The results indicated that those taking the survey had discussed the honor system with 250 faculty and students. The combined faculty and student population of the university is approximately 15,000. The students surveyed were primarily drawn from leadership positions in student organizations on campus. The persons constructing the survey concluded that virtually all members of the university community agreed that having an honor code was a good idea. Do you believe the conclusion was justified? Why or why not?

3. State U. recently released the results of a survey on drinking. It reported that 80 percent of the student body consumed fewer than two drinks per week. An investigation found that the sample on which the survey was based consisted of students studying in the library on successive Friday and Saturday nights. Should you accept the results of the survey? Why or why not?

4. Should you accept the conclusion of the following argument? Why or why not? Last Thursday evening, between the hours of 5:00 and 6:00, 150 students entering the college dining hall were asked, "Is Pearl Jam your favorite rock group?" The total student population of the university is approximately 15,000. Thirty answered yes. So, we may conclude that a fifth of the college community prefers Pearl Jam to any other musical group.

5. It is Friday night and you are doing an informal survey of the drinking habits of students on campus. You visit ten parties and notice that everyone attending was drinking liberally. You wander down the halls of your dormitory and find that four out of five students surveyed have alcoholic beverages in their rooms. You visit the library and discover that, other than the library staff, the only person there was a befuddled philosophy professor puffing on his pipe in the smoking lounge. Which of the following conclusions is best supported by the evidence (pick a letter): (A) All students drink. (B) At least 80 percent of the student body drinks. (C) The majority of students drink. (D) Many students drink. (E) Some students drink.

6. You are planning to construct a survey of your tennis club to see which brand of tennis ball is most popular. There are 200 members in your tennis club. Fifty members are males above thirty, and fifty members are males below thirty. Fifty members are females above thirty, and fifty members are females below thirty. Assuming that you plan to survey twenty people, how would you choose them to increase the probability that your survey is random? What other issues might be relevant to your choice of polling technique?

7. When Alfred Kinsey's reports on sexual behavior in males and females were published in 1948 and 1953, critics questioned the statistics presented. Since the sample consisted of voluntary informants, why might such questioning be reasonable?

8. Conservative groups sometimes claim that polls have a liberal bias. According to one caller to the Rush Limbaugh Program, pollsters never call people in North Dakota and Wyoming, since people in those states are too conservative. Assume that the *adult* population of the United States is 150 million, the *adult* popula-

tion of North Dakota is 450,000, and the *adult* population of Wyoming is 375,000. If the caller's claims were true and a national poll consists of 1,000 responses, do you believe that ignoring North Dakota and Wyoming makes a *significant* difference in the statistics? If it is a telephone poll, is there reason to believe that ignoring North Dakota and Wyoming introduces less bias than the fact that it is conducted by telephone?

9. A number of years ago, a beer company advertised that it was preferred in a nationwide taste test. The commercial showed several people tasting two cans of beer, each wrapped in paper so the brand could not be seen, and showed the drinkers' surprise when the preferred beer was that being advertised. Do you have any reason to believe that the taste test was biased? If the test had been focused on only two brands of beer, would the same suspicions have been raised?

10. In 1967, Stanley Milgram sent 300 letters to randomly selected people in Omaha, Nebraska, asking them to contact a target person through a chain of social contacts. He discovered that in the overwhelming majority of cases, the target could be reached through a chain of six or fewer acquaintances. This led to the "Six Degrees of Separation" hypothesis, according to which any two people in the world could be reached by a chain of six or fewer acquaintances. To test this hypothesis, a study was set up in which Internet surfers were given a name and location, and asked to respond by sending the email address of a person they believed would be most likely to know the target person or know someone who would be a link in a chain leading to that person. The sample is indefinitely large. Is it biased? Why or why not?

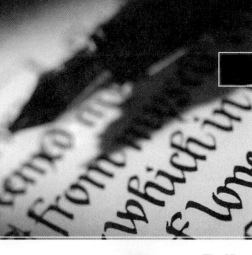

Hypotheses, Explanations, and Inference to the Best Explanation

The View: We often argue from the fact that we can explain a phenomenon to the claim that our explanation must be correct. This is done in the sciences as well as in much of the "troubleshooting" we do every day. In this chapter we examine criteria for evaluating such arguments. We also notice that arguments of the same kind are used in such nonscientific activities as literary interpretation.

How do we evaluate explanations? How do we judge among alternative explanations? How can we use explanations to solve problems?

As we saw in Chapter 5, explanations answer the questions Why? or How? Explanations increase our understandings of the world. When we do not know why something happened, we propose a **hypothesis**. A hypothesis is a proposed answer to a question or solution to a problem. The hypothesis, if true, would explain why the **phenomenon**, the event or circumstance to be explained, is as it is.

In this chapter we examine the criteria for evaluating explanations. We discuss the criteria for evaluating hypotheses. We begin with explanatory hypotheses. We examine how the criteria apply in various circumstances and examine several cases. Finally, we look at how the same criteria can be applied in cases outside the sciences. Of course, in applying these criteria you assume that the hypothesis has all the properties for which you look for in *any* discourse: (a) The hypothesis must not merely redescribe the phenomenon in other words. (b) The hypothesis must be free from ambiguities. (c) The hypothesis must be consistent; that is, the hypothesis must not entail self-contradictory statements. (d) The hypothesis and the predictions made on the basis of the hypothesis must be precise.

Hypotheses explain why a phenomenon is as it is. Hypotheses provide the basis for **predictions** and **retrodictions**. A prediction is a claim that some phenomenon will occur in a specified set of circumstances. A retrodiction is a claim that some phenomenon has occurred in a specified set of circumstances. Retrodictions are common in historical studies. Predictions and retrodictions provide the basis for testing a hypothesis. So, the first criterion for the adequacy of a hypothesis is

H1: A hypothesis must be testable.

How do you do you test a hypothesis? Assume one morning I get into my car, turn the key, and nothing happens. Why will my car not start? I propose a hypothesis: The battery is dead. If the battery is dead, this would explain why the car will not start. If I am going to test my hypothesis, there must be a procedure. Knowing a bit about cars, I propose the following conditional:

**If the battery is dead and I connect my battery by jumper cables
to the battery of a functioning car, then my car will start.**

So, I connect jumper cables between my car and my son's car, start his car, and try to start mine. *Voilà!* The car starts. Have I discovered the cause of my problem? Probably. Although we will see there are additional considerations that strengthen the evidence, the test tends to **confirm** my hypothesis. The evidence tends to show that my hypothesis is true. It reflects the second criterion for the acceptability of a hypothesis:

H2: If predictions based upon a hypothesis are true, this tends to show that the hypothesis is true.

Hypotheses are cheap. The only hypotheses that are valuable are those that can be tested. For example, if my hypothesis had been, "The gods of General Motors are frowning upon me this morning," I could not have tested the hypothesis. But the value of the hypothesis is not primarily in the fact that I made a prediction that worked. The value of the hypothesis is in the fact that if my prediction had failed, I would have shown that the hypothesis is false. Remember, I *do not* know that the problem is with the battery. All I know is that *if the hypothesis is true,* then the test procedure will result in a functioning car. The test procedure, when successful, provides some evidence that the battery is dead. You are arguing from the effect (the running car) to the supposed cause (the dead battery). It is a case of affirming the consequent.[1]

What happens if the car does *not* start? Then I have shown that the hypothesis is false. It is a case of denying the consequent. The argument goes like this:

If the battery is dead and I connect my battery by jumper cables to the battery of a functioning car, then my car will start.

The car did not start.

So (by denying the consequent), it is not the case that both the battery is dead and I have connected my jumper cables to the battery of a functioning car.

So (by De Morgan's theorem), either the battery is not dead or I have not connected by jumper cables to the battery of a functioning car.

I have connected by jumper cables to the battery of a functioning car.

So (by double negation and disjunctive syllogism), the battery is not dead.

---

[1] The problem might not have been that the battery was dead. For example, it might have been that the terminals on the battery were corroded, and while connecting the jumper cables I scraped off enough corrosion for the connections to be made.

This is sufficient to **falsify** the hypothesis, that is, to show that the hypothesis is false.[2] Notice that since there is no procedure to test the hypothesis "The gods of General Motors are frowning upon me," it is impossible to falsify that hypothesis.

A third criterion for evaluating a hypothesis is

H3: A hypothesis is more probably true if it has a broader explanatory scope, that is, if it explains more phenomena than alternative hypotheses.

Before rousing my son from his sonorous slumbers to start his car, I might ask whether my hypothesis will explain more than the fact that my car will not start. Knowing a bit about the electrical system of the car, I propose a number of hypotheses.

If the battery is dead and I turn on the lights, then the lights will not shine.

If the battery is dead, I turn the switch to auxiliary, and turn on the radio, then the radio will not work.

If the battery is dead, I turn the switch to on, and try to lower my electric windows, then the windows will not go down.

If the battery is dead, I turn the switch to auxiliary, and turn on the windshield wipers, then the windshield wipers will not work.

I do the appropriate tests. Each prediction is realized. These tests, together with the jumper cable test, reflect **consilience**. Consilience is the tendency of several forms of inductive evidence to point to the same conclusion.

You should notice that throughout this example I have been concerned *only* with the assumption that the battery was dead. I *could* have had a more complex hypothesis, for example, the battery is dead and the fuel pump is not functioning. My dead-battery hypothesis was simpler in the sense that it involves fewer theoretical assumptions. Generally speaking,

H4: If either of two hypotheses will explain a phenomenon and one involves fewer theoretical assumptions, the hypothesis that involves fewer assumptions is more probably true.

This is sometimes known as the **principle of parsimony** or **Ockham's razor**, for the thirteenth century English philosopher who championed the principle. The principle of parsimony, like considerations of scope, tends to unify our understanding of a phenomenon or a collection of phenomena. Further, the smaller the number of theoretical assumptions, the easier it is to falsify the hypothesis (theory). So, if it is possible to explain why my car will not start on the basis of a dead battery alone, that is more probably the cause than a dead battery *and* something else. A more interesting case is this: If it is possible to explain all psychological phenomena on the basis of physiological phenomena (states of the nervous system), it is likely that a physiological explanation of psychological states is true.

---

[2]At least it is sufficient in this simple case. In a complicated case, such as a hypothesis that is related to a scientific theory, predictive failure shows that either the hypothesis *or* some element of the theory is false. We look at examples of this below.

You also should notice that my hypotheses did not occur in a vacuum. Like almost anyone who has driven a car for a few years, I know a little bit about how they work. I know, for example, that cars are *not* powered by squirrels running on a treadmill. My hypotheses were consistent with theories of automotive mechanics. Generally,

H5: A hypothesis is more probably true if it is consistent with the best theoretical explanations available.

This requires a couple remarks: (1) The theory guides you regarding what are *probably* relevant hypotheses. I might know little about the workings of cars, but I know that when a car does not start, it is usually a problem with either the electrical system or the fuel system. I might also know that a dead battery is one of the most common reasons a car will not start. So, I start there. (2) Theories explain. If there is a widely confirmed theory—theories of electronics, or chemistry, or mechanics, for example—and it explains why your hypothesis is reasonable, you have reason to believe that your hypothesis is true. As we will see below, one of the grounds on which hypotheses are accepted is that they fit into an established theoretical framework. This is a matter of theoretical consistency. (3) Theoretical explanations are conservative. If there is already an explanation of a phenomenon, a novel explanation must be shown to be superior to the accepted theory on the basis of the other criteria for accepting a hypothesis. In particular, it must explain something that the accepted theory does not explain.

There is one more theoretical virtue that should be mentioned, a virtue that I cannot tie to my dead-battery case.

H6: A hypothesis is more probably true if it is fruitful, that is, if it predicts previously unknown phenomena.

A hypothesis is fruitful if it correctly predicts previously unknown phenomena. Among the phenomena predicted by Einstein's general theory of relativity was that light rays near massive bodies appear to be bent. This prediction could be tested during a solar eclipse. During a solar eclipse the moon blocks the sun's light and stars very close to the sun's edge become visible. It is the light from these stars that passes through the sun's gravitational field. If Einstein's general theory is correct, then it should correctly predict the apparent position of these stars during a solar eclipse. Observations made during a total eclipse in 1919 showed that the apparent positions of the stars were exactly as Einstein had predicted. His theory was fruitful.

Since we propose hypotheses to solve everyday problems, let's start with a few cases of troubleshooting before turning to the confirmation of scientific theories.

We engage in troubleshooting every day. For many people, it is an integral part of their daily jobs—they call it diagnosis. When troubleshooting, criteria **H1**, **H2**, and **H5** play the principal roles, with **H3** playing a subordinate role. Typically, you are looking for *one* cause of the phenomenon, so **H4** (simplicity) is implicit. For example, assume you walk into your apartment one evening and turn on a lamp. Nothing happens. Immediately, a number of hypotheses come to mind, any one of which would explain why the lamp will not work:

(1) The electricity is off in the city.

(2) The electricity is off to your house.

(3) The bulb burned out.

(4) The switch is broken.

(5) There is a short in the cord.

Each of these is based on your theoretical understanding of how lamps work (**H5**). If you have evidence that is inconsistent with the hypothesis, the hypothesis must be rejected. You glance out the window, and notice that the streetlights are on, as are the lights in the house next door. So, (1) is rejected. You click on the switch on another lamp. Behold, there is light! So, (2) is rejected. Given your experience with light bulbs, (3) is the favored hypothesis. So you test the hypothesis (**H1**). You change the bulb. It still does not work. So, you reject (3). Now things become serious. To test (4) you would have to go to a store to buy a new switch, and then install it. So, you might skip (4) and go to (5). If there is a short in the cord, *sometimes* that causes the circuit breaker to click off. So, you test that hypothesis by visiting the breaker box (**H3**). The breaker is on. If there is a short in the cord, *sometimes* jiggling the cord in various ways causes the lamp to flicker. You try it, and nothing happens. So, you are relatively confident that the problem is in the switch. You replace the switch and install the original bulb. The lamp works. So, the problem was the switch, right?

One day, while listening to my favorite tape, my boombox stopped. My experiences with boomboxes suggested three hypotheses.

(1) There is a short in the electrical cord.

(2) There is a short inside the machine, either (a) in the tape player or (b) at some other place in the machine.

(3) The belt running the tape player broke.

I did an easy test. I flipped the switch from tape to radio and heard the appropriate noises. This tended to show that there was not a short in the cord (not hypothesis 1) and that there was not a short in some part of the machine distinct from the tape recorder (not hypothesis 2b). Of course, I have had experience with power cords. I know that *sometimes* a short in a power cord can be reconnected by a gentle nudge. So, I nudged, twisted, and tugged on the power cord a few times. The radio stayed on. I had better reason to believe that the problem was not in the power cord (not hypothesis 1). So, I was reduced to hypotheses (2a) and (3). If it was an electrical short in the tape player, I would have to buy a new machine. *I* don't know how to find electrical shorts or defective transistors. My favorite stereo repairperson's motto is, "I don't fix boomboxes, since it would be cheaper for you to buy a new one." But testing hypothesis (3) was easy. After letting the boombox sit for a few days—there are always warnings about electrical build-up, so one must be careful!—I opened the back. The belt was broken. So, I installed a new belt, closed the back, and popped in a tape. The tape player ran, but the tape did not sound quite right. Why was that? There were three hypotheses:

(1) The heads are dirty. (They had not been cleaned for some time.)

(2) The tape was bad.

(3) I had messed up the repairs.

Cleaning the heads made no difference. So, I put in a newish, commercially produced tape. Things sounded find. So, I concluded (a) the problem with the boombox had been a broken belt, (b) I had solved the problem by replacing the belt, and (c) there is at least one defective tape in my house.

In each of these cases we have considered alternative hypotheses. We rejected hypotheses when the predictions we made on the basis of them proved false. When the predictions we made on the basis of a hypothesis were true, we took that as a reason for believing the hypothesis was true. It is important to be open to alternative hypotheses when diagnosing the cause of a problem.

One day I was walking across my deck when I experienced a sharp pain in my foot and noticed blood flowing from a wound. I put a Band-Aid on the wound and thought little of it—except when I walked. Since the nails holding down the boards on my deck had worked their way up, I assumed I had caught the head of a nail with my heel. My tetanus shots were up to date, so I was not concerned. After a few days, the wound became filled with pus. The medical book I consulted was very illuminating: "If a wound becomes filled with pus, you should visit a doctor." So, I visited my doctor and stated my nail hypothesis. I also mentioned that in some of the pus that had oozed out there appeared to be gray flecks. "Could the large grayish spot in the wound be a wooden sliver?" "No," he said, "that's just the infection." He prescribed an antibiotic salve and pills.

Was the doctor right? Yes and no. After a few days on the pills, there was no more pus. So, I assume the wound was infected. The large grayish spot remained. It also felt as if I was walking on a small board. After a couple weeks, I clipped away the dead skin and removed a large gray piece of wood. I am convinced that stating my nail hypothesis blinded the doctor to alternatives.

Exercises

I. For each of the following, state a hypotheses or a series of hypotheses that would explain why the phenomenon occurs. Develop a test procedure to determine which hypothesis is most likely correct. Explain why you place confidence in your procedure.

1. It is 10:00 in the morning. You missed the test in your 8:00 class. You intended to go but did not hear your alarm clock. How did that happen?

2. Assume you own a Hewlett-Packard inkjet printer. Recently, you have noticed that the documents you print often are smeared. There are lines of ink where there should not be such lines. You consult the manual, and it suggests three possible causes. (1) The inkjets are clogged. (2) You are using the wrong paper. (3) Ink has accumulated on various parts of the printer and must be washed off with warm water. You are using the same kind of paper you have always used. How would you test the hypotheses?

3. The toilet in your apartment occasionally runs. You flush it, and everything is fine, but about an hour later there is the sound characteristic of the tank filling, a sound which lasts for about thirty seconds. The tank never overflows. You examine the objects inside the tank and conclude that the problem is with either (1) the float, (2) the flush valve, (3) the tank ball, or (4) the ball seat (the gasket under the tank ball). You know that the tank ball is raised when you flush. The tank fills until the float reaches a certain level, at which point the flush valve closes. How would you determine the probable cause of the problem?

4. You taped a movie on your VCR. After watching the movie, you popped the cassette out and put it away. You did not rewind, since you wanted to tape another movie in a few days. When you taped the second movie, you discovered that the tape had rewound a bit, and in taping the second movie, you taped over the last minute or two of the previous movie. You are puzzled. You had programmed the VCR to tape two television shows on the same night, with an hour between the end of the first and the beginning of the second, and there had been no problem. What probably happened? How can you prevent such problems in the future?

5. Your automatic drip coffee maker occasionally pours coffee grounds into the carafe. When it does so, the coffee filter has collapsed. Usually, there is no problem. Usually, when you are done, the wet filter is neatly sticking to the sides of the basket. You usually have problems with grounds in your coffee only when you are near the bottom of your box of filters, and the filter doesn't sit neatly in basket with its sides uniformly along the sides of the basket. How can you solve the problem?

Cases of troubleshooting provide illustrations of arguments to the best explanation. You propose alternative hypotheses which, if true, would explain the phenomenon. You test them. When you reach the desired result, you figure your hypothesis was correct. Troubleshooting assumes the don't-mess-with-success approach to choosing the best explanation. If you are successful, doesn't that mean your hypothesis was correct? No. Sometimes by "fixing" one thing, you inadvertently change something else that was the actual cause of the problem. We have all "fixed" something at one time or another, only to find that the problem reappears a few days or weeks later. This suggests that the hypothesis we accepted was false or that our explanation of the phenomenon was incomplete. Replacing a blown fuse might explain why your toaster will not work. But if you pop a slice of bread in the toaster and another fuse blows, you would need to find out why the circuit is overloaded.

Knowledge develops slowly over time. We propose and test hypotheses. Hypotheses are explained in terms of more general hypotheses, or **theories**. An explanatory theory consists of a number of well-confirmed, interrelated hypotheses which explain phenomena of a certain kind. More general hypotheses or statements of natural law explain the less general hypotheses. Theories unify diverse phenomena. They are broad in scope (**H3**). So, let us look at the possible explanations of an airplane crash and some cases confirming scientific hypotheses. We will conclude by asking whether accounts of best explanation can apply beyond natural phenomena.

On August 2, 1947, the British airliner *Stardust* left Buenos Aires, Argentina. Its destination was Santiago, Chili. It never arrived. The experienced crew of four contacted air traffic control in Santiago four minutes before it was due to arrive, suggesting that it was on course. It sent another message in Morse code: S-E-N-D-E-C. When the tower requested clarification, the same message was sent twice more. Then the plane disappeared. This was a period before commercial flights were tracked by radar and before there were radio guidance systems. It was a period when air-to-ground communications could be made only in Morse code except when a plane was very close to its destination.

An air search was undertaken. Nothing was found. This led to various hypotheses: (1) Sabotage was suggested. It was suggested that this would also explain the disappearance of two other planes from the same airline within months of each other (**H3**). (2) Since one of the passengers on the plane was a messenger of King George VI, and since Britain and Argentina were not on good terms at the time, it was suggested that the plane had been blown up. (3) And there was the UFO hypothesis: The plane had been abducted by aliens. This, it was said, might also explain *Stardust*'s mysterious final message (**H3**).

None of the explanations was very good. If the plane had been sabotaged or blown up, you would expect that some remnants of the plane would be found. None was. There is a further problem with sabotage. If the plane had been sabotaged—if there had been a conspiracy to destroy the plane—there would need to be evidence of a conspiracy. Conspiracy theories are very popular. Historians say that conspiracy theories usually make for bad history. If there is a conspiracy, you need to show that various people worked together toward a specific end. To show that this is *possible*, there must be a way for the conspirators to communicate. You would expect some of the conspirators to be in the same area at the same time. Without evidence that the conspirators met together, it is *improbable* that there was a conspiracy. Even if the alleged conspirators were acquaintances and met together, one has no ground for claiming that there *probably* was a conspiracy unless there is further evidence. Written evidence (letters and papers) or known active participation in the act itself are evidence of a conspiracy. Given these considerations, there is good evidence of a conspiracy to assassinate President Lincoln and to destroy the World Trade Center Towers. There is far less evidence that there was a conspiracy to assassinate President Kennedy.[3] There was *no* evidence of a conspiracy to sabotage the *Stardust*. No possible conspirators were identified. There was no physical evidence of sabotage, since the plane literally disappeared. The sabotage hypothesis was pure speculation.

The UFO hypothesis is dubious on theoretical grounds. Plausible explanations are always conservative. They are based on the best available theories (**H5**). Alien beings do not fit into current scientific accounts of the world. Further, introducing alien life forms into explanatory theories would yield a far more complicated theory than is currently available. So, considerations of simplicity (**H4**) suggest that *if* the phenomenon could be explained without the introduction of extraterrestrials, it would be a superior explanation by criteria **H4** and **H5**. Further, although the UFO hypothesis might explain other odd phenomena (**H3**)—such as crop circles, accounts of alien

---

[3]One reason for this is a dispute regarding facts. Were all the shots fired from the textbook depository building, or were some shots fired from the grassy knoll? If shots were fired from several places, there is *some* evidence of a conspiracy, but it would be consistent with the facts to claim that there were independent plots to kill the President.

Source: The Far Side *by Gary Larson* © *1985 FarWorks, Inc. All rights reserved. Used with permission.*

abduction by the alleged victims, strange lights in the sky—it was not testable (**H1**) nor could it provide the basis for predictions (**H2**) in the case of the *Stardust*. The UFO hypothesis was pure speculation.

Fifty-three years after its disappearance, pieces of the *Stardust* and some human remains were found on Mount Tupangato, fifty miles from Santiago. This called the UFO hypothesis further into question. An expedition by the Chilean army found about ten percent of the plane in an area about one kilometer square. The spread of the wreckage was *inconsistent* with what should be found if the plane had been destroyed by a bomb, which called hypotheses related to sabotage further into doubt. Further, the damage to the propellers indicated that the plane had flown directly into the mountain.

Finding the wreckage fifty miles off course at the bottom of a glacier on one of Chili's highest peaks raised a number of questions. How could the plane have been that far off course? Was the place the wreckage was found the place that the plane crashed?

A World War II fighter plane had been discovered in Greenland under 250 feet of ice. It had been deserted there with five other planes, and as the snows accumulated, the plane was frozen into the Greenland glacier. If the *Stardust* had crashed higher on the mountain, the wreckage eventually would have become part of the glacier. Glaciers move down mountains by gravitational attraction. As the glacier reaches more temperate areas of the mountain, it melts, thereby disgorging the objects it contains. So, investigators framed the hypothesis that the *Stardust* crashed high on the mountain, caused an avalanche, and became part of the glacier. The hypothesis can be tested by determining whether—as is predicted—more pieces of the plane and remains of the passengers and crew will be found at the bottom of the glacier in coming years. So, the hypothesis is testable (**H1**) by predicting events that will occur (**H2**) in the future. Further, it is consistent with the best scientific theory available (**H5**). And if it is correct, it explains something else as well (**H3**). The area near the top of Mount Tupangato was scanned for wreckage after the *Stardust* disappeared. Nothing was seen. Loud noises and shocks in glacial regions often cause avalanches. So, it is quite probable that crashing a plane into a glacier would cause an avalanche, covering the wreckage. This would explain why searches flying over the area in 1947 saw no signs of the wreckage. So, on criteria **H1, H2, H3**, and **H5**, the new hypothesis is superior to the speculative hypotheses introduced in the aftermath of the disappearance. In addition, it is a theoretically simpler hypothesis than any of the alternatives (**H4**). So, it is currently the best explanation of the disappearance of *Stardust*. But that doesn't explain why the plane was fifty miles off course.

August 2, 1947, was a stormy day. On stormy days, pilots fly above the clouds. The *Stardust* was a converted Lancaster bomber. It was one of the most powerful airplanes of its time, and therefore capable of flying over high mountains. The jet stream flows at high altitudes above storms. The jet stream was unknown in 1947. So, the effects of the jet stream were not a part of navigational calculations made on the *Stardust*. This would explain the navigational error. Is it the only explanation? No, but it is probably the best explanation. Can you explain why?

Of course, none of this explains the mysterious Morse code message, S-E-N-D-E-C, which remains a mystery.[4]

Let's turn to some scientific discoveries and see how the criteria were used to confirm the hypotheses. Consider Marie Curie's discovery of radium.

Madame Curie.   By the early nineteenth century, both physics and chemistry followed a mathematical model. Laws of nature, such as Newton's laws of motion, were described mathematically. Mathematical equations must be balanced. After Henri Becquerel's discovery of the radioactive nature of uranium, the use of an electrometer allowed scientists to determine the amount of radiation given off by a sample of uranium of a given size. Marie Curie developed an interest in uranium and examined

---

[4]For a more complete discussion of the *Stardust*, see http://www.pbs.org/wgbh/nova/vanished/resources.html and follow the links.

samples of pitchblende, a uranium ore. The equations did not balance. Given the amount of uranium in the ore and other known components, the radioactivity was higher than it should have been. This was the occasion for Madame Curie's hypothesis that there was another, unknown radioactive element in pitchblende, an element she called radium. Her hypothesis provided the basis for a prediction and test procedure (**H1**). If she could purify the uranium ore, she would be able to isolate an element with properties that would explain why the equations did not balance. Her hypothesis was simple. She *initially* contended that the difference in radioactivity could be explained by the presence of one element (**H4**). Pierre and Marie Curie spent three years extracting one decigram (1/10 gram) of pure radium from several tons of pitchblende. Her hypothesis had to be revised, however. There were two elements that accounted for the difference in radioactivity. Several months before isolating radium, they isolated polonium, which was also unknown at the time. Since her prediction was true, this tended to confirm her hypothesis (**H2**). Her hypothesis was fruitful (**H6**). As her later work confirmed, it extended the domain of inquiry in numerous directions, including medicine.

But the confirmation of her hypothesis is not merely a case of extracting the elements from several tons of pitchblende. It also involved showing the place of her discovery within ongoing scientific theory (**H5**). Ongoing theory provided the basis for claiming that her radium hypothesis was plausible even before she isolated the element.

The periodic table of the elements, developed by Dmitri Ivanovich Mendeleyev in the late nineteenth century, provided a systematic understanding of the known elements. This allowed Mendeleyev correctly to predict the existence and chemical properties of gallium, germanium, and scandium in 1871, elements that were subsequently discovered. It also allowed Marie Curie to place radium within a general scheme and to describe its chemical properties in a systematic way. This **external consistency**, that is, consistency between claims made by Madame Curie's hypothesis for which there appeared to be evidence and the ongoing theoretical assumptions of the science of the time, was partially responsible for the acceptance of the discovery of polonium and radium.

Barry Marshall.   There are times when a hypothesis is contrary to "common knowledge"—and therefore seems to violate **H5**—but turns out to be true. In some cases there are alternative explanatory models, and the issue is whether an explanatory model that has been successful in some other area can be extended to the case under examination.

Consider gastric ulcers (ulcers of the stomach). Twenty years ago, little was known of their cause.

> A stomach ulcer is a raw spot, often about 30mm (more than one inch) wide, that develops in the lining of the stomach. The exact cause of such ulcers is not known. There is evidence, however, that irritation of the stomach lining from bile juices from the duodenum is sometimes a factor.[5]

---

[5]Jeffrey R. M. Kunz, editor-in-chief, *The American Medical Association Family Medical Guide* (New York: Random House, 1982), p. 465.

The cause of ulcers was assumed to be some combination of genetic and environmental factors,[6] and either stress or how persons react to stress was assumed to contribute to the occurrence of ulcers.[7] The typical treatment for ulcers was antacids and rest. About 95 percent of those so treated relapsed within two years.

Enter Drs. Barry Marshall and J. Robin Warren. In 1982 Drs. Marshall and Warren studied biopsies of 100 ulcer patients and found the presence of bacteria resembling *Campylobacter* in 87 percent of them. They never found such bacteria in patients without ulcers or gastritis (a common precursor of ulcers). They proposed the hypothesis that the bacteria were the cause of ulcers in at least the overwhelming majority of patients. Through a litera-

> "Fifteen hundred years ago everybody *knew* the earth was the center of the universe. Five hundred years ago, everybody *knew* the earth was flat. Fifteen minutes ago you knew that people were alone on this planet. Imagine what we'll *know*... tomorrow."
>
> —Agent K in *Men in Black* (Columbia Pictures, 1997).

ture search, Marshall discovered that as early as 1893 scientists had known of the presence of bacteria in the stomach, and a 1940 article indicated that the over-the-counter drug bismuth seemed to heal some ulcers. Eventually, he discovered that a regimen of bismuth and antibiotics cured ulcers—without a relapse within two years—in about 75 percent of all patients. Convincing the medical community, however, took nearly another decade.[8]

Notice the initial problem. There was a widely accepted account of the cause of ulcers. Marshall's hypothesis was inconsistent with that. So, on the basis of **H5**, it was deemed improbable. On the other hand, the germ theory of disease has proven very fruitful since the time of Pasteur (**H6**). Since Marshall's hypothesis was closely tied to a fruitful *general* theory, it should be deemed probable (**H5**). In theory, these two considerations regarding **H5** might be expected to cancel one another. In practice, any hypotheses that are contrary to common knowledge face an uphill battle. The cause of this seems to be based more on what might be called "psychological inertia" than purely theoretical considerations.[9]

Marshall's hypothesis was that ulcers, like many other diseases, are caused by bacteria. If the hypothesis is true and the correct combination of antibiotics could be found, then patients treated with the antibiotics will be cured of ulcers (**H1**). The results of the tests were favorable (**H2**), indeed, more favorable than the standard treatment for ulcers. His hypothesis is no more complex than the stress hypothesis (**H4**). And the scope of the hypothesis is broader than the stress hypothesis (**H3**).

---

[6]Editors of *Prevention* Magazine Health Books, *Everyday Health Tips: 2000 Practical Hints for Better Health and Happiness* (Emmaus, PA: Rodale Press, 1988), p. 19.

[7]Sharon Faelton, David Diamond, and the editors of *Prevention* Magazine, *Take Control of Your Life: A Complete Guide to Stress Relief* (Emmaus, PA: Rodale Press, 1988), pp. 205–208.

[8]For some of the details of Marshall's research, see Suzanne Chazin, "The Doctor Who Wouldn't Accept No," *Reader's Digest*, October 1993, pp. 119-24, as well as the medical journal articles cited therein.

[9]A physicist once told me that the acceptance of quantum mechanics depended upon the death of a generation of physicists who were trained prior to the introduction of quantum.

Marshall's hypothesis explains why a certain bacterium is found in the stomach when, and only when, one has ulcers or gastritis. It was only after Marshall convinced others to engage in clinical trials, and the results of those trials were consistent with Marshall's, that his hypothesis was accepted.

Barbara McClintock.   Now consider an issue in the sociology of science. Barbara McClintock (1902–1992) was an American geneticist who won the 1983 Nobel Prize in physiology for her work on plant genetics. Throughout her career, her research focused on the genetics of maize (*Zea mays*). Her early work was very well received. Her early papers are among the classics of genetic theory. In 1944 she began an investigation on unstable mutations in maize. Her hypothesis was that some mutations arise not from the gene on the DNA strand that is usually associated with the trait but from adjacent genes. Her hypothesis was new. It was radical. And it was ignored for over a decade.

Why was her work ignored? Consider three hypotheses: (1) McClintock was a victim of gender discrimination. (2) Her hypothesis was implausible. (3) No one cared. Which of these provides the best explanation and why? To answer this question, we need to look at a few more historical facts.

Seen within its historical context, McClintock's hypothesis was theoretically implausible (**H5**). She presented her hypothesis in a paper in 1951. At that time, most genetic research focused on fruit flies and bacteria, notably *E. coli*. At the time, it was assumed that any genetic modification that occurred in fairly simple organisms was paralleled in more complex organisms, such as maize. Further, it was a *fundamental assumption* of genetic research that genetic information in DNA was not subject to modification except by means of mutation. McClintock's research was not only focused on a less-than-popular subject (maize), it also flew in the face of the fundamental working assumption of genetic research at the time.

In the early 1960s François Jacob and Jacque Monod argued that protein synthesis in bacteria is not regulated by the structural DNA gene itself but by two genes lying adjacent to the structural gene. This was a rejection of the fundamental assumption of a decade earlier, and it brought McClintock's work into the mainstream of genetic research.

So what is the best explanation of McClintock's temporary fall from scientific grace? Is it (1) that she was a woman in a field dominated by men and was therefore a victim of gender discrimination? Let us grant the unhappy fact that women, particularly in certain fields, are victims of discrimination. But the discrimination hypothesis explains neither the widespread acceptance of McClintock's early work nor her subsequent

> But by now I was deeply involved in my love affair with old Volvos. One was a 1967 Model 122 with a balky twin-carbureted engine. When something went wrong that I could not figure out right away, I would retreat to my study in Quarters 10 and pull out the manual. I would sit there, schematics of the fuel and electrical systems spread out in front of me, and through the process of elimination trace the problem. When I had eliminated every explanation but one, I would go back to the garage and say, all right, you little SOB, I've got you. I cannot exaggerate the satisfaction it gave me to analyze and solve a car problem by reading a book.
>
> —Colin Powell with Joseph E. Persico, *My American Journey* (New York: Random House, 1995), pp. 403–404.

acclaim. Hence, hypothesis (1) does *not* seem to be the best explanation of the temporary rejection of the work McClintock undertook in the 1940s and 1950s. Is it (2), that her hypothesis was deemed implausible? This certainly is at least part of the explanation. Her hypothesis flew in the face of a fundamental assumption of

Is the Following Reasonable?

"...once you get the correct solution, all of the evidence fits into place. Or, looking at it the other way, once you fit all the evidence into place, you have the solution."

—Perry Mason, in Erle Stanley Gardner, *The Case of the Lonely Heiress* (New York: Ballantine Books, 1948), p. 215.

genetic research at the time. In this respect, McClintocks's hypothesis is like Marshall's ulcer hypothesis. Given the state of knowledge when the hypothesis was proposed, it was implausible. This explains why McClintock's hypothesis was rejected. It also explains why it ultimately was accepted. In the early 1960s her hypothesis regarding the genetic behavior of maize was shown also to explain the genetic behavior of bacteria. Her hypothesis provided the best available explanation of the genetic behavior of both kinds of organisms, and with this the assumption that the information on the DNA strand was not subject to modification was rejected. So, this would seem to be a better explanation than (1) for two reasons. First, it explains why her hypothesis was initially rejected but ultimately accepted. Second, the history of science provides many examples of cases in which the acceptance of the correct hypothesis requires a significant period of time and a shift in some of the underlying theoretical assumptions.

Is it a better explanation than (3), that no one cared? It would seem so. Certain discoveries that were later deemed significant were ignored for a period of time. Alexander Fleming announced his discovery of penicillin in 1929. It was ignored for a decade. The potential importance of penicillin was recognized only when World War II loomed on the horizon. McClintock's hypothesis was purely theoretical. By itself her hypothesis would not save lives, it would not produce a better hybrid corn, it would not have any immediate economic or humanitarian effects. It was a hypothesis that would be of interest *only* to those involved in genetic research—and they were all looking in a different direction, because McClintock's hypothesis was inconsistent with the leading theoretical assumptions in the genetics of the time. For these reasons, hypothesis (2) seems to provide the best explanation for McClintock's temporary fall from scientific grace.

So far our concern with providing the best explanation of a phenomenon—and therefore claiming that the explanation in question was the most probably true—has focused on scientific issues. The central claim of an argument to the best explanation is that, of a set of possible explanations, the explanation is best that provides the most coherent account of the phenomenon, that takes into account the greatest amount of data, and that shows the relationships among those bits of data. The data are observational and theoretical. Our six criteria for evaluating a hypothesis provide guidance in determining which explanation is best, although, as we have seen, there are numerous cases in which the plausibility condition (**H5**) might require a shift in the theoretical basis for deeming a hypothesis plausible or implausible. Recognizing the need for such a shift is often the basis for a scientific discovery. The earlier cases—the dead battery hypothesis and Marie Curie's discovery of radium—can be reconstructed in terms of an argument to the best explanation. Each hypothesis makes the phenomenon under investigation coherent, and the best explanation is the one that yields the greatest degree of coherence (it specifies the relationship among the greatest amount of data). Each of the situations we have considered is causal. In each we were looking for the cause of a specific kind of phenomenon. Can we generalize the procedure? That is, does the same procedure work in cases that are not causal, such as literary interpretation?

Yes. If you are going to develop an interpretation of a part of *Gulliver's Travels,* for example, you will need to consider a number of hypotheses (alternative interpretations), one of which will be your own. Your hypotheses will allow you to predict things you will find in the text or in other of Swift's writings. You test your hypotheses by looking for those elements (**H1** and **H2**). You will need to know exactly what is said in the text, where there are textual ambiguities, where commentators are in general agreement (**H5**), and something of the history of the British Empire at the time, since it is a common assumption that *Gulliver's Travels* is an allegory, an elaborate analogy. You will need to show how your interpretation (hypothesis) makes better sense of the texts and the historical situation than is provided by other interpretations. That is, you will need to show that your interpretation is broader in scope (**H3**), simpler (**H4**), or more fruitful (**H6**) than the alternative interpretations. If you are very fortunate, it will manifest several of the previous virtues. If your interpretation makes a text more coherent than the alternatives—and if your arguments show that it makes the text more coherent than other interpretations—you have grounds for claiming that your interpretation (hypothesis) should be accepted. Here we are concerned with what might be called an argument to the best interpretation, but the strategies used exactly parallel those used in an argument to the best explanation. Indeed, if your interpretation is adequate, it *explains why* certain elements of the text you are examining are as they are.

Exercises

II. Follow the instructions for each of the following.

1. Choose the best explanation. Give reasons for your answer.

   Dana was eating breakfast at a restaurant at 8:50 one Monday morning and noticed a number of United Parcel Service trucks turning left from Trabine Road onto Hillard-Rowe. In twenty minutes, she saw over eighty trucks, including several double semitrailer trucks. The best explanation of this phenomenon would seem to be (A) the trucks are driving in circles; (B) all the UPS drivers attend early morning prayer services at St. James Lutheran, which is on Trabine Road; (C) all the UPS drivers eat breakfast at the Cracker Barrel, which is just off Trabine; (D) the UPS depot is on Trabine Road; or (E) the UPS depot is either on Trabine Road or a road that intersects with Trabine.

2. Why might the following be considered an argument to the best explanation? Using the criteria for evaluating hypotheses, is there an alternative explanation? Is there a better explanation?

Fred came running up to the hunting campsite, out of breath. "Harry," he said panting, "are all the guys out of the woods yet?"

"Yes," Harry said.

"All six of them?"

"Yes."

"And everybody's safe?"

"Yes," Harry said.

"In that case," Fred said proudly, "I just shot a deer!"   (*The Random House Book of Jokes and Anecdotes*, Joe Claro, Ed. [New York: Random House, 1990], p. 182)

3. Is the following an argument to the best explanation? Why or why not?

"So, we're back to square one on Day's killing," she added.

"No. I know who did it."

She looked at him. "Who?"

"The Russian. Plekhanov."

She thought about it for a second. "How did you come to that?"

He said, "It was part of his plan all along, to give Net Force something else to look at while he pulled off his power grab. The attacks on Day, our listening posts, all the rascals he threw in our paths all over the world. He wanted us busy, so we wouldn't notice what he was doing. It all makes a kind of warped sense."

"I don't know, Alex. It's possible, but—"

"It's him. I know it. He was willing to crash systems that caused deaths. It's not that big a leap to hiring a shooter. We were looking in the wrong direction— right where Plekhanov wanted us to look. He's smart."   (Tom Clancy and Steve Pieczenik, *Tom Clancy's Net Force* [New York: Berkley Books, 1998], pp. 342–343)

4. Is the following an argument to the best explanation? Why or why not?

Given the apparent close relationship between CO_2 and temperatures in the past, it hardly seems reasonable—or even ethical—to assume that it is probably all right to keep driving up CO_2 levels. In fact, it is almost certainly *not* all right. Isn't it reasonable to assume that this unnatural and rapid change in the makeup of a key factor in the environmental equilibrium could have sudden and disastrous effects? Indeed, rising CO_2 levels may well lead to the kind of unwelcome surprise we received with the sudden opening of the ozone hole after a rapid and unnatural increase in the concentration of chlorine in the atmosphere.   (Al Gore, *Earth in the Balance* [Boston: Houghton Mifflin Company, 1992], p. 96)

5. Is the following passage an argument to the best explanation? Why or why not?

". . . It suddenly became perfectly apparent. It had to be Andover."

"Why?"

"Because," Mason said, "Andover got the fifteen thousand dollars for Dewitt, the fifteen thousand dollars that was to be the bait he was using in order get Lorraine to take her thirty-five thousand dollars in cash. He stood on the curb and handed the envelope containing the money to Dewitt when Lorraine drove the car to the place which Dewitt had designated for the meeting."

"Go on," Della Street said, "I still don't see it."

"Remember," Mason said, "that Andover had only known Dewitt as Weston Hale, according to his story. And he didn't know that Weston Hale had an artificial eye. Yet at the same time Andover handed over the money, Hale was masquerading as Dewitt and had the black patch over his eye.

"If Andover had been on the square and had been telling the truth, the first thing he would have mentioned was that he was surprised when he saw his friend to see the black patch over his eye."   (Erle Stanley Gardner, *The Case of the Amorous Aunt* [Roslyn, NY: Walter J. Black, 1963], p. 182)

6. Is the following passage an argument to the best explanation? Why or why not?

It is sometimes forgotten in considering medieval religion that it had adapted its method for the service of a society where the majority could not read or write. Most people were peasants, countrymen, small craftsmen, and illiterate: there was a much larger cultural gap between them and the medieval university student than there would be between corresponding classes today. Popular illiteracy was not the fault of the church, which did educate the masses as far as she could, but it was the necessary accompaniment of the stage of civilization to which Europe had so far advanced. National education depends on marginal national energy: on the balance of leisure and effort left over when primary needs have been satisfied: and this in the middle ages was too small to allow it. England did not get national education till 1870: three quarters of the native population of India are today [1925] illiterate, after two hundred years of our rule. Ninety-five per cent of the population of Russia was illiterate in 1914. It was not the printing press which made national education possible, for that was discovered in the fifteenth century: it was coal. The industrial revolution brought many evils, but it made national education possible, by increasing the balance of energy after primary needs were satisfied. In the middle ages the winds on the sea, the ox for ploughing, the horse for traveling, the stream for grinding, were the only sources of power additional to the energy of the human body. Life was physically tiring, not only for the peasant reaping his corn with a sickle, but even for the king, traveling endlessly about on horseback. There was not margin for general eduction. (M. Deanesly, *A History of the Medieval Church, 590-1500* [London: Methuen & Co., 1925], pp. 210-11)

7. Why is the following an argument to the best explanation?

Spock: An ancestor of mine maintained that if you eliminate the impossible, whatever remains, however improbable, must be the truth."

Uhura: What exactly does that mean?

Spock: It means that if we cannot have fired those torpedoes, someone else did.

Scott: Well, they did not fire on themselves, and there are no other ships present.

Spock: There was an enormous neutron energy surge.

Scott: Not from us.

Chekov: A neutron energy surge that big could only be produced by another ship.

Uhura: *Kronos One?*

Spock: Too far away. Very near us. Possibly beneath us.

Scott: If there were a ship beneath us, the Klingons would have seen her.

Spock: Would they?

Valeris: A Bird of Prey

Spock: A Bird of Prey.

Chekov: Cloaked?

Scott: A Bird of Prey cannot fire when she's cloaked.

Spock: All things being equal, Mr. Scott, I would agree. However, things are not equal. This one can.

Valeris: We must inform Starfleet Command.

Scott: Inform them of what, a new weapon that is invisible? Raving lunatics, that's what they'll call us. They'll say we're so desperate to exonerate the captain that we'll say anything.

Spock: And they would be correct. We have no evidence, only a theory which happens to fit the facts. (*Star Trek VI: The Undiscovered Country*, Paramount Pictures, 1991)

8. Is the following an argument to the best explanation? Does it seem plausible? Why or why not?

   Deep inside our intelligence services and even within the President's own cabinet were cadres of career government officials working—some knowingly, some not—for the Soviet Union by carrying out policies devised inside the KGB. Some of the position papers that came out of those offices made no sense otherwise. We also knew the CIA had been penetrated by KGB moles, just as we also knew that some of our own policy makers were advocating ideas that would only weaken the United States and lead us down the paths that served the best interests of our enemies. (Col. Philip J. Corso [Ret.], *The Day After Roswell* [New York: Pocket Books, 1997], p. 37)

9. Why is the following passage from the chapter "The Science of Deduction" in Sir Arthur Conan Doyle's *A Study in Scarlet* better described as an argument to the best explanation than as a case of deduction?

   Sherlock Holmes remarks: "I have a lot of special knowledge which I apply to the problem, and which facilitates matters wonderfully. Those rules of deduction laid down in that article which aroused your scorn are invaluable to me in practical work. Observation with me is second nature. You appeared to be surprised when I told you, on our first meeting, that you had come from Afghanistan."

   "You were told, no doubt."

   "Nothing of the sort. I knew you came from Afghanistan. From long habit the train of thoughts ran so swiftly through my mind that I arrived at the conclusion without being conscious of intermediate steps. There were such steps, however.

The train of reasoning ran, 'Here is a gentleman of a medical type, but with the air of a military man. Clearly an army doctor, then. He has just come from the tropics, for his face is dark, and that is not the natural tint of his skin, for his wrists are fair. He has undergone hardship and sickness, as his haggard face says clearly. His left arm has been injured. He holds it in a stiff and unnatural manner. Where in the tropics could an English army doctor have seen much hardship and got his arm wounded? Clearly in Afghanistan.' The whole train of thought did not occupy a second. I then remarked that you came from Afghanistan, and you were astonished."

10. Is the following an argument to the best explanation?

It takes considerable courage to work in an environment in which one is compensated according to one's performance. Most affluent people have courage. What evidence supports this statement? Most affluent people in America are either business owners or employees who are paid on an incentive basis. Remember, whether their parents were wealthy or not, most of the affluent in America acquired their wealth on their own. They had the courage to undertake entrepreneurial and other business opportunities that were associated with considerable risk. (Thomas J. Stanley and William D. Danko, *The Millionaire Next Door: The Surprising Secrets of America's Wealth* [Atlanta: Longstreet Press, 1996], p. 171).

11. Why is the following an argument to the best explanation?

"The radiator fan is not working," he told me after about fifteen seconds. He showed it to me and explained that ordinarily it only comes on when start-and-stop city driving makes the engine overheat.
"Could it be a blown fuse?"
"Could be," he said. But he ruled that out by trying a new one, which did no better than the old one. He said, "Hold on," and fetched a pen-type probe, which he used to test the plug that connected the fan to the electrical system. "You got fire to the fan," he told me, "so it looks like it's the fan itself that's shot." (Daniel Quinn, *Ishmael: An Adventure of the Mind and Spirit* [New York: Bantam/Turner Books, 1992], p. 258)

12. Is Spong's explanation more plausible than alternative explanations? Why or why not?

There is also a strong possibility that Abraham, Isaac, and Jacob, far from being the founding ancestors of Israel, were in fact Canaanite holy men, connected with the religious shrines at Hebron, Beersheba, and Bethel. Did the marauding Hebrews simply take over these shrines and their stories, adapt them to Israel's history, link these patriarchal figures together as father, son, and grandson and then use them to legitimize their invasion and conquest of Canaan? From the Canaanite point of view, the claim that God had promised Canaanite lands to the forefathers of the Israelite people some five hundred years earlier must have had a strange sound. It was in Israel's political interest, then, to claim ancestors associated with these Canaanite holy places and to show how the Hebrew people left this area for Egypt to avoid famine only to fall into the oppression of slavery from which they now escaped to reclaim their ancestral lands. (John Shelby Spong, *Rescuing the Bible from Fundamentalism: A Bishop Rethinks the Meaning of Scripture* [New York: Harper, 1991], p. 42)

13. Using the criteria for evaluating arguments to the best explanation, evaluate the following:

> Far Eastern influences permeated the Beatles recordings from 1965 to 1967 like the pungent aroma of incense. George Harrison introduced the droning sounds of the sitar into Beatles' compositions. For the first time, the Beatles experimented with backward recordings and introduced metaphysical themes. However, not everyone was happy with the sudden change in the group.
>
> The American public, it seemed, refused to allow change in its heroes. If there really was change in the Beatles, there had to be a reason for it. After the release of the Beatles' albums from 1967 to 1969, these adoring fans of the past became inquisitors of the present. A scapegoat was demanded, and when the "Paul is dead" rumors surfaced in October 1969, those fans, filled with insecurity, were only too eager to search for the clues that provided the answer for this strange change in the Beatles' behavior.
>
> The answer was obvious: Paul McCartney had indeed died, and an imposter had taken his place. (R. Gary Patterson, *The Walrus was Paul: The Great Beatle Death Clues* [New York: Fireside Books, 1998], p. 37)

14. In 1962 General Dynamics, a company that recently had suffered serious financial setbacks, was awarded a multibillion dollar contract to develop a tactical fighter plane for the navy. Its primary competitor was Boeing. In an elaborate evaluation process throughout 1961 and 1962, Boeing's design was consistently chosen by the military. The Navy was strongly opposed to the General Dynamics design. In this passage from his *The Dark Side of Camelot* (Boston: Little Brown, 1997, pp. 316–318) Seymour M. Hersh provides a possible explanation of the choice. Do you believe it constitutes the *best* explanation? Why or why not?

> Jack Kennedy's womanizing had repeatedly put his career at risk, but until now the potential loss had always been his. The affair with Exner posed a much broader danger: to the well-being of the nation's security. The Kennedy-Exner relationship apparently became known in the late summer of 1962 to the General Dynamics Corporation, one of two defense firms intensely competing for the right to manufacture a new generation of air force and navy combat plane known as the TFX (Tactical Fighter Experimental). General Dynamics may have used that knowledge to win the contract and force the government to spend billions of dollars to build a navy version of TFX that many in the military knew would not work.
>
> J. Edgar Hoover's lunch in March 1962 with Jack Kennedy had not left the FBI director reassured enough to stop the Los Angeles field office from continuing its round-the-clock surveillance of Exner's apartment from a nearby undercover observation post. Hoover's hunch paid off in an unexpected way late on August 7, 1962, when the FBI's William Carter watched as two young men climbed onto

a balcony at Exner's apartment on Fontaine Avenue, in west Los Angeles; one man watched as the other slid open a glass door and entered. After fifteen minutes or so—more than enough time to sort through records or install a wiretap—the pair fled. . . . "We were absolutely stunned," Carter told me. . . .

Carter's role in the Exner break-in ended at that point. His supervisors did not tell him that within three days they tracked the break-in team to a getaway car rented by a former FBI special agent named I. B. Hale, of Fort Worth, Texas. The two men who entered Exner's apartment were identified by the FBI as Hale's twin sons, Bobby and Billy, twenty-one years old. I. B. Hale, who died in 1971, was in charge of security for General Dynamics.

At the time of the break-in, the company's chances of winning the immensely lucrative TFX contract were precarious, as the men running General Dynamics were only too aware. To improve the company's odds, nothing could be ruled out in the summer of 1962, including the utilization of a high-priced former FBI agent who might be in a position to accumulate information on the Kennedy administration. The Hale family's criminal entry into Judith Campbell Exner's apartment. . . raises an obvious question: Was Jack Kennedy blackmailed by a desperate corporation?

15. In 1692 in Salem Village, Massachusetts, a number of young women brought charges of witchcraft against numerous women and men in the village and the surrounding area. Nineteen people were convicted of and hung for the crime of witchcraft.

Below are three explanations of the phenomenon. Using the criteria for evaluating a hypothesis, which is the best explanation of that phenomenon? Why? If you are uncertain, explain how you would go about determining what the best explanation is.

(1) Cotton Mather (1663–1728) was the son of Increase Mather and grandson of John Cotton and Richard Mather. A third-generation Puritan, Cotton Mather was noted for both his theological studies and his interests in science. In 1692 he published a book entitled *On Witchcraft*. The book is a compilation of numerous theories on witchcraft and the identification of witches. Among the characteristics he lists as showing that a person is probably a witch are the following: (a) the testimony of the person(s) bewitched, (b) unusual body marks, (c) cursing and living a "lewd and naughty kind of Life," (d) inconsistent testimony, (e) pacts with the devil and rejection of divine worship, (f) certain gestures, (g) talking to their familiars (cats and other animals), (h) possessing pictures and dolls, (i) periods of ecstasy, and (j) confessing their own witchcraft and denouncing others as witches. All those convicted of witchcraft exhibited *some* of these characteristics. The accused were witches.

(2) The playwright Arthur Miller proposed an alternative explanation in his play *The Crucible* (1953). This was written during the period of the McCarthy Hearings, a period when numerous notable people were called before the Senate to answer to charges of being Communists or Communist sympathizers. Miller suggested that there was a parallel to witchcraft trials. He wrote,

The Salem tragedy, which is about to begin in these pages, developed from a paradox. It is a paradox in whose grip we still live, and there is no prospect yet that we will discover its resolution. Simply, it was this: for good purposes, even high purposes, the people of Salem developed a theocracy, a combine of state and religious power whose function was to keep the community together, and to prevent any kind of disunity that might open it to destruction by material or ideological enemies. It was forged for a necessary purpose and accomplished that purpose. But all organization is and must be grounded on the idea of exclusion and prohibition, just as two objects cannot occupy the same space. Evidently the time came in New England when the repressions of order were heavier than seemed warranted by the dangers against which the order was organized. The witch-hunt was a perverse manifestation of the panic which set in among all classes when the balance began to turn toward greater individual freedom. (*The Crucible*, Act I [New York: Penguin Books, 1954] pp. 6–7)

(3) Mary L. Starkey was a journalist who taught at schools, including the University of Connecticut at New London. Her book, *The Devil in Massachusetts: A Modern Enquiry into the Salem Witch Trials* (New York: Doubleday Anchor Books, 1949) attributed the phenomenon to hysteria.

There was nothing new, nothing peculiar to Salem Village in the outbreak. Similar examples of mass hysteria and on a far more enormous scale had occurred repeatedly in the Middle Ages, and always like this one in the wake of stress and social disorganization, after wars or after an epidemic of the Black Death. There had been the Children's Crusades, the Flagellantes, the St. Vitrus' Dance, and again and again there had been outbreaks of witchcraft. Sweden had recently had one, and on such as scale as to make what was going on in Salem Village look trivial.

Nor has susceptibility to "demonic possession" passed from the world. A rousing religious revival will bring out something like what Salem Village was experiencing; so will a lynching, a Hitler, so will a dead motion-picture star or a live crooner. Some of the girls were no more seriously possessed than a pack of bobby-soxers on the loose. The affliction was real enough, deserving of study and treatment, but not of the kind of study and treatment it was about to receive.

In the long run what was remarkable here was less the antics of the girls than the way the community responded to them. It was the community—extended in time to include the whole Bay Colony—that would in the end suffer the most devastating attack of possession, and not only the ignorant, but the best minds. The nearly universal belief in devils and witches could not alone explain the capitulation of reason which took place. The fact was that the commonwealth no less than the girls craved its Dionysiac mysteries. A people whose natural instincts had long been repressed by the severity of their belief, whose security had been undermined by anxiety and terror continued longer than could be borne, demanded their catharsis. Frustrated by the devils they could not reach, they demanded a scapegoat and a full-scale lynching. And they got it.

Yet surely no one was "plotting," least of all the hapless Mary [Warren]. The community at large had become bewitched, magistrates no less than the girls—bewitched by a kind of mad hypnosis, expressed in panic on the one hand and crusading fervour on the other. At such moments the voice of reason always sounds like blasphemy and dissenters are of the devil. The wonder was not that Mary's defection was denounced, but that it should have been treated with mercy. (*The Devil in Massachusetts*, pp. 46–47, 102)

16. In the late 1960s, Erich von Däniken published a book entitled *Chariots of the Gods? Unsolved Mysteries of the Past.* His hypothesis was that various historical mysteries—the building of the pyramids, certain biblical accounts (such as the exodus from Egypt and Ezekiel's chariot ride into heaven), accounts of giants, and so on—could be explained by the visitation of extraterrestrial beings. This would also explain the various UFO sightings that were common in the 1950s and 1960s. His account has two virtues not found in religious accounts. (1) His account is possible, given our scientific knowledge of the universe. Ezekiel's supposed chariot ride, for example, is not consistent with a scientific understanding of the universe. (2) Extraterrestrials, although mysterious beings, would fit into a purely naturalistic account of the world. Däniken's hypothesis is simpler than explaining some events on the basis of a religious hypothesis and most events on the basis of science. Is this sufficient to deem Däniken's hypothesis probable?

17. Between 1844 and 1848 numerous women at the Vienna General Hospital died shortly after childbirth. The cause of death was called childbed fever. The hospital had two maternity divisions. In the First Division, 8.8 percent of mothers died of childbed fever between 1844 and 1847. In the Second Division, only 2.33 percent died of childbed fever during the same period. Medical students were trained in the First Division. Midwives were trained in the Second Division. Ignaz Semmelweis (1818–1865) was charged with investigating the phenomenon.

There were numerous hypotheses. (1) It was simply an epidemic. But this would explain neither why it was more prevalent in the First Division than in the Second, nor why the death rate from childbed fever was lower among those giving birth outside the hospital than among those giving birth in the First Division. (2) Overcrowding and poor ventilation were proposed hypotheses, but there were no differences regarding these factors between the First and Second Divisions. (3) It was suggested that the examination techniques of medical students were rough, but the techniques did not differ from those of the midwives in the Second Division, and injuries resulting naturally from the birth process were more extensive than those caused by the examinations. (4) In the First Division, but not the Second, priests offering last rites were preceded by an attendant ringing a bell. The bell-ringing practice was stopped with no change in death rates. (5) In the First Division, women delivered on their backs. In the Second Division, women delivered on their sides. Changing the delivery position in the First Division resulted no change in death rates.

In 1847 one of Semmelweis's colleagues died. The symptoms of his final illness corresponded to those of childbed fever. Prior to the illness, the colleague's hand had been punctured by a scalpel while performing an autopsy. The medical students regularly dissected cadavers before attending to the women in the First Division. Semmelweis proposed a new hypotheses and a test. The hypothesis was that the students were carriers of an infectious material from the cadavers. He tested the hypotheses by requiring medical students to wash their hands in a solution of chlorinated lime before making examinations. In 1848 the death rate in the First Division dropped to 1.27 percent compared to 1.33 percent in the Second Division.

Why was Semmelweis's hypothesis more probably true than the alternatives?

18. There is an area off the southeastern coast of the United States popularly known as the Bermuda Triangle. It is an area noted for unexplained disappearances of ships, small boats, and aircraft. A popular explanation of the disappearances claims the missing craft are spirited away by extraterrestrial beings. The U.S. Navy suggests the mysterious disappearances can be explained by environmental factors. They cite the following: (1) The Bermuda Triangle is one of two places on earth where magnetic compasses do not point north. They can be off by as much as 20 degrees. The second place which exhibits the same phenomenon is an area off the coast of Japan known as the Devil's Sea. The Devil's Sea is also known for disappearances. (2) The Gulf Stream is strong in the Triangle, which would explain the rapid disappearance of the craft. (3) Weather patterns are violent and unpredictable in the Triangle. (4) A significant number of the craft which disappeared were pleasure craft, which suggests human error may have played a significant role in the disappearance of the craft.

Which is the better explanation? Why?

19. In 1857 Louis Pasteur attempted to discover why some batches of wine and beer turned bad. At the time, wine was produced by crushing grapes in vats and simply allowing the juice to ferment. The process differed from brewing beer insofar as beer could be brewed only if yeast were added from a previously successful batch. A generation before Pasteur there was good evidence that yeast was some kind of living being. His studies of beer brewing showed that the amount of yeast in the batch increased greatly until the sugar was consumed, then fermentation stopped. He concluded that the presence of yeast was necessary for the production of alcohol, and his hypothesis was that "bad" batches of beer and wine were caused by unwanted microorganisms. He did parallel studies on the souring of milk. Later in life he developed vaccines to fight anthrax and rabies.

Prior to Pasteur, diseases were believed to be caused by chemical reactions and little was understood about the role of microorganisms in brewing. Explain why Pasteur's hypothesis that fermentation is the result of the actions of microorganisms can be deemed fruitful.

20. A friend of mine believes in astrology. He said that when he was young, an astrologer had constructed his horoscope, and the predictions had been exceptionally accurate. It had predicted that he would fight in a war, which he did. It predicted that he would have two children, a boy and a girl, which he did. It predicted that he would move away from his homeland, which he did.

It is unquestionable that *some* astrological predictions come true. Taking the criteria for confirming a hypothesis into account, what reasons are there to believe that astrology does *not* provide the best explanation of the events in my friend's (or anyone's) life?

III. Do a bit of research. How do each of the following show that a hypothesis was confirmed on grounds of best explanation?

1. William Hershel's discovery of Uranus.

2. Walter Reed's discovery of the means by which yellow fever is transmitted.

3. Arnold J. Toynbee's hypothesis that history is the development of civilizations rather than the development of nations.

4. Wolfgang Pauli's discovery of the neutrino.

5. Murry Gell-Mann and Yuval Ne'eman's hypothesis that quarks are the ultimate components of matter.

IV. The following are common quotations stated in "code." By using the principles of argument to the best explanation, break the code and determine what is said in each. For example,

❾★■✳ ❑✳ ▼✳✳ ⑩❑▲▼ ▲▼❑✳✳✳■✳ ✳✳✳✳✳❑✳■✳✳▲ ❍✳▼❉✳✳■ ❍ ✳❍▼ ❍■✳ ❍ ●✳✳ ✳▲ ▼✳❍▼ ✳❍▼ ✳❍▲ ❑■❍■ ■✳■✳ ●✳❖✳✳▲❦ ✢★❍❑✳ ✳❉❍✳■ ⓧ ☆◆✳✳⦿■✳✳❍ ✳✳●▲❑■⑩⑩

is "One of the most striking differences between a cat and a lie is that a cat has only nine lives. (Mark Twain, *Pudd'nhead Wilson*)

1. Βυτ, σοφτ! ωηατ λιγητ τηρουγη ψονδερ ωινδοω βρεακσ?
   Ιτ ισ τηε εαστ, ανδ ϑυλιετ ισ τηε συν.
   Αρισε, φαιρ συν, ανδ κιλλ τηε ενϖιουσ μοον,
   Ωηο ισ αλρεαδψ σιχκ ανδ παλε ωιτη γριεφ, ... ──Σηακεσπεαρε, *Ρομεο ανδ ϑυλιετ*

2. [coded symbols]

3. [coded symbols]

PART VII

Informal Fallacies

In the last three parts we examined arguments. In addition to examining techniques for evaluating deductive and inductive arguments, we examined a number of common formal fallacies. An argument commits a formal fallacy if it is possible for all the premises to be true and the conclusion false. All inductive arguments are formally fallacious. In this part we examine some mistakes in reasoning that are commonly called **informal fallacies** or material fallacies. As we use the term in this part, a **fallacy** is a defective argument. Many informal fallacies can be treated as unsound deductive arguments, often an argument with a false implicit premise. Much of our effort will be devoted to asking whether the missing premise is true or might reasonably be taken to be true.

Dealing with informal fallacies requires careful thought. In some cases, the *only* difference between a sound deductive argument and its fallacious counterpart is that one of the premises is false. The false premise often is unstated.

We examine twenty-five distinct informal fallacies. This is not a magic number. In some cases we look at alternative ways in which the named fallacy can be committed and give names to those different ways. In some cases we look at a single discourse and suggest reasons why the argument could be understood as committing more than one informal fallacy. In some cases *you* will look at an argument and suggest that there is something wrong with it that does not fit into any one of the categories we consider. This is as it should be. In terms of critical-thinking skills, it is more important to know the ways in which arguments can go wrong than to know the names of the individual informal fallacies. (Your instructor, however, might test you by playing a game of "name the fallacy.") There are four general types of informal fallacies: fallacies of ambiguity (Chapter 28), fallacies of relevance (Chapter 29), fallacies of presumption (Chapter 30), and fallacies of weak induction (Chapter 31). By considering fallacies under these general headings, you probably can think of other ways in which an argument can go wrong that are not explicitly listed.

Fallacies
of Ambiguity

The View: Fallacies of ambiguity are based upon an ambiguous use of terms or phrases. We examine five kinds of fallacies of ambiguity. Equivocation rests upon two meanings of a term. Amphiboly is based on two meanings of a phrase. Accent rests upon unusual stress placed on a word in a common claim or the use of a quotation out of context. Division is based on a shift from the meaning of a term which is true of a whole or a set to a part or member of a set. Composition is based on a shift from the meaning of a term which is true of a part of a thing or a member of a set to the whole thing or a whole set. In the last two cases you will need to ask whether the shift from a part to a whole or a whole to a part is legitimate.

How can ambiguities in language mislead our reasoning?

Fallacies of ambiguity rest upon multiple meanings of words or phrases. We have seen a special case of this kind of fallacy when examining categorical syllogisms, namely a violation of the first rule for evaluating syllogisms (an **equivocation** on one of the terms). But there are a variety of ways in which a word or a phrase can be ambiguous.

Equivocation

To equivocate—literally, to speak in two voices—is to use a word in two senses. Equivocations can occur in ordinary discourse as well as in arguments. If you tell your boss that your paycheck does not reflect the quarterly bonus that had been promised and she flips you a quarter, there is an equivocation on the word 'quarter'. There is no *fallacy* of equivocation here, however, since there is no argument. *Fallacies occur only within the context of arguments.* A **fallacy of equivocation** is committed when there is a shift in the meaning of a word from one premise to the next or from a premise to the conclusion. As we observed in Chapter 15, the following syllogism contains four terms and therefore violates the first rule for judging the validity of syllogisms:

> All cats are small domestic animals.
>
> <u>All lions are cats.</u>
>
> So, all lions are small domestic animals.

Here the word 'cat' is used in one sense in the first premise and in a different sense in the second. But equivocations do not occur only in categorical syllogisms. Consider the following hypothetical syllogism in which there is also an equivocation on the word 'cat':

> If Jess owns a product of the Caterpillar Corporation, then Jess owns a Cat. If Jess owns a cat, then Jess owns a small furry creature. So, if Jess owns a product of the Caterpillar Corporation, then Jess owns a small furry creature.

Here the word 'cat' is used in two distinct ways. While it might be true that Jess owns both a small furry creature and a product of the Caterpillar Corporation, the fact that the argument equivocates on 'cat' ('Cat') does away with any deductive connection between the premises and the conclusion. Both the categorical syllogism and the hypothetical syllogism are *formally* fallacious. In the first case it breaks rule 1 for evaluating categorical syllogisms. In the second case you have what resembles a hypothetical syllogism due to the equivocation, but which actually has the following form:

> If *p*, then *q*.
>
> <u>If *r*, then *s*.</u>
>
> So, if *p*, then *s*.

If the second argument had been stated as follows, there would have been no temptation to accept the conclusion:

> If Jess owns a product of the Caterpillar Corporation, then Jess owns a piece of earth-moving equipment. If Jess owns a cat, then Jess owns a small furry creature. So, if Jess owns a product of the Caterpillar Corporation, Jess owns a small furry creature.

Source: Seth Casana, Academia Nuts. *Used with permission of the author.*

Amphiboly

Amphiboly is like equivocation except there is a phrase that is ambiguous and the apparent meaning of the phrase shifts either among the premises or from a premise to the conclusion. The problem is generally one of loose sentence construction. Sometimes, by adding the proper punctuation or a few more words, the ambiguity disappears. Consider a sign found near an elevator in a university building:

In case of fire elevators are out of service. Use stairs.

We all know what the sign means. If there is a fire, then the elevators *will be* out of service. But what the sign *seems* to say is that the elevators are *now* out of service on the chance that there is or will be a fire at some time. Reading the sign in the latter way can provide the basis for an amphibolous argument:

> You can't take the elevator down to the first floor, since the elevator is out of service. Notice that the sign says, "In case of fire elevators are out of service."

Now consider this one: Methodists certainly are not doctrinaire. Indeed, they encourage their members to be skeptics (to engage in doubt), for the call to worship at a recent service read:

> Leader: Rise and greet the morning.
>
> People: Cast off your sleep and doubt.

The intended meaning of the second line of the call to worship is almost certainly *not* an invitation to skepticism. The scripture for the day concerned "Doubting Thomas," whose doubts are not considered virtuous. The intent of the imperative might more clearly be stated as, "Cast off your sleep and cast off your doubt."

Accent

The fallacy of **accent** occurs when either you place an unusual stress on a word in a common phrase or you quote a passage incompletely or out of context and, in so doing, shift its meaning. Consider the commandment, "Thou shalt not steal." Normally, the emphasis is on "not steal," but by placing the emphasis on 'thou' it could provide the basis for an argument with an unexpected conclusion:

> The commandment says that "*thou* shalt not steal," so it's okay for me to pilfer.

After Richard Roeper deemed *Little Nicky* his choice for the worst movie of 2000, Roger Ebert commented: I haven't had a whole lot of enthusiasm for a lot of Adam Sandler's movies, and you may recall that on this show I said that I thought *Little Nicky* was actually the *best* Sandler movie, even though I gave it Thumbs Down. And amazingly in the ads they just quoted, "'The best movie Adam Sandler has ever made.' Roger Ebert," you know.

Roeper: Well, you said that though.

Ebert: But it was bad, you know. I wasn't able to get that in, so I'm glad you gave me an opportunity to set the record straight.

—"The Worst Movies of 2000," *Ebert and Roeper and the Movies,* January 2001.

The more common version of this fallacy occurs when a passage is quoted incompletely or out of context. Consider what arguments could be constructed by dropping the *not* from "Thou shalt not steal."

> The commandment says, "Thou shalt . . . steal," so it's perfectly fine to steal the hubcaps from Smith's car—indeed, it's divinely commanded.

Or, consider what can happen if Emily is arguing against abortion, and she raises an objection to which Brandon offers a reply. Assume Emily began the objection by saying, "But some will object that a woman's right to choose what happens to her body exceeds any supposed rights of the fetus." In his response to Emily's argument, Brandon says,

> A woman's right to choose is absolute. Why, even Emily, who is critical of abortion, said, ". . . a woman's right to choose what happens to her body exceeds any supposed rights of the fetus."

Brandon has quoted Emily's words, but the shift in context completely shifts the meaning of what Emily said. Ellipsis points (. . .) can cover a multitude of sins. If you are reading a discussion of a literary figure, and a passage from that person's works is quoted that does not seem quite right, you should either check the context from which the passage is taken or see what was "covered up" by the use of ellipsis points.

The fallacy of accent is fairly common. In 1992 Hillary Rodham Clinton's comment that she was not "some little woman standing by her man like Tammy Wynette" was taken as insulting to women who did not work outside of the home. But, taken within its context, the meaning was entirely different. Deborah Tannen describes the situation as follows:

> When the Clintons agreed to discuss their personal relationship on *60 Minutes,* the interviewer, Steve Kroft, suggested that their decision to remain married was an "arrangement." Protesting this insulting evaluation, Mr. Clinton said, "It's not an arrangement. It's a marriage." And Mrs. Clinton said, "I'm sitting here because I love him and I respect him and I honor what he's been through and what we've

Source: Cathy Guisewite, Cathy. *Used with permission of Universal Press Syndicate.*

been through together." The sound bite that was picked up, however, was the phrase she used to reject the "arrangement" idea: She said that she was not "some little woman standing by my man like Tammy Wynette." This phrase was repeatedly quoted as if it were the first move in a conversation, interpreted as an insult to women who stay home rather than work outside the home. The fact that the remark had been provoked by an insult to her marriage was lost.[1]

So, if you are presenting an argument, be certain that you are aware of the context in which anyone you quote made a certain statement and be certain your audience knows the context as well. If you are examining an argument of another, check the context from which any quoted material is drawn. It is easy to commit the fallacy of accent, either wittingly or unwittingly, but it is never fair to the person quoted.

Division

You commit the fallacy of **division** if you apply a claim that is true of an entire class of things or of a whole to a single member of that class or a part of the whole. For example, if you argued that Jean, who is a member of Δ Δ Δ sorority, is wealthy because Δ Δ Δ is the richest sorority on campus, you would commit the fallacy of division.

Consider this one:

On a recent news broadcast, it was said that the cars on the road today are safer than they were ten years ago. I found this very encouraging, since it means that my 1976 Chevy Nova is safer than it was ten years ago.

The claim made in the news broadcast was true. It applied to the entire class of cars on the road today. The conclusion is probably false. If—as is high unlikely—my old car is safer than it was ten years ago, that has nothing to do with the fact that the entire class of cars—as a class—on the road today are safer than they were ten years ago.

Consider one more:

On the day following the 1998 national congressional elections, a reporter on a Virginia television station remarked that the outcome of the elections were good news for Virginia's liberal senator, since the elections showed that there was a shift away from conservative politics toward a more moderate position, and the senator's most probable opponent in the next election was a conservative.

The shift toward the middle occurred at the *national* level. All the conservative congressional representatives in Virginia had been reelected. The reporter had applied a general trend to a particular case, a case to which there was evidence it did not apply. The reporter committed the fallacy of division.

---

[1]Deborah Tannen, *The Argument Culture* (New York: Random House, 1998), pp. 65–66.

Source: Seth Casana, Academia Nuts. *Used with permission of the author.*

While you should be aware of cases in which an arguer moves from a property of a whole to a property of a part, you should *not* assume that all such moves are fallacious. The following is a nonfallacious case of division:

My computer weighs fewer than twelve pounds. So, the processor in my computer weighs fewer than twelve pounds.

Weight is an additive property. The weight of a whole is a function of the weight of its parts. So, if the whole is a given weight, each part of the whole must weigh no more than that. *Pay attention: In cases of division, you must ask whether the move is legitimate.*

Composition

The fallacy of **composition** is the mirror image of the fallacy of division. The fallacy of composition is committed if you infer that a whole or an entire class of objects has a certain property because one of the parts of that whole or one of the members of that class has that property. This is a fairly common fallacy. You have almost certainly fallen victim to it on many occasions. Consider the last time you saw news reports of rioting in Jerusalem or Belfast, or flooding in Texas or the Midwest. Did you conclude that the city in question was a dangerous place to be, or that virtually all of Texas or the Midwest was under water? It *might* be more dangerous than the municipality in which you live; but, then again, it might not. The news clip shows you that in one small area of a city for one period of about thirty seconds on a given day people were throwing rocks, or bombs were exploding. This does *not* show that riotous acts continued all day or that the entire city was under siege. The news clip shows that there was flooding in Texas or the Midwest, but it does not show how widespread the flooding was. Were you taken in?

As in the case of division, there are cases in which you can legitimately go from a property that is true of a part to ascribing the same property to the whole. If the engine in my car weighs more than 300 pounds, then my car weighs over 300 pound, since weight is an additive property. If the processor in a *new* computer costs over $100, you can be pretty sure the new computer will cost over $100. But if replacing the processor costs over $100, this *might not* imply that my old computer with a new processor will have a value that exceeds $100. Old computers are not terribly valuable.

Exercises

I. What fallacy of ambiguity, if any, is committed in each of the following passages? If no fallacy is committed, write, "No fallacy." Remember: If there is no argument, there is no fallacy.

1. If Jennifer spent the night in Moscow, Idaho, then she experienced midnight in Moscow. "Midnight in Moscow" is a popular song from the 1960s. So, if Jennifer spent the night in Moscow, Idaho, she experienced a popular song from the 1960s.

2. "Gracie, why should I give your mother a bushel of nuts? What has she ever given me?"

   "Why George, she gave you me. And I'm as good as nuts." (George Burns, *Gracie: A Love Story* [New York: G. P. Putnam's Sons, 1988], p. 12)

3. It is okay to get slightly tipsy during a communion service, since the preacher says, "Drink ye all of it" before passing around the large chalice of wine.

4. After the Republican Party won control of the Virginia Legislature in the 1999 election, the head of the National Republican Party claimed that this indicated that the Republican Party would do well nationally in the 2000 congressional elections.

5. The mean value theorem makes a claim about an entire class of functions, and so a claim about the processes that they represent, and so ultimately a claim about a determinate aspect of the world. (David Berlinski, *A Tour of the Calculus* [New York: Vantage Books, 1995], p. 206)

6. Next year Hotentot has a booming year—net income before interest and taxes advances to $40,000. Let's see what this means to profits under both conditions (full $100,000 in cash and borrowing $70.000):

	All Cash Purchase	Borrowing $70,000
Net income before taxes	$ 40,000	$ 40,000
Less interest expense	None	4,200
Net income before taxes	$ 40,000	$ 35,800
Less income taxes (50%)	20,000	17,900
Net income	$ 20,000	$ 17,900
Cash investment made	$100,000	$ 30,000
Return on original cash investment	20%	59.5%

Fantastic! You have tripled the return on your money by going into debt (by "leveraging" your investment as they say in investment circles'). (Claude N. Rosenberg, Jr., *Stock Market Primer,* rev. ed. [New York: Warner Books, 1981], p. 128)

7. According to an article in *The Breeze: James Madison University* (March 20, 2000, p. 1), "JMU students' weekly alcohol consumption is double that of students nationwide". That's a lot of booze! And the claim has to be false. However much JMU students drink, it is part of consumption of students nationwide. So, if the claim were true, JMU students would need to drink twice as much as they drink, and were they able to do that, they would still have to drink twice *that* amount for the statement to be true, and so on. JMU students cannot drink an infinite amount of booze—or twice an infinite amount of booze, or four times an infinite amount of booze—so the claim in *The Breeze* has to be false.

8. On September 9, 2000, Paul Harvey reported that if we had gone to the movies the weekend before we would have found slim pickin's. But that has to be wrong, since Slim Pickens died in 1983, and there are no recent revivals of such classic films as *Dr. Strangelove* or *Blazing Saddles.*

9. A local pet store's motto—which it uses to try to convince us that we should shop there—is, "We care for your pets as much as you." But they have given me no reason to believe they care for me. So, they have given me no reason to shop at their store.

10. Alice sighed wearily. "I think you might do something better with the time," she said, "than wasting it in asking riddles that have no answers."

"If you knew Time as well as I do," said the Hatter, "you wouldn't talk about *it*. It's *him*."

"I don't know what you mean," said Alice.

"Of course you don't!" the Hatter said, tossing his head contemptuously. "I dare say you never even spoke to Time!"

"Perhaps not," Alice cautiously replied; "but I know I have to beat time when I learn music."

"Ah! That accounts for it," said the Hatter. "He won't stand beating." (Lewis Carroll, *The Adventures of Alice in Wonderland*, Chapter 7)

11. The parking officials at the University are not concerned with safe driving. The back of the hang-tag says, "Permit must be removed when vehicle is in motion," and everyone knows that such an activity can distract the driver from attending to the traffic conditions, which is dangerous!

12. For those of you who have children and don't know it, we have a nursery downstairs. (Cal and Rose Samra, *More Holy Humor: Inspirational Wit and Cartoons* [Carmel, NY: Guideposts, 1997] p. 75)

13. The Constitution says all Americans have the right to keep and bear arms. So there can be no objection to having the members of the Senate speak without a suit coat while wearing short-sleeved shirts.

14. The news media are liberal in political orientation. So, Paul Harvey, of *Paul Harvey News and Comment,* is a liberal.

15. The hood of my Pontiac is red, so my Pontiac is red.

16. **John:** I like bratwurst better than you.

    Joan: If that's the way you feel, I never want to see you again!

17. The average American family has 2.5 children. So, the Joneses, an average American family, have 2.5 children.

18. Crumbs have virtually no calories. So, if you break your favorite food up into crumbs and eat the crumbs, you ingest virtually no calories.

19. The teller will give you $1,000 if and only if you go to the River Bank. But if you go to the riverbank, your feet will get muddy. Therefore, if the teller gives you $1,000, your feet will get muddy.

20. **Alf:** I see no good reasons to go to Chicago. I do not intend to go.

    Agnes: So, you admit that there are "good reasons to go to Chicago"—those are your very words. I'm glad that you "intend to go."

21. Chris claims she interviewed for a job as an auto mechanic in the personnel office. She must not have been telling the truth, since no automobiles are repaired in the personnel office.

22. The United States of America is the richest country in the world. So, every American is wealthy.

23. A medical doctor had taken a couple years off from his practice to do graduate work. When he returned to his practice, he commented, "When I returned to my practice I felt a bit rusty. I just didn't have all those facts at my finger tips." His patient replied, "That's no problem, Doc. Just keep practicing and eventually you'll get it right."

24. Priests take a vow of poverty. The Church is a corporate body composed of priests. Therefore, the Church should not own property.

25. Caring for the basic needs of every convicted felon in this state costs the tax-payers about $20,000 per year. Since we have a multibillion-dollar budget, no one can complain about the cost of the prison system.

26. There has been a great deal of public interest in the private life of the .44-caliber killer. The press has an obligation to publish what is in the public interest. Therefore, the press has an obligation to print the details of the killer's private life.

27. A penny saved is a penny earned. So, save those pennies, but feel free to spend your silver and paper money.

28. John saw a picture in Sonia's locker. Since the volume of Sonia's locker is only about three cubic feet, John must be very small.

29. The master bedroom in the house I'm planning to buy is large and spacious, so the whole house is large and spacious.

30. In 1990, Arkansas was one of the poorest states in the United States. So, Sam Walton, the Arkansan who started Wal-Mart, was one of the poorest men in the United States.

Fallacies
of Relevance

The View: Arguments committing fallacies of relevance assume a false premise or reach a conclusion that is not supported by the premises. The fallacy of appeal to force assumes a threat of force is a sufficient reason to engage in an action or hold a belief. The fallacy of personal attack occurs in the context of a reply to an argument. The person rather than the argument is attacked. The fallacy of mob appeal assumes that some kind of popular appeal is a sufficient reason to engage in an action or hold a belief. The fallacy of appeal to pity assumes that the fact that someone is suffering from some kind of distress is a sufficient condition to engage in an action or hold a belief. The fallacy of accident assumes a general rule that does not apply in a particular situation. Stereotyping involves an appeal to a false but widely held general claim. The genetic fallacy is a special case of stereotyping in which you argue that given the cause or origin of a claim, the claim should not be taken seriously. You commit the straw person fallacy if you misrepresent another person's argument and criticize the argument you have misrepresented. You commit the red herring fallacy if you reply to another person's argument by confusing the issues, if you distract someone from the content of another person's argument. You commit the fallacy of irrelevant conclusion if you draw a conclusion from an argument that is *not* suggested by the premises. In all but the last three cases, the fallacy is based *strictly* on a false assumed premise.

What are some common ways in which the premises of an argument fail to support the argument's conclusion?

In an argument the premises are said to provide evidence for the truth of the conclusion. Sometimes people attempt to persuade us to believe a statement or do something by bringing up issues that are not relevant to the conclusion of the argument. In this chapter we examine eleven fallacies of relevance.

Appeal to Force

The fallacy of appeal to force *(argumentum ad baculum)* occurs when an argument includes an implicit but unwarranted (or inappropriate) threat. If your boss says, "You should make a contribution to the Democratic Party if you want to continue working here," the argument is simple:

> If you want to keep working here, then you should make a contribution to the Democratic Party.
>
> You want to keep working here. (implicit premise)
>
> So, you should make a contribution to the Democratic Party.

The argument is valid. The *reason* why you should make a contribution to the Democratic Party is not of the right sort. There *should* be no connection between your political contributions and your job status. So, there is an (illegitimate) appeal to force.[1]

The example above is rather blatant. Often an appeal to force is more subtle—often the *conditional* is left unstated. The same argument is assumed in the following words: "You should make a contribution to the Democratic Party. After all, you *do* want to remain employed here" or "You should make a contribution to the Democratic Party. After all, you are *currently* an employee of this company."

Now contrast this with a road sign that poses an implicit threat: "Watch your speed. We are ✈ ." The suggestion is that if you speed, we will see you (from our airplanes), and if we see you, you will be fined. So, if you do not want to be fined, do not speed. Is this a threat? Sure, but anyone who has driven for any period of time knows that if you speed, you might be fined. Whether you like it of not, enforcing traffic laws is one of the legitimate jobs of the government. So, while there is an appeal to force, it is legitimate. There is no fallacy.

So, it is not enough to simply find a threat, implicit or explicit. You need to know whether the person making the threat is in a position legitimately to do so. But it is not even that simple. Sometimes there will be an appeal to force made by someone who has no legitimate authority to make such an appeal, but which is still not a fallacious appeal to force. Consider the following passage from *The Godfather*:

> The next day Don Corleone went to see the band leader personally. He brought with him his two best friends, Genco Abbandando, who was his *Consigliori,* and Luca Brasi. With no other witnesses Don Corelone persuaded Les Halley to sign a document giving up all rights to all services from Johnny Fontane upon payment of a certified check in the amount of ten thousand dollars. Don Corelone did this by putting a pistol to the forehead of the band leader and assuring him with the utmost seriousness that either his signature or his brains would rest on that document in exactly one minute. Les Halley signed. Don Corleone pocketed his pistol and handed over the certified check.[2]

---

[1] Even if you were working for the money-raising arm of the Democratic Party, the appeal would be illegitimate, *unless* making such a contribution were part of your job description.

[2] Mario Puzo, *The Godfather* (Greenwich, CT: Fawcett Publications, 1969), p. 43.

Source: Seth Casana, Academia Nuts. *Used with permission of the author.*

This is *not* an argument. It is a description of a situation in which an appeal to force is made. *One* way to construe the implicit argument is as follows:

> You want either your signature or your brains on the line.
>
> <u>You do not want your brains on the line.</u>
>
> So, you want your signature on the line.

Understood in this way the argument is valid but unsound and may be construed as an instance of appeal to force. Les Halley wanted neither his brains nor his signature on the line. But, viewed from the perspective of the band leader, the argument might be construed in a different way:

> All things being equal, you should act in ways that preserve your life.
>
> <u>Signing is a way to preserve my life.</u>
>
> So, I should sign.

The general principle is true. The exceptions—when all things are not equal—might occur when one's loved ones are in danger or when one wishes to make a very important religious or political point. There is reason to believe the second premise is true. So, *here* there is no fallacy. (It is always wise to choose your fights with care.)

Personal Attack

The fallacy of **personal attack** (*argumentum ad hominem*) occurs when *replying* to an argument. The fallacy occurs when the person or the person's character rather than the argument is attacked. This can take several forms. The **abusive** form is a direct attack on the person or the person's character.

Assume that Danielle and Jeb are involved in a debate concerning the need for a balanced budget amendment. Danielle has presented the following argument:

> The government is like a family unit. If a family unit consistently spends more money than it brings in, it must continually bring in more money simply to retain

Source: Scott Adams, Dilbert. *DILBERT reprinted by permission of United Feature Syndicate, Inc.*

a stable standard of living, since an ever-increasing amount of money must be spent on interest. For the same reason, if a government consistently spends more than it obtains in tax revenues, it must obtain ever-increasing tax revenues so it can provide the same level of government services. But just as a family unit cannot consistently engage in deficit-spending without going bankrupt, the same holds for a government. Since a balanced-budget amendment would prevent an ever-increasing deficit, we should support the amendment.

Jeb replies as follows:

> We've all known Danielle for years. We all know she's seldom inclined to tell the truth. You never should accept the word of a liar. So, we should reject her conclusion.

Notice that Jeb has attacked the arguer rather than the argument. There *might* be problems with the argument—for example, it *might* be that Danielle's analogy between spending patterns in a family unit and spending patterns by a government are not sufficiently similar—but Jeb has attacked the person offering the argument rather than the argument itself. Jeb commits the abusive form of the fallacy of personal attack.

Fallacies are tricky. They always resemble legitimate forms of argument. If Danielle had been a discredited witness at a trial or she had told you that ghosts are haunting her dorm room, the fact that she had proven an unreliable witness in the past would provide reasons to questioning her claims.[3] But in *this* case we are dealing with an argument, not simply with testimony. The only acceptable reply to an argument is an attack on the argument. You must show that the analogy is weak or that one of the premises is (probably) false. Since Jeb ignored the argument and attacked the arguer, he committed the fallacy of personal attack.

The **circumstantial** version of personal attack focuses on either the situation in which an arguer finds himself or herself, or there is an argument that the present

---

[3]See the criteria for evaluating testimony in Chapter 11.

position defended is inconsistent with what the person had argued at some other time.

Assume Father O'Roark, a Roman Catholic priest, has presented an argument against abortion. Merle replies by saying, "He's a Catholic priest. The Catholic Church is officially opposed to abortion. What would you expect him to say?!" Here Merle implicitly claims that Father O'Roark's "reasons" for opposing abortion are mere rationalizations.[4] Since there was no examination of the argument presented, it is fallacious.

Or, assume that Jen, who for many years had argued against euthanasia, presents an argument favoring euthanasia in very specific circumstances. Doug replies to the argument by saying, "Ten years ago Jen published a paper called 'Euthanasia? *Never!*' in which she provided very strong arguments against euthanasia. Now she's arguing that euthanasia is okay. Since she's defended inconsistent positions, we can't believe anything she says." Again, Doug attacks the person rather than the argument presented, so it is an instance of the fallacy of personal attack.

Of course, if a person actually defends inconsistent positions, both positions cannot be true. If a person defends inconsistent positions within the context of a single work, pointing that out is sufficient to show that the author has suffered from some kind of conceptual confusion: It is a very serious criticism. Pointing out a case of *actual inconsistency* is sometimes known as a Lockean *ad hominem,* named after the seventeenth century English philosopher John Locke, who alludes to such criticisms in his *Essay concerning Human Understanding.*[5] So, when George Berkeley (1685–1753), pointed to an inconsistency in one of Locke's discussions of abstract ideas, Berkeley was presenting a Lockean *ad hominem.*[6] Berkeley was *not* guilty of a *fallacious* personal attack.

A final version of personal attack is called *tu quoque* (literally "you too"). It is a special form of the circumstantial version of the fallacy. You commit this form of the fallacy if you reply to someone's argument by saying, in effect, "You do it, so why shouldn't I?" For example, assume one of your relatives has given you a standard argument against smoking: It's hard on your health, it discolors your teeth, it leaves a foul odor on your clothes and in your room, it's hard to stop if you start, and so forth. Let us assume that this relative is a person who has smoked for forty years. If you replied, "But you've smoked as long as I've known you, so why should I take your argument seriously?" you commit the *tu quoque* version of personal attack. It is an attempt to discount the premises of the argument without giving reasons to believe that the premises are false; instead, you are attacking the credibility of the person giving the argument.

---

[4]This is sometimes known as **poisoning the well.**

[5]See John Locke, *An Essay concerning Human Understanding,* P. H. Nidditch, Ed. (Oxford: Clarendon Press, 1975), book 4, Chap. 17, Sec. 21, p. 686.

[6]See George Berkeley, *Essay towards a New Theory of Vision,* §125, in George Berkeley, *The Works of George Berkeley, Bishop of Cloyne,* A. A. Luce and T. E. Jessop, Eds., 9 volumes (London: Thomas Nelson and Sons, 1948–1957), Vol. 3, p. 221. While Berkeley is not guilty of the fallacy of personal attack, he *might* be guilty of the fallacy of accent, since the passage Berkeley quotes is *not* taken from Locke's principal discussion of abstraction.

Mob Appeal

The fallacy of **mob appeal** *(argumentum ad populum)* occurs when you assume that some kind of popular appeal is a sufficient reason to engage in an action or hold a belief. Often, this appeals to your sense of self-worth on the basis of your membership in some group.

Appeals to emotions often occur in political speeches, religious tracts, and sales promotions. In 1916 Woodrow Wilson was reelected president on the slogan, "He kept us out of war!" Insofar as there was an argument, it went like this:

All presidents who have kept us out of war should be reelected. (implicit premise)

Wilson kept us out of war.

So, Wilson should be reelected.

Consistent with American isolationist tendencies, the First World War was unpopular with Americans during the first two years of the conflict. Wilson's slogan was popular, and it was, at least in part, responsible for his reelection. But is the implicit premise true? The United States entered World War I on April 2, 1917, within about a month of Wilson's second inauguration. Had the United States entered the war earlier, it is likely the war would have ended sooner. It was the entrance of the United States into the war that ended the deadlock by shifting the balance of power. Similarly, had President Franklin Roosevelt convinced Congress to declare war on the Axis powers in 1937, or had the French stopped Hitler's march into the Rheinland in 1936, or had British Prime Minister Neville Chamberlain taken a firm stand against the Nazis' move on Czechoslovakia rather than declaring "Peace for our time!" in 1938, it is likely that the Second World War would have been shorter.[7] So, is the premise, "All presidents who have kept us out of war should be reelected" true? Probably not, although the premise "All things being equal, presidents who kept us out of war should be reelected" might be true.

There are many cases in which appeals are made to your emotions. Political conventions, religious revival meetings, and sales conventions are examples of meetings that are rife with emotional appeals. There often are songs, chants, or slogans that rouse the emotions of those present. The desired effect is to cause you to believe or act in certain ways. The general form of mob appeal may be put this way: Doing x (supporting the political candidate, believing that you will be saved, being part of a certain sales team) makes you feel good, so you should do x (with enthusiasm!). Is the fact that engaging in a certain kind of activity or having a certain belief or being part of a certain group makes you "feel good" a good reason to do or believe something? No. To be caught up in the emotions of a crowd can have disastrous effects. If you have any doubts, watch Leni Riefenstahl's movie *Triumph of the Will*, which depicts the 1934 Nuernberg rallies in Nazi Germany. Much of a nation was caught up in fun-

---

[7]As we all know, however, historical hindsight is always 20-20: Without considerable information, it would have been impossible to predict the effects of any of those actions.

damentally emotional appeal, which had disastrous consequences for the entire world. As is typical in cases of mob appeal, those to whom the appeal was made were led to believe that they are special—"the master race"—and as such, there were certain things they deserved, including world dominance.

Mob appeal does not generally take the extreme forms found in Nazi Germany, but appeals to the emotions of the crowd are common in everyday life. We all want to be loved and accepted. We all want to be special in some way. If "everyone is doing it," whatever 'it' might be, and you take that as a reason for you to do it, you have fallen victim to the fallacy of mob appeal.[8] Is the fact that everyone is doing something any reason why you should? If everyone were jumping off tall office buildings, is that any reason why you should?

The fallacy is common in advertising, where it often takes a form that may be called "snob appeal." You should buy a certain brand of mustard because the ad depicts persons driving very expensive cars stopping and asking for that brand of mustard. Certainly, only very special people use that brand of mustard, and if you bought it you would be among those elite. Or an ad depicts attractive people drinking a certain brand of soda or beer. Or a store advertises its goods as for persons of discriminating taste.[9] Or you are told that you *deserve* something, or that you *owe it to yourself* to have something. Each of these is a case of mob appeal.

Does this mean you should rid yourself of all emotional attachments? No, of course not. But you *should* be aware of attempts to persuade you to believe or do something on the basis of an appeal to your emotions. Should you buy a certain brand of computer because it is the most popular brand in America (because "everyone is buying it")? Not for that reason alone, but if you did some research, you might discover that the computers made by that company are extremely reliable—then again, you might discover that they have nothing more than a very aggressive advertising campaign.

Appeal to Pity

The fallacy of **appeal to pity** *(argumentum ad misericordium)* assumes that the fact that someone is suffering from some kind of distress is a sufficient condition to engage in an action or hold a belief. When disaster strikes, you are certain to see live television coverage followed by some relief organization asking for a contribution. Or you see a public service announcement showing a child in squalid conditions, followed by a request to send your dollars to an organization that claims to help such children. Or you receive a phone call at suppertime—they *always* come at suppertime—asking you for a contribution to send some poor deprived children to some cultural event or camp, for example. Shouldn't you open your heart—and your checkbook—and respond to each of these appeals? No, of course not.

---

[8]Some call this particular form of the fallacy **bandwagon:** "Everyone is voting for George, so you should jump on the bandwagon and do so too."

[9]These also could be seen as cases of **false cause** (see Chapter 31), since they may be taken as indicating that buying a certain product will cause you to be special.

Source: Seth Casana, Academia Nuts. *Used with permission of the author.*

There might be good moral or religious reasons for aiding persons in distress. It might be, as some have argued, that these moral reasons rest ultimately on one's emotional dispositions. But there are several reasons why a rational person will not respond to all of these appeals. First, it would be impossible. No amount of wealth is sufficient to allow you to contribute to every cause. Second, some contributions would be "bad investments." All charitable organizations devote a certain sum to soliciting contributions. In some cases, the bulk of your contribution might be used to solicit more contributions.[10] Further, every organization has certain administrative costs. If you believe it is your duty to contribute to a certain cause, do some research. Find out which organization is most efficient in delivering the money *you* contribute to the cause *you* want to support. Make sure that there is no evidence that the organization to which you would contribute has a history of "bait and switch" tactics, that is, convincing you to contribute by appealing to one disaster while using the bulk of your contribution for some other project. Third, do some research to find out whether it is likely that your contribution will actually make a difference. Some relief organizations have delivered food and other necessities to the *country* in which a disaster happened, but little of the aid reached the victims due to the lack of a distribution system or the political situation in the country. Finally, *never,* ***never,*** ***NEVER!!!*** give your credit card number to a telephone solicitor unless you know the person making the call. If you do not know the person, there is no guarantee (a) that the request for funds is legitimate, so (b) your credit card *could* be used to purchase any number of things, and you would not know until your next bill came due—by which time the "solicitor" would be untraceable.[11]

While charitable appeals might involve appeals to pity, they are fallacious appeals only if one assumes that the fact that someone is suffering from some kind of distress

---

[10]Some organizations hire companies to solicit contributions by telephone. Hiring an outside firm to solicit contributions is costly. In such cases it often happens that a very significant portion of your contribution goes to the company soliciting the funds.

[11]"I'm sorry, but I can't help you this year" followed by hanging up the phone is polite. Of course, there are more interesting replies. My favorite is, "Will you marry me?" In the moment of shocked silence that follows, you add, "I wouldn't give my credit card number to anyone to whom I'm not married." Then hang up.

is a sufficient condition for acting or believing that one should act in a certain way. The general form of the argument is

> If *x* is suffering from a certain kind of distress, then we should contribute to organization *o* to provide relief to *x*.
>
> <u>*X* is suffering from a certain kind of distress.</u>
>
> So, we should contribute to organization *o*.

Even if we should do something to help *x*, contributing to organization *o* might not be the best way to provide the relief—in some cases, there might be no good *means* to the end of helping *x*.

But not all cases of a fallacious appeal to pity are cases in which the end is proper but the means to that end are incorrect. Sometimes the problem is with the end itself. Someone appeals to pity when there is no reason why the person should be pitied. For example, a student who has devoted little effort in a course and comes to her professor at the end of semester saying, "You've gotta give me a B in the course, because if I don't receive at least a B in your course, I won't be able to take any courses in my major next semester" is requesting pity when none is deserved. The student might be confronting a dire situation, but it is a situation she has brought upon herself. Legitimate appeals to pity—cases in which it is reasonable to claim that someone deserves some aid—are cases in which the situation is beyond the control of the sufferer. Drawing a line between what is and is not a legitimate end is often difficult. If a student requested extra time on a project because his dog had had a difficult pregnancy, he probably is not worthy of pity. If a student requested additional time on a project because a close relative died or her parents were getting a divorce, a situation which had been very emotionally trying, she *might* be worthy of pity.

So, there are two questions to be asked when confronted with an appeal to pity. First, is the *end* of the right sort to be worthy of pity? Second, if the end is of a sort that is worthy of pity, are the means to that end of the right sort? A negative answer to either of these questions is a ground for claiming that the appeal to pity is fallacious.

Problems with Principles —————————

We often argue from general principles to singular conclusions. As in all cases of arguing from premises to a conclusion, you must determine whether the premises are true. The next three fallacies make appeals to general principles which are either false or improperly applied. In most of the cases below, the general principle is unstated. Your first job is to figure out what is assumed. Once you have done that, you should ask whether the assumed premise is true or reasonable.

Accident

The fallacy of **accident** occurs if you apply one of a pair of a general principles in a situation where it does *not* apply but the other principle does. "You should keep your promises" is a general principle. Usually, you can apply the principle without any problem. But there are times when other considerations override the principle.

Assume you have promised to meet me for lunch at my favorite restaurant. While driving along a deserted road on your way to the Burger Shack, the car in front of you veers off the road into the ditch. It is ten minutes to noon. You promised to meet me for lunch at noon, and by your best calculations, you might already be a few minutes late for our luncheon date. So, you should just drive on, right? Probably not. There is another principle: "You should aid people in distress." Does that principle take precedence over "You should keep your promises"? In this case it probably does. If you do not stop, the person in the car might suffer permanent injuries or die. If you are late for lunch, there probably will be no long-term unfavorable consequences, and even if there were—"That's the last time I'll invite *you* to lunch!" I say—they would not be as disastrous as letting the person in the auto accident die. So the principle "You should aid people in distress" is more compelling. To argue, "I can't stop, since that would violate the principle 'You should keep your promises' and I promised to meet you for lunch," would commit the fallacy of accident.

The fallacy of accident arises when there are two principles that conflict in a particular situation. To *avoid* the fallacy, you should ask yourself two questions: (1) In a given situation, is there more than one principle that applies? (2) If there is more than one principle that applies, which takes precedence? In some cases the choice is clear. In some cases you might need to weigh the alternatives and give reasons why one should be chosen over the other. One issue regarding euthanasia concerns the conflict between the principles "Do not kill" and "Relieve suffering."[12] To see that things are not always clear-cut, consider the following familiar story:

> A certain *man* went down from Jerusalem to Jericho, and fell among thieves, which stripped him of his raiment, and wounded *him,* and departed, leaving *him* half dead. And by chance there came down a certain priest that way: and when he saw him, he passed by on the other side. And likewise a Levite, when he was in the place, and looked *on him,* and passed by on the other side. But a certain Samaritan, as he journeyed, came where he was: and when he saw him, he had compassion *on him.* And went to *him,* and bound up his wounds, pouring oil and wine, and set him on his own beast, and brought him to an inn, and took care of him. And on the morrow when he departed, he took out two pence, and gave *them* to the host, and said unto him, Take care of him; and whatsoever thou spendest more, when I come again, I will repay thee.[13]

Virtually anyone familiar with the story knows that the Samaritan is the hero, but that ignores the conflict of principles confronted by the priest and Levite. The priests and the Levites performed religious functions in the society. They could perform these functions only if they where ceremonially clean. If they were to touch a corpse or human blood, they would be ceremonially unclean for a period of seven days,[14] and

---

[12]And euthanasia is not the only such case. Consider abortion. Let us say that there is a principle that is unproblematic, namely, "All things being equal, you should not intentionally kill other human begins." Here the problem is with the premise, "All human fetuses are human beings," or the premise "Abortion is a case in which not all things are equal."

[13]Luke 10: 30–35, King James Version.

[14]Numbers 19: 11–17.

therefore they would be unable to perform their duties at the temple. Of course they, like all others in their religious community, had a duty to aid the afflicted.[15] So, which was the greater duty? The priest and the Levite were fulfilling *a* duty by riding past on the other side of the road. It will not do to simply claim that the priest and the Levite committed the fallacy of accident in arguing, "Poor guy. But I can't stop, since I have a duty to remain ceremonially clean so I can perform my duties at the temple." Reasons must be given for holding that their principal duty in this case was to render aid to the man who was robbed.[16]

Stereotypes

A **stereotype** is a false, though commonly made, general claim about a certain group of people. The argument "You can understand why Dan has a bad temper; after all, he's a redhead" assumes the general proposition, "All redheads are bad tempered." Insofar as the assumed general proposition is false, the argument is unsound. Often, if you make the implicit generalization explicit, you will recognize its falsehood. Do you know any redhead who is *not* bad tempered? If you do, the general claim that all redheads are bad tempered is false. Are there *proportionately* more bad tempered redheads than blondes, brunettes, people with gray hair, or people with no hair? And make sure your survey is unbiased; after all, redheads get very angry when they are stereotyped![17]

Genetic Fallacy

The **genetic fallacy** is a special case of stereotyping based on the origins of a person or thing. Consider the argument, "Our instructor cannot be very bright, since he was raised in a small town." The general principle assumed is "No one raised in a small town is very bright," a principle that is false.[18] If you weaken the principle to "Most people raised in a small town are not very bright," you will confront vagaries in the expressions "not very bright" and "small town." If you weaken it to "Many people who were raised in a small town are not very bright," you can say the same of many people raised in New York City or Los Angeles.

---

[15]See Job 6:14, Psalms 82:3, Proverbs 22:22.

[16]Remember, they had a particularly strong duty to remain ceremonially clean in virtue of their duties at the temple. Special duties often arise from one's job or status in a society; for example, psychiatrists and lawyers have an obligation to hold such information in confidence as is told them by their patients or clients. So, in the case of the priest and the Levite, their duty to remain ceremonially clean was particularly pronounced.

[17]For what it's worth, such hair as the author of this book has is (mostly) red.

[18]You want evidence? John R. Mott, the 1955 Nobel Peace Prize winner, spent his boyhood in Postville, Iowa, a town of fewer than 2,000 residents. Norman Borlaug, who won the 1970 Nobel Peace Prize for his work in plant genetics, was from Cresco, Iowa, a town of fewer than 4,000 residents. Former President Bill Clinton hailed from Hope, Arkansas, which boasts a population of fewer than 10,000 residents. While few small towns can claim Nobel prize winners or presidents, pick almost any small town and you'll discover that it has produced medical doctors, lawyers, university professors, and various other rogues who have some claim to intelligence.

Straw Person

You commit the **straw person** fallacy if you misrepresent another person's argument and criticize the argument you have misrepresented. You either suggest that the argument presented was enthymematic and attack the allegedly suppressed premise or you misrepresent the conclusion and attack that alleged conclusion. It is called a straw person fallacy because, rather than attacking a real full-blooded argument, you are attacking a weak imitation of it. To understand how this works, consider an example.

> Sheila has presented an argument to the conclusion that the federal government should impose certain regulations on the medical profession. In particular, she has argued that laws need to be made that will guarantee that (a) when a person leaves a certain job, he or she will have the option of retaining his or her health insurance, and (b) when a person obtains a new job, he or she will not be deprived of group insurance coverage because of a pre-existing condition. Albert replies to Sheila's argument by claiming that Sheila has proposed a system of socialized medicine, and since the experiences with socialized medicine in Canada and Europe tend to show that government-run medical care results in increased bureaucracy and a decrease in the quality of medical services, Sheila's argument should be rejected.

Albert has committed the straw person fallacy. Sheila did *not* argue that the federal government should take over the medical insurance industry—which happens in countries with socialized medicine. She has merely argued that the government should impose laws that would guarantee that no person would be deprived of the possibility of obtaining or retaining insurance coverage. The conclusion Albert attacked was different from and stronger than the conclusion Sheila drew, and therefore Albert has committed the straw person fallacy.

The stress placed in earlier chapters on the need to *very carefully* reconstruct the arguments of others—to reconstruct as strong an argument as possible—was made to avoid being charged with the straw person fallacy. To commit the fallacy is to treat someone else's argument with insufficient respect. If you commit the fallacy with any regularity, you will gain a reputation as someone who does not reason carefully; that is, you will lose credibility as an arguer.

Red Herring

You commit the **red herring** fallacy if you reply to another person's argument by confusing the issues, if you distract someone from the content of another person's argument. Consider the following example:

> Joan has argued that the local factory is a dangerous place to work and that the factory should be closed for six months so that it can be renovated and modernized. James replies as follows: "We can't take Joan's argument seriously. The factory is the largest employer in the city; it employs over 1,200 people. If the

factory were closed for renovations, each of those 1,200 people would be out of work for six months. If they were out of work for six months, it would have a devastating effect on the local economy. We can't afford to have the factory closed! So you must reject Joan's argument."

There is a confusion of issues. Joan argued that the factory is unsafe and proposed a way to deal with that problem. James's reply does not touch that issue—Joan might agree that closing the factory for six months would have dire economic effects, but that is irrelevant to the content of her argument. James has not attacked Joan's argument. He has focused on a different issue. James has committed the red herring fallacy.

Irrelevant Conclusion

You commit the fallacy of **irrelevant conclusion** (*ignoratio elenchi or non sequitur*) if you draw a conclusion from an argument that is *not* suggested by the premises. Sometimes this takes the form of a discussion to which a conclusion is unexpectedly attached—and once you think about what was said, you are still puzzled.

The most pronounced case of an irrelevant conclusion is found in a clearly invalid deductive argument. Consider the following:

All aardvarks are mammals. All mammals are vertebrates. So, some aardvarks are good pets.

Obviously, the conclusion has nothing to do with the premises. There are four terms: the term *pet* does not appear in the premises, and so it cannot be contained in the conclusion.

Sometimes the problem is not one of deductive entailment. It is merely that there seems to be no connection between the premises and the conclusion of an argument. Consider the following passage from René Descartes's "Discourse on Method":

Good sense is the best distributed thing in the world: for everyone thinks himself so well endowed with it that even those who are the hardest to please in everything else do not usually desire more of it than they possess.[19]

"So what?" you might say. What is the connection between the alleged fact that everyone has as much good sense as he or she might wish and the claim that "Good sense is the best distributed thing in the world"? The conclusion is not supported by the premise. The conclusion is irrelevant.[20]

---

[19]René Descartes, "Discourse on Method," in *The Philosophical Writings of Descartes*, translated by John Cottingham, Robert Stoothoff, and Dugald Murdoch, with portions of vol. 3 trans. by Anthony Kenny, 3 vol. (London: Cambridge University Press, 1985, 1984, and 1992), vol. 1, p. 111.
[20]You also could argue that this is an appeal to authority, namely, the authority of popular opinion. The fact that Descartes continues, "In this it is unlikely that everyone is mistaken" (*The Philosophical Writings of Descartes*, volume 1, p. 111) might be taken as evidence for an appeal to popular opinion.

Exercises

I. Identify the fallacies of relevance in each of the following. If no fallacy occurs, explain why not. If a fallacy occurs, explain why it occurs.

1. A recent news broadcast reported research tending to show that the calcium in milk is ineffective in preventing or treating osteoporosis. A representative of the dairy industry responded, "Milk is still the cheapest source of calcium."

2. On behalf of the TIME-LIFE Board of Editors, I am pleased to inform you that you have been selected as one of a small group of discerning readers invited to preview the Premiere Edition of our new OUR AMERICAN CENTURY book series. (Letter from Time-Life Books, September 1999)

3. "Last night Clinton allowed himself to put pressure on Russia. It seems that he forgot, at least for a few seconds, what Russia is. Russia has a full nuclear arsenal at its disposal, but Clinton decided to flex his muscles," Yeltsin said. "I want to tell Clinton that he should not forget what kind of world he is living in. There never was and never will be a time when he alone dictates to people how to live and how to relax." (Boris Yeltsin, quoted in "Atomic Tongue," *ABCNEWS.com*, December 9, 1999)

4. Selby turned from Worthington to the members of the grand jury. "Men, we're working on these cases. There are a lot of things we haven't been able to solve. I don't think *you* can solve them. It's a lot more dangerous to get off on the wrong foot than it is to wait. As district attorney I deem it my duty to tell you that. I'm fully aware Worthington wouldn't adopt the position he has unless he'd already made an informal canvas of this body and learned its sentiments. I'm also aware that Roper has been doing a lot of talking. It's a lot easier to stand on the side lines and criticize than it is to get in and do something. Any time I'm unable to discharge the duties of this office, I'll resign. Any time I need help, I want someone who will give me *help* rather than someone who will use the opprotunity to stick a political knife in my back."

   One or two of the members nodded. One of them said to Worthington, "You've got to admit that's right, Mr. Foreman. Roper's had a lot of experience, but if he got in there, he wouldn't be trying to help Selby."

   Worthington sneered, "On the basis of Selby's promise to resign if he can't solve this case," he said, "we'll leave Roper out of it."

   "That wasn't what he said," one of the members protested. (Erle Stanley Gardner, *The D.A. Goes to Trial* [New York: Pocket Books, 1940], p. 148)

5. Speaking of Jesus: Nicodemus, who had gone to him before, and who was one of them said to them [the Pharisees]: "Does our law judge a man without first giving him a hearing and learning what he does?" They [the Pharisees] replied, "Are you from Galilee too? Search and you will see that no prophet is to rise from Galilee." (John 7: 50–52, Revised Standard Version)

6. We are free to do what we want to do, as long as [if and only if] we don't hurt somebody else. So if Dracula asks to drink a pint of your blood, indicating that

he'll die if he doesn't get to drink it, you're *not* free to refuse him. (Based on Richard Bach, *Illusions: The Adventures of a Reluctant Messiah* [Delacorte Press, 1977], pp. 105–109)

7. **Calisto:** What do you think of this sickness of mine?

   Sempronio: You're in love with Melibea. But it's a sad thing to see you held captive by one lone woman.

   Calisto: You know little of constancy.

   Sempronio: Perseverance in evil is not constancy; rather, in my country they call it stubbornness or pig-headedness. You philosophers of Cupid may call it what you will.

   Calisto: It's a wicked thing to lie when you pretend to be teaching another. Don't you praise your mistress Elicia [the prostitute Sempronio is keeping]?

   Sempronio: Follow my good advice and not my bad example. (Fernando de Rojas, *The Celestina: A Novel in Dialogue*, trans. Lesley Byrd Simson [Berkeley: University of California Press, 1955], Act 1, Scene 2, p. 6)

8. On September 29, 2000, presidential candidate George W. Bush criticized his rival, Al Gore, for supporting the release of oil from the strategic oil reserves the previous week. Gore replied that Bush was beholding to his former employers, the oil interests.

9. "A number of questions will be directed to me. From a wide spectrum of influential people. I should have answers."

   "I'll tell Mr. Green."

   "He should *know* it." Webster watched himself. He didn't want to appear desperate.

   "I'll remind him."

   He *was* being excluded, and in a manner that was far too cavalier, thought Webster. The White House was being excluded. It was a moment for audacity.

   "Do more than 'remind' him. Make it clear that there are a few of us down here who wield pretty big sticks. There are some areas of Genessee Industries that we're more knowledgeable about than anyone else. We like to think of them as our insurance policies."

   The man from Green abruptly looked up from the table and locked his eyes with Webster's. "I'm not sure that's an apt term, Bobby. 'Insurance policies,' I mean. Unless you're thinking about double indemnity; that's expensive." (Robert Ludlum, *Trevayne* [New York: Bantam Books, 1973], pp. 349–350)

10. On December 5, 2000, Judge N. Sanders Sauls ruled that there were no grounds in law or in fact for the selective recounts of the Florida vote that had been requested by the Al Gore for President Campaign. This ruling was considered adverse to the Gore interests and was immediately appealed. In responding to the ruling, Gore attorney David Bois said, "The ballots were the best evidence. And, unfortunately, this ruling comes without the judge having looked at a single ballot. Even though those ballots were admitted into evidence, none of those ballots have been reviewed." (From *Nightline*, December 5, 2000)

11. GALILEO'S CHILDREN In the early 1600s, Galileo looked up into the starry night and decided to make some sense of the unknown. His revolutionary findings opened the doors to an entire galaxy of discovery (not to mention cheesing off a whole bunch of know-it-alls.) Take a lesson from the man. Seek your own truth. Make your own discoveries. With the advent of the Internet, there's never been more to learn. We bring it to you without limits or restrictions. That's the real Internet. And we're the #1 provider of it. So go on, **get linked**, you visionary you. **Earthlink**™ **1-800-EARTHLINK**.   (Used with permission of Earthlink)

12. You tell me that I should buy a small, fuel-efficient car. Then why do you drive that old gas-guzzling Cadillac?

13. A Lutheran College in the Midwest forbids the use of alcoholic beverages, including wine, on campus. We may conclude, therefore, that they do not use wine in their communion services.

14. And if any man shall take away from the words of the book of this prophecy, God shall take away his part out of the book of life, and out of the holy city, and *from* the things which are written in this book.   (Revelation 22:19 [King James Version]).

15. How do you spell 'bonds'? T-a-x-e-s! Vote NO on the bond issue!

16. All politicians are liars. No liars should be elected to public office. So, an absolute monarchy is preferable to a democracy.

17. Opponents of monopolies claim that they are unfair insofar as they limit competition. But when AT&T was synonymous with the telephone company, we had the most efficient telephone system in the world. When Standard Oil dominated the petroleum industry, there was cheap gasoline for everyone. When 'Carnegie' meant steel, America dominated steel production. So, obviously, monopolies are extremely efficient.

18. General Jack D. Ripper has argued that it is absolutely essential to our future security that we immediately start mass production of the RS-100 long-range bomber. But his arguments hardly deserve serious consideration, for in a couple of weeks General Ripper will retire from the Air Force and become CEO of the Hawk Corporation, which manufactures the RS-100.

19. Meg A. Bucks, president of the Noxxe Petroleum Company, has argued that the government should provide petroleum companies with economic incentives for oil exploration. Her argument is reasonable only if she assumes that it is in the national interest to remain dependent on oil for the next century. But the oil reserves will be depleted within the next fifty years. So, we must reject her argument.

20. Ambassador: Mr. Prime Minister, it would be fairer if your country increased its contribution to our mutual defense, for in order for us to continue paying our present contribution, it will be necessary to raise the tariff on imports such as those we have been purchasing from your country.

21. The Cynics claimed that . . . if it is lawful to know one's wife, it is lawful to know one's wife in public. Now, it is lawful to know one's wife; therefore, it is lawful to

know her in public.   (Pierre Bayle, *Historical and Critical Dictionary,* s.v. "Hipparchia," trans. Richard H. Popkin [Bobbs-Merrill, 1965], p. 98)

22. The Pigeon accepts the general proposition that anything that eats eggs is a serpent, and says to Alice:

    "You're a serpent; and there's no use denying it. I suppose you'll be telling me next that you never tasted an egg!"

    "I *have* tasted eggs, certainly," said Alice, who was a very truthful child; "but little girls eat eggs quite as much as serpents do, you know."

    "I don't believe it," said the Pigeon; "but if they do, why, then they're a kind of serpent: that's all I can say." (Lewis Carroll, *Alice in Wonderland* [Chapter 5])

23. The gasoline tax should not be raised. Everyone drives. Everyone needs to eat. If the gasoline tax were raised, the poor, those who generally drive the least efficient cars, would become poorer. Since the additional cost of production and transportation of food would be passed on to the consumer, the poor would be hit hardest again. Certainly, many would starve. So, all calls to raise the gasoline tax should be rejected.

24. Medical evidence tends to show that a diet low in cholesterol and saturated fats leads to a greater life expectancy. So, if you want to live a long life, you can't eat anything tasty.

25. Professor Smith can't be a very good professor, since she did *not* receive her doctorate from an Ivy League school.

26. This product contains/produces chemicals known to the State of California to cause cancer and birth defects or other reproductive harm.

27. Ms. Kai contends that terminally ill patients have a right to die with dignity. But murder, whether self-inflicted or other-assisted, is still murder. And murder is wrong!

28. Father to son: "Go ahead. Go to law school. Do whatever you like with your life! But if you don't come back and run the family business, I'm going to disinherit you!"

29. Senator McMurphy argued that more money should be devoted to the space program. But the space program is part of the military-industrial complex. With the end of the Cold War, it's time to decrease military spending and decrease the size of the military. So McMurphy's argument to increase funds for the space program should be rejected.

30. Glassoff Crystal: the ultimate expression of your good taste.

31. George *claims* that he was in Chicago on June 4. But George is a drug addict. He has been convicted of numerous misdemeanors. He has defaulted on numerous loans. So there is no reason to believe he was in Chicago on June 4.

32. The more formal education a person receives, the higher that person's lifetime income potential. So, since Thomas Alva Edison had little formal schooling, he must not have made much money.

33. Maggie has argued that the system of letter grades should be abolished. But such a position assumes that there are no genuine differences in the quality of work

done by students, which is absurd. So, the system of letter grades should not be abolished.

34. Dr. Stark has argued that the petrochemical plant in town should be closed, since it poses major health risks to the community. With over 300 employees, that plant is the second largest employer in town. Closing the plant would throw the town into an economic recession. So, we cannot afford to close the plant.

35. The political polls indicate that the Democratic presidential candidate will win the election. When economic times are tough, the incumbent usually loses. Economic times are tough, and the incumbent is a Republican. So, the Republican candidate will win.

II. Identify the fallacies of ambiguity or fallacies of relevance in each of the following. If there is no fallacy, write "No Fallacy." Give reasons for your answers.

1. All people who favor a democratic form of government are democrats. No Republicans are Democrats. So, no Republicans are people who favor a democratic form of government.

2. Water extinguishes fire. Oxygen is a part of water. So, oxygen extinguishes fire.

3. German-Austria must return to the great German mother country, and not because of any economic considerations. No, and again no: even if such a union were unimportant from an economic point of view; yes, even if it were harmful, it must nevertheless take place. One blood demands one Reich. (Adolph Hitler, *Mein Kampf,* translated by Ralph Mannheim [New York: Houghton Mifflin, 1943], p. 3)

4. Everyone has the right to say what he or she wishes. So, George has the right to make slanderous remarks about his professor.

5. Ms. DeMark has provided evidence that children who watch more than two hours of television daily do not perform as well in school as those who watch no television. But who would want to give up television? It is a source of news and weather reports. It provides large varieties of entertainment for little more than the cost of the set. Surely, her conclusions are flawed.

6. Cleo read a book on zebras in the wild. So, obviously, Cleo has been traveling in Africa.

7. Oscar tells me that I should always drive within the speed limit. But Oscar regularly drives at speeds of well over eighty miles per hour on the interstates. So there is no reason to believe anything Oscar says.

8. Francesca claims that the government should not interfere with the personal lives of the governed. But this is just another version of the old saw that the government that governs least governs best, which implies that the best government does not govern at all. But if there were no government, there would be anarchy. Anarchy is untenable. So, we obviously must reject Francesca's claim.

9. The commandment says, "Thou shalt not bear false witness against thy neighbor." Since Jerusha lives 200 miles from here, she is not my neighbor. So, I can say anything about her that I wish.

10. Since buses and trains take more fuel than cars, we will not save any energy by switching from private cars to public transportation.

11. Joan contends that it is wrong to support the euthanasia movement. But people have rights everywhere. So, certainly, young people in the Far East have as many rights to their movement as anyone else.

12. Professor, you should have no trouble accepting my paper six weeks late. My parents are getting a divorce. My roommate has a drinking problem. And my dog had a very difficult pregnancy. All these things have been very trying, and I just don't know how I could survive if you didn't accept my paper late.

13. Father to son: Your grades are going to improve, or I'm going to quit paying for your college education.

14. All sorority members are women. So, Josephine, a member of Sigma Alpha Psi sorority, is a woman.

15. Sheriff: We were all fond of Billy, and we want the person who killed him to be brought to justice. Jake is only being held for questioning. So far there isn't a shred of evidence that points to him.

(The sheriff enters the jail.)

Bad Jack: We all know how special Billy was. Pete, who took you in when your house burned down? Billy, that's who. And Mack, remember that spring when you broke your leg? Your crops would never have been planted if Billy hadn't done it. He did something like that for each and everyone of us. And what did he ask in return? Not a thing! Now we have a chance to do something for the finest man who ever lived in this town, a man who was shot in the back by that coward in jail. For Billy's sake, let's go and string him up.

16. Professor Egalf claims that a bit of skepticism with respect to one's beliefs is the mark of a rational, educated person. What would you expect from him? Egalf is a self-professed skeptic!

17. Hunting is a safe and exhilarating sport, for thousands of people go hunting every year.

18. Dr. Fernandez claims that learning a second language increases our understanding of and eases our communications with people in other cultures. But English is taught in more countries around the world than is any other language. It is virtually the universal language of commerce and scholarship. So there is nothing to be gained by learning a second language.

19. "This is a pretty pass," he fumed, "when they send a businessman to a preacher. I suppose you are going to pray with me and read the Bible," he said irritably. . . .

He proved most sullen and uncooperative until finally I was forced to say to him: "I want to tell you bluntly that you had better cooperate with us or you're going to be fired."

"Who told you that?" he demanded.

"Your boss," I replied. "In fact, he says that unless we can straighten you out, as much as he regrets it, you are going to be through." (Norman Vincent Peale, *The Power of Positive Thinking* [New York: Fawcett, 1956], p. 158)

20. "Who did you pass on the road?" the King went on, holding out his hand to the Messenger for some more hay.

"Nobody," said the Messenger.

"Quite right," said the King: "This young lady saw him too. So of course Nobody walks much slower than you."

"I do my best," the Messenger said in a sullen tone. "I'm sure nobody walks much faster than I do!"

"He can't do that," said the King, "or else he'd have been here first." (Lewis Carroll, *Through the Looking Glass*)

Fallacies
of Presumption

The View: Arguments committing fallacies of presumption either assume the conclusion as a premise or assume that the premises contain all the relevant information while they do not. The fallacy of begging the question occurs if you assume the conclusion as a premise. The fallacy of complex question is committed when you ask a question that assumes that another question already has been answered and conclusions are drawn regarding the assumed question. The fallacy of suppressed evidence occurs when relevant evidence contrary to the position for which one is arguing is intentionally concealed. The fallacy of false dichotomy is committed when a disjunctive premise is taken as exclusive and exhaustive when it is not exhaustive, that is, when not all the possibilities are considered.

Do some arguments assume too much? Of what kinds of "hidden" assumptions should we be beware?

In this chapter we look at the fallacies of presumption. Arguments committing fallacies of presumption either assume what is to be proved or incorrectly assume that that all the relevant information is given.

Begging the Question

Deductive arguments are sometimes described as arguments in which the conclusion is found in the premises. In a valid categorical syllogism, the "parts" of the conclusion are contained in the premises, but the whole of the conclusion is contained in neither premise. You commit the fallacy of **begging the question** if you assume the conclusion—often restated in synonymous terms—as one of the premises. If the conclusion is assumed as a premise, the argument is formally valid—every statement entails itself—but it proves nothing. If you have already assumed the conclusion as a premise, the argument provides no additional evidence for the conclusion. The following is a blatant case of begging the question:

Henry VIII was a king of England, since Henry VIII was a king of England.

Here the conclusion is nothing but a restatement of the premise, and were you to confront such an argument, you would be likely to say, "So what?"

It is rare to find so blatant a case of begging the question. It is far more common to find a case in which a conclusion is nothing but a restatement of the premise in synonymous terms. But that makes no difference. If you confronted the argument,

> Henry VIII was a king of England, since Henry VIII was a male monarch who ruled England.

you would still have a case of begging the question, since the expressions 'king' and 'male monarch' are synonymous. At most, the argument tells you how the words are used. An acceptable argument provides substantive (nontrivial) reasons for claiming that a conclusion is true. Mere verbal agreement is a trivial reason for claiming that a conclusion follows from a premise. Hence, like the original version of the argument, the argument above begs the question.

But you have to be careful in criticizing apparent cases of begging the question. You must still avoid charges that your criticism is a straw person argument. For example, is the following argument an instance of begging the question?

> Children, it is the last hour; and as you have heard that antichrist is coming, so now many antichrists have come; therefore we know that it is the last hour.[1]

This *appears* to be a case of begging the question, since it *appears* that the writer is saying, "It is the last hour, so we know it is the last hour." Is that the argument, or part of the argument? Perhaps, but the presence of the word 'know' in the conclusion *suggests* that the author had something more in mind. If the argument is reconstrued as follows, the appearance of a question-begging argument disappears:

> If the antichrist has come (or a number of antichrists have come), then it is the last hour.
>
> A number of antichrists have come.
> _____
> So, it is the last hour.

Is this the implicit argument? Perhaps. If it is, then there are grounds for claiming that you can *know* that this is the last hour, even if you might question the truth of the premises. If this is the intended argument, the example also shows why it is important to state your own arguments as clearly as possible. By clearly stating your arguments, you can avoid possible charges of fallacious reasoning.

There is a variation on begging the question called **circular argument,** or **arguing in a circle,** in which there are several arguments arranged in such a way that the conclusion of the last is a premise of the first. Consider the following:

> We know that everything the Bible says is true, since it is the inspired word of God. And we know that the Bible is the inspired word of God, since everything the Bible says is true.

---

[1] I John 2:18, Revised Standard Version.

The arguments can be stated formally as follows:

> The Bible is the inspired word of God. _____
>
> Therefore, everything the Bible says is true.
>
> Everything the Bible says is true. _____
>
> Therefore, the Bible is the inspired word of God.

It might be that the conclusions of both the first argument and the second argument are true, but the pair of arguments provides no reason to believe that either premise is true. The pair of arguments constitutes an argumentative circle.

A third version of begging the question is called a **question-begging epithet**. An epithet is a descriptive word or phrase. If Honest John Cribbs is on trial for grand larceny and the prosecutor, in her closing arguments, alludes to "that crook Cribbs," her use of the epithet 'crook' begs the question of Cribbs's guilt.

Complex Question—————————————————————

A complex question assumes that a previous question has been answered. If I asked you, "When did you start cheating in this course?" the question assumes that at some time you have cheated in this course. It is a special case of begging the question.

A complex question by itself does not constitute a fallacy. It must occur in the context of an argument. So, if you answered my complex question, it would provide the basis for a fallacious argument:

> "When did you start cheating in this course?"
>
> "On January 28."
>
> "Aha! So you admit cheating in this course!"

While you might seldom see a complete argument based on a complex question, it is reasonable to suggest that there is an implicit argument when you see a complex question. Have you ever discussed the question, "What are we going to do about the illegal immigration crisis?" Did you notice that the question is complex? Is there a crisis? Is there even a problem? What is the evidence that there is a problem, let alone a crisis? If you answer the complex question—or proceed as if it must be answered—without showing that there is a problem, you have committed the fallacy of complex question. On the other hand, if you are writing a paper, devote the first part to an extended argument that illegal immigration *is* a problem, and *then* ask the question, there is no fallacy.

Complex questions are common in politics and advertising. If you confront a question, ask yourself whether it is complex, and if it is, whether the *assumed* answer to the *implicit* question is supported by evidence.

Of course, there are cases of complex questions that do not yield fallacies. Assume you are a witness in a jury trial. While on the stand, an attorney asks you, "Where were you on the evening of last June twenty-fifth?" Is the question complex? Sure. It assumes you were *somewhere* on the evening of June twenty-fifth. Should you, the critical thinker, object, "Aha! You've asked a complex question!"? No. If you are old enough to be a witness, you *were* somewhere last June twenty-fifth.

So, whenever you confront a complex question, divide it. Ask whether the question that has been assumed has been satisfactorily answered. If it has, answer the question. If it has not, reply, "Before I can answer *that* question, I must answer *this* question."

Suppressed Evidence

When we construct a persuasive argument, we seldom marshal all the evidence on all sides of an issue. Sometimes issues are so complex that it is virtually impossible to examine all the evidence in anything short of a very long book. Many times we may not know what all aspects of an issue are, and so we do not know what will count as evidence. There is no fallacy so long as you make a diligent effort to examine the issue thoroughly, and you show that your conclusion is the most reasonable conclusion. This requires that you have positive arguments for your conclusion and strong criticisms of alternative positions on the same issue. You commit the fallacy of **suppressed evidence** when you ignore evidence that is contrary to your own position.

Assume you are at a town meeting. The XYZ Corporation has proposed a new factory for your community. The object of the town meeting is to discuss the issue and decide whether or not the town should allow the factory to be built. Mr. Big, president of XYZ, proposes the following argument:

> Our factory, when completed, initially will provide employment for 600 people, and it is likely that we will expand further within the next decade. In addition, several hundred people—people from your community—will be involved in constructing the factory. More employment will yield a great boost to the local economy, both immediately and in the long term. So, you should allow us to build our factory.

Are those the only effects the factory would have on the town? Are those the only effects of which Mr. Big is likely to know? Probably not. Let us assume that if the factory is built, the town will need to construct a large new water treatment plant. Let us assume that wherever else XYZ has built a factory, there were very serious problems with water and air pollution. Let us assume that XYZ has a company policy of bringing in cheap immigrant labor, so relatively few of the residents of the community found jobs at XYZ's factories. Let us assume that wherever else XYZ has built a factory, the crime rate has increased markedly. Mr. Big is in a position to know all of these things—as the president of the company, he *should* know all of these facts. By not revealing them, Mr. Big is guilty of the fallacy of suppressed evidence.

Of course, you never know what another person actually knows, so establishing that evidence has been suppressed requires some homework. Further, if someone is attempting to persuade you to believe or do something, it is unlikely that she will go out of her way to point out all the possible negative implications of the belief or action. When was the last time a salesperson said to you, "Of course, you can buy the same thing at the store down the street for $50 less" or "Since the company that manufactures this well-known brand I'm trying to sell you was taken over by the Schlock Corporation, the quality has really gone down the tubes"? So, if you are going to be a careful consumer, you should do some research. If a company wants to build a new factory in your town, find out what has happened when it has built factories in other towns. Was the impact, on balance, an improvement? If your research yields questions, ask them! If you are planning to buy a late-model used car, check the prices in the *Kelly Auto Market Report (Blue Book)* at your public library and have a trusted independent mechanic inspect the car before you put down any money. If you are planning to buy a new consumer product, check *Consumer Reports* or other publications that provide an *independent* evaluation of the product you are considering. If *you* are well informed, it is unlikely that you will fall victim to the fallacy of suppressed evidence.

False Dichotomy

A disjunctive syllogism is a valid deductive argument in which, given a disjunctive ("or") statement and the denial of one of its disjuncts, the truth of the other disjunct follows with necessity. While the form of the argument is valid, you can know the truth of the conclusion only if the disjunctive premise is true. A disjunction is true if and only if at least one of its disjuncts is true.[2] If the disjunctive premise in a disjunctive syllogism is false, the argument commits the fallacy of **false dichotomy**. Consider the following argument:

> Tristan is either in the school band or in the choir.
>
> He is not in the band.
> _____
>
> So he is in the choir.

Is the disjunctive premise true? You will have to check. If Tristan attends a school where all students are required to be in either the band or the choir, and he is not in the band, the argument is sound. In most schools, however, there is no requirement that a student be a member of *either* the band or the choir. So, you have to check whether the disjunctive premise is true.

In general—and especially when someone is trying to persuade you of something—check the disjunctive premise to see if it is true. An initial step in checking the truth of the disjunctive premise is to ask whether there are additional alternatives that reasonably could be included in the disjunctive premise. If the disjunctive premise is false, the argument commits the fallacy of false dichotomy.

In the 1950s and 1960s, when the Cold War was at its chilliest, some anti-communists boldly set forth the motto "Better dead than red!" The implicit argument was

> Either it is better to be a living communist or it is better to be a dead noncommunist.
>
> It is not better to be a living communist.
> _____
>
> So, it is better to be a dead noncommunist.

___
[2]See Chapter 20.

Source: *Jim Davis,* Garfield. *Used with permission of Universal Press Syndicate.*

Those who suggested that the disjunctive premise was false, that the motto involved a false dichotomy, responded, "Better pink than extinct."

Exercises

I. Identify the fallacies of presumption in each of the following. If no fallacy is committed, write "No Fallacy." Give reasons for your answers.

1. "What are we going to do about the health-care crisis in America?" (William Jefferson Clinton, 1992)

2. Eating peanut butter is heart-healthy, since peanut butter contains no cholesterol.

3. What he had asked, seemingly out of the blue, was whether she had any strong feelings about her employer's "underhanded corporate tactics." As if it were an obvious *given* that there was something wrong with the manner in which Marcus Caine did business. The sky is blue, the sea is wide, Marcus Caine is an unscrupulous crook. Elementary my dear Kirsten. (Tom Clancy and Martin Greenberg, *Tom Clancy's Power Plays: ruthless.com* [New York: Berkley Books: 1998], p. 58)

4. Master Pangloss taught the metaphysico-theologo-cosmolonigology. He could prove to admiration that there is no effect without a cause; and, that in this best of all possible worlds, the Baron's castle was the most magnificent of all castles, and My Lady the best of all possible baronesses.

   "It is demonstrable," said he, "that things cannot be otherwise than as they are; for as all things have been created for some end, they must necessarily be created for the best end." (Voltaire, *Candide*)

5. "In *that* direction," the Cat said, waving its right paw round, "lives a Hatter: and in *that* direction," waving the other paw, "lives a March Hare. Visit either you like: they're both mad."

   "But I don't want to go among mad people," Alice remarked.

   "Oh, you can't help that," said the Cat: "we're all mad here. I'm mad. You're mad."

   "How do you know I'm mad?" said Alice.

"You must be," said the Cat, "or you wouldn't have come here." (Lewis Carroll, *Alice's Adventures in Wonderland*, Chapter 6)

6. We should drill for oil in the Alaskan Wildlife Refuge, because that's where the oil is.

7. "Mulder, you're paranoid," Scully said with wry amusement.
   "Only because everybody's out to get me," he said. (Kevin J. Anderson, *The X-Files: Gound Zero* [New York: HarperPrism, 1995], p. 174)

8. So you think we should discuss whether to buy a new car. Very well, shall we buy a Ford or a Chevy?

9. Drug addiction is bad because it is bad to become physically or psychologically dependent upon drugs.

10. Voting for the state bond issue will not raise taxes, since all costs of administering the bonds will be drawn from the lottery fund.

11. The evidence shows that the testimony of that pathological liar Marduk is false, so he should be convicted of perjury.

12. Given the medical evidence regarding the relationship between cholesterol and heart disease, the choice is clear: Give up meat or die of a heart attack!

13. Why did you steal the painting?

14. You must obey the law because it is right to do so. And we know it is right to do so because it is the law.

15. You should vote Yes on the referendum to legalize dog racing, for it provides a means of increasing state revenues without raising the income tax.

16. Furniture is expensive. Either you spend your money on the furniture itself, or you spend your money on the tools and wood to make it. In either case, you will spend thousands of dollars on furniture.

17. You have a simple choice: Either take our speed-reading course or fall behind on your reading assignments.

18. How did you conceal your identity for all these years?

19. Why do I know more than other people? Why, in general, am I so clever? I have never pondered over questions that are not really questions. I have never wasted my strength. (Frederich Nietzsche, *Ecce Homo*)

20. When did David write the Twenty-Third Psalm?

II. Identify the fallacies of ambiguity, relevance, or presumption committed in each of the following passages. If no fallacy is committed, write "No Fallacy." Give reasons for your answers.

1. Anyone who cannot keep his or her personal finances in good order cannot keep public finances in good order. Alexander Hamilton, the first U.S. Secretary of the Treasury, could not keep his personal finances in good order. Therefore, Alexander Hamilton must not have been a good Secretary of the Treasury.

2. The call for a national health-care program should be rejected, for nothing the government does can assure that human life will be lengthened indefinitely.

3. All men are mortals. So, all the immortals of stage, screen, and television must be women.

4. Bumper sticker: If you tease me about my age, I'll beat you with my cane.

5. Sue claims that bicycling is a good form of exercise. But bicycles are hard to see, and when a bicycle collides with a car, the bicycle always loses. Many cyclists are injured every year because of their own negligence or unseen road hazards. Maybe Sue doesn't value her life, but bicycling is too dangerous for me.

6. Either the defendant knew what was going on in his house but did nothing about it, in which case he is lying, or he knew nothing and is a fool.

7. Ms. Merple has argued that a civilized society cannot condone capital punishment, since it is inhumane and there is always the chance of putting an innocent person to death. But consider the facts. Each convicted felon costs the taxpayer over $20,000 per year. When felons appeal their sentences, it is again the taxpayer who pays. And our prisons are overcrowded, and you know who will have to pay for the solution to that problem! Economic viability requires that the sentences of death row inmates be speedily carried out!

8. You shouldn't take the religious arguments of John Wesley, the founder of Methodism, seriously, for Wesley was a scholastic quibbler and a critic of such modern works as John Locke's *Essay Concerning Human Understanding*.

9. When we worked through a practice examination as a group, the class completed it in less than an hour. So, any student in the class should be able to complete a comparable test within an hour.

10. How do we know that "The Ride of the Valkyries" is a better piece of music than the theme from *The Sound of Music?* Because of the unanimous opinion of the experts. And how do we know who these experts are? They are the ones who hold that "The Ride of the Valkyries" is a better piece of music than the theme from *The Sound of Music.*

11. Elkie has argued that a national sales tax is a reasonable way to raise additional revenues for the federal government. Her argument is plausible only on the assumption that such a form of taxation is equitable. But a sales tax is not equitable. People are not taxed on the basis of their ability to pay. So, her argument must be rejected.

12. Little girl: "My daddy says that Churchill Downs is a place where people race horses. I'm sure few people go to Churchill Downs, because it doesn't take too long to figure out that the horses always win."

13. MacMurphy's Mausoleum, the choice of the finest families in our community for over a hundred years.

14. You shouldn't take Mrs. Jones's arguments in favor of farm subsidies seriously, since she manages one of the largest agricultural enterprises in the state.

15. They are just one of a growing number of homeless families in our community. The Smythes are a family of ten. They live in an unheated bus. Finding employment of any kind is a hit-or-miss proposition, and steady employment is little more than a dream. Winter is setting in, and the eight children have nothing warmer than T-shirts. Shouldn't you give to the Community Homeless Drive to help this family and others like it? It could be a matter of life and death.

16. I'm not backward. If I were backward, I would eat with my feet, and I don't eat with my feet.

17. At the trial of La Vale and Windshield on charges of grand larceny, the District Attorney asked a prosecution witness: "What, precisely, was your job when working for those crooks LaVale and Windshield?"

18. The first musical notation was invented in about CE 200. We may conclude that before then everyone was a monotone.

19. Each of the atomic bombs dropped during the Second World War killed more people than were killed by any conventional bomb. So, more people were killed by atomic bombs during the Second World War than by conventional bombs.

20. It's the party of the people! Vote Democratic!

21. Obviously, we should support the continued construction and use of nuclear-powered electrical-generating plants, for in the past thirty years there have been fewer accidents at nuclear generating plants than at conventional power plants.

22. Dr. Swenson has provided evidence that diets high in fiber and low in polyunsaturated fats and cholesterol tend to result in fewer deaths from cancer and heart disease. But diets high in fiber have all the gustatory appeal of tree bark. Low-fat and low-cholesterol foods have no flavor at all. So, unless you want to spend your life eating cardboard, you'll ignore Dr. Swenson's dietary advice.

23. Either you favor a conservative fiscal program and vote Republican, or you favor an increase in social programs and vote Democratic.

24. Try, dear friends, to make the civilized world and particularly the French people clearly hear your Fatherland's voice. Struggle to frustrate the ignominious slanders unleashed by the French colonists. In order to oppress our people once more, the French colonists have killed women and children. They have asked for the help of the British, Indian, and Japanese forces, using airplanes, tanks, cannons, and warships. But however modern an army is, it is powerless before the determined attitude of a whole people. Wherever we go, they will find scorched earth and the hatred of a people who are only waiting for an opportunity to drive them out of the country. (Ho Chi Minh, "Appeal to Vietnamese Residents in France" [November 5, 1945], in *Ho Chi Minh on Revolution*, Ed. Bernard B. Fall [Signet Books, 1967], p. 151)

25. Help protect an endangered species! Vote Communist!

Fallacies of Weak Induction

The View: Fallacies of weak induction are inductive arguments that provide insufficient evidence to show that the conclusion is probably true. An appeal to authority is committed when one cites a person or group or practice as an authority in a field in which that person, group, or practice does not have the credentials necessary to establish that it is an authority in that field. An appeal to ignorance is committed when you say that since there is no evidence that a certain proposition is true, it must be false, *or* when you say that since there is no evidence that a certain proposition is false, it must be true. A hasty generalization occurs when you reach a general conclusion—whether universal or statistical—on the basis of insufficient evidence, especially when the sample from which the conclusion is drawn is atypical. The fallacy of false cause occurs if you claim that something is a cause when it is not. The slippery slope fallacy occurs if there is a chain of causal claims—often in which things begin with bad consequences and grow progressively worse—in which one or more of the causal claims is false. A weak analogy is an analogical argument in which the points of comparison are insufficient to support the conclusion or in which there are significant disanalogies among the things compared, so the conclusion is not well supported.

Are there any problems peculiar to inductive arguments?

An inductive argument with true premises provides some, but not conclusive, evidence for the truth of its conclusion. The fallacies of weak induction are committed if the inductive evidence cited is weak or incomplete, or evidence contrary to the conclusion is ignored.[1]

---

[1]If you have read all the previous chapters, you will find that there is virtually nothing new in this chapter. Hence, references will be made back to chapters where most of these fallacies have been discussed before.

Appeal to Authority

Much of what we learn is based on authoritative statements of others. You may assume that what your computer science professor tells you about computers is true, since she has several degrees in (and extensive experience with) computer science. You commit the fallacy of **appeal to authority** when you assume that because a person is an authority in one field, he or she is also an authority in an unrelated field, or when you appeal to something as an authority—common practice, popular opinion, tradition—when it is not an authority.[2]

Appeals to authority are common in advertising. Jack Nicklaus advertises heart medicine. Tiger Woods advertises Buicks. Are they authorities on these subjects? You should check *Who's Who in America* to find out. It will tell you that Nicklaus was a student at Ohio State University, and Tiger Woods was a student at Stanford. There is no indication that either completed a degree, let alone that Nicklaus has a degree in medicine or Woods has a degree in automotive engineering. The implicit argument in the Woods commercial seems to go like this:

If Woods is an expert on golf, then he is an expert on cars.

If Woods is an expert on cars, then you should believe what he says about cars.

Woods is an expert on golf.

So, you should believe what Woods says about cars.

The first premise is probably false. There is no reason to believe that being an expert on golf automatically makes you an expert on cars. So, the implicit argument is unsound. Barring additional evidence that Woods has stronger credentials than you or I have on what makes a quality car, the implicit argument should be rejected as an appeal to authority.[3]

But if the commercials concerned golf equipment, the situation might be different. Both Nicklaus and Woods have outstanding credentials in the game of golf. So, if they advertise golf equipment, should you believe them? You still should be skeptical. While Nicklaus and Woods know more about golf equipment than I will ever know, there might be a conflict of interest. People making commercial endorsements are *paid*. Are they pushing the product because they believe it is the best? Or are they pushing the product because they are paid to do so? If they use the equipment they advertise, you might have some reason to take the endorsement seriously. If they have an outstanding reputation for integrity, you might have additional reasons to believe them. But the best endorsement might be by an independent source, such as *Consumer Reports*.

---

[2]You may wish to review the criteria for evaluating testimonial evidence in Chapter 11, since these criteria provide guidelines for determining who or what is an authority on a particular topic.

[3]In many cases of advertising, one might argue that there is *not* an implicit appeal to authority. The person in the commercial is glamorous or charismatic, and some of this glamour is transferred to the product. One might argue that they are cases of mob appeal or false cause. By buying the product, you become someone special.

Appeals to authority are not limited to advertising. Consider your favorite social cause. Whether you are interested in funds for AIDs research, or revising the drug laws, or any other cause, you probably can find a public service announcement or a gathering in which famous persons make a plug for the cause. Does being a famous person make someone an expert on social issues? No. But it does make for a good appeal to authority—which should be rejected.

These might be blatant cases. Appeals to authority can be far more subtle. In 1970 Linus Pauling published a book called *Vitamin C and the Common Cold*.[4] He contended that large doses of vitamin C can *prevent* colds. Pauling was a very intelligent person. He won the 1954 Nobel Prize in chemistry and the 1962 Nobel Peace Prize. Surely you can believe him, right? Wrong. Chemistry and medicine are distinct sciences. Someone can know a great deal about chemistry and still know relatively little about medicine. Pauling's hypothesis was proven false, even though many people initially believed it due to Pauling's reputation.

People are not the only authorities to which we appeal. Popular opinion is taken as an authority. Several years ago Ford Motor Company advertised that the Ford Taurus was the most popular car sold in America. What can you infer from this? You can infer that more Ford Tauruses were sold than any other any model car made that year—which is what it means to say it was the most popular car. Can you infer that the Taurus was the best-built car in America? No. This would be like saying that because Richard Nixon (1972) and Bill Clinton (1996) received more popular votes than any previous presidential candidates, they were two of the greatest presidents in the history of the United States. History might judge that Nixon and Clinton were great presidents, but popularity has nothing to do with that. Similarly, the Taurus might have been the best-built American car during the relevant model year, but the fact that it was popular does not show that. The only clear inference you can make from popularity is that something was popular.

Tradition is sometimes taken as an authority. We have always done it that way, so it is right. That will not work either. The story is told of a man who was going to roast a ham, and before placing it in the roaster, he ceremoniously cut several inches off the end of it. His wife saw this and asked, "Why did you cut the end off the ham?"

"That's the way my father did it."

"But why did he do that?"

The husband had no answer, so they called Dad.

"That's the way my mother did it," Dad replied.

"But why did she do that?" the inquisitive wife asked again.

Dad had no answer, so the couple called Granny.

"I cut the end off the ham because my roaster was too short to hold the whole thing," Granny replied.

Was there a good reason to cut the end off the ham? *Granny* had a good reason. Dad and son did it simply because "that's the way it's done in our family," which was less than a great reason.

---

[4]Linus Pauling, *Vitamin C and the Common Cold* (San Francisco: W. H. Freeman, 1970).

Appeal to Ignorance

An **appeal to ignorance** is committed when you say that since there is no evidence that a certain proposition is true, it must be false, *or* when you say that since there is no evidence that a certain proposition is false, it must be true. For example, if I said, "There is no evidence that there are not intelligent extraterrestrial beings living in New York City, so there are intelligent extraterrestrials that live in New York City," I would commit the fallacy of appeal to ignorance. I would need some kind of *positive* evidence to reach that conclusion, including criteria for detecting intelligent extraterrestrials. Further, by changing the position of 'not', I can provide equally strong evidence for the contrary of the original conclusion: "There is no evidence that there are intelligent extraterrestrial beings living in New York City, so there are not intelligent extraterrestrials that live in New York City."

As with many informal fallacies, there are cases in which an argument that looks like an appeal to ignorance is perfectly acceptable. If you told me that there is no evidence that your roommate smokes, I should accept your conclusion. Smoking is a habit that is hard to hide. There are the lingering aromas in the air and on clothes, the telltale stains on the teeth, and the various sorts of paraphernalia that smokers generally have around—smoking materials, ash trays, and so on. If there are none of these "marks" of a smoker, you have good reason to believe your roommate does not smoke.

Similarly, if after careful examination a scientist reports that there is no reason to believe that a certain phenomenon occurs, you have good reason to accept her conclusion. Here there is an appeal to evidence. The evidence tends to show that the phenomenon in question does not occur. Further, if accepted scientific theory cannot explain the occurrence of the alleged phenomenon, there is further evidence that the phenomenon did not occur. Finally, if there is an alternative explanation of the occurrence of the *apparent* phenomenon, which is consistent with scientific theory, you have more evidence that the phenomenon in question did not occur. For example, scientific evidence suggests that what was described as "cold fusion" was actually a chemical reaction. This is *not* an appeal to ignorance.

Notice that this ties appeal to ignorance to questions of authority. If an authority in a field claims that there is no evidence for a phenomenon in his or her field, the person is not speaking out of ignorance. On the other hand, if the person making the "no evidence" claim is *not* an authority in the relevant area and the apparent evidence on both sides of the issue is approximately equal, then the person commits the fallacy of appeal to ignorance.

Hasty Generalization

A **hasty generalization** occurs when you reach a general conclusion—whether universal or statistical—on the basis of insufficient evidence, especially when the sample from which the conclusion is drawn is atypical. If I claim that Sony does not make good tape recorders because my Sony doesn't work well, I could be charged with a hasty generalization for two reasons. First, I am generalizing from one case. There are lots of Sony tape recorders. To generalize, you need to have a fairly large sample. Second, my Sony tape recorder is probably not typical. It is a reel-to-reel tape recorder, which I bought used something over a decade ago. (Old things wear out. It used to work very well.)

Typicality is a curious requirement. Clearly, if you conclude that all redheads are temperamental because you know only one redhead and he is temperamental, you haven't looked at enough redheads. The problem is, if you do not have a large enough sample, there is no way for you to know whether or not the case from which you are generalizing is *typical*. So, the requirement that you have a fairly large sample *should* take care of problems of typicality.[5]

False Cause

The fallacy of false cause is committed when either you take something to be a cause when it is not (*non causa pro causa,* "not a cause as a cause") or you contend that just because one event occurred before another, the first event is the cause of the second (*post hoc ergo propter hoc,* "before therefore because").

We all look for causal relations all the time. We recognize that whatever causes something must occur prior to that which is caused. We also recognize that when two kinds of things are causally related, the first and second occur together or in a regular succession. So, if the claim is made that one phenomenon causes another, but you do not have all the conditions necessary for the second to occur, you have a case of a false cause. Consider the following:

> The barometer is falling in the Sahara Desert, so it is going to rain there. Taken at face value, it is a false cause. The actions of meteorological instruments have no effect on the weather. "But," you will say, "what's meant is that the atmospheric pressure, as measured by the barometric scale, is decreasing. When the atmospheric pressure decreases, it rains. That's why some barometers have rain icons in the low-pressure range." So understood, we have a genuine cause, right? Maybe. Maybe not. And maybe it depends where you are. Two conditions are needed if it is going to rain. There must be moisture in the air, and the atmospheric pressure must be low enough that it will not prevent the moisture from falling. When we (imprecisely) talk about *the* cause of rain, we commonly refer to whichever of the two is most commonly needed to trigger a shower *in a particular place.* In the Florida Everglades, where the air is moisture-laden, the factor that triggers rain is a decrease in the atmospheric pressure. In the desert, the factor that triggers rain is the presence of sufficient moisture—the daily heating expands the air and reduces the air pressure, but it usually doesn't rain. So, in the desert, appealing to a drop in atmospheric pressure as *the* cause of rain might reasonably be deemed a false cause.

Superstitions are cases of appeals to a false cause. Your friend who says, "I've always sung a chorus of Bach's 'Death, Death, I Do Not Fear Thee'[6] before a college

---

[5]See Chapter 26 for a more thorough discussion of the criteria for evaluating a generalization.
[6]J. S. Bach, *Jesu, Priceless Treasure (Jesu Meine Freund)*, Number 5, Verse 3.

Source: Seth Casana, Academia Nuts. *Used with permission of the author.*

exam, and I've always done well on my college exams," probably would have done well without the vocalization. But superstitions are not the only cases of false causes.

Sometimes someone gives an explanation in which the claimed causal relation simply does not hold. This is another case of false cause. Consider the following:

> "I always wanted to be a real singer, the kind that comes out on stage all dressed up. But I didn't have no education and I didn't know the first way about how to start being a stage singer. Mind your job, my mother told me. You don't know how lucky you are to have work, she said. So I drifted into the singing waiter business. It's not steady work. I'd be better off if I were just a plain waiter. That's why I drink," he finished illogically.[7]

Might the fact that the person in the previous paragraph had a disappointing career have caused him to drink? Sure, but surely it is not the complete cause. Many people have professional disappointments but avoid alcoholism. Some people become alcoholics without any professional disappointments. How you react to an adverse situation depends upon at least your upbringing and the social conditions in which you find yourself. And some people take disappointments as an *excuse* to drink. In the latter case, the causal appeal would be false. In any other, it is at best incomplete.

There are clearly causal claims that are false. If I said that Napoleon invaded Russia in 1812 because Julius Caesar invaded northern Europe during the first century BCE, you would probably be hard-put to find any clear causal connection between the two events. If I said that Hermann the Great invaded Rome because the Roman emperors had been attempting to conquer the Germanic territories for several centuries, I am probably making a true claim. The Roman conquests were probably at least a necessary condition for Hermann's actions; that is, if the Romans had not tried to conquer the Germanic states, Hermann would not have invaded Rome. But there are many causal claims which, while true, leave a lot out.

Consider this one: If the Treaty of Versailles (which ended World War I) had not imposed reparations on the Germans, Hitler would not have risen to power. Is that claim true? Historians claim that *part* of the political and economic problems in

---

[7]Betty Smith, *A Tree Grows in Brooklyn* (New York: Harper and Brothers Publishers, 1943), p. 29.

Germany after World War I were caused by the terms of the Treaty of Versailles. German reparations were a partial cause of economic problems in Germany. Economic problems were a partial cause of German political instability. But another element was that a democratic form of government was imposed upon Germany, while the Germans did not have a tradition of democratic government. So, if the causal claim is understood to mean that *the* (one and only) cause of Hitler's rise to power was the reparations imposed by the Treaty of Versailles, the claim is false. It is too simplistic. Complex causal phenomena generally require fairly complex explanations. Hitler might have risen to power even if there had been no reparations.

Similarly, the statement, "Hitler rose to power because his mother didn't have an abortion" states a necessary condition for his rise to power. If Hitler's mother *had* had an abortion, Hitler would *not* have risen to power. But prenatal decisions are sufficiently remote to have little or no bearing on Hitler's rise to power.

Appeals to false causes are fairly common in advertising. As we noted in Chapter 29, many cases of mob appeal might also be deemed cases of false cause. The beer commercials featuring "beautiful people" might be seen as appealing to your desire to join the beautiful people by joining the beer drinking crowd. They also may be seen as suggesting that drinking beer will cause you to become a beautiful person. The first is a case of mob appeal. The second is a false cause. But these are not the only cases. Sometimes what is claimed might be true, but there are reasons to suspect that the whole causal story was not told.

Old people (such as the author of this book) spend a great deal of time worrying about their cholesterol levels. A recent oatmeal commercial featured a senior citizen who claimed that she had started eating oatmeal every morning for breakfast and her cholesterol levels had dropped nine points in thirty days. Was it the oatmeal that did it? Perhaps. But there might have been other factors as well. Consider this case:

> Dan, a man in his late forties, visited his doctor for his annual physical. The doctor decided to do a cholesterol screening. The last time Dan had had a physical—some twelve years and thirty pounds ago—his cholesterol number had been 127, which is quite good. This time his cholesterol number was 270, which is quite high. So Dan switched to a breakfast of oatmeal every morning and within six months his cholesterol number had dropped down to 180, which is within the normal range. Was it the oatmeal that did it?

When an old person receives a high cholesterol number, it is usually understood to mean, *You're going to die!* So, Dan switched from breakfasts of bacon and eggs to oatmeal—it couldn't hurt. He also lost fifteen pounds and switched from a diet that was high in fats to a fairly low-fat diet. The huge bowl of ice cream he had eaten every night became little more than a pleasant memory. And he vowed he would refrain from eating four batches of homemade caramels in the space of a month.[8] Did the oatmeal *cause* the drop in his cholesterol number? It certainly didn't hurt, but the more probable cause was a general shift in his eating habits. If you are to believe the claims in the

---

[8]Homemade caramels consist of brown sugar, corn syrup, sweetened condensed milk, a dash of salt, a teaspoon of vanilla, and *butter*, lots and lots of butter. (Nothing but butter will do!)

oatmeal commercials, you must also *assume* that the *only* shift in the person's diet was *adding* oatmeal. If the person shifted from a high-fat diet to a low-fat diet, the oatmeal might be only a minor factor in the change in cholesterol numbers.[9]

Looking for causes is a complicated activity. Many times, if you claim that there is a false causal appeal, you might need to explain why the proposed cause is causally irrelevant or why it is only one element in a complex causal situation.

Slippery Slope (Wedge)

The **slippery slope fallacy** occurs if there is a chain of causal claims—often in which things begin with bad consequences and they grow progressively worse—in which one or more causal claim is false. This is sometimes known as the **wedge fallacy**. A type of action is seen as the thin edge of a wedge. As the wedge is driven further into a block of wood, it causes a continually wider split. Similarly, the consequences that follow from an action become worse and worse.

"Don't smoke cigarettes, because if you smoke cigarettes you'll try marijuana, which will lead to hashish, which will lead to cocaine, which will ruin your life." Is there a problem here? Sure. It might be true that most people who became drug addicts smoked cigarettes before trying other drugs, but many cigarette smokers never try other drugs. The first claimed causal relation usually does not hold. So, the supposed causal train derails.

Of course there *are* causal chains that hold, and some of these causal trains lead to increasingly terrible consequences. So, finding such a chain does not guarantee that you have found a fallacious slippery slope. The person who gives you the following advice probably should be heeded: "Don't tailgate. If you tailgate, you'll eventually run into the vehicle in front of you. If you run into the vehicle in front of you, your auto insurance rates will increase. If your auto insurance rates increase, you'll have less money for enjoyable endeavors. So, don't tailgate." What you need to do is determine whether the alleged causal relations hold. If they do, there is no fallacy. If they do not, then you should indicate where the causal chain breaks down.

This does not mean it is always an easy job. Consider the following slippery slope argument that was once proposed by opponents to abortion. "We cannot legalize abortion. If we legalize abortion, there will be a move to legalize euthanasia. If we legalize euthanasia, a general disregard for human life will follow. Since you can see what the consequences will be if we legalize abortion, you can see that we should not do so." Abortion was legalized about thirty years ago. Euthanasia is a hot moral and political topic. Various states have passed laws allowing euthanasia under specifiable conditions. Does this mean that the doomsayers were right? Not necessarily. Abortion has been practiced for centuries, whether legally or otherwise. Euthanasia was openly practiced by the ancient Greeks and Romans. At least the removal of extraordinary care was commonly practiced in many hospitals long before the question of the legalization of euthanasia was openly debated. One question you need to

---

[9] If the people in the oatmeal commercial are like Dan, then questions of suppressed evidence as well as false cause might be involved.

ask is whether there is an increase in the frequency of cases of abortion and euthanasia, or whether the issue is simply much more publicly discussed. If there are more cases of abortion and euthanasia than there were thirty years ago, is there a causal relation between the legalization of abortion and the legalization of euthanasia? And if there is a causal connection between these two, does this cause a decreased regard for human life? These are not easy questions to answer.

Weak Analogy

Weak analogy is based on an analogical argument in which the points of comparison are insufficient to support the conclusion or in which there are significant *disanalogies* among the things compared. As we noted in Chapter 25, one of the problems with many arguments by analogy is that the points of comparison are not fully stated. You may need to dig a bit deeper and determine how similar or different the things compared are and whether the similarities or differences are relevant to the conclusion.[10] Consider some examples.

Assume you are comparing universities. A recruiter is attempting to convince you to attend Notmuchofa University (founded six months ago) by comparing it to Yale. The recruiter argues:

> Both Notmuchofa and Yale have comprehensive programs. Yale graduates get great jobs. So, Notmuchofa graduates will get great jobs too.

You are not convinced, are you! What are the differences? Yale has been around for about three hundred years. Notmuchofa is new. Yale has a marvelous reputation in most academic areas. Notmuchofa is too young to have any reputation. *Because* Yale has a reputation for excellence that Notmuchofa lacks, most employers will give Yale graduates more attention than they give graduates of a fairly unknown school. *Because* Yale has been around for a long time, there is a network of Yale graduates who tend to prefer Yale graduates to graduates of other schools. So, the analogy is quite weak. The schools are different in relevant respects.

A few years ago a professor I know was concerned about grade inflation. He had taught for a year at a prestigious four-year liberal arts college in the upper Midwest, a school we shall call PC. He commented,

> At PC nearly a quarter of the senior class graduated with honors. If a quarter of the seniors here at State College graduated with honors, we would be guilty of grade inflation in the extreme. So, obviously, grade inflation is completely out of control at PC.

Is the conclusion warranted? Perhaps. Perhaps not. State College has a fairly open admissions policy. Anyone graduating in the top 50 percent of his or her high-school class is guaranteed admission to State College. PC has very high admission standards. Admission to PC requires that the applicant be in the top 5 percent of his or her high-school class

---

[10]Review the criteria for evaluating analogies in Chapter 25.

and that he or she have high SAT or ACT scores. State College is very concerned with student retention. If 3,000 students are admitted in a given fall, State College believes it has fulfilled its mission only if at least 2,700 of those students graduate within four to five years. PC admits only 700 students in any given year, and they expect no more than 60 percent of those students to graduate. Forty percent of a freshman class will fail out or transfer to other schools, generally to schools that have lower academic standards. So, is grade inflation out of control at PC? Probably not. If you were to claim that grade inflation is out of control at PC, you must assume that *any* school that graduated more than a certain percentage of its students with honors was guilty of grade inflation.

Of course, it is not always easy to tell whether an analogy is weak or strong. Consider the following:

> "You were trying to collect money?"
> "Of course I was trying to collect money. I was trying to collect money due to me."
> "Who was helping you?"
> "That's none of your business."
> "Don't you know that you can't use the telephone for that purpose?"
> "I don't know why not."
> "Haven't you ever heard that it's against the law to demand money on a postal card?"
> "Yes, I've heard of that."
> "And yet you have the nerve to sit there and claim that you don't know it's against the law to ring up a man and demand that he pay you money?"
> "We didn't do that," she said.
> "Didn't do what?"
> "Didn't ring him up and demand that he give us money—not in so many words."[11]

The argument goes like this. Demanding money by phone is like demanding money by a postcard. Demanding money by a postcard is illegal. So, demanding money by phone is also illegal. Is it a weak analogy or a strong analogy? It is hard to say. Both postcards and telephones are means of communication, so they are similar. But that *might* be the extent of the similarity. While the post office is a federal agency, the telephone company is not. There are laws regarding what can be transmitted both by post and by phone. On the face of it, it is not unreasonable to suggest that if a certain kind of message cannot legally be transmitted by mail, it cannot be transmitted by phone. But reasonable similarities do not always translate into parallel laws. If a request for money is an illegal request—such as extortion or blackmail—then the means of transmitting the request is irrelevant. If the kind of request for funds was *not* illegal, then there *might* be regulatory differences between the two industries. So, without further information, it is impossible to determine whether the cases are parallel. It is impossible to determine the strength of the analogy.

---

[11]Erle Stanley Gardner, *The Case of the Curious Bride* (Mattituck, NY: Aeonian Press, 1934), pp. 181-182.

Exercises

I. Which of the following passages commit a fallacy of weak induction? If the passage commits a fallacy, name the fallacy and explain why the fallacy is committed. If the passage commits no fallacy, explain why it does not.

1. A young woman from Columbus, Ohio: "I'd like to know what each of you thinks of the proposition that Kennedy had to be killed because he was about to order a withdrawal of our troops from Vietnam."

   Drury signed [University of Texas history] Professor Trabue to answer first, and the professor said, "There is no evidence whatsoever of that. None whatever. In the absence of evidence, I am not prepared to believe any such preposterous accusation." (William Harrington, *Columbo: The Grassy Knoll* [New York: A Tom Doherty Associates Book, 1993], p. 23)

2. "Ghosts don't haunt us. That's not how it works. They're present among us because we won't let go of *them*."

   "I don't believe in ghosts," I said, faintly.

   "Some people can't see the color red. That doesn't mean it isn't there," she replied. (Sue Grafton, *M is for Malice,* a Marion Wood book [New York: Henry Holt and Company, 1996], p. 280)

3. "We didn't have any problems going from BC to AD, so why should we have any problems going from Y1K to Y2K?" ("Italy's Y2K Worries," *Morning Edition,* National Public Radio, December 14, 1999)

4. "Surely," Dail said, "when a man has been in your employ, suddenly leaves without a word of explanation, and there's a shortage of twenty-five thousand dollars, it's at least a reasonable inference that he's guilty of embezzlement," (Erle Stanley Gardner, *The Case of the Substitute Face* [New York: Ballantine Books, 1938], p. 111)

5. In reply to its critics, the tobacco industry recently has proposed the following argument. If tobacco is held fiscally responsible for the diseases and deaths that arise from using tobacco, then next the makers of alcoholic products will be held responsible for diseases and deaths that arise from using their products. Who will be next? The meat and dairy industries for deaths arising from using their products? Then motorcycle makers? Then auto makers? But it would be absurd to hold auto makers responsible for auto accidents. So, it's absurd to hold the tobacco industry responsible for diseases and deaths that arise from the use of tobacco.

6. I have been a preacher for a good number of years, and whenever the pictorial church directories were delivered, eight to ten people died—and they were always people whose pictures were not in the directory. So, for your good health, you will want to make sure your picture is in the new directory.

7. Historically, the direction of the stock market between September 1 and election day corresponds with the results of a presidential election. If the market goes up, the incumbent party retains control of the White House. If the market goes down, the incumbent party loses. So, if you like the President's party, the best way to keep it controlling the White House is to buy a lot of stock.

8. The American West was settled primarily by veterans of the Civil War. They all had guns. Except for saloon fights, the crime rate was quite low in the American West. So, if we want to reduce the crime rate today, we should make guns are available to virtually everyone.

9. I've always reckoned that looking at the new moon over your left shoulder is one of the carelessest and foolishest things a body can do. Old Hank Bunker done it once, and bragged about it; and in less than two years he got drunk and fell off of the shot tower and spread himself out so that he was just a kind of a layer, as you may say; and they slid him edgeways between two barn doors for a coffin, and buried him so, so they say, but I didn't see it. Pap told me. But anyway, it all come of looking at the moon that way, like a fool. (Mark Twain, *The Adventures of Huckleberry Finn*, Chapter 10)

10. Great artists are seldom recognized as great before they die. So, if you want to be recognized as a great artist, die.

11. There is no evidence that capital punishment is a deterrent to murder, so it is not a deterrent.

12. Chevrolets are not safe cars, for Joan drove her 1952 Chevy I at a high speed on a mountainous road, the brakes gave out, and she was killed.

13. We should not worry about protecting the spotted owl and the various other so-called endangered species. To claim these species must be preserved in their pure genetic state is like arguing for racial purity. But the arguments for racial purity are morally pernicious. So, the arguments for preserving endangered species are also morally pernicious.

14. If I don't get a B in this course, I won't be able to register for courses in my major next semester. If I can't register for courses in my major next semester, completing my degree will take an additional year. Since I can't afford to spend an extra year in college, I won't be able to finish, and my fourteen children (all under the age of six) will certainly starve.

15. When I go to church, I seldom have trouble sleeping. But when I go to bed at night, I frequently suffer from insomnia. So, I've decided to replace my bed with a church pew.

16. There is no evidence that the presidential primary system yields the most qualified presidential candidates, so obviously it doesn't.

17. Jocelyn put her money in Gambler's Savings and Loan. Gambler's Savings went broke, and Jocelyn lost all her money. So, no savings and loan institutions are safe places to put your money.

18. As a parent, you must be a strict disciplinarian. If you allow your child to get by without eating her brussels sprouts, she will expect you to allow her to ignore liver. If you allow her to ignore liver, she will assume she can get by without cleaning her room. If you allow her to get by without cleaning her room, she will start staying out late with her friends. If she starts staying out late with her friends, she is certain to fall in with the wrong crowd. If she falls in with the wrong crowd, she will eventually be picked up and sent to prison for life. So, you see how important it is to be strict and make your child eat those brussels sprouts!

19. Since St. Paul advised Timothy, "Do not drink water only, but take a little wine to help your digestion, since you are sick so often" (1 Timothy 5:23), we may conclude that no churches object to the consumption of wine.

20. Father Murphy performed last rites for Monique, and she died. Father Murphy performed last rites for Roderick, and he died. Father Murphy performed last rites for Zadrick, Caroline, Hilda, Isadora, Kelvin, Glendon, Conway, and Amber. They all died. So, if you don't want to die, don't let Father Murphy perform last rites.

21. It would be no crime in me to divert the *Nile* or *Danube* from its course, were I able to effect such purposes. Where then is the crime in turning a few ounces of blood from their natural channel? (David Hume, "Of Suicide")

22. The members of this family have always voted Republican. So, obviously, the Republican candidate is the one you will want to support with your vote!

23. No one has shown that using alcoholic beverages for medicinal purposes only is dangerous. So, the purely medicinal use of alcoholic beverages is perfectly safe.

24. According to the surgeon general, women should not drink alcoholic beverages during pregnancy because of the risk of birth defects.

25. Father Rizzini is a Roman Catholic priest, and he is married. So, all Catholic priests can now be married.

26. The only proof capable of being given that an object is visible is that people actually see it. The only proof that a sound is audible is that people hear it; and so of the other sources of our experience. In like manner, I apprehend, the sole evidence it is possible to produce that anything is desirable is that people do actually desire it. (John Stuart Mill, *Utilitarianism,* Chapter 4)

27. If you develop a taste for ice cream, you will want to try chocolate sauce as a topping. If you try chocolate sauce as a topping, you will develop a taste for candy bars. If you develop a taste for candy bars, you are certain to eat them to excess. If you eat candy to excess, you will grow fat. If you grow fat, you will almost certainly die prematurely of a heart attack. So, you certainly don't want to develop a taste for ice cream.

28. The President says we are coming out of our current economic slump, so it must be true.

29. During the Second World War, the Nazis murdered over 6 million Jews, and much of the world stood idly by. Since the *Roe* v. *Wade* decision in 1973, American abortionists have murdered over 40 million innocent babies. Can we afford to stand idly by and allow such a holocaust?

30. Cigarette smokers have a life expectancy that is two years less than that of nonsmokers. Pipe smokers have a life expectancy that is two years greater than that of nonsmokers. So, if you want an extra couple years, you should take up a pipe.

II. Consider all the fallacies covered in this part of the book. Which of the following passages commit an informal fallacy? If the passage commits a fallacy, name the fallacy and explain why the fallacy is committed. If the passage commits no fallacy, explain why it does not.

1. **Roger Murtaugh:** George.

   George: Yes, sir?

   Roger: Home. Out.

   George: But, sir. . . .

   Roger: George, I got a gun.

   George: Yes, sir. [George leaves.]   (*Lethal Weapon 2* [Burbank: Warner Bros., 1989])

2. A recent report by the Department of Agriculture reports that over 10 percent of all food consumed in the United States is from the inside of cars. So, you shouldn't be surprised if you find large bites taken from your car's seats.

3. "Of course Thomas Jefferson would have been a member of WMRA, had he been around at this time." (Announcer on WMRA-FM, Harrisonburg, VA, July 3, 1998)

4. It's not snowing, so it's not cold.

5. It's the party of peace and prosperity! Vote Republican!

6. The federal government has no right to control the production of wine, for wine is made by pressing grapes and the First Amendment guarantees that "Congress shall make no law . . . abridging the freedom . . . of the press."

7. **Hitchhiker:** "I stood on Route 150 for three hours without getting a ride. As soon as I put on my stocking cap, I got a ride all the way to Capital City. So, it was the cap that got me the ride, and now I always wear it when I hitch."

8. Everyone should spend a couple of years in the Army, for it certainly helped a guy in my high-school class who used to be lazy and a drug-user.

9. **Boss:** Is that harebrained scheme of yours going to have detrimental effects on company profits?

   Employee: No, my study suggests it will improve profits.

   Boss: Nonetheless, since you admit it's a harebrained scheme, we're going to have to make some changes around here!

10. Ms. Margroff argues that the government's deficit spending is an economic time bomb that will ultimately destroy the country. But the American people have demanded a national health-care system. We have obligations to retired people, the unemployed, and the underemployed. Defense is still a pressing need. And the tax revenues simply will not cover everything. So, deficit spending is here to stay.

11. It was a unique briefcase that Ms. Nehrer lost, for her ad in the paper reads, "Lost: American Tourister briefcase with eyeglasses."

12. We must have a free press, for we must not restrict the rights of our news media to inform us of the facts as they see them and to voice their opinions on the central issues of the day.

13. We must not allow children to play with firecrackers, for Colonel Oakdale, the head of the Army Demolition Squad, says that their fuses burn erratically.

14. My new car is well designed. Therefore, its radiator is well designed.

15. Boss to employee: You will want to increase your giving to the United Way this year. After all, you should be thankful that you're *currently* in a position to be charitable.

16. To claim that the government should decrease the size of its welfare program is like claiming that parents ought to decrease the amount of time, energy, and money they devote to the care of their children. Since it is ridiculous to suggest that parents should reduce their support of their children, it is equally ridiculous to suggest that the government should decrease its welfare program.

17. It would be terrible if the government decreased the size of its welfare program. Think of all those children who would suffer from malnutrition and exposure to the cold.

18. It is improper to charge persons bail to get out of jail, since the Eighth Amendment to the Constitution asserts that ". . . bail shall not be required."

19. Alicia has argued that recycling paper is beneficial to the environment. But her argument is reasonable only if one assumes that there are recycling centers in every city and town across the country. But any town of less than 2,500 residents is unlikely to have its own recycling center. So, we must reject her argument.

20. We should reject arguments for tighter environmental controls on industry, since such controls are certain to reduce the numbers of people employed in existing industries.

21. Given the federal deficit, the choice is clear: Either we cancel our foreign aid program or the national debt will double in the next four years.

22. Block's Granulated Sugar must be the best sugar on the market: Granny Smerad has been using it for years.

23. Senator Rockingham has argued that we should increase the minimum wage. What would you expect from a senator whose primary source of campaign funds comes from labor-union war chests?

24. Professor Sun has argued that genetic manipulation holds the key to curing numerous diseases. But genetic engineering is dangerous. The bacteria used in gene manipulation experiments are hard to contain. Several scientists have died as a result of their own genetic experiments. If some of those things they are working on escaped from the labs, they could destroy human life as we know it.

25. Each and every American citizen has the right to keep and bear arms. So, the United States is militaristic.

26. The First Amendment forbids the government from prohibiting the free exercise of religion. Therefore, the government cannot prohibit religions from engaging in human sacrifice.

27. You don't want to smoke. Smoking is old-fashioned, passé. It's not an activity condoned by those who are with it.

28. If God is everywhere, [as] I had concluded, then He is in food. Therefore, the more I ate the godlier I would become. Impelled by this new religious fervor, I

glutted myself like a fanatic. (Woody Allen, *Getting Even* [New York: Random House, 1971], pp. 86–87)

29. Anaytus: Socrates, I think that you are too ready to speak evil of men: and, if you will take my advice, I would recommend you to be careful. Perhaps there is no city in which it is not easier to do men harm than to do them good, and this is certainly the case at Athens, as I believe that you know. (Plato, *Meno*, translated by Benjamin Jowett)

30. We should always help a friend in need. So, we should help our friends who become stumped during an examination.

31. The Roman Catholic Church has declared that gender discrimination is a sin. So, the Catholic Church has no objection to ordaining women as priests.

32. It makes no difference what your occupation is: Either you commit yourself to it fully or you fail.

33. Never let your kids play in the snow. If they play in the snow, they will want to go sledding. If they want to go sledding, they will want to go skiing. If they take up skiing, they will either crash into a tree while careening down a slippery slope, or they will want to enter Olympic competition. If they enter Olympic competition, they will either win the gold or they will not. If they win, it will go to their heads and you will not be able to live with them. If they do not win, they will be so depressed you won't be able to live with them. So, unless you do not want to live with your kids, do not let them play in the snow.

34. Chemistry for the Consumer was an easy course. I had always thought that chemistry courses were some of the most difficult courses in the university. I now see that they are really quite simple.

35. Caffeine is an addictive drug, and its use is not prohibited by law. Alcohol is an addictive drug, and its use is not prohibited by law. Nicotine is an addictive drug, and its use is not prohibited by law. Cocaine is an addictive drug. So, its use should not be prohibited by law.

36. The Sixth Amendment to the Constitution asserts that "In all criminal prosecutions, the accused shall enjoy . . . a speedy and public trial. . . ." But I talked with George, and it was clear that he didn't enjoy his murder trial at all, and it took a full twenty weeks. So, his conviction should be overturned on constitutional grounds.

37. How did you manage to pull off the perfect bank robbery?

38. Jessica says she hopes to be married one day. Thus, I suspect Jessica will pay her divorce lawyer a retainer even before the wedding.

39. John has argued that retaining a strong military provides the best prospect for world peace. If he is correct, we must assume that members of the military are primarily peacemakers. But the military consists of soldiers, men and women trained to fight wars. So, as professional warriors, members of the military are certainly not peacemakers, and we must reject John's argument.

40. There is no evidence that a system of letter grades improves the quality of education, so the grading system should be rejected.

41. The majority of members of the Senate and the House believe that there should be relatively few restrictions on campaign contributions, so there must be good reasons not to restrict contributions.

42. A mob is no worse than the individuals in it.

43. You can tell that Dave has a high moral character by the character of his friends, for people who hang out with Dave must be of the highest moral type, or they wouldn't associate with him.

44. You should support the referendum for a state lottery, for a lottery provides a means of generating state revenues without raising taxes.

45. First Fundamentalist Church believes in predestination—it is one of the doctrines upon which the church was founded. So, Ginger, who is a member of First Fundamentalist, believes in predestination.

46. Minister: You may believe that there is no harm in an exaggerated claim of youth or cheating the scale of a few pounds. It's just a little white lie you tell yourself. But let sin in the door, and you're on your way down the road that leads to hell and damnation! The little white lie becomes comfortable. So, it's easier to tell a large lie—indeed, the lies are certain to get larger, for the only way to cover one lie is with another. You will lose all sense of guilt. Cheating on your income tax, you will tell yourself, is just a little lie. Cheating the butcher, the baker, the candlestick maker are just little lies. Cheating on your spouse is just a little lie. Taking the life of another is little more than a little lie. So you see what will inevitably follow from those little white lies: hellfire and damnation!

47. Perhaps there may be some one who is offended at me, when he calls to mind how he himself on a similar or even less serious occasion, prayed and entreated the judges with many tears, and how he produced his children in court, which was a moving spectacle, together with a host of relations and friends; whereas I, who am probably in danger of my life, will do none of these things. The contrast may occur to his mind, and he may be set against me, and vote in anger because he is displeased at me on this account. Now, if there be such a person among you—mind, I do not say that there is—to him I may fairly reply: My friend, I am a man, and like other men, a creature of flesh and blood, and not "of wood or stone," as Homer says; and I have a family, yes, and sons, O Athenians, three in number, one almost a man, and two others who are still young; and yet I will not bring any of them hither in order to petition for an acquittal. (Socrates, in Plato's *Apology*, translated by Benjamin Jowett)

48. Letter to a hair-product manufacturer:

    I'm writing to tell you what a wonderful dandruff shampoo you produce. I know you claim that it works, but you should know that the longer you use it, the better it works. I've been using your shampoo every day for the last thirty years. When I was twenty, I had a serious case of dandruff, and it helped keep it under control. By the time I was thirty, and my hair was beginning to thin a bit, it was considerably more effective. Now that I'm fifty, I no longer have any problem with dandruff.

    Recently, I've also been using your new head wax. It's all I expected: it really keeps that old chrome dome shining. Thank you for these wonderful products!

49. McCool presents the following account of the origin of the counterculture of the late 1960s:

> "The '50s was a generation of Dull," said McCool. "We were running around trying to be F. Scott Fitzgerald characters. The only difference between us and our parents was we were young and they were not. I have a theory on what got things moving: the high school dress codes."
>
> "Oh, stop."
>
> "Hear me out. I just want to try on an idea. The Beatles came along when?—about 1963?—and kids start wearing their hair a little long. Principal says 'no.' Then some of the kids start playing in rock bands on weekends and making more money than the Principal makes all week. They say they need long hair for their work, and they have real lawyers to say it louder. The youth culture is born and the lines are drawn. Dress codes come out of the Principal's office carved in granite, but the kids peck away at them: a little more hair here, a little less skirt there, and the dress code turns to mush. Aha! Authority is successfully defied."
>
> Rene exploded into a coughing fit, thumped his chest, "Greedy, greedy," he said.
>
> McCool continued. "It becomes a real test of wills. The kids are treated to the spectacle of a red-faced coach in a flattop marine haircut ranting at them about how the All-American football team wears its hair short and the All-American football team is clean, decent, brave, manly and, especially, American. This is being said in front of a portrait of George Washington wearing powdered curls. . . ."
>
> "You may have a point."
>
> "So a generation of kids learn a great lesson in school: if authority is stupid and arbitrary and won't explain itself rationally, you can tell it to . . . itself and, by George, it will. Then these same kids come right out of high school and into the Vietnam War, and they get to try it out for real. And next thing you know, the whole system is coming apart." (Denison Andrews, *How to Beat the System: The Fiftieth, Last and True Success Book of Lionel Goldfish* [Sag Harbor, New York: Permanent Press, 1987], pp. 75–76)

50. U.S. imperialism invaded China's territory of Taiwan and has occupied it for the past nine years. A short while ago it sent forces to invade and occupy Lebanon. The United States has set up hundreds of military bases in many countries all over the world. China's territory of Taiwan, Lebanon and all military bases of the United States on foreign soil are so many nooses round the neck of U.S. imperialism. The nooses have been fashioned by the Americans themselves and by nobody else, and it is they themselves who have put these nooses round their own necks, handing the ends of the ropes to the Chinese people, the peoples of the Arab countries and all the peoples of the world who love peace and oppose aggression. The longer the U.S. aggressors remain in those places, the tighter the nooses round their necks will become. (Mao Tse-Tung, Speech at the Supreme State Conference [September 8, 1958], in *Quotations from Chairman Mao Tse-Tung* [New York: Bantam Books, 1967], p. 41)

PART VIII

Reading and Writing Essays

An argumentative essay is a discourse presenting an extended argument to show that a certain statement, the **thesis**, is true. The thesis is the conclusion of an argument. As an extended argument, an essay is like a sorites. It is composed of several distinct arguments—arguments for distinct **subordinate theses**—that jointly support the main thesis. Not all essays are argumentative. Some essays describe. Others explain. Nonetheless, most of the essays you read or write in college—whether you are interpreting literature or experimental data, exploring the causes of the Great Depression, or arguing that an investment in XYZ Corporation will probably prove profitable—are argumentative essays.

To use an orchestral analogy, to this point we have been engaged in sectional rehearsals. Now we bring the entire ensemble together. To give a stunning performance of Beethoven's Fifth Symphony, each section—each individual part—has to be right. But you will not pay to hear the violin sectional, let alone to hear the third trumpet practice her part. All the preperformance efforts are a necessary means to a successful performance. Similarly, everything to this point has been "practice." Now we assemble the orchestra. And just as a single orchestral rehearsal does not guarantee a stunning performance, our critical-thinking orchestra must also be willing to "practice the piece" several times: Rereading and rewriting are essential to the process.

In Chapter 32 we examine techniques for reading essays. In Chapter 33 we examine techniques for writing argumentative essays.

How
to Read
an Essay

The View: When reading an essay, you should ask the following questions: What do you know about the author? What theses are being defended? Does the author tell you how the essay is structured? What rhetoric is used in setting forth the theses and outlining the structure of the essay? Regarding any collection of one or more sentences, what linguistic or rhetorical function does it fulfill? If you find an argument, is it inductive or deductive? Are the premises of the argument true? Are there any words that have emotive content? Are there words introduced that might convince you to accept the truth of a premise but which do not themselves provide any evidence—for example, words like 'of course' or 'surely'? Are there any words that suggest the author has a certain bias? Has the author succeeded in proving the truth of the conclusion or in providing good inductive evidence for the probable truth of the conclusion?

How do the skills covered in this book help us understand what we read? Do some of those skills play a larger role than others?

Many critical-thinking skills come together when reading or writing an essay. While essays are of various sorts—there are descriptive essays and "photo essays" as well as argumentative essays—our focus will be on argumentative essays. There are several reasons for this. First, most of the essays you will read during your college career are argumentative essays. Such essays try to convince you that a certain claim is true or to act in a certain way. Second, argumentative essays are more complex than descriptive essays. While there are purely descriptive elements in *any* essay, the argumentative essay requires that you employ more of your critical-thinking skills. Third, most of the essays you will write during your college and postcollegiate career will be argumentative essays. By analyzing essays written by others, you should learn various techniques that will improve your writing.

You will be asking questions. Foremost among these are the questions, (1) What does this mean? (2) Is a given claim true? and (3) Are the claims made coherent? Do they make sense? Question 1 occasionally will be asked regarding words. At other times, question 1 will be asked regarding sentences, clauses, or phrases. Question 2 always will be directed toward sentences or parts of sentences that constitute statements. Question 3 will take several forms: (3a) Does a certain conclusion follow from a given statement or set of statements? What is the argument? How strong is the argument? (3b) Are there implicit contradictions found within the essay? Does the essay defend both a statement and its denial (internal incoherence)? (3c) Are the conclusions reached in the essay consistent with other things we know (external coherence)? If the conclusions reached in the essay are inconsistent with other things we know or believe we know, how are we to resolve this apparent inconsistency?

> Carefully examining essays is like analyzing a piece of music. By examining the chordal progressions in a piece of music, you come to understand why things sound as they do—which chords resolve into which others, how musical swells are produced, and so on. By analyzing a piece of music, you also see how the great composers applied and occasionally "bent" the rules of musical composition. By taking apart an essay, you see how the individual arguments support a general thesis, how the strength of the general thesis depends upon the strength of the individual arguments, and how occasionally the proponent of an argument will attempt to persuade you to accept a conclusion by using faulty arguments.

In what follows we set forth a number of questions that should be asked regarding essays. Questions of meaning are *always* in the background.

If you are going to do a careful analysis of an essay, you will read the essay several times. For the first reading, you read the essay rather quickly to get the "general flavor" of it. You might look for the drift of the argument, but not the details. Does anything really stick out? Bad arguments? Bias? For the second reading, you read it very slowly and carefully, and look for the details. The questions that follow focus *primarily* on the second and subsequent readings, although having them in mind during the first reading will be helpful. In third and subsequent readings (often undertaken several days after the previous reading) you read it again, slowly and carefully, double-checking the details noted in the previous reading. If there are very few or no changes made in your analysis, you may consider yourself finished. If there are any significant changes, you should plan additional readings until you are satisfied that you have missed nothing. It is useful to place some time between the second and subsequent readings. Being away from the essay—and your analysis of it—for a few days between readings often helps you to see things you did not see before.

Source: Bill Watterson, Calvin and Hobbes. *Used with permission of Universal Press Syndicate.*

Source: Seth Casana, Academia Nuts. Used with permission of the author.

RE1. What do you know about the author? There are several reasons why it is often helpful to know a bit about the author. (1) It tells you what kinds of credentials the author has. Is the author an expertise on the topic under discussion? (2) Knowing what the author has done in the past might *suggest* what the author will be doing in the present essay. *Never assume*, however, that the author will present arguments like those presented in the past. *Never assume* that the author will defend the same thesis that she defended in the past. People occasionally change their positions on a certain issue, and each argument should be judged on its own merits. (3) Knowing a bit about the author might help you recognize her biases. *Determining whether* the author has a particular bias *must* be tracked down through a careful reading of the essay. What information does the author include? What is left out? Are there emotionally charged terms? For example, if you are studying the religious reformation of the sixteenth century, you might expect a Protestant historian to view the events somewhat differently from a Roman Catholic historian, *but you must not assume that a historian has a certain bias simply on the basis of his or her religious or other affiliation.* If a person has defended a conservative economic agenda in the past, do not assume she is doing the same in the essay you are examining. If the author has defended a conservative economic agenda, do not assume she will also defend a conservative social agenda. People's views sometimes change. In the 1940s and 1950s, Ronald Reagan was a liberal Democrat. President Ronald Reagan was a conservative Republican.[1]

RE2. What theses are being defended? An essay is an extended argument defending a conclusion, the *thesis*. In most essays, a writer defends a main thesis and subordinate theses that support the main thesis. The thesis is often stated within the first few paragraphs of the essay. In a *short* essay, it is reasonable to expect the thesis statement in the first or second paragraph. In some cases, the thesis is stated in or suggested by the title of the essay. In a longer essay—one divided into sections, for example—several paragraphs might be devoted to placing the problem in context before

---

[1]Were you to suggest that a person's views should not be taken seriously, since at one point he or she supports a certain position, and at another time he or she supports a position that is inconsistent with the first, you would commit the fallacy of personal attack. See Chapter 29.

stating the thesis. Sometimes the author will use words that point to the thesis: "This paper shows that . . . " or "In this paper I argue that . . . ". In other cases, the main thesis simply is stated. And in some cases, particularly in short essays, there is no thesis statement. If there is no explicit thesis indicator, but you have a little background on the topic, you probably will be able to pick out the main thesis and the subordinate theses without much trouble.

RE3. Does the author tell you how the essay is structured? This question is related to the second. In some essays, the author will lay out the structure of the argument before proceeding to the arguments themselves. Often this is no more than stating the main thesis and the subordinate theses: "In this paper I show that *thesis*. To do so, I first argue that *subordinate thesis 1*. Next I show that *subordinate thesis 2*. Finally, I argue that *subordinate thesis 3*." Why is it important to notice this? (1) It provides the first set of "road signs" that help you find your way through the essay. You know what to expect, and you should recognize the arguments for the various subordinate theses when you come upon them. (2) Insofar as it lists the theses the author defends, it gives you insight into the general argument set forth in the essay.

RE4. What rhetoric is used in setting forth the theses and outlining the structure of the essay? Rhetoric, the words used and the way they are used, can tell you a number of things. (1) It gives you insight into the author's biases. (2) It gives you insight into the author's position on an issue relative to the generally accepted position. Assume you are reading an interpretive essay on *Moby Dick*. Assume further that there is general agreement among most Melville scholars that certain elements of the text have a certain symbolic function—though you might not know what this "standard interpretation" is. If the author uses tentative language—"there is some evidence that . . . " or "the texts might be taken to suggest . . . "—you will have reason to believe that the author is opposing a standard interpretation. (It is also possible that the author is skeptical of any interpretation, including her own.) Tentative language might entice a reader to continue. The more forceful "I show" might raise skeptical red flags. There is a certain amount of politics involved in the publishing game. This often is reflected in the rhetoric of the thesis statement.

RE5. Regarding any collection of one or more sentences in the body of the essay, what linguistic or rhetorical function does it fulfill? Is the sentence purely descriptive? There always will be some purely descriptive sentences in an essay. Such sentences set the stage for an argument. Does a collection of sentences constitute an argument?

RE6. If you find an argument, is it inductive or deductive? This is not always a simple question to answer. The most common deductive argument forms in most essays are affirming the antecedent, denying the consequent, hypothetical syllogism, disjunctive syllogism, and constructive dilemma. Often a premise is assumed but not stated. Is there a premise that will yield a valid argument? If so, is it true? If not, assume that the argument is inductive and judge its strength. Always give reasons for your judgment.

RE7. Are the premises of the argument true? Give reasons to support your judgment of truth.

RE8. Do any words have emotive content? If there are emotionally charged words, will the persuasive force of the argument remain the same if those words are replaced by emotionally neutral terms? If not, (a) the argument is *not* deductive, and (b) it is a weak inductive argument: You are being carried along by the emotive connotations of the term rather than by questions of evidence and truth.

RE9. Are there words introduced that might convince you to accept the truth of a premise but which do not themselves provide any evidence—for example, words like 'of course' or 'surely'? Cross out the words and ask yourself whether the premise should be accepted as true. Give reasons for your judgment.

RE10. Do any words suggest the author has a certain bias? What are those words? What reasons do you have for claiming that they reflect a certain bias? Does this bias blind the author from considering certain available pieces of evidence? (Every author has some bias; only some are blinded by that bias. Sometimes a bias allows the author to see things that others don't. So bias by itself is not a terrible shortcoming.)

Work through the essay sentence by sentence, paragraph by paragraph, showing where the arguments are, what the nature of each argument is, and judging whether the premises are true. In *some* cases, you will need to do some research to find out whether a premise is true or whether it is reasonable to hold that a premise is true. Each argument should be set forth in a systematic way, evaluated in terms of deductive validity or inductive strength, and the truth of the premises should be judged. Next, you must ask how the several arguments in the essay link together. Does each argument individually support the main thesis of the essay or one of the subordinate theses? Does the cumulative effect of the several arguments provide inductive or deductive evidence for the truth of the main thesis? If it is inductive evidence, how strong is the argument? In other words, you must ask the "Big Question":

RE11. Has the author succeeded in proving the truth of the conclusion or in providing good inductive evidence for the probable truth of the conclusion? If you judge that the main argument fails, why does it do so? If you judge that the main argument succeeds, explain why.

In constructing your analysis of an essay, it might be useful to number each paragraph and sentence in the paragraph. This will allow you to allude to the relevant sentence by paragraph and sentence numbers and to construct an elaborate diagram of the sort we examined in Chapter 9.

In what follows, we will take apart essays. We begin with a letter to the editor. Next, we turn to an editorial. Finally, we examine a more involved essay.[2]

A Letter to the Editor

Drug war is a failure; other solutions for drug problem should be explored

To the Editor:

¶1 (1) It is with much interest that I have followed the issue of increased marijuana use on college campuses. (2) I feel compelled to share another viewpoint often overlooked and ignored by mainstream America. (3) As the Clinton administration

---

[2]You will see that I am critical of a number of the arguments. This should *not* be taken as a reason to conclude that I oppose the measures the author of each article supports. *Nor* should you conclude that I *favor* those measures. We are concerned only with the strength of the arguments for their respective conclusions.

has admitted, the "drug war" is a multibillion dollar failure. (4) Dumping more government money into antidrug programs will never solve the problem, especially when the emphasis is on apprehension and incarceration.

¶2 (1) Constitutionally speaking, the government cannot legislate morality. (2) This is the case with all consensual crimes including gambling, prostitution, suicide, homosexuality, as well as drug use. (3) Furthermore, history has proven that attempts to do so have not been successful. (4) The government has no business protecting individuals from themselves.

¶3 (1) Many prominent leaders and entertainment professionals now advocate a new approach—decriminalization. (2) It is impossible to convey all of the benefits of drug decriminalization in this short space. (3) I encourage everyone to educate himself/herself by checking out the variety of literature published on the issue. (4) The time has come to end the drug war.

Oscar R. Brinson

Class of 1993

(*The Breeze*, James Madison University, September 1, 1997. Used with permission of *The Breeze*)

Following is an analysis of "Drug war is a failure; other solutions for drug problem should be explored."

The title tells us one of two theses for which the author argues (**RE2**), namely that the war on drugs is a failure. If you have read the letter, you will know that the second thesis is that drug use should be decriminalized (¶3).

Paragraph 1 presents two arguments:

Argument 1: (3) The Clinton Administration has admitted that the Drug War is a failure. Therefore, the drug war is a failure.

This is an appeal to authority (inductive). The Clinton administration should be in a position to know whether recent efforts against the use of illegal drugs have been successful, so it is a reasonable conclusion that recent battles in the drug war failed.

Argument 2: The drug war—as it has been waged in recent years—is a failure. Therefore, (4) dumping more government money into antidrug programs will never solve the problem, especially when the emphasis is on apprehension and incarceration.

This argument is incomplete. It might be better stated as follows:

a. The government's program to limit the use of illegal drugs has focused on apprehension and incarceration of drug users and salespersons.

b. The government's program to limit the use of illegal drugs has been ineffective.

c. Therefore, the best means to limit the use of illegal drugs is *not* to focus on apprehension and incarceration of drug users and salespersons.

Notice what we have done: The term 'drug war' is emotionally loaded. The term has been replaced with an emotionally neutral description (**RE8**). Further, the description indicates the means that have been used in an attempt to limit the use of illegal drugs.

It is *that* program that has proven ineffective (**RE8**). Assuming the premises are true (**RE7**), we have some reason to believe that the conclusion is true. This is an inductive argument; it is an argument to the best explanation. Were you to challenge the conclusion while granting the premises, you would need to show that while efforts were made to limit the use of drugs by means of apprehension and incarceration, such efforts were insufficiently rigorous. (There is a shift in the burden of proof.)

In paragraph 2 argument in sentences 1 and 2 might be restated as follows:

  a. All cases of legislating morality are instances of unconstitutional acts.

  b. All cases of placing legislative limits on drug use are instances of legislating morality (in this way it is like—analogous to—the "sins" listed in sentence 2).

  c. Therefore, all instances of placing legislative limits on drug use are unconstitutional acts.

This is a valid deductive argument (**RE6**). Further, let us assume that the premises are true (**RE7**), even though the claim made in (a) is dubious at best. So, we must accept the conclusion, right? Indeed, we should accept the general conclusion stated in paragraph 2, sentence right?

If we are concerned *solely* with the legislation of morality, the conclusion must be accepted, but there are government interests that have nothing to do with morality. Public health is one such interest. A nonmoral reason for enacting laws against prostitution is public health: Prostitutes can be carriers of venereal diseases. So, if drug use is similar to prostitution, then public health issues might justify laws prohibiting drug use. (We leave open questions regarding the analogies between drug use and the other sins listed in sentence 2, as well as what national interests might be limitations on any of them.)

Paragraph 2, sentence 3, presumably means that attempts to legislate morality have failed. From this you are to conclude that attempts to place legislative limits on drug use will fail. What does this mean? Presumably, the author is concerned with prohibition. His argument could be rephrased this way:

  Prohibition was an attempt to legally prevent the consumption of alcohol, and it failed.

  Attempts to legally limit the use of drugs are similar to prohibition.

  Therefore, attempts to legally limit the use of drugs also will fail. (The author might also be concerned with the *fact* that attempts to limit drug use have failed.)

If this is the author's argument, and if there are significant similarities, the conclusion seems reasonable. But you might challenge the analogy. You might suggest, for example, that the legal limitation of drug use is analogous to other forms of legal prohibition. For example, the government establishes speed limits on its roads. Speed limits do not guarantee that no one will exceed them. But if there were no speed limits, the average speeds on American highways would be much greater. If there are nonmoral reasons for the legal limitation of drug use, the laws might check drug use even if they do not abolish it. The author does not make the nature of the analogy clear. Therefore, he provides limited evidence for accepting his conclusion.

Paragraph 3 presents the argument for the decriminalization of drugs and the end of the 'drug war.' It is an appeal to authority:

Prominent leaders and entertainment professionals advocate the
    decriminalization of drugs.

Therefore, drugs should be decriminalized.

There are two problems with the argument: (1) There is no indication who these "prominent leaders" are, so we cannot examine the credentials of these "leaders." (2) Entertainment professionals might be authorities on the entertainment industry, but they have, *as such,* no expertise regarding drug-use issues. Hence, the argument is a fallacious appeal to authority.

Beyond this appeal, the author recommends that the reader acquaint himself or herself with the literature on the topic. He gives no allusions to what pieces of literature one should examine. His allusion to the literature *suggests* that the literature would provide good reasons to decriminalize drugs. But the appeal provides no reason to conclude that "The time has come to end the drug war."

Should you accept the author's conclusion? Probably not. The arguments seem weak.

An Editorial

King holiday deserves recognition

¶1 (1) Today, the University Council will vote on an issue that is important to many people—whether or not to make Martin Luther King, Jr., Day an official university holiday.

¶2 (1) Proponents of JMU's observance of the holiday cite numerous reasons why it should be observed. (2) In the April 12 issue of *The Breeze,* SGA President Tim Emry said, "About 80 percent of schools in the nation have off [for this day]. . . . (3) It's just the right thing to do."

¶3 (1) While this is a valid and important reason to institute the holiday, even better arguments exist.

¶4 (1) The day in question is a nationally recognized holiday. (2) For many, it is not just another day off from work or school, it is a day to reflect upon and pay respect to the work and teachings of King. (3) It is also a time to realize what contributions this man made to our society and what it would be like today had he never existed.

¶5 (1a) Those opposed to observance of this holiday need to realize that as an institution of higher learning, we have a responsibility to respect the feelings of others and (1b) to respect what King Day represents. (2) The fact the holiday would make the semester one day longer is both trivial and ridiculous.

¶6 (1) As it is, many professors already devote their class instruction time to the study of King rather than to typical classwork on this day. (2a) By declaring an official holiday, we are in essence getting an extra day of classroom instruction, (2b) since we'll be able to devote the entire day to Dr. King and make up regular coursework on another date.

¶7 (1) Lately, JMU has been extremely concerned with ways to increase minority enrollment and promoting a more diverse campus. (2) However, not observing King Day cannot speak highly for JMU's multicultural awareness.

¶8 (1) Why would many minority students choose to come to a school that, unlike 80 percent of other universities, refused to officially recognize a day allotted to the remembrance of a key leader of the Civil Rights Movement?

¶9 (1) Many clubs and organizations already have their own activities and ways of celebrating during the day, but this isn't enough. (2) We must have an official university recognition as well.

¶10 (1) Just think of the benefits gained by observing this holiday. (2) First and foremost, the rights of those who wish to honor Dr. King will no longer be infringed upon. (3) Everyone else will have a day to relax.

¶11 (1) Both minorities and majorities, supporters and nonsupporters will have lost nothing, but gained something instead. (2) It's a win-win situation.   (*The Breeze*, James Madison University, April 15, 1999. Used with permission of *The Breeze*.)

Following is an analysis of "King holiday deserves recognition."

The title tells us the thesis of the editorial: Dr. Martin Luther King, Jr.'s birthday should be recognized as a university holiday (nonclass day). The editorial is drawn from a student newspaper. It is unsigned, so no hypotheses can be posed regarding the possible bias of the author.

Paragraph 1 sets the stage for the topic of the editorial. Paragraph 2 contains the following argument:

> Eighty percent of colleges and universities in the United States recognize
> <u>   Martin Luther King's birthday as a college holiday.   </u>

So, (3) it's the right thing to do (we should do it too [paragraph 3, sentence 1]).

This argument commits the bandwagon fallacy: Everyone is doing it, so we should too. The fact that "everyone" or a significant majority of people engage in an action does not show that there are good reasons to do so. Hence, the conclusion in paragraph 3, sentence 1, is unwarranted.

Paragraph 4 contains no explicit argument. Sentence 1 might be taken to imply an argument: Martin Luther King Day is a national holiday, so we should not have class on King Day. But such a move would make it *disanalogous* other national holidays at the same school on which classes are held: Columbus Day, Veterans' Day, Presidents' Day, Labor Day, and Memorial Day. Sentences 2 and 3 might be taken as reasons to declare King Day a university holiday, but it is unclear why a university holiday (nonclass day) is necessary to reflect on and pay attention to King's contributions to our society.

In paragraph 5, sentence 1a is a curious claim. Declaring King Day a university holiday would show respect to the feelings of some. Declaring Alan Greenspan's birthday a university holiday *also* would show respect to the feelings of some—perhaps people in the College of Business. Choose your favorite person or cause. Declaring a day a holiday will respect your feelings regarding that person or cause. Is that a sufficient reason to declare it a holiday? More needs to be said about what makes Dr. King's birthday *special* and *worthy* of recognition—appeals to feelings will not do that. And much the same can be said about sentence 1b.

The conclusion in paragraph 6 is that King Day should be a holiday. The premises are (2a), we could have spent the entire day reflecting on Dr. King's work and, since (1) many professors already devote King Day to Dr. King's work, (2b) the class-work-makeup day would effectively be an extra day of instruction. The operative word in sentence 2a is 'could'. *Would* all or the majority of students "spend the entire day reflecting on Dr. King's work"? Probably not. If (1) is true, and if the objective in declaring King Day a university holiday is to reflect on Dr. King's work, it is likely that the objective is better served by in-class discussions on that day than it would be served by individual reflection.

Paragraphs 7 and 8 involve mob appeal, including another bandwagon appeal. Do students, in fact, choose their college or university on the basis of the symbolic nature of their recognized holidays?

Paragraph 9 involves the fallacy of irrelevant conclusion.

> Many organizations celebrate King Day with special activities.
>
> Organizational celebrations are not enough. _____
>
> Therefore, we need a university holiday.

Why does the conclusion follow? What reasons are given for accepting the second premise? Even if you grant the premises, what reason is there to believe that it follows that we need a university holiday? If some organizational activities are not enough, why not *require more* organizational or departmental activities? Why not *require* that professors devote the day the works of Dr. King? What would be gained by a recognized university holiday?

In paragraphs 10 and 11 the argument seems to go like this:

> If we have the holiday, those who wish to honor Dr. King will benefit by not having their rights infringed upon, and those who do not wish to honor Dr. King will benefit by having a day to relax.
>
> Everyone either wishes to honor Dr. King or not. (Implicit premise) _____
>
> So, if we have the holiday, everyone will benefit.
>
> We should do what benefits everyone. _____
>
> So, we should have the holiday.

The arguments are plausible if the premises are true. The second premise in the first argument is a tautology, so it is true. Questions might be asked regarding the conditional premise in the first argument and the premise "We should do what benefits everyone" in the second argument.

The first premise is a conditional statement. A conditional statement is true except when the antecedent is true and the consequent is false. The consequent is a conjunction, and a conjunction is false if either of its conjuncts is false. The first conjunct is curious. What does it mean to claim that "those who wish to honor Dr. King will benefit by not having their rights infringed upon"? What rights are infringed upon? Must we assume that we have a right to have all our heroes honored with a university holiday? The absence of a holiday does *not* mean that there is a prohibition against celebrating Dr. King's accomplishments. The editorial indicates that without a class holiday, many professors and organizations had devoted the day to studying Dr. King's works and celebrating his accomplishments. At best, the first conjunct needs clarification and defense. Apart from that, there is no reason to accept it as true.

Nor is the second conjunct less problematic. It is not clear that a day to relax is, as such, beneficial. Since the holiday would be early in the second semester, it is unclear that having *that* day "to relax" is more beneficial than it would be to have a nonclass day later in the semester to prepare for final exams.

So, it is unclear that either conjunct in consequent of the conditional premise is true. At best, both conjuncts stand in need of elaboration and argument.

Nor is it clear that the premise "We should do what benefits everyone" is true. Everyone would benefit if all members of the university community were required to give blood regularly. Were this the case, those who need blood would be relatively certain of its availability. Those who give blood would benefit by the mini-physical that is required before giving blood and the various tests the blood undergoes after it is drawn. (There is also evidence that giving blood regularly increases the body's ability produce blood cells.) But giving blood is a (minimally) invasive procedure, and it is a generally accepted moral principle that no one should be required to undergo invasive procedures. So, there are reasons why everyone should not be *required* to give blood regularly, even though everyone would benefit. So, the truth of the premise is dubious, and the argument provides no ground for accepting the conclusion.

Thus, none of the arguments in the editorial provides a good reason for claiming that King Day should be a holiday.

Does this show that King Day *should not* be a recognized university holiday? *No!* All the analysis shows is that the arguments given are weak. To show that a set of arguments is weak does *not* show that the denial of the conclusion should be accepted. It *does not* show that the cause supported by the arguments is not a worthy cause. All it shows is that further work must be done if you are to have good grounds for accepting the conclusion.

An Essay

Deconstructing the Dead
By Michael Shermer

¶1 (1) Like all other animals, we humans evolved to connect the dots between events so as to discern patterns meaningful for our survival. (2) Like no other animals, we tell stories about the patterns we find. (3) Sometimes the patterns are real; sometimes they are illusions.

¶2 (1) A well-known illusion of a meaningful pattern is the alleged ability of mediums to talk to the dead. (2) The hottest medium today is a former ballroom-dance instructor, John Edward, star of the cable television series *Crossing Over* and author of the *New York Times* best-selling book *One Last Time*. (3) His show is so popular that he is about to be syndicated nationally on many broadcast stations.

¶3 (1) How does Edward appear to talk to the dead? (2) What he does seems indistinguishable from tricks practiced by magicians. (3) He starts by selecting a section of the studio audience, saying something like "I'm getting George over here. George could be someone who passed over, he could be someone here, he could be someone you know," and so on. (4) Of course, such generalizations lead to a "hit." (5) Once he has targeted his subject, the "reading" begins, seemingly using three techniques:

¶4 (1) **1. Cold reading,** in which he reads someone without initially knowing anything about him. (2) He throws out lots of questions and statements and sees what sticks. (3) "I'm getting a 'P' name. (4) Who is this, please?" (5) "He's showing me something red. (6) What is this, please?" (7) And so on. (8) Most statements are wrong. (9) If subjects have time, they visibly shake their heads "no." (10) But Edward is so fast, they usually have time to acknowledge only hits. (11) And as behaviorist B. F. Skinner showed in his experiments on superstitious behavior, subjects need only occasional reinforcement or reward to be convinced. (12) In an exposé I did for WABC-TV in New York City, I counted about one statement a second in the opening minute of Edward's show, as he riffled through names, dates, colors, diseases, conditions, situations, relatives, and the like. (13) He goes from one to the next so quickly you have to stop the tape and go back to catch them all.

¶5 (1) **2. Warm reading,** which exploits nearly universal principles of psychology. (2) Many grieving people wear a piece of jewelry that has a connection to a loved one. (3) Mediums know this and will say something like "Do you have a ring or piece of jewelry on you, please?" (4) Edward is so facile at determining the cause of death by focusing either on the chest or the head area and then working rapid-fire through the half a dozen major causes of death. (5) "He's telling me there was a pain in the chest." (6) If he gets a positive nod, he continues. "Did he have cancer, please? Because I'm seeing a slow death here." (7) If the subject hesitates, Edward will immediately shift to a heart attack.

¶6 (1) **3. Hot reading,** in which the medium obtains information ahead of time. (2) One man who got a reading on Edward's show reports that "once in the studio, we had to wait around for almost two hours before the show began. (3) Throughout that time everybody was talking about what dead relative of theirs might pop up. (4) Remember that all this occurred under microphones and with cameras already set up."

¶7 (1) Whether or not Edward gathers information in this way, mediums generally don't. (2) They are successful because they are dealing with tragedy and finality of death. (3) Sooner or later we all confront this inevitability, and when we do, we may be at our most vulnerable.

¶8 (1) This is why mediums are unethical and dangerous: They prey on the emotions of the grieving. (2) As grief counselors know, death is best faced head-on as a part of life. (3) Pretending that the dead are gathering in a television studio in New

York to twaddle with a former ballroom-dance instructor is an insult to the intelligence and humanity of the living.

(*Source:* "Deconstructing the Dead: 'Crossing over' to expose the tricks of popular spirit mediums." Michael Shermer. *Scientific American*, August 2001, p. 29. Used with permission of *Scientific American*. Michael Shermer is the founding publisher of *Skeptic* magazine (www.skeptic.com) and the author of *How We Believe* and *The Borderlands of Science*.)

Following is an analysis of "Deconstructing the Dead"

The author, Michael Shermer, received a B.A. in psychology from Pepperdine University, an M.A. in experimental psychology from the California State University, Fullerton, and a Ph.D. in the history of science from the Claremont Graduate School. He is the publisher of *Skeptic* magazine and director of The Skeptics Society. His column, "Skeptic," appears monthly in *Scientific American*. He has written numerous books debunking pseudoscience, as well as a number of books on cycling.[3]

Scientific American is a monthly publication devoted to reporting developments in science and technology, often with articles written by the scientists who made the discoveries. While written with the nonscientist in mind, it has a reputation for accuracy.

Like many short essays, "Deconstructing the Dead" contains no explicit thesis statement. The implicit thesis is suggested in the subtitle, namely, that the claims of spiritual mediums are unfounded. A significant portion of the article is devoted to explaining how spiritual mediums in general—and John Edward in particular—are able to give the appearance of talking with the dead. Shermer's general argument takes the form of an argument to the best explanation. Since we can give a purely naturalistic explanation of the alleged ability of John Edward to "talk to the dead" on the basis of recognized psychological principles, the psychological explanation is more probable than the claims made by the medium.

Paragraph 1 makes three claims about the tendencies of animals to discern meaningful patterns. Humans tell stories about the patterns they perceive, and sometimes those patterns are illusions.

In paragraph 2, after asserting that the medium's claim to talk to the dead is a well-known illusion—which reflects the main thesis of the paper—Shermer gives a biographical sketch of John Edward. There is no explicit argument in this paragraph, although the fact that Edward is "a former ballroom-dance instructor"—a point Shermer repeats in paragraph 8—suggests that Edward's experiential background provides no basis for granting him credibility as a medium. (Of course, it is unclear what would give one credibility as a medium.)

Paragraph 3 begins Shermer's discussion of Edward's procedure. The juxtaposition of the question in (1) and the remark in (2) suggest that Edward's alleged abilities can be explained by procedures like those by which magicians misdirect the attentions of their audiences in performing "tricks." Since everyone grants that a magician's tricks are illusions that can be explained naturalistically, if there are simi-

---

[3](Source: The Skeptics Society Web page.)

lar naturalistic explanations of the apparent results of mediums, there is good reason to believe that they also are illusions.

Edward targets a subject by making various general claims. Since the claims are general, and most of those present are inclined to believe Edward has the power to speak to the dead (which Shermer assumes but does not say), it is virtually guaranteed that someone will respond.

Paragraph 4 concerns cold readings. In a cold reading, Edward makes a rapid series of statements (as many as one per second, according to sentence 12). Most of the statements are wrong (8). Some, due to the sheer number of statements, are "hits." Because of the occasional hits, the subject believes Edward is talking to the departed, that this is the source of Edward's knowledge. The belief, however, can be explained on accepted psychological principles. As Skinner showed (11), an occasional reinforcement (correct statement) is sufficient to engender superstitious belief. (Remember, an authority should be believed if and only if he or she generally makes correct statements.) Since there is a naturalistic explanation of the engendered belief, there is little reason to believe that the medium is actually speaking to the dead. This naturalistic explanation parallels the ways a magician creates an illusion, so there is reason to believe the medium also is creating an illusion.

Paragraph 5 concerns warm readings. Warm readings employ something owned by the dear departed. (The medium might suggest that such items possess an "aura" of the departed.) The medium's procedure is the same as in a cold reading, and the same psychological principles explain the engendered belief.

Paragraph 6 concerns hot readings. In this case, the medium obtains information in advance by means of microphones and so forth. This, of course, is a simple and plausible explanation of how the medium can have knowledge of the information he claims to obtain by talking with the dead.

Thus, paragraphs 4, 5, and 6 show that there are naturalistic explanations of why the grieving are inclined to believe the claims of a medium. Insofar as there are naturalistic explanations of the alleged paranormal phenomena, and insofar as naturalistic explanations are more plausible than the alternative, the claims of the medium should be rejected.

Paragraph 7 notes that when we confront the death of a loved one, we are psychologically vulnerable; that is, we are inclined not to think clearly and can fall prey to those who would take advantage of our psychological state.

In paragraph 8 Shermer claims that mediums are unethical and dangerous. His argument seems to go like this:

Mediums profit from (prey upon) the emotions of the grieving.

Grieving persons are vulnerable to deception.

It is immoral (and dangerous?) to profit from persons who are vulnerable.
    (Implicit premise)
_____

Therefore, the actions of mediums are immoral (and dangerous).

The conclusion that the actions of mediums are immoral seems plausible.[4] One might question why they are also dangerous. Perhaps his ground for claiming it is dangerous is that it is always dangerous to hold irrational beliefs (beliefs that are contrary to the best evidence available).

Shermer's final statement, while strong on rhetoric, may be taken to contain an implicit argument:

> If it is reasonable to accept Edward's claims that he talks with the dead, then it must be plausible that the dead gather in a television studio in New York "to twaddle with a former ballroom-dance instructor."
>
> It is not plausible that the dead gather in a television studio in New York "to twaddle with a former ballroom-dance instructor."
> _____
>
> So, it is not reasonable to accept Edward's claims that he talks with the dead.

While Shermer's conclusion seems reasonable insofar as naturalistic explanations of Edward's apparent ability to talk with the dead are more plausible than the alternative, this argument might misrepresent the views of the medium. Few of those who believe in the reality of paranormal phenomena contend that spirits of the dead are located at a particular point in physical space.

In general, Shermer's arguments and explanations seem more plausible than the alternative explanation of Edward's "knowledge" of facts of the dead. So, Shermer's conclusion that Edward lacks the ability to converse with the dead should be accepted.

Essays for Analysis

Monica What's-Her-Face and "Responsible" Journalism

By Tom Magliozzi

I have long suspected that "responsible" journalists were just a bunch of schlocks with very few smarts and not much in the way of good taste (seems you can seldom trust those with highfalutin' titles like the Fourth Estate). And we need no longer suspect, for now we know for sure.

There I was in the checkout line at the supermarket, and there was everybody's favorite trashy newspaper—the *Weekly World News.* Now, nobody actually believes anything that's printed in the *Weekly World News* (in my opinion), but you must admit that it's fun to see what those guys find to report on. I mean, it really does take a certain brand of creativity.

---

[4]There might be a counterargument to this. Shermer assumes that Edward is intentionally deceiving his subjects. It is *possible* that Edward is himself deceived and sincerely believes that he is speaking with the dead—cases of self-deception are not terribly uncommon. If Edward is a victim of self-deception, then he is not intentionally deceiving others. The ground for claiming a self-deceived medium is immoral for (unintentionally) deceiving others would seem to be that the medium does not subject the assumption that there are paranormal phenomena to critical scrutiny.

Lo and behold, the headline—something to do with Monica What's-Her-Face—was the same as the cover stories in the more respectable papers: *Time, Newsweek,* and that last bastion of what's fit to print—the *New York Times!* Well, guys, you've finally shown yourselves for exactly what you are—and the word "responsible" does not leap to mind. Same goes for radio and TV newsrooms everywhere. You're all nothing but a bunch of jerks looking to fill another half hour with anything you can get your hands on—as long as you can keep those Nielsen ratings up to help pay your ridiculously exorbitant salaries.

Get this for rationalization! As I was channel surfing one night, I ran across one of those pseudo news programs where "responsible" journalists sit around and discuss what they're doing. I tuned in too late to know who any of these schlocks were, but one of them was from *Time* or *Newsweek,* I forget which. Here's how he justified his magazine's coverage of this Monica story: "This is what people are talking about, so it's our responsibility to write about it," he says.

You jerk! Don't you have it bass ackwards? Aren't people talking about it because you're writing about it? How would we even know about it if YOU hadn't decided that it was news? It's not news, stupid. And just because you've got a bigger vocabulary than I, it obviously doesn't qualify you to decide what's "fit to print."

I now have before me the latest issues of *Time, Newsweek,* and the *New York Times.* I'm canceling my subscriptions to them all.

My cancellation won't mean much. It won't mean anything to the network news shows if I don't watch. It will matter, however, if you happen to be a Nielsen family. If you are, I strongly urge you to avoid them all like the plague. But I do have to thank them all for proving quite conclusively what I have long suspected.

(*Source*: From *In Our Humble Opinion: Car Talk's Click and Clack Rant and Rave* by Tom Magliozzi and Ray Magliozzi, copyright © 2000 by Tom Magliozzi and Ray Magliozzi. Used by permission of Perigee Books, a division of Penguin Putnam Inc. Tom Magliozzi received his bachelor's degree from M.I.T. and his Ph.D. from Boston University. He is co-host of the PBS program *Car Talk*.)

Titanic

Jack Dawson: **Leonardo DiCaprio**
Rose DeWitt Bukater: **Kate Winslet**
Cal Hockley: **Billy Zane**
Molly Brown: **Kathy Bates**
Brock Lovett: **Bill Paxton**

Written and directed by **James Cameron**. Running time: 194 minutes. Rated PG-13 (for shipwreck scenes, mild language, and sexuality).

BY ROGER EBERT   Like a great iron Sphinx on the ocean floor, the *Titanic* faces still toward the West, interrupted forever on its only voyage. We see it in the opening shots of "Titanic," encrusted with the silt of 85 years; a remote-controlled TV camera snakes its way inside, down corridors and through doorways, showing us staterooms built for millionaires and inherited by crustaceans.

These shots strike precisely the right note; the ship calls from its grave for its story to be told, and if the story is made of showbiz and hype, smoke and mirrors—

well, so was the Titanic. She was "the largest moving work of man in all history," a character boasts, neatly dismissing the Pyramids and the Great Wall. There is a shot of her, early in the film, sweeping majestically beneath the camera from bow to stern, nearly 900 feet long and "unsinkable," it was claimed, until an iceberg made an irrefutable reply.

James Cameron's 194-minute, $200 million film of the tragic voyage is in the tradition of the great Hollywood epics. It is flawlessly crafted, intelligently constructed, strongly acted and spellbinding. If its story stays well within the traditional formulas for such pictures, well, you don't choose the most expensive film ever made as your opportunity to reinvent the wheel.

We know before the movie begins that certain things must happen. We must see the *Titanic* sail and sink, and be convinced we are looking at a real ship. There must be a human story—probably a romance—involving a few of the passengers. There must be vignettes involving some of the rest and a subplot involving the arrogance and pride of the ship's builders—and perhaps also their courage and dignity. And there must be a reenactment of the ship's terrible death throes; it took two and a half hours to sink, so that everyone aboard had time to know what was happening, and to consider their actions.

All of those elements are present in Cameron's "Titanic," weighted and balanced like ballast, so that the film always seems in proportion. The ship was made out of models (large and small), visual effects and computer animation. You know intellectually that you're not looking at a real ocean liner—but the illusion is convincing and seamless. The special effects don't call inappropriate attention to themselves but get the job done.

The human story involves an 17-year-old woman named Rose DeWitt Bukater (Kate Winslet) who is sailing to what she sees as her own personal doom: She has been forced by her penniless mother to become engaged to marry a rich, supercilious snob named Cal Hockley (Billy Zane), and so bitterly does she hate this prospect that she tries to kill herself by jumping from the ship. She is saved by Jack Dawson (Leonardo DiCaprio), a brash kid from steerage, and of course they will fall in love during the brief time left to them.

The screenplay tells their story in a way that unobtrusively shows off the ship. Jack is invited to join Rose's party at dinner in the first class dining room, and later, fleeing from Cal's manservant, Lovejoy (David Warner), they find themselves first in the awesome engine room, with pistons as tall as churches, and then at a rousing Irish dance in the crowded steerage. (At one point Rose gives Lovejoy the finger; did young ladies do that in 1912?) Their exploration is intercut with scenes from the command deck, where the captain (Bernard Hill) consults with Andrews (Victor Garber), the ship's designer and Ismay (Jonathan Hyde), the White Star Line's managing director.

Ismay wants the ship to break the trans-Atlantic speed record. He is warned that icebergs may have floated into the hazardous northern crossing but is scornful of danger. The Titanic can easily break the speed record but is too massive to turn quickly at high speed; there is an agonizing sequence that almost seems to play in slow motion, as the ship strains and shudders to turn away from an iceberg in its path—and fails.

We understand exactly what is happening at that moment because of an ingenious story technique by Cameron, who frames and explains the entire voyage in a modern story. The opening shots of the real Titanic, we are told, are obtained during an expedition led by Brock Lovett (Bill Paxton), an undersea explorer. He seeks precious jewels but finds a nude drawing of a young girl. Meanwhile, an ancient woman sees the drawing on TV and recognizes herself. This is Rose (Gloria Stuart), still alive at 101. She visits Paxton and shares her memories ("I can still smell the fresh paint"). And he shows her video scenes from his explorations, including a computer simulation of the *Titanic's* last hours—which doubles as a briefing for the audience. By the time the ship sinks, we already know what is happening and why, and the story can focus on the characters while we effortlessly follow the stages of the Titanic's sinking.

Movies like this are not merely difficult to make at all, but almost impossible to make well. The technical difficulties are so daunting that it's a wonder when the filmmakers are also able to bring the drama and history into proportion. I found myself convinced by both the story and the saga. The setup of the love story is fairly routine, but the payoff—how everyone behaves as the ship is sinking—is wonderfully written, as passengers are forced to make impossible choices. Even the villain, played by Zane, reveals a human element at a crucial moment (despite everything, damn it all, he does love the girl).

The image from the *Titanic* that has haunted me, ever since I first read the story of the great ship, involves the moments right after it sank. The night sea was quiet enough so that cries for help carried easily across the water to the lifeboats, which drew prudently away. Still dressed up in the latest fashions, hundreds froze and drowned. What an extraordinary position to find yourself in after spending all that money for a ticket on an unsinkable ship.

(*Source*: Copyright © The Ebert Co., Ltd. Used with permission of Roger Ebert. Available online: http://www.suntimes.com/ebert/ebert_reviews/1997/12/121904.html. Roger Ebert received a Bachelor of Science degree from the University of Illinois. He is a Pulitzer Prize-winning film critic for the *Chicago Sun-Times* and the author of numerous books. He is the co-host of *Ebert and Roeper and the Movies*.)

Half-Baked Science

By Ray Magliozzi

For the record, I would like to state the following: I think the global warming "crisis" is utter bull feathers.

There, I've said it. Want to take a guess on how many scientists who are currently working on global warming actually believe it's a problem or even fixable? It's only about 30%.* So, you may ask, whom do we have to blame for this hysteria? Well, that 30% and maybe Al Gore, the father of the Internet.

---

*This may be complete BS. I made it up. There is absolutely no statistical or scientific evidence to support this claim or any of the scientific principles put forth in this essay. You are, however, free to believe anything you wish.

A few years ago, the scientific community approached the world leaders and said, "Look, we've got a problem with chlorofluorocarbons getting into the upper atmosphere and eating away at the ozone layer." Where do these chlorofluorocarbons come from? Well, one place they come from is refrigerants, like R12. So we have to ban R12 and come up with a new refrigerant that won't damage the ozone layer. And we'll begin to use this in all the cars and all the air-conditioning systems all over the world. And we have to ban aerosol cans that use chlorofluorocarbons as a propellant, because that's getting into the atmosphere, too. Well, I just don't buy it. They don't mention the fact that the chlorine from these chlorofluorocarbons that's wrecking the ozone layer is overshadowed tremendously by the amount of chlorine introduced into the atmosphere every day by volcanoes. We have no control over volcanoes. And as far as I know, we never have. What are we going to do? Ban volcanoes? OK, we're going to cap all the volcanoes. We'll outlaw volcanoes. No more volcanic action on the planet, and we'll have no more chlorine going into the atmosphere.

Now, I know some scientists say, "Well, that chlorine that's coming out of those volcanoes, that's just CL_2 and not a danger to the ozone layer." Well, I believe that enough of that chlorine comes out as free-radical chlorine (CL-minus), and that's the very stuff they claim is doing the damage. Well, if that's doing the damage, then banning spray cans of Right Guard isn't going to help very much, because the chlorine of volcanic origin is bajillions of times greater than the amount of chlorine that's coming out of our spray deodorant cans.

Now, don't get me wrong, there are lots of good reasons, perhaps, to ban things, but I'm just afraid that our replacement for chlorofluorocarbons may turn out in years to come to be even more of a threat to mankind than the stuff it replaced. The jury's still out on that. We'll see. Now, if we really want to ban something, I'd like to suggest that we consider cows. This may be news to some of you, but bovine flatulence, which is mostly methane, is believed by some scientists to be another leading cause of global warming. Geez!

I guess we humans just find it hard to accept the fact that there are certain ecological and environmental factors beyond our control. Let's not forget that the planet had gone through cycles of warming and cooling long before mankind was here to screw up the environment, and what caused those? We don't know. There are forces at work that are so complex we can't possibly understand them, and even if we could, we certainly couldn't control them. Let's not let the scientific community lead us astray. The problem with science is scientists. For the most part, they're intelligent, they're articulate, and they're convincing. Furthermore they don't seem to be in it for the money. So when they tell us something, we believe it because they've been studying this subject and we haven't. And everyone wants to believe in something. Everyone wants someone to give him the answer. The scientists always seem to have the answers.

And is it any surprise that most of our prominent, or at least most vocal, scientists are men? Men have answers for all the questions, and many of those answers have been proven wrong throughout history. Let's look at a few examples. One of the earliest, and maybe even greatest, scientists of the ancient world was Aristotle. He had everyone believing that Earth was the center of the universe and that everything revolved around our planet. Hmm. Guess we found that wasn't true, but mankind believed it for a long, long time. I think something like 15 centuries. Let's not forget how many scientists had everyone convinced that the earth was flat.

Here's one of my personal favorites, and I think this has been in just about every science book that I've ever read. Heat radiating from the earth's core is the result of a long-term cooling process that started when the earth was a molten mass. Remember this one? We were taught that the heat from the core of the earth was created at the earth's beginning and has been slowly released ever since. I don't believe it. I don't give a damn how high an R value our planet has, after 4 billion years, the core of the earth should have cooled off completely. I don't think you need a Ph.D. to figure that out. I think scientists now know, after foisting this harebrained theory on us for years, that this is complete nonsense. There is—there must be, a nuclear reaction taking place at the center of our planet, and probably every planet that is something more than a frozen glob of interstellar rock. And yet the scientific community had us believing that this was, in fact, the absolute truth and it was not to be disputed. And now we know the truth; it's baloney. I mean, come on, we know that there is radioactivity all through the planet, and this radioactivity is what's keeping the core of the earth molten, not heat that was trapped in there 4.2 billion years ago. Let's get serious.

Here's another one I love. Imagine how many dinosaurs it would take, standing shoulder to shoulder in a place like Saudi Arabia, just so those Saudis could pump 9 billion gallons of oil out of the ground every 10 minutes. It's just impossible. The truth is, there is no such thing as "fossil" fuel. We were taught in school that we get oil out of the ground because billions and billions of dinosaurs all decided to die in the same place and were then covered up by rock and dust and falling trees, and under tremendous pressure over millions and millions of years those decaying dinosaurs turned into oil! We all fell for that one. What we do know is that geologists have found oil in certain places on Earth where they know dinosaurs never existed. 'Splain me that, Lucy. A more reasonable explanation is that oil is constantly being manufactured from the elemental components of the earth. Carbon and hydrogen atoms, trapped beneath the earth's crust, are being combined by the heat generated from that aforementioned molten mass of 4.2 billion years ago. That's where oil comes from—in my humble opinion. Now if you really believe that oil came from decomposing pterodactyl wings, you know what? We should have run out about 112 years ago.

So what's my point? Well, I'm glad you asked. I propose that we're just too quick to accept what the scientific community is telling us. We figure they must be telling us the truth because they've explained so many things correctly in the past and they don't seem to be trying to sell us something. When someone is trying to sell you a vacuum cleaner, you know he's lying because he's in it for the money. But the scientific community seems to be above that, and therefore we've made the mistake of elevating scientists to the level of gods. Why? Because they explain the things to us that we can't explain to ourselves. And you know what? We're too quick to believe them, if only because they always sound like they know what they're talking about. And they look like they know what they're talking about, too. They've got that wild hair and that wide stare and all those college degrees. They just can't be wrong. (By the way, don't believe me either, even if I sound like I know what I'm talking about.) It's high time we stopped believing all these bogus theories that a bunch of half-baked scientists are spoon-feeding us.

Look at it this way—even if all the doomsayers are right about global warming, so what? There was an article in the *Boston Globe* (the major newspaper in Our Fair City) last year about life on our planet just after the last ice age. (By the way, what caused that ice age, anyway? We don't know.) In any event, scientists say that after that ice age, temperatures in some parts of the planet rose 19 degrees in just a few decades. Well, I don't believe that either, because I don't believe they have the means to really measure that. But let's assume for the time being that it's true. How did that happen? And wouldn't that have seriously altered any life that was on the planet at that time? Well, it certainly did, and that's part of the process; life on Earth gets altered by climatic changes. And certainly life, as we know it now, will get altered by global warming. And when it does, we will not have caused it; it's part of the ever-changing nature of planet Earth. We've simply attached too much importance to our impact on this giant planet. Let's get serious. Now, I don't know where you're living, but another 19 degrees in Boston would look just about perfect to me. That's my opinion. I'm probably wrong, but I'm sticking with it.

(*Source*: From *In Our Humble Opinion: Car Talk's Click and Clack Rant and Rave* by Tom Magliozzi and Ray Magliozzi, copyright © 2000 by Tom Magliozzi and Ray Magliozzi. Used by permission of Perigee Books, a division of Penguin Putnam.
Ray Magliozzi received his bachelor's degree in humanities and science from M.I.T. He is co-host of the NPR program *Car Talk*.)

Verbicide

By David W. Orr

He entered my office for advice as a freshman advisee sporting nearly perfect SAT scores and an impeccable academic record—by all accounts a young man of considerable promise. During a 20-minute conversation about his academic future, however, he displayed a vocabulary that consisted mostly of two words: "cool" and "really." Almost 800 SAT points hitched to each word. He could use them interchangeably, as in "really cool" or "cool . . . really!" He could also use them singly. When he was a student in a subsequent class I later confirmed that my first impression of the young scholar was largely accurate and that his vocabulary, and presumably his mind, consisted predominantly of words and images derived from overexposure to television and the new jargon of computer-speak. He is no aberration but an example of a larger problem, not of illiteracy but of diminished literacy in a culture that often sees little reason to use words carefully, however abundantly. Increasingly, papers from otherwise good students have whole paragraphs that sound like advertising copy. Whether students are talking or writing, a growing number have a tenuous grasp on a declining vocabulary. Excise "uh . . . like . . . uh" from most teen-age conversations, and the effect is like sticking a pin into a balloon.

In the past 50 years, by one reckoning, the working vocabulary of the average 14-year-old has declined from some 25,000 words to 10,000 words (Spretnak 1997). This is not merely a decline in numbers of words but in the capacity to think. It also signifies there has been a steep decline in the number of things an adolescent needs to know and to name in order to get by in an increasingly homogenized and urbanized consumer society. This is a national tragedy that goes virtually unnoticed in the media. It is no coincidence that in roughly the same half century the average person has come to recognize over 1,000 corporate logos but can now recognize fewer than 10 plants and animals native to his or her locality. That fact says a great deal about why the decline in working vocabulary has gone unnoticed: Few are paying attention. The decline is surely not consistent across the full range of language but concentrates in those areas having to do with large issues such as philosophy, religion, public policy, and nature. On the other hand, vocabulary has probably increased in areas having to do with sex, violence, recreation, and consumption. As a result we are losing the capacity to say what we really mean and ultimately to think about what we mean. We are losing the capacity for articulate intelligence about the things that matter most. "That sucks," for example, is a common way for budding young scholars to announce their displeasure about any number of things that range across the spectrum of human experience. But it can also be used to indicate a general displeasure with the entire cosmos. Whatever the target, it is the linguistic equivalent of duct tape, useful for holding disparate thoughts in rough and temporary proximity to some vague emotion of dislike.

The problem is not confined to teenagers or young adults. It is part of a national epidemic of incoherence evident in our public discourse, street talk, movies, television, and music. We have all heard popular music lyrics that consisted mostly of pre-Neanderthal grunts. We have witnessed "conversation" on TV talk shows that would have embarrassed intelligent 4-year olds. We have listened to politicians of national reputation proudly mangle logic and language in less than a paragraph, although they can do it on a larger scale as well. However manifested, our linguistic decline is aided and abetted by academics, including whole departments specializing in various forms of postmodernism and the deconstruction of one thing or another. They have propounded the idea that everything is relative, hence largely inconsequential, and that the use of language is primarily an exercise in power, hence to be devalued. They have taught, in other words, a pseudo-intellectual contempt for clarity, careful argument, and felicitous expression. Being scholars of their word they also write without clarity, argument, and felicity. Remove the arcane constructions from any number of academic papers written in the past 10 years and the argument—such as it is—evaporates. But the situation is not much better elsewhere in the academy, where thought is often fenced in by disciplinary jargon. The fact is that educators have all too often been indifferent trustees of language. This explains, I think, why the academy has been a lame critic of what ails the world, from the preoccupation with self to technology run amuck. We have been unable to speak out against the barbarism engulfing the larger culture because we are part of the process of barbarization that begins with the devaluation of language.

The decline of language, noted by commentators such as H. L. Meneken, George Orwell, William Safire, and Edwin R. Neuman, is nothing new. Language is always coming undone. Why? First, it is always under assault by those who intend to control others by first subverting the words and metaphors that people would otherwise use to describe their world. The goal is to give partisan aims the appearance of inevitability by diminishing the sense of larger possibilities. In our time, language is under assault by those whose purpose it is to sell one kind of quackery or another: economic, political, religious, or technological. It is under attack because the clarity and felicity of language, as distinct from its quantity, are devalued in an industrial-technological society. The clear and artful use of language is, in fact, threatening to that society. As a result we have highly distorted and atrophied conversations about ultimate meanings, ethics, public purposes, or the means by which we live. Because we cannot expect to cope with problems that we cannot name, one result of our misuse of language is a growing agenda of unsolved problems that cannot be adequately described in words and metaphors derived from our own creations such as machines and computers. The words and metaphors derived from our own creations, in other words, are inadequate to describe the major flaws in these same creations.

Second, language is in decline because it is being Balkanized around the specialized vocabularies characteristic of an increasingly specialized society. The highly technical language of the expert is, of course, both bane and blessing. It is useful for describing fragments of the world but not for describing how these fit into a coherent whole. But things work as whole systems whether we can describe them or not, whether we perceive it or not. And more than anything else, it is coherence our culture lacks, not specialized knowledge. Genetic engineering, for example, can be described as a technical thing in the language of molecular biology. But saying what the act of re-arranging the genetic fabric of Earth means requires an altogether different language and a mindset that seeks to discover larger patterns. Similarly, the specialized language of economics does not begin to describe the state of our wellbeing, whatever it reveals about how much stuff we may buy. Over and over again the simplistic and seductive language of the specialist displaces that of the generalist—the specialist in whole things. A result is that the capacity to think carefully about ends, as distinct from means, has all but disappeared from our public and private conversations.

Third, language reflects the range and depth of our experience. But our experience of the world is being impoverished to the extent that it is rendered artificial and prepackaged. Most of us no longer have the experience of skilled physical work on farms or in forests. Consequently, as our reality becomes increasingly artificial, words and metaphors based on intimate knowledge of soils, plants, trees, animals, landscapes, rivers, and oceans have declined. "Cut off from this source," Wendell Berry writes, "language becomes a paltry work of conscious purpose, at the service and the mercy of expedient aims" (Berry 1983). Our nonparticipatory experience within the confines of a uniform and ugly artificial environment is engineered and shrink-wrapped by the recreation and software industries and pedaled back to us as "fun" or "information." We've become a nation of television watchers and Internet browsers, and it shows in the way we talk and what we talk about. More and more we speak as if we are voyeurs furtively peeking at life, not active participants, moral agents, or engaged citizens.

Fourth, we are no longer held together, as we once were, by the reading of a common literature or by listening to great stories, and so we cannot draw on a common set of metaphors and images as we once did. Allusions to the Bible and other great books no longer resonate because they are simply unfamiliar to a growing number of people. This is so in part because the consensus about what is worth reading has come undone. But the debate about a worthy canon is hardly the whole story. The ability to read serious things in a serious way is diminished by over-stimulation by television and computers, with their rapidly changing images that mock concentration. The desire to read is jeopardized by the same forces that would make us a violent, shallow, hedonistic, and materialistic people. As a nation we risk coming undone because our language is coming undone, and our language is coming undone because one by one we are being undone.

The problem of language, however, is a global problem. Of the roughly 5000 languages now spoken on Earth, only 150 or so are expected to survive to the year 2100. Language everywhere is being whittled down to conform to the limited objectives of the global economy and homogenized in accord with the shallow imperatives of the "information age." The languages being lost, in Vine Deloria's words, often "convey deeper and more precise meanings than does English" (Delori 1999:176). This represents a huge loss of cultural information and a blurring of our capacity to understand the world and our place in it. And it represents a losing bet that a few people armed with the words, metaphors, and mindset characteristic of a transient, failing industry and technology can manage the Earth, a vaster, infinitely more complex, and longer-lived thing altogether.

Because we cannot think clearly about what we cannot say clearly, the first casualty of linguistic incoherence is our ability to think well about many things. This is a reciprocal process. Language, George Orwell once wrote, "becomes ugly and inaccurate because our thoughts are foolish, but the slovenliness of our language makes it easier for us to have foolish thoughts" (Orwell 1981:157). In our time the words and metaphors of the consumer economy are often a product of foolish thoughts as well as evidence of bad language. Under the onslaught of commercialization and technology we are losing the sense of wholeness and time that is essential to a decent civilization. We are losing, in short, the capacity to articulate what ought to be most important to us. And the new class of corporate chiefs, global managers, genetic engineers, and money speculators has no words with which to describe the fullness and beauty of life or to announce their role in the larger moral ecology. They have no way to say how we fit together in the community of life, indeed no idea beyond that of self-interest about why we ought to protect it. They have, in short, no language that will help humankind, including themselves, navigate through the most dangerous epoch in its history. On the contrary, they will do all in their power to reduce language to the level of utility, management, self-interest, and the short term. Evil begins not only with words used with malice but also with words that diminish people, land, and life to some fragment that is less than whole and less than holy. The prospects for evil, I believe, will grow as those for language decline.

We have an affinity for language, and that capacity makes us human. When language is devalued, misused, or corrupted, so too are those who speak it and those who hear it. On the other hand, we are never better than when we use words clearly, eloquently, and civilly. Language can elevate thought and ennoble our behavior. Abraham Lincoln's words at Gettysburg in 1863, for example, gave meaning to the terrible sacrifices of the Civil War. Similarly, Winston Churchill's words moved an entire nation to do its duty in the dark hours of 1940. If we intend to protect and enhance our humanity, we must first decide to protect and enhance language and fight everything that undermines and cheapens it.

What does this mean in practical terms? How do we design the right use of language back into the Culture? My first suggestion is to restore the habit of talking directly to each other, whatever the loss in economic efficiency. To that end I propose that we begin by smashing every automated answering machine. Messages like "Your call is important to us ..." or "For more options, please press five," or "If you would like to talk to a real person please stay on the line," are the death rattle of a coherent culture.

Second, the proper use of language is a slowly acquired art that is easily corrupted by technological contrivances that increase the volume and velocity of communication. Whatever the gains in speed and convenience provided by the Internet, I seldom receive any email message that could pass a sixth-grade composition exam. Worse, many people are simply overwhelmed by the volume of email. We cannot disinvent the Internet, but for our sanity we can and should limit the use we make of it.

My third suggestion is to restore the habit of public reading. One of my most distinctive childhood memories is attending a public reading of Shakespeare by the British actor Charles Laughton. With no prop other than a book, he read with energy and passion for 2 hours and kept a large audience enthralled, including at least one 8-year-old boy. No movie has ever been as memorable to me. Further, I propose that adults should turn off the television, disconnect the cable, undo the computer, and once again read good books aloud to their children. I know of no better or more pleasurable way to stimulate thinking, encourage a love of language, and facilitate a child's ability to form images.

Fourth, those who corrupt language ought to be held accountable for what they do—beginning with the advertising industry. In 1997 it spent an estimated $187 billion to sell us an unconscionable amount of stuff, much of it useless, environmentally destructive, and deleterious to our health. Often using only seductive imagery, advertising fuels the fires of consumerism that are consuming the Earth and our children's future. Advertisers regard the public with utter contempt—as little more than sheep to be manipulated to buy whatever at the highest possible cost and at any consequence. Dante would have consigned them to the lowest level of hell, only because there was no worse place to put them. We should too. If we lack the gumption to do that we ought to require by law full disclosure of the damage consumer products do to other people, to the environment, and to the buyer.

Fifth, language, I believe, grows from the outside in, from the periphery to center. It is renewed in the vernacular by the everyday acts of living, doing, and speaking. It is renewed in the streets, shops, farms, and rural places where human life is most authentic. It is, by the same logic, corrupted by contrivance, pretense, and fakery. The center, where power and wealth work by contrivance, pretense, and fakery, does not create language so much as exploit it. To facilitate control, the powerful would make our language as uniform and dull as the interstate highway system. To preserve the places where language grows, we must protect the independence of local newspapers and local radio stations by forbidding nonlocal ownership. We need to support regional publishing houses and small, independent bookstores. We need to protect local culture and local dialects from highbrow ridicule. We need to teach the young to honor difference in speech and dialect. And we must protect those parts of our culture where memory, tradition, and devotion to place still exist, because it is there that language is often most vibrant.

Finally, because language is the only currency wherever men and women pursue truth, there should be no higher priority for schools, colleges, and universities than to defend the integrity and clarity of language in every way possible. We must instill in our students an appreciation for language, literature, and words well crafted and used to good ends. As teachers we should insist on good writing. We should assign books and readings that are well written. We should restore rhetoric—the ability to speak clearly and well—to the liberal arts curriculum. Our own speaking and writing ought to demonstrate clarity and truthfulness. And we too should be held accountable for what we say.

In terms of the sheer volume of words and data of all kinds, this is surely an information age. But in terms of understanding, wisdom, spiritual clarity, and civility we have entered a darker time. We are drowning in a sea of words with nary a drop to drink. We are in the process of committing what C. S. Lewis once called "verbicide." The volume or words in our time is inversely related to our capacity to use them well and to think clearly about what they mean. It is no wonder that, in a century of gulags, genocide, global wars, and horrible weapons, our use of language has been increasingly dominated by propaganda and advertising and controlled by language technicians. "We have a sense of evil," Susan Sontag has said, but we no longer have "the religious or philosophical language to talk intelligently about evil" (Miller 1998:55). If that is so for the twentieth century, what will be said at the end of the twenty-first century, when the stark realities of climatic change and biotic impoverishment will become fully manifest? Can we summon the clarity of mind to speak the words necessary to cause us to do what ought to have been our obvious course all along?

David W. Orr

Oberlin College, Oberlin, OH 44074, U.S.A.

Literature Cited

Berry, W. 1983. Standing by words. North Point Press, San Francisco.

Delori, V., Jr. 1999. For this land. Rutledge, London.

Miller, S. 1998. A note on the banality of evil. Wilson Quarterly 22(4):54–59.

Orwell, G. 1981. A collection of essays. Harcourt, Brace, Jovanovich, New York.

Spretnak, C. 1997. The resurgence of the real. Addison-Wesley, Reading.

(*Source:* From *Conservation Biology* 13 (1999): 696–699. Used with permission of Blackwell Sciences.)
David Orr is a Professor of Environmental Studies at Oberlin College.

CHAPTER 33

Writing an Argumentative Essay

The View: An argumentative essay is an extended defense of a thesis and several subordinate theses. A clear presentation requires that you tell your reader where you are going (state your theses) and remind your reader where you have been. You might need to show your reader why your topic is significant. You must develop arguments based on premises that your reader accepts as true. You should plan on writing several drafts of your paper, seeking criticisms between drafts.

How can my critical-thinking skills improve my writing?

If you worked through several essays following the guidelines in the last chapter, you probably concluded that many essays are not clearly written. You might have had difficulty finding the main thesis or the subordinate theses of some essays. You might have needed to search long and think hard to figure out what some of the arguments in the essay were. You might have had to figure out whether there were unstated premises for some arguments, what those premises might be, and whether any possible premises were true or plausible. You might have had to think hard about the connections among the conclusions of the arguments in the essay. You might have found yourself saying, "This is hard work!"

If you are to write an effective argumentative essay, you should do all in your power to avoid the shortcomings you find in the writings of others. You should try to make *reading* your essay as easy as possible. To write an effective essay requires the use of virtually all the critical-thinking skills covered in this book.

Our focus will be on one intellectual virtue—**clarity**—a virtue which may be deemed central to any effective writing. Why clarity? Your teachers have a certain bias. They believe that the best indicator of clarity of thought is clarity of writing and speaking. So, you probably have been bombarded with a number of old proverbs: "Clarity is a virtue." "Clarity begins at home." And didn't even Saint Paul write, "Though I speak with the tongues of men and of angels and have not clarity, I am become *as* sounding brass, or a tinkling cymbal" (I Corinthians 13:1)?[1] The emphasis on clarity is

---

[1]No, but he should have.

quite reasonable, since two people will benefit from clear writing. Your reader will benefit, since he or she will be able to follow your argument with ease. More importantly, *you* will benefit because you are likely to see, and therefore be able to fix, weak points in your arguments. This implies that *sometimes* you will recognize that your thesis is implausible—so you will need to approach your topic in a different way—and other times you will notice that your arguments do *not* show that your thesis is true or probably true.

So, what are the elements of clarity? What can you do to assure that the argumentative essay you write is clear?

Getting Started: Know Where You Are Going!

Consider the difference between going for a drive and going on vacation. In the early days of America's romance with the motor car, it was fairly common for people to simply "go for a drive." If you went for a drive, you had no particular destination in mind. Little time was devoted to a careful examination of maps before you started the drive. If you carried a map, it was only to make sure you could find your way back home. On the other hand, vacations take careful planning. You have to decide where to go. Once you have decided where to go, you might need to examine various maps or call the AAA to determine the best route to your destination. Even then you might need contingency plans in case the roads you choose are closed. You might calculate how far you will travel in a single day, where you will stay, what you will see along the way. While "going for a drive" is a fairly carefree activity, going on vacation is serious business!

Writing an argumentative essay is like going on vacation. You need to know *exactly* where you are going—you need to define your thesis. If you are planning to vacation at Disney World, you plan your vacation in such a way that you will *arrive at* Disney World. No one plans to vacation "somewhere in Florida." Similarly, if you are planning to write an essay on the role of the ghost of Hamlet's father in Shakespeare's *Hamlet,* your thesis should state *precisely* what you intend to show. The thesis is the *destination* of your essay. Your thesis might be that Shakespeare intended the appearances of the ghost of Hamlet's father to show that Hamlet was insane.[2] How do you state your thesis? The same way you tell someone where you are going on vacation: tell 'em! If someone asked, "Where are you going on vacation?" you would respond, "I'm going to Disney World." In *reading* an essay, the reader is asking a similar question, "Where is this going to go?" You should answer that question in the same way: "In this paper I show that Shakespeare intended the appearances of the ghost of Hamlet's father to show that Hamlet was insane" (or whatever your thesis happens to be). Similarly, just as you would respond to inquiries regarding your planned route to Disney World by saying, "I'll start by going south on Interstate 35 to Oklahoma City, then I'll turn east on . . .," you trace the "route" to your thesis by stating your subordi-

---

[2]This would be a very difficult thesis to establish, since it is always difficult to establish the *intent* (purpose, objective) of an author.

nate theses:"First I argue that.... Next I show that.... Finally I argue that...." By doing
this you inform your reader where you are going and how you are going to get there.

After reading the previous paragraph, some will respond, "Ah! I see what's coming. You're going to propose that old structuring technique commonly expressed as
'Tell them what you are going to say. Tell them. And tell them what you said.' But that's
not merely old, it's old fashioned, out-of-date, boring, passé." I plead guilty on all
counts, but I deny that being "old fashioned, out-of-date, boring, passé" is any reason
to reject the structure. We are concerned with *clarity*. Clarity requires that you know
what—and that your reader be able to perceive—the links in your argumentative
chain are and how they fit together. From the perspective of the reader, a clear essay
is one that is easy to follow. An essay that is easy to follow is largely a matter of structure. It requires that the author tell what the arguments are, what conclusions are
drawn, and how the several intermediate conclusions "hang together" in support of
the main thesis. The *content* of the essay might be very complex—many readers
might question whether the premises of your arguments are true, so you will need to
give arguments in support of those premises—but *one* element of clarity consists of
a carefully articulated structure. If you "tell them what you're going to say"—state
your main theses and immediately subordinate theses—"tell them"—carefully
develop the arguments in support of your main and subordinate theses—and "tell
them what you said"—conclude with a summary of your arguments—both you and
your reader will know where the argument is going and where it has been. Think
about the essays you analyzed in the previous chapter. Wouldn't they have been easier to follow if they had had such a structure?

But there is a real sense in which we are getting ahead of ourselves. To state and defend a thesis, you must first decide what thesis you wish to defend. How do you do that?

The answer to that question depends on the type of argumentative essay you are
writing. If your teacher asks you to write on the theme "why your favorite pastime is
a worthwhile activity," you have a thesis. Assume your favorite activity is coin collecting. Your thesis would be, "Coin collecting is a worthwhile activity." Your subordinate theses would consist of all the reasons why you believe that coin collecting is
worthwhile. Your opening paragraph might look like this:

> In this paper I argue that coin collecting is a worthwhile activity. I begin by argu-
> ing that coins are aesthetically interesting. Next, I show that coin collecting
> enriches one's knowledge and appreciation of history. Third, I show that coin col-
> lecting is a profitable hobby. Finally, I show that coin collecting can even enrich
> one's social life. Since any one of these reasons can be a sufficient condition for
> deeming an activity worthwhile, the fact that coin collecting can result in all
> these desirable consequences implies that virtually everyone would deem coin
> collecting a worthwhile activity.[3]

---

[3]Not all stylists maintain that one should be as blunt as I have been in this paragraph. In his *The
Practical Stylist*, second edition (New York: Thomas Y. Crowell, 1969), Sheridan Baker suggests
that your opening paragraph should be like a funnel: You should start with a broad generalization and "funnel down" to a thesis statement (pp. 18–19). In many cases that might be reasonable. But regardless how you do so, there *must* be a clear statement of your thesis, and it is very
helpful to your reader if you state your subordinate theses as well.

The remainder of the essay would consist of arguments for the subordinate theses. Notice that by stating your main thesis and your subordinate theses, you have effectively given an outline of the paper.

Typically, of course, you won't simply sit down and ask yourself, Why do I like coin collecting (or stamp collecting, or collecting beanie babies, or hunting, or reading novels, etc.)? Typically, you will be given an assignment to write an essay on the causes of World War I, or the role of imagination in René Descartes's *Rules for the Direction of the Mind,* or the symbolic function of the whale in *Moby Dick,* or the most important element in mitosis (cell division). To develop your thesis, you will need to do some research. What do the experts say regarding your topic? What kinds of evidence do they give? Are their arguments cogent? When there are disagreements among the experts—as there will be—which position seems to have better support? Why? Is there something that the experts have missed? If so, is that important?

Once you have done your research, you must decide upon a thesis. *Choosing a thesis is the most difficult and the most important element of writing an argumentative essay.* It is the most important element because it focuses your attention and your reader's attention on a specific issue. It is the most difficult because it must be narrow enough to defend completely. If your thesis is too broad, it is like vacationing somewhere in Florida: You can expect to see a lot of sites, but you will never arrive at your destination because there *was no* explicit destination. A narrow thesis focuses both your attention and your reader's attention on a specific issue. And a narrow thesis is much easier to defend than a broad thesis.

In his book *Zen and the Art of Motorcycle Maintenance*, Robert Pirsig tells the story of a girl who was going to write a five-hundred-word essay on the United States. She couldn't get started, so the instructor told her to limit her essay to the main street of Bozeman, Montana. Again, she couldn't get started. The instructor became angry and said, "Narrow it down to the *front* of *one* building on the main street of Bozeman. The Opera House. Start with the upper left-hand brick."[4] That did it! "She came in the next class with a puzzled look and handed him a five-*thousand*-word [my emphasis] essay on the front of the Opera House on the main street of Bozeman, Montana."[5]

If you start with a narrow thesis, your essay will be easier to write. If you start with a narrow thesis, you can always broaden it—although generally you should resist that temptation.

Exercise

I. Write a 500-word essay on a topic of your instructor's choice. Begin with a paragraph in which you state your thesis and at least two subordinate theses. Next, defend each of your subordinate theses with an argument of at least one paragraph. Construct an argument showing how the subordinate theses support the main thesis. Conclude with a summary paragraph.

---

[4]Robert M. Pirsig, *Zen and the Art of Motorcycle Maintenance* (New York: Bantam Books, 1974), p. 185.
[5]Pirsig, *Zen and the Art of Motorcycle Maintenance*, p.185.

The Body: The Road and Its Guideposts

The body of an argumentative essay consists of a set of arguments defending your subordinate theses and thereby defending your main thesis. In addition, there generally will be a number of paragraphs that do nothing more than provide information. If your first paragraph states your main thesis and your subordinate theses, all you need do is fill out the arguments for your subordinate theses. Use sound deductive arguments whenever possible. State all the premises so your reader will not become lost and so you can see the form of the argument. If you cannot present a sound deductive argument, present a strong inductive argument with true premises. In principle this is easy. In practice it calls all of your critical-thinking skills into play.

Assume you are writing the essay on coin collecting mentioned above. Your first subordinate thesis is that coins are aesthetically interesting. How do you develop the argument? You might start with something like this:

All coins are aesthetically interesting objects, since all artifacts are aesthetically interesting objects, and all coins are artifacts.

The argument is valid. Is the argument sound? Perhaps, but your reader probably won't find the premise "All artifacts are aesthetically interesting objects" plausible. If it were plausible, you would have to grant that everything made by humans is aesthetically interesting. Coins—at least some coins—might be aesthetically interesting. But for your reader to *accept* the premise as true, she would need to grant that the labels on generic cans of green beans are aesthetically interesting. Such labels consist of white paper with "GREEN BEANS" printed on them. Generic green bean labels do not seem to have as much aesthetic appeal as paintings by Rembrandt or Van Gogh or Picasso. Nor is it evident that all coins are aesthetically interesting. Few people paying for groceries with disks engraved with portraits of dead presidents take themselves to be parting with *objets d'art*. So, even if the deductive argument were sound, your reader would not find it convincing. Your reader probably would not accept the major premise. Truth is fine. But in an argumentative essay you are attempting to show that your thesis (or subordinate thesis) is true. Your reader will not be *convinced* of the truth of your conclusion unless she *accepts* the premises as true. So you must be concerned with three distinct issues: (1) Are the premises of your argument true? (2) Do the premises, if true, provide reasons for granting that the conclusion is true? (3) Will your reader recognize the truth of the premises?

What do you need to show in order to establish the thesis that coins are aesthetically interesting? Do you have to show that *all* coins are aesthetically interesting? Or will it do to show only that *some* of them are interesting? Few coin collectors grant that all coins are aesthetically interesting. The evidence for this is that no coin collectors build their collections by going to the bank, buying rolls of coins, and placing these unopened rolls in their coin vaults. So, it would seem that establishing your thesis requires only showing that *some* coins are aesthetically interesting. How would you do that? Choose several of your favorite coins and explain (give reasons) why you find them aesthetically interesting. Your explanation will consist of a detailed description of, let us say, an 1850 large cent, an 1873 three-cent piece, and a 1936 liberty standing quarter. Just as you might try to convince someone that Cézanne's *The Card Players* is an excellent work of art by pointing to the vibrant colors, the various elements of Cézanne's technique, and the relationships among the various elements of the painting—thereby explaining why *you* find it an excellent painting—you might point to the delicate lines in the liberty standing quarter, the visual symmetry of the reverse of the three-cent piece, and the strength and optimism portrayed in the figure on the large cent. By pointing to these elements, the reader might come to see these coins as works of art.

Ask yourself what you need to show in order to demonstrate that your theses are true or plausible. Use a sound deductive argument if you have good reason to believe that your reader will grant the truth of the premises, since that will *require* your reader to grant the truth of your conclusion. If there are no valid deductive arguments with premises your reader will recognize as true, construct a strong inductive argument. And be certain to recognize what is required for your argument to work. Do you need to show that *all* things of type *a* are things of type *b,* or only that *some* of them are? While it might be easy to show that some coins are aesthetically interesting, it might be impossible to show that all coins are aesthetically interesting. What is required? Why is that—and only that—required? In other words, if you focus on the claim that *some a*'s are *b*'s is sufficient to establish your thesis, you may need to provide an argument that (reasons why) the weaker claim is sufficient to establish your thesis. For example, you might need to note that *no* coin collectors consider all coins of equal aesthetic value.

If you follow this procedure, you might conclude that the body of an essay is little more than one argument followed by another, with a few additional arguments thrown in to establish that the premises of the main arguments are true. If this were so, then the body of an essay might be outlined like this:

Argument for subordinate thesis 1.

Argument for subordinate thesis 2.

Argument for the first premise of the argument for subordinate thesis 2.

Argument for subordinate thesis 3.

Sometimes such an approach is very effective. Generally, your reader would fault you for "lack of style." Clarity requires that your reader be able to follow your argument. If you do nothing but state one argument followed by another, your essay will be "choppy." At the least, you need some **transitional narrative** to take you from one argument to another. If you have just completed your argument that (some) coins are aesthetically interesting, you need something to move you smoothly to your next argument. You might include a sentence such as, "But the aesthetic value of coins is not the only reason coin collecting is worthwhile." Or, "Aesthetic considerations show that coin collecting is worthwhile, but that is not the only reason. Coin collecting is also historically interesting." Such transitional narratives smoothly move you from one argument to another, a point your reader will appreciate.

The second example is a transition narrative I call a **guidepost**. It tells your reader where you have been and where you are going. If you are writing a 500-word essay, you might believe that your reader will be able to keep the various destinations listed in your first paragraph in mind throughout the essay. As essays become longer, it becomes increasingly beneficial to tell your reader where you have been and where you are going. *Part* of this can be done by dividing your essay into sections corresponding to your subordinate theses. If you are writing a ten-page essay, introducing divisions effectively says, "This is my argument for the first subordinate thesis," "This is my argument for the second subordinate thesis," and so on. Even then, it is helpful to introduce guideposts. The first paragraph of your second section might begin with a summary of your previous argument, a statement of the subordinate thesis defended in the second section, and some indication of how the two subordinate theses are related to one another and to the main thesis. Such guideposts keep your reader focused. In a very short essay, a short piece of transitional narrative is sufficient to "slide" your reader comfortably from the argument for one subordinate thesis to the argument for another. In a long essay, guideposts not only yield smooth transitions from one topic to another, they help the forgetful reader—all readers are forgetful— remember where you have been, where you are going, and why you are taking a particular route to your destination.

Keep the Audience in Mind

Assume you have constructed an introductory paragraph in which you state your major thesis and your subordinate theses. You have constructed a series of arguments to support your subordinate theses, introduced some transitional narratives to move your reader from one point to the next, and even capped off the essay with a paragraph summarizing your conclusions. Does this mean you have successfully written an essay?

No. Your reader must understand your arguments. Your reader's interest must be maintained. Your reader must know why the topic under discussion is significant. Your reader must not be "put off" at any point in your essay.

In an argumentative essay, your objective is usually to convince your reader that your thesis is true.[6] *You must pay attention to your audience.* How sophisticated is your audience? What claims will your audience grant on first sight? Should they grant the truth of those claims? What words can you expect your audience to understand? Does your audience recognize that your *topic* is significant? What is the relationship between your thesis and that of others discussing the same topic?

Keep It Simple

For many years you have heard that one of the marks of an educated person is a large vocabulary. Let us assume that is true. Does that mean you should flaunt your superior vocabulary when writing an essay? No. The vocabulary you use should be

---

[6]There are cases in which you are your only reader, that is, cases in which you might write an essay to explore the implications of *assuming* that a statement is true. In such cases, the issues we examine in this section are of less relevance than when your essay is presented to an external audience.

appropriate for your audience. Obviously, you would not use the same words in writing an essay addressed to fourth graders that you would use in an essay addressed to your local chapter of Phi Beta Kappa. Members of Phi Beta Kappa might appreciate appeals to "incontrovertible evidence" or "indubitable truths"; elementary students would not. If the vocabulary is either too advanced or demeaning for your audience, you are guaranteed to put off your audience. But how do you decide what is appropriate?

> One of the really bad things you can do in your writing is to dress up the vocabulary, looking for long words because you're maybe a little bit ashamed of your short ones. This is like dressing up a household pet in evening clothes. The pet is embarrassed, and the person who committed this act of premeditated cuteness should be even more embarrassed. Make yourself a solemn promise right now that you'll never use "emolument" when you mean "tip". . . .
>
> —Stephen King, *On Writing: A Memoir of the Craft* (New York: Pocket Books, 2000), p. 117.

Know as much as you can about your audience. If you do not know by what audience your essay will be read, go for simplicity. Further, if you want to be understood—if you value clarity—simplicity is always a good idea. Generally, short words are better understood and understood by more people than are long words. Remember, your efforts as a writer are in vain if no one reads your essay. If your reader has to look up every other word in one of your sentences, it is likely that your essay will remain unread. So, all things being equal, go for short, common words.

The same holds for sentences. Convoluted sentences may be "impressive," but there is little reason to believe your readers will find their way through them. So, keep your sentences short. Keep them to the point. Always be certain your sentences are grammatically correct. Ungrammatical sentences will distract the reader, as will misspelled words.

Having said this, we must note the exceptions. Your words must say *exactly* what you want them to say. As Mark Twain once observed, "The difference between the almost right word and the right word . . . [is] the difference between the lightning bug and the lightning." This means that sometimes you will use a longer word rather than a shorter word, since the longer word says *precisely* what you want to say. This, however, is the exception rather than the rule. Generally, you will be more clearly and widely understood if you use shorter words.

Another exception, of course, is when you are dealing with a very sophisticated audience or perhaps when writing an essay for an instructor who places a very high value on complicated words. If your verbiage is very simplistic when addressing a

Source: Charles M. Schulz, Peanuts. *PEANUTS reprinted by permission of United Feature Syndicate, Inc.*

sophisticated audience, your reader will assume you are "talking down" to him or her and might be put off. So, knowledge of your audience increases the chances of successful communication.

There is another issue that concerns verbiage. You should *not* use **sexist language**. Sexist language does not treat members of both sexes equally. Some of your readers will find sexist language offensive. When referring to members of both sexes, use the pronoun 'one' or the construction 'he or she' rather than the word 'he'. If you are writing a long essay, you might alternate the use of 'he' and 'she'. For example, rather than writing, "Everyone must do his homework," write "Everyone must do his or her homework" or "One must do one's homework."[7] Use constructions such as "husband and wife" rather than "man and wife." Avoid racist language and any other terms that your audience might find offensive. For example, never refer to a German as a *Kraut*. Similarly, avoid **stereotypes**. A stereotype is a false, though commonly made, general claim about a certain group of people. For example, *never* write something like this: "You can understand why Dan has a hot temper, since he's a redhead." There is no evidence that redheads have tempers that are worse than those of people with other hair colors, and the assumption that they do will offend a number of your readers. An offended reader is unlikely to continue reading your essay.

And you must attend to your audience's broader linguistic sensitivities. While characters in novels might allude to male-bovine excrement, such allusions have no place in a formal paper. Linguistic crudeness is often associated with crudeness of thought. Crude language will distract many readers from the content of your argument. And the point always can be made in unoffensive language. If you write that you wouldn't do something until it's "a brisk day in a bad place,"[8] your reader will get the point—and smile at your eloquence.

Capture Your Audience's Interest

In the last section I suggested that you should start your essay with a thesis statement and an enumeration of your subordinate theses. While there should be an explicit statement of your thesis and subordinate theses early in your essay, there are times when something else should be done in the first paragraph. Assume you are going to write an essay on the role of the ghost in Shakespeare's *Hamlet*. Assume that there are two widely received but conflicting interpretations of the role of the ghost in the scholarly literature. Assume, finally, that you are going to offer a third interpretation, one that will reconcile the apparent conflicts between the two popular interpretations. If you begin by saying "In this paper I argue that . . .," your audience might assume that you are unfamiliar with the current interpretations, which might be a put off. What you might do instead is begin with a paragraph that points to the common interpretations and indicates that both cannot be true. You might begin as follows:

---

[7]Some would suggest that the locution, "Everyone must do *their* homework" is equally acceptable. The problem with the plural pronoun is that the word 'everyone' is singular, and some readers will find such a mixture of a singular pronoun and a plural modifying pronoun distracting and a mark of an uneducated person.

[8]Katie Kania, "Boat Out of Water," *Guideposts*, July 1999, p. 38.

What is the role of the ghost of Hamlet's father in Shakespeare's *Hamlet*? According to one popular interpretation, the ghost represents. . . . [Here you would have a footnote to several people championing this interpretation.] According to another, the ghost represents . . . . [Here you would have a footnote to several people championing the second interpretation.] But both interpretations cannot be correct, since . . . . Further, the first interpretation seems inconsistent with Hamlet's remark in in Act 1, Scene 1 that ". . . .," while the second interpretation seems inconsistent with Hamlet's remarks in Act 3, Scene 1 that ". . ." and that ". . . ." Is there a way these two interpretations can be reconciled with each other and with the texts of the play?

Yes. In this paper I argue that . . . .[9]

The first paragraph tells your reader what the topic is and why there is a problem in answering the question of the role of the ghost. If your reader is a student of *Hamlet,* he or she probably will be familiar with the interpretative debate. By stating your thesis in contrast with two popular interpretations, you have shown that you are an informed writer. You have set your discussion in a context with which your reader might be familiar. If the conflict between these two popular interpretations is well known, you will have generated some interest in the topic of your paper.

Should you then proceed, as is suggested above, by boldly stating your thesis? Probably not. The first interpretation was set forth by the eminent Professor Smith. The second was set forth by the distinguished Professor Jones. Here you are, Dr. Nobody, claiming to see things that neither of these highly respected scholars noticed. Academic politics requires that you, the lowly unknown scholar, be appropriately humble. So, rather than the brash, "Yes!" you might begin, "I believe there is some evidence that they can." This alternative is mild. It will not immediately offend your reader. After that, you state your subordinate theses in a similarly modest way. You might use expressions such as 'I argue', but rather than saying "I show" or "the evidence shows," you should soften the verbiage to "the texts might be taken to mean . . ." or "some evidence tends to show . . . ." Stating your theses tentatively increases the probability that your reader will continue reading.

Know Your Topic Thoroughly

When writing an argumentative essay, you are trying to show that your thesis is true. Generally, you are also trying to persuade your reader that your thesis is true. Your research should acquaint you with what scholars on the topic are generally willing to grant as "common knowledge." Common knowledge is a double-edged sword. Sometimes you will be convinced that "what everyone knows" is false. In such cases, you will need to proceed with caution. You should cite prominent scholars who hold the common view and be tentative in the tone you use to state your conflicting the-

---

[9]The author confesses to having *read Hamlet* at one time. He does not maintain that he has any understanding of the play or its various interpretations. This example is strictly for purposes of illustration.

sis. The argument for your thesis will need to be very tight.[10] You will need to provide careful arguments in support of the premises of your arguments for the thesis and the subordinate theses. You must be willing to follow the argument "down" to premises that even your opposition will grant.

At other times, you will be perfectly willing to grant what is common knowledge. In such cases, you need do little more than cite scholars who hold the common view. In such cases, to develop an argument for the common view would be pointless, and to rehearse common arguments for the common position would suggest that you do *not* know the topic well.[11] Pick your fights with care.

What should be clear from the previous two paragraphs is that *at some point* you and your audience will agree that a proposition is true. If you are writing on *Hamlet,* this point of agreement might be nothing more than that a character in the play made a certain claim.[12] If you are writing on a piece of literature in translation, there might be disagreements regarding the translation. If the seventeenth-century philosopher Descartes used the Latin term *tanquem,* should that term be translated as 'as' or as 'as if'? Does it make a difference? Why? Has anyone acknowledged the ambiguity and its importance? Such questions can be answered only if you have a thorough acquaintance with the secondary literature.

Objections and Replies

Regardless what topic you choose, someone has written on the topic and has proposed arguments that support a position contrary to yours. You should acknowledge this—it shows that you are an informed writer. But you should not only acknowledge that there are disagreements, you should reply to them. Pose objections to your own position and reply to those objections. Assume you are writing an essay on abortion. Assume that you are arguing that a woman's right to abortion exceeds any presumptive rights of the fetus. Whatever your arguments might be, there will have been a "right to lifer" who proposed a contrary argument.

Acknowledge that fact. Either state an objection that is commonly made to one element of your position and cite a number of people who have developed that argument, or quote such an objection and cite others who have proposed arguments along the same lines. *If you take the first approach, be certain to give a fair rendering of the argument. If you can think of a stronger variant on the argument*

---

[10]Your arguments should *always* be as tight as possible, but if you are defending a variant of a popular interpretation of *Hamlet,* there will be more common ground between you and your reader. At the very least, you will not need to defend as many of your premises as when you are going against a widely accepted interpretation.

[11]The exception to this is when you have an *original* argument for the common position. In such a case, you might briefly rehearse the common argument as a prologue to your own, introducing your thesis with such verbiage as, "There is an additional reason why one should accept this claim."

[12]Even *there* one might find potential disagreements. For example, it might be an issue among scholars whether the words in question were originally a part of the play. So, one must be well acquainted with the secondary literature to be certain that the presumptive data (the words in a particular edition of the play) are taken as correct.

than is generally offered, an argument that provides better reasons to accept the conclusion you oppose, *use that. Such procedures should insure that you will not be charged with the straw person fallacy.* Then take the argument apart. Show either that the premises of the argument are weak or that the conclusion does not follow even if you were to grant the truth of the premises. (Typically, you will do the former.) By showing that arguments contrary to your position will not stand up to careful scrutiny, you strengthen your own case. So, raise objections to the theses you defend and reply to them. By so doing, you will strengthen your own case.

Keep Focused

Regardless what topic you examine, regardless what thesis you defend, there will always be topics that are closely related to it. There is always a temptation to digress and discuss those topics. *Resist that temptation.* Acknowledge that there are related issues that you *do not* discuss, issues that are not directly relevant to the topic of your essay. Use a phrase such as "but to discuss this is beyond the scope of the present paper" to excuse yourself from discussing the topic.

Throughout your essay, you must remain focused on the thesis. You must determine what is and what is not relevant to establishing your thesis. Even if you are writing a *long book,* you cannot cover everything that is related to your topic, although you should cover everything that is needed to establish your thesis. Focus on your thesis. Never let your thesis become subordinate to other considerations. Be willing to say, "This is not germane to my thesis."

And Revise, and Revise, and Revise ———

Writing an essay is not something you do in one sitting. There are always arguments you did not consider. There are always ways more clearly to state your arguments. There are often grammatical issues that you might have overlooked during your first writing. You should always plan your writing so that you can subject your essay to *at least three* revisions. What does that mean? Plan your writing so that you have several days—or better, several weeks—between the time you complete your first draft and the time the essay must be given to your teacher. If your essay sits on the shelf for a few days, you will see it with different eyes when you next look at it. Anyone who has written essays knows that there are strange forces in the universe, forces which can "change" your brilliant insights into unintelligible babble in the space of three or four days. Once you have given yourself some temporal distance from your own work, you will

> How long you let your book rest—sort of like bread dough between kneadings—is entirely up to you, but I think it should be a minimum of six weeks. During this time, your manuscript will be safely shut away in a desk drawer, aging, and (one hopes) mellowing. Your thoughts will turn to it frequently, and you'll likely be tempted a dozen times or more to take it out, if only to reread some passage that seems particularly fine in your memory, something you'd like to go back to so you can re-experience what a really excellent writer you are.
>
> Resist temptation.
>
> —Stephen King, *On Writing: A Memoir of the Craft* (New York: Pocket Books, 2000), p. 211.

see it in a new way. At the least, you will see new ways in which to express your thoughts. You will see ways to make your prose clearer. You might notice that your arguments could be improved. Or, alas, you might notice that some of your arguments are fallacious or that some of your premises are false. So, you revise. You think through the topic again. Reexamine your arguments. Take the position of your opponent seriously and see if you can make the objections to your thesis stronger. Typically, you should plan to work through your own essay several times, critically examining your work each time. If you have a friend who is willing to examine your essay, allow him or her to do so. Your friend will almost certainly see things that you have missed, and then you can revise again in accordance with your friend's comments.

Writing is hard work. Take it seriously. Plan your writing projects so that you will have time to work through each draft of your essay several times. The more often you think it through, the more often you are willing to critically examine what you have said, the better the end product will be. So, do the research. Write multiple drafts. Polish. Revise. Rewrite. The more critical-thinking skills you employ in your writing, the better the end product will be.

A Checklist for Writing Essays

1. Do I have to show that my topic is significant?

2. Have I clearly and unambiguously stated my main thesis and my subordinate theses? Consistent with this, have I taken the politics of the situation into account? For example, if my thesis is contrary to common knowledge on the subject, have I stated my thesis and subordinate theses tentatively rather than boldly?

3. Have I presented arguments for my main thesis? for my subordinate theses? for the premises supporting my subordinate theses?

4. Are the premises, conclusions, and relations between premises and conclusions in my arguments clear?

5. Have I carried my arguments down to a point that the reader will acknowledge the truth of my premises?

6. Have I provided transitional narrative to move the reader smoothly from one argument to the next?

7. Have I provided guideposts so my reader knows where I have been and where I am going?

8. Have I chosen my words with my audience in mind? Is the verbiage sufficiently simple so that it will be clear to all readers? Is it sufficiently sophisticated so that no reader will take it to be condescending? Have I chosen words that are sufficiently precise to avoid ambiguities? Have I avoided sexist and racist language? Have I avoided stereotypes?

9. Is the construction of each sentence easy to follow? Are my sentences grammatically correct? Have I double-checked all my spellings? Have I followed standard styles of reference and footnotes or endnotes?

10. Have I taken measures to retain the interest of my audience?

11. Have I demonstrated that I have good working knowledge of the topic under discussion? of the issues? of the primary and secondary literature on the topic?

12. Have I raised objections to my arguments and replied to them?

13. Have I retained focus on the thesis throughout the essay? Have I been willing to acknowledge related topics that are beyond the scope of the present paper?

14. Have I sought criticisms from my peers or "experts" on the topic?

15. Have I worked through the essay at least three times, reexamining the arguments, checking the grammar, and taking each of the first thirteen of the previous issues into account?

SOLUTIONS

Solutions to the Odd-Numbered Problems

CHAPTER 1, I

1. bookmaker: a person who makes books (publisher), a person who takes bets
3. name: that by which one is called, one's reputation
5. horse: the animal, sawhorse
7. mad: angry, insane, rabid
9. mouse: a rodent, a pointing device for a computer

CHAPTER 1, II

1. It is unclear whether the lecture or the causes of cancer are in the biology building.
3. Is the topic of the book zebras in the wild, or is Juan reading the book while he is seated on zebras in the wild?
5. Was Angelica's interview in the personnel office, or is that where the computer programmer job is?
7. Was the announcement a mistake, or was the marriage a mistake?
9. Is the church going to help you with your worry, or is the church going to help kill you?

CHAPTER 1, III

1. Did he rob someone else, or did he rob himself?
3. Is this the number of (people) killed by the deer or the number of deer killed?
5. Are milk drinkers themselves turning to powder, or are milk drinkers' tastes switching from liquid milk to powdered milk?
7. Will we be invited to a funeral, or is this a piece of legislation?
9. Are the lawmen guests at a barbeque, or do they cook their guests?

CHAPTER 1, IV

1. The number of people is unclear. Is it twenty or thirty? Two hundred?
3. Is doing well receiving an A, or at least a B, or a passing grade?
5. What does it mean for an exercise to be difficult? Does it mean that it can be done in a matter of minutes? Does it mean they require little thought?
7. Is the author of the book over thirty, or over forty, or over fifty, or over sixty, or even older?
9. Does this mean Norman has a bachelor's degree, or a master's degree, or a Ph.D.? Or does it mean Norman has a degree from a prestigious university? Or does it mean Norman has accumulated a great deal (however much that might be) of

information about a particular subject or subjects, regardless of his educational background?

CHAPTER 1, V

1. The word 'liberal' is ambiguous: It can deal with either fiscal policy or social policy, and not all social liberals are fiscal liberals. The kind of liberal should be noted. 'Liberal' is also vague, since it is unclear what degree of support for either kind of policy is necessary for one to be deemed a liberal.
3. The word 'bald' is vague. How much hair-loss is necessary to be deemed bald? It might be clearer to say, "Professor Smith is developing a bald spot on the back of his head," or "Professor Smith has no hair (or virtually no hair?) on the top of his head."
5. The word 'dogs' is ambiguous: It is not clear whether George sells frankfurters or canine pets.
7. The word 'airplane' is ambiguous. Are they drones (remote-control planes) or planes that can be occupied? Either can be built from a kit. The ambiguity could be eliminated by specifying the kind of plane.
9. The word 'harmful' is vague: How dangerous does something have to be before it is harmful? The word 'health' is ambiguous: Is it harmful to your physical health, your mental health, both? Clear up the ambiguity, and then indicate what counts as being harmful to the relevant type of health.
11. 'Big man' is both ambiguous and vague. John might be physically large or socially prominent. In either case, the criteria for determining "bigness" are unclear.
13. 'Wooden' is ambiguous. It might mean that the face was literally made of wood. It might mean that the face was expressionless.
15. 'Long way' is both ambiguous and vague. The context should show whether the distance is physical, or social, or intellectual, or some other kind of distance. Depending on the kind of distance, one should be able to develop criteria for determining what would be *long*.

CHAPTER 1, VI

1. This is a verbal dispute. Merle is talking about degrees Fahrenheit, while Maud is talking about degrees Celsius.
3. This is a factual dispute. Both Jan and Jean have the facts wrong.
5. This is a verbal dispute. Jim's comparison is based on a comparison of prices unadjusted for inflation, while Jen is concerned with buying power.
7. This is a factual dispute. Juanita appeals to a moral principle and the assumed fact that by aiding victims we might save a life. Jorge appeals to a different moral principle and the fact that those who have aided victims in the past became victims themselves.
9. This is a verbal dispute. Brodie and T. S. disagree about the meaning of the term 'food court'.

CHAPTER 2, I

1. 'Glass' might be vague. It would be more precise to say "Drink at least three 8-ounce glasses of milk every day. The American Dairy Association is not neces-

sarily the best authority on how much milk you should drink daily. You might want to consult a respected authority on health.

3. There might be some vagueness in the term 'pushup': The sergeant might not count each of your attempts. *Assuming* you are in the military, your drill sergeant would have the authority to command you to do pushups.

5. The expression 'the theater' might be ambiguous—there might be several theaters. Presumably, the context of your conversation with Fred would alleviate the ambiguity. Whether Fred has the authority to make such a command is an open question.

7. 'Vegetarian' is at least ambiguous, if not vague. Some vegetarians eat neither meat nor fish nor eggs nor dairy products. Some abstain only from meat. Your ethics teacher might be an authority on this issue, *but only if* she provides sound arguments to support vegetarianism.

9. 'Love' is vague. 'Neighbor' is both ambiguous and vague. Whether the Bible is deemed authoritative is a matter of debate.

CHAPTER 2, II

1. Drive on the right side of the road.
3. Respect your roommate's possessions.
5. Vote.
7. Look after your own interests.
9. Write carefully.

CHAPTER 2, III

1. You are legally obligated not to trespass.
3. You are prudentially obligated not to take drugs. (You should not take drugs if you want to further your health.)
5. If you do not want to lose in the long run, you always should read the fine print. (You are prudentially obligated to read the fine print.)
7. If you wish to be cured of your disease, then it is in your best interest to take two pills before bedtime. (You are prudentially obligated to take two pills before bedtime.)
9. It is financially prudent always to keep two month's wages in a savings account.

CHAPTER 3, I

1. works
3. read
5. rerun
7. fan, lover
9. liar
11. state, say forcefully
13. spit
15. writing
17. selfishness
19. pen name

CHAPTER 3, II

1. car
3. rainforest, forest primaeval
5. challenged
7. pudgy, plump
9. speech
11. grace-challenged and/or mentally challenged
13. critic
15. persistent
17. comedian
19. speech

CHAPTER 3, III

1. 'Restrictive' suggests that the author is opposed to the current drinking laws.
3. 'Dangerous' and 'rot-encouraging' indicates that Avery opposes the position of the Center for Food Safety.
5. 'Bloated' means little more than "large and complex." 'Bureaucratic' has negative connotations. Ms. Dole is opposed to the size of government.
7. 'Go completely crazy' indicates that the author is opposed to at least some kinds of science and technology. The focus of concern is genetic modification of organisms.
9. 'Propaganda' shows a negative disposition toward the Global Climate Coalition.

CHAPTER 4, I

1. Who: Ben Coon, the narrator, a group of miners, and others. When: 1865. Where: Angel's Camp in the Rockies. What: Most are gathered to while away a wintry afternoon; Ben Coon is telling stories. How: The stories are not told well.
3. Who: Siddhartha. When: As he left the grove where Buddha and Govinda were. What: Siddhartha is thinking about his life and experiences. How: He's thinking deeply and seriously.
5. When: The first Monday in April, 1625. Where: Meung (in France), near the hostelry of the Frank-Meunier. Who: The townspeople. What: Running about the street and gathering weapons. How: The movements were rapid; the town appeared as if it were in a state of revolution.
7. Who: Lady Lynn, Mrs. Dent, and the narrator (Jane). What: Jane is describing the physical characteristics of the two women, their bearing, their attire, and her (Jane's) reactions to each.
9. When: Eight o'clock. Where: Stoke Poges Club. Who: Lenina and Henry (although they are little more than window dressing). What: Light was fading, the courses were closing, there were various sounds.

CHAPTER 4, II

1. The description is incomplete. The French and Indian War was the American phase of the Seven Years War between Britain and France. It occurred between 1754 and 1763.

3. There are many stories about "Honest Abe." It is likely that either the event did not happen or, if it did, that the distance was less or the amount of change greater.

5. The statement is accurate, but incomplete. It fails to mention that he was assassinated.

7. Quite possibly, it is "or what." Assuming the information is accurate, you would still want to know what the yearly fee for the card is after the first year. More importantly, you would want to know that *you* would qualify for the 4.8 percent rate and what the rate on the outstanding balance would be after the first six months. Even if those numbers were favorable, you also would want to know at precisely what time the balances on your other cards would be transferred to the new card so you could avoid paying extra interest and late fees on your current cards.

9. Since the number of miles per gallon you receive from a car depends upon a number of factors, you might question the gas mileage. The information is sufficiently complete if you know you *don't* want to buy a Volvo, or a four-door, or a car with a four-cylinder engine. If you would consider buying the car, you would want to know about at least its general condition, its mileage, and its service record.

CHAPTER 5, I

1. **My car would not start this morning.** The battery was dead.

3. **Your juries do not hang murderers.** They are afraid the man's friends will shoot them in the back, in the dark—and it is just what they would do.

5. **You managed to get hold of all this stuff.** It is all Inner Party stuff. Waiters and servants pinch things.

7. **You constantly accuse me of being the warden's friend.** Your cheeks are shaven. Your coat is brushed, your linen is clean. Someone is feeding you well. You are too poor to offer bribes. You are in the warden's quarters nearly every day.

9. The look is unmistakeable in its nostalgic appeal. Yet, well beyond its retro inspiration, this car's styling is an innovative mix of past, present, and future, melding its classic shape with a unique new-millennium influence, along with the current realities of 5-mph bumpers and side airbags. Yet, most significant of all, the New Beetle is much more than just a clever design. This VW delivers throughout. It's genuinely fun to drive. It has segment-leading safety features, as well as a surprisingly roomy interior for its class size. Plus, with a base price of under $16,000 that includes a long list of standards more typical of higher-cost models, it's an outstanding value.

    We're proud to name the Volkswagen New Beetle as *Motor Trend*'s '99 Import Car of the Year.

CHAPTER 5, III

1. Explanation. **I think Watanye liked me a good deal**, because <u>he often used to take me out alone to fish or hunt, and he was always teaching me things</u>. Also, <u>he liked to tell me stories</u>, mostly funny ones when he did not have sore lips. *'Funny ones' tells what kind of stories they were.*

3. Explanation. **Perry was held in high regard by the acting community.** Rather, <u>it was her efforts as an activist, organizer, and promoter of causes that benefited and uplifted her Broadway "family."</u>

5. Explanation. **I'm closer to my notebook computer than to some of my friends.** That may sound sick, but think about it: <u>No matter where I am, my portable PC is there to help keep track of my thoughts, to tell me jokes, to educate and entertain me. It keeps me on schedule and within my budget. And it knows when to stay out of the way too. When my buddies come over for Monday-night football, I simply slip my computer out of sight in a desk drawer.</u>

7. Description. What: Characteristics of orgiastic union contrasted to conformity.

9. Explanation. **The band almost didn't survive long enough to enjoy this moment.**

   <u>There were tumultuous times last year when Aerosmith seemed to have used up all nine lives and a few bonus rounds to boot.</u>

   (*The previous sentence is the explanans with respect to the sentence before it. It is the explanadum with respect to the following sentences.*)

   <u>Between a publicly traumatic group/manager split, the exit of one member in the throes of depression, squabbling over musical direction, a producer change, an entire scrapped album, and—most damningly and doggedly—rumors about renewed drug use, 1996 was the Year of Recording Dangerously.</u>

CHAPTER 6, I

1. Some Pontiacs are Grand Ams.
   <u>No Fords are Pontiacs.</u>
   Some Grand Ams are not Fords.

3. All laptops are computers.
   <u>Some laptops are IBM products.</u>
   Some IBM products are computers.

5. Either today is Monday or today is Tuesday.
   <u>Today is not Monday.</u>
   Today is Tuesday.

7. Dan writes books.
   <u>Sally sells seashells.</u>
   Dan writes books and Sally sells seashells.

9. If John goes to the dance, then Sallie goes to the game, and if Uma is an actress, then Dirk plays pool.

Either John goes to the dance or Uma is an actress.
Either Sallie goes to the game or Dirk plays pool.

CHAPTER 6, II

1. All cars are motorized vehicles.
   No motorcycles are cars.
   No motorcycles are motorized vehicles.
3. *Assumption for the argument: Assume your critical-thinking class meets on Monday, Wednesday, and Friday, and assume that today is Wednesday.* If it is Monday, then we have critical thinking today. It is not Monday. So, we do not have critical thinking today.
5. All unicorns are mythical animals. All mythical animals are animals that do not exist. So, some unicorns are things that do not exist.
7. Not both Abraham Lincoln and Bill Clinton were Democrats. So, Bill Clinton was not a Democrat.
9. No cats are dogs. No cats are collies. So, no collies are dogs.
11. Some Fords are not Chevrolets. Some Monte Carlos are not Fords. So, some Monte Carlos are not Chevrolets.
13. All professors are members of the campus community. All students are members of the campus community. So, all students are professors.
15. There are *two* arguments. One is valid. From the two conditional statements in the first paragraph, you may conclude, "If there had been a gun there, I naturally would have demanded what Edward was doing with a gun." The *invalid* argument is of the same form as that in question 3: If there had been a gun, then I would have seen it. There was no gun. So I didn't see it. (Or, if you use the conditional statement above that follows from what is in the first paragraph, the conclusion would be "I didn't demand what Edward was doing with a gun.") See question 3 for the counterexample.

CHAPTER 7

1. inductive generalization
3. best explanation
5. analogy
7. inductive generalization
9. best explanation

CHAPTER 8, I

1. Since Heinrich Böll won the Nobel Prize for Literature in 1972, we may conclude that his books and short stories are significant.
3. The fact that today is Friday implies that I'll have two relatively uninterrupted days to study for the test on Monday.
5. Assuming that the clock runs properly, it follows that the current time is 10:50, for the clock was set to the correct time yesterday.

7. The fact that Tom Clancy has published a new novel |means that| Jack Ryan is still "alive and well," (since) Jack Ryan is a major character in the novel.

9. (Because) the old educational wing of the church was torn down, and (since) a basement was dug, and (insofar far as) cement, bricks, and other building materials were delivered to the site, |we may conclude that| the church is building a new educational wing.

CHAPTER 8, II

1. These men are not drunk, as you imagine; (for) it is only nine in the morning. It is either an inductive argument or a deductive argument with the suppressed premise, "No one is drunk at nine in the morning," a premise which is false.

3. "I believe in a journeyman period in any profession. It was so in the Army. It was. . . ."

    This is like the Nash case above. Jones *explains* why he holds a belief by giving an argument by analogy, an inductive argument.

5. This is an argument by analogy, an inductive argument. No premise or conclusion indicators are given.

7. "Visby [is the best pastor], and I will tell you why." Kierkegaard explains why he believes that Visby is the best pastor. *Holst* might have taken Kierkegaard's *explanans* as premises supporting the claim that Visby is the best pastor.

9. |Therefore,| all should work. (First,) because it is impossible that you have *no* creative gift. (Second,) the only way to make it live and increase is to use it. (Third,) you cannot be sure that it is not a *great* gift.

    This is an inductive argument. There might be other reasons why you should work (write). For example, writing is fun.

11. Description

13. "I have always believed in the death penalty for murderers, and I still do." The author explains why he believes in the death penalty.

15. This is a deductive argument. There are no indicators. The argument is used to determine the precise reason the car will not start.

17. This is an inductive argument. No indicators are given. The *unstated* conclusion is that sexual license in Africa is at least *no greater than* in New York City. The evidence might be increased by comparative statistics regarding, perhaps, birth rates regarding single mothers.

19. This is an inductive argument—notice the analogy to golfing. No indicators are given. The conclusion is in the first sentence.

CHAPTER 9, I

1. (1) Either I'll figure out argument trees without much trouble, or I'll become perplexed. (2) I won't become perplexed. So, (3) I'll figure out argument trees without much trouble.

    (1) Either I'll figure out argument trees without much trouble, or I'll become perplexed.

    (2) I won't become perplexed.

(3) I'll figure out how to figure out argument trees without much trouble.

3. (1) Everyone who studied for an hour mastered argument trees, for (2) Angel studied for an hour and mastered argument trees. (3) Leticia studied for an hour and mastered argument trees. (4) Dimitri studied for an hour and mastered argument trees. (5) Solvig studied for an hour and mastered argument trees.

(2) Angel studied for an hour and mastered argument trees.
(3) Leticia studied for an hour and mastered argument trees.
(4) Dimitri studied for an hour and mastered argument trees.
(5) Solvig studied for an hour and mastered argument trees.
(1) Everyone who studied for an hour mastered argument trees.

5. (1) We should go to the movie, since (2) it's based on a Robert Ludlum book, (3) it stars Demi Moore, and (4) Woody Allen has a cameo appearance. Further, (5) *I'll* buy the popcorn.

(2) The movie is based on a Robert Ludlum book.
(3) The movie stars Demi Moore.
(4) Woody Allen makes a cameo appearance in the movie.
(5) [If we go to the movie,] I'll buy the popcorn.
(1) We should go to the movie.

7. (1) Everyone who goes to the movie will receive a free mask. (2) No one who receives a free mask will be able to eat popcorn. Therefore, (3) no one who goes to the movie will be able to eat popcorn.

(1) Everyone who goes to the movie will receive a free mask.
(2) No one who receives a free mask will be able to eat popcorn.
(3) No one who goes to the movie will be able to eat popcorn.

9. (1) Giralda likes sports cars. (2) Giralda is like Ackley insofar as they are both students at the same school. (3) Giralda is like Ackley insofar as they both play in the orchestra. (4) Giralda is Ackley insofar as they both water ski. (5) Giralda is like Ackley insofar as they both like to vacation on the French Riviera. We may conclude, therefore, that (6) Ackley likes sports cars.

(1) Giralda likes sports cars.

(2) Giralda is like Ackley insofar as they are both students at the same school.

(3) Giralda is like Ackley insofar as they both play in the orchestra.

(4) Giralda is Ackley insofar as they both water ski.

(5) Giralda is like Ackley insofar as they both like to vacation on the French Riviera.

(6) Ackley likes sports cars.

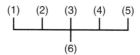

CHAPTER 9, II

1.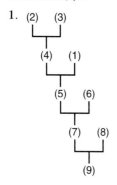

3.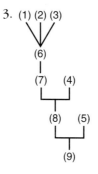

5.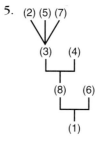

7.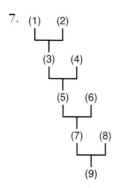

9.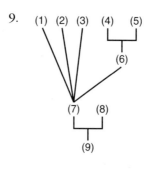

CHAPTER 9, III

1. (1) Reusable goods reduce pollution.
   (2) You should do what you can to reduce pollution.
   So, (3) you should use reusable goods.

```
(1)    (2)
 └──┬──┘
    (3)
```

3. (1) Our bodies are 70 percent water.
   (2) So, when you pollute a body of water, you may eventually pollute your own body.
   [(3)] You should not engage in activities that will pollute your own body.
   (4) So, you should not pollute bodies of water.

```
        (1)
         |
   (2)   [(3)]
    └──┬──┘
      (4)
```

5. (1) Joining Army ROTC will help fuel your desire to be the best.
   [(2)] You want to fuel your desire to be the best.
   (3) So, you should join Army ROTC.

```
  (1)   [(2)]
   └──┬──┘
     (3)
```

7. (1) Snapping out of depression is as likely as talking yourself out of a heart attack.
   (2) It is not likely that you will talk yourself out of a heart attack.
   (3) So, it is not likely you will talk yourself out of depression.
   (4) So, depression is a serious illness that needs medical attention.
   (5) So, if you or someone you know is suffering from depression, he or she should seek medical help.

```
  (1)   [(2)]
   └──┬──┘
    [(3)]
      |
     (4)
      |
     (5)
```

CHAPTER 9, IV

1. (1) Hirsch is identical with Lancaster.
   (2) Hirsch is identical with Easter.

Therefore, (3) Lancaster is identical with Easter.

3. (1) Glazer and Cuaron never discovered what *Great Expectations* is about.
   (2) Glazer and Cuaron created a movie that is so lost in its own ambiguity and obsessed with its own beauty that the emptiness at its center is crystal clear.

5. (1) He is speaking the truth.
   (2) If we are not with God, we are in hell.
   (3) That is what Mark is preaching.

7. (1) Never taste other people's cones.
   (2) If the cone tastes good, you'll wish you had it.
   (3) If it tastes bad, you'll have had the taste of something that tastes bad.
   (4) If it doesn't taste either good or bad, you won't have missed anything.
   [(5) Either the cone will taste good, or it will taste bad, or it will taste neither good nor bad.]
   [(6) Either you'll wish you had it, or you'll have had the taste of something that tastes bad, or you won't have missed anything.]
   [(7) Each of these alternatives is a reason not to taste other people's cones.]

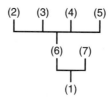

9. (1) Swine are miraculously efficient converters of grain to meat.
   (2) Swine help farmers hold grain off the market until its price improves.
   (3) Grains seldom fetch their cost of production.
   (4) A hog's fatal walk helps keep food affordable and agriculture solvent.

11. (1) Equity markets should benefit from steady or declining rates, and earning will drive divergence in the market.
    (2) As currency devaluations make American goods more expensive, large multinational companies will likely find reduced demand for their products in Asia.
    (3) Less expensive imports from Asia will put pressure on American companies to lower their prices on goods such as automobiles.
    (4) Small and medium-sized companies would benefit.
    (5) Lower prices for imported goods increase real disposable income.

13. (1) I am moved.
    (2) To move is to stir.
    (3) To be valiant is to stand.
    (4) If thou art moved, thou runn'st away.
    (5) A dog of that house shall move me to stand.
    (6) I will take the wall of any man or maid of Montague's.
    (7) That shows thee a weak slave.
    (8) The weakest goes to the wall.
    (9) Women are the weaker vessels.
    (10) Women are thrust to the wall.
    (11) I push Montague's men from the wall and thrust his maids to the wall.

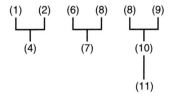

15. (1) She and her grooms and her maid had passed by in the forest two days previously.
    (2) Adelais must have arrived here that same day.
    (3) They would have no need to halt for a night between Chenet and Elford.

(4) On horseback the distance was easy.

[(5) Adalais is the woman's son.]

(6) She must already have seen and talked with her son.

(7) What she had to communicate to him now, as soon as he returned from riding, might well have to do with whatever was new this day at the manor of Elford.

(8) Nothing was new but the arrival of the two monks from Shrewsbury, and their reason for being here, a reason she would interpret with discretion for his ears.

[(9) She must have communicated the reason the monks from Shrewsbury were there.]

(10) Adelais had been here at Elford when his sister died at Hales, for the world's ears—and her brother also?—of a fever.

(11) That must be all he had ever known of it, a simple, sad death, such as may happen in any household, even to one in the bloom of youth.

(12) The woman was strong and resolute

(13) The woman would never have let her son into the secret of his sister's death.

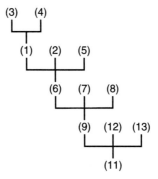

17. (1) There have always been apostles of peace and men who have risked a bold and quotable word against war.

(2) The poet Opitz, who during the Thirty Years' War—how vainly, we know—attempted to foment peace.

(3) Old Man Bebel gave an antiwar speech in the spring of 1913.

(4) In religious songs and philosophical treatises peace has been sung, longed for, spun into allegory, and meditated upon *ad nauseam*.

(5) No one ever tried seriously to resolve the conflicts of human society while forswearing the categories of masculine thinking.

(6) Nothing was ever accomplished beyond protestation of peaceful intent and sophistical distinctions between just and unjust wars.

(7) Crusaders have always managed to massacre people in the name of brotherly love.

(8) Wars of liberation are still very much in vogue.

(9) The principle of the free market has meant undernourishment for millions of people.

(10) Hunger, too, is war.

19. (1) We've been making mesh shirts for about fifteen years now.
    (2) Fifteen years is long enough to perfect everything—from buttons to bottom vents and all seams in between.
    [(3) We have had time to perfect everything—from buttons to bottom vents and all seams in between.]
    (4) Most of our competitors use single-piqué mesh rather than our airier, more luxurious double-piqué.
    (5) Some of our competitors use fabric softeners and get stiff and "boardy" after a wash or two.
    (6) Some of our competitor's shirts fade easily.
    (7) All but one of our competitors have chosen a less expensive, less stylish placket than we have.
    (8) None of our competitors have our same clean-finished "treetop" side vents.
    (9) Our shirts have elegant single-needle topstitching.
    [(10) Our competitor's shirts are inferior to ours.]
    (11) Some of our competitors ask you to pay more than twice our price.
    (12) We are confident we offer you the best mesh at any price.

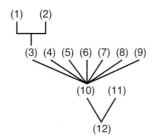

CHAPTER 10

1. (O1) She was in the right place at the right time. (O2) Observation conditions were far from ideal. (O3) Assuming Solvig has good eyesight, or that her vision is corrected by glasses, we may assume she had the appropriate technology to make the observation. (O4) Bigfoot sightings are fairly rare—the existence of Bigfoot is doubtful. If Solvig knows this, she probably would not claim to have seen Bigfoot. O5 is an open question. In any case, given O2 and O4, she should not conclude that she saw Bigfoot, indeed, given O2, she might be well advised not even to claim to have seen a person or something like a person.

3. (O1) I was in a position to see the garden. (O2) Assuming it was early in the morning, the lighting might have been less than ideal. O2 suggests that I should

not draw any conclusions. (O3) Since I'm nearsighted and was not wearing my glasses, I have little reason to believe what I "see." (O4) Given that there are ordinances against keeping livestock in the city, it makes little sense to say that I saw an ox. Further, in most places, oxen are fairly rare. O5 remains an open question. All in all, I probably should not conclude that I saw an ox.

5. Assume the convention was televised and Natalie watched the convention. Assuming she has normal eyesight, it is plausible to suggest that she saw Horace at the convention. The probability might be increased if Horace always wore a red coat, and the person that looks like Horace was wearing a red coat. It might be increased further if Horace was one of the speakers at the convention, which would virtually assure that Natalie had a good look at the person she identified as Horace.

7. Night vision goggles are useful on a moonless night. Bob apparently knows how to use this technology, since he has gone hunting with night vision goggles in the past and (apparently) has been successful. Whether or not I would be willing to go hunting with Bob probably has more to do with my belief that he is a careful hunter than with questions of observation conditions. Assuming he is a careful hunter, I would go along.

9. If Sharon is one of my fellow BIO101 students, I would not accept her conclusions. O3 is doubtful. While she has the appropriate technology, there is some question whether she knows how to use it. Further, (O4) she almost certainly does not have the appropriate background knowledge that would allow her to correctly interpret what she sees.

11. There is a problem with O1. While under ordinary conditions Jan might have the background necessary to identify the characteristics of the person (O4), and while under ordinary conditions the general observation conditions might have been favorable, here the conditions are questionable. If Jan saw the person "out of the corner of his eye," he did not get a good look at the person. Even if Jan was knocked down by the person, everything happened very quickly, and it is unclear that Jan could have gotten a good enough look at the person to provide such a detailed description. So, Jan's story should be believed only if it is consistent with the descriptions of other witnesses.

13. O1 suggests that Felicia did not get a good look at the object, certainly not a good enough look at the object to positively determine that it was her neighbor's car. It could very well have been a red car that was not Fred's.

15. Seeing Sydney at the concert is consistent with various things Carter knows about Sydney and Jorge (O4). The fact that Carter has 20-20 vision tends to strengthen the case. But if she *seemed* to see Sydney just before the lights dimmed, the observation conditions were not ideal (O2). So, there might be some reason to believe that Carter saw Sydney at the concert, but before you believe Sydney was there, you might want to do a little more investigating.

CHAPTER 11, I

1. You might want to check with your professor to see what the reputation of G. I. M. Smart is among Goethe scholars. You might want to read a number of reviews of the book. You also might want to check a citation index: If the book is cited

by numerous other experts—whether or not they agree with the author—there would be some reason to believe that Smart's work should be taken seriously.

3. The problem is that both statements cannot be true—it has nothing to do with testimony. The statements are *contraries*: it is possible that both are false—Duracell and Energizer might be equally good—but both claims cannot be true.

5. (a) Jordan has a lot of experience with basketball shoes (T1). So, he should be a reliable source. But (b) Jordan is offering a paid endorsement, so there could be a conflict of interest.

7. Given his reputation and his long-term position in the community, there is reason to believe that Dr. K. is generally reliable (T1). As a medical doctor, he has the background and training necessary to make the diagnosis even if he has never diagnosed the disease before (T2). He stands to lose in terms of reputation if he is wrong (T4), and he will gain nothing if he is right—he will be paid in any case (T2). There is no reason to believe that the doctor is biased (T6).

9. There is hearsay evidence—evidence passed from person to person, which might change in the passing. It is inconsistent with other evidence you have regarding Joan's romantic intentions (T5). So, you have good reasons to question John's claims.

11. Dr. Jones has a conflict of interests (T3): If the drug is approved, he will stand to gain financially and perhaps in prestige. This is probably sufficient to call into question the positive aspects of Dr. Jones's expertise (T2).

13. While Twain had no conflict of interest (T3), he also had no training in medicine (T2). Other sources tend to suggest that Scotch and toothache are not causally related (T5). So, Twain probably should not be believed regarding the medicinal virtues of Scotch.

15. He has training and background in the general area, but his previous work was not on Descartes, so T2 probably comes to a draw. If Dr. F. is wrong, he will stand to lose in terms of prestige in his area (T4). The fact that Dr. F. will gain financially from the book seems to make little difference: If he had published a book in some other area, the same effects would occur (T3). The fact that Dr. F's work conflicts with that of others might count against it (T5), but the arguments would need to be carefully examined on both sides to reach a conclusion. And he is "biased" in the same way that virtually any scholar is biased: His hypothesis leads him to look at various pieces of evidence rather than others. All in all, it is not clear whether the question can be answered.

17. This is hearsay evidence. So, it is not a generally reliable source.

19. The main question is whether email from a person who is not an authority on computer problems should be taken seriously (T2). There is also an internal problem. What is described is a Trojan horse, not a virus, although that error might not be significant. The main problem is that the source probably does not have sufficient background to judge whether the message she received should be taken at face value.

CHAPTER 11, II

1. You probably have good reason to believe John. The observation conditions he reports were favorable. He says he observed the pink elephant with both the

It was taken outside the Miss Marquette Supper Club, the former site of the Pink Elephant Supper Club, in Marquette, Iowa. (Photograph by Dana Flage.)

sense of sight and the sense of touch. He was where he said the pink elephant was. And it is consistent with the philosophers' claim that there are not pink elephants to assert that there are pink elephant statues. Since John is generally honest and does *not* behave in the way he typically does when he is trying to "pull the wool over your eyes," he probably should be believed. On the other hand, if his testimony were not sufficient, showing you a black and white photograph, such as that above, would not guarantee that he had seen a *pink* elephant. And had John shown you a color photograph of a pink elephant, it would not bolster his story, since it is possible that the picture was "touched up."

3. In the fifty-eighth row, without binoculars, John and Joe do not have ideal observation conditions. Add to that the fact that they apparently are midgets, and it is likely that they would not be able to see the actions on the field if the rest of the crowd came to its feet. Finally, they were not paying attention to the game. So, they probably are not a good source of testimony on the "big play."

5. Elwood was at the right place at the right time, but Elwood probably had been having a bit to drink, so observation conditions were not ideal. There is the problem that, as experience suggests, six-foot, three-and-a-half-inch talking rabbits are not commonly found leaning against lampposts.

CHAPTER 13

1. All (cats) are <u>pets</u>. **A** False.

3. Some (horses) are <u>palominos</u>. **I** True.

5. No (mutts) are <u>purebred Afghan hounds</u>. **E** True.

7. All (teachers at this school) are <u>people born before 2000</u>. **A** True.

9. No (aardvarks that occasionally enjoy a tasty ant) are <u>kangaroos</u>. **E** True.

11. All products that are featured in infomercials are products that are useful around the house. **A** False.

13. Some insomniac is a person who would like to have a full night's sleep. **I** True.

15. Some plays by William Shakespeare are not tragedies. **O** True.

17. Some light bulb is a light bulb that has lasted more than three years. **I** True.

19. All people who have robbed a bank are people who have been caught. **A** False.

21. All people who write in the margins of library books are people who can expect a cross word from the librarian if they are caught. **A** True.

23. Some person who is not President of the United States is a person who sells books in London. **I** True.

25. All people who understand everything that's in this chapter are people who are prepared for the next chapter. **A** True (we hope).

CHAPTER 14, I

1. All **collies** are dogs, so no **collies** are cats, since no cats are dogs.

3. No **pampered pets** are portly pooches, since some portly pooches are massive mastiffs, and all massive mastiffs are **pampered pets**.

5. Some **wise wombats** are wretched rascals, so no **wise wombats** are portly pooches, since no portly pooches are wretched rascals.

7. Some **fastidious felines** are ambitious Angoras, and some ambitious Angoras are cantankerous kitties, so some **fastidious felines** are cantankerous kitties.

9. All ferocious fruit flies are preposterously persistent pests. Therefore, no **dastardly dangerous dogs** are preposterously persistent pests, because some ferocious fruit flies are not **dastardly dangerous dogs.**

CHAPTER 14, II

1. Some cows are pets.
   Some Herefords are pets.
   All Herefords are cows.

3. All spiders are eight-legged animals.
   No aardvarks are spiders.
   Some aardvarks are not eight-legged animals.

5. Some studious stenographers are not practitioners of pecuniary peccadilloes.
   All serious scribes are studious stenographers.
   Some serious scribes are practitioners of pecuniary peccadilloes.

7. All attenuated attendants are folks who have wasted away.
   <u>No hefty humans are attenuated attendants.</u>
   Some hefty humans are folks who have wasted away.

9. Some restive rodents are not solitary sheep.
   <u>Some restive rodents are not gregarious goats.</u>
   No gregarious goats are solitary sheep.

11. Some lecherous leopards are animals that talk turkey with turtles.
    <u>Some animals that talk turkey with turtles are not elegant elephants.</u>
    Some elegant elephant is not a lecherous leopard.

13. All tumultuous tigers are cool cats.
    <u>No perplexed primate is a cool cat.</u>
    Some perplexed primate is not a tumultuous tiger.

15. Some boisterous buffalo are animals that elicit emotions from elegant elk.
    <u>No cantankerous carnivore is a boisterous buffalo.</u>
    All cantankerous carnivores are animals that elicit emotions from elegant elk.

17. Some burnished brass is not tarnished titanium.
    <u>No amalgamated aluminum is tarnished titanium.</u>
    Some amalgamated aluminum is not burnished brass.

19. Some malicious madmen are writers of exasperating exercises to torment tenacious tutees.
    <u>No malicious madmen are awful authors.</u>
    Some awful authors are writers of exasperating exercises to torment tenacious tutees.

CHAPTER 15, I

1. Invalid, violates rules 2, 4
3. Valid
5. Invalid, violates rules 2, 4
7. Invalid, violates rules 3, 4
9. Valid
11. Invalid, violates rules 3, 6
13. Invalid, violates rules 2, 3, 4, 6
15. Invalid, violates rules 3, 5
17. Invalid, violates rules 2, 4
19. Invalid, violates rules 2, 4
21. Invalid, violates rules 3, 5
23. Invalid, violates rules 2, 5
25. Valid
27. Invalid, violates rules 3, 4, 5, 6
29. Invalid, violates rules 3, 4, 5, 6

CHAPTER 15, II

1. Invalid, violates rule 1: equivocation on 'cool cats'
3. Invalid, violates rules 2 and 5.

5. Invalid; it either violates rule 1 (equivocation on 'anteaters') or it violates rules 2 and 6. In any case, the conclusion is false.
7. Invalid, violates rules 2 and 6
9. Invalid, violates rules 3 and 4

CHAPTER 15, III

1. No C^D are F^D.
   <u>All L^D are F^U.</u>
   Some L^U are not C^D.
      Invalid, violates rules 4 and 6
3. No D^D are C^D.
   <u>No C^D are A^D.</u>
   All A^D are D^U.
      Invalid, violates rules 2, 3, and 5
5. All C^D are R^U.
   <u>All C^D are M^U.</u>
   No M^D are R^D.
      Invalid, violates rules 2, 3, 4, and 5
7. All P^D are M^U.
   <u>All M^D are S^U.</u>
   Some S^U are P^U.
      Invalid, violates rules 3 and 6
9. No P^D are M^D.
   <u>No B^D are M^D.</u>
   Some B^U are P^U.
      Invalid, violates rules 2, 3, 4, 5, and 6
11. No A^D are M^D.
    <u>Some D^U are not M^D.</u>
    Some D^U are not A^D.
      Invalid, violates rules 2 and 5
13. Invalid, violates rule 1 (equivocation on 'bookmakers')
15. All C^D are G^U.
    <u>Some C^U are E^U.</u>
    Some E^U are G^U.
      Valid
17. Some P^U are not L^U.
    <u>All A^D are P^U.</u>
    Some A^U are L^U.
      Invalid, violates rules 2, 3, 4, and 5
19. Some P^U are G^U.
    <u>Some G^U are not A^D.</u>
    No A^D are P^D.
      Invalid, violates rules 2, 3, and 6

CHAPTER 16, I

1.

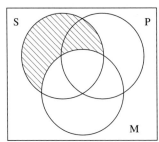

3.

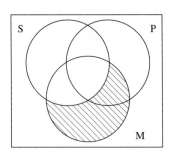

5.

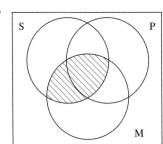

7.

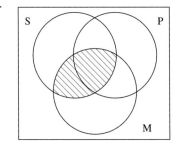

9.

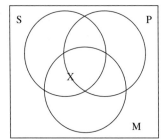

If another premise shaded either of the two areas where the S and M circles overlap, the X would be forced into the unshaded area.

11.

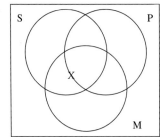

If another premise shaded either of the two areas where the S and M circles overlap, the X would be forced into the unshaded area.

13.

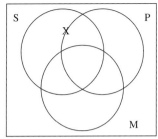

If another premise shaded either of the area that is P but not M, or the area that is S but not M, the X would be forced into the unshaded area.

15.

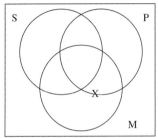

If another premise shaded either the area that is P but not S, or the area that is M but not P, the X would be forced into the unshaded area.

CHAPTER 16, II

1.

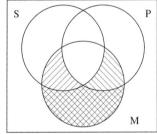

Invalid

3.

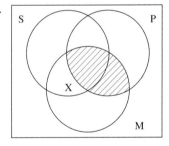

Valid

5.

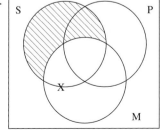

Invalid

7.

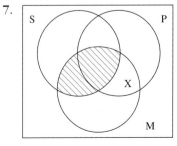

Invalid

9.

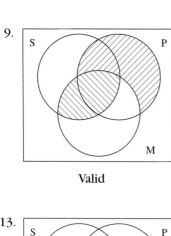

Valid

11.

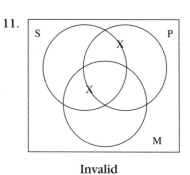

Invalid

13.

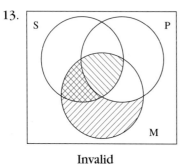

Invalid

15.

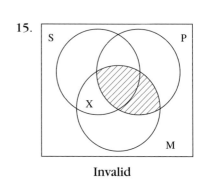

Invalid

17.

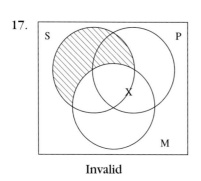

Invalid

19.

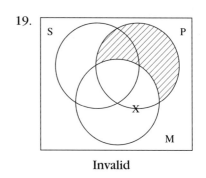

Invalid

21.

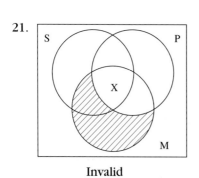

Invalid

23.

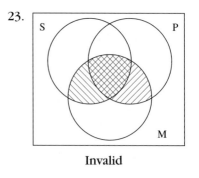

Invalid

25.

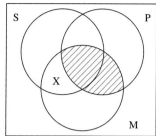

Valid

27.

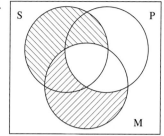

Invalid

29.

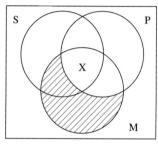

Invalid

CHAPTER 16, III

1. Invalid: equivocation on 'cool cats'

3.

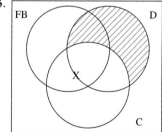

Invalid

5. Invalid: equivocation on 'anteater'
    or

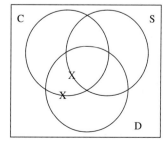

7.

Invalid

9.

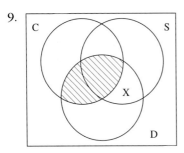

Invalid

CHAPTER 16, IV

Go to the solutions for Chapter 15, III to examine the arguments in standard form.

1.

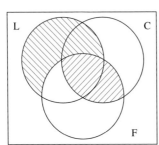

Invalid

3.

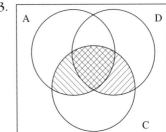

Invalid

5.

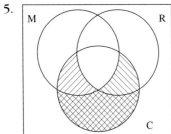

Invalid

7.

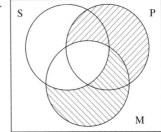

Invalid

9.

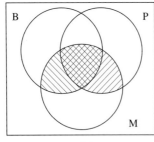

Invalid

11.

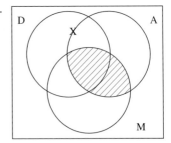

Invalid

13. Invalid: equivocation on 'bookmaker'

15.

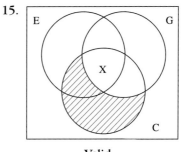

Valid

17.

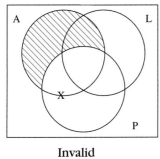

Invalid

19.

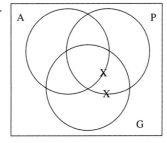

Invalid

CHAPTER 17

1. Some stingy people are not poor. The premise is true.

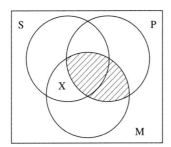

3. All spiders are arachnids. The premise is true.

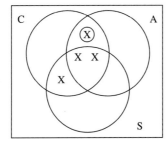

5. All Methodists are Lutherans. The premise is false.

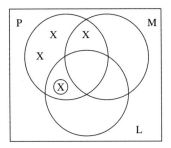

7. Some utterly perplexed persons are players, or some players are utterly perplexed persons. The premise is true.

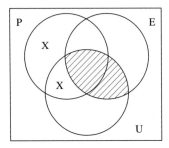

9. All Presbyterians are Protestants. The premise is true.

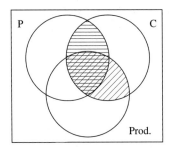

11. Nothing follows. Violates rules 2 and 5.

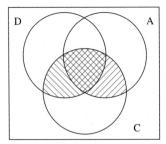

13. All aardvarks are mammals. The premise is true.

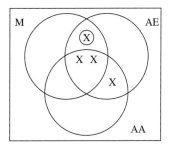

15. All dogs are schnauzers. The premise is false.

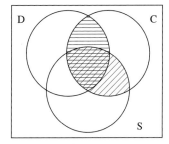

17. No confused people are students, or no students are confused people. The premise is false.

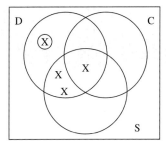

19. All confused people are aardvarks. The premise is false.

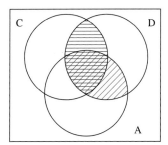

21. All people who do not work fewer than fifteen hours per day are authors. The premise is false.

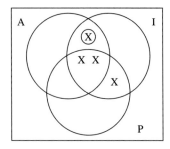

23. Nothing follows. Violates rule 2.

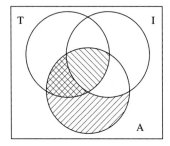

25. No premise. Violates rule 4.

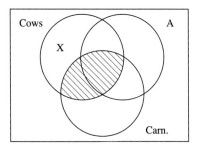

27. No conclusion. Violates rules 2 and 6.

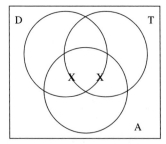

29. Some jazz-lovers are classical music buffs or Some classical music buffs are jazz-lovers. The premise is true.

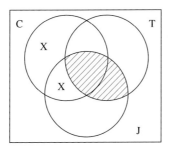

31. No premise. Violates rules 4 and 6.

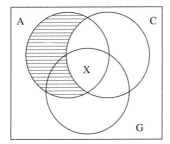

33. All trombone-players are musicians. The premise is true.

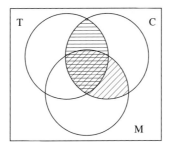

35. Some singers are not trumpeters. The premise is true.

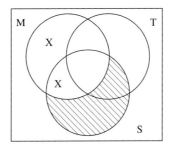

37. No premise. Violates rule 3.

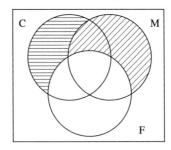

39. Some physicists are not alchemists. The premise is true.

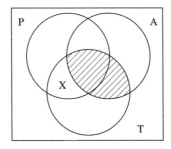

CHAPTER 18, I

1. False
3. False
5. False
7. Nothing
9. True
11. Nothing
13. Nothing
15. True

CHAPTER 18, II

1. Nothing
3. Nothing
5. Nothing
7. Nothing
9. Nothing
11. Nothing
13. Nothing
15. Nothing

CHAPTER 18, III

1. False
3. False

5. False
7. False
9. True
11. True
13. True
15. True

CHAPTER 18, IV

1. False
3. Nothing
5. Nothing
7. True
9. True
11. Nothing
13. True
15. Nothing

CHAPTER 19, I

1. No W^D are I^D.
   <u>All A^D are I^U.</u>
   No A^D are W^D.   Valid

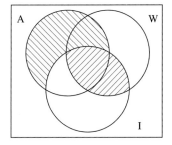

3. Some S^U are not C^D.
   <u>Some C^U are not D^D.</u>
   Some D^U are not S^D.   Invalid, rules 3, 4, 5, and 6

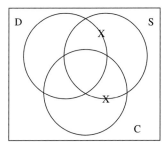

5. All F^D are T^U.
   Some P^U are not T^D.
   Some P^U are not F^D.   Valid

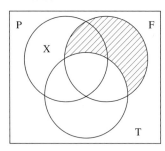

7. Invalid, rule 1: equivocation on 'viper' ('Viper').
9. Some L^U are T^U.
   Some M^U are L^U.
   Some M^U are T^U Invalid, rules 2 and 6

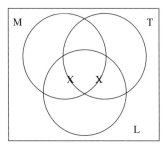

   Some L^U are T^U.
   Some M^U are not L^D.
   Some M^U are T^U.   Invalid, rules 5 and 6

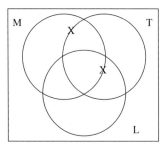

CHAPTER 19, II

In each case there are other ways to reword the premises and conclusion to yield a valid syllogism. So, if your answer isn't here, see whether conversion, obversion, and contraposition will yield the given form of the syllogism.

1. No dogs that do tricks^D are kangaroos^D.
   Some kangaroos^U are zoo animals^U.
   Some zoo animals^U are not dogs that do tricks^D.

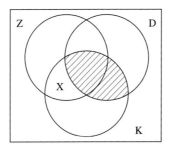

3. No scholars^D are cowards^D.
   (Some) John^U is a coward^U.
   _____
   (Some) John^U is not a scholar^D.

No scholars^D are cowards^D.
(All) John[s]^D are cowards^U.
_____
(No) John[s]^D are scholars^D.

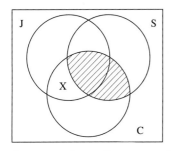

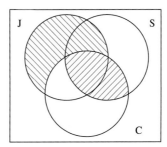

5. Some racehorses^U are not winners at Belmont^D.
   All racehorses^D are thoroughbreds^U.
   _____
   Some thoroughbreds^U are not winners at Belmont^D.

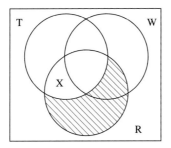

7. All misers^D are hoarders^U.
   Some counting-house executives^U are misers^U.
   _____
   Some counting-house executives^U are hoarders^U.

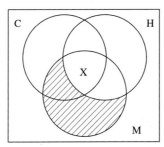

9. All humane persons^D are nice persons^U.
   All nurses^D are humane persons^U.
   All nurses^D are nice persons^U.

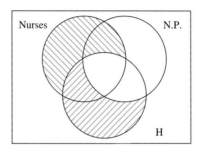

11. All people who cow to authority^D are people who are weak of will^U.
    Some prison inmates^U are not people who are weak of will^D.
    Some prison inmates^U are not people who cow to authority^D.

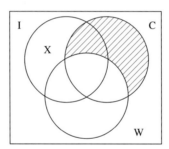

13. All people who freely and willingly do these problems^D are logicians^U.
    Some workers^U are people who freely and willingly do these problems^U.
    Some workers^U are logicians^U.

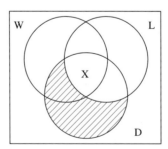

15. All times when I have a writ of *habeas corpus* for Mrs. H^D are times when Mrs. H. must be brought out^U.
    (All/Some) This time$^{D/U}$ is a time when I have a writ of *habeas corpus* for Mrs. H^U.
    (All/Some) This time$^{D/U}$ is a time when Mrs. H. must be brought out^U.

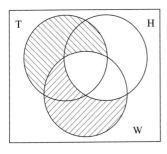

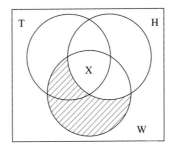

CHAPTER 19, III

If your answer is not below, see if it is equivalent to one of those below (convert, obvert, contrapose).

1. All cats^D are mammals^U.
   (No) This cat^D is a tabby^D.
   ___
   (No) This tabby^D is a mammal^D.
   Invalid, all universals: rules 2, 3; particular minor and conclusion: rules 3, 4.

   All cats^D are mammals^U.
   (Some) This cat^U is not a tabby^D.
   ___
   (Some) This tabby^U is not a mammal^D.

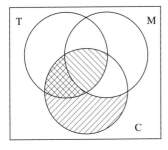

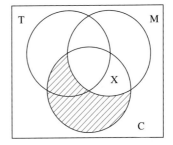

3. Invalid: rule 1, equivocation: 'Democrats' and 'democrats'
5. Some rats^U are not cats^D.
   No dogs^D are rats^D.
   ___
   No dogs^D are cats^D.
   Invalid: rules 5 and 6

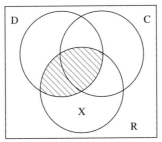

7. Invalid: rule 1, equivocation: 'Lincoln' the President and 'Lincoln' the car.
9. All Roman bridges^D are stone bridges^U.
   Some bridges in Koblenz^U are stone bridges^U.
   ___
   Some bridges in Koblenz^U are Roman bridges^U.
   Invalid: rules 2, 3

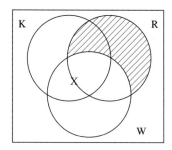

11. All news watchers[D] are people interested in current events[U].
    All presidential candidates[D] are people interested in current events[U].
    All presidential candidates[D] are news watchers[U].
    Invalid: rules 2, 3

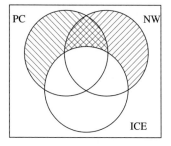

13. All lies[D] are pieces of fiction[U].
    All pieces of fiction[D] are works of art[U].
    All works of art[D] are lies[U].
    Invalid: rules 3, 4

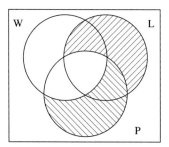

15. All murderers[D] are criminals[U].
    No soldiers[D] are criminals[D].
    No soldiers[D] are murderers[D].
    Valid

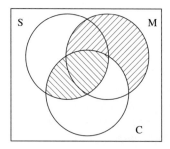

CHAPTER 19, IV

1. (1) All my tin things are saucepans.
   (3) No saucepans are useful things.
   No useful things are tin things.
   (2) All presents from you are useful things.
   No presents from you are tin things.
3. (3) No nice things are wholesome things.
   (1) All puddings are nice things.
   No puddings are wholesome things.
   (2) (All) This dish are puddings.
   (No) This dish is a wholesome thing. (This dish is unwholesome.)
5. (3) No ostriches are things that live on mince pies.
   (1) All birds that are nine feet high are ostriches.
   No birds that are nine feet high are things that live on mince pies.
   (4) All birds of mine are birds that are nine feet high.
   No birds of mine are things that live on mince pies.
   (2) All birds in this aviary are birds of mine.
   No birds in this aviary are things that live on mince pies.
7. (1) All interesting poems are poems popular among people of taste.
   (4) No affected poems are poems popular among people of taste.
   No affected poems are interesting poems.
   (2) All modern poems are affected poems.
   No modern poems are interesting poems.
   (5) All poems on the subject of soap-bubbles are modern poems.
   No poems on the subject of soap-bubbles are interesting poems.
   (3) All poems of *yours* are poems on the subject of soap-bubbles.
   No poems of *yours* are interesting poems.
9. (4) No animals that kick are animals easy to swallow.
   (1) All excitable animals are animals that kick.
   No excitable animals are animals easy to swallow.
   All nonbuffaloes are excitable animals.
   No nonbuffaloes are animals easy to swallow.
   (3) All animals that cannot toss one over a gate are nonbuffaloes.
   No animals that cannot toss one over a gate are easy to swallow.
   (5) All hornless animals are animals that cannot toss one over a gate.
   No hornless animals are animals easy to swallow.
   (2) All donkeys are hornless animals.
   No donkeys are animals easy to swallow.

CHAPTER 20

1. $D \lor C$ False
3. $D \rightarrow I$ False
5. $\sim(H \rightarrow C)$ False
7. $M \rightarrow G$ False

9. H → (P → C) True
11. (D ↔ N) → B True
13. S ∨ (N ↔ M) True
15. [(P & N) → C] ∨ A True
17. [(~P & ~S) → T] → ~D or [~(P) ∨ S) → T] → ~D False
19. (L → M) ∨ (J → ~B) True

CHAPTER 21, I

1.

p	q	p & q	p	
T	T	T	T	
T	F	F	T	
F	T	F	F ✓	
F	F	F	F ✓	Valid

3.

p	q	p → q	~q	~p	
T	T	T	F	F ✓	
T	F	F	T	F ✓	
F	T	T	F	T	
F	F	T	T	T	Valid

5.

p	q	p ∨ q	p	~q	
T	T	T	T	F ✗	Invalid
T	F	T	T	T	
F	T	T	F	F ✓	
F	F	F	F	T	

7.

p	q	p ∨ q	~q	p	
T	T	T	F	T	
T	F	T	T	T	
F	T	T	F	F ✓	
F	F	F	T	F ✓	Valid

9.

p	q	r	p →	(p & q)	q → r	~r	→	~p	
T	T	T	T	T	T	F	T	F	
T	T	F	T	T	F	T	F	F ✓	
T	F	T	F	F	T	F	T	F	
T	F	F	F	F	T	T	F	F ✓	
F	T	T	T	F	T	F	T	T	
F	T	F	T	F	F	T	T	T	
F	F	T	T	F	T	F	T	T	
F	F	F	T	F	T	T	T	T	Valid

11.

p	q	r	(~p ∨ q)	&	(q→r)	p→r	
T	T	T			T	T	
T	T	F			F	F	✓
T	F	T			F	T	
T	F	F			F	F	✓
F	T	T			T	T	
F	T	F			F	T	
F	F	T			T	T	
F	F	F			T	T	Valid

13.

p	q	r	s	(p→q)	&	(r→s)	p∨q	r∨s	
T	T	T	T		T		T	T	
T	T	T	F		F		T	T	
T	T	F	T		T		T	T	
T	T	F	F		T		T	T	✓ Invalid
T	F	T	T		F		T	T	
T	F	T	F		F		T	T	
T	F	F	T		F		T	T	
T	F	F	F		F		T	F	✓
F	T	T	T		T		T	T	
F	T	T	F		F		T	T	
F	T	F	T		T		T	T	
F	T	F	F		T		T		
F	F	T	T		T		F	T	
F	F	T	F		F		F	T	
F	F	F	T		T		F	T	
F	F	F	F		T		F	F	✓

15.

p	q	r	s	(p→q)	&	(r→s)	~q ∨ ~s	~p ∨ ~r	
T	T	T	T		T		F F F	F F F	✓
T	T	T	F		F		F T T	F F F	✓
T	T	F	T		T		F F F	F T T	
T	T	F	F		T		F T T	F T T	
T	F	T	T		F		T T F	F F F	✓
T	F	T	F		F		T T T	F F F	✓
T	F	F	T		F		T T F	F T T	
T	F	F	F		F		T T T	F T T	
F	T	T	T		T		F F F	T T F	
F	T	T	F		F		F T T	T T F	
F	T	F	T		T		F F F	T T T	
F	T	F	F		T		F T T	T T T	
F	F	T	T		T		T T F	T T F	
F	F	T	F		F		T T T	T T F	
F	F	F	T		T		T T F	T T T	
F	F	F	F		T		T T T	T T T	Valid

CHAPTER 21, II

1. A → C
    C → L
    A ∨ L /∴ C

A	C	L	A → C	C → L	A ∨ L	C
T	T	T	T	T	T	T
T	T	F	T	F	T	T
T	F	T	F	T	T	F ✓
T	F	F	F	T	T	F ✓
F	T	T	T	T	T	T
F	T	F	T	F	F	T
F	F	T	T	T	T	F ✓ Invalid
F	F	F	T	T	F	F ✓

3. (A → C) & (C → L)
    ~L /∴ ~A

A	C	L	(A → C)	&	(C → L)	~L	~A
T	T	T	T	T	T	F	F ✓
T	T	F	T	F	F	T	F ✓
T	F	T	F	F	T	F	F ✓
T	F	F	F	F	T	T	F ✓
F	T	T	T	T	T	F	T
F	T	F	T	F	F	T	T
F	F	T	T	T	T	F	T
F	F	F	T	T	T	T	T Valid

5. (A & ~C) ↔ L /∴ (A → L) & (~L → C)

A	C	L	(A & ~C)	↔ L	(A → L)	&	(~L → C)
T	T	T	F F	F	T	T	F T
T	T	F	F F	T	F	F	T T ✓ Invalid
T	F	T	T T	T	T	T	F T
T	F	F	T T	F	F	F	T F ✓
F	T	T	F F	F	T	T	F T
F	T	F	F F	T	T	T	T T
F	F	T	F T	F	T	T	F T
F	F	F	F T	T	T	F	T F ✓

7. H → [A → (C & L)]
    H & ~A /∴ ~C

H	A	C	L	H → [A	→	(C & L)]	H &	~A	~C	
T	T	T	T	T	T	T	F	F	F	Invalid
T	T	T	F	F	F	F	F	F	F ✓	
T	T	F	T	F	F	F	F	F	T	
T	T	F	F	F	F	F	F	F	T	
T	F	T	T	T	T	T	T	T	F ✓	
T	F	T	F	T	T	F	T	T	F ✓	
T	F	F	T	T	T	F	T	T	T	
T	F	F	F	T	T	F	T	T	T	
F	T	T	T	T	T	T	F	F	F ✓	
F	T	T	F	T	F	F	F	F	F ✓	
F	T	F	T	T	F	F	F	F	T	
F	T	F	F	T	F	F	F	F	T	
F	F	T	T	T	T	T	F	T	F ✓	
F	F	T	F	T	T	F	F	T	F ✓	
F	F	F	T	T	T	F	F	T	T	
F	F	F	F	T	T	F	F	T	T	

9. S → (A ∨ J)
   ~A & P   /∴   S → (J & P)

S	A	J	P	S →	(A ∨ J)	~A	& P	S →	(J & P)	
T	T	T	T	T	T	F	F	T	T	
T	T	T	F	T	T	F	F	F	F ✓	
T	T	F	T	T	T	F	F	F	F ✓	
T	T	F	F	T	T	F	F	F	F ✓	
T	F	T	T	T	T	T	T	T	T	
T	F	T	F	T	T	F	F	F	F ✓	
T	F	F	T	F	F	T	T	F	F ✓	
T	F	F	F	F	F	F	F	F	F ✓	
F	T	T	T	T	T	F	F	T	T	
F	T	T	F	T	T	F	F	T	F	
F	T	F	T	T	T	F	F	T	F	
F	T	F	F	T	T	F	F	T	F	
F	F	T	T	T	T	T	T	T	T	
F	F	T	F	T	T	F	F	T	F	
F	F	F	T	T	F	T	T	T	F	
F	F	F	F	T	F	F	F	T	F	Valid

CHAPTER 21, III

1.

p	*p* → *p*	
T	T	
F	T	Tautology

3.

p	q	p →	(p & q)
T	T	T	T
T	F	F	F
F	T	T	F
F	F	T	F

Contingent

5.

p	q	(p → q)	&	(q → p)
T	T	T	T	T
T	F	F	F	T
F	T	T	F	F
F	F	T	T	T

Contingent

7.

p	q	[(p ∨ q)	&	(~p ∨ q)]	&	[(p ∨ ~q)	&	(~p ∨ ~q)]
T	T	T	T	F T	F	T F	F	F F
T	F	T	F	F F	F	T T	T	F T
F	T	T	T	T T	F	F F	T	T T
F	F	F	F	T T	F	T T	T	T T

Contradiction

9.

p	q	r	~{	(~p & r)	&	[(p ∨ q)	&	(q → r)]}
T	T	T	T	F F	F	T	T	T
T	T	F	T	F F	F	T	F	F
T	F	T	T	F F	F	T	T	T
T	F	F	T	F F	F	T	T	T
F	T	T	F	T T	T	T	T	T
F	T	F	T	T F	F	T	F	F
F	F	T	T	T T	F	F	F	T
F	F	F	T	T F	F	F	F	T

Contingent

CHAPTER 21, IV

1.

p	q	~(p ∨ q)	↔	(~p & ~q)
T	T	F T	T	F F F
T	F	F T	T	F F T
F	T	F T	T	T F F
F	F	T F	T	T T T

Logically equivalent

3.

p	q	~(p ∨ q)	↔	(~p ∨ ~q)
T	T	F T	T	F F F
T	F	F T	F	F T T
F	T	F T	F	T T F
F	F	T F	T	T T T

Not logically equivalent

5.

p	q	(p → q)	↔	(~p ∨ q)
T	T	T	T	F T
T	F	F	T	F F
F	T	T	T	T T
F	F	T	T	T T

Logically equivalent

7.

p	q	(p ↔ q)	↔	[(p & q)	∨	(~p & ~q)]
T	T	T	T	T	T	F F F
T	F	F	T	F	F	F F T
F	T	F	T	F	F	T F F
F	F	T	T	F	T	T T T

Logically equivalent

9.

p	q	r	[p → (q → r)]	↔	[(p & q) → r]
T	T	T	T T T	T	T T
T	T	F	F F T	T	T F
T	F	T	T T T	T	F T
T	F	F	T T T	T	F T
F	T	T	T T T	T	F T
F	T	F	T F T	T	F T
F	F	T	T T T	T	F T
F	F	F	T T T	T	F T

Logically equivalent

CHAPTER 22

1. E, simplification
3. D, disjunctive syllogism
5. G, constructive dilemma
7. C, hypothetical syllogism
9. H, destructive dilemma
11. I, denying the antecedent
13. J, affirming the consequent
15. A, affirming the antecedent
17. G, constructive dilemma
19. E, simplification
21. H, destructive dilemma
23. A, affirming the antecedent
25. H, destructive dilemma
27. I, denying the antecedent
29. D, disjunctive syllogism
31. D, disjunctive syllogism
33. B, denying the consequent
35. C, hypothetical syllogism; the assumed conclusion is, "If you don't serve your people well, you can't serve your shareholders well."

CHAPTER 23, I

1. C, hypothetical syllogism
3. B, denying the consequent
5. B, denying the consequent; "The instructor is not kind."
7. D, disjunctive syllogism; "The instructor is not a mean old man."
9. G, constructive dilemma
11. I, fallacy of denying the antecedent; "We are not nearly free."

13. Notice that the last sentence contains both premises for a constructive dilemma (G). Conclusion: "Either Benjamin Addicks' story to the police is false, or someone else surreptitiously removed them."

15. B, denying the consequent

17. B, denying the consequent; "Calico serves the purpose of covering a corpse for burial." Notice that the second to last sentence is the denial of the consequent of the previous conditional.

19. G, constructive dilemma; "Either we'll send the letter when we reach Para or we won't." Conclusion: "Either this letter will be a mail ahead or it will reach London on the very day that I do."

21. G, constructive dilemma, "Either I will tell you the tale or I will lie." Conclusion: "Either you will kill me, or you will kill me" (which is equivalent to "You will kill me").

23. Two arguments: (1) A, affirming the antecedent (sentence 1). (2) G, constructive dilemma with three disjuncts. Premise: "Either they are anxious to see you happily married, or they wish to have you settled in the same country and circle which they have chosen to place you in, or their only object is that you should, in the common phrase, be well married." Conclusion: "Either here is a man whose amiable character gives every assurance of it, or here it will be accomplished, or here is the comfortable fortune, the respectable establishment, the rise in the world which must satisfy them."

25. G, constructive dilemma. Conclusion: "Either there is no reason to pray to them or instead of praying to be granted to be spared such-and-such a thing, you should pray to be delivered from dreading it, or lusting for it, or grieving over it." You could suggest that the conditional premises are implicitly conjoined to form the premise.

27. D, disjunctive syllogism. Premise: "Either you look like Don Raphael [your father] or you look like your mother."

29. D, disjunctive syllogism: "Either we laugh because we are happy, or we are happy because we laugh (implicit premise). We do not laugh because we are happy [the second paragraph tends to support this]. So, we are happy because we laugh."

CHAPTER 23, II

1. If today is Friday, the instructor will spend the weekend grading.
   1. $F \rightarrow T$
   2. $T \rightarrow I$
   3. $F \rightarrow I$ 1,2 HS

3. Either we have a test or we can sleep late.
   1. $(F \rightarrow T) \& (S \rightarrow W)$
   2. $F \vee S$
   3. $T \vee W$ 1,2 CD

5. It is not the case that both the instructor is sane and there are no trick questions.
   1. $(S \& \sim T) \rightarrow E$
   2. $E \rightarrow G$
   3. $\sim G$

4. (S & ~T) → G   1,2 HS   or   4. ~E   2,3 DC
5. ~(S & ~T)   4,3 DC   5. ~(S & ~T)   1,4 DC

7. I'll pay seven bucks to sleep for two hours.
   1. M ∨ D
   2. (M → P) & (D → H)
   3. ~H
   4. D → H   2 Simp.   or   4. P ∨ H   2,1 CD
   5. ~D   4,3 DC   5. P   4,3 DS
   6. M   1,5 DS
   7. M → P   2 Simp.
   8. P   7,6 AA

9. The "Festive Overture" is a classic of contemporary Russian music.
   1. ~E
   2. H ∨ S
   3. S → C
   4. H → E
   5. (H → E) & (S → C)   3,4 Conj.   or   5. ~H   4,1 DC
   6. E ∨ C   5,2 CD   6. S   2,5 DS
   7. C   6,1 DS   7. C   3,6 AA

11. "Lincolnshire Posy" has a light and breezy air about it.
    1. G → L
    2. G ∨ S
    3. L → A
    4. ~S
    5. G   2,4 DS   or   5. G → A   1,3 HS
    6. L   1,5 AA   6. G   2,4 DS
    7. A   3,6 AA   7. A   5,6 AA

13. Either Ana does not play poker or Eve does not work in a cattle drive.
    1. (A → B) & (C→ D)
    2. E → F
    3. ~B ∨ ~F
    4. A → B   1 Simp.
    5. (A → B) & (E → F)   4,2 Conj.
    6. ~A ∨ ~E   5,3 DD

15. Either Cassandra catches calico cats in cavernous caves, or Francois fences furiously for fifty francs.
    1. (A → B) & (~A → C)
    2. (D → E) & (~D → F)
    3. ~B ∨ ~E
    4. A → B   1 Simp.
    5. D → E   2 Simp.
    6. (A → B) & (D → E)   4,5 Conj.
    7. ~A ∨ ~D   6,3 DD
    8. ~A → C   1 Simp.
    9. ~D → F   2 Simp.

10. $(\sim A \to C) \;\&\; (\sim D \to F)$ 8,9 Conj
11. $C \lor F$ 10,7 CD

CHAPTER 24, I

1. C, hypothetical syllogism. The second premise is equivalent to "If Luis went to the dance, then Chris went to the dance."
3. E, simplification. The premise is equivalent to "If Sam enjoys these problems, then Jan enjoys these problems; and if Jan enjoys these problems, then Sam enjoys these problems."
5. G, constructive dilemma. The first premise is equivalent to "Either Sam does not expect to ace this course or Chris does not expect to ace this course."
7. B, denying the consequent. The second premise is equivalent to "It is not the case that it is not the case that either Sam is perplexed or Lynn is perplexed," which is equivalent to "It is not the case that Sam is not perplexed and Lynn is not perplexed."
9. "John enjoys these exercises if and only if Jen enjoys these problems" is equivalent to "If John enjoys these exercises, then Jen enjoys these problems; and if Jen enjoys these problems, then John enjoys these exercises." By E, simplification, you obtain, "If Jen enjoys these problems, then John enjoys these exercises." Given this and the other premise, the conclusion follows by b, denying the consequent.

CHAPTER 24, II

1. Joan will stay home alone.
   1. $C \to (J \lor F)$
   2. $\sim F \;\&\; C$
   3. C   2 Simp.
   4. $J \lor F$ 1,3 AA
   5. $\sim F$ 2 Simp.
   6. J   4,5 DS
3. Jean went to the movies.
   1. $J \leftrightarrow A$
   2. A
   3. $(J \to A) \;\&\; (A \to J)$ 1 Equiv.
   4. $A \to J$ 3 Simp.
   5. J   4,5 AA
5. Belinda did not go to the dance.
   1. $M \to (B \leftrightarrow C)$
   2. $M \;\&\; \sim C$
   3. M   2 Simp.
   4. $B \leftrightarrow C$ 1,3 AA
   5. $(B \to C) \;\&\; (C \to B)$ 4 Equiv.
   6. $B \to C$ 5 Simp.
   7. $\sim C$ 2 Simp.
   8. $\sim B$ 6,7 DC

7. Juan passed the course.
     1. $(F \leftrightarrow A) \rightarrow J$
     2. $(A \rightarrow F) \& (F \rightarrow A)$
     3. $F \leftrightarrow A$ 2 Equiv.
     4. J   1,3 AA
9. John is not a student in this class.
     1. $(S \vee H) \& \sim(S \& H)$
     2. H
     3. $\sim(S \& H)$ 1 Simp.
     4. $\sim S \vee \sim H$ 3 DeM
     5. $\sim\sim H$ 3 DN
     6. $\sim S$ 4,5 DS
11. Either Lucinda believes she needs to study for this exam or George will not receive an A.
     1. $\sim L \rightarrow \sim J$
     2. $A \rightarrow S$
     3. $J \vee \sim S$
     4. $J \rightarrow L$ 1 Trans.
     5. $\sim S \rightarrow \sim A$ 2 Trans.
     6. $(J \rightarrow L) \& (\sim S \rightarrow \sim A)$ 4,5 Conj.
     7. $L \vee \sim A$ 6,3 CD
13. Sam did not have lunch in D-Hall.
     1. $(S \rightarrow J) \& (C \rightarrow L)$
     2. $\sim J$
     3. $S \rightarrow J$ 1 Simp.
     4. $\sim S$ 3,2 DC
15. R. W. will not have a perpetual hit and Siegfried should have bathed under a tree. Or, it is not the case that either R. W. will have a perpetual hit or Siegfried should not have bathed under a tree.
     1. $\sim(W \vee S)$
     2. $(R \rightarrow W) \& (\sim B \rightarrow S)$
     3. $\sim W \& \sim S$ 1 DeM
     4. $\sim W$ 3 Simp.
     5. $\sim S$ 3 Simp.
     6. $R \rightarrow W$ 2 Simp.
     7. $\sim B \rightarrow S$ 2 Simp.
     8. $\sim R$ 6,4 DC
     9. $\sim\sim B$ 7,5 DC
    10. B   9 DN   or   10. $\sim R \& \sim\sim B$ 8,9 Conj
    11. $\sim R \& B$ 8,10 Conj.   11. $\sim(R \vee \sim B)$ 10 DeM
17. The concert will be a sellout.
     1. $(U \& I) \rightarrow T$
     2. $(D \rightarrow I) \& D$
     3. $T \rightarrow S$
     4. U
     5. $D \rightarrow I$ 2 Simp.

    6. D   2 Simp.
    7. I   5,6 AA
    8. U & I 4,7 Conj.
    9. T   1,8 AA   or   9. (U & I) → S 1,3 HS
  10. S   3,8 AA   10. S   8,9 AA

19. I have time to study for my test.
    1. (M → E) & (W → I)
    2. ~E ∨ ~I
    3. (~M → T) & (~W → P)
    4. ~P
    5. ~M ∨ ~W   1,2 DD
    6. T ∨ P   3,5 CD
    7. T   6,4 DS

CHAPTER 25, I

1. describe
3. describe
5. argue
7. describe
9. explain   13. describe
11. inquire/describe   15. argue

CHAPTER 25, II

1. She is again planning to serve a German dinner like the earlier one. She cooked the previous meals herself, and she will cook this meal as well.
3. We use computers for the same kinds of tasks. We care for our computers in approximately the same ways.
5. People in Iowa have approximately the same tastes your friends have. Information you have obtained from the *Washington Post* in the past—perhaps, particularly recipes—have been well received, and this recipe is in the *Washington Post*.
7. The similarities between the coffee maker and the *tools* I have purchased are, at most, that they are things powered by electricity—the Workmate is *not* even an electrical tool. The coffee maker will be used quite heavily, while the tools were used infrequently. These are significant disanalogies, so the argument is weak.
9. Industrial managers attempt to increase the profit margin for their companies; professors are not interested in profits. Industrial managers will probably receive a bonus if they can increase productivity; professors usually will not profit by teaching more students.

CHAPTER 25, III

1. Kings can do no wrong, presidents can. Kings cannot be named in a debate; presidents can. So, presidents are not entirely like kings. The argument is strong, since the disanalogies are significant and the conclusion is rather weak.

3. Adults in the 1950s and 1960s did not understand rock music; adults in the 1990s do not understand hip-hop music. Adults in the 1960s took rock music to be loud, undifferentiated noise; so, adults in the 1990s take hip-hop to be loud, undifferentiated noise. The argument seems strong, since even though there are only two *types* of things compared, there are indefinitely many instances of music of each type, it is clear to those of us who were around in the 1960s that adults took rock to be "loud, undifferentiated noise," and it is likely that adults of the 1990s look at hip-hop in the same way.

5. Goals in life are like the guidance system on a missile. If the guidance system on a missile is not targeted, the missile it will not hit anything. So, if goals are not set, your life will not hit anything (get anywhere significant). Here there are only two types of things compared—guidance systems on missiles and goals. There are lots of disanalogies—missile guidance systems are made of electrical circuits and wire and have to be set by intelligent beings, while human goalsetters are not made of wire and electrical circuits, and ultimately the "goal" of a missile is a human goal. Nonetheless, the analogy seems fairly strong, since we have all known enough unguided humans who are unable to accomplish anything.

7. The comparison is between decisions one must make as a physician and decisions one must make as a starship captain. Both are decisions that can have life-and-death implications. Both often need to be made rather quickly and with only limited information. Both are decisions the decision-maker must be able to live with after they are made. So, since a doctor's decision is a decision made to save lives, McCoy's plan to send a rescue mission is also a decision made to save lives. The number of respects in which the two cases are similar is significant, and the points of comparison seem relevant. There are indefinitely many cases compared. There are differences between the cases, since a doctor's decision generally affects only one person, while the decision made regarding the actions of a starship can directly affect a fairly large number of people. The conclusion is fairly strong. The argument is probably acceptable, even though it is not terribly strong.

9. The points of comparison are carefully spelled out in the second paragraph. There are numerous respects in which the success of evolutionary theory and the success of Newtonian are similar. Of course—a point the author does not note—there were phenomena that Newton's theory could not explain, which resulted in the replacement of Newtonian physics with Einsteinian physics and quantum mechanics. So, the argument provides fairly good reason to believe that evolutionary theory will evolve to the point that it will explain the emergence of sexual reproduction, but of course that might be an "evolution" from the current theory to some more advanced theory, just as Einstein's theory is a physical theory that is "more advanced" than Newton's.

11. Two specific cases are being compared. The number of respects in which the two cases are similar is significant. There are no relevant dissimilarities. The argument seems strong.

13. The argument is weak. The alleged similarity is between types of behavior. The contention seems to be that if I worship as Ishmael worships, then Ishmael will

worship as I worship, where there is little or no similarity between the types of worship.

15. The alleged similarity is between overindulgence in molasses and overindulgence in reading pieces of humorous writing. It is said that both forms of overindulgence can make you ill. The molasses manufacturer is not responsible if you are foolish enough to eat too much molasses. So, by analogy, the humorist is not responsible if you foolishly read too much humorous literature in one sitting. Assuming this is to be taken as a *serious* argument (it was probably intended to be an opening foray into Twain's humor), and assuming that it might have been a reasonable argument in 1910, it will not hold today, when numerous people sue for damages they have brought on themselves by their own actions (smoking, owning or using guns, etc.).

17. Comparisons are being made between magnetic forces on paper clips and friendships. Magnets attract paper clips, which then attract additional paper clips—things that are similar. The contention is that personality types attract similar personality types, and by associating with desirable personality types, you will be converted into a person with that personality type just as a magnet converts paper clips into magnets. The conclusion might be true, but there are few explicit similarities between personality types and the behavior of magnets. So, the argument is weak.

19. Technology is like the genie in the lamp. Aladdin's problems arose, not because of the genie, but because of the choices Aladdin made in asking (magical) favors from the genie. Similarly, problems in technology arise from the uses to which it is put. So, just as there is no reason, as such, to put the genie back into the lamp and dispose of the lamp, there is no reason to attempt to squelch technology; rather, it must be used reasonably. Here there could be a good number of analogies involved, although they are not explicitly stated. The speaker could have talked about comparisons between Aladdin and old technologies to make his point and gone from there to more recent (developing) technologies. If this is implicit, the argument might be seen as fairly strong. If there are no implicit appeals to older technologies, that is, if the similarities are *strictly* between Aladdin's use of the genie's magical powers and the magical powers of computer technology, the argument is fairly weak, since you then have a comparison between real cases (technology) and a merely hypothetical (literary) case.

CHAPTER 25, IV

1. a. weaken, 4
    b. strengthen, 5
    c. weaken, 4
    d. strengthen, 1
    e. strengthen, 1
    f. weaken, 6
    g. weaken, 4
    h. strengthen, 1

    i. In principle, the time of the class is irrelevant, 2. In practice, it might weaken the argument, 4.

    j. Quite possibly weaken, 4. In principle, it should be irrelevant, 2.

3. a. strengthen, 1
   b. weaken, 4
   c. strengthen, 1
   d. weaken, 6
   e. strengthen, 1
   f. neither, 2
   g. neither, 2
   h. strengthen, 5
   i. strengthen, 1
   j. weaken, 4

5. a. strengthen, 1
   b. strengthen, 2
   c. neither, 2; some of the games the previous year's team played were almost certainly on astroturf.
   d. strengthen or neither, 2
   e. weaken, 6
   f. weaken, 4
   g. weaken, 4
   h. neither, 2 (although we all know that being a preseason favorite "jinxes" a team)
   i. weaken, 4
   j. neither, 2

7. a. probably neither, 2
   b. strengthen, 1
   c. weaken, 4
   d. strengthen, 1
   e. strengthen, 5
   f. weaken, 4
   g. neither, 2
   h. strengthen, 1
   i. strengthen, 1
   j. strengthen, 6 (This would mean it would be less successful than the previous book, and his current standard of living is based largely on the previous book.)

9. a. neither, 5
   b. stronger, 3
   c. stronger, 1
   d. stronger, 1
   e. probably neither, 2
   f. neither, 2
   g. stronger, 5
   h. weaker, 4
   i. weaker, 4
   j. stronger, 1

CHAPTER 26, I

1. (B), (C) assuming I haven't observed the same raven twice, and (D).
3. Blood circulates throughout the body. So, there is no reason to believe that the blood in my arm differs from the blood in my foot.
5. The sample is small. The predictions were vague.

CHAPTER 26, II

1. Fewer Americans have Internet access than have telephones. The poll will *not* tell anything about the views of Americans.
3. The survey was biased. It tells you little about the drinking habits of all students on campus.
5. (E)
7. Some people believe questions concerning their sexual habits are too personal to respond to a survey.
9. One might suspect that beers other than that advertised were not equally represented.

CHAPTER 27, I

1. It might be that the electricity was off, but the clock records the correct time. It might be that my roommate turned it off—he hates alarm clocks. It might be that I slept through it, but I have never done that, and the alarm is turned off. It might be that I turned it off without waking up, but I have never done that. The roommate hypothesis seems most plausible.
3. If either the float or the flush valve were the problem, there would be water on the floor: The water would not have stopped flowing. A common problem is with the tank ball. If it were not aligned with the ball seat, this would explain the seepage of water and, the fact the water comes on for a short period of time. So, you might try adjusting the tank ball so it is aligned with the ball seat. If that works, it was probably the problem. If not, you will have to replace the ball seat. Chlorine is hard on rubber. So, if the chlorine content in your water is high, it provides further reason to believe that the problem was with either the tank ball, the ball seat, or both.
5. You probably could solve the problem by wetting the filter all the way around the basket. It will then adhere to the sides of the basket and not collapse.

CHAPTER 27, II

1. (E), since it is broader than (D). (D), of course, is more easily refutable.
3. It is a plausible explanation, since it explains the facts.
5. It is a plausible explanation insofar as it explains a number of facts. It also seems to be the only explanation of Andover's lack of surprise in seeing his friend with an eye patch.
7. It is an explanation, and even though it is inconsistent with standing assumptions, it is the only available explanation that explains the phenomenon.
9. There is no deduction. Holmes is showing how the assumption that Watson was in Afghanistan explains a number of observable properties.

11. The defective fan explains why the fan is not working, as would a blown fuse. But if the fuse hypotheses were true, replacing the fuse should have yielded a working fan. It did not. So, the fan hypothesis is the best hypothesis available.

13. The hypothesis would explain the change in the Beatles' behavior, but it was implausible insofar as there were incontrovertible tests (such as fingerprinting) showing that Paul McCarthy was still alive.

15. Mather's witch hypothesis is least good, since we can *now* explain the behavior of the girls in other ways, as we can virtually any other phenomena that were once attributed to witchcraft. The choice between Miller's hypothesis and Starkey's hysteria hypothesis is more difficult. The hysteria hypothesis explains other, similar phenomena, as does Miller's societal evolution hypothesis. They are, in fact, compatible. The choice between the two would need to be made on the basis of the fruitfulness of each in predicting and explaining other historical phenomena.

17. The transference of infectious materials hypothesis was best because it was testable, the test yielded the predicted outcome, and it was fruitful: It could be used to predict causes of other diseases.

19. Pasteur's hypothesis explained fermentation on the basis of the effects of living beings. It placed serious doubt on the chemical explanation of disease that was prevalent at the time. It was fruitful insofar as it allowed him to predict that human diseases were also the result of the actions of microorganisms.

CHAPTER 27, IV

1. But, soft! what light through yonder window breaks?
   It is the east, and Juliet is the sun.
   Arise, fair sun, and kill the envious moon,
   Who is already sick and pale with grief. . . . (Shakespeare, *Romeo and Juliet*)

2. The only way to get rid of a temptation is to yield to it. Resist it, and your soul grows sick with longing for the things it has forbidden to itself. (Oscar Wilde, *The Picture of Dorian Gray*)

CHAPTER 28

1. equivocation
3. amphiboly
5. no fallacy
7. amphiboly
9. amphiboly
11. amphiboly
13. equivocation
15. composition (although the "color of a car" is the exterior color exclusive of the trim, and if you have a single-color car, the fact that the hood is red would indicate that the whole car is red)
17. division
19. equivocation
21. amphiboly

23. equivocation
24. composition
26. equivocation on 'public interest'
28. amphiboly
30. division

CHAPTER 29, I

1. red herring
3. appeal to force
5. genetic fallacy
7. personal attack
9. appeal to force
11. mob (snob) appeal
13. accident
15. mob appeal
17. red herring
19. straw person
21. accident
23. appeal to pity
25. stereotype
27. red herring
29. personal attack
31. personal attack
33. straw person
35. irrelevant conclusion

CHAPTER 29, II

1. equivocation
3. mob appeal
5. red herring
7. personal attack
9. equivocation on 'neighbor'
11. equivocation
13. appeal to force
15. mob appeal
17. irrelevant conclusion: The fact that thousands of people hunt does not show that it is safe.
19. appeal to force

CHAPTER 30, I

1. complex question
3. complex question
5. begging the question
7. begging the question
9. begging the question

11. begging the question (epithet)
13. complex question
15. suppressed evidence
17. false dichotomy
19. complex question

CHAPTER 30, II

1. accident
3. equivocation
5. red herring
7. red herring
9. division
11. straw person
13. mob (snob) appeal
15. appeal to pity
17. begging the question (epithet)
19. composition
21. suppressed evidence
23. There is a false dichotomy, but there is no argument, so there is no fallacy.
25. To the extent that this appeals to emotions, it might be deemed a mob appeal. But to the extent that an appeal to protect endangered species provides the reason to vote for the communist candidate, it rests on the general principle that "We should do what we can to protect endangered species." This principle applies to biological species. In applying the general principle to a political species, it is being applied to an exceptional case, which makes it a fallacy of accident. Similarly, it might be claimed that 'species' is being used in two senses—biological species and political species—so it might be an equivocation.

CHAPTER 31, I

1. No fallacy. The person making the reply should be in a position to know the evidence. So, it is not a fallacious appeal to ignorance.
3. weak analogy
5. slippery slope
7. false cause
9. false cause
11. appeal to ignorance
13. weak analogy
15. false cause
17. hasty generalization
19. hasty generalization
21. weak analogy
23. appeal to ignorance
25. hasty generalization
27. slippery slope
29. weak analogy

CHAPTER 31, II

1. appeal to force
3. mob (snob) appeal
5. mob appeal
7. false cause
9. complex question
11. amphiboly
13. no fallacy; Colonel Oakdale has the credentials that make him an authority on fuses.
15. appeal to force
17. appeal to pity
19. straw person
21. false dichotomy
23. personal attack
25. composition
27. mob appeal
29. appeal to force
31. accident
33. slippery slope
35. weak analogy
37. complex question
39. straw person
41. appeal to authority
43. begging the question
45. division
47. appeal to pity
49. false cause

GLOSSARY

accent, fallacy of Accent is one of several informal fallacies. In one form, it consists of placing an unusual stress on a word and drawing a conclusion on the basis of that stress. Example: "Thou shalt not steal" is a moral law, presumably applying to everyone. But you commit the fallacy of accent if you argue, "The commandment is that '*thou* shalt not steal,' so it is okay if *I* do a bit of pilfering." In another form, it consists of taking claims out of context and, as a result, shifting the meaning of the claim. Example: Joan had been arguing against euthanasia. In the course of her argument, she raised an objection to her position, part of which was the principle, "It is a moral principle that we never should allow people to suffer needlessly." If you reply to her argument by saying, "Even Joan says it is a moral principle that we never should allow people to suffer needlessly. Opposing euthanasia is a case of allowing people to suffer needlessly. So, on Joan's principles we should not oppose euthanasia," the appeal to the principle apart from the context is an instance of the fallacy of accent. In yet another form, which is related to the second, it consists of incomplete quotation, where the incompleteness shifts the meaning. Example: "It is a divine commandment that 'Thou shalt . . . commit adultery,' so fooling around a bit is morally correct—indeed, we are commanded by God to do it!"

accident, fallacy of The fallacy of accident occurs if you apply one of a pair of general principles in a situation where it does *not* apply but the other one does. Example: It is a general principle that you should aid others when you can. It is also a general principle that you should not aid others during a test. To attempt to justify giving your friend the answer to a test question by appealing to the first principle would be an instance of the fallacy of accident.

accuracy Accuracy is a critical-thinking virtue. It is a freedom from error.

act-deontology Act-deontologists maintain that there is a method whereby one can determine the moral value or obligation of a specific action without appealing to rules. The consequences of an action can play *some* role, but not the only role, in determining the moral property of an action or state.

affirming the antecedent Affirming the antecedent *(modus ponens)* is a valid argument form. Where p and q are variables that can be replaced by any statement, affirming the antecedent is an argument of the following form: If $p,$ then $q. p.$ Therefore, $q.$

affirming the consequent Affirming the consequent is a fallacious argument form. Where p and q are variables that can be replaced by any statement, an argument commits the fallacy of affirming the consequent if it has the following form: If $p,$ then $q. q.$ Therefore, $p.$ While the argument form is invalid, arguments of this form provide some inductive evidence for the truth of the conclusion.

ambiguous, ambiguity A word is ambiguous if it has more than one meaning.

ampersand (&) The ampersand represents conjunction. A statement of the form p & q is true if and only if both p and q are true.

amphiboly Amphiboly is an informal fallacy of ambiguity that rests upon loose sentence construction, sentence construction that may be interpreted in more than one way.

Example: You can't take the elevator down to the first floor, since the elevator is out of service. Notice that the sign says, "In case of fire elevators are out of service."

analogy An analogy is a comparison between two or more objects. Analogies can be used to illustrate points—"the desert sizzled like bacon in a pan"—to explain—"validity is like a conventional light switch: just as the switch is either on or off, so a deductive argument is either valid or invalid"—or to argue, that is, to provide reasons for believing that since two or more objects are similar in a certain number of ways, it is likely that they are also similar in additional ways. *See also* **basis of an analogy**, **ground of an analogy**, **objective extension of an analogy**, *and* **problematic extension of an analogy**

analytic proposition An analytic proposition is a proposition whose truth depends only on the meaning of the words in the proposition.

antecedent In a conditional statement of the form "If p, then q," the antecedent is the *if* clause.

appeal to authority The fallacy of appeal to authority is committed when one cites a person or group or practice as an authority in a field in which that person, group, or practice does not have the credentials necessary to establish that it is an authority in that field. Examples: John Madden endorses Ace Hardware, so Ace Hardware must be good. *Warning:* There are times when a person is known for his or her work in one field, but he or she has significant credentials in another field as well. So, before screaming "appeal to authority," you should check out the person's background.

appeal to force The fallacy of appeal to force assumes some implicit threat of force is a sufficient reason to engage in an action or hold a belief.

appeal to pity The fallacy of appeal to pity assumes that the fact that someone is suffering from some kind of distress is a sufficient condition to engage in an action or hold a belief.

argument An argument is a discourse in which the presumed truth of certain statements, the premises, are taken as evidence for another statement, the conclusion. All arguments are either valid deductive arguments or inductive arguments. Examples: (1) Each crow I have observed over the past ten years has been black, so all crows are black (inductive argument). (2) Your car and my car are of the same make, model, and year. Your driving habits and my driving habits are very similar. I needed a valve job at 80,000 miles. Therefore, it is likely that you will need a valve job sometime after your car reaches the 75,000 mile mark (analogy: inductive argument). (3) All humans are mortals. Socrates is a human. Therefore, Socrates is a mortal (categorical syllogism: deductive argument).

argument to the best explanation An argument to the best explanation is an inductive argument based on a comparison of alternative explanations of an event.

argumentum ad hominem *See* **personal attack**

argumentum ad baculuum *See* **appeal to force**

argumentum ad misericordium *See* **appeal to pity**

argumentum ad populum *See* **mob appeal**

Aristotelian interpretation of categorical propositions According to the Aristotelian interpretation of categorical propositions, both universal and particular propositions have existential import.

arrow ($\rightarrow$) The arrow represents material conditionality. A statement of the form $p \rightarrow q$ is true *except* when p is true and q is false.

assumption In an argument an assumption is an unstated premise.

authority An authority is a person or reference work whose credentials—based on training or experience—are sufficient with respect to a particular issue that his or her word can be accepted as (very probably) true. Examples: Former University of Iowa head football coach Hayden Fry is an authority on collegiate football. Albert Einstein was an authority on nuclear physics.

average *See* **mean**, **mode**, **median**, *and* **midrange**

bandwagon The bandwagon fallacy is a special case of mob appeal that takes the form "Everyone is doing it, so you should do it too."

basis of an analogy The basis of an analogy consists of those properties know to be common to the ground and the objective extension of the analogy. For example, if you have three objects, A, B, and C, all which are known to share properties a, b, and c, and the question is whether there is an additional common property, a, b, and c are the basis of the analogy.

begging the question The informal fallacy of begging the question occurs when you assume as a premise the conclusion to be established by an argument. Generally, the premise and the conclusion are *not* stated in the same words, but the meaning of both is the same: "We know that Chris is a bachelor, since he is an unmarried man" begs the question, since the words 'bachelor' and 'unmarried man' are synonymous. A second version of the fallacy occurs in a chain of arguments in which the conclusion of the last is a premise of the first. "We know that everything the Bible says is true, since it is the inspired word of God. And we know that the Bible is the inspired word of God, since the Bible says it is the inspired word of God and everything the Bible says is true" argues in a circle. A third version is a question-begging epithet. It involves a descriptive term that ascribes a property to a thing in a premise that you are trying to establish in a conclusion. In the statement, "That crook John Cribbs should be found guilty of grand larceny," the word 'crook' is an epithet that begs the question of Cribbs's guilt.

belief, to believe A belief is a proposition one accepts as true. One might or might not have evidence to support one's belief that the proposition is true. Examples: Clara believes that it will rain tomorrow. Fodsworth believes that God exists.

bias, biased A survey is said to be biased when there are unequal chances that any given member of a population be selected for the survey. A person is said to be biased when he or she is more favorably inclined to one kind of thing than another, often without having reasons for such a favoritism. A person's bias is often shown by the descriptive words he or she uses.

biconditional statement A biconditional is a statement of the form p if and only if q.

Boolean interpretation of categorical propositions According to the Boolean interpretation of categorical propositions, particular propositions have existential import, but universal propositions do not have existential import.

burden of proof The burden of proof is the responsibility of showing that a claim is true. If Ashley makes a claim or presents an argument, she assumes the burden of proof. Once the argument is presented, the burden of proof *shifts* to any would-be critic. If someone shows that there are reasons to question Ashley's argument, the burden of proof shifts back to Ashley.

categorical statement, categorical proposition A categorical statement is a statement expressing the relationship between two classes of objects.

categorical syllogism A categorical syllogism is a deductive argument composed of two premises and a conclusion, each of which is a categorical proposition, and which has, or can be reduced to, three categorical propositions having exactly three distinct terms.

cause A cause is that without which a certain phenomenon would not occur, or that which, when given, a certain phenomenon will occur, or both. The term 'cause' is ambiguous.

charity, principle of The principle of charity is the principle that whenever you are trying to state a person's argument, you always state it in as strong a form as you can justify. For example, treat the argument as a deductive argument with a missing premise if the premise you propose is true and will yield a valid deductive argument. If you cannot find a premise that is both true and will yield a valid deductive argument, treat the argument as an inductive argument.

circular argument *See* **begging the question**

civility Civility is a critical-thinking virtue. To be civil is to treat the works of others with tolerance and respect.

clarity Clarity is a critical-thinking virtue. It is a commitment to avoiding confusion and ambiguity.

cognitive meaning of a term The cognitive meaning of a term is either the objective, conventional, or subjective connotation of a term. It consists of those properties in virtue of which a term can be correctly applied to a thing.

coherent, coherence A set of propositions is coherent if it "makes sense," that is, if it consistent and shows that there is some determinate relationship(s) among the objects discussed. For example, a theoretical framework will often make a certain set of data coherent by showing the relationships among the data.

complement, complementary class, complementary term The complement of any class is the class containing all those things *not* in a given class. The complement of the class of all red things contains all things that are not red. The complement to the term "red things" is "nonred things."

complex question A complex question asks two or more questions at once. In answering the explicit question, you also answer the assumed questions. The *fallacy* of complex question occurs when a conclusion is drawn on the basis of an answer to the complex question. Example: "When did you start cheating in the course?" "On January 28." "Aha! So you admit you have been cheating in this course!"

composition Composition is an informal fallacy in which a claim that is true of a member of a class or of a part of a whole is applied to the class or the whole. Example: The steering wheel of my car weighs fewer than ten pounds, so my car weighs fewer than ten pounds. You should be careful in claiming that an argument commits the *fallacy* of composition, since there are cases in which a property of a part is also a property of the corresponding whole. For example, if a disjunct is true, the disjunction of which it is a part is also true.

compound statement A compound statement is any statement that has another statement as a component. Examples: "Today is Tuesday, and it is raining." "John believes that Elise likes pizza." *See also* **truth-functionally compound statements** and **nontruth-functionally compound statements**

concept A concept is the meaning of a word.

conceptual framework A conceptual framework is a set of assumptions operative in presenting an argument or explanation. Example: The conceptual framework operative in scientific explanations is naturalistic; that is, it assumes that all natural phenomena can be explained on the basis of other natural phenomena, including natural laws.

conclusion The conclusion of an argument is the statement the argument is taken to establish as true or probably true.

conclusion indicator A conclusion indicator is a word such a 'thus' or 'therefore', which is commonly found before a statement that is the conclusion of an argument.

conditional statement A conditional statement is statement of the form, "If . . ., then. . . ." It is also known as a hypothetical statement.

confidence level In a survey the confidence level is the degree of accuracy which experience indicates can be assumed on the basis of a sample of a certain size for a population of a certain size.

confirm, confirmation Evidence that tends to confirm a hypothesis tends to show that the hypothesis is true.

conflict of interest A person has a conflict of interest if he or she has, or appears to have, mixed motives in making a claim. Example: In any commercial featuring a famous personality, the person is giving a *paid* endorsement. Because the person stands to gain financially from the endorsement, you might question whether the person is making the endorsement *only* because he or she is paid to do so.

conjunct A conjunct is one of the statements in a conjunction.

conjunction A conjunction is a statement in which the main connective is the word 'and' or 'but'. Example: "Today is Tuesday, and today it is sunny."

connectives In propositional logic there are one-place and two-place connectives. The tilde ($\sim$) is a one-place connective. The ampersand (&), wedge ($\vee$), arrow ($\rightarrow$), and double arrow ($\leftrightarrow$) are two-place connectives.

connotation The connotation or intension of a term consists of those properties a thing of a kind has in virtue of which it is a thing of that kind. The *objective connotation* consists of all those properties a thing *actually has* in virtue of which it is a thing of a certain kind. The *conventional connotation* consists of those properties the speakers of a language deem sufficient to classify a thing as a thing of a certain kind. Dictionary definitions usually state the conventional connotation of a term. The *subjective connotation* consists of those properties a particular speaker of a language deems sufficient to classify a thing as a thing of a certain kind.

consequent In a conditional statement of the form "If p, then q," the consequent is the *then* clause.

consequentialism, consequentialist Consequentialism is a moral theory holding that one's moral obligation to engage in or refrain from engaging in an action is based solely upon the consequences (results) of that action. Consequentialist moral theories are sometimes known as teleological moral theories.

consilience Consilience is the tendency of several forms of inductive evidence to point to the same conclusion.

consistent Consistency is a critical-thinking virtue. Two propositions are consistent if it is possible for both to be true at the same time, that is, if their conjunction does *not* yield a contradiction. For example, the propositions "Today is Tuesday" and "Today it is raining" are consistent. The two propositions "It is raining" and "It is not raining" are inconsistent. *See also* **external consistency** *and* **internal consistency**

context A context is either (1) a *domain of discourse,* that is, a set of assumptions operative in an argument (*see* **domain of discourse**), or (2) the more general discussion from which a sentence or argument is taken. In the second sense, when a passage is "taken out of context," its meaning can change. If the meaning shifts by taking a passage out of context, you commit the informal fallacy of accent. Example: Assume Fred was raising an objection to his own argument. If you quote the objection without acknowledging that it was an objection, you have taken the passage out of context.

contingent truth A contingent truth is a statement whose truth or falsehood depends on facts in the world. It is *not* a necessary truth.

contradiction, contradictory Two propositions are contradictory if and only if it is logically impossible for both to be true and it is logically impossible for both to be false. For example, the statements "It is raining" and "It is not raining" are contradictory statements. It is logically impossible that both statements be true under the same conditions, *and* it is logically impossible for both to be false under the same conditions.

contrapositive, contraposition The contrapositive of a categorical proposition is formed by switching the subject and predicate terms and replacing each with its complement. Example: The contrapositive of "All professors are intelligent beings" is "All non-intelligent beings are nonprofessors." Only the contrapositive of a universal affirmative proposition and a particular negative proposition are logically equivalent to the original proposition.

contrary, contraries Two statements are contraries if they cannot both be true at the same time and in the same place. It is possible for contrary statements both to be false. Example: The following two statements are contraries which might both be false: "All critical-thinking textbooks are interesting pieces of literature," and "No critical-thinking textbooks are interesting pieces of literature."

converse, conversion You form the converse of a categorical proposition by switching the places of the subject and the predicate term. Example: The converse of "No cats are dogs" is "No dogs are cats." Only the converse of universal negative propositions and particular affirmative propositions are logically equivalent to the original propositions.

counterexample (1) A counterexample to a given deductive argument is an argument of the same form in which all the premises are true and the conclusion is false. Sometimes known as a deductive counterexample, this is sufficient to show that the form of the given argument is invalid. (2) A counterexample to an inductive generalization or a definition is a single instance that shows that the generalization is false. For example, if you found a gray crow, it would be a counterexample to the general claim that all crows are black. It would be sufficient to show that the statement "All crows are black" is false.

criterion, criteria A criterion is a standard for judgment. Example: The criteria for judging the value of a diamond include weight, cut, and color.

critical thinking Critical thinking is careful reasoning. It is a careful, deliberate, efficient, and effective means for determining whether a statement or claim is, or is probably, true or false.

cultural relativity of morals The cultural relativity of morals refers to the *fact* that different cultures accept different codes of morals.

curiosity Curiosity is a critical-thinking virtue. It is the desire to learn.

deduction, deductive argument A valid deductive argument with true premises, a sound argument, provides conclusive evidence for the truth of its conclusion. Please note that this is *not* equivalent to the popular definition of 'deduction' in terms of going from particular premises to a general conclusion: There are arguments that virtually anyone would deem valid deductive arguments which are inconsistent with the popular definition. Note also that this is *not* equivalent to the uses of 'deduction' and 'deduce' in many mysteries: Sherlock Holmes's description of his elaborate deduction at the end of *A Study in Scarlet* is primarily an inductive argument, although there are deductive arguments that play a role in his elaborate argument.

deductive counterexample You construct a deductive counterexample to an argument of a given form by constructing another argument of the same form in which all the premises are true and the conclusion is false. A deductive counterexample shows that any argument of that form is invalid.

denial A denial is a compound statement containing the word 'not' or one of its synonyms. This is also known as a negative statement.

denotation The denotation or extension of a term consists of those objects to which a term is correctly applied.

denying the antecedent Denying the antecedent is a fallacious argument form. Where p and q are variables that can be replaced by any statement, an argument commits the fallacy of denying the antecedent if it has the following form: If p, then q. Not p. Therefore, not q.

denying the consequent Denying the consequent *(modus tollens)* is a valid argument form. Where p and q are variables that can be replaced by any statement, denying the consequent is an argument of the following form: If p, then q. Not q. Therefore, not p.

deontological moral theory *See* **nonconsequentialist moral theory**

dependence In calculating the probability of events, two events are dependent if calculating the probability of the first event affects the probability of the second event.

depth Depth is a critical-thinking virtue. To understand something in depth is to understand most of its aspects or implications.

detachment Detachment is a critical-thinking virtue. It is the ability to set aside your own interests and emotional attachments in seeking truth.

disjunct A disjunct is one of the statements in a disjunction.

disjunction A disjunction is a statement in which the main connective is a word such as 'or' or 'unless'. Example: "Either Sally likes chocolate or she likes caramels."

distribution A term is distributed in a categorical proposition if it refers to all members of a class. The subject term of all universal propositions is distributed. The predicate of all negative propositions is distributed.

divine command theory The divine command theory of morals holds that the source of moral obligation is the commands of God.

division Division is an informal fallacy in which a claim that is true of a class or a whole is applied to a member of a class or a part of the whole. Example: My car weighs over 2,000 pounds, so the steering wheel of my car weighs over 2,000 pounds. Please note that there *are* cases in which properties of the whole or class are also properties of the parts or the individuals in the class. For example, if a conjunction is true, then each of its conjuncts is true.

domain of discourse A domain of discourse is a set of assumptions operative in a discussion or argument. For example, when discussing the Sherlock Holmes stories, Sir Arthur Conan Doyle's stories specify a domain of discourse, that is, the subject matter of the discussion.

double arrow (↔) A double arrow represents material biconditionality. A statement of the form $p \leftrightarrow q$ is true if and only if p and q have the same truth value.

economy Economy is a critical-thinking virtue. It is demonstrated in reducing verbiage by being precise and recognizing that simpler explanations (those with fewer theoretical assumptions) are probably true.

end An end or objective or purpose is that which one seeks in engaging in an action. Example: Joan's end in crossing the street was to purchase cigars in the tobacco shop.

enthymeme, enthymematic argument An enthymeme is a deductive argument with a missing premise or an unstated conclusion.

ethical egoism Ethical egoism is a consequentialist moral theory holding that you always ought to act in such a way that it maximizes your own interests.

equivocate, equivocation You equivocate if you use the same word with two different meanings in the course of an argument. All arguments that equivocate on the meaning of one or more terms and the acceptance of the conclusion depends upon the equivocation are invalid.

essay An essay is a piece of writing in which the author provides evidence that a statement—the thesis—is true. An essay is often a fairly long discourse, and in addition to the main thesis, there are subordinate theses that support the main thesis, which in turn are supported by argumentative evidence.

ethical egoism Ethical egoism is a theory of moral obligation based on the principle "Act in such a way that the action maximizes your self-interest."

evaluative description An evaluative description maintains something is good or bad (or evil) or that an action is one you are obligated to perform or refrain from performing. Evaluative descriptions are made in terms of moral or aesthetic qualities as well as in terms of nonmoral and nonaesthetic qualities.

evidence Evidence consists of reasons to believe that a proposition is true. Example: General Schwarzkopf's testimony before the Senate committee provided evidence that a significant amount of care was taken to protect the soldiers during Operation Desert Storm.

existential import A statement has existential import if and only if its truth assumes that there is at least one object of which the proposition is true. On the Boolean interpretation of categorical logic, only particular propositions have existential import. On the Aristotelian interpretation of categorical logic, both universal and particular propositions have existential import.

experimental question An experimental question is one whose answer depends upon experience.

expert choice sampling Expert choice sampling is a form of purposive sampling that assumes that experts in a certain area have some special understanding of what is typical.

explanandum In an explanation, the explanandum is a sentence describing an event or phenomenon that is known or believed to have occurred.

explanans In an explanation, the explanans consists of one or more sentences that answer the question, Why did the event or phenomenon described by the explanandum occur?

explanation An explanation is a complex discourse composed of two or more statements in which one statement describes an event or phenomenon which is known or believed to have occurred (the explanandum), and the remaining statement or statements (the explanans) answer the question why the event or phenomenon described in the explanandum is as it is.

explanatory scope The explanatory scope of a hypothesis consists of that class of phenomena a hypothesis will explain.

extension *See* **denotation**

external consistency In the sciences, external consistency is the consistency between claims made by a hypothesis for which there appears to be evidence and the ongoing theoretical assumptions of a science.

factual disagreement A factual disagreement is a disagreement about how things are in the world. For example, Jen and Jeff disagree about the number of people who live in the apartment upstairs.

fallacy, fallacious A fallacy is a defective argument. A deductive argument is fallacious or commits a formal fallacy if it is invalid, that is, if it is possible for all the premises of the argument to be true and the conclusion false. Informal or material fallacies arise when the content of an argument (the material) fails to support the truth of the conclusion.

fallacy, formal *See* **fallacy**.

fallacy, informal or material *See* **informal fallacy**

false, falsehood A statement or proposition is false if and only if it does not correspond to the way the world is.

false cause The informal fallacy of false cause occurs if you claim that something is a cause when it is not. Sometimes there is a cause, but it is not the cause cited (this is sometimes known as *non causa pro causa,* "not the cause for the cause"). Example: "It rained because John washed and waxed his car." Sometimes one assumes that one event is the cause of another simply because the first occurred first (this is sometimes known as *post hoc ergo propter hoc,* "before, therefore because"). Example: "The Boy Scouts went camping on Friday night, so it rained early Saturday morning."

false dichotomy An argument commits the fallacy of false dichotomy if it presents a disjunction as exhaustive when it is not. Example: Dana is either a Republican or a Democrat. She is not a Democrat. So, she is a Republican. Were it the case that Dana is a member of the Green Peace Party, the disjunctive premise would have been false.

falsify, falsification Evidence falsifies a hypothesis when it shows that the hypothesis is not true. Example: If your hypothesis is that "If A occurs, then B occurs," and you find a case in which A occurs but B does not occur, then that instance falsifies the hypothesis.

form The form of an argument is the structure or pattern found in an argument. More than one argument can have the same form. For example, the following two arguments have the same form (affirming the antecedent): (1) If today is Tuesday, then tomorrow is Wednesday. Today is Tuesday. Therefore, tomorrow is Wednesday. (2) If interest rates are dropping, then the Dow Jones Industrial average is rising. Interest rates are dropping. Therefore, the Dow Jones Industrial average is rising. Validity is a formal property of an argument. It is a property of its form, not its content.

genetic fallacy The genetic fallacy is a special case of arguing from a stereotype based on the origins of a person or thing. Example: "Our professor isn't very bright, since he was raised in a small town" assumes the *false* premise that "All (or most) people raised in a small town are not very bright."

Gettier paradox The Gettier paradox, named for Edmund L. Gettier, who originally raised the puzzle, arises when one has a belief, there is evidence that supports the belief, and the belief is true, but the evidence you cite does not show that the belief is true. Example: You believe that Smith now owns a brown 1955 Ford. Your evidence for that is (1) last Friday

Smith told you she owns a brown 1955 Ford, (2) you saw her driving a brown 1955 Ford when she left work that day, and (3) Friday night you had a friend in the police department check the license number of the brown 1955 Ford Smith was driving to see to whom it was registered: It was registered to Smith. You have very good evidence that, as of 5:30 Friday, Smith owned a brown 1955 Ford. But there was a tragic accident on Saturday morning, and her classic car was totaled. She sold her car to a salvage yard, but had the great good fortune to find and purchase another brown 1955 Ford on Saturday afternoon. So, your belief that she now owns a brown 1955 Ford is true, but your evidence is irrelevant: Under the circumstances, none of the evidence supports the belief that Smith *now* owns a brown 1955 Ford.

ground for an analogy The ground for an analogy are those objects having *all* the properties under consideration. For example, if you have three objects, A, B, and C, both A and B have properties *a, b, c,* and *d,* and the question is whether C also has property *d,* A and B are the ground for the analogy.

grouping indicators In propositional logic the grouping indicators are parentheses, square brackets ([]), and braces ({}). They show which two statements are grouped together by a sentential connective.

guide columns In a truth table the guide columns show all possible combinations of the truth values of the same statement in an argument.

guidepost In an essay a guidepost is a paragraph that tells your reader where you have been and where you are going. It summarizes the arguments you have given to that point and indicates which subordinate thesis you will examine next.

haphazard survey A haphazard survey is a purposive survey limited to subjects that fortuitously present themselves.

hasty generalization The informal fallacy of hasty generalization occurs when you reach a general conclusion, whether universal or statistical, on the basis of insufficient evidence, especially when the sample from which the conclusion is drawn is atypical. Example: Fred is a redhead and he has a bad temper, so all redheads have a bad temper.

hearsay evidence Hearsay evidence is second-hand evidence (rumor), often based on nothing more than the testimony of an individual. All things being equal—assuming that other types of evidence are available—it is weak evidence. Example: Sam said that Lynn said that she would not be going to the party on Saturday.

humor Humor is a critical-thinking virtue. A critical thinker is willing not to take himself or herself seriously.

hypothesis A hypothesis is a proposed answer to a question or solution to a problem. It is typically the starting point of an investigation—a search for *evidence*—that will tend to *confirm* or *falsify* the hypothesis.

hypothetical statement *See* **conditional statement**

ignorance, appeal to The informal fallacy of appeal to ignorance is committed when you say that since there is no evidence that a certain proposition is true, it must be false, *or* when you say that since there is no evidence that a certain proposition is false, it must be true. Examples: (1) Since there is no evidence that extraterrestrial intelligent life does not exist, extraterrestrial intelligent life exists. (2) Since there is no evidence that extraterrestrial intelligent life exits, it does not exist. **Warning:** There are cases in which the lack of evidence that a proposition is true provides good reason to believe that the proposition is false. Example: There is no reason to believe that my neighbor is the Atlanta Ax Murderer, so she is not the Atlanta Ax Murderer.

ignoratio elenchi *See* **irrelevant conclusion**

independence In calculating the probability of two or more events, the events are independent if and only if the probability of the first event does *not* affect the probability of the second and subsequent events.

indifference, principle of In classical probability theory, the principle of indifference is the assumption that all possibilities are equally probable.

inductive argument An inductive argument with true premises provides some, but not conclusive, evidence for the truth of its conclusion. There are several types of inductive arguments. In some you argue from particular instances to a general proposition. In analogies, your argument is based on a comparison of two or a small number of objects. Here you argue that since objects A and B share a certain number of properties (*a, b, c, d,* and *e*), and since A has an additional property *f*, it is likely that B also has the property *f*.

industriousness Industriousness is a critical-thinking virtue. It is the tendency to work diligently to obtain a goal.

inference An inference is a psychological state in which you draw a conclusion on the basis of a certain body of information. Sometimes the word 'inference' is used to represent an argument or an argument form. *See* **reasoning**

informal fallacies Informal fallacies are mistakes in reasoning that arise from the content of the argument, that is, the materials from which the argument is constructed. They are also known as material fallacies. Informal fallacies occur when the premises of an argument are irrelevant to the argument's conclusion, or the premises are ambiguous and the move from the premises to the conclusion exploits that ambiguity, or the premises rest on unwarranted assumptions, or the premises provide only weak inductive evidence for the truth of the conclusion.

intension *See* **connotation**

internal consistency A theory, or any other kind of discourse, is internally consistent if there are *not* two or more propositions in the theory that can be combined to form a contradiction.

invalid, invalidity Invalidity is a formal characteristic of an argument. An argument is an invalid deductive argument if and only if it is possible for all its premises to be true and its conclusion false.

irrelevant conclusion You commit the fallacy of irrelevant conclusion if you draw a conclusion from an argument that is *not* suggested by the premises.

knowledge, to know Knowledge is often defined as justified true belief. So understood, a true belief can be deemed knowledge only if there is good evidence that the belief is true. Example: You believe that Smith owns a brown 1955 Ford, and your evidence for that is (1) Smith told you she owns a brown 1955 Ford, (2) you have seen her driving a brown 1955 Ford, and (3) you had a friend in the police department check the license number of the brown 1955 Ford Smith was driving to see to whom was registered: It was registered to Smith. You have good evidence that your belief is true; you seem justified in claiming to *know* that Brown owns a brown 1955 Ford. *See also* **Gettier Paradox**

logically equivalent propositions Two propositions are logically equivalent if and only if they are true under exactly the same conditions.

loose derivation A loose derivation is an inductive argument that differs from a valid deductive argument only insofar as a universal premise is replaced with a less than universal premise.

major premise In a categorical syllogism, the major premise is the premise that contains the major term.

major term In a categorical syllogism, the major term is the predicate term of the conclusion.

margin of error In a survey, the margin of error is the percentage by which past experience suggests actual behavior might deviate from the results of a survey within a certain confidence level.

material biconditionality *See* **biconditional** *and* **double arrow**

material conditionality *See* **conditional** *and* **arrow**

mean The mean is the arithmetic average calculated by dividing the sum of the individual values by the total number of values in a reference class.

means The means are the actions undertaken to reach a certain end or objective. Example: Jan attended college as a means to obtaining a job as an accountant. Often a means-end statement is given in the form of a conditional. For example, in the statement "If you want to pass this course, then you should study hard every day," the antecedent specifies an end to which the consequent is the means.

median The median is a meaning of 'average'. It is the number that occurs in the middle when the numbers are placed in ascending order.

metaphor A metaphor is an analogy in which an implicit comparison is made between two things. The statement "Language is a picture of the world" is a metaphorical statement.

metaphorical usage A word is used metaphorically when it is used outside of its normal domain but there is an implicit assumption that the meaning is somehow similar to the standard meaning.

middle term In a categorical syllogism, the middle term is the term found in the premises but *not* in the conclusion.

midrange The midrange is a meaning of 'average'. The midrange is the point in the arithmetic middle of the range. It is calculated by adding the highest number in the range to the lowest number and dividing by two.

minor premise In a categorical syllogism, the minor premise is the premise containing the minor term.

minor term In a categorical syllogism, the minor term is the subject term of the conclusion.

mob appeal The fallacy of mob appeal assumes that some kind of popular appeal is a sufficient reason to engage in an action or hold a belief.

mode The mode is an average consisting of the number that occurs most frequently in a reference class.

modus ponens *See* **affirming the antecedent**

modus tollens *See* **denying the consequence**

moral relativity Moral relativity is the thesis that there are no universal moral rules, that actual moral rules vary from culture to culture.

moral rule A moral rule is a statement of moral obligation.

natural law A natural law is a general statement describing the way the world is. Examples: "All pure water heated to 212°F at standard atmospheric pressure boils." "For every action there is an equal and opposite reaction." Natural laws, to the extent they are known, are known on the basis of inductive evidence. Hence, what we take to be a natural law at any given point in time is subject to revision as our knowledge of the world increases.

naturalistic explanation A naturalistic explanation is an explanation based upon facts about nature. It assumes that *if* certain natural events occur, then they will be followed by other natural events or other natural events will occur at the same time. All scientific explanations are naturalistic.

necessary and sufficient condition A necessary and sufficient condition for some event *E* is a condition which, if present, will guarantee that *E* will occur, and which, if absent, will guarantee that *E will not* occur.

necessary condition A necessary condition for some event *E* is a condition which, if absent, will guarantee that the event *E* will not occur. Example: The presence of oxygen, combustible materials, and heat are necessary conditions for fire.

necessary truth A necessary truth is a statement whose falsehood is impossible. Necessary truths are of several kinds, including logically necessary, conceptually necessary, and epistemically necessary. The proposition "All bachelors are unmarried male adult human beings" is a conceptually necessary truth.

negative statement A negative statement is a compound statement containing the word 'not' or one of its synonyms. This is also known as a denial.

non causa pro causa *See* **false cause**

non sequitur *See* **irrelevant conclusion**.

nonconsequentialist moral theory A nonconsequentialist moral theory maintains that either the consequences of an action are irrelevant to the evaluation of a moral claim (rule-deontology) or that they are not the only considerations that are relevant to the evaluation of a moral claim (act-deontology).

nontruth-functionally compound statement A compound statement is a nontruth-functionally compound statement if and only if the truth value of the statement does not depend solely upon the truth values of the component statements. Example: "John believes that Elise likes pizza." The statement might be true even if Elise hates pizza.

normal probability distribution The normal probability distribution is obtained when the mean, mode, median, and midrange averages approximate one another. It is graphed as a bell curve.

objective An objective or end is that which a human being might seek by engaging in an action. Example: Joan's objective in playing college football was to land a job with the National Football League after graduation.

objective extension of an analogy The objective extension of an analogy is the object compared to the ground of the analogy and which is known to have a number of properties in common with the objects in the ground. For example, if you have three objects, A, B, and C, both A and B have properties *a, b, c,* and *d,* and the question is whether C also has property *d,* C is the objective extension of the analogy.

obscure, obscurity *See* **vague**

obverse, obversion The obverse of a categorical proposition is formed by changing the quality of a proposition from affirmative to negative and replacing the predicate term with its complement. Example: The obverse of "Some dogs are collies" is "Some dogs are not non-collies." Every categorical proposition is logically equivalent to its obverse.

Ockham's razor *See* **parsimony, principle of**

open question An open question is a question that is not answered.

open-mindedness The virtue of open-mindedness is a willingness to consider new ideas or hypotheses.

opinion The word 'opinion' has at least three meanings: (1) a belief, (2) a belief that has not been supported by an argument, and (3) a belief that *cannot* by its nature be supported by an argument. The locution "It's only an opinion" seems to take 'opinion' in the third way. What is then needed is an *argument* to show that there is no way to show that the belief is true or false. Once that is attempted, you usually will find that there are ways to clarify the meaning so that you can at least provide some justification for your belief.

oxymoron An oxymoron is a figure of speech by which a locution produces the effect of seeming self-contradiction. Example: cruel kindness.

paradigm, paradigmatic A paradigm is a perfect example. Joan took collies to be her paradigm of doghood.

parsimony, principle of If either of two hypotheses will explain a phenomenon and one involves fewer theoretical assumptions, that hypothesis is more probably true. Also known as Ockham's razor.

particular affirmative proposition A particular affirmative proposition asserts that some members of the subject class are members of the predicate class. Example: Some professors are redheads.

particular negative proposition A particular negative proposition asserts that some members of the subject class are *not* members of the predicate class. Example: Some professors are not redheads.

particular proposition A particular proposition asserts that *some* members of a class are (or are not) members of another class.

performative utterances A performative utterance is a sentence used to bring some state of affairs into being. Examples: You make a promise by saying, "I promise that. . . ." A minister makes two people husband and wife by saying, in the correct ceremonial context, the words, "I now pronounce you husband and wife." A person becomes President of the United States by repeating the oath of office in the context of an inauguration ceremony.

personal attack The fallacy of personal attack occurs when replying to an argument. The person or the person's character is attacked rather than the argument.

persuasion, persuasive Persuasion is the art of convincing someone to accept a conclusion. Persuasive arguments are not always strong arguments: They can be invalid, or weak, or based on a false premise. Some persuasive arguments appeal to emotions rather than to facts.

phenomenon A phenomenon is an event or a state of affairs. In an explanation, that which is to be explained (the explanandum) often is called a phenomenon.

plausibility *See* **reasonableness**

poisoning the well *See* **personal attack**

population A population is the group of people or animals or things about which a person constructing a survey wishes to attain some information.

post hoc ergo propter hoc *See* **false cause**

precision Precision is a critical-thinking virtue. Precision concerns the degree of accuracy. For example, it is accurate to claim that Columbus discovered America in 1492. It is more precise to say he discovered America on October 12, 1492.

predicate term In a proposition, the predicate term is that which is said about the subject. Example, in the proposition "All professors are insane persons;" the term 'insane persons' is the predicate term.

prediction A prediction is a claim that some phenomenon will occur in a specified set of circumstances.

premise A premise is a statement in an argument that is taken as providing evidence for the truth of the argument's conclusion.

premise indicator A premise indicator is a word such as 'since' or 'because', which is commonly found before a statement that is the premise of an argument.

presumption A presumption is something that is assumed but not stated (*see* **assumption**). Fallacies of presumption are based on the unstated assumption that all the relevant information is given.

primary literature If you are writing an interpretive essay on *Hamlet,* the primary literature is the play itself and anything else written by Shakespeare—for example, his letters. If you are writing an essay on the causes of the War of 1812, the primary literature consists of documents written during the War of 1812 by participants in that war. In general, primary literature consists of works written by contemporaries of an event about the event or the piece of literature under examination and other writings by the same author. *See also* **secondary literature**

principle of parsimony *See* **parsimony, principle of**

principle of the uniformity of nature *See* **uniformity of nature, principle of**

probability sampling *See* **random survey**

probability theories There are three probability theories. (1) Classical probability theory assumes that all probabilities are taken into account and all possibilities are equally probable. (2) Relative frequency probability theory is based on empirical data for determining frequencies. This is common in the sciences. (3) Subjective probability theory is based on individual beliefs. This is common at the race track.

problematic extension of an analogy The problematic extension of an analogy is that property common to objects in the ground but not known to be a property of the objective extension. For example, if you have three objects, A, B, and C, both A and B have properties *a, b, c*, and *d*, and the question is whether C also has property *d*, the question whether C also has property *d* is the problematic extension of the analogy.

proposition A proposition is what is meant by a declarative sentence. Technically, only propositions are true or false. Example: The proposition expressed by the statement "Today is Friday" is true if and only if today is Friday. The same proposition can be expressed by declarative sentences in several languages. The proposition expressed by the English sentence "It is raining" is the same proposition expressed by the French sentence "*Il pleut*" and the German statement "*Es regnet.*"

purpose A purpose or end or objective is the result a person has in mind when engaging in an action. Example: John's purpose in taking GPHL120 was to fulfill a graduation requirement. Sometimes we talk about the purposes of nonhuman objects, for example, "The purpose of a hammer is to drive nails." When we attribute purposes to inanimate objects, we are implicitly concerned with either the purpose of the inventor in making the object or the purpose of the user in using the object.

purposive sampling A survey based on purposive sampling is nonrandom (biased).

quality The quality of a categorical proposition is affirmative (positive) or negative.

quantity, quantifier Quantity is concerned with how many. In a categorical syllogism, the quantifiers 'all', 'no', and 'some' tell you with how many objects of a certain kind you are concerned.

question-begging epithet *See* **begging the question**

quota sampling Quota sampling is a form of purposive sampling that divides a population into relevant groups and samples the population in proportion to its prevalence in a population.

random survey, randomness A survey is random when every member of a given population has an equal chance of being chosen for inclusion in the survey.

reasonableness It is reasonable to accept the conclusion of an argument (or the conclusion you reach by the process of inference) if the information presented—as well as any other evidence that might be available—tends to show that the conclusion is true. *Inductive* arguments or inferences are deemed reasonable or plausible. *Deductive* arguments are deemed valid or sound.

reasoning Reasoning is a psychological process by which a person reaches a conclusion on the basis of a body of information taken as evidence. Reasoning is often expressed in the form of an argument. *See* **argument**

recognition Recognition is an act of perceiving something as a thing of a certain kind or as an individual previously perceived. Examples: He recognized that the object in the abstract painting was a cow. She recognized the sixth man in the police lineup as the man who committed the robbery.

reconstructing an argument You reconstruct an argument when you attempt to restate it in such a way that the implicit reasoning process is made explicit. Example: You are given "Students going to college have to start budgeting their money, so everyone in this critical-thinking class needs to budget his or her money, for everyone in this critical-thinking class is a college student." You might reconstruct it as follows:

All college students are people who have to start budgeting their money.
All students in this critical-thinking class are college students.
Therefore, all students in this critical-thinking class are students who have
    to start budgeting their money.

But your reconstruction might be in error. Is the first premise true? You might need to reexamine your reconstruction to see whether all of your premises are true.

red herring fallacy You commit the red herring fallacy if you reply to another person's argument by confusing the issues, that is, if you distract someone from the content of another person's argument.

rehearse an argument To rehearse an argument is to state or summarize an argument, typically an argument set forth by someone else.

relevance Relevance is a critical-thinking virtue. Evidence is relevant to a conclusion if and only if it tends to show that the conclusion is true.

retrodiction A retrodiction is a claim that some phenomenon has occurred in a specified set of circumstances.

rhetoric, rhetorical Rhetoric is the art or science of communication in words. The rhetorician often is at least as concerned with persuasion as with argumentative strength.

rhetorical question A rhetorical question is a question that assumes an answer. It is a statement in the form of a question. Example: Who can doubt that critical thinking is the most important skill you learn in college? Implicit statement: Critical thinking is the most important skill you learn in college.

sample In constructing a survey or attempting to reach a generalization, the sample is the group of objects examined.

scope *See* **explanatory scope**

secondary literature If you are writing an essay on *Romeo and Juliet,* the secondary literature consists of books and articles written about the play *Romeo and Juliet.* If you are writing an essay on the causes of the Thirty Years War, the secondary literature consists of any other books or essays written on the causes of the Thirty Years War. In general, secondary literature consists of essays written on the same topic you are discussing. *See also* **primary literature**

sexist language Sexist language is language that does not treat both sexes equally. For example, if you are choosing a pronoun that applies to both women and men, use the construction "he or she," rather than "he." Use the expression "husband and wife" rather than "man and wife."

simile A simile is an analogy in which the word 'like' or 'as' makes the comparison between two or more things explicit.

simple random sample with replacement In a simple random sample with replacement any individual that is drawn from the population is sampled (interviewed, examined) and then returned to the population from which the sample is drawn. In a simple random sample with replacement an individual can be sampled multiple times. This is commonly used for an indefinitely large population.

simple random sample without replacement In a simple random sample without replacement any individual that is drawn from the population is sampled (interviewed, examined) and *not* returned to the population from which the sample is drawn. In a simple random sample without replacement no individual can be sampled multiple times. This is commonly used for a finitely large population.

simple statement A simple statement is any statement that does not have another statement as a part.

singular proposition A singular proposition makes a claim about an individual person or thing.

skeptic, skeptical, skepticism A person is skeptical regarding the truth of a statement if he or she provides reasons to question the statement's truth. Example: David Hume (1711-1776) was a skeptic with respect to our beliefs in causal reasoning, for he argued that there are no unquestionable grounds for establishing the truth of our belief that two kinds of things, for example, fire and heat, always stand in causal relations to each other.

slippery slope The slippery slope (wedge) fallacy is an informal fallacy in which there is a chain of causal claims—often in which things begin with bad consequences and grow progressively worse—in which one or more of the causal claims is false.

snowball samples In a snowball sample, you begin with members of the relevant group and ask for names of additional members.

sound argument A sound argument is a valid deductive argument with true premises.

squares of opposition A square of opposition is a chart showing the immediate inferences that can be drawn given the truth or falsehood of a categorical proposition. There are distinct squares for the Aristotelian and the Boolean interpretations.

standard-form categorical proposition A categorical proposition is said to be in standard form if it is composed of a standard quantifier (*all, no,* or *some*) followed by a subject term, followed by a form of the verb *to be,* followed by a predicate term. For example, the categorical proposition "All fire trucks are red things" is a standard-form categorical proposition. The categorical proposition "Every living tree grows" is *not* a standard-form categorical proposition.

standard-form categorical syllogism A categorical syllogism is said to be a standard-form categorical syllogism if each of its component propositions is a standard-form categorical proposition and it is arranged major premise first, followed by the minor premise, followed by the conclusion. It must contain *exactly* three terms used in the same sense throughout the syllogism.

statement A statement is a declarative sentence. Examples: "Today is Friday," "*Heute ist Freitag.*"

stereotype A stereotype is a false, though commonly made, general claim about a certain group of people. Example: "You can understand why Dan has a hot temper, since he's a redhead." The stereotype, the general principle that is assumed in the previous argument, is "All redheads are hot tempered." Arguments based on stereotypes are unsound.

stratified random survey In a stratified random survey, the population is divided into categories (strata), and each stratum is surveyed randomly.

straw person fallacy You commit the straw person fallacy if you misrepresent another person's argument and criticize the argument you have misrepresented.

structural samples Structural samples are purposive surveys made regarding relationships in a structure. You need to construct such surveys regarding numerous kinds of groups to provide evidence that the relationship in question holds independently of the kind of group to which each structural sample is constructed.

subaltern, subalternation On the Aristotelian interpretation of categorical logic, subalternation is a relation between a universal and its corresponding particular such that if the universal is true, the corresponding particular is also true. For example, if you know that "All jazz musicians are cool cats" is true, you can infer that "Some jazz musicians are cool cats" is true.

subcontrary Two statements are subcontraries if it is possible for both to be true, but it is not possible for both to be false. On the Aristotelian interpretation of categorical logic, this is the relation between a particular affirmative and a particular negative with the same content.

subject term The subject term of a proposition is that about which something is claimed. Example: In the proposition, "All professors are insane persons," the subject term is 'professors'.

sufficient condition A sufficient condition for some event E is a condition in the presence of which event E is *guaranteed* to occur. Example: The presence of oxygen, combustible materials, and sufficient heat are jointly sufficient conditions for fire.

suppressed evidence, fallacy of The fallacy of suppressed evidence occurs when someone intentionally ignores evidence contrary to the position he or she is defending.

Example: Ms. Salesperson is trying to sell you a widget, pointing out all its virtues while ignoring the fact that since Widgets Inc. was taken over by the Schlock Corporation, the quality of its products has decreased significantly.

survey A survey is an investigation undertaken to discover the current distribution of something in the world. Public opinion surveys are used, for example, to discover the current approval rating of the President or to determine the group with whom a certain product is most popular.

syllogism A syllogism is a deductive argument having two premises and a conclusion.

synthetic statement A synthetic statement is a statement in which the predicate provides information in addition to what is known in knowing the meaning of the subject term.

systematic sampling Systematic sampling consists of choosing every so-manyeth object after a random choice of the first object.

tautology, tautologous statement A tautology is a statement that is true in virtue of its form. "Either it is raining or it is not raining" is an example of a tautologous statement.

teleology, teleological Something is teleological if it is end-directed. On teleological moral theories, see **consequentialism**.

term A term is a word or phrase that can function as the subject of a sentence.

testimony Testimony is a claim made by a person.

theory An explanatory theory consists of a number of well-confirmed, interrelated hypotheses that explain phenomena of a certain kind.

thesis In an essay the thesis is the statement the author is attempting to establish as true. A thesis is to an essay what a conclusion is to an argument.

tilde (~) The tilde represents negation. A statement of the form $\sim p$ is true if and only if p is false, and $\sim p$ is false if and only if p is true.

transitional narrative In an essay transitional narrative is a sentence or a number of sentences that move you from one argument to the next.

true, truth A statement or proposition is true if and only if it corresponds with the way the world is. Example: The statement "Winter officially begins on December 20, 21, or 22" is true.

truth table A truth table is a chart representing all possible combinations of truth values of the premises and conclusion of a propositional argument. Truth tables allow you to determine whether there could be any case in which all the premises are true and the conclusion is false.

truth-functionally compound statement A compound statement is a truth-functionally compound statement if and only if the truth value of the whole rests entirely upon the truth value of each of the statements of which it is composed. Example: "Today is Tuesday, and it is raining." The statement is true if and only if it is true that today is Tuesday and it is true that it is raining.

truth value The truth value of a statement is its truth or falsehood.

uniformity of nature, principle of The principle of the uniformity of nature is the assumption that, *at some level*, the future will resemble the past. This is reflected in the fact that any natural law, for example, Einstein's theory, has always held and will always hold.

universal affirmative proposition A universal affirmative preposition asserts that all members of the subject class are members of the predicate class. Example: All collies are dogs.

universal negative proposition A universal negative proposition asserts that no members of the subject class are members of the predicate class. Example: No cats are dogs.

universal proposition A universal proposition asserts that either all members of one class are members of another or that no members of one class are members of another.

unpacking a metaphor You unpack a metaphor when you spell out the ways in which the objects compared are similar and different from each other.

utilitarianism Utilitarianism is a consequentialist moral theory based on the principle that one ought act in such a way that it yields the greatest good (or pleasure or happiness) to the greatest number of people.

vague A word is vague if its meaning is unclear, if there are no clear criteria for the application of the word.

validity, invalidity Validity is a formal characteristic of deductive arguments. An argument is valid if and only if it is impossible for all its premises to be true and its conclusion false. If an argument form is invalid, it provides no more than inductive evidence for the truth of its conclusion.

variable A variable is letter used to represent a term or a proposition in an argument. It is a placeholder. We often represent the form of an argument by replacing common terms or propositions with variables. Notice how variables are used to represent the form of the following argument:

Argument	Form
If today is Tuesday, then tomorrow is Wednesday.	If p, then q.
Today is Tuesday.	p.
Therefore, tomorrow is Wednesday.	Therefore, q.

verbal disputes A verbal dispute is a disagreement between two or more people that rests on ambiguities in language rather than questions of fact. The disputants assign different meanings to a key word, and any apparent disagreement is resolved once the alternative meanings of the word are recognized.

weak analogy Weak analogy is an informal fallacy based on an analogical argument in which the points of comparison are insufficient to support the conclusion or in which there are significant disanalogies among the things compared so the conclusion does not follow.

wedge (v) The wedge represents disjunction. A statement of the form $p \vee q$ is true *except* when both p and q are false.

wedge fallacy *See* **slippery slope**

INDEX

A